OZIAS LEDUC
An Art of Love and Reverie

Ozias Leduc (1864-1955)

OZIAS LEDUC

An Art of Love and Reverie

MUSÉE DU QUÉBEC

THE MONTREAL MUSEUM
OF FINE ARTS

Ozias Leduc: An Art of Love and Reverie was published
in conjunction with the exhibition presented at the
Montreal Museum of Fine Arts from February 22 to May 19, 1996,
at the Musée du Québec, Quebec City, from June 12 to September 15, 1996,
and at the Art Gallery of Ontario, Toronto, from October 18, 1996, to January 15, 1997.
The exhibition was mounted by the Montreal Museum of Fine Arts
and the Musée du Québec, with financial support from the
Museums Assistance Program, Department of Canadian Heritage,
and the Quebec Ministère de la Culture et des Communications.

Publication of this catalogue was co-ordinated by the Montreal Museum of Fine Arts.
A production of the Publications Service, Department of Communications.

Production co-ordination: Denise L. Bissonnette
Editorial co-ordination: Donald Pistolesi
Translation and revision: Jill Corner, Judith Terry and Donald Pistolesi
Photo credits: see p. 318
Graphic design and typesetting: Dufour et Fille Design inc.
Photo-engraving and printing: Richard Veilleux imprimeur

Frontispiece:
Ozias Leduc, in front of *Christ Blessing Little Children*, about 1893
(photo by Ozias Leduc, printed from glass negative No. 100, BNQ 327/13/1.80)

Legal deposit - 1st quarter 1996
Bibliothèque nationale du Québec
National Library of Canada
ISBN: 2-89192-207-7

THE MONTREAL MUSEUM OF FINE ARTS
P.O. Box 3000, Station "H"
Montreal, Quebec H3G 2T9

PRINTED IN CANADA

The exhibition *Ozias Leduc: An Art of Love and Reverie* was organized by PIERRE THÉBERGE, Director of the Montreal Museum of Fine Arts, and JOHN R. PORTER, Director of the Musée du Québec.

The organization of the exhibition was co-ordinated by YVES LACASSE

Guest Curator: LAURIER LACROIX
assisted by

                     MONIQUE LANTHIER
                     and
                     ARLENE GEHMACHER

The exhibition catalogue was prepared under the editorship of
                     LAURIER LACROIX

Contributors: ANDRÉ G. BOURASSA
                     FRANÇOIS-MARC GAGNON
                     ARLENE GEHMACHER
                     YVES LACASSE
                     LAURIER LACROIX
                     PIERRE L'ALLIER
                     MONIQUE LANTHIER
                     GINETTE LAROCHE
                     ESTHER TRÉPANIER

Note to the reader

Wherever possible, titles correspond to those provided by the artist at the first known mention of a work. Parenthetical additions to the titles *Still Life* and *Landscape* are for convenience of identification only. Alternative titles by which some works are well known are also noted.

In dimensions, height precedes width.

Multiple inscriptions are separated by a semicolon. Attached labels are listed, but their contents have not generally been transcribed.

A work's Provenance begins with "studio of the artist" only when its complete history of ownership is known.

The Leduc papers (Fonds d'archives Ozias-Leduc) are held by the Division des archives privées of the Bibliothèque nationale du Québec (BNQ), in Montreal, where they are classified as MSS 327. These documents were inventoried by Monique Lanthier in conducting the preliminary research for this exhibition.

Abbreviations
AGO, Art Gallery of Ontario, Toronto
ANQQ, Archives nationales du Québec, Quebec City
BNQ, Bibliothèque nationale du Québec, Montreal
NAC, National Archives of Canada
NGC, The National Gallery of Canada, Ottawa
MMFA, The Montreal Museum of Fine Arts
MQ, Musée du Québec, Quebec City

Table of Contents

Lenders to the Exhibition

BRITISH COLUMBIA
Victoria
Art Gallery of Greater Victoria
NEW BRUNSWICK
Fredericton
The Beaverbrook Art Gallery
ONTARIO
Hamilton
Art Gallery of Hamilton
Kingston
Agnes Etherington Art Centre,
Queen's University
Ottawa
House of Commons
The National Gallery of Canada
Toronto
Art Gallery of Ontario
Windsor
Art Gallery of Windsor
QUEBEC
Joliette
Musée d'art de Joliette
Longueuil
Sœurs des Saints Noms de Jésus
et de Marie du Québec
Montreal
Bibliothèque nationale du Québec
McCord Museum of Canadian
History
Messieurs de Saint-Sulpice

The Montreal Museum of
Fine Arts
Musée d'art contemporain de
Montréal
Musée des Sœurs Grises de
Montréal
Université de Montréal
Quebec City
Assemblée nationale
Musée de la civilisation
Musée du Québec
Saint-Hyacinthe
Centre d'archives du Séminaire de
Saint-Hyacinthe inc.
Sherbrooke
Corporation Archiépiscopale C.R.
du Diocèse de Sherbrooke
Musée des beaux-arts de
Sherbrooke
Musée du Séminaire de
Sherbrooke
Trois-Rivières
Musée des arts et traditions
populaires du Québec
Musée Pierre-Boucher
SASKATCHEWAN
Regina
Mackenzie Art Gallery
Saskatoon
Mendel Art Gallery

PRIVATE COLLECTORS
Céline and Paul J. Audette
Chrystian Beaudoin
Renée Bergeron
Luc Choquette
The Cordier-MacAllister family
Béatrice Coulombe
Madeleine Darche
Suzette Dorval-Cardinal
The Farley family
Pierrette Filion-Véronneau
François-Marc Gagnon
Yvan Gauthier/KPMG
Paul Gouin
Françoise Goulet
Dr. and Mrs. Byrne Harper
Noëlla Lagacé
Jeanne L'Archevêque-Duguay
Germain Lavallée
Gérard and Gisèle Lortie
Jean-Paul Riopelle
Jean-Pierre Valentin

and others who wish to remain
anonymous

"Take Good Care of Me"

THE output of Ozias Leduc is rooted in the art and culture of late nineteenth-century Symbolism, as was demonstrated by its inclusion in the exhibition *Lost Paradise: Symbolist Europe*.[1] Its effect was apparent in the enormous enthusiasm it aroused among the young artists of the Automatiste generation who were his contemporaries. Indeed, Leduc was a leader by example in their immense cultural revolution that still, almost fifty years after the publication of *Refus global*, represents a living source of inspiration for the Quebec of today.

Ozias Leduc always worked not on his style or manner but on content, the inner meaning of what he painted and drew. "Your painting", he said to a young artist, "must have a *soul*."[2] For Leduc, art was not just what he depicted; it had another wider and deeper significance, and it is in this sense that his influence has been most intensely felt.

There was, in this respect, no distance between Leduc and the younger generation of Borduas, Riopelle and the signatories of the 1948 manifesto, for despite differences in plastic approach, they were in agreement on the power, mysterious but real, of art to embody ideas and convey thoughts.

Is there, then, any great distance between Leduc's *Three Apples* of 1887, which he gave to Borduas in 1942, and the latter's undoubted masterpiece *The Black Star*, from 1957?[3] That there is not was the conclusion of Riopelle, who often said that his work, like, let us say, Leduc's, sprang entirely from his direct experience of nature in all its infinitely rich complexity.

Thus it was that in the company of Ozias Leduc, Quebec's greatest artists left the nineteenth century behind and have traversed the twentieth century in the absolute conviction that art has a meaning, and that

1 As Paul-Émile Borduas wrote, "Leduc is the sweetest European fruit to ripen in Canada" ("Paul-É. Borduas nous écrit au sujet de Ozias Leduc", *Arts et pensée*, vol. 3, no. 18 [July-August 1954], p. 177; quoted in English from Paul-Émile Borduas, *Écrits/Writings*, trans. François-Marc Gagnon and Dennis Young [Halifax: The Press of the Nova Scotia College of Art and Design, 1978], p. 134).

2 Quoted in Gilles Corbeil, "Ozias Leduc, peintre de natures mortes", *Arts et pensée*, vol.3, no. 18 (July-August 1954), p. 170.

3 The Montreal Museum of Fine Arts' purchase of *The Three Apples* from Mme. Gabrielle Borduas in 1988 has brought these two great paintings together once again in the same collection.

art history is much more than just a mechanical series of images that vary in interest according to the mood of the place or moment.

There is, then, more than sufficient reason for the Montreal Museum of Fine Arts and the Musée du Québec to have jointly invested considerable resources for over four years in preparing the most comprehensive exhibition ever of the work of Ozias Leduc. The organization was entrusted to an outstanding team of experts headed by Laurier Lacroix, Professor at the Art History Department of the University of Quebec at Montreal. It includes Yves Lacasse, Curator of Canadian Art (painting and sculpture before 1970) at the Montreal Museum of Fine Arts and, since November 1995, Assistant Chief Curator at the Musée du Québec; François-Marc Gagnon, Professor in the Department of Art History, University of Montreal; Monique Lanthier, project research director at the Montreal Museum of Fine Arts; Arlene Gehmacher, lecturer in the Department of Art History, University of Toronto; Pierre L'Allier, Curator of Modern Art at the Musée du Québec; Esther Trépanier, who teaches in the Department of Art History, University of Quebec at Montreal; and from the Montreal Museum of Fine Arts, Mayo Graham, Chief Curator, and Hélène Lamarche, Head of Education and Public Programmes.

This huge and complex project vividly illustrates the manner in which our two institutions carry out their mandates, which include the duty to promote the cultural heritage of Quebec and, in the case of the Montreal Museum of Fine Arts, that of the Montreal region.[4]

Following the retrospectives devoted to his juniors, Paul-Émile Borduas in 1988 and Jean-Paul Riopelle in 1991, this exhibition of the work of Ozias Leduc in 1996 seems to us an answer to that "slight reproach" the artist made one day to Borduas – "Take good care of me, Paul-Émile!"[5]

PIERRE THÉBERGE, C.Q.
Director
The Montreal Museum of Fine Arts

4   "That while upholding its universal mandate, the Museum nonetheless devote particular attention to the art of Quebec and Canada, emphasizing as well, though its activities, Montreal's contribution to the development of the arts across Canada" ("Recommendations of the Museum's Policy Advisory Committee", July 1994).

5   Paul-Émile Borduas, "Quelques pensées sur l'œuvre d'amour et de rêve de M. Ozias Leduc", *Canadian Art*, vol. 10, no. 4 (Summer 1953), p. 158. This essay has been published in English in Borduas 1978, pp. 131-134.

A Painter of the Soul's Seasons

Leduc's paintings do not put themselves forward, but await us and move us to our depths. There is nothing loud or showy, but a brilliant glow of intensity like that of smouldering embers. Individuality is forgotten in the move towards the universal.

Fernand Leduc[1]

IT is clear from the critics' writings on Ozias Leduc that his work was admired by many artists among his contemporaries, including younger painters such as Paul-Émile Borduas, Fernand Leduc and Jean-Paul Riopelle. The same was true of the intelligentsia, even though the discerning evaluations of people like Jean-Marie Gauvreau, Olivier Maurault and Robert de Roquebrune are now little read. After Leduc's death, his output continued to attract informed art lovers and museum curators alike, as can be seen from the perceptive remark made by the late Guy Viau shortly before he became Director of the Musée du Québec: Ozias Leduc "centred his dream on the most everyday of objects. The stuff of his imagination was what he saw, touched and lived, what was around him. He captured all these transient things by using that most transient of elements – light."[2]

I still remember how deeply impressed I was by the exhibition *Ozias Leduc: Symbolist and Religious Painting*, organized by the National Gallery of Canada in 1974. Although this show did not claim to be a retrospective, it presented a good selection of important works and opened the way for many promising new avenues of research. Since then, many scholars have helped to illuminate the various aspects of the artist's life and work, producing an ever greater body of visual and documentary research. It was in the light of this growing interest that, in the winter of 1991, I suggested to Pierre Théberge a major retrospective on Leduc like the outstanding exhibition on Paul-Émile Borduas he had organized in 1988. From the very start, it was agreed to invite Professor Laurier Lacroix to curate the show, to make use of contributions from a number of Leduc experts in many fields and to ask the Musée du Québec to join in organizing the exhibition.

1 Fernand Leduc, "Ozias Leduc, peintre exemplaire", *Arts et pensée*, vol. 3, no. 18 (July-August 1954), p. 176.

2 Guy Viau, *La peinture moderne au Canada français* (Quebec City: Ministère des Affaires culturelles, 1964), p. 13.

Five years later, after research, lists, inventories, discoveries, brain-waves and analyses of every kind, the results have far surpassed our expectations. Once again, it has been demonstrated that the pooling of intellectual and material resources is the solution to the future; this approach produces a ripple effect, thus benefiting not only our museums and universities but also art lovers and the public as a whole.

Through a concatenation of circumstances, I have had the pleasure of being associated with the Leduc project from two points of view, initially as Chief Curator of the Montreal Museum of Fine Arts, and latterly as Director of the Musée du Québec. Given its mandate to promote the art of Quebec from earliest times to the present day, it was clearly appropriate for the Musée to become actively involved in this project. In the event, as in the case of a number of Quebec artists, it turned out that the Musée du Québec held the largest collection in Quebec or Canada of works by Leduc: 137 paintings and works on paper. We are all very happy that the Musée du Québec and the Montreal Museum of Fine Arts have collaborated yet again, to honour a painter of world stature whose work and memory both institutions hold dear.

JOHN R. PORTER
Director
Musée du Québec

Acknowledgements

THE initial impetus for mounting this exhibition came from Pierre Théberge, Director of the Montreal Museum of Fine Arts, and from John R. Porter, then the Museum's Chief Curator, who in 1991 invited me to prepare a retrospective representing every aspect of the oeuvre of Ozias Leduc. When appointed Director of the Musée du Québec, an institution representing the whole of Quebec, Mr. Porter wished the Musée to be fully involved in the project, and so the two museums combined efforts to organize this major exhibition.

Without the ongoing co-operation of a host of people – museum professionals, collectors and those who provided information on the artist – this project could not have come to fruition. From the very outset, it was my desire to work closely with a Research and Organizing Committee that would discuss and decide upon all aspects of this undertaking. I am delighted that Monique Lanthier, a doctoral student at the University of Montreal, and Arlene Gehmacher, who was working on a doctorate at the University of Toronto, were able to join in this adventure, which has brought us together for the past four years. Monique Lanthier, an expert on Leduc's portraits, was in charge of regularly updating files, going through Leduc's papers and preparing an inventory of the Leduc archive held by the Bibliothèque nationale du Québec. Arlene Gehmacher, who had previously studied the artist's still lifes, completed her doctoral thesis on the critical reaction to Leduc that gave rise to the myths surrounding the painter from Saint-Hilaire. Her bibliographical and chronological research provided many insights, as did her examination of comparative iconography. Both of these colleagues were most generous with their time and expertise, and their contribution to the exhibition is apparent from the texts published here. I am particularly grateful for their friendship and support throughout this venture.

The activities of this Committee were followed up, supported and validated by the project's equally dedicated Advisory Board, who took part in our discussions on the approach to be taken and offered valuable suggestions: art professors and historians Esther Trépanier of the University of Quebec at Montreal and François-Marc Gagnon of the University of Montreal, and Mayo Graham, Chief Curator, and Hélène Lamarche, Head of Education and Public Programmes at the Montreal Museum of Fine Arts. Committee member Pierre L'Allier, Curator of Modern Art at the Musée du Québec, also acted as co-ordinator between the staffs of the Montreal and Quebec City museums. The confidence Didier Prioul, Chief Curator of the Musée du Québec, showed in us greatly facilitated our task. Yves Lacasse, Curator of Canadian Art (Painting and Sculpture before 1970) at the Montreal Museum of Fine Arts until November 1995 and then Assistant Chief Curator of the Musée du Québec, was in charge of organizing the preparations for the exhibition; we benefited greatly from his experience, and his sense of humour enlivened many a work session. Finally, I wish to thank the authors of the catalogue for giving us the benefit of their scholarship and wholehearted teamwork.

Bringing together so many works by Leduc required the co-operation of dozens of lenders. We are, of course, particularly indebted to public institutions, but also and above all to those private collectors who consented to share their treasures with us for a few months. To those who chose to remain anonymous, as well as to those named in these pages, I wish to express our liveliest gratitude. Thanks are also due to the administrators and staff of the lending institutions, from the technicians and curators to archivists, who responded promptly to our many requests and whose devoted professionalism enabled this major exhibition to take place.

Special mention must be made of those many individuals who have been kind enough over the past several years to share with us information and documentation regarding Leduc, and in particular the painter Gabrielle Messier, the artist's collaborator, whose remarkable memory helped us verify innumerable data. Gabrielle was an unfailing source of information, and her contribution towards perpetuating Leduc's memory, evidenced on so many occasions, was most useful. I should also like to thank others who graciously consented to share their reminiscences with us, especially Sister Berthilde Germain, Rollande Bengle, Jeannette Bergeron, Florence Bindoff, Thérèse Chabot, Thérèse Clerk, Suzette Dorval-Cardinal, Juliette Doyle, Alice Gagné, Claire Lavoie, Gertrude Leduc, Louise Morissette, Fernande Préfontaine,

Rolande Raymond, Michel Clerk, Luc Choquette, Maurice Church, Jean-Claude Dufresne, Wilbrod Faucher, Guy Fortin, Yvon Handfield and Raoul Viens. Msgr. Jean-Marie Fortier, Sister Lucille Potvin, Father Aurèle Beauregard, Monique Gauthier, Huguette Pinard Lachance, Hélène Sicotte, Michèle P. Tremblay, Michel Biron, Alain Côté, Jean-Noël Dion, Michel Doyon, Serge Joyal, Jean-René Lassonde, Robert Lebeau, Jean-René Ostiguy and David Passmore, as well as the staff of the Galerie Bernard Desroches, the Dominion Gallery, the Galerie Jean-Pierre Valentin, Klinkhoff Gallery, the Galerie Michel-Ange, Waddington & Gorce and the Hôtel des Encans have all done everything possible to put us in touch with collectors and to provide information.

Monique Lanthier, Arlene Gehmacher and I wish to express our deepest gratitude to all our correspondents and to the many people who gave us help and hospitality with such alacrity and goodwill.

A special vote of thanks goes to the staff of the Administrator, Curatorial and Communications Departments of the Montreal Museum of Fine Arts, who helped us at every stage of the project, in assembling and restoring the works, mounting the exhibition and preparing it to travel to Quebec City and Toronto, preparing this catalogue, and disseminating and interpreting Leduc's oeuvre. I would particularly like to recognize the contribution of the Archives, Conservation, Exhibitions and Collections, and Publications Services, whose patience and dedication in carrying out the countless tasks imposed by this project enhanced our efforts. The Volunteer Guides, the staff in Education and Public Programmes, the Library, Reception and the Museum Shop, have also been most generous with their time and help, as have the staff of the painting laboratory of the Centre de conservation du Québec, who carried out major restoration in consultation with the Musée du Québec. We are also sincerely grateful to the staff of the Musée for their efficient co-operation in assembling, photographing and documenting the works.

Faithful to their mandate, the Museums Assistance Program of the Department of Canadian Heritage and the Quebec Ministère de la Culture et des Communications provided funding to enable the exhibition to be mounted. Once again, we thank all those who shared with us the pleasure of presenting the exhibition *Ozias Leduc: An Art of Love and Reverie*.

LAURIER LACROIX
Guest Curator

Introduction

As Ozias Leduc himself acknowledged, no doubt with some amusement, understanding and explaining his work is no easy task. While this first assembling of a large number of his paintings and drawings may not accomplish the mission entirely, we hope that it will suggest a new way of approaching, perceiving and appreciating this important oeuvre.

It is perhaps worth wondering why Ozias Leduc the painter, dead now for over forty years, has never before been the object of a retrospective. And, moreover, why such an exhibition is being held now. Perhaps there is a need today to look again at this body of work, to go beyond celebration and commemoration and make certain aspects of Leduc's art part of our own lives.

It could certainly be claimed that his turn has come, that after - presentations focussing on other artists who were Leduc's contemporaries – Morrice, Laliberté, Milne, Carr and several members of the Group of Seven – it is time to explore more fully the significance of a practice whose author contemporary history has remembered primarily as the first master and mentor of Paul-Émile Borduas.

All the studies of the history of painting in Canada published over the past thirty years have given a large place to Ozias Leduc, often presenting him as an isolated monument in the landscape of Canadian artistic production and thus perpetuating the marvellous portrait of him sketched by critic Maurice Gagnon in 1940.

> This noble figure of our art is remarkable, and truly exceptional in his eminence. There is not another painter in this country who possesses the same conscience, serenity of spirit, brilliance of mind, equanimity of character.
>
> The ceaseless questioning of self, the passionate reflection of a philosopher

who dwells outside the world but has his own small universe, his mountain, his orchards, his vast, horizon-filled sky, is all too rare in this prosaic century. So many are drawn to him in search of peace, joy, tranquillity …"[1]

All the events devoted to Leduc's work – the exhibitions organized by Jean-René Ostiguy at the National Gallery of Canada in 1955 and 1974, the one of drawings I presented in 1978 at Sir George Williams University (Concordia) and the exhibition of his landscapes mounted by Louise Beaudry at the Montreal Museum of Fine Arts in 1986 – have contributed, within the confines of their respective missions, towards keeping our memory of the artist alive and deepening our understanding of the painter from Saint-Hilaire. In addition, during the past twenty years there have been five masters' theses and more recently a doctoral dissertation that have taken Leduc as their theme, further enhancing our interpretation of his work.

Is this new research alone enough to justify the major undertaking that this retrospective exhibition represents? The question bears within it at least part of the answer. Without the ideas propounded in these studies, our understanding of Leduc would be sketchy indeed. These analyses have enabled us to further our knowledge of the artist and his art, and this exhibition and its accompanying catalogue will help disseminate these new perspectives.

The reading that emerges from this exhibition shows Leduc as paradigmatic of a dichotomy that lies at the heart of cultural experience in French-speaking Quebec. We find an artist formed by a society both Catholic and nationalist, who was drawn by art towards a spiritual and intellectual world of greater breadth. His work is seen to occupy an ambiguous position between rigour and sensuality, spirituality and materiality. In this, Leduc's art carries a message that can enlighten our own era, providing it, if not with specific examples, at least with the historical model of an artist who defined his role in society by adhering to the very highest standards and aiming for the very highest goals. Leduc's painting focusses on the importance of knowledge and ideals. As well as mirroring his philosophical development, however, it is also and primarily a meditation on painting and art in general. Leduc talks painting, thinks painting. Beyond their immediate charm, his pictures embody a vision whose significance – manifest in both the choice and rendering of their subjects – is inexhaustible.

Apart from the obvious logistical and organizational hurdles, every exhibition represents a challenge: that of deciding what its central proposition is to be. Will the selection of works and the way they are presented succeed in touching spectators' minds and stirring their feel-

1   Maurice Gagnon, *Peinture moderne* (Montreal: Éd. B. Valiquette, 1940), p. 201.

ings? The works chosen for this exhibition cover the whole of Leduc's career. All the various genres he practised are represented, as are all the media he employed. Our efforts to be comprehensive have nevertheless been hampered by certain circumstantial limitations. A few major paintings that would unquestionably have completed and modulated the view presented have not been located. Moreover, we are very conscious of the impossibility of presenting as part of such a retrospective a vital facet of Leduc's work: his church murals. This aspect of his production can be glimpsed, though, in a number of preparatory sketches that are a fascinating reflection of the artist's creative process, iconographical priorities and formal techniques. We have focussed on three ensembles, deliberately omitting the interior of the baptistry in Montreal's Notre-Dame Church, on which Jean-René Ostiguy published a monograph in 1970 and of which he included ten preliminary drawings in his 1974 exhibition. Without placing too much emphasis on Leduc's church interiors, there seems little reason to accept the sharp division generally drawn between Leduc's easel painting and his murals. Format and support were not, for him, distinct elements, and it would be a mistake to analyze a single aspect of his oeuvre in isolation on the grounds that its themes are apparently drawn from the secular realm.

The exhibition divides into four periods a career that was actually remarkably free of definitive change. There are, however, certain concrete events, such as trips away from home, commissions or the commencement of a new series of works, that suggest different stages in the artist's life. Early in his career, Leduc gained a reputation as a painter of still lifes and portraits. The artist's visit to France in 1897 marked a turning point in his aesthetic experience. Eighteen ninety-seven was also the year in which he was commissioned to undertake his first large-scale decorative project – the interior of the Church of Saint-Hilaire – and thus marks the transition between the two first periods. The second period was characterized by a growing preoccupation with landscape and the creation of a number of allegorical compositions. The years between 1913 and 1921 stand out particularly, for they gave rise to the large Symbolist landscapes, the portraits of close friends and the interior of the Sacred Heart Chapel at the Saint-Enfant-Jésus Church in the Montreal district of Mile-End. Leduc's religious painting subsequently evolved, and the works in Sherbrooke, Montreal's Notre-Dame Church, Lachine and Shawinigan-Sud show signs of a new philosophical approach and a growing synthesism that are also strikingly reflected in the "Imaginations" series.

In the exhibition, each of the four periods is highlighted by the exploration of a sub-theme that relates Leduc's work to that of his contemporaries and helps viewers grasp how the artist fitted in to his era and his milieu. His work cannot be classed along with that of other painters; but it shares with it many common components – ideological, methodological, iconographical and stylistic – that prompt re-examination within a broader context.

Because it is part of a pictorial tradition and the creation of one of that tradition's most important figures, the work of Ozias Leduc acts as the link between two centuries of Quebec art. But it can also be seen from a more international perspective, since it was produced at a time when artists everywhere were energetically searching for new ways to translate intellectual and imaginative experience in visual terms. In 1954, the critic Rodolphe de Repentigny described Leduc as "the most Canadian and the most universal of our painters".[2] While the meaning of the terms he employed may have altered, this statement retains all of its impact; for, within his own highly specific cultural context, Leduc was the source of artistic propositions that still challenge and touch us today.

L.L.

2 Rodolphe de Repentigny, "Le plus canadien et le plus universel de nos peintres, Ozias Leduc: fruit mûr de 3 siècles d'isolement", *La Presse*, [Montreal] June 23, 1954, p. 48. De Repentigny, also a well-known painter working under the name of Jauran, was a member of the first group of Plasticiens.

"A Dream of a Garden of Beauty"

The supreme art might possibly be the harmonious interdependence of matter arranged in the form of a universe.[1]

LAURIER LACROIX

OZIAS LEDUC's goal of creating a major pictorial oeuvre appeared relatively early in his life, took shape slowly, and was gradually defined and developed until it became the focus of his existence and his career, both of which were long and fruitful. The still lifes and the early genre portraits bear the seeds of an artistic practice whose subject is primarily the creative process itself. On the surface of these works are condensed, with rare complexity, objects that symbolize a network of cultural and social activities. The disposition of the objects, however, despite the powerful materiality with which they are rendered, carries both philosophical and spiritual connotations. Later paintings whose handling and subjects still charm and delight – the large landscapes from the 1910s, for example – also spark contemplation of the conditions that gave rise to this art and prompt the spectator to reflect upon the aesthetic ideas propounded by the painter. Starting in 1903, Leduc's writings offered regular formulations of different aspects of his artistic approach and provided clues to his concept of art.

Surprisingly, given the period in which he lived and his social background, Leduc succeeded in pursuing this vision without undue compromise. His often enigmatic works can be read on numerous levels and are fully immersed (not, occasionally, without contradiction) in all the major issues of his time.[2] Leduc's living and working expenses were slight and, deriving a modest revenue from his church decoration projects and the produce of his orchard, he was able to execute his art relatively free of financial cares.[3] His notes clearly indicate that he did not perceive his ecclesiastical commissions as a burden or a diversion from his easel painting, but rather as a means through which to develop

1   Lecture given by Ozias Leduc to the Saint-Hilaire chapter of the Union catholique des cultivateurs in about 1928, BNQ 327/4/3.

2   See, for example, Arlene Gehmacher's essay in this catalogue, "Authenticity' and the Rhetoric of Presentation", p. 43, and my introductions to Sections III and IV, "The Struggle between the Material and the Intellectual" p. 175 and "Between Symbolism and Nationalism", p. 225.

3   As Leduc wrote in a letter dated March 18, 1941, "I am not a martyr to art – everything has always been very easy for me. Labour and Discipline have been my collaborators all through life, together with an enduring good fortune that favours me still." (Private archive.)

his artistic thinking while earning a living. Aware of the importance of history painting and its role in society, Leduc always committed himself wholeheartedly to these projects and maintained a close connection between his studio work and the iconographical, stylistic and formal investigations undertaken for his murals.

Leduc was thus able to create his easel paintings in response to inspiration and his own needs, unhindered by the necessity to attract buyers; his only obligations were those imposed by the rare opportunities to exhibit and the demands of the circle of acquaintances and friends who were his principal collectors.

This comparative freedom encountered occasional obstacles,[4] but these did not prevent Leduc developing the ideas that were central to his vision of art, his art. My aim here is to summarize the elements underlying Leduc's efforts to define and realize the ideal beauty of art through painting,[5] although I am conscious of the abridgements such a schematic and systematic account necessarily involves. I shall quote the artist's own words frequently, for the organization of his thoughts into a sustained discourse would not do justice to his ever-evolving view.

Leduc's thinking, firmly rooted in the Thomist philosophy that then held sway among Catholic intellectuals in Europe and Canada, was the source of his idealistic concept of art.[6] He may have been influenced, too, by the writings of more contemporary art theorists – J.-K. Huysmans, Émile Mâle and Maurice Denis, for example – who were a good deal preoccupied with Symbolism. His view of art also possessed a more pragmatic dimension that owed something to the British artist William Morris (1834-1896), founder of the Arts and Crafts movement, whose theory of "aesthetic socialism" the painter shared.[7] Leduc's convictions concerning art and his confidence in the importance of his work were reinforced by the form of nationalism that began to develop in Quebec late in the second decade of this century.[8]

For Leduc, art is founded essentially on the will and the capacity to "penetrate the order of Nature". To achieve this end, the artist must understand and master the matter of which the natural world is composed, which will then reveal itself to be an infinite source of nourishment in the creation of an oeuvre. The painter is entrusted with a mission to seek knowledge and truth, his own truth. These are made manifest, through the poetic transpositions of the artist, in a form of painting designed to transmit his transcendent vision of the world and of his ideal:

4 For example, some commissioned portraits were refused (cats. 131, 132), while others were accepted only reluctantly by their models (cats.165, 171). Certain submissions for church interiors were turned down (see Chronology), sometimes for financial reasons (price too high), sometimes because other conditions, such as submission deadlines, were not met. As Leduc confided to Olivier Maurault (cats. 161-163), another cause of refusal was a certain lack of understanding of his work, which was not like that of his competitors.

5 For more on Leduc's artistic approach, see, for example, Victoria Baker, "On Art, Beauty, and Imagination: Currents of Thought in the Writings of Ozias Leduc", in Laurier Lacroix *et al.*, *Ozias Leduc the Draughtsman*, exhib. cat. (Montreal: Concordia University, 1978), pp. 125-135; Arlene Gehmacher, "In Pursuit of the Ideal: The Still Life Paintings of Ozias Leduc", Master's thesis, University of Toronto, 1986; and Barbara Ann Winters, "The Work and Thought of Ozias Leduc in the Intellectual and Social Context of His Time", Master's thesis, University of Victoria, May 1990.

6 The aesthetic theories of Thomas Aquinas underwent a revival in the mid-nineteenth century and remained popular in Catholic circles. Early in the twentieth century, Jacques Maritain attempted to reconcile Aquinas's views with modern art. On the presence of religious thinking in nineteenth-century aesthetic definitions, see J. Pierre N. L'Abbé, "Catholic Critics on Religious Art in France, 1870-1920", Master's thesis, University of Toronto, 1990, especially pp. 139-143 and Bibliography.

7 See Janice Seline, "The Real and the Ideal: Progress and the Landscapes of Ozias Leduc", in Lacroix *et al.* 1978, pp. 107-124. For Leduc, art becomes part of reality and fulfils fundamental needs if it is motivated by the will and passion that should inspire all human activity. The artist wrote, "To apply oneself with all one's heart to a useful task is to make art. It is the struggle between rebel matter and thought. It is through this struggle that human beings perfect their intelligence and penetrate even further into the order of Nature." (From a typescript at the Beaverbrook Art Gallery, acquired from a Fredericton collector in 1971. This document, whose original is not among the Leduc papers at the BNQ, is considered to be by the artist since there exists a partial transcription of it in notes [now in the Archives of the Montreal Museum of Fine Arts] taken by Gilles Corbeil from Leduc's archives during the artist's lifetime.)

8 Messianism was one of the peculiarities of French-Canadian nationalism as developed by Lionel Groulx during the twenties and thirties. Groulx revived the idea that certain peoples have a special mission to fulfil. Earlier, in *La France aux colonies* (1859), Rameau de Saint-Père had offered French Canada the following suggestion:
   Pay less attention to industry and trade, devote greater time to agriculture, more useful perhaps in terms of the real power of nations, and certainly less foreign to intellectual development, give the greatest care not only to spreading learning, but to improving its quality and raising the general level of intelligence, combine the elevation of ideas with the most serious science, and enhance through the beauty of form the community of thought: this is the goal Canadians should set themselves, and the very essence of the national character, revealed by their aptitudes and

... another word [on the artist] to show him to you now, on the glorious but obstacle-barred trail of the ideal whose realization he pursues, to show him to you in his flight towards Beauty, supreme model of his art. Here, he seems part of a kind of priesthood. His mission is to reveal to his delighted contemporaries his splendid conception of a world made iridescent by the prism of his intelligence, celebrating the Cause of causes, to show them within themselves unsuspected riches, grounds for more love, more clarity in their actions ... the artist's mission, noble and great, is worth a few sacrifices on his part, he tirelessly pursues the perfecting of his intelligence, he strives to acquire all possible skills to make it, this mission, ever more effective in its increasing penetration of total life. No matter the difficulties he encounters if he succeeds in stimulating truth, in fashioning a little beauty, towards the good.[9]

The creation of a work of art is thus an ethical and moral undertaking. For the artist, it means a lifelong commitment to the execution of a body of work that goes beyond him in translating his thinking, making it manifest in the form of a painting. Art is a means of attaining the ideal of the Beautiful, of reaching God, via the path of knowledge.

Mastering the Material Substance of Painting

All works of art should be governed by this basic principle: "Adapt matter to its particular purpose." This means treating a substance according to its requirements and its capacity.[10]

An artist's first aim in the accomplishment of his mission must be to identify and master the elements that will enable him to produce his work. Leduc did not give a painting's subject or its moral value the foremost place in his artistic approach.[11] For him, the vital first step was the evaluation and appreciation of the picture's elements – its physical and formal constituents. These are the source of the work, and its genesis depends on their combinations on the canvas.

The subject of several of the still lifes (cats. 12, 13, 185) is that blend of drawing, colour and composition that Leduc was to claim as the three constitutive elements of the "Painter-Creator" (cat. 90). To execute his paintings, the artist must possess knowledge of the science of colour and of the physical properties of pigments and binders, as well as command of the techniques of drawing from observation and of ordering the pictorial surface – all skills related to the organization of the elements that compose his discourse. These fundamental notions are acquired though study of what Leduc saw as the foundations of art, rooted in the material character of the work. Art is a product of the

tastes, carries them towards it together. (Quoted in Jean-Pierre Gaboury, *Le Nationalisme de Lionel Groulx: aspects idéologiques* [Ottawa: Éditions de l'Université d'Ottawa, 1970], p. 56.)

The idea of messianic nationalism was passed on by Msgr. Laflèche and Msgr. Paquet, and later by the group known as L'Action française, of which Groulx was the guiding light. He wrote, "What is demanded of nations, even the greatest, is to express, to describe for the world, original patterns of thought and life, a distinct humanity, and it is thus that a people attains civilization." ("Notre mission française", in Lionel Groulx, *Constantes de vie* [Montreal and Paris: Fides, 1967], p. 73) and quoted in Gaboury 1970, p. 57.

Although relations between Leduc and Abbé Groulx were not fruitful – the plan to illustrate *Les Rapaillages* came to nothing – Leduc had more regular contact with several other members of L'Action française, who were also the source of a number of commissions: Abbé Philippe Perrier, Olivier Maurault (cat. 163), Édouard Montpetit, Adélard Dugré and Yves Tessier Lavigne. See Susan Mann Trofimenkoff, *Action française: French Canadian Nationalism in the Twenties* (Toronto: University of Toronto Press, 1975).

The notion of the fulfilment of a special mission is basic to the concept of messianism. The passion with which Leduc tried to direct his contemporaries towards a new idealism, whose source lay deep within the artist's own natural and cultural surroundings, was marked by the same mysticism that runs through messianic nationalism.

9 From the lecture by Leduc cited in note 1.

10 From the typescript cited in note 7.

11 Romanticism had given precedence to expression over subject. For the Thomists, however, means of expression were less important than a work of art's theme and the ideas that lay behind it. All of an artist's work "strives towards this close and concrete union; towards this fusion of thought in the expression of what it objectifies; towards this mutual penetration of two elements of the work. And of the many-faceted sketch that thought moulds, it is not the idea that emerges but the idea incorporated in and informing the expression; and the expression embodying and materializing the idea." (V.-M. Breton, o.f.m., "Du sujet dans l'œuvre d'art", *Le Devoir* [Montreal], April 20, 1918, p. 7.)

exploitation of the finality of matter, and a work is successful to the degree that it is in a state of symbiosis with the physical elements that compose it.

Leduc chose, moreover, to structure his compositions using only a limited number of parameters – essentially a sharply contoured drawing style and a mood-creating light rendered in a technique of highly controlled brushwork. His paintings are composed on regular lines, defined by the format and dimensions of the picture. The painter generally employs a shallow spatial field reflecting the two-dimensionality of the canvas, and a high horizon line that also accentuates the picture plane. The still lifes are spatially arranged in a staggered, receding fashion around a central axis. The portraits are closed off by coloured grounds; the landscapes, though, are often composed of disconnected planes that suggest depth and perspective while making it impossible to apprehend real space.

The inclination to see a painting in this way, in terms first and foremost of its technical and formal elements, has its source in a questioning of the act of painting itself. The transference that operates between observation, imagination and physical procedures generates an image capable of registering perceptions, sensations and information. Leduc's preoccupation with the models in his portraits of readers (cats. 21-23) seems to mirror a process of learning and assimilation of knowledge through concentration and active reflection. These readers provide an example of the effort and application required to develop understanding. Leduc thus offers a meditation on the importance of education, which is seen not only as the foundation of all human activity but also as a "precondition of aesthetic pleasure".[12] This intellectual exercise is contrasted with that of the young musician (cat. 15), who, equally absorbed, allows inspiration more freedom in guiding the action of his breath and lips upon the harmonica. The acts of learning and creating are ways of surpassing oneself, of expressing the thoughts and feelings that arise when a sentient being communes with nature. In more general terms, Leduc defines matter as "a provoker of thoughts; it is the tool of all thoughts expressing themselves."[13] It is characterized not only by its form, but above all by its essence, which is to stimulate the act of creation.

Art is an autonomous act based on the relations between the material means of realizing the work and the imagination governing the creative faculty.

12 Maurice de Wulf, *La valeur esthétique de la moralité dans l'art* (Brussels: Corné-Germon, 1892), p. 36. De Wulf, a Thomist at the University of Louvain, also wrote, "Intelligence is not an isolated faculty in man. When it undertakes its act of aesthetic contemplation, the other activities do not remain passive. The self is not a juxtaposition of sense, imagination, emotion, will ... It is continuous in its unity; everything in it is subordinated towards the end" (p. 37).

13 Ozias Leduc, "Remarques sur l'art", about 1936, BNQ 327/4/1.

The substance of my art as a creator comes from the wide-open world of dreams, substance of living imagination, rendered almost palpable by token of a play of lines, shapes, colours, so also substance of the universe. A somewhat unreal world, then; but with a particular appearance, incarnation of subtlety, magic, infinity, contemplation. The contemplation that precedes creation."[14]

For Leduc, intelligence is not the sole seat of beauty: another fundamental ingredient is imagination. He dwells on the subjectivity and individuality that dominate the creative process. Knowledge is a subjective factor, and the infinite combinations it suggests to the mind find a means of expression in the materials of art.

The artist creates a Universe from which he cannot exclude himself. The magic of his most far-fetched conceptions, it seems, of the ordinary order of things and beings, always emerges, undoubtedly, from a greater, more fantastic magic whose laws escape us and are lost, beyond our reach, in the confusion of an imagination tied to appearances alone.[15]

The substance of creation resides in an act of communication;[16] it is a way of allowing an inner world to advance towards the Other, of uniting two minds. The work of art is an altruistic venture, the act of a consciousness detached from itself and in search of another voice.

Paint what is imagined? Models? What I know to be, *what I see*. I can imagine an object, in the atmosphere created for it by my eyes, without any need for understanding what it is essentially. Imagining a World, lines, shapes and colours, means creating a World – a spiritualized World. Realizing this World means going beyond one's egoism. Awareness – image…[17]

Mastering Nature

Intelligence and feeling are the two paths open to the artist in furthering his understanding of the world and developing the associations that will sustain his thinking. While Leduc sometimes assigned to nature the role of absolute source of artistic inspiration ("Nature is more daring in its realities … than man's imagination in its fantasy!"),[18] he perceived it primarily as a whole from which the artist cannot divorce himself: "Nature is the master of masters, so they say. Is it a model? The artist draws upon it, from it comes the matter of which the work's body is formed, matter that he masters, it seems, as if it were outside, above nature; which is not the case."[19]

14 From the typescript cited in note 7.

15 BNQ 327/3/15.

16 "We seek the revival of love, reason for the continuity of the world and of Art, of Art as exaltation of matter and life" (notes for the magazine *Arts et pensée*, no. 14, BNQ 327/3/17). This idea recalls the views of the poet Rudhyar who, in 1919, published the following advice to French Canadians: "All that we achieve through Love, by identifying with the matter and spirit of the special creation undertaken, all that we recognize within ourselves, and by ourselves alone. All this is fertile, and beautiful because directly expressive of the Soul … What I wish to say to you is primarily this: You have everything in you. Deepen yourselves. Come to know yourselves. Be not 'memories' but 'creators'. The only sublime thing is Love, which leads to Knowledge. Create. Attend no school but the school of nature, of life and of yourselves." ("Le devoir d'art et la race canadienne-française", *Le Canada*, April 15, 1919.)

17 Ozias Leduc, "Peindre ce qui est penser", Textes poétiques, undated, BNQ 327/3/17.

18 BNQ 327/3/15.

19 BNQ 327/3/18.

20 Leduc actually borrows a sentence from Maritain's *Art et Scolastique* (1920): "The imitative arts aim neither at copying the appearance of nature nor at depicting 'the ideal', but at making something beautiful by the display of a *form* with the help of visible symbols." (Jacques and Raïsa Maritain, *Oeuvres complètes* [Paris: Éditions Saint-Paul/Fribourg: Éditions universitaires, 1986], p. 680; quoted in English from Jacques Maritain, *Art and Scholasticism, with Other Essays*, trans. J. F. Scanlan [New York: Charles Scribner's Sons, 1947], p. 48.) In his version, Leduc stresses the importance of the imagination: "Art aims neither at copying the appearance of nature nor at depicting the ideal; but only at making something beautiful by the display of a form with the help of visible symbols. To achieve this single goal he [the artist] will invent them and they will thus lend themselves to the transfiguration of the material appearance of nature" (BNQ 327/3/17).

Fashioned in nature's image, the work of art is also an integral part of nature. But it neither mirrors nor imitates it:[20] through its close association with the artist and his view of the world, it is a part of nature itself. The "matter" of nature, of the artist and of art is inextricably interwoven.

The beauty that we seek and find.

The beauty we are given has its source in the very depths of the acknowledged resemblance between Creator and created. Beauty is a concrete fact, it exists resplendent as part of the order that governs the relations between matter and spirit.

The order desired by Him who can make worlds, who brings in stages the being evolving towards its ideal form, towards its perfection. Similarly for all things that are beautiful.[21]

Underpinned by this desire to learn and to penetrate more deeply into the mysteries of nature, art becomes a lifework. It answers an essential need: it is the means by which to seek and attain the ideal that each of us defines and that allows us to know ourselves and to discover our environment.[22] For Leduc, then, the act of creation is an exercise in definition and an effort to understand oneself and the world.

The Artist: A God Dispossessed

At the heart of this creative approach there is intelligent and sentient matter: the artist, whose mission is to communicate his knowledge and perception of the world. Leduc makes the artist's individuality the focus of the drive to master matter. Art becomes possible if man succeeds in imposing on it some kind of order.

To this end, the artist must discover the rules that govern nature and identify the principles according to which the world is organized. He adopts a sovereign position, analogous to that of the Creator vis à vis the infinity of possible worlds. He conceives and regulates a creation,[23] gives it a meaning, whether he understands it himself or not.[24] He structures it according to the rules of proportion, clarity and balance that govern knowledge.[25] The artist faces an enormous undertaking, with few pointers to guide him through the infinite spatio-temporal possibilities of his consciousness as a being. Again, Leduc:

Existence

Nonexistence

The Intelligence at the centre of the Universe radiates in all directions,

Man or God becoming aware of himself through his creation,

The boundless Container of a world without limit, without end.

21 BNQ 327/3/17.

22 Leduc clearly wished to imbue his work with the immediacy of time and place. His early secular works are compositions inspired by his studio and portraits of family and friends. Many of his religious paintings offer information about the natural or architectural settings in which the scenes take place. The sacred thus takes on a significance that appeals more directly to spectators or believers, involving them in the narrative by means of a concrete symbol. It was not a new idea: over the centuries, many artists had given a timeliness to religious art by situating it in the present. In Leduc's painting, it is images taken from the natural world, physical landmarks, that ensure a link between the sacred message and the contemporary spectator.

23 The image of the nebula is particularly rich in Leduc's iconography (e.g., interiors of the baptistry in Montreal's Notre-Dame Church and the Bishop's Chapel in Sherbrooke, the "Imaginations" series). It represents primal energy, the universe in its embryonic form; fusing order and chaos, it is capable of eternal rebirth. "Nebulas. Abundant diffuse matter, faintly lit, perhaps the first substance, the chaos out of which are ordered by condensation worlds, stars? Or possibly the radiation emitted by these bodies, the residue of the gradual attrition that, little by little, disorganizes them and causes them to disappear in space. This substance may be the source of the marvellous oscillation that, in an eternal cycle, runs through the suns of space, which move ceaselessly from chaos to order, and from there, through other transformations of matter, attain new forms of chaos. Endless new developments …" (BNQ 327/3/15).

24 "The superior artist is not the most aware. The genius knows no restraint, if he is clear, he is so mysteriously; you will interpret his work" (from the typescript cited in note 7).

25 "The True, the Good, the Beautiful trouble Intelligence equally in its march towards ultimate perfection. What is chaos tends to order itself and fall into rhythms of beauty. An instant of the world in a state of becoming is captured forever by art, its power over matter results in this marvel." ("Sur la beauté", typescript cited in note 7.) Leduc specified on several occasions that the laws of beauty are similar to musical harmony and are consequently linked to emotion.

26 "Existence, Inexistence", BNQ 327/3/15.

Freedom of time and space.

Matter as radiation of the Spirit.

Matter, seat of intelligence, of the soul

All is matter in the Universe

Man in the centre, a self-shackling god.[26]

The very essence of the creative act resides in the struggle of matter to free itself, in the tension of human nature yearning towards the divine state. This emancipating introspection compels the artist to recognize himself as a fallen god.[27] A god dispossessed, he recalls an earlier heavenly and enlightened state that he longs to recapture. Art is a way of penetrating the secret of nature, of transcending appearances and of glimpsing God, whose principal attributes Leduc perceives as beauty and truth. The artist is capable of understanding and of attaining this objective. But he is restricted: he discovers the bipolarity of his nature, the good and evil to which he is shackled. Despite the everlastingness of evil, art allows man to move towards the good.[28] Art's role is to provide the human race with the means to recover its original state.

Leduc's work reflects this principle through the particular emphasis in his painting on means of communication, forms of passage and transitional states as subjects for meditation.[29] Some works deal specifically with passage from one place to another – *The Ferryman's House* (cat. 226), for example. Water, moreover, has a particular significance for Leduc; its magnetic fluidity links it to the sources that presided over the creation of the universe, and its movement is invariably present at key moments in human history.

The concept of transition runs through Leduc's painted and drawn production like a leitmotif. It gives concrete form to the passage between the material and spiritual worlds. Both the image of the Assumption and the trance-like state of a person in ecstasy are frequently used to symbolize a sublime manifestation of the reunion between man and God (cats. 12, 196). The notion of passage often takes the form of a landscape (cats. 154, 186) – the one that humanity must traverse in order to regain Paradise. In *Mary Hailed as Co-redeemer*, in the Bishop's Palace in Sherbrooke, Adam and Eve kneel at the foot of the fruit-laden Tree of Knowledge (cat. 176). The ground is rough, but it is Adam's proximity to a rocky gorge that is the real key to the earthly environment. Man can hope to re-enter Paradise by following this narrow, obstacle-strewn path. In *Day's End* (cat. 144), Leduc expressed the possibility of rising towards heaven – an ideal as yet only barely sug-

27 Several texts written between the 1920s and 1940 deal with this notion of man as a fallen god:

Man in the centre is God. Powerful, he constructs his work, he is its master, it seems. But he is subjected to it, it dominates him and even rejects him. What force it possesses! Powerful man is weak, he admires his work and admires himself in it.

Man in the centre – a god who crawls.

Man in the centre, a god: but weak, he judges his work, that he admires. He sees it as bigger than himself and attributes to it a mysterious power that he did not put there. Man in the centre? A god subjected – outside his realm.

Man at the centre admires himself in his work, he is God. And his work bears his stamp, and the stamp of nature that surrounds man. The power and weakness of man, here, beckon one another – Man only creates in obedience – he has seen himself as god – and wears shackles. (Typescript, dated June 8, 1935, cited in note 7.)

28 "Before there was no man
And the disorder of heaven was created because of him.
This being who once was not, sinned
Justice, mercy
An angel in hell
A Redeemer for a day-long Paradise, lost."
("Comprendre", BNQ 327/3/16.)

29 The constant recurrence in Leduc's work of the notion of passage seems to undermine a reading that perceives him as a painter of calm, stillness and immutable values.

gested – by evoking the act of struggling painfully up a narrow rope ladder to reach the top of a rocky cliff.

Within Leduc's vision, creative activity is often exemplified by a metaphor of alteration, the transformation of one form of matter into another: of intelligence and imagination into the concrete matter that is the work of art.

> The mind at work. Organization by the discipline of a creation rooted in the subconscious. A first idea? A gift that the artist will endeavour to develop, to transmute into a work, his image.
>
> The mind at work under the influence of the impulse to order: an escape to a true joy, the work at last crowned; a glory of the creative self.[30]

The artist's task is to bring about a transformation of matter. The subject of a number of Leduc's paintings is this operation itself, the moment of transfer from a natural to an idealized state. He shows art in the process of being made. Some of his portraits (cats. 131, 194, 231) depict their models emerging from a magma of warmly lit coloured matter, while the subject of his still lifes is often the act of creation itself (cats. 12, 90). His religious paintings focus on manifestations of the purifying effect of grace. In the major artistic legacy represented by the interior of Notre-Dame-de-la-Présentation, in Shawinigan-Sud (cats. 237-253), Leduc links the sacrifice of Christ to those of Abraham and Melchizedek. He also features the labour of the parishioners themselves, who achieve transcendence by working wood and earth, by making paper and forging metal. In the various forms of manual labour depicted, Leduc centres on the moment of transformation, the passage from one state to another: soil becomes fertile; impure ore becomes usable metal; wood fibre becomes paper. All these metamorphoses are linked to the sacrifice of the Eucharist, in which bread and wine are transformed into the body and blood of Christ. Qualitative change is likened to the process of creation, which also effects permutations: through knowledge, matter becomes a work of art.

Constantly seeking formal perfection, art is an ascent, a series of victories – over matter, nature and self.

Constantly pursuing an ideal, art is an exploration, a ceaseless quest to recapture the radiance of the Knowledge that once illuminated the human race and of which it retains both a memory and a need. With the tools at his disposal, the artist fashions the trophies of the struggle and points the way to the ascent. He opens up to us the walkways of a heavenly place, the garden where we long to live.

30 BNQ 327/3/17.

I had a dream
A dream of a Garden of beauty
as beautiful as Paradise Past.
The one before the Sin.
A garden of avenues
and winding paths,
travelled
by my haloed dream,
a dream of pasts long gone,
I had a dream,
A dream of a garden in paradise,
a paradise, a mirror in which Being dwells
Today, as long ago, I wandered through it.[31]

31 "J'ai fait ce rêve", BNQ 327/3/15. This poem was written in 1952 according to a letter dated September 17 of that year (private archive).

Leduc and Modernism

François-Marc Gagnon

THE person primarily responsible for the Quebec art world's unqualified alignment of Ozias Leduc with the modernist movement was undoubtedly Borduas. He was speaking, of course, of his personal debt to the old master of Saint-Hilaire; but in so doing, he revealed how Leduc had shown the way. "I owe to him", he wrote, "… the freedom to pass from the spiritual and pictorial atmosphere of the Renaissance to the power of the dream which opens upon the future".[1] Given that for Borduas the "Renaissance" was virtually synonymous with "academism" (for in striving to re-create Antiquity, he felt, the Renaissance had invented nothing), this statement amounts to a declaration of Leduc's total allegiance to the camp of "living art". And in fact, within Borduas's view, the "dream which opens upon the future" could only be surrealism.

Borduas's conviction gains additional weight when we realize that he did not, as many have since, see Leduc's religious and secular production as separate, mistakenly believing that ensuring the artist's position in the "modernist camp" depends on discounting his religious work. It should be recalled that Borduas's first real contact with Leduc occurred in Sherbrooke, where he acted as assistant to the master on a church decoration project. In fact, one of the three examples Borduas later offers of the "magic of the dream" from which Leduc's life "streamed" – this is his word – actually concerns religious painting and, more specifically, the interior of the Bishop's Chapel in Sherbrooke, in which he had played a modest part. Borduas wrote, "I see him fashioning an irretrievably blind peep-hole, stuck flatly on the full panel of the door to his studio; sealing with the point of a pencil, twenty five feet high in a chapel vault, the tiny white holes left in plaster by the needles used to

1 Paul-Émile Borduas, "Quelques pensées sur l'œuvre d'amour et de rêve de M. Ozias Leduc", *Canadian Art*, vol. 10, no, 4 (Summer 1953), p. 161; quoted in English from Paul-Émile Borduas, *Écrits/Writings 1942–1958*, trans. François-Marc Gagnon and Dennis Young (Halifax: The Press of the Nova Scotia College of Art and Design, 1978), p. 132.

hold the stencils in position; filling with sweet toil, over years, the smallest picture."[2]

The first example is fascinating, for it focusses not on a painting but on an object – better, a simulacrum of an object: a fake peephole. Making a peephole usually consists of piercing a small hole in a floor, a wall or more frequently a door, in order to see without being seen. These days, peepholes are fitted with a one-way lens that allows a dwelling's occupant to see who has come knocking without themselves being under surveillance. If the visitor is unwelcome, one simply has to lie low until they retreat, congratulating oneself the while on this small exercise of power. But of what conceivable use is a blind peephole? It would be as if Duchamp had constructed the entire mechanism of *Étant donnés* only to render it inaccessible by representing the small holes – through which we now view the spectacle – in trompe-l'oeil.[3] In other words, with a blind peephole, illusionism blocks the gaze and frustrates (thus exacerbating) the desire to see and transform the "for self" of the voyeur into "in itself", just as surely as if the voyeur were himself seen, as in Sartre's example, by another person.[4] Except that here the other person is not really "another", since the person likely to be frustrated by the peephole is the very one who created it! There must be some other reason for its existence. In truth, making a blind peephole means renouncing that small power over the person mentioned earlier who comes knocking at one's door, welcome or not. A blind peephole is thus the perfect symbol of welcome, of a heart open to all. The eye of the painter rejects the role of voyeur, and while it may seem absorbed by the surface of things, we should understand that it is more interested in what appearances hide than in what they reveal. Leduc's painting cannot be simply illusion. It aims much higher. A curious reversal, then, in which the resources of illusionism are employed in its own denunciation.

Borduas's second example seems to denote a rare rigour of craftsmanship: what is the point of filling in holes that are invisible from the spectator's position below? But, more important, what does such an act have to do with the "magic of the dream"? Are we to assume that this meticulous finishing work was accomplished to satisfy some dream self, capable of gliding twenty-five feet above the ground? In fact, here again the act is of significance not to the potential spectator, but to the painter himself. The spectator will never know whether the holes are filled or not, unless someone tells him. But the painter would be unable to forget. It is not so much that the ornamental stencilled band with its pin holes is an unfinished work that the artist, as a matter of conscience,

2   *Ibid.*

3   Anne de Harnoncourt and Walter Hopps, *Étant Donnés: 1° la chute d'eau 2° le gaz d'éclairage. Reflection on a New Work by Marcel Duchamp* (Philadelphia Museum of Art, 1987).

4   Sartre in the chapter on "The Look" in *Being and Nothingness*, quoted by Rosalind Krauss, *The Optical Unconscious* (Cambridge, Massachusetts and London: MIT Press, 1993), p. 112.

feels obliged to complete. It is that the ceiling, which from below appears finished without actually being so, is a false thing. It creates the illusion of being finished, but is actually not. For Leduc, the imperatives of being were always more urgent than the mirages of appearance. Once again, illusionism is denounced, this time not by itself, but by the absurd task, by the pencil point that blackens each white speck where the plaster shows through.

And what, finally, can we say about the "sweet toil" of Borduas's third example, which involved the reworking "over years" of his smallest pictures? Do we deduce that Leduc was subject to a never entirely satisfied desire to recreate reality, a desire foiled by the endless transformation of his subjects? This, certainly, is what is suggested by the anecdote recounted often by Riopelle, which has Leduc redoing the same painting over and over.

> The most important influence on me was certainly Ozias Leduc. When I visited him, he was an old man. He lived in a hut and everyone thought he was crazy. He was a great painter. He could spend three, four years on a painting. When he painted a tree, he followed its progress meticulously through the seasons. In the spring, he put buds on the branches; in the autumn, he made the leaves fall; in winter, he put snow on it. Gradually, a thick crust would be formed – and then, he would work on the painting again for twenty minutes and finish it, and it would be a masterpiece.[5]

Although probably apocryphal, this story possesses a certain charm. It depicts Leduc as a sort of Canadian Douanier Rousseau – a notion that would have appealed to Borduas, who called him "a distant brother of Douanier Rousseau, or of Facteur Cheval. But", he added, "a brother who would have hesitated to abandon the rational." But is it so naïve, this idea of capturing all the various forms of a subject in a single painting? It seems rather to echo something that the academic American painter Frederick Edwin Church wrote in his diary in 1857: "I commenced to sketch the effect as rapidly as possible but constant changes took place and new beauties revealed themselves as the setting sun turned the black smoke into burnished copper and the white steam into gold … I was so delighted with the changing effects that I continued making rapid sketches."[6] But the evocation of Church's glowing landscapes takes us very far from Leduc, whose works in this genre are, by comparison, discretion itself.[7]

In fact, what Borduas describes in his final example was filmed by Abbé Albert Tessier. In the footage, we see the old painter sitting on a window sill, running his fingertips over the rough surface of a small painting, retouching what has already been worked on countless times

5 Jean-Louis Prat, ed., *Jean-Paul Riopelle*, exhib. cat. (Montreal: Montreal Museum of Fine Arts, 1991), pp. 193-194.

6 Quoted in Barbara Novak, "The Meteorological Vision: Clouds", *Art in America*, vol. 68, no. 2 (February 1980), p. 112.

7 See for example Church's *Twilight in the Wilderness*, 1860, Cleveland Museum of Art.

before. Nothing seems further from the artist's mind than resemblance to the real world. He does not look out. He shows no interest in the tree that was purportedly his model. He looks at the canvas. Perhaps he is looking inside himself, seeking yet again the truth that lies beyond appearances. Reworking a small picture, covering it with a new layer of paint, means sacrificing something that corresponded only approximately to the idea originally aspired to. It also means that one's primary concern is not likeness to a subject, but realization of an idea.

The "dream which opens upon the future" is thus the opposite of illusion. It is the quest for a truth that invariably transcends appearances. But what truth is this? We might imagine that it is that sublime truth lying within the mysteries of faith. And in a way, we would be right. (Most of Leduc's career was, after all, devoted to church decoration projects.) But only in the sense that faith presupposes the existence of an invisible world that matters more than the visible one, of presences more intense than those we see, of a depth to sensual experience. In short, a soul behind each face. For Leduc, faith itself becomes a metaphor for art.

So how do we explain Leduc's fascination with photography and trompe-l'oeil? At first view, there seems to be a perfect affinity between these two interests. A photograph, explains Barthes, "is never distinguished from its referent (from what it represents), or at least it is not *immediately* or *generally* distinguished from its referent". Admittedly, certain professionals are able to perceive the photographic signifier, but for ordinary people, in a photo "a pipe ... is always and intractably a pipe".[8] And this is surely also the case with a trompe-l'oeil painting, whose goal is to become so transparent to the spectator that its existence as a painting is forgotten. There is nevertheless an enormous difference between photography and painting, trompe-l'oeil or otherwise. Trompe-l'oeil does not "deceive the eye" for long. As the philosopher Richard Wollheim has explained, we are capable of a kind of "seeing-in" that permits us to see the subject of the paintings we look at without losing sight of what it is in them we are being shown.[9]

In concrete terms, the spectator only needs to shift a little when standing before the work to realize that a particular shadow is painted, not real, that a particular mark is represented, not carved. In other words, however transparent it might try to be, a trompe-l'oeil painting soon reveals itself to be exactly that – a painting. Only a photograph, says Barthes, remains unencumbered by "the way in which the object is simulated", so close is its link to the referent. Trompe-l'oeil is, by contrast, so encumbered by representation that it denies itself the spatial

8 Roland Barthes, *La chambre claire. Notes sur la photographie* (Paris: Cahiers du cinéma, Gallimard Seuil, 1980), pp. 16-17; quoted in English from *Camera Lucida: Reflections on Photography*, trans. Richard Howard (New York: Hill and Wang, 1981), p. 5.

9 Richard Wollheim, *Painting as an Art* (London: Thames and Hudson, 1987), pp. 46-51.

devices used to suggest depth and, as a result, an infinity of possible subjects. The "best" examples of the genre, like those by the American painter William Harnett, are most successful when they portray simply letters and pieces of paper attached to a wall with tape and thumb tacks.[10]

The way Leduc employed the two mediums indicates that he was aware of the fundamental difference between them. It is my view that he perceived them as diametrically opposed activities – the one as more or less auxiliary to his painting and the other as a form of meta-painting. Photography seems to have been for Leduc a quick way of taking notes – of indicating the position of an ornamental element, of exploring a model's pose in preparation for a portrait, of recording the best location for the Choquette farm in a landscape (cat. 121) – never an end in itself. From a semiotic point of view, Leduc perceived the photograph as an analogon of reality, a site of pure denotation, a codeless message. The painting, on the other hand, and especially the trompe-l'oeil painting (and hence the series of still lifes) is invariably, for Leduc, a site of maximum connotation.

And what of Leduc's still lifes? Many of us are familiar with the small still life from 1887 that represents three apples in a shallow bowl sitting on the end of a bench (cat. 1). But at every attempt to examine it critically, one's head begins to spin. What is there to say about this little work? It seems hardly to require analysis. Yet its significance is not that obvious. Is it usual to put a bowl of apples on a bench? Are they not less accessible positioned thus than they would be on a table? Leduc thus forces us to see something that normally we would glance at only distractedly, just long enough to put out a hand in the right direction, take an apple and eat it. But the painter has been careful to place the apples beyond the reach of people in a hurry. The relationship with the spectator is therefore not as simple as it first appears. In fact, Leduc is not interested in the real relationship between an everyday object and its user. He "enunciates" the position of a painting's viewer in relation to the objects represented, which is not the same thing. This concept of the work's "enunciated subject" played an important role in literary and film criticism of the seventies and eighties.[11] Leduc's paintings, especially his portraits and landscapes, invariably include features intended to determine the spectator's ideal position, such as the swirling background of the *Portrait of Guy Delahaye* (fig. 49) and the shattered tree stump in the foreground of *Blue Cumulus* (cat. 143). These elements do not simply capture our attention – they provide us with the key to the painting. By closing off his composition on the left side with a highly

10 See, for example, Harnett's *The Artist's Letter Rack*, 1879, Metropolitan Museum of Art, reproduced in Doreen Bolger, Marc Simpson and John Wilmerding, *William M. Harnett* (New York: Amon Carter Museum and Metropolitan Museum of Art, 1992), p. 15.

11 See Johanna Drucker, *Theorizing Modernism: Visual Art and the Critical Tradition* (New York: Columbia University Press, 1994), pp. 141ff.

elaborate decorative ground whose symbolism various writers, following on from Jean-René Ostiguy,[12] have done their best to decipher, Leduc forces the spectator to reflect on the character of the poet portrayed. In the landscape, we perceive that the blue cumulus cloud magnificently filling the heavens is also the source of the thunderbolt that destroyed the great tree. Hence the significance of the splintered stump in the foreground.

But let us return to the three apples. Leduc has tackled his subject with all the enthusiasm of a minor seventeenth-century Dutch master, giving himself up to the pleasure of "description" in the sense that Svetlana Alpers uses the word.[13] Three textures of decreasing reflectivity are explored: the waxy skin of the apples, the more matte surface of the rough earthenware bowl and the even humbler wood. The three surfaces react differently to light: the apples reflect; the pottery partially reflects and partially absorbs; while the wood, with its dents, cracks and dowel-pin, simply absorbs. Painters never employ reflecting surfaces unthinkingly. Painting is often defined as the mirror of reality. Leduc is also fascinated by surfaces that bear marks: the wood of a bench or table, a letter with a used stamp, a beautiful and frequently handled book whose plates are protected with sheets of tissue paper. This motif will come up again.

Finally, in this small still life with three apples, the dark ground discourages any distraction of the eye. Here, Leduc shares a device employed by Zurbarán, who also thwarted all temptation to wander outside the visible field by giving his still lifes backgrounds of the deepest black. It is a practice, though, that Leduc did not pursue. In fact, he generally filled his backgrounds in, clearly perceiving them as surfaces too precious to be left empty.

It could be claimed that for Leduc there are two important paradigms of painting – the mirror and writing (or books) – that are only glimpsed in this work but that become much clearer in the later still lifes.

In *Still Life, Onions* (cat. 16), owned by the Musée d'art de Joliette, the reflection of the onions in the copper pot is already very explicit. It is a veritable tour de force, in fact, for the surface is convex and the mirror therefore distorts, offering an alternative scene to the one portrayed in the foreground. In *Phrenology* (cat. 12), the head of the compass, the base of the glass and the metal cap of a paint tube are reflected in the varnished surface of the table. But it is the little *Still Life (with Lay Figure)* (cat. 90) that pushes this device the furthest: in its centre is a mirror that reflects the contents of the studio, including the very paint-

12 Jean-René Ostiguy, *Ozias Leduc: Symbolist and Religious Painting*, exhib. cat. (Ottawa: National Gallery of Canada, 1974), pp. 143-144.

13 Svetlana Alpers, *The Art of Describing: Dutch Art in the Seventeenth Century* (Chicago: University of Chicago Press, 1983).

ing we are in the process of contemplating! But for Leduc, the painting is the mirror of reality, just as the eyes are the mirror of the soul. Or, if you will, the painting reflects in both senses of the word. Obviously, it presents a reflection of objects, but it also offers a reflection on the nature of painting itself. The following inscription is hidden beneath the edge of the frame of *Still Life (with Lay Figure)*: "Osias Leduc painted this picture in February and March 1898 in Saint-Henri de Montréal. Drawing, colour, composition: the painter's trinity." It is not by chance, then, that in the backgrounds of most of these still lifes can be seen reproductions of much-admired paintings – W. E. Frost's *Sabrina*, for example, which appears in at least two of them (see cat. 12). For the reflection on painting embodied in the still lifes is present throughout his oeuvre, including the ecclesiastical works.

Still Life (Three Pennies) (cat. 13), with its inclusion of a *Cupid* by the eighteenth-century German painter Anton Raffael Mengs and Guido Reni's *Saint Michael Slaying the Dragon*, contains allusions to painting as an art; but also, in its portrayal of various humble tools and materials – hinged ruler, pencil, pen and inkpot, bottles of linseed oil and varnish – as a craft. In this "classical" example of trompe-l'oeil, whose three coins spark a certain spontaneous cupidity (we recall the painted dollar bill of some American trompe-l'oeil works), the theme is extremely complex. And in fact the obvious subject is not so much the three pennies as the letters and their evocation of the to-and-fro between writer and receiver. For Leduc, the letter is a paradigm of the painting, not because a letter bears a stamp and a stamp is an image, but, more fundamentally, because a letter is a means of communicating thoughts through writing. For the Protestant theologian Comenius, the development of the letter rivalled the invention of printing and gunpowder in importance – and even Christopher Columbus's voyages to America. To support his view, he cited the Amerindian reaction to the European practice of exchanging letters: "Nor could the American Indians comprehend how one man is able to communicate his thought to another without the use of speech, without a messenger, but by simply sending a piece of paper. Yet with us a man of the meanest intelligence can understand this."[14]

The letter is a bearer of truth that operates at a distance. The same could be said of the books so often depicted by Leduc. And, indeed, of the greatest book of all, from which, as a church painter, he so often drew inspiration.

Leduc's religious painting is always contrasted with his still lifes – the major genre compared to the humbler one that developed late in the history of painting. Leduc's intensive practice of the two incompatible

14 Quoted in *ibid.*, p. 198.

forms is seen as paradoxical, an undermining of the eighteenth-century theoreticians who judged still life to be an ideal pursuit for those who had failed to achieve success in one of the great genres. But this is to forget that for Leduc, still life was the site of a critical assessment of painting, of his own painting, which is essentially a form of religious painting. This is not to say that his still lifes – or his landscapes, for that matter – embody some kind of religious symbolism similar to that required by his religious commissions. But it is hardly surprising that a painter who spent his life translating the written word into images should have investigated in his paintings the respective scope of the text and the figure. In all religious painting, there are two distinct levels: the "discursive" and the "figural". The first is related to the text and determines the theme; the second refers to what enables the discursive to be rendered in painting.

To be understood, the subject portrayed must be recognizable and therefore to some extent already known. The subjects of religious painting were drawn from the Old and New Testaments, the lives of the saints and traditional teachings. They were recognizable not because the works' commissioners and their audiences – the clergy and their flocks – knew the Bible and the lives of the saints by heart, but because they were already familiar with the stories and a particular way of telling them through painting. In other words, the spectators Leduc was addressing were in possession of a code that enabled them to immediately recognize a naked couple in a grove as Adam and Eve being tempted by the serpent (cats. 241-244), a young woman being carried skyward by angels as an Assumption (cat. 8), and an elderly bishop bringing a dead child back to life as Saint Hilary (cats. 24-27) – on the condition that the painter included a few additional conventions, such as the serpent curled around the Tree of the Knowledge of Good and Evil, the haloes, the angels' wings and the bishop's mitre.

Iconographical codes are not foolproof, of course. It is perfectly possible for a particular spectator to make a mistake in his iconographical decoding of a painting and to assign it the wrong subject. Or simply not to know the code. Nevertheless, by definition a code can be learned, and in the case of a religious code, it can be learned from books. These themes have, indeed, been so regularized by tradition and teaching that it is not hard to arrive at the right interpretation.

But the meaning of a painting is not exhausted when we have discovered its subject. A painting always contains elements that enable us to transcend this first level of iconographical interpretation. A painting always presents us with an excess of information that is semantically neutral. This excess information is extremely important, for it is at this level that the painter's originality can be expressed, that Leduc could leave his mark, transmit his way of thinking. The further this type of information seems to move away from the first level, the more an effect of verisimilitude is created in the painting, because this movement is read as movement towards the real. Verisimilitude is not an automatic result of the pictorial procedure, as in photography. It is achieved in part through the painter's skill, but above all by his use of the four "codes" that determine the figures' facial features, poses and clothing, and the setting in which they are placed. For example, nothing in traditional accounts of the Assumption stipulates that the Virgin must have her eyes raised towards Heaven and her hands clasped on her breast, or that she be wearing a long, flowing dress and be surrounded by clouds. Or that she be pictured minus the crescent moon generally shown beneath her feet in representations of the Immaculate Conception. Nevertheless, all these clues are an integral part of the image. When, in addition, the painter decides to portray the Virgin's age, her facial features, the colour of her gown and the number of accompanying angels, he moves even further from the textual data and, in so doing, imbues the image with even greater verisimilitude. In religious painting, each detail not supplied by the text but confirming it and giving it substance produces what has been called the "effect of the real".[15]

It would be possible to define still life and landscape as genres in which references to reality take on such importance that the text disappears altogether. This is only partially true in Leduc's case, however, for he invariably succeeds in giving a symbolic meaning to his still lifes and landscapes, thereby establishing a link if not with a specific text at least with a form of decodable discourse, which in the case of the still lifes focusses on the art of painting itself.

By opening a book at a page showing a reproduction of a Botticelli Madonna, and particularly by concealing the printed text under a protective sheet of tissue paper, Leduc shows how, in attaining the figural, the discursive must necessarily be transcended. Hardly surprising, then, that he should place behind this beautiful book a pile of old, greenbacked journals, like a collection of now useless tools. In *Phrenology*, a treatise on art anatomy even serves as a base for the phrenological head portrayed; and in *Still Life (with Lay Figure)*, a sketchbook predominates over the magazines[16] on which the model and letter opener are placed.

We must now conclude by weaving together the three threads we have identified in the work of Ozias Leduc: the awareness of the limits

15 See Norman Bryson, *Vision and Painting: The Logic of the Gaze* (New Haven and London: Yale University Press, 1983), p. 62.

16 The dates on the spines – April 1897 and June 1897 – indicate that they are copies of an English-language publication, possibly *The Studio*.

of pictorial illusionism, the critical assessment of painting, and the predominance of the figural over the discursive. Leduc's "trinity", one might be tempted to suggest! But (a fact often overlooked), also the "trinity" of modernist painting itself. For the practitioners of modernism rejected illusionism and embarked on the inexorable pursuit of innate truth, reflected ceaselessly on the act of painting and freed us from all the old ties that linked iconography to mythological and religious texts. This is what made Leduc's oeuvre of such vital importance in Quebec's move towards modernism and justifies our returning to it frequently as a basic source. That Leduc was able to point the way to the path "which opens upon the future" while working as an ecclesiastical painter – leaving his mountain only reluctantly and returning always, to Correlieu – is truly extraordinary. It proves, in fact, that he was one of the subtlest and most intelligent figures in the history of Quebec painting. It was Borduas's good luck to have encountered him very early in his development. "I owe to him", Borduas wrote, "that rare permission to pursue one's own fate."[17] May Leduc's other successors acknowledge the same debt.

17 Borduas 1978, p. 132.

"Authenticity" and the Rhetoric of Presentation

The Bibliothèque Saint-Sulpice Exhibition of 1916
and the Critical Reception of Ozias Leduc

ARLENE GEHMACHER

1 Lucien de Riverolles, "Chronique artistique: O. Leduc", *L'Opinion publique* [Montreal], vol. 1, no. 18 (April 14, 1893), p. 284.

2 Gilles Corbeil *et al.*, "Hommage à Ozias Leduc", special issue of *Arts et pensée*, vol. 3, no. 18 (July-August 1954).

3 For critical discussion of Romantic aesthetic theory, see M. H. Abrams, *The Mirror and the Lamp: Romantic Theory and the Critical Tradition* (New York: Oxford University Press, 1953); Raymond Williams, *Culture and Society, 1780-1950*, revised edition (New York: Columbia University Press, 1983); August Wiedmann, *Romantic Art Theories* (Oxfordshire: Gresham Books, 1986); and Charles Taylor, *The Malaise of Modernity* (Concord, Ontario: Anansi Press, 1991; subsequently published as *The Ethics of Authenticity* [Cambridge, Massachusetts: Harvard University Press, 1992]).

4 This simile was used by Hippolyte Taine (1828-1893) in "De la production de l'œuvre d'art", Chapter 2 of his *Philosophie de l'art* (Paris, 1865; 2nd edition, enlarged, Paris, 1880; ed. Stéphane Douailler [Paris]: Fayard, 1985), pp. 43-47. For an investigation of the concept of environmental determinism and its basis in nineteenth-century German philosophy, see Timothy Mitchell, "Bound by Time and Place: The Art of Caspar David Friedrich", *Arts Magazine*, vol. 61, no. 3 (November 1986), pp. 48-53.

5 On organicism, see Wiedmann 1986, pp. 89-100.

I F there is a leitmotif in the critical reviews of Leduc's work throughout his career, it would surely be the concept of "authenticity". From the earliest monographic article on Leduc (1893)[1] right up to the special 1954 issue of *Arts et pensée*[2] devoted entirely to the artist, this concept has played various roles. For along with validating Leduc's artistic production and characterizing its essence, the concept has frequently assumed the status of a rhetorical device, used by commentators and critics of varying ideological persuasions to address different and at times competing concerns and issues specific to the shifting social landscape of French Quebec. But the spate of reviews triggered by Leduc's first solo exhibition, held at the Bibliothèque Saint-Sulpice in Montreal from February 20 to March 15, 1916, expressed the concept of authenticity most forcefully and provided a source for all subsequent invocations of the theme. The critics applied the notion to the sincerity and originality of Leduc's artistic expression, generally ascribing these qualities to his close relationship to nature. In accordance with nineteenth-century Romantic aesthetic theory, this relationship was understood basically in two ways.[3]

The first approach, "environmental determinism", held that the artist, like all human beings, is formed by his natural environment: the artist springs from the soil like a plant.[4] In Leduc's case, reference was usually made to the predominant influence of his immediate surroundings of Saint-Hilaire.

The second theoretical approach, generally called "organicism",[5] maintained that an artist seeks out the path to his innate creative forces by looking to the creative forces of nature. The artist's role is not to reproduce visible nature but to tap the primal energy within, his creative impulses thus emulating those of nature. In 1893, Leduc is quoted as saying, "Art cannot be taught … Nature is suggestive, containing the idea and the means of expressing it."[6] Thus, by downplaying the role of artistic tradition in the formation of the artist and elevating the inner workings of nature in the creative process, Leduc aligned himself with the organicist view.

Depending on whether the environmental determinist or the organicist way of thinking was emphasized, the notion of authenticity, as expressed in the intimate connection between artist and nature, could be adapted to suit the individual points of view of commentators promoting quite divergent agendas. This adaptability is markedly evident in the four essays written in response to Leduc's first retrospective exhibition at the Bibliothèque Saint-Sulpice.

This exhibition took place during a period when French Quebec was seeking ways to strengthen its cultural identity. However, there were varying, even conflicting, approaches to the common goal of defining the character of French-Canadian society. On the one hand were those who promoted a clerico-regionalist ideology that embraced the traditional morals, customs and values of French-Canadian culture. This point of view was embodied in the time-honoured notions of *le terroir*, or rural tradition, and *la patrie*, the attachment to one's native soil. On the other hand were those who, rejecting the collective traditionalist approach, turned to France and the United States for the modern values that accompanied the rise of the metropolis and the push to engage in free enterprise. For them, individual liberty and self-expression were the ideals to which contemporary French-Canadian society should aspire.[7] Both ideologies – traditionalist and progressive – are evident in the reactions to Leduc's exhibition at the Bibliothèque Saint-Sulpice. Although the critics' presentations of Leduc and his art had much in common, when one considers the authors' background and relation to the cultural milieu, it becomes apparent that, with one exception, each emphasized one ideology or the other.

The article showing the most pronounced progressive leanings was by Leduc's friend the author Robert LaRoque de Roquebrune (cat. 155). Roquebrune was sympathetic to a small group of francophile French-Canadian poets and writers in Montreal whose literary ideals, rooted in the Symbolist aesthetic, challenged the conventions of regionalist French-Canadian literature in both style and content.[8] Promoting the expression of universal subjects, such as "man" and "the passions", whose inspiration originated from within the artist, they espoused a modernist ideal of a French-Canadian artistic culture.[9] Roquebrune's essay was

6 Riverolles 1893. Environmental determinism is also integral to Riverolles's consideration of Leduc as an essential artist: "Born in a parish where picturesque sites abound," he informed his readers, "he began to love nature at a tender age. Without the help of any teacher, without a single lesson, he became an artist … The place where he was born no doubt greatly aided this young artist's vocation. Accustomed early on to admiring nature, he later applied himself to reproducing it."

7 These ideals were promoted by the likes of economist Édouard Montpetit, a professor at the University of Montreal. See Laurier Lacroix, "Entre l'Érable et le Laurier", *The Journal of Canadian Art History*, vol. 13, no. 2 (1990)/vol. 14, no. 1 (1991), pp. 154-172. Leduc admired Montpetit, to whom he was introduced by Olivier Maurault (cats. 161-163), possibly as early as 1918.

8 The debate between the literary "regionalists" and the "exotics" is addressed in Annette Hayward, "Le Conflit entre les Régionalistes et les 'Exotiques' au Québec (1900-1920)", Ph.D. dissertation, McGill University, 1980.

9 Throughout 1918, these ideals found their most eloquent expression, and defence, in the periodical *Le Nigog*. See, for example, Fernand Préfontaine, "L'art et le régionalisme", *Le Nigog*, vol. 1, no. 11 (November 1918), p. 378. The monthly was published by the group of the same name, whose membership included, in addition to Préfontaine, such progressives as Roquebrune, Léo-Pol Morin, Marcel Dugas and Guillaume Lahaise. Leduc executed the drawing for the cover of the magazine (fig. 111). Regarding the group and the periodical, see *Le Nigog* (Montreal: Fides, 1987), "Archives des lettres canadiennes", vol. 7.

published in the newspaper *L'Action* the day before the exhibition's official opening;[10] an abbreviated version appeared in the pamphlet-catalogue. The second paragraph of the newspaper version, in characterizing Leduc's art as "original", evoked both the environmental determinist and the organicist aspects of Romantic thought, the latter more strongly.

> We feel entirely justified in declaring Leduc, along with Cullen and Adrien Hébert, the most original of the exhibitors at the latest painting Salons. His art is free of those eccentricities of technique by means of which many painters since Manet have been trying to capture the attention of critics and the public. The quest for novelty may result in something fine, like Impressionism, but it may also lead vision totally awry, as with the recent Cubism, whose endeavours must not however be entirely condemned, for they may yet produce some better works. Leduc has none of these curiosities or preoccupations with style. A landscapist, he has translated nature with a moved soul and an idealist brush. Having lived an existence, a very noble existence, amid art and nature, he has subjected the latter to the former, ennobling it in the process. There are those who like to take nature by surprise and brusquely transcribe it in the raw. Nature is beautiful enough to remain so in copies made in this manner. But there are others who wish to arrange nature according to an ideal, according to a dream, and this is what Leduc does. His large panel … *Green Apples* is a breathtakingly magnificent composition that reveals the artist's decorative mastery. The painting of a poet. In fact, an intense lyricism emanates from this painter's most recent works. A high-minded lyricism, precise and devoid of artifice and false accessories.
>
> The small canvas from the most recent Salon represents nothing, pictorially, but a viaduct in the gathering night. But a night charged with mystery, shimmering and rustling, where the great span of a bridge assumes the appearance of a triumphal arch awaiting the sun's rays.[11]

Roquebrune justifies his reference to Leduc as "original" by dissociating the artist both from the more radical of recent developments, which he finds overly self-conscious, and from the work of painters who simply record nature as they see it. Leduc rises above these poseurs and transcribers because his art idealizes nature. This approach, stemming from a consonance with nature, results not in stylistic gratuitousness or slavish copying but in pictorial poems, subjective responses to nature that originate deep within the artist's self. They are, it would appear, the ultimate in authentic artistic expression.

10 Robert de Roquebrune, "L'exposition Leduc", *L'Action* [Montreal], February 19, 1916, p. 1.

11 *Ibid.* "The small canvas from the most recent Salon" refers to *The Concrete Bridge* (cat. 149), which Leduc exhibited at the Royal Canadian Academy Exhibition of 1915 in Montreal.

Roquebrune's recognition of the significance of Leduc's interiority – his "moved soul", his "dream" – to the creative process contributed to his placing of Leduc in the modern camp. This classification is re-inforced by the critic's decision to refer only to Leduc's Symbolist landscapes, even though the exhibition included several other genres in a wide range styles. It is further reinforced by the terminology he employed to discuss them. The word "decorative", for example, used in describing *Green Apples* (cat. 148), connotes an absence of anecdote or other readily identifiable subject; "mystery", characterizing the essence of *The Concrete Bridge* (cat. 149), implies the vague and intangible. Neither word would appear in the aesthetic vocabulary of the clerico-nationalist sympathizers, who preferred pictures like those by Clarence Gagnon, Suzor-Coté and E.-J. Massicotte – pictures that celebrated *le terroir* and *la patrie*, nostalgically affirming the traditional values of French-Canadian society, in a direct and naturalistic manner.[12]

The implication that Leduc's art was "modern", however, did not necessarily suggest that Leduc was divorced from tradition. Using the concept of authenticity to promote a more progressive visual culture, Rocquebrune nevertheless presented it in such a way as to reassure his readers that the traditional values of French-Canadian society would not be hopelessly subverted by a modernist approach. Although Roquebrune's preference may have been for Symbolist landscape, the primary significance of such painting lay in its being landscape, pure and simple. In calling Leduc a landscapist, in setting his work apart from the self-indulgent whimsies of contemporary art, in linking the notion of the intimacy between nature and Leduc's artistic impulses to a discussion of two of the painter's landscapes (regardless of their Symbolist or modern qualities), Roquebrune could soften his rhetori-cal stance by evoking the rural tradition and attachment to the soil. In so doing, he was promoting Leduc as a modernist while keeping him and his art palatable to French Canadians who held to traditional values.

The divergence in the interpretation of authenticity revolved around the question of how art could best help to perpetuate the French-Canadian community, whose survival had been of increasing concern owing to political developments that were perceived as posing a threat to the culture of French Quebec.[13] In fact, *L'Action*, in which Roquebrune's essay appeared, dealt largely with nationalist concerns.[14] The critic begins his article by positing art as a means for affirming identity.

The day when French Canadians will be in possession of an authentic artistic voice is when they will be on the point of being saved. An art

12 Olivier Maurault, though he privately displayed liberal tendencies (he was a contributor to *Le Nigog*), publicly promoted such traditional values. Writing in the conservative periodical *Action française*, where he toed the clerico-nationalist line, he acknowledged the achievements of artists who had been inspired by "a subject about this place, about where we live … our country and the things of our coun-try … our fine history, our rich and varied seasons, our truly picturesque country folk." He refers to Gagnon's "winter landscapes", Suzor-Coté's "heads of robust Canadians" and E.-J. Massicotte's "scenes of daily customs". (Olivier Maurault, "Tendances de l'art canadien", *Action française*, vol. 2, no. 8 [August 1918], pp. 371-372.)

13 Consider, for example, Ontario's Regulation 17, in effect from 1915, which restricted instruction in and of the French language, as well as the tensions between English and French Canada raised by the issue of Canada's participation in the war effort. See Robert Rumilly, *Histoire de la Province de Québec*, vol. 20: *Philippe Landry* (Montreal: Montréal Editions, undated), especially Chapter 6, "Que devons-nous à l'Angleterre?" (pp. 125-142), which highlights the close connection between French Canada's resistance to Regulation 17 and enlistment propaganda. See also Robert Craig Brown and Ramsay Cook, *Canada, 1896-1921: A Nation Transformed* (Toronto: McClelland and Steward Ltd., 1974), Chapters 13 and 14 (pp. 250-293).

14 Robert de Roquebrune, *Cherchant mes souvenirs (1911-1940)* (Montreal: Fides, 1968), p. 99, refers to *L'Action* (without, however, naming it) as a "political" newspaper, explaining how it "attacked those it judged wrongdoers or stupid".

devoid of clichés, conventional stereotypes and pastiche, a truly ethnic art, if we may say so, will be the clearest evidence of a strong race, brimming with intellectual vitality and activity. Architecture, literature, visual art and music born of the French-Canadian genius would speak up clearly for a race that would become more and more difficult to betray and persecute. It is thus of immediate practical concern – almost a duty, even – to encourage the efforts of national artists. It behooves even those who are strangers to art to take an interest in the work being done by the French architects, writers and painters of Canada. In the presence of a painting like that of D. [*sic*] Leduc, it becomes essential that everyone understand and like it.

The question of race entirely apart (and it is certainly surprising to find it intervening in a discussion of such matters), we feel entirely justified in declaring Leduc, along with Cullen and Adrien Hébert, the most original of the exhibitors at the latest painting Salons.[15]

Roquebrune makes a case not for the mere preservation of traditional modes of artistic expression, but for the development of a vital and truly French-Canadian visual culture. He holds up the work of Leduc and two fellow artists as shining examples, superior to the mass of English-Canadian artists with whom they had recently exhibited. His exhortation against "eccentricities of technique" also takes on a nationalistic flavour when one considers that three years before, the Annual Spring Exhibition of the Art Association of Montreal had featured several English-Canadian disciples of Post-Impressionism, whose works, especially those of John Lyman, A. Y. Jackson and Randolph Hewton, were considered offensive and duly ridiculed in the press.[16]

But attempts like Roquebrune's to propose that the surest way to cultural survival was the path of modernism – that is, the expression of universal ideas through the free expression of the artist's self – were roundly criticized by the traditionalists as tantamount to antinationalism. Whereas Roquebrune advocated the encouragement of nontraditional views of art and artists, the ruralists feared that succumbing to the allure of "novelty" would lead society away from its roots, at the expense of its identity. "We must react and struggle against novelty," Abbé Camille Roy advised, "or else we must alter the soul of our native land. That is why it is always a failing and a betrayal of the race to forget traditions. We French Canadians do cultivate respect for traditions, but less so today than in the past. We are too overrun with foreign influences – English, French and American. It will always be of value to remind French Canadians that remaining faithful to tradition is a sacred duty."[17]

The articles that followed Roquebrune's essay were all in one way or another indebted to it, but not all shared his ideological bent. The

15 Roquebrune 1916.

16 See, for example, "Post-Impressionists Shock Local Art Lovers at the Spring Art Exhibition", *The Montreal Daily Witness*, March 26, 1913, p. 5; and S. M[organ]-Powell, "Art and the Post-Impressionists", *Montreal Daily Star*, March 29, 1913, p. 22.

17 Quoted from "Revenons au culte des traditions nationales", *Le Canada* [Montreal], December 15, 1916, p. 8. The quotation is from a speech Roy delivered to the "parish circle" of the Church of Saint-Enfant-Jésus, Mile-End, Montreal, whose curé, Philippe Perrier, was a well-known Ultramontanist.

concept of authenticity wears a more traditional, less overtly political guise in the article entitled "Un peintre de 'chez nous'", by Leduc's fellow Saint-Hilairean Ruth Bohème (pseudonym of Fernande Choquette, daughter of Ernest Choquette, whose rural novel *Claude Paysan* Leduc had illustrated in 1899).[18] Although Bohème was not an established critic like the others who responded directly or indirectly to the exhibition, her expression of the concept was the one most consistently adopted by later commentators.[19] She offers a vivid, highly romanticized account of the effect of the Saint-Hilaire environs on Leduc's evolution as an artist, thus identifying the idea of authenticity in Leduc's work in terms of a symbiosis of art and nature. She presents the artist as isolated on his mountain, an autodidact who was the exclusive product of his natural environment and who acquired a profound and vast knowledge from communing with the land. Purity, sincerity and life imbue his work.

> Mr. Leduc grew up with a painter's soul and came to be an artist by virtue of having breathed in the scent of hay and from hearing, on balmy evenings, the sound of water gurgling through the gully. The rhythm of the blacksmith's hammer from the nearby forge rang all the way to their orchard, and the drowsy sound of the great millwheel proved to him that there is nothing in the world like one's native soil, no greater life than that of simply continuing to extol, in words and deeds, the old earth that nurtured his father and his father's father.
>
> One day, he took up a pencil and, at first naïvely, then with greater control over the results, captured on paper the beloved images, the most beautiful peaks … and the time came when, to his amazement, he discovered that he had transferred to his canvases his own heart and mind.[20]

Bohème goes on to equate humility with truth and to maintain it is to the land that Leduc owes his sincere and gentle soul.[21] The author takes her cue from Roquebrune in referring to the absence from Leduc's work of ephemeral, if fashionable, stylistic approaches. "These are not the futuristic and neurotic images conceived by certain hallucinating intellects," she asserts. No, Leduc is firmly grounded, in harmonious existence with his environment. The miraculous transformation of the surrounding landscape into images resonant of the artist's soul springs from his being nurtured and cultivated by the land of his ancestors – the French-Canadian soil. In Bohème's word's, he is a "child of the earth and of the mountain."[22] In other words, he grew – like a plant – in Saint-Hilaire; his art is intrinsically French-Canadian.

Referring to "our mountains" in a simple but forceful echo of the "chez nous" in the article's title, Bohème makes it clear that she too

18 Ruth Bohème, "Un peintre de 'chez nous'", *La Patrie* [Montreal], March 11, 1916, p. 19.

19 In 1928, Arthur Lemay concentrated on the artist-*terroir* analogy, invoking both Leduc's life as an apple farmer and his art. Reaching back to Leduc's earlier work (cats. 95, 120, 122), Lemay used it to promote the clerico-nationalist colonization programme that encouraged the clearing and settling of land as a way of perpetuating the traditional rural way of life. (Arthur Lemay, "Un artiste du terroir à St-Hilaire de Rouville: l'œuvre du peintre Osias Leduc", *Le Terroir*, vol. 8, nos. 11-12 [March-April 1928], cover, pp. 186-187.) That same year, Jean Chauvin, a progressive at heart, interviewed Leduc, who presented himself as a renewer of church decoration, leading Chauvin to present him as a priestly figure – as had Bohème – who built his studio stone by stone in the tradition of medieval artisans (it was actually made of wood). See Jean Chauvin, *Ateliers: études sur vingt-deux peintres et sculpteurs canadiens* (Montreal and New York: Louis Carrier and Co., 1928), pp. 118-126.

20 Bohème 1916, p. 19.

21 *Ibid.*

22 *Ibid.*

hails from around Saint-Hilaire. On one level, this creates the sense of an intimate, closely knit community within the *terroir-patrie* of Saint-Hilaire. But at the same time, it broadens the title, situated directly beneath *La Patrie*'s page banner, from a "chez nous" meaning Saint-Hilaire, to a "chez nous" meaning Quebec.

Though Bohème's prime concern may not have been to promote a political agenda, the particularization of the artist-land relationship on this more literal level would seem to tend towards the espousal of the *petite patrie* that informed the conservative clerico-nationalist ideology. Indeed, Bohème's narrative image of Leduc's immediate surroundings in the countryside could be read as an endorsement of regionalist ideology and is perhaps itself an example of regionalist journalism. The author also describes the isolation of this "countrified" artist, claiming that his solitude within his surroundings is what makes him what he is: "Born far from the city in this remote landscape; child of the land and of the mountain; doubly countrified, his work, it goes without saying, is healthy and fresh."

By portraying Leduc as solitary as well as geographically isolated, Bohème goes beyond the usual regionalist scenario.

> If one day you are passing through our mountains and you spy, in the shady distant corner of an orchard, set far back from the main road, a house that should be called "Peace", push open the wooden gate in the fence and make your way silently down its short grassy path and knock at the door of this lovely retreat where a great artist hides.[23]

Free of external influences, the artist can be wholly himself. Furthermore, Bohème suggests that Leduc was not only geographically isolated – spiritually, too, he dwelt in another world. She would make his home a pilgrimage site: "You will surely thank me for having pointed out the happy abode surrounded by calm silence." The author assures the reader that "there you will spend … the most lucid hour of your whole life."[24] The sense of visionary mysticism evoked is heightened in her subsequent casting of Leduc as "priest" and "poet". Given the overwhelming sense of *terroir* and *patrie* that infuses the article, the identification of Leduc as an authentic seems to result more from idealizing the conduciveness of Saint-Hilaire's rural quietude to artistic creation than from any reference to the modernist self. And the very term "priest" suggests the clerical tradition.

The article "L'exposition Leduc" by Émile Vézina, an artist who doubled as art critic, was no doubt a direct response to Roquebrune's critique.[25] But Vézina evinces no ideological bent, progressive or otherwise; rather, his concern is first and foremost for matters artistic. He

23 *Ibid.*

24 *Ibid.*

25 Émile Vézina, "L'exposition Leduc", *Le Devoir* [Montreal], February 21, 1916, p. 1. Vézina was known primarily as a portraitist and illustrator. See Léon Lorrain, "Une toile d'Émile Vézina", *Le Nationaliste* [Montreal], January 29, 1911, p. 1; "M. Émile Vézina", *Le Nationaliste* [Montreal], April 23, 1911, p. 6; and "M. Émile Vézina", *L'Action* [Montreal], May 25, 1912, p. 1.

does not invoke the symbiosis of "the artist's soul" and the "soul of nature";[26] nor does he portray Leduc as a mystical progressive. Vézina seems to accept Roquebrune's intimation of Leduc's sincerity; however, his aim was to bring the ideologue's overly lofty praise of the Saint-Hilaire artist down to earth. For Vézina, Leduc's work inspires no particular understanding of an ethnic French-Canadian art or any stated or unstated defence of modernism. He acknowledges Leduc's talent, praising the landscapes, portraits, still lifes and church decoration projects – but with reservations. To Vézina, Leduc was not an exceptional artist. Leduc's work was sincere in the most prosaic sense of the word, marked above all by sheer conscientiousness. The critic makes no concessions to Roquebrune's implicit analogy between sincerity, authenticity and originality. By comparison, Vézina's matter-of-fact appraisal of the paintings *Green Apples*, *The Concrete Bridge* and *Day's End* (cat. 144) shows just how rhetorical Roquebrune's article is:

> It does seem to us to be in his best manner, always thoroughly upright and absolutely sincere. No air of the revolutionary about this painter, no outrageous affectations. He is a traditionalist. There is no need of lyrical turns of phrase to suitably praise what we see here. It is always the same very conscientious effort, combined with a somewhat distinct handling of the brush, a sober, admirably restrained brush stroke.[27]

The same day Bohème's appreciation of Leduc's exhibition appeared in *La Patrie*, a review by liberal author and art critic Albert Laberge appeared in *L'Autorité*.[28] He casts the painter in the role of a poet, drawing upon his earlier (unsigned) review of the 1915 Annual Spring Exhibition at the Art Association of Montreal (perhaps also the source of Roquebrune's phrase "the painting of a poet" and its association with original artistic expression).[29]

Laberge affirmed the identification of Leduc as an authentic and original poet on these same grounds. He cited the artist's major Idealist-Symbolist landscapes as "the impressions of a poet, a great poet", and it is no surprise that *Green Apples* and *The Concrete Bridge*, the works at the crux of Roquebrune's interpretation, were at the top of his list, too. In his description of Leduc's isolation, however, Laberge went one step beyond Roquebrune and Bohème in actually employing the word "isolated":

> Of our artists, Mr. Leduc is one of those who have the strongest, most pronounced personality. He has always lived off the beaten path, isolated in his corner; he has not had the company of his peers – other artists – to stimulate him, but on the other hand, he has remained himself, he has not undergone the influence of any fashionable or successful painter.[30]

26 See G.-Albert Aurier, "Les peintres symbolistes", *Œuvres posthumes* (Paris: Édition du Mercure de France, 1893), p. 303.

27 Vézina 1916.

28 Albert Laberge, "L'œuvre d'un artiste", *L'Autorité* [Montreal], March 11, 1916, p. 2. Laberge was the author of *La Scouine*, a realist novel published privately in 1918, of which segments had appeared in various newspapers and periodicals beginning in 1903. In 1909, it was censored by Msgr. Bruchesi, Archbishop of Montreal, who labelled it "base pornography". See the critical edition of *La Scouine* by Paul Wyczynski (Montreal: Les Presses de l'Université de Montréal, 1986), p. 30. On Laberge's activities as an art critic, see Esther Trépanier, "Deux portraits de la critique d'art des années vingt. Albert Laberge et Jean Chauvin", *The Journal of Canadian Art History*, vol. 12, no. 2 (1989), pp. 141-172, followed by a summary in English.

29 [Albert Laberge], "Une exposition d'art canadien", *La Presse* [Montreal], November 20, 1915, p. 21.

30 Laberge 1916, p. 2.

By saying that Leduc – in rejecting all interaction with other artists and remaining "isolated" – was true unto himself, the critic identified the artist as progressive; for his aesthetic sensibilities and achievements were not the result of external influences, but were drawn entirely from his innermost being.

Laberge completed his positioning of Leduc as a progressive by framing his review with references to a self-portrait and the two portraits of the artist's friend, the Symbolist poet Guy Delahaye. The self-portrait is that from 1899 (cat. 107).[31] The artist's face, "with a high forehead that seems to radiate light", emerges from the dark space of infinity, the piercing intensity of the right eye – the focus of the picture – commandingly engaging the viewer. It is the very image of the romantic genius, enlightened from deep within. "The portrait of a poet and thinker", as Laberge sums it up.

The same comment applies to the *Portrait of Guy Delahaye*, from 1911 (cat. 138), which Laberge chose to close his discussion of Leduc's works. This critic, who had supported Leduc's friend's poetry in all its mysticism, subtlety and radical originality when the collection *Les Phases* appeared in 1910,[32] was now implying an analogy between the artist and the poet: the "strong spirituality" with which the *Portrait of Guy Delahaye* was imprinted is just as evident in Leduc's self-portrait; Leduc is as much the Symbolist painter as Delahaye is the Symbolist poet; Delahaye had been as isolated as Leduc was now. In this way, Leduc, whose work was much more accepted by the public as authentically French-Canadian than that of his literary counterpart, is used to validate the progressive ideas of the "avant-garde".

Taken together, these four reviews are a strong and concentrated invocation of the notion of authenticity, and they set the tone for Leduc's subsequent critical reception through to the very end of his career. In 1954, the year before his death, the artist was positioned by the much-maligned Automatiste Paul-Émile Borduas and his abstractionist cohorts as a link between them and tradition: the venerable Leduc, having ripened at the foot of the mountain, had progressed by means of his dream to a stage where, as the teacher of Borduas, he stood at the threshold of abstraction, thereby validating these young artists as authentically French-Canadian and therefore worthy of respect.[33] Although it is this characterization of Leduc as a progressive link to modernism that has persisted in the literature since the artist's death, the concept of authenticity was also applied to Leduc and his art during his lifetime in defence of the competing cause of traditionalism.

31 No. 22, *Portrait du peintre*. On a handwritten list of the exhibited works and their dimensions, Leduc indicated that *Mon Portrait* was 10 3/4 x 13 [inches] (width precedes height, as can be determined from identifiable works like *Mater Dolorosa*: 9 x 12 1/2"). These dimensions roughly correspond to the *Self-portrait* in the National Gallery of Canada (cat. 107).

32 Albert Laberge, "'Les Phases'", *La Presse* [Montreal], April 23, 1910, p. 18.

33 Rodolphe de Repentigny, "Le plus canadien et le plus universel de nos peintres – Ozias Leduc: fruit mûr de 3 siècles d'isolement", *La Presse* [Montreal], June 23, 1954, p. 48; Paul-Émile Borduas, "Paul-É. Borduas nous écrit au sujet de Ozias Leduc", *Arts et pensée*, vol. 3, no. 18 (July-August 1954), pp. 177-179. See also Paul-Émile Borduas, "Quelques pensées sur l'œuvre d'amour et de rêve de M. Ozias Leduc", *Canadian Art*, vol. 10, no. 4 (Summer 1953), pp. 158-161, 168. An English version of this article has been published in Paul-Émile Borduas, *Écrits/Writings* (Halifax: The Press of the Nova Scotia College of Art and Design, 1978.)

This essay has been adapted from my doctoral dissertation, "The Mythologization of Ozias Leduc, 1890-1954", University of Toronto, April 1995.

CATALOGUE

I. BEFORE 1897

The Schooling of an "Autodidact"

Ozias Leduc (1864-1955) (fig. 1) liked to say that he was an auto-didact, that his work owed nothing to any particular school or teacher. As he confided to Suzette Dorval,

> I went to school and I drew, like the other pupils. I liked it. That's all. I had no masters. I visited various foreign cities as an Art pilgrim and went to a number of places in Canada for my work, stopping in museums when the occasion arose, taking advantage of everything that pleased my mind, delighting my eyes with what I felt were the most beautiful images, those that appealed to me.[1]

The reality, however, was somewhat different. It is certainly true that Leduc's own intellectual curiosity was his most effective guide and that throughout his life he drew much from the books and journals he pored over so assiduously and from the exhibitions and museums he visited with such interest. Leduc had nonetheless benefited from two enriching apprenticeships – one with Luigi Capello (1843-1902), which brought him into contact with the European academic tradition, and the other, more vernacular in nature, under the guidance of Adolphe Rho (1839-1905).

Leduc describes Rho as an artist with a "natural talent ... always changing – trying everything – by turns a photographer, carpenter, ironsmith, painter and sculptor, inventor of countless refinements to everything he touched".[2] This inventiveness no doubt contrasted with the more restrained and meticulous approach of Capello, who had studied for some years at the Academy in Turin before emigrating to Montreal, where he earned his living as a painter and church decorator. Capello married Leduc's cousin, Marie-Louise Lebrun, and soon

Fig. 15   Ozias Leduc, March 4, 1899
(photo: P. F. Pinsonneault, BNQ 327/13/1.3).

1   Suzette Dorval, "Interview d'Osias Leduc", *Amérique française*, vol. 7, no. 3 (March–May 1949), p. 21.

2   Letter from Ozias Leduc to Augustin Arce, o.f.m. [August 1939?], BNQ 327/9/2. On Rho, see the special issue of *Les Cahiers Nicolétains*, vol. 6, no. 1 (March 1984), ed. Denis Fréchette.

became an example for the budding artist, who visited Montreal frequently at this period.[3]

It could also be claimed, however, that the only school Leduc really attended was the school of Nature.[4] The Saint-Hilaire region where he was born represented an endless source of instruction and wonder. The proximity of the Richelieu River and Mount Saint-Hilaire creates a varied terrain that was a constant inspiration to the painter. The fertile farms and rich soil that had nourished a history and traditions still very much alive provided countless object lessons. By 1920, Leduc's attachment to the region and his defence of local culture had become almost legendary: he was often perceived as indissolubly linked to Saint-Hilaire – the hermit of the mountain.

The first group of catalogue entries deals principally with the initial ten years of Leduc's career, focussing on the results of his apprenticeship and his earliest works. Between 1864, the year of Leduc's birth, and the late 1880s, when, at the age of twenty-two or twenty-three, he could seriously consider making a career as an artist, the Montreal and Canadian art scenes had changed considerably. The development of the illustrated press, the influence of photography, the establishment of a number of institutions dedicated to art education, the growing dissemination of art and a new appreciation of artists all combined to completely alter the conditions under which art was practised.

The classes offered by Abbé Chabert's École spéciale des beaux-arts, by the Art Association of Montreal (now the Montreal Museum of Fine Arts) starting in 1881, and by the Council of Arts and Manufactures of the Province of Quebec at the Monument National beginning in 1893 provided artists with the opportunity to develop their talents locally, before considering embarking on a study trip to Europe. Such trips were nevertheless frequent after 1885 and by 1890 had become virtually mandatory. The increase in exhibition spaces presenting both permanent collections and temporary exhibitions (ranging from Laval University's Pinacothèque, opened in 1875, to the Numismatic and Antiquarian Society, starting in 1887) reflected a trend that gained major impetus from the inauguration in 1879 of the building housing the Art Association of Montreal. The city's first commercial galleries began to open their doors, and competition between collectors and dealers became more intense than ever. The founding of the Royal Canadian Academy of Arts in 1879 was a major step in the growing recognition of Canadian artists, both socially and professionally.

As this excerpt from a contemporary newspaper article indicates, the keynote was optimism.

3 On Luigi Capello, see Alexandra Shtychno, "Luigi Giovanni Vitale Capello, a.k.a. Cappello (1843-1902), Itinerant Piedmontese Artist of Late Nineteenth-century Quebec", Master's thesis, Concordia University, March 1991.

4 "Ozias Leduc had no masters … He constructed his work alone, far from salons and discussions on aesthetics … Leduc … in the splendid landscape of Saint-Hilaire, was enraptured by his mountain and the orchards that brought a blush to its slopes." (Henri-M. Guindon, s.m.m., "À propos d'un dessin: Ozias Leduc, peintre marial", *Messager de Marie Reine des Cœurs*, vol. 46, no. 5 [January 1949], p. 2.)

One of the truest pleasures of life is the sense of progress and development in the things around us. Perhaps it has been similarly felt in former ages, but this nineteenth century seems to claim for itself a very special property interest in the law of progress … One thing which is making apparently very great advances in our day is the art of painting … But a thing which is certain is that the Canadian artists are making great progress from year to year in the standard of work they are able to present to the public at their annual exhibition.[5]

The Art Association and the Royal Canadian Academy organized annual exhibitions of contemporary works, thus stimulating the interest of collectors and the development of art journalism. Most daily newspapers carried exhibition reviews, and specialized magazines began to make a tentative appearance – among them *Arcadia* (1892-1893), to which Leduc was a faithful subscriber.

While the major collectors – for the most part wealthy financiers – preferred to acquire works by celebrated European artists,[6] Leduc's early career offers proof that the professional and merchant elite included art enthusiasts who were ready to encourage young Canadian artists.[7] Support for artists was still precarious, however, and remained a much-discussed issue.

Among the French Canadians, several artists warrant attention.

These are people with an inborn vocation, developed by very serious study; they offer ample proof to anyone who cares to see that they are the stuff great artists are made of. Unfortunately, these young people's financial circumstances do not permit them to pursue their studies but force them to devote more time to their *profession*, to making a living, than to pure art…

There are four or five of them, struggling tenaciously, all young and bursting with life.

Soon, the fatal hour will come when they'll be obliged to choose their path once and for all, *their line*, to the exclusion of all others.

But they're poor, very poor! Hard-working, self-made, having offered to all proof of perseverance, industry, skill, capability, they find their development brought to a standstill by the eternal and wretched problem of money, and barring the unforeseen, their burgeoning talent is destined, through lack of nourishment, to *languish*, to wither.

Why not help these young people, so full of potential and confidence?

Why shouldn't the government do something, for the honour and glory of us all?[8]

5   "The Canadian Artists at the Art Gallery", *The Montreal Daily Witness*, April 20, 1891, p. 6.

6   On Montreal collections of European works, see Janet M. Brooke, *Discerning Tastes: Montreal Collectors, 1880–1920*, exhib. cat. (Montreal: Montreal Museum of Fine Arts, 1989).

7   Artists targeted this market by producing small-format landscapes: "Canadian scenery has received a fair share of attention, and a few of the pictures are remarkably fine. Smaller works predominate, the tendency of the age for condensation having evidently crept into the art circle." ("From Canadian Brushes: The Work of Our Artists on Exhibition", *The Montreal Daily Witness*, April 23, 1894, p. 6.)

8   G. de Werthemer, "Le Salon de l'« Art Association »: conclusions", *Les Nouvelles* [Montreal], April 18, 1897, p. 5.

The 1880s were a particularly vital period for the development of religious mural painting in Quebec. This art form reflected the importance of the Church, which, reinforced by Ultramontanist ideology, was consolidating its power by becoming involved in political and social causes. Under the motive force of first-generation artists like Capello and local artists like Napoléon Bourassa (1827-1916), who completed the Notre-Dame-de-Lourdes Chapel in 1880, numerous decoration projects were undertaken.[9] In 1890, the now well-established trend was confirmed with the commissioning by the Sulpician Father Sentenne of several artists – Henri Beau (1863-1949), Joseph-Charles Franchère (1866-1921), Joseph Saint-Charles (1868-1956), Ludger Larose (1868-1915) and Charles Gill (1871-1918) – to work on the major project of the Sacred Heart Chapel of the Church of Notre-Dame in Montreal.

Following a traditional studio apprenticeship and before his trip to Europe, Leduc produced a few paintings that were immediately recognized as masterpieces. His career was well launched: he began obtaining ecclesiastical commissions and attracting the attention of critics and collectors. He had mastered the techniques of easel and mural painting, and was already practising the various forms that absorbed him subsequently: still life, portraiture, genre scenes and history painting. Moreover, by 1897 or even earlier, his paintings embodied an artistic and theoretical approach that would prove of major importance to the development of Canadian art.

9   Delphis-Adolphe Beaulieu (1860-1908), Charles Huot (1855-1930), François-Xavier Meloche (1855-1914), Sinaï Richer (1865?-1947), Louis Saint-Hilaire (1860-1922) and Joseph-Thomas Rousseau (1852-1896) – this latter introduced Suzor-Coté (1869-1937) to painting in Arthabaska – were some of the players in the swiftly expanding market in which Leduc would have to compete.

L. L.

1
The Three Apples

1887

Oil on heavy cardboard

22.7 x 31.7 cm

Signed and dated lower right: *O. Leduc 87*

The Montreal Museum of Fine Arts, purchase,
Harriette J. MacDonnell, Gilman Cheney,
Dr. F. J. Shepherd, and Horsley and Annie
Townsend Bequests, inv. 1988.11

INSCRIPTIONS

Verso, labels: *MBAM, Mexican exhibition, Oct. 5
1960 no. 51*; *MBAC, catalogue no. 1, boîte 7*;
*Panorama 1 de la peinture au Québec, OKanada,
Berlin 1982-1983*

PROVENANCE

Studio of the artist; Paul-Émile Borduas collection,
Montreal, 1942; Gabrielle Borduas, Montreal;
Montreal Museum of Fine Arts, 1988

ONE of the earliest known paintings
by Leduc, *The Three Apples* was executed when the artist was twenty-three
years old. A simple composition of three
apples nestled in a shallow bowl set upon
a bench in low light, the painting heralds
life-long aesthetic concerns of Leduc.

The objects depicted are of naturalist
inspiration, suggested by the artist's
home region of Saint-Hilaire as well as
his personal history and alluding to the
pomiculture and carpentry from which
his family made a living. The articulation of the forms underlines this
naturalism. The apples are shaped by the
modulation of their surface through red,
orange, yellow and green, the minute
directional brush strokes reinforcing
their contour. The effect is a palpable
sense of the shiny, ripe fruit. Similarly,
directional strokes articulate the grain of

the rough-hewn bench in a highly realistic way.

The light in the painting, however,
has a mystical quality to it that adds a
supernatural dimension to the ensemble.
It seems to illuminate the objects from
above while at the same time glowing
from within the apples. Combined with
the trinitarian formation of the perfect
spheres of the apples encompassed in
the circle of the bowl, this painting of
workaday objects assumes religious
overtones.

This interplay between the spiritual
and the natural suggests a parallel
between the creative effort of nature and
the manual effort of the worker on the
one hand, and the artist's effort in aesthetic creation on the other. Just as the
mystical fruit bespeaks nature's labour,
and the nicks on the bench make us

aware of the worker's labour, so does the painstaking detail of the painting point to the labour of the artist. Not only do the objects within the painting become symbols of creativity, but the very painting itself becomes a metaphor for the creative process.

The notion of the creative act is one that Leduc addressed throughout his career, in a number of still-life paintings – the heirs of *The Three Apples* – executed throughout the 1890s, and in his writings from the 1930s.

The Three Apples held great sentimental value for the artist. Only in 1942 did he part with it, giving it up to his friend and former student Paul-Émile Borduas (1905-1960) and receiving in exchange the small oil *Les écureuils*. The younger artist's possession of Leduc's painting marks the beginning of its dissemination to the wider public. The reproduction of *The Three Apples* in 1955 on the cover of the catalogue of the National Gallery of Canada's Leduc retrospective (the first after the artist's death), and the work's subsequent illustration in virtually every history of Canadian art, has guaranteed its present status not only as one of Leduc's best-known paintings but also as one of the icons of Canadian art.

A. G.

2
Study of Sky
1887
Oil on cardboard
32 x 22.5 cm
Private collection
INSCRIPTIONS
Verso: *OZIAS LEDUC ÉTUDE DE CIEL 1887*
PROVENANCE
Sold at auction, about 1970; private collection

THE "discovery" of this study suggests new avenues of exploration in understanding the early work of Ozias Leduc. The known works from this period are mostly still lifes, religious paintings and portraits, and the existence of this oil sketch indicates that Leduc's later preoccupation with the direct observation of nature was actually present at the very start of his career. Although landscape did not become one of his major themes until after 1910, the recurrence of local features in his works is proof of an ongoing concern for the study of nature.

The composition of this painting is extremely simple. The eye is drawn to a point above the trees that fill the lower third of the picture. The thin paint layer appears to have been applied rapidly, although the palette employed is broad. All the varying shades of the dense foliage are rendered with just a few brushstrokes in a range of greens. The pastel tones of blue, white and pink that represent the cirrocumulus clouds offer a highly poetic vision of a late afternoon sky.

The practice of painting from reality began to develop seriously in Canada following the immigration around the 1870s of a number of British and German artists like J. A. Fraser (1838-1898), J. H. Sandham (1842-1910), O. R. Jacobi (1812-1901) and A. Vogt (1843-1871). Their works, presented regularly to the Montreal public, probably encouraged Leduc to draw the settings for his historical and genre paintings directly from the natural world.

L. L.

3
Portrait of My Father

About 1888

Oil on cardboard

31.7 x 22.8 cm

Signed lower right: *OZIAS LEDUC*

Private collection

INSCRIPTIONS

Verso: *Fernande Clerk Saint-Hilaire, P.Q.; From S. Clerk, Mont Saint-Hilaire Ro 139-2-73; Portrait de mon père. Ébauche faite à Saint-Hilaire « Les Trentes », vers 1888, alors que mon père Antoine Leduc menuisier-charpentier, avait à peu près 48 ans - Ozias Leduc; […] Letter […] Cabaillot Lassalle*

PROVENANCE

Studio of the artist; Mr. and Mrs. Édouard Clerk, Saint-Hilaire, 1953; Stephen Clerk, Saint-Hilaire, 1982; private collection, 1986

4
My Mother in Mourning

About 1890

Oil on canvas

40 x 35 cm

Signed lower right: *OZIAS LEDUC*

Ottawa, The National Gallery of Canada, inv. 37488

INSCRIPTIONS

Verso: *Ma mère en deuil. Ce portrait, esquisse à l'huile, a été fait à Saint-Hilaire, <u>Chemin des Trente</u> vers 1890. Ma mère née Émilie Brouillette avait épousé mon père vers 1861 - Ozs L.; The National Gallery of Canada O. Leduc Ex. cat. no. 2 n° de caisse 1; Ma Mère en deuil - Leduc h.t. 15 ½" x 13 ½"; The Montreal Museum of Fine Arts from Mr & Mrs E. Clerk Ozias Leduc « Ma Mère en deuil » 11 artists in Mtl exhibition = 1860-1960; La Mère de l'artiste Mde Edouard Clerk Saint-Hilaire, P.Q.*

PROVENANCE

Studio of the artist; Mr. and Mrs. Édouard Clerk, Saint-Hilaire, 1953; collection Pierre Clerk, New York, 1982; National Gallery of Canada, 1994

I N about 1888, Leduc undertook his first portraits, choosing to represent his father and mother, and his old school-master, Jean-Baptiste Nectaire Galipeau (cat. 5). A later inscription on the back of *Portrait of My Father* tells us that the work is a "Sketch made at Saint-Hilaire 'Les Trentes', about 1888, when my father Antoine Leduc, joiner-carpenter, was around 48 years old". Antoine Leduc (1837-1921) is shown smoking his pipe. The artist describes the portrait as a sketch, and in fact only the head has been treated in any detail; the clothes are just barely roughed in with charcoal over the primed surface. The model is seen against a neutral ground, in a close-up three-quarter view. The informal pose is reinforced by the tight framing of the image. The modelling of the face and beard is rendered by sharp contrasts between the warm tones and the areas of shadow. The hat, represented by light

Fig. 2   Fig. 3

Fig. 2   Ozias Leduc, *My Father*, about 1895, charcoal and graphite on paper, 29.2 x 18.5 cm (Quebec City, Musée du Québec, inv. 56.34).
Fig. 3   Ozias Leduc, *My Mother*, about 1895, charcoal on brown paper, 43 x 38.1 cm (Quebec City, Musée du Québec, inv. 56.35).

brush strokes applied in a circular motion around the model's head, looks almost like a halo. The expression is pensive. In about 1895, Leduc executed another portrait entitled *My Father* (fig. 2).[1]

My Mother in Mourning also carries a handwritten inscription on the back: "This portrait, an oil sketch, was made at Saint-Hilaire *Chemin des Trente* about 1890. My mother born Émilie Brouillette married my father in about 1861."[2] Émilie Leduc (1840-1918) is depicted here at the age of fifty, wearing mourning clothes in memory of her daughter Eugénie, who died in 1888 at three and a half years old. The model is represented face on, positioned in the middle plane against an indeterminate background; the light coming from the left concentrates attention on the face. While the frontal pose makes contact with the spectator possible, the model's expression strikes us as meditative, even introspective. Both the black veil and clothes and the bistre-coloured ground are rendered broadly in quick, deliberately uneven strokes. The work's classical composition – a perfectly centred pyramid – and sombre palette emphasize the power of the sitter's personality. At around the same time, Leduc also executed another portrait of his mother (fig. 3), in which the model's expression of calm melancholy is very similar to the one

depicted in this oil. Leduc kept the second work, a drawing, pinned on the wall of his studio. René Bergeron was very fond of this portrait, which he felt emanated feelings of "such gentleness and goodness" and "inner peace"[3] – qualities also conjured up by the oil painting.

These two paintings might be described as "reference" portraits, in that they provide us with information about the painter's origins. In executing them, Leduc was imitating the many artists who have, in their youth, made portraits of their parents as a way of showing that their educational efforts had not been in vain. The portraits convey his parents' physical and psychological characteristics without dwelling on their social status, while the inscriptions provide further details about the couple. Like his father before him, Leduc was an apple grower, and he continued to tend the family orchard in spite of the extensive travelling required by his church decoration contracts. The orchard was, for him, a constant source of inspiration. As well as being a fine seamstress, Émilie Leduc was known as a person of great sensitivity, possessed of a lively intellectual curiosity – qualities that she passed on to her painter son.

M. L.

1   This extremely simple drawing – it consists of an outline and some hatching for the shadows – does not create the same intimist feeling as the oil sketch: the model is further away and seems more constrained by his Sunday clothes.

2   Émilie Brouillet married Antoine Leduc on November 25, 1861. (The other members of the family spelled the name Brouillette.)

3   René Bergeron, *Art et Bolchévisme* (Montreal: Fides, 1946), p. 92.

5

*Portrait of the Schoolmaster of
Saint-Hilaire*

About 1888

Pastel on paper

58.2 x 46.1 cm

Signed lower left: *OZIAS LEDUC*; upper right:
O. Leduc

Quebec City, Musée du Québec, inv. 54.150

PROVENANCE

Studio of the artist; Graziella Galipeau-Lemay-
Poirier; Pâquerette Lemay-Charbonneau; Ozias
Leduc; Musée du Québec, 1954
Exhibited at the Musée du Québec

T HE drafts of two letters from Leduc
to Gérard Morisset, then curator at
the Musée de la Province (now the
Musée du Québec), indicate why the
young artist chose to paint *Portrait of the
Schoolmaster of Saint-Hilaire*.[1] Leduc
explains that the painting represents
Jean-Baptiste-Nectaire Galipeau (1848-
1918), his master at the Model School
during 1880 and 1881, who recognized his
talent for drawing and encouraged him
"by providing him with beautiful pictures to copy". A few years later, the
artist executed this portrait and presented it to his one-time teacher as a token
of gratitude. Leduc may have been
prompted to make the painting in the
wake of a party held in November
1888 to celebrate the schoolmaster's
fortieth birthday, which sparked some
controversy: a number of detractors
wanted the Conseil de l'Instruction
publique to conduct an enquiry into the
master's behaviour.[2] Leduc may have
taken this opportunity to let Galipeau
know that his talents as a dedicated and
enlightened teacher were appreciated by
his former pupils.

Jean-Baptiste-Nectaire Galipeau was
born in Sainte-Rosalie and educated at
the Seminary of Saint-Hyacinthe. He
worked as a teacher in his native village
before settling in Saint-Hilaire in 1873.
Among the subjects he taught his Model
School pupils were practical arithmetic,
mental arithmetic, single-entry book-
keeping, algebra, weights and measures,
letter writing, agriculture and the rules of
English and French grammar. He also
instructed them in singing and instrumental music[3] and, in 1882,
established the village's first
brass band.[4] Galipeau also
seems to have possessed a
sense of civic pride – inherited by Ozias Leduc – for he
had his pupils plant trees on
the land belonging to their
school.

According to Leduc, this
pastel was executed "with
extreme care, in a manner
similar to some of my still
lifes, *Onions* [cat. 16], for
example".[5] And, indeed, all
the details of the model's
physiognomy have been
meticulously rendered. The
static pose and high degree
of realism would seem to
indicate that Leduc used a
photograph in making the
portrait. A clear line traces
the facial features and the
details of the clothing – shirt
collar, tie and suit. Deep
shadows mark the hollows of
the cheeks and emphasize the broad,
prominent forehead, while the greys of
the clothes and background highlight
the brilliant white of the collar. The
darker tone of the ground behind the
model's head focusses attention on the
face. The head is turned slightly away
from the spectator, which creates a certain feeling of distance, despite the
frontal pose. The obvious desire to create
a likeness, the sober colours and the discreet lighting all combine to create an
overwhelming impression that the model
is a man of exemplary respectability.

M. L.

1 BNQ 327/9/17. In both the letters, one dated July 5,
   1954, and the other almost certainly sent in late July of
   the same year, Leduc offers to sell the drawing to the
   Musée du Québec on behalf of the model's grand-
   daughter. In the first letter, Leduc writes, "This
   life-size portrait is signed with my name. It is the only
   existing pastel that bears my signature." This is not, in
   fact, true. Leduc executed at least three other pastel
   portraits: the 1916 *Portrait of J. E. Wilfrid Lecours*
   (cat. 158), and the pictures of his nephew and niece as
   children, *Portrait of Noël Leduc*, about 1918, and *Portrait
   of Gertrude Leduc*, about 1920 (reproduced in Jean-René
   Ostiguy, *Ozias Leduc: Symbolist and Religious Painting*,
   exhib. cat. [Ottawa: National Gallery of Canada, 1974],
   p. 158).

2 Several articles and letters were published at the time.
   See *L'Union*, November 3, 1888; *Le Courrier de Saint-
   Hyacinthe*, December 27, 1888, and January 8 and
   24, 1889.

3 J. Craig Stirling, *Ozias Leduc et la décoration intérieure
   de l'église de Saint-Hilaire* (Quebec City: Ministère des
   Affaires culturelles, 1985), "Civilisation du Québec"
   series, p. 35.

4 "Ozias Leduc", *Les Cahiers d'histoire de la Société d'histoire de Belœil – Mont-Saint-Hilaire*, no. 21 (October
   1986), p. 28.

5 Draft of a letter from Ozias Leduc to Gérard Morisset
   of July 5, 1954, BNQ 327/9/17.

6

Mater Dolorosa

1890

Oil on wood

30.2 x 22.5 cm

Signed and dated upper left: *O. Leduc 1890*

Ottawa, The National Gallery of Canada,
inv. 35058

INSCRIPTIONS

Verso: *1890 Commencée à Montréal et terminée à St.
Hilaire pendant la construction de mon atelier en
1890 O. Leduc; Ozias Leduc 1890; Madone
douleureuse; 9946; Musée de la Province de Quebec
'cat. no. 32 Propriété de Monsieur Luc Choquette,
4497 rue Saint Denis, Montréal Mater Dolorosa,
1890. par Ozias Leduc'; 'Lycée Pierre Corneille
Exposition Ozias Leduc 12-15 juin 1954; Artist: O.
Leduc Title: Mater Dolorosa, 1890 From: M. Luc
Choquette, Hampstead ro 37-2-69 'H8726'*

PROVENANCE

Studio of the artist; Mr. and Mrs. Luc Choquette,
Montreal, 1944; National Gallery of Canada, 1990

M ATER DOLOROSA marks Leduc's first
participation in a public exhibition. Begun in Montreal but finished in
Saint-Hilaire in the artist's studio (then
under construction) in 1890, it was featured in the Exposition des Beaux-Arts
held in the city in September that same
year.[1] The painting seems to have served
as an assertion of his status as a young
independent professional artist entering
the commercial market. This interpretation is supported by his submission of
Mater Dolorosa, an original work, alongside *Christ on the Cross* (fig. 105), which,
as a copy,[2] was a typical product of a
nineteenth-century French-Canadian
religious painter's apprenticeship. This
pairing was a tactical move, a visual
demonstration of his professional artistic
progress; by comparison, the copy
emphasized the *Mater Dolorosa*'s "original" qualities.

The painting was upheld as an "original" by one reviewer of the exhibition,
who nonetheless suspected a certain
dependence on the popular Italian master Guido Reni (1575-1642).[3] Though
Leduc replied in gratitude to the critic's
comments, later writings reveal that he
was actually offended by this veiled
charge of plagiarism.[4]

Mater Dolorosa is iconic in conception. While the theme of the Mother of
Sorrows is often depicted as a grand nar-

rative with Mary grieving for her son at
the foot of the cross, Leduc's painting
focusses solely on the draped head of
Mary. Soft light enters the enveloping
darkness to fall on the left side of her
face, accentuating the depth of her dole-
ful eyes lifted heavenward. This dramatic
chiaroscuro enhances the pervasive sense
of sorrow.

Leduc's treatment of the theme was
perceived as somewhat unconventional.
Was it the too-youthful face or the omission of tears that led the writer of one
critique of the Art Association of
Montreal's 1891 Spring Exhibition to
suggest that the work might have been
differently titled?[5] The question remained twenty-five years later. In
reviewing Leduc's retrospective at the
Bibliothèque Saint-Sulpice in 1916, one
critic mused whether the image – still
called *Mater Dolorosa* in the catalogue –
was of a despairing Mary who has spent
all her tears at the foot of the cross or a
Mary fraught with anxiety over the
crying of the infant Jesus.[6]

Despite its religious subject, *Mater
Dolorosa* can be set apart from the large-
scale works that Leduc had produced
and would continue to produce as a
church decorator (fig. 4; cats. 24-56, 136-
137, 166-167, 175-182, 237-253). Its intimate
scale suggests that it was intended for
the home, where it would be either used
for private devotion or appreciated strictly for its aesthetic value.

The attention accorded the painting
prompted Leduc to exhibit his works
regularly over the next ten years and
again from 1912 to 1917, recording many
sales. *Mater Dolorosa* itself, however,
occupied as firm a place in Leduc's heart
as it did in the launching of his career.
He held onto it until 1944, when, one
year after agreeing to sell it to Luc
Choquette, the son of his friend
Dr. Ernest Choquette (cat. 92), he finally
relinquished possession.

A. G.

Fig. 4   Ozias Leduc, advertising card, about 1898
(photo by Ozias Leduc, printed from glass negative
No. 94, BNQ 327/12/6.15).

1   For the commercial aspects of the Exposition des
    Beaux-Arts, see Arlene Gehmacher, "The
    Mythologization of Ozias Leduc", Ph.D. dissertation,
    University of Toronto, April 1995, pp. 33-35.

2   After the popular image by French painter Léon
    Bonnat (1833-1922). The copy was probably based on an
    engraving like the one in *L'Opinion publique*, vol. 12,
    no. 15 (April 14, 1881), p. 174.

3   G. A. Dumont, "L'Exposition des beaux-arts III", *Le
    Monde illustré* [Montreal], October 11, 1890, pp. 374,
    376.

4   See O[zias] Leduc, "À propos de l'exposition des
    beaux-arts" (letter to the editor dated October 16, 1890,
    from Bécancour), *Le Monde illustré* [Montreal],
    December 13, 1890, p. 511; Dr. [Ernest] Choquette,
    "Un artiste de mon pays", *La Patrie* [Montreal],
    December 3, 1898, p. 2; Jean Chauvin, *Ateliers: études sur
    vingt-deux peintres et sculpteurs canadiens* (Montreal and
    New-York: Louis Carrier and Co., 1928), p. 125.

5   W. M., "Canadian Art" (letter to the editor),
    The Gazette [Montreal], April 29, 1891, p. 7.

6   Ruth Bohème [pseudonym of Fernande Choquette-
    Clerk], "Un peintre de « chez nous »", *La Patrie*
    [Montreal], March 11, 1916, p. 19.

7

Study for *The Assumption*

About 1889

Graphite on paper

29 x 22.5 cm

Signed lower right: *Ozias Leduc*

Musée d'art de Joliette, on deposit from the Clercs
de Saint-Viateur, Joliette, inv. 1978.072
INSCRIPTIONS
Verso: *O. Leduc Montréal Jonas dans la baleine 1889*
PROVENANCE
Wilfrid Corbeil, c.s.v.; Musée d'art de Joliette, on
deposit from the Clercs de Saint-Viateur, 1978

8

The Assumption

About 1890

Oil on prepared cardboard

25.4 x 17.7 cm

Private collection
PROVENANCE
Studio of the artist; Mr. and Mrs. Fred Bindoff,
Montreal, 1940; Sotheby's, Toronto, May 11, 1994,
lot 135; private collection

THE idea that art serves to elevate the body and the soul was a notion dear to Ozias Leduc. The communion of spirit and matter with Beauty, at the very heart of his creative thinking, was manifested in various ways in his work.[1] He employed the subject of the Assumption as one of the metaphors for this union between creation and Creator, this desire for fusion between the work and an infinity of "love and beauty".

Early in his career, Leduc used the theme of Mary's ascension to Heaven on three occasions in his church interiors, in Joliette, Saint-Hilaire (cats. 30-33) and Rougemont. It is a subject closely linked to the following and final scene of the cycle, which depicts the Coronation of the Virgin and her reunion in Heaven with her Divine Son. (This scene is included in the decoration of the churches in Joliette, Farnham [cat. 135], Notre-Dame-de-Bonsecours in Montreal and Shawinigan-Sud). Leduc's oeuvre also demonstrates a predilection for portraying the apotheosis of female saints (Julia, Joan of Arc, Genevieve, Theresa [cat. 196]) – another expression of his desire to translate by a state of mystical ecstasy the union of the material and the spiritual. In one of his poems, entitled "Assumption", the artist even goes so far as to put himself in the Virgin's place in the voyage towards the God of his desire.

In my flight
Along the pathway
That I climbed
To reach my God
Heart and soul bedazzled
Love and beauty
Followed me
And no one knows
How from rise to rise,
By love and beauty moved,
I arrived,
At the threshold of the empire whence
    leads my destiny,

Advancing along a trail
Outlined against the blue clarity
Of a sky
All studded with stars
To, at the end of the road,
Exhausted,
See open, awaiting me, the arms of God,
My God,
The God of my desire,
The God of love and beauty
And sink myself within him
Forever!
In my flight,
My flight.[2]

These two works are not related to any known commission or decorative programme of the period. The drawing belonging to the Musée d'art de Joliette (cat. 7) is dated 1889 on the verso, and the oil painting can be linked to the *Christ on the Cross* after Bonnat (private collection), dated 1890. Moreover, a photo of Leduc's studio (fig. 105) seems to indicate that these two small paintings formed a pair.

The compositions of these two *Assumption*s, although extremely different, both testify to the knowledge and artistic skill already possessed by Leduc. The drawing, which shows a concern for perspective, bears an inscription on the back – "Jonah in the whale" – and traces of watercolour that hint at certain iconographical and pictorial explorations. The small oil contrasts the background sky, which combines spirited brushwork with a highly economical treatment, and the painting's main subject, which is rendered with all the detail and chromatic harmony required by a far larger painting.

The studies of nude figures that recur throughout Leduc's artistic production[3] are evidence that Leduc learned this academic method of composition from Luigi Capello. They also imply that the artist had access to live models. Here, however, the concentration on the outline and the absence of light effects may be an indication that the drawing was executed after engravings or other drawings. The slim-winged angels are set back, a discreet accompaniment to the swift flight of the Virgin who, arms spread and head thrown back, ascends yearningly skyward.

The scenic arrangement of the drawing contrasts with that of the oil: in the painting, the Virgin, arms open wide in a gesture of acceptance and comfortably enveloped in the folds of her shroud, is carried by three angels.[4] The ascension is well under way; the group has left death and the gloomy lower part of the painting behind and rises towards the glory of a sky shaped by clouds into a brilliant vault.

Leduc kept this painting of *The Assumption* until May 1940, when he gave it to his friends Fred and Florence Bindoff (cats. 194-195).[5]

L. L.

1 See the essay "A dream of a Garden of Beauty" in this catalogue (pp. 23-31).

2 Published in *Arts et pensée*, vol. 3, no. 17 (May-June 1954), p. 139.

3 For example, for the church decoration projects in Joliette (see Laurier Lacroix *et al.*, *Ozias Leduc the Draughtsman*, exhib. cat. [Montreal: Concordia University, 1978], p. 18),and Saint-Hilaire (cat. 33).

4 There is a photograph of a preparatory sketch for this painting (BNQ 327/11/7.30; reproduced in *ibid.*, p. 156). An examination of the painting shows that the angels originally had long wings, as in the drawing. The National Gallery of Canada has a drawing of a *Head of an Angel* inscribed "Assumption" and dated July 4, 1883 (photo, BNQ 327/11/7.42). Thus, Leduc had used this subject early in his career.

5 Details about the circumstances of this acquisition are given in two letters (BNQ 327/7/12; 327/9/3).

9

The Enshrouding of Christ

1891

Oil on canvas

180 x 135 cm

Monogrammed and dated lower left: *-18OL91-*

Musée des Sœurs Grises de Montréal,
inv. 1973-A-001

INSCRIPTIONS

Recto, lower left: *D'APRÈS ARY SCEFFER*
Verso: *M. LE CURÉ AUCLAIR SJB+*
1-43 4 1286 MI-J.BTU CHAM[…]; *Ensevelissement
de Jésus copie de Paul Delaroche; N. RHÉAUME &
BRO. Manufacture of […] & Looking Glasses
[…]erers of Glass […] in lithograving, painting,
chromos Picture Framer's Supplies 75 St-Laurent Street
Montreal; Les Sœurs Grises de Montréal 12376*

PROVENANCE

Church of Notre-Dame-de-la-Paix, Verdun;
Communauté des Sœurs Grises, Montreal, about
1950; Musée des Sœurs Grises de Montréal, 1973

THE Dutch-born French painter Ary Scheffer (1795-1858) was enormously popular in nineteenth-century Catholic circles, and paintings like his *Holy Women at the Sepulchre* (1845, Manchester City Art Galleries) were well known in Quebec.[1]

Leduc was attempting to break into the religious painting market by making copies,[2] still a common practice in Quebec. In this case, he was faced with the task of adapting the much-reproduced original to the format of the canvas and of interpreting Scheffer's palette.[3] Execution of the work was an excellent academic exercise for Leduc, particularly the depiction of the holy women of varying ages, with their subtly different expressions of grief. The cross that closes off the upper left-hand corner, in contrast to the tomb, creates a trompe l'oeil effect.

The fame of the painting on which the work was modelled and the opportunity to practise technique were perhaps not the only reasons for Leduc's selection of the subject, for he often chose themes focussing on grief-stricken mothers (cats. 25-26) or dead children (cats. 4, 101).

The disposition of the central group in *The Enshrouding of Christ* can be related to other symbolic figures that no doubt held meaning for Leduc.

Scheffer's composition isolates Christ's head against the folds of the shroud, where Mary clasps it in a gesture of affection. The bodiless head recalls those of John the Baptist and Orpheus, two "initiates" who are often associated with Christ.[4] The composition of this painting is similar to the *Orpheus* by Gustave Moreau (1865, Musée d'Orsay), in which a disciple of the Orphic cult holds the poet's head on a lyre.

L. L.

1   Scheffer was also the best-known French painter in England (see Edward Morris, "Ary Scheffer and His English Circle", *Oud Holland*, vol. 99, no. 4 [1985], pp. 294-323) and was among the artists whose works were the most reproduced during the nineteenth century. "These prints are extremely popular with all those who wish to have on view, in their living room, a sentimental or pious image. With Paul Delaroche, Ary Scheffer is certainly the most frequently 'framed' painter." (H. Béraldi, *Les Graveurs du XIXe siècle. Guide de l'amateur d'estampes modernes* [Paris, 1892], vol. 12, p. 14.)

   There exists a photograph of *The Entombment of Christ* in the "Album de comptoir" Livernois photography studio, Quebec City (ANQQ N79-2-40 CM211); the painting was often reproduced in religious journals (for example in an unidentified clipping, BNQ 327/14/13). Jean-René Ostiguy, *Ozias Leduc: Symbolist and Religious Painting*, exhib. cat. (Ottawa: National Gallery of Canada, 1974), p. 110, suggests that Leduc may have based his work on the engraving published in France by A. Goupil et Cie in 1855.

   The error in the transcription of Scheffer's name at the lower left is an indication that Leduc worked from a rather carelessly produced edition.

   There is another version of the subject by Scheffer, dated 1854, in the National Gallery of Victoria, Melbourne.

2   Other examples are the *Saint Charles Borromeo* after Charles Le Brun (1619-1690) (1891, destroyed), acquired by the church of Lachenaie, and the *Christ on the Cross* after Bonnat (1890, private collection), which is more a modello. The interior of the church in Joliette (cat. 18) is largely dependent on this kind of adaptation.

3   It is not known whether the painting was a commission or if Leduc executed it without knowing its destination. Its large size seems to indicate it was intended for a public place. The work was first mentioned in 1937, by Gérard Morisset and Jules Bazin, as being in the Church of Notre-Dame-de-la-Paix in Verdun (see Ostiguy 1974, p. 110).

4   The syncretic association of Christ and Orpheus goes back to the beginning of Christianity. In the late Middle Ages and during the Renaissance, Neo-Platonist theory established a clear link between the two figures. Not only does Orpheus himself sometimes take the form of a priest or the Good Shepherd, but his journey to the underworld can be related to Christ's harrowing of hell. See Dorothy M. Kosinski, *Orpheus in Nineteenth-century Symbolism* (Ann Arbour and London: UMI Research Press, 1989), especially pp. 7-10, 193-197.

10

Child with Helmet Guarding a Treasure

1891

Oil on cardboard

22.8 x 16.1 cm

Signed and dated lower right: *O LEDUC 1891*

Toronto, Art Gallery of Ontario, purchase, 1983, inv. 83.236

PROVENANCE

Studio of the artist; Crevier family; Robert-Henri Falbord; Sœur Marguerite Falbord; Frère Joseph-Henri Falbord; Oliva and Rose Bouchard; Bouchard estate; Art Gallery of Ontario, 1983

VARIOUS first-hand reports of Leduc describe him as something of a humorist, a poker face who always had a witty remark at the ready. Our first reaction to this enigmatic painting is to laugh. It appears to be a caricature or a puzzle to which we have, as yet, no solution.

Wearing a helmet and armed with a sword, traditional attributes of Mars, the child stands confidently on a dollar bill bearing the likeness of Lady Dufferin. The scale of the bill and of the small

stack of coins on the right indicates that the child is an imaginary creature, a Lilliputian. Moreover, this odd personage is clearly on a stage, whose heavy red curtain trimmed with a gold fringe can be seen in the background. It must, then, be in a theatre that this fantastic figure keeps watch over his treasure, which is either ridiculously small or – given the hero's size – quite enormous. Is the whole thing a trick, a mockery of the over-ingenious interpretation of pictures? Or is it a fantasy on the value of the artist's work?

In fact, the joke might have been commissioned by Montreal architect Robert-Henri Falbord, but the circumstances surrounding the work's execution are not known.[1] Much later, Leduc described the painting as "a panel of only a few inches depicting a little boy wearing a metal helmet, sword in hand, guarding a treasure".[2] He omitted, however, to unveil the mystery surrounding the image.

L. L.

---

1   The stage curtain can be linked to a series of sketches executed by Leduc in 1897 for the Cercle Montcalm theatre troupe of Saint-Hyacinthe (fig. 99); McCord Museum of Canadian History, reproduced in Laurier Lacroix *et al.*, *Ozias Leduc the Draughtsman*, exhib. cat. [Montreal: Concordia University, 1978], pp. 21-22). Might Falbord have had some connection with the design of these sets?

In 1896, the architect was given the contract for the roof and interior decoration of the Church of Saint-Hilaire (*Le Prix courant*, April 24, 1896, p. 382).

Leduc's correspondence with Falbord's son Joseph-Henri offers evidence of the friendly relations that existed between the two men (letter from J.-H. Falbord to Ozias Leduc, September 9, 1930, BNQ 327/7/2).

2   Letter from Ozias Leduc to J.-H. Falbord, April 1, 1940, BNQ 327/9/3.

11

Still Life, Books

1892

Oil on canvas

32 x 40.1 cm

Signed and dated lower left: *O. LEDUC 1892*

Private collection

INSCRIPTIONS

Verso: *To darling […] from Mother Oct. 13th 1907 Montreal*; labels: *Nature morte (livres) O. Leduc 202 St-Martin Montréal*; *The Montreal Museum of Fine Arts 11 Artists in Montreal: 1860-1960 Exhibition*; *The Montreal Museum of Fine Arts "Doctors and Art" Exhibition*; unindentified newspaper clipping

PROVENANCE

Studio of the artist; R[obert] Pinkerton, 1892; given to an unidentified person October 13, 1907; Dominion Gallery, Montreal; private collection

"CHARMINGLY done, it comes off marvellously";[1] "Of all these pictures … the most perfect … the whole, admirably natural";[2] Leduc "has, perhaps, no equal, for who else would spend so much labor on those books?";[3] "As a copy of still life [it is] a masterpiece … The work is a marvel of true copy";[4] "This work is wonderfully natural … The painter attains the acme of realism in this painting."[5] Such were the accolades bestowed upon *Still Life, Books* when it was exhibited at the Art Association of Montreal in 1892. It was further honoured by winning the first prize of $100 for a painting by a non-Association member under thirty years of age.

This litany of praise, it is clear, was prompted by the convincing depiction of books, one of which is opened to display a reproduction of a painting largely obscured by a protective tissue, the others, only some of whose titles are legible, arranged in a row behind.[6] The image has for the most part been rendered with a high degree of minute detail painted in slick, virtually imperceptible brush strokes to create the illusion of three dimensions. In certain areas, however (for example, the bottom edge of the pages of the book), the paint has been built up to effect an actual three dimensionality.

The highly tactile illusionism that results beckons seductively. As one reviewer put it, "The tissue paper leaf

lying loosely on the open book is so real that the spectator feels inclined to blow it off to see the picture underneath."[7] Such comments are responding to Leduc's technical virtuosity in achieving the illusionary realism of trompe l'oeil. But Leduc is not merely "tricking the eye". Rather, his aim is to lure viewers like this critic into the painting on a quest for deeper understanding, to see beneath the veil as it were.

Though the partially obscured image in the open book seems to be a of studio in which an artist paints from a live model, the overlying tissue is just opaque enough to preclude any absolute visual identification of the scene. Similarly, the titles of several of the books, which at first glance appear to be legible, upon closer scrutiny turn out to be indecipherable. Ultimately there is no easy resolution to the painting, only prolonged inquiry.

Leduc has combined high realism and the juxtaposition of literary with pictorial sources of knowledge in order to challenge the authority of material reality. What seems tangible and accessible, what seems to be nature, is not: such is art.

Thus *Still Life, Books*, in form and content and in the paradoxical way it simultaneously engages and frustrates the viewer, is a commentary on the relationship of art to nature. One writer remarked, "And as if to challenge art, an open book allows the viewer to barely discern, under a sheet of tissue paper yellowed with age, one of the engravings contained in the volume."[8] In portraying apparent reality as facile illusion, this painting challenges one to search beneath the surface of the material world to perceive, however dimly, the outlines of a deeper truth.

A. G.

1 Domino, "Exposition de peinture", *Le Monde* [Montreal], April 23, 1892, p. 1.

2 Françoise [pseudonym of Robertine Barry], "Chronique du lundi", *La Patrie* [Montreal], May 16, 1892, p. 1.

3 "The Art Gallery: Exhibition of Canadian Artists", *The Montreal Daily Witness*, April 18, 1892, p. 6.

4 "Spring Exhibition", *Montreal Daily Star*, April 21, 1892, p. 5.

5 "The Canadian Art Exhibition", *The Montreal Daily Witness*, April 20, 1892, p. 6.

6 For example, the New Testament, an *Anatomie artistique*, *Forestiers et Voyageurs*, Charles Bayet's *Précis d'histoire de l'art*, Johnson's *Natural History* and Aubert de Gaspé's *Les anciens canadiens*.

7 From the article cited in note 5.

8 Françoise 1892.

12

Phrenology

1892

Oil on wood panel

33.8 x 27.2 cm

Signed and dated lower right: *O. Leduc 1892*

Musée d'art contemporain de Montréal, Lavalin
Collection, inv. A 92 644 P 1

INSCRIPTIONS

Verso: *17D*; *DV 450 per in ft*; *1470*; National Gallery
of Canada label: *O. LEDUC No de catalogue: 8 No
de la caisse: 7; 1470 Corbeil S/R*

PROVENANCE

Studio of the artist; Honorius Leduc; Maurice and
Andrée Corbeil; Lavalin Collection; Musée d'art
contemporain de Montréal, 1992

T HE plaster head that is the focus of
this small painting is clearly no
ordinary bust, for the skull is divided
into numbered zones. It also bears the
partially effaced label "PHRENOLOGY" on
its base and sits on a treatise on anatomy.
In the foreground, Leduc has arranged
the tools of his art. To the left are drawing instruments: a lead pencil, chalk in a
holder, an eraser, a stump and a pair of
compasses; on the right, three paintbrushes in a glass and a few tubes of
paint – the instruments of painting.
Between the two, curling against the
base of the head, are several sheets, no
doubt engravings or drawings. The background is filled by a painting depicting a
number of draped women.

At first view, this little painting constitutes something of a puzzle. The title
Phrenology, which offers only a partial
clue to the work's true meaning, is an
allusion to a psychological system
invented by the German Franz Joseph
Gall (1758-1828), who claimed that it is
possible to assess a subject's intelligence
(*phren* is the Greek for "mind") and even
their personality and talents by a careful
examination of the bumps on their skull.
In fact, Gall was on the track of an
important discovery – that of cerebral
localization – but mistakenly believed
that the external shape of the head
reflected the convolutions of the brain.
His book *On the Functions of the Brain
and Each of Its Parts*, first published in
1808, was enormously successful in
Europe and North America,[1] but because

his was an essentially materialistic
approach, based on the correspondence
between matter and spirit, the book was
placed on the *Index* by the Catholic
Church!

But what is a phrenological bust
doing surrounded by tubes of paint and
drawing instruments?

Another of the enigmas associated
with this still life centres on the difficulty
historians have experienced in correctly
identifying the painting in the background. It is a work to which Leduc was
evidently attached, for it appears in a
photo of the interior of his studio
(fig. 105) and in another of his still lifes
(fig. 5). It is actually a painting by the
English artist W. E. Frost (1810-1877),
entitled *Sabrina* (1843).[2] Sabrina is the
Latin name for the Severn, a river in
Britain. In his picture, Frost apparently
represented the Severn by a young
woman attended by a group of nymphs
as numerous as the river's tributaries.[3]
But how does this help in the interpretation of Leduc's painting? Let us attempt
to unravel the thread.

It seems that we must start with the
humblest elements – the pencil, chalk,
eraser and stump, the tubes of paint and
glass containing paintbrushes. These
objects suggest that the work may be primarily a meditation on painting itself. It
is presented first as a craft – whence the
painting and drawing instruments. But
painting is not only a craft; it is also a
science – whence the treatise on anatomy
and the phrenological bust. Moreover,
might not phrenology, which claims to
be capable of perceiving evidence of the
mind in matter, be a metaphor for painting, especially the form of symbolic
painting practised by Leduc? Is a painting not a material object into which we
read an intellectual content?

Painting, then, is both craft and science. But it is also inspiration. And it is
on this level that Frost's picture becomes
significant. Leduc has represented water
three times in his painting: in the glass,
entirely realistically; in the rolled drawing in the foreground, which is probably
based on a work by Corot (1796-1875), a
frequent portrayer of mist and lakes; and

Fig. 5   Ozias Leduc, *Still Life (with Weeping Lay
Figure)*, 1907 (whereabouts unknown; photo by
Ozias Leduc, printed from glass negative No. 251,
BNQ 327/12/2.17).

in the background, in Frost's somewhat
byzantine river allegory, which nevertheless appealed to Leduc. So it is water,
that most mobile of elements, that the
artist has employed to convey the idea
that painting is not merely the representation of reality but also a creative
endeavour in which imagination plays
just as important a role as observation.

F.-M. G.

1   On the influence of phrenology see, among others,
L'âme au corps, arts et sciences 1793-1993, exhib. cat.
(Paris: Réunion des musées nationaux, 1993),
pp. 196-393, and Charles Colbert, "'Each Little Hillock
Hath a Tongue': Phrenology and the Art of Hiram
Powers", *The Art Bulletin*, vol. 68, no. 2 (June 1986),
pp. 281-300.

2   It was Michael Pantazzi of the National Gallery of
Canada who finally identified this painting.

3   Arlene Gehmacher, "In Pursuit of the Ideal: The Still
Life Paintings of Ozias Leduc", Master's thesis,
University of Toronto, 1986, p. 43, note 27, traces the
legend of Sabrina to Milton's masque *Comus*. It should
be noted how the side of the glass acts like a prism,
fragmenting the spectrum.

13
Still Life (Three Pennies)
1892

Oil on canvas

36.9 x 29.2 cm

Signed and dated lower left: *O Leduc 1892*

Private collection

PROVENANCE

Studio of the artist; E. M. Chadwick, Toronto (21st Annual Exhibition, Ontario Society of Artists), 1893; Dr. D. McLeish, Toronto; Sotheby's, Toronto, May 19, 1977, lot 60; Laing Galleries, Toronto, 1977; private collection

Exhibited at the Montreal Museum of Fine Arts and the Musée du Québec

ALTHOUGH advised by one critic in April 1892 to forego painting still lifes and do "more ambitious work" worthy of his obvious skill,[1] Leduc thought otherwise. As an essay in that genre painted from nature in a high realism that borders on trompe-l'oeil, *Still Life (Three Pennies)* – along with the slightly earlier *Still Life, Books* (cat. 11) and two others from the same year, *Phrenology* (cat. 12) and *Still Life, Onions* (cat. 16) – is the artist's pictorial response to the insinuations of plagiarism of Guido Reni that had been levelled against *Mater Dolorosa* (cat. 6) in 1890.[2] These paintings were Leduc's proof that his artistic inspiration came from nature rather than from another artist's work. In *Still Life (Three Pennies)*, Leduc answers to these charges in an ironic way, including in this work "from nature" reproductions of mythologically and biblically based paintings by other artists (among them, the infamous Guido Reni himself) and crowning it with a similar work of his own.

Leduc's embrace of trompe-l'oeil illusionism has led some commentators to link his work with his American contemporaries, the most representative of whom was William Harnett (1848-1892).[3] Whereas Harnett's use of trompe-l'oeil also involved issues of originality and imitation, he seems to have revelled more in the technique for its own sake, while Leduc sublimated it into his iconographic enquiry into such philosophical issues.

Leduc here once again uses trompe-l'oeil illusionism to "hook" the spectator and then engage him in the act of looking in a way that reinforces the meaning of the style and iconography of the painting in its questioning of materialism and its questing after a more spiritual reality. The objects are arranged on levels reflecting a hierarchy of values. The eye, drawn first to the coins and letters in the foreground by their trompe-l'oeil treatment, is swept up from these brightly lit objects of everyday life, through images of mythological figures representing intangibles (love and goodness)[4] to the realm of artistic creativity symbolized by artists' and writers' tools and as-yet-untouched paper to rest finally on a drawing, veiled in semidarkness, by Leduc himself of an *Assumption* (cat. 8), signifying the ideal to which life and art should aspire.

The prominence of the three pennies suggests that Leduc was wrestling philosophically with the material aspects of art (and life) in which he was engaging by painting and exhibiting this work for commercial gain. Not hidden away in his "remote" Saint-Hilaire studio as some have contended, but frequenting Montreal (as shown by the address on the envelope)[5] and trying to make a name for himself, Leduc was here moved to examine the role of art and artist in society.

As usual, all of such a philosophical inquiry was lost on the general public. Cited by one reviewer as an "example of industry and unusual skill"[6] and by another as "an excellent piece of work" that "could not be fully appreciated until closely inspected",[7] *Still Life (Three Pennies)* is one of those paintings that appealed to the gallery-going public because of its preoccupation with minutiae. Such paintings were popular with upper middle class art lovers, as the work's purchase from the 1893 Ontario Society of Artists exhibition by E. M. Chadwick, "one of the most prominent barristers"[8] in Toronto, attests.

A. G.

1 Domino, "Exposition de peinture", *Le Monde* [Montreal], April 23, 1892, p. 1, regarding *Still Life, Books* (cat. 11).

2 Arlene Gehmacher, "The Mythologization of Ozias Leduc," Ph.D. dissertation, University of Toronto, April 1995, pp. 49-57.

3 Evan H. Turner, "From the Collections", *Canadian Art*, vol. 19, no. 3 (May/June 1962), p. 231; Jean-René Ostiguy, *Ozias Leduc: Symbolist and Religious Painting*, exhib. cat. (Ottawa: National Gallery of Canada, 1974), p. 115.

4 Represented, respectively, by *Cupid Sharpening His Arrow* by Mengs (1728-1779) and *Saint Michael Subduing Satan* by Guido Reni.

5 The "Martin" discernible on the envelope with the cancelled stamp refers to 202 Saint-Martin Street, Leduc's address at the time. The uppermost envelope, addressed to "Mr. A[ntoine?] Leduc, [Saint-]Hilaire, P.Q." would also indicate that the artist is absent from his Saint-Hilaire studio.

6 "Ontario Art Exhibition", *The Globe* [Toronto], April 29, 1893, p. 17.

7 "Art and Artists", *Toronto Saturday Night*, April 29, 1893, p. 15.

8 Letter from Robert F. Gagen to Ozias Leduc, May 22, 1893, BNQ 327/5/3.

14

Study for *Boy with Bread*

1892

Charcoal and graphite on buff wove paper

47.7 x 54.3 cm

Initialed lower right: *OL*

Ottawa, The National Gallery of Canada, inv. 15858

INSCRIPTIONS

Recto: *M[ULTU]M-IN-PARVO; 21 x 19*

PROVENANCE

Studio of the artist; Mr. and Mrs. Luc Choquette, Montreal; National Gallery of Canada, 1969

15

Boy with Bread, also known as *The Little Musician*

1892-1899

Oil on canvas

50.7 x 55.7 cm

Monogrammed and dated upper right: *.92. LEDUC .99.* encircled with an *O*

Ottawa, The National Gallery of Canada, inv. 15793

PROVENANCE

Studio of the artist; Mr. and Mrs. Édouard Clerk, Saint-Hilaire; National Gallery of Canada, 1969

PRIOR to 1900, apart from a number of still lifes, Leduc executed several genre scenes depicting his brothers and sisters pursuing the intellectual activities of music and reading. The first picture in this series, begun in 1892, is the work known as *Boy with Bread* or *The Little Musician*. The model was Leduc's brother Ulric, sixteen years his junior.[1] The child sits playing a harmonica, the remains of his breakfast or snack on the table before him. The scene is highly simplified: the young musician is posed against a bare wall,[2] and there are few identifying features. The painter has concentrated on reproducing the diverse textures that make up the image: wood, cloth, bread, earthenware and pewter. The scene is lit by a warm, natural light, and the space is structured by the chair, table and baseboard. The seated figure of the young boy – back curved and one foot propped on the chair rail – is contained within an oval form that finds echoes in the brim and ribbon of the hat, the suspenders, the trouser waistband, the right elbow, the left heel and the rim of the bowl. All these curved lines are counterbalanced by the slight diagonals of the furniture and baseboard. The centre of the painting is located just above the child's left hand, at the point where the light is strongest and the contour line becomes slightly blurred.

Several critics and art historians have interpreted this image as a representation of the "poor and rustic life of nineteenth-century French Canadians",[3] or an expression of "the interest Leduc took in themes from peasant life".[4] But *The Little Musician* is far more than simply an evocation of rural existence. The painting's interest does not lie in the remains of the frugal meal, or the ragged clothes. The repetition of the oval shape that encloses the child suggests another reading. The egg is a universal symbol, container of the germ of all potentiality. In spite of the impression of poverty, Leduc sees the curved figure of this boy as the embodiment of all possibilities. Moreover, on the preparatory drawing (cat. 14), done to scale, the artist wrote *Multum in parvo* (Much in little). The painting focusses on a moment of pleasure: the child savours the peace of being briefly alone. The work can be read as an allegory on the senses, with the bowl and piece of bread evoking taste and smell; the harmonica, hearing; and the various textures, touch. The egg, associated with domesticity, is also a symbol of rest. It is in this atmosphere of creative leisure that the adolescent's personality is constructed. The whole painting is an appeal for discretion, a plea not to shatter this magic moment. Even the brush stroke is so smooth we are scarcely aware of it. The artist has nonetheless created a work of some depth; he captures our attention by an effect of trompe l'oeil and then directs it beyond the anecdotal towards a meditation on the conditions of creation. *The Little Musician* is a reminder that we have need of nourishment not only for the body but also for the mind, nourishment like music and painting, which provide both instruction and delight.

M. L.

1 Ulric A. Leduc (1880-1965) later became an electrical contractor. Leduc commissioned his brother to make various items based on his own designs: in 1926, a cross and a triangle made of lights for the Church of Sainte-Geneviève in Pierrefonds (BNQ 327/6/11), and in 1929, light fixtures for the Church of Saint-Hilaire and for Notre-Dame in Montreal (BNQ 327/8/35).

2 The atmosphere and composition are reminiscent of genre scenes by Chardin (1699-1779) – for example, *The Young Draftsman* (1737, Louvre) and *The House of Cards* (1741, National Gallery, London) – even though in these works the children's clothes place them in a different social class from the little French-Canadian boy. Also, the bowl and spoon can be compared to the utensils in Chardin's still life *The Silver Goblet* (about 1765, Louvre).

3 Gilles Corbeil, "Le silence et le calme des objets, complices du rêve chez Ozias Leduc", *La Presse* [Montreal], January 13, 1956, p. 38.

4 Jean-René Ostiguy, *Ozias Leduc: Symbolist and Religious Painting*, exhib. cat. (Ottawa: National Gallery of Canada, 1974), pp. 118-119.

16
Still Life, Onions

1892

Oil on canvas

36.5 x 45.7 cm

Signed and dated lower right: *O. Leduc 92*

Musée d'art de Joliette, bequest of the Reverend
Father Wilfrid Corbeil, c.s.v., inv. 1974.015

INSCRIPTIONS

Verso: *Corbeil C.S.V. Noviciat Joliette PQ Canada*

PROVENANCE

Wilfrid Corbeil, c.s.v., 1933; Musée d'art de
Joliette, 1974

STILL LIFE, ONIONS relates to Leduc's very first still life, *The Three Apples* (cat. 1), for it too offers up the bounty of the earth set upon a rough-hewn wooden table. It does so in a way that is strongly evocative of "the simple life".

A mound of onions fills a deep, round container while others are scattered around its base and across the surface of the table. The resulting cascade of onions is halted by one freshly halved onion; its singular brightness, contrasting with the pervasive subdued tones of the rest of the painting, causes a visual arrest. This jolt, heightened by the enticing realism of the painting – right down to the onions' distorted reflection in the convex surface of the metal pan – focusses the viewer's gaze. Thus are the rural connotations of the scene, as well as its naturalist inspiration, insistently presented.

This at least seems to have been the effect of the painting on Lucien de Riverolles, author of the earliest known monographic article on Leduc.[1] Familiar with the artist's still-life paintings and writing on the heels of the 1893 Royal Canadian Academy exhibition in Montreal, in which *Still Life, Onions* (along with *Still Life, Study by Candlelight* [cat. 17]) was featured, the author is moved to relate how Leduc's home region of Saint-Hilaire inspired the artist to love and appreciate nature, thus effectively causing him to become an artist.

Other contemporary commentators, however, made no such connections between *Still Life, Onions* and Leduc's immediate surroundings. In fact, the subject of onions was so common that one critic of the 1893 RCA exhibition referred to it as "hackneyed" and its appearance there as "inevitable".[2] Rather, the discussion regarding Leduc's work focussed on the "accuracy" of his rendition. Leduc's onions seemed so real that one could "almost pick [them] off the canvas",[3] or submit them to a "microscopic test."[4] Such responses were typical of the many art lovers who were drawn to and impressed by artists who, like Leduc, could seemingly capture nature perfectly in paint. It is perhaps not surprising that such a crowd-pleaser would be chosen for inclusion in the Canadian art exhibit at the World's Columbian Exposition in Chicago that same year.

A. G.

1   Lucien de Riverolles, "Chronique artistique: O. Leduc", *L'Opinion publique* [Montreal], April 14, 1893, p. 284.

2   "The Art Gallery: Still Life in the Canadian Academy Pictures", *Montreal Daily Star*, March 6, 1893, p. 1. According to this article, Joseph-Charles Franchère also exhibited a still life of onions (No. 59).

3   "Royal Academy Exhibit", *The Gazette* [Montreal], March 1, 1893, p. 2.

4   From the article cited in note 2.

17

Still Life, Study by Candlelight,
also known as *The Farmer's Meal*

1893

Oil on canvas

36.1 x 46.2 cm

Signed and dated lower right: *O. Leduc 1893*

Ottawa, The National Gallery of Canada, inv. 6402
PROVENANCE
Studio of the artist; R. Ostiguy, Saint-Hyacinthe,
about 1900; Mrs. Ostiguy, Marieville; Dominion
Gallery, Montreal, 1955; National Gallery of
Canada, 1955

ALTHOUGH more popularly known as *The Farmer's Meal*, the title given this painting by Leduc when he first exhibited it in 1893 at the Royal Canadian Academy was *Still Life, Study by Candlelight*. This was abbreviated to *Candle Light Study* when the work was exhibited with the Ontario Society of Artists in 1894.

By titling it thus, Leduc intimated that his intent was to capture the effect of the candlelight on the various objects arrayed across the table's surface. Indeed, the visual centre of the painting is the aureole of the candle flame, the sole light source, whose rays reflect off the candlestick, earthenware jug, glass, spoon, pottery bowl and onions, accentuating their individual forms as well as their textures.

The evocative realism of *Still Life, Study by Candlelight* was remarked upon, though not as extensively as with *Still Life, Onions* (cat. 16), exhibited in the same show. Like the reviewer who wanted to pick the onions off the latter canvas, one reviewer of Leduc's candlelit scene also recorded a physiological response: it "makes one blink after looking steadily at the candle that almost flickers".[1] Another was impressed with this "very interesting and clever study in shadows".[2] The attempt to capture light

effects was not an unknown endeavour, however; it was observed that Leduc's painting was "killed" by its placement near a painting featuring a firelight effect.[3]

If both artist and contemporary commentary have indicated that the identity of the objects plays a subordinate role to the light effect, then how did the painting come to be known as *The Farmer's Meal*? This title first appeared in the National Gallery of Canada's travelling Leduc retrospective, which opened a few months after the artist's death and gave the broad Canadian public its first exposure to his work. In an essay on the still lifes, Gilles Corbeil presented them as going beyond reflecting the personal world of Leduc's studio to represent the poor and rustic life of nineteenth-century French Canada.[4] *The Farmer's Meal*, a title evocative of rural living, is much more appropriate to such an interpretation than the academic *Study by Candlelight*. The new title and Corbeil's viewpoint set the tone for much subsequent commentary, which has echoed the focus on the subject's humbleness.[5]

A. G.

1   "Art Notes: The Ontario Society of Artists…",
    The Week [Toronto], May 4, 1894, pp. 543-544.

2   "Of the Brush and Palette", *Toronto Daily News*, April
    25, 1894, p. 5.

3   "The Art Gallery: Still Life in the Canadian Academy
    Pictures", *The Montreal Daily Star*, March 6, 1893, p. 1.

4   Jean-René Ostiguy and Gilles Corbeil, *Ozias Leduc,
    1864-1955*, exhib. cat. (Ottawa: National Gallery of
    Canada and Musée de la province de Québec, 1955),
    No. 3.

5   J. Russell Harper, *Painting in Canada: A History*, 2nd
    edition (Toronto and Buffalo: University of Toronto
    Press, 1977), p. 220. Barry Lord, *The History of Painting
    in Canada: Toward a People's Art* (Toronto: NC Press,
    1974), p. 147, uses the painting, which he calls *The
    Settler's Meal*, to promote a Marxist ideology.

18
Study for *The Resurrection*

1893

Oil and graphite on cardboard

19.1 x 22.5 cm

Toronto, Art Gallery of Ontario, purchase, 1985,
inv. 85.10

PROVENANCE

Studio of the artist; Mr. and Mrs. Édouard Clerk,
Saint-Hilaire; Édouard Clerk estate, Saint-Hilaire;
Art Gallery of Ontario, 1985

THE circumstances surrounding the granting to Leduc of the major commission that resulted in his executing, in 1893-1894, twenty-five paintings for the new Church of Saint-Charles-Borromée, in Joliette, remain a matter of some conjecture. The artist had recently collaborated on the interior of the church of the neighbouring parish, Saint-Paul-l'Ermite. Also, Leduc's much-remarked participation in Montreal exhibitions may explain in part how the priest of Saint-Charles-Borromée, Prosper Beaudry, came to know of him.

In 1888, Father Beaudry took advantage of the relative prosperity of Joliette, a town of over three thousand inhabitants, to undertake the construction of a new church. The building was done by contractor D. A. Dostaler according to plans drawn up by the firm of H.M. Perrault et Mesnard. The paintings were paid for by public subscription.[1]

The series' main iconographical programme focusses on the fifteen Mysteries of the Rosary. These images are accompanied by eight other scenes from the life of Christ and completed by a *King David* and a *Saint Cecilia* installed near the organ loft (1896). In the summer of 1893, Leduc began by painting the Glorious Mysteries for the chancel; he executed them in situ "because of the concavity of the vault where they are".[2] The paintings for the chancel vault were already in place in November 1893 when the Stations of the Cross by Georges Delfosse (1869--1939) were installed.[3] The paintings of the Sorrowful Mysteries were put in position on the left side of the nave vault in February 1894, and the marouflage, or process of cementing the painted canvas

to the wall, was supervised by Leduc's future partner Eugène L. Desautels (d. 1937) of Saint-Hyacinthe. The Joyful Mysteries were installed in October 1894.[4] The transept paintings were the last to be completed except for the two for the organ loft, and Leduc signed the ensemble by inserting his own portrait among the disciples in the scene showing *Jesus Calming the Waves* (fig. 6).

A letter from Leduc to Abbé Eugène Martin, dated August 16, 1932, throws light on the spirit in which the artist undertook this first ecclesiastical commission and on some of the problems he had to contend with:

One might say that the paintings are, rather than copies, arrangements after photographic or engraved reproductions of works by artists, for the most part well known. Or, in a few cases, that they are very free interpretations, as to drawing and colour, of the selected masters.

These arrangements and interpretations, to which the author added his own inventions to a quite considerable degree in some cases, were all executed on the same scale, in order to adapt them to the format of the panels to be filled.

This initial unification, continued and completed by the application of a uniform technique and the choice of a general colour scheme, was intended, according to the artist's plan, to create an overall harmony, a complete concordance between these "remade" paintings and the existing decoration. However, this piecemeal approach, although at the time it might have been appropriate to the amount Father Beaudry had budgeted for the work, affords little glory to its author, who would rather remain in the background.[5]

In accordance with the financial resources provided by Father Beaudry, Leduc drew inspiration from a collection of engravings and photographs "of pictures by European painters of different schools and periods".[6] This saved him from having to conceive an original composition for each scene. He did, however, face the task of adapting the images to the architecture and creating a certain unity in the colouring and scale of the figures in the various paintings. Moreover, the base of the barrel vault and the half

dome of the chancel posed particular problems, not the least of which was making the paintings "readable" from the height at which they were to be placed.

The format of the paintings in the chancel of the church of Joliette is complex, being composed of three geometric forms one inside the other: a horizontal rectangle, a circle and a square. In the Art Gallery of Ontario study, Leduc has meted out the various episodes that compose the story of the Resurrection. The fallen soldiers fill the right-hand part of the composition. In the centre, the angel guarding the tomb seems to support Christ, who floats above. Mary Magdalene, on the left, serves as a strong foreground element. The final painting would employ the same composition, although with greater emphasis on the Christ figure.

L. L.

---

1   *L'Étoile du Nord* [Joliette], March 21, 1894. The consecration of the church took place in February 1892 (*L'Étoile du Nord*, February 11, 1892). The wall paintings, begun in October 1891 by Joseph-Thomas Rousseau of Saint-Hyacinthe, were already finished at that time (*L'Étoile du Nord*, October 8, 1891).

2   Letter from Ozias Leduc to Wifrid Corbeil, c. s. v., September 3, 1932, BNQ 327/8/38.

3   *L'Étoile du Nord*, November 2, 1893. This information is confirmed by Brother Louis Vadeboncœur, c.s.v., choir master and draftsman, who saw the installation of Leduc's paintings, which began on October 30, 1893 (letter to Ozias Leduc, BNQ 327/5/3).

4   *L'Étoile du Nord*, February 8 and October 18, 1894.

5   BNQ 327/8/38.

6   List of works made for churches by Ozias Leduc, BNQ 327/2/1. For example, the figure of Christ in *The Resurrection* is derived from a painting by Ernst Deger (1809-1885) at the Maximilianeum in Munich. This figure was used again in the decoration of the original Church of Saint-Michel, Rougemont (fig. 129). The figure of the Magdalene in the foreground is derived from Bernhard Plockhorst (1825-1907).

Fig. 6   Ozias Leduc, *Jesus Calming the Waves*, 1894, oil on canvas, glued in place (Joliette, Cathedral of Saint-Charles-Borromée).

19
Night

About 1893

Oil on cardboard

22.8 x 15.8 cm

Signed lower right: *OZIAS LEDUC*

Private collection

INSCRIPTIONS

Verso: *Mr & Mme Édouard Clerk 36 Chemin Ozias Leduc Mont Saint Hilaire P.Q. « Ozias Leduc » « La Nuit »; Galerie Michel-Ange: Ozias Leduc La Nuit huile 1900 8¼ x 6 BB01 Sonia Denault; Exposition « Petits formats » 1987 Bruens 1988; Ozias Leduc huile La nuit 1900 8¼ x 6; Encadrements Marcel; à paraitre dans le livre de Broquet*

PROVENANCE

Studio of the artist; Mr. and Mrs. Édouard Clerk, Saint-Hilaire; Marc Clerk; Galerie Michel-Ange, Montreal, 1987; unidentified owner; Galerie Michel-Ange, 1992; private collection

L EDUC's good friend Olivier Maurault (cats. 161-163) once wrote to Leduc, "Your friends think that in your little house by the mountain, you have a back room where we are never admitted but from which you bring us out things that utterly astound us."[1] The apparent lack of any mention of *Night* in Leduc's personal papers or elsewhere, combined with the Victorian attitude towards depicting nudity, suggests he may have kept the painting hidden in this imaged room.

Here, Night is personified as a semi-nude woman perched on an ominous, billowing cloud that casts much of the picture in darkness. Her arm is raised in a gesture protective of her children as she moves to draw her drapery to shield them from the encroaching blinding light of dawn. The female figure and one child, both in a posture of anticipation, bear the impact of the fiery light of the rising sun. The highlights on her forehead and arm and those on the child's uplifted face enhance the chiaroscuro contrast between the areas of night and dawn. The atmospheric effect created by the luminous rays of the sun that bleed into the stratified clouds and tinge them with soft pink is one that Leduc would embrace more consistently, and perhaps to even greater effect, in his symbolist landscapes of the 1910s.

The dating of about 1893 is based on the research of Gabrielle Messier

(b. 1904), Leduc's assistant at the time of his death, who later compiled a catalogue of his works. If this date is correct, *Night* predates Leduc's other nudes, such as *Erato (Sleeping Muse)* (cat. 89) and *Repentant Magdalene* (cat. 125), by as much as five years. *Night* is as much an enigma today as it no doubt would have been to those few of Leduc's friends privileged enough to have the artist bring it out to them from his secret cache.

A. G.

1 Letter from Olivier Maurault to Ozias Leduc [27 March 1917], BNQ 327/6/2.

20
Still Life with Open Book

1894

Oil on canvas

38.5 x 48 cm

Signed and dated lower right: *O. Leduc 1894*

The Montreal Museum of Fine Arts, purchase, with contributions from the Government of Canada through the Cultural Property Export and Import Act and a gift from the Volunteer Committee of the Montreal Museum of Fine Arts, inv. 1985.7

INSCRIPTIONS

Recto: *Madonna and Child Sandro Botticelli*
Verso: *Still Life [...] book O. Leduc St-Hilaire; W.H. Rowley; Mr. W.H. Rowley 140 Bay; W.H. Rowley Ottawa April 94 50*

PROVENANCE

Studio of the artist; Colonel W. H. Rowley, Ottawa (15th Annual Exhibition, Royal Canadian Academy), 1894; Colonel W. H. Rowley estate, Ottawa; W. S. Walker, Ottawa; Paul-Émile Morin, Sarasota, Florida, 1949; Montreal Museum of Fine Arts, 1985

THE acquisition of *Still Life with Open Book* by the Montreal Museum of Fine Arts in 1985 was the occasion for its rediscovery, for the work had never been seen by those interested in the painter from Saint-Hilaire.[1] It was known to have been presented in Ottawa, at the Royal Canadian Academy's 15th Annual Exhibition in 1894. A photograph of the hanging illustrates the painting's unenviable fate during this show: enclosed in the heavy gold frame still in evidence today, the work was relegated to a position in the corner of the gallery, a bare thirty centimetres from the floor (fig. 7).[2]

The young Leduc's painting nevertheless succeeded in attracting the attention of a Toronto journalist, who recorded "a very painstaking study of still life, 'Open Book', which must have cost [the artist] many hours of labour". The critic felt, however, that "the brilliant red cloth foreground injures this work much and would be better away or subdued".[3] This reservation was clearly not shared by all, for the work found an immediate buyer, as the secretary of the RCA, James Smith, wrote to inform Ozias Leduc on April 2, 1894.[4]

The virtuosity with which Leduc has rendered each element of *Still Life with Open Book* is still a source of astonishment and delight. The open book that occupies the centre of the painting has been depicted with such scrupulous attention to detail that we are able to read the caption of the illustration on the left-hand page: "Madonna and Child Sandro Botticelli". In fact, the image is the central group from the painting in the Louvre entitled *Virgin and Child with Saint John the Baptist (Madonna of the Rosebush)* (fig. 8). We have the feeling that if we could just remove the tissue paper placed in the book to protect the engraving, we should also succeed in reading what is printed at the right. The exquisitely accurate rendering of virtually every leaf of the preciously jacketed volume represents one of Leduc's most masterful achievements in the art of trompe l'oeil.

The same perfectionism is evident in the treatment of the pile of books propping up the central volume and the folded newspaper inserted among them; this ensemble is topped by a magazine, a few letters and what looks like a curious little half-open box, or perhaps an optical instrument whose function remains something of a mystery. Between this monument to knowledge and learning – it is possible to decipher that one of the books is an art history textbook – and the open book, which is an invitation to introspection and meditation, Leduc has placed, parallel to the pictorial surface, a violin and bow.

On the right can be seen a stick of rosin and a candlestick, while to the left a partially visible rolled parchment effectively balances the composition. The background is almost entirely filled by the lower half of a grisaille after *The Presentation in the Temple* by Rubens

Fig. 7   Installation of the National Gallery of Canada's north gallery, 15th Annual Exhibition of the Royal Canadian Academy of Arts, Ottawa, March 1894 (photo: William James Topley/NAC).

Fig. 8   Sandro Botticelli (1444-1510), *Virgin and Child with Saint John the Baptist*, about 1468, oil on panel, 91 x 67 cm (Louvre).

Fig. 9   Fig. 10   Fig. 11

Fig. 9 Peter Paul Rubens, *The Presentation in the Temple*, before 1638, oil on panel, 62 x 47 cm (whereabouts unknown).
Fig. 10 Pierre-Henri Lebrun in Leduc's studio (BNQ 327/13/2.23).
Fig. 11 Ozias Leduc, *Raphael Album*, 1900, oil on canvas, 24.8 x 30.5 cm (whereabouts unknown; photo by Ozias Leduc, printed from glass negative No. 113, BNQ 327/12/2.13).

(1577-1640) (fig. 9).[5] Strangely, Leduc has concealed the central subject of this work – the Infant Jesus himself. His presence is merely suggested by the figure of the Virgin, who, arms outstretched, has just presented the child to Simeon. Joseph, kneeling at the latter's feet, proffers two doves, while to his right stands a male figure holding a taper. A photograph taken in Leduc's studio towards the end of the nineteenth century (fig. 10) reveals that he owned a large reproduction of the Rubens. The image had to be considerably reduced to serve as the background for this still life.

Still Life with Open Book is one of Leduc's most ambitious works of this type from the last decade of the century. There are nonetheless a number of features that link it to these other paintings, including its highly finished style and the subject depicted. The central motif of the open book also appears in *Still Life, Books* of 1892 (cat. 11) and the *Raphael Album* of 1900 (fig. 11), as well as *Still Life with Books and Magnifying Glass*, from after 1924 (cat. 185). In the two latter cases, the book is placed on the same red tablecloth, which, moreover, appears again in *Still Life (Three Pennies)* of 1892 (cat. 13). In addition, the illustration that figures in the *Raphael Album* also shows a Virgin and Child. Finally, a violin was the main subject of a still life exhibited at the Art Association of Montreal in 1891 (whereabouts unknown).

Are these duplications fortuitous, or do they contain clues that can help us understand *Still Life with Open Book*? How, in fact, should we "read" this

painting by Leduc? Although nothing appears to have been left to chance in the choice and arrangement of each of the composition's elements, are we obliged to assume that each object possesses a particular and precisely defined meaning? It has been suggested that Leduc was attempting to establish here a parallel between God, creator of the universe, and the artist – himself – creator of a personal universe.[6] It has also been claimed that the work constitutes something of a manifesto on the role of the artist as mediator between the phenomenal and noumenal worlds.[7] Another possibility, supported by the juxtaposition of the Virgin and Child theme with that of the Presentation in the Temple, is to see the work as a meditation on the notion of offering and, by extension, on the dispossession it entails: the dispossession experienced by the artist, who offers for judgement to his peers, his critics and his public the fruits of his labour, his research and his doubts.

Y. L.

1   The work had at that time never been reproduced, and although its existence and precise location were known to Louis Portugais, director of production at the National Film Board, he was not, as he had hoped, able to borrow it for the shooting of Jean Palardy's 1959 film *Correlieu* (letter from Louis Portugais to Paul-Émile Morin, May 26, 1958, MMFA Archives, work file).

2   This may have had something to do with the fact that Leduc was not at that time a member of the RCA.

3   "Art Notes: The Royal Canadian Academy's Exhibition", *The Week* [Toronto], April 6, 1894, pp. 448-449.

4   "I am pleased to inform you that your Picture, 'Open Book' has been sold to W. H. Rowley Ottawa for $50.00" (BNQ 327/5/4). A second letter from Smith to Leduc, dated April 17, 1894, accompanied Rowley's cheque (BNQ 327/5/4). The amount paid in 1894 for *Still Life with Open Book* was only slightly less than the prices asked by the artist the same year for two of his best-known works: $55 for *Still Life, Study by Candlelight* (cat. 17) and $60 for *The Young Student* (cat. 23).

5   Reproduced in Julius S. Held, *The Oil Sketches of Peter Paul Rubens: A Critical Catalogue*, vol. II (Princeton, New Jersey: Princeton University Press, 1980), pl. 327.

6   Arlene Gehmacher, "In Pursuit of the Ideal: The Still Life Paintings of Ozias Leduc", Master's thesis, University of Toronto, 1986, pp. 36-37.

7   Barbara Ann Winters, "The Work and Thought of Ozias Leduc in the Intellectual and Social Context of His Time", Master's thesis, University of Victoria, May 1990, pp. 97-98.

21
Girl Reading
1894

Oil on canvas

29.6 x 25.6 cm

Monogrammed and dated upper left: *18 O.L. 94*

Quebec City, Musée du Québec, inv. 77.212

PROVENANCE

Studio of the artist; René Bergeron, Chicoutimi, 1943; Fraser, Montreal, January 1971, lot 667; René Gagnon; Musée du Québec, 1977

22
The Reader
1894

Charcoal on laid paper

39.6 x 46.4 cm

Monogrammed and dated upper left: *18 OL 94*

Private collection

PROVENANCE

Studio of the artist; Émile Filion, p.s.s., 1940; private collection 1963

23
The Young Student
1894

Oil on canvas

36.7 x 46.7 cm

Monogrammed and dated upper right: *18 OL 94*

Ottawa, The National Gallery of Canada, inv. 18023

INSCRIPTIONS

Verso: *St H. Nov 1894 O.L.*

PROVENANCE

Henri Lemaître Auger; Jacques Auger, Montreal; National Gallery of Canada, 1974

A LONG with the products of the earth (cats. 1, 16-17) and the instruments and materials of the artist (cats. 12-13, 90), books are among the objects that figure most frequently in Leduc's still lifes (cats. 11, 20, 185, 236). Indeed, in the early 1890s, the fruits of nature, items related to the practice of painting and printed matter were the basis of his pictorial production.

A group of four works combine portraiture with some of these elements to underscore the merits of reading and create an allegory on art.[1] Adolescents are depicted reading, not casually, as a pastime, but with unusual concentration, completely enthralled by the page before them. Clearly, the process taking place is a genuinely instructional and formative one. Although each of the models can be identified, the works are not so much portraits as edifying parables.[2] The highly finished style and attention to detail make us immediately conscious of their narrative and prescriptive content. What should our approach to reading be? Leduc suggests it is a habit that must be instilled during youth, when it can nourish and guide.

Several clues indicate that we are in the painter's own space: the green tablecloth, the magazines and the glass with its brushes serve to locate the scenes in Leduc's studio. Moreover, the sitters are all members of his family. *Girl Reading* features his sister Ozéma (1878-1956)

(fig. 12), whom he was to represent again in a charcoal drawing, where she is seen in profile, again reading (fig. 13). More notably, though, she was his favoured model for the figure of the Virgin in *The Assumption* in the Church of Saint-Hilaire (cats. 31-32). Leduc's brother Honorius posed for *The Reader* and *The Young Student*.[3] In fact, the artist made no attempt to hide the identity of his models even though he exhibited the works under the general title of "reader" (fig. 14).[4] In each version of the theme, Leduc has varied the pose and components, and altered the lighting to create the different atmospheres associated with different times of day.

It is possible to see these scenes as evocations of the adolescent Leduc himself, absorbed by a fascinating passage, copying out texts that interested him, discovering the world of images through the printed reproductions of illustrated magazines. Later, when he served as a school commissioner, Leduc had the opportunity to reiterate in another way his faith in the didactic potential of books and illustrations (cat. 172).[5]

Various critics noted the contrast between the models' youth and beauty

Fig. 12   Leduc's sister Ozéma reading in front of the painting *Saint Hilary Writing His Treatise* for the Church of Saint-Hilaire (photo by Ozias Leduc, printed from glass negative No. 153, BNQ 327/13/2.2).

Fig. 13   Ozias Leduc, *My Sister (Ozéma)*, undated, charcoal on paper, 45 x 30 cm (private collection).

21

22

23

Fig. 14   *Reader*, about 1894, oil on canvas mounted on cardboard, 54.6 x 45 cm (whereabouts unknown).

and the seriousness of their intellectual involvement.[6] The act of reading seems to have induced a kind of trance: the model is completely engrossed, and the space between the page and the face seems charged with a mysterious density. This mystery is rooted partially in the fact that what is being read remains hidden, for Leduc deliberately does little or nothing to reveal the subject of their scrutiny. The reader holds his almost transparent newspaper up to the light; the characters on the page before the girl reading are so delicate they apparently cannot be reproduced; and the studying boy concentrates on an illustrated journal of which not even the image can be deciphered. It is thus not what the young people are reading that is the subject of these works, but the importance of the act of reading itself and how it should be approached. Here, the printed page becomes, like a painting, a surface to be examined and interpreted, one whose full import depends on the degree of the reader-observer's involvement. Leduc illustrates the absorption of the reader, and in so doing offers a mirror image of the spectator attempting to grasp the meaning of the painting.

L. L., M. L.

1   The whereabouts of the fourth painting, *Reader*, about 1894, is unknown (Sotheby's sale, Toronto, May 28, 1985, lot 864) (fig. 14). The model for this work was Ernest Lebrun (1871-1950), Leduc's cousin and future brother-in-law. Lebrun married Leduc's sister Adélia (1870-1946), and the artist married Ernest's sister Marie-Louise (1859-1939).

2   Several critics remarked on the realism and conservatism of *The Young Student*: "Mr. O. Leduc's 'Young Student' is almost microscopic in its attention to detail and will be studied with pleasure and relief, after seeing some of the 'slap dashery' that is striving to pass as 'art'" ("Art Exhibition: Some Vicissitudes of Criticism", *The Montreal Daily Witness*, April 1, 1897, p. 1); "Rather curious, nevertheless, this small pile of books, the open magazine, and the shirt sleeve. We are tempted to touch it to make sure that it is actually a painting" (Louis Fréchette, "Le Salon", *La Presse* [Montreal], April 10, 1897, p. 4).

3   Honorius Leduc (1876-1959) assisted on a number of Leduc's religious interiors: 1896-1899, Church of Saint-Hilaire; 1902-1903, Saint Ninian's Cathedral, Antigonish, Nova Scotia (BNQ 327/2/5); 1903, chapel of the Dames du Sacré-Cœur Convent, Halifax, Nova Scotia (BNQ 327/2/9); 1905-1907, Church of Saint-Romuald, Farnham (BNQ 327/2/17); 1906, Church of Sainte-Marie, Manchester, New Hampshire (BNQ 327/2/12); 1942-1944, Church of Notre-Dame-de-la-Présentation, Shawinigan-Sud (BNQ 327/9/7).

4   This is clear from the contents of a letter dated August 15, 1894, sent to Leduc by Robert Lindsay, secretary of the Art Association. Following the inclusion of *Girl Reading* in the 15th Spring Exhibition, a collector expressed interest in acquiring a painting on the same theme: "Have you got such a painting on hand for sale, or if not will you paint one on commission? I do not mean of course another portrait of your sister, but a fancy head" (BNQ 327/5/4).

5   See, for example, the draft of a letter from Ozias Leduc to Father Barré of Saint-Hilaire, asking him to stress the importance of school attendance. Leduc adds, "We hope to make [the schools] more appealing and to attract children by carefully chosen pastimes, images calculated to develop the intellectual and physical faculties" ([early January 1919], BNQ 327/8/25).

6   For example, Ruth Bohème [pseudonym of Fernande Choquette-Clerk], "Un peintre de « chez nous »", *La Patrie* [Montreal], March 11, 1916, p. 19, and René Bergeron, *Art et Bolchévisme* (Montreal: Fides, 1946), p. 93: "But the beautiful exterior does nothing to hide the intellectuality of the model's activity."

24
Study for *Saint Hilary Raising the Child Who Died without Baptism*

About 1894

Pen and brown ink with graphite on pink wove paper

15.8 x 23.3 cm

Ottawa, The National Gallery of Canada, inv. 9723
INSCRIPTIONS
Verso: *Étude pour une tête de Saint-Hilaire. Un tableau qui était autrefois dans l'église de la paroisse*; M
PROVENANCE
Studio of the artist; Pierre de Ligny Boudreau; National Gallery of Canada, 1961

25
Study for *Saint Hilary Raising the Child Who Died without Baptism* (first version)

About 1894

Graphite and blue pencil with pen and black ink on wove paper

31 x 21.6 cm

Ottawa, The National Gallery of Canada, gift of Gabrielle Messier, Saint-Hilaire, Quebec, 1972, inv. 17014
PROVENANCE
Studio of the artist; Gabrielle Messier, Saint-Hilaire; National Gallery of Canada, 1972

26
Study for *Saint Hilary Raising the Child Who Died without Baptism* (second version)

About 1894

Graphite and blue pencil with pen and black ink on laid paper (watermark: "ED & Cie")

30.3 x 20.9 cm

Ottawa, The National Gallery of Canada, gift of Gabrielle Messier, Saint-Hilaire, Quebec, 1972, inv. 17015
PROVENANCE
Studio of the artist; Gabrielle Messier, Saint-Hilaire; National Gallery of Canada, 1972

24

25

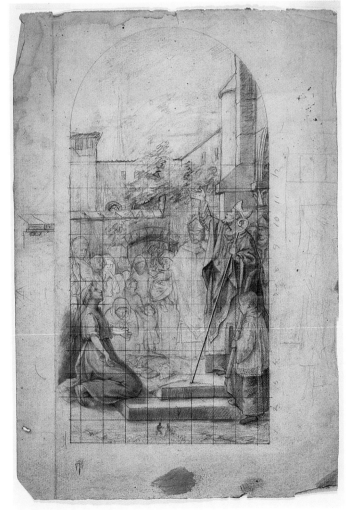

26

Before 1897

IN the many lists of his paintings drawn up by Ozias Leduc, there is never any mention of *Saint Hilary Raising the Child Who Died without Baptism*. However, an inscription on the back of the drawing of Saint Hilary's head leaves no doubt concerning the identification, execution and destination of the work: "Study for a head of Saint Hilary. A painting that was previously in the church of the parish." The picture was apparently removed and donated to "a mission church in Manitoba"[1] when a new decorative ensemble was created for the Church of Saint-Hilaire in 1898 (cats. 27-56).

There are no extant documents related to this commission, but it probably came from Louis-Cléophas Blanchard, parish priest of Saint-Hilaire from 1889 to 1894, who undertook renovations in the church and ordered construction of a luxurious presbytery.

The Bibliothèque nationale du Québec holds a rough sketch[2] that shows an early idea for the composition of *Saint Hilary Raising the Child Who Died without Baptism*. The scene as compared to the National Gallery drawings is reversed, and the group of mother and child is on the same level as the Bishop of Poitiers. Two of the Ottawa sheets are full compositional studies with partial squaring off. Here, the action takes place in a church square. The architecture and the disposition of the figures enable us to determine the rank and function of the various protagonists. The Romanesque building closes the composition off and concentrates attention on the foreground. The crowd merges into the wall, while the dramatic gesture of the weeping mother echoes the Bishop's prayer. The head study is an indication of the care with which Leduc conceived each character. The gaunt features and contemplative demeanour make this image of the miracle worker both convincing and inspiring.

Of all the events in the life of Saint Hilary, Leduc chose to depict this scene of the bringing back to life of a dead child. The death in November 1887, during an epidemic of fever, of the five-year-old twin daughters of Luigi Capello and Marie-Louise Lebrun, and the deaths of four of his own brothers and sisters[3] (cat. 4), must have made this episode in the life of his native parish's patron saint especially poignant for the artist. In his 1898 interior of the Church of Saint-Hilaire, Leduc depicted the Bishop of Poitiers in another role – that of inspired writer (cat. 27).

L. L.

---

1   Jean-René Ostiguy, *Ozias Leduc: Symbolist and Religious Painting*, exhib. cat. (Ottawa: National Gallery of Canada, 1974), p. 112.

2   BNQ 327/9/38. An entry dated June 8, 1953, in Leduc's Diary mentions the sale of a "Head of a woman (detail of a painting formerly in the Church of Saint-Hilaire)" to Roger Laflamme (BNQ 327/3/12).

3   The oldest, Célestine, died in 1863, before Leduc was born; Théodore died in 1869; another child named Célestine in 1879; and Eugénie in 1888.

"Drawing, Colour, Composition: The Painter's Trinity"

1 Maurice Cullen (1866-1934), James Wilson Morrice (1865-1924) and Marc-Aurèle de Foy Suzor-Coté are some of the Canadian artists who brought back from their studies in Europe influences that enabled them to better defend the values of modern art.

2 "Moreover, the supreme object of Art is to instruct; and whenever it has forgotten this object, history shows us it in decay. Its glory is bound up with the ideas it calls forth. In spite of the beautiful form, the perfect technique, the magnificent colouring with which it has been clothed at certain periods of its evolution, it has often remained void. It has drawn attention merely by its exteriors, and the mind has grown quickly tired of it; for the mind has other eyes than the easily fascinated eyes of the flesh." (Ozias Leduc, "The Decorations of St. Ninian's Cathedral", *The Casket* [Antigonish, Nova Scotia], September 3, 1903, p. 2.)

3 See Laurier Lacroix *et al.*, *Ozias Leduc the Draughtsman*, exhib. cat. (Montreal: Concordia University, 1978), p. 104.

4 Dante, *Paradiso*, Canto 1: 103-105, noted by Ozias Leduc in "Transcriptions de citations", BNQ 327/4/14. Quoted in English from the translation by Dorothy L. Sayers and Barbara Reynolds (Baltimore: Penguin Books, 1962).

WHILE new art movements and avant-garde theories raged in Europe, Ozias Leduc (fig. 15), with his usual reserve, quietly went about painting a *Still Life (with Lay Figure)* (cat. 90) as a sort of understated manifesto. Beneath the frame's rabbet, he concealed what is openly conveyed in the painting itself: the creative elements of his art. Leduc proclaimed the primacy of drawing, colour and composition as the fundamental elements of the artist's work. The terms he used show Leduc as a forerunner of modernism in Quebec,[1] a champion of painterly qualities as opposed to the subject and idea represented, but they also carry a more classical, traditional meaning.[2]

Leduc was certainly conscious of the importance of plastic values in painting, as is apparent from the accomplished works produced at this time, but he also used these three terms in a particular way. The subject is not rejected but remains the central element in each painting. The term "drawing" carries the idea of the concept of the work, of the choices the artist must make in terms of specific shapes. These may present themselves during the execution of the work, and the artist must pay them heed,[3] but they are not constrained to fit into an overall notion, nor are they to be considered as spontaneous upwellings from the subconscious, in the Automatistes' sense of the pictorial object. "Colour" is what reveals light, embodies the emotion expressed by the painting, and is therefore the painter's most vital tool. "Composition" refers to the ordering of the elements of the subject. In recasting Dante's "All beings great and small / Are linked in order, and this orderliness / Is form which stamps God's likeness on the All,"[4] Leduc claims that the structure of an artwork is based on rules that correspond to those found in nature and which it is the artist's business to discover or to reinvent.[5] Imagination shaped by knowledge is the path to beauty.

This sense of a natural order of things "around which the human soul circles, trembling and in fear, with its unappeasable thirst for happiness" is apparent in the list Leduc made in 1906 of the ten paintings he would choose for his ideal picture gallery. Corot, Whistler, Millet, Poussin, Ingres, Puvis de Chavannes, Watts, Delacroix, Claude Lorrain and Turner constitute the pantheon of artists in whose work colour and design meld together on the canvas to evoke an idealized vision.[6] The artists of the Renaissance, whose influence on his earlier work is undoubted, have been replaced by artists of the nineteenth century, with the exception of Claude Lorrain and Poussin.

For Leduc, the years 1897-1911 constituted a period in which to further his knowledge.[7] His time in London and Paris in 1897 had given him direct contact with European paintings and enabled him to amass "the largest possible amount of materials and information, and it will be upon these foundations that I shall build my craft, which I pray may bear some resemblance to the purest ideal that each of us harbours within".[8] It was in the year 1911 that Leduc's Symbolist bent became apparent, translated into an even more private vocabulary of images drawn from landscape.

During this period, Leduc's work became better known, not so much through exhibitions as had previously been the case, but mainly as a result of commissions for churches in Quebec, the Maritime Provinces and the United States.[9] Antigonish, Halifax, Dover and Manchester were perhaps not well-known centres for art, but commissions from these towns – and from Saint-Hilaire, Rougemont, Sainte-Julie, Farnham, Saint-Barnabé, Saint-Hyacinthe and Coaticook – made Leduc more widely known and appreciated. In his designs for churches, he stressed the importance of drawing, colour and composition, but never at the expense of the central idea, the message of the work: "My only object is to show clearly the importance of the *meaning* underlying a work of this sort. And it is my earnest desire to see this principle, and others also, such as *unity*, in *variety*, *adaptation*, *association*, which are the criteria of beautiful things, a little less misunderstood whenever there is a question of making a useful application of Art."[10]

At the same time, some of Leduc's still lifes (cats. 90, 103), landscapes (cats. 120-122), portraits (cats. 123, 126) and illustrations (cats. 93-102, 127) attracted the attention of people with a certain social, intellectual or political standing, albeit at the regional rather than the

5 Leduc often spoke of the importance of rules in using the materials and methods that will culminate in a work of art. Writing about the decoration of Saint Ninian's Cathedral, he said, "Everyone knows that in order to realize an artistic decoration, it is not enough to give rein to one's imagination, to conceive lines, to evoke forms, to arrange colours. Lines, forms, colors, are only the elements; it is necessary to coordinate them, to arrange them after certain fixed principles, in order to produce an harmonious effect. Every Art must have rules." (Leduc 1903.) Speaking of the church at Saint-Hilaire, he wrote, "Beauty is the result of measured proportions, of rules governed by that order which seems to be, must be, the pivot around which the human soul circles, trembling and in fear, with its unappeasable thirst for happiness. Beauty is part of happiness. It is through order that art achieves beauty." (Ozias Leduc, "Pourquoi nous aimons notre église", undated manuscript, BNQ 327/2/38.)

6 In reply to a request from the Boston publishers Bates & Guild dated September 18, 1906 (BNQ 327/15/16). The paintings' titles are given in the Chronology, at 1906.

7 This coincides with Sir Wilfrid Laurier's successive terms of office as Prime Minister of Canada, from 1896 to 1911. The Liberals were also in power in Quebec during the same period, which ended with the rise of Quebec nationalism under the leadership of Henri Bourassa.

8 Letter from Ozias Leduc to Father Laflamme, dated Paris, June 24, 1897 (Service des archives de l'Archidiocèse de Sherbrooke, Msgr. Desranleau papers, P2/7.4.1A).

9 Leduc benefited from the spread of Quebec Catholicism through emigration. An estimated half-million French Canadians moved to the United States between 1861 and 1901. Leduc believed, as did the clergy who ministered to the immigrants, in the importance of fostering nationalist values associated with faith and language. "The observance of the laws of God is not opposed to the veneration which we have for whatever has been handed down to us by our ancestors. After Faith, its language is what a nation holds most dear." (Leduc 1903.)

While learning as much as he could about his art, Leduc was also becoming an established painter of religious subjects. In the summer of

1899, he began to teach the nuns of the Saints Noms de Jésus et de Marie congregation at Saint-Hilaire, and later in Longueuil. In June 1904, at the request of Father Laflamme Leduc became acquainted with the Sisters of the Precious Blood at Saint-Hyacinthe; he gave them classes and executed for the convent his painting *Jesus in the House of Martha and Mary* (whereabouts unknown). In 1906 and 1907, he painted the portraits of the Abbé Vincent (cat. 132), Leduc (cat. 131) and Desnoyers (destroyed 1963).

10 Leduc 1903.

11 The earliest examples of illustrated books published in Canada include Catherine Parr Trail's *Canadian Wild Flowers, Painted and Lithographed by Agnes Fitzgibbon* (Montreal, 1868), and *Picturesque Canada*, published in serial form in Toronto from 1882. The latter was largely illustrated by Lucius O'Brien (1832-1899) together with a team of illustrators in the United States. On the subject of book illustration during this period, see Yves Chèvrefils, "John Henry Walker (1831-1899), artisan-graveur", *The Journal of Canadian Art History*, vol. 8, no. 2 (1985), pp. 178-225.

12 F. S. Coburn illustrated W. H. Drummond's *Phil-o-rum's Canoe and Madeleine Verchères*, published in 1898, and the following year illustrated the same author's *The Habitant and Other French Canadian Poems*, as well as Louis Fréchette's *Christmas in French Canada* (by the same publisher). See Elizabeth H. Kennell, "Frederick Simpson Coburn's Illustrations for the Poetry of Dr. W. H. Drummond", Master's thesis, Concordia University, 1985.

13 Other notable illustrated books published at this time include Dr. Eugène Dick's *Un Drame au Labrador*, illustrated by Edmond-J. Massicotte (1875-1929) (Montreal: Leprohon & Leprohon, 1897?); J. O. Chauveau's *Charles Guérin: roman de mœurs canadiennes*, illustrated by Jean-Baptiste Lagacé (Montreal: la Cie de publication de la Revue canadienne, 1900); and Rodolphe Girard's *Florence: légende historique, patriotique et nationale*, illustrated by Georges Delfosse (Montreal, 1900). On Canadian English-language illustrated publications, see Sybille Pantazzi, "Book Illustration and Design by Canadian Artists, 1890-1940", *National Gallery of Canada Bulletin*, no. 7 (1966), pp. 6-24.

provincial level. These included members of literary and political circles such as the Choquette family (cat. 92, fig. 104), Gustave Ouimet, Louis-Philippe Brodeur (cat. 123), Joséphine Marchand-Dandurand and Arsène Bessette.

A number of these new contacts came about as a result of Leduc's part in the boom in illustrated novels. Although from the 1880s onwards, original illustrations were to be found in some magazines and books with Canadian content,[11] it was still unusual for illustrations to be commissioned for works by Canadian authors. Among the finest editions of the period were the volumes of William H. Drummond's poetry published by the American company of G.P. Putnam's Sons and illustrated by Frederick Simpson Coburn (1871-1960).[12] Leduc's illustrations for Dr. Choquette's novel *Claude Paysan* (cats. 92-102) show him to have been one of the first Canadian artists with limited means and training to take up the challenge of book illustration.[13]

L. L.

Preparatory Drawings for the Decoration of the Church of Saint-Hilaire (Cats. 27-56)

27
Study for *Saint Hilary Writing His Treatise*

About 1897-1899

Graphite on buff wove paper

25.2 x 15.8 cm

Signed lower right: *OZIAS LEDUC*

Ottawa, The National Gallery of Canada, inv. 28108.4

PROVENANCE

Studio of the artist; Gabrielle Messier; Edward Bourbeau; private collection; National Gallery of Canada, 1982

28
Study for *The Adoration of the Magi*

About 1897-1899

Graphite on cream wove paper

9.8 x 12.2 cm

Signed lower right: *OZIAS LEDUC*

Private collection

INSCRIPTIONS

Verso: *No 47*

PROVENANCE

Galerie Rodrigue Lemay, Ottawa; Maurice Chagnon, Ottawa, about 1982; private collection

29
Study for *The Ascension*

About 1897-1899

Graphite on buff wove paper

20.3 x 13 cm

Ottawa, The National Gallery of Canada, inv. 28108.3

INSCRIPTIONS

Verso: *Saint-Hilaire; Adoration des Mages; 19.9 x 8.2 ³/₈*

PROVENANCE

Studio of the artist; Gabrielle Messier; Edward Bourbeau; private collection; National Gallery of Canada, 1982

27

28

29

30

Study for *The Assumption*

About 1898

Charcoal on beige laid paper

24.2 x 31.4 cm

Initialed lower right: *OL*

Françoise Goulet collection

INSCRIPTIONS

Verso, label: *Morency (no 1472)*

PROVENANCE

Cécile Baillargeon; Françoise Goulet, about 1970

31

Study for *The Assumption*

1898

Charcoal and traces of white chalk on laid paper

30.9 x 25.9 cm

Signed and dated lower right: *Ozias Leduc 1898*

Private collection

INSCRIPTIONS

Recto, lower right: *Ressemblance de ma sœur – Ozema*

Verso: labels of ABC Frame & Gallery Ltd; Galerie d'art Michel Bigué

PROVENANCE

Studio of the artist; Galerie l'Art canadien, Chicoutimi; Galerie Michel Bigué; Galerie Vinant, Ottawa; private collection

30

31

32

33

33
Study for *The Assumption*

About 1897-1899

Graphite on buff wove paper

25 x 15.9 cm

Signed lower right: *OZIAS LEDUC*

Ottawa, The National Gallery of Canada, inv. 28108.5

PROVENANCE

Studio of the artist; Gabrielle Messier; Edward Bourbeau; private collection; National Gallery of Canada, 1982

32
Study for *The Assumption*

1898

Charcoal on laid paper

41.4 x 30.6 cm

Initialed and dated lower right: *O.L. 98*

Private collection

PROVENANCE

Studio of the artist; Stephen Clerk, Saint-Hilaire; private collection, 1970

34

Study for *The Baptism of Christ*

About 1897-1899

Graphite on buff laid paper

16.1 x 21 cm

Ottawa, The National Gallery of Canada,
inv. 28108.6

INSCRIPTIONS

Verso: Studies for *Christ Giving the Keys to Saint
Peter* and *Saint Hilary Writing His Treatise*

PROVENANCE

Studio of the artist; Gabrielle Messier; Edward
Bourbeau; private collection; National Gallery of
Canada, 1982

35

Study for *The Baptism of Christ*

About 1897-1899

Graphite on buff wove paper

12.5 x 7.5 cm

Initialed lower right: *OL*

Ottawa, The National Gallery of Canada,
inv. 28108.7

INSCRIPTIONS

Verso: Study for *The Baptism of Christ*

PROVENANCE

Studio of the artist; Gabrielle Messier; Edward
Bourbeau; private collection; National Gallery of
Canada, 1982

36

Study for *The Baptism of Christ*

About 1897-1899

Graphite on buff wove paper

21.4 x 12.5 cm

Ottawa, The National Gallery of Canada,
inv. 28108.8

PROVENANCE

Studio of the artist; Gabrielle Messier; Edward
Bourbeau; private collection; National Gallery of
Canada, 1982

34

35

36

38

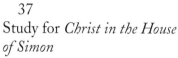

37

1811.5 B

39

O. LEDUC

40

37
Study for *Christ in the House of Simon*
About 1897-1899

Graphite on buff wove paper

21.2 x 14.4 cm

Initialed lower left: *OL*

Ottawa, The National Gallery of Canada, inv. 28108.9

INSCRIPTIONS

Recto, lower right: *S. Luc. VII*

PROVENANCE

Studio of the artist; Gabrielle Messier; Edward Bourbeau; private collection; National Gallery of Canada, 1982

38
Study for *The Supper at Emmaus*
About 1897-1899

Graphite on buff laid paper

16.6 x 11 cm

Ottawa, The National Gallery of Canada, inv. 28108.10

INSCRIPTIONS

Verso: Studies of cherubim

PROVENANCE

Studio of the artist; Gabrielle Messier; Edward Bourbeau; private collection; National Gallery of Canada, 1982

39
Study for *The Supper at Emmaus*
About 1897-1899

Graphite on blue wove paper

21.4 x 10.1 cm

Ottawa, The National Gallery of Canada, inv. 28108.11

PROVENANCE

Studio of the artist; Gabrielle Messier; Edward Bourbeau; private collection; National Gallery of Canada, 1982

40
Study for *The Supper at Emmaus*
About 1897-1899

Graphite on paper

21.4 x 10.2 cm

Signed lower right: *O. LEDUC*

Quebec City, Musée du Québec, inv. 85.21

INSCRIPTIONS

Verso: *O. Leduc No 13*

PROVENANCE

Studio of the artist; Gabrielle Messier, 1955; Otto Bengle, Montreal, late 1950s; Musée du Québec, 1985

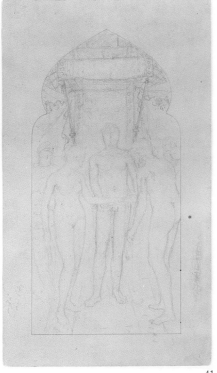

41

42

41
Study for *The Marriage of the Virgin*

About 1897-1899

Graphite on buff wove paper

21.3 x 12.6 cm

Ottawa, The National Gallery of Canada, inv. 28108.13

INSCRIPTIONS

Verso: *9*

PROVENANCE

Studio of the artist; Gabrielle Messier; Edward Bourbeau; private collection; National Gallery of Canada, 1982

42
Study for *The Marriage of the Virgin*

About 1897-1899

Graphite on buff wove paper

22 x 15.9 cm

Signed lower right: *OZIAS LEDUC*

Ottawa, The National Gallery of Canada, inv. 28108.14

PROVENANCE

Studio of the artist; Gabrielle Messier; Edward Bourbeau; private collection; National Gallery of Canada, 1982

44

43
Study for *Christ Giving the Keys to Saint Peter*

About 1897-1899

Graphite on buff wove paper

21.4 x 10.1 cm

Ottawa, The National Gallery of Canada, inv. 28108.15

PROVENANCE

Studio of the artist; Gabrielle Messier; Edward Bourbeau; private collection; National Gallery of Canada, 1982

44
Study for *Christ Giving the Keys to Saint Peter*

About 1897-1899

Graphite on blue paper

19.3 x 8.6 cm

Musée des beaux-arts de Sherbrooke, Sylvio Lacharité collection, inv. 90.8.21aG

PROVENANCE

Sylvio Lacharité, Sherbrooke; Musée des beaux-arts de Sherbrooke, gift of Luc Lacharité, Saint-Lambert, 1990

45

46

45

Study for *Christ Giving the Keys to Saint Peter*

1897

Oil over graphite sketch on canvas

20.2 x 9.1 cm

Signed lower right: *OZIAS LEDUC*; dated upper right: *1897*

Musée des beaux-arts de Sherbrooke, Sylvio Lacharité collection, inv. 90.8.21bG

INSCRIPTIONS

Recto, upper left: *Paris*

PROVENANCE

Sylvio Lacharité, Sherbrooke; Musée des beaux-arts de Sherbrooke, gift of Luc Lacharité, Saint-Lambert, 1990

46

Study for *Christ Giving the Keys to Saint Peter*

About 1897-1899

Pen and black ink with graphite on buff wove paper

22.8 x 16.5 cm

Ottawa, The National Gallery of Canada, inv. 28108.16

INSCRIPTIONS

Verso: Study for *Christ Giving the Keys to Saint Peter*

PROVENANCE

Studio of the artist; Gabrielle Messier; Edward Bourbeau; private collection; National Gallery of Canada, 1982

47

48

49

50

51

47
Study for *Pentecost*
About 1897-1899

Graphite on buff wove paper

14 x 13 cm

Ottawa, The National Gallery of Canada,
inv. 28108.12

INSCRIPTIONS

Verso: *Jesus*; *S. Pierre*; *Jean*; *Jacques*; *André*; *Philippe*;
Thomas; *Barthélemi*; *Mathieu*; *Jacques-fils d'Alphée*;
Simon; *Jude frère de Jacques*; *O.L.*

PROVENANCE

Studio of the artist; Gabrielle Messier; Edward
Bourbeau; private collection; National Gallery of
Canada, 1982

48
Study for *The Death of Joseph*
About 1897-1899

Graphite on buff wove paper

13.6 x 13.1 cm

Ottawa, The National Gallery of Canada,
inv. 28108.20

PROVENANCE

Studio of the artist; Gabrielle Messier; Edward
Bourbeau; private collection; National Gallery of
Canada, 1982

49
Study for *The Death of Joseph*
About 1897-1899

Graphite on buff wove paper

14.1 x 12.8 cm

Ottawa, The National Gallery of Canada,
inv. 28108.18

INSCRIPTIONS

Verso: Study for a decoration

PROVENANCE

Studio of the artist; Gabrielle Messier; Edward
Bourbeau; private collection; National Gallery of
Canada, 1982

50
Study for *The Death of Joseph*
About 1897-1899

Graphite on buff wove paper

14 x 12.7 cm

Ottawa, The National Gallery of Canada,
inv. 28108.19

PROVENANCE

Studio of the artist; Gabrielle Messier; Edward
Bourbeau; private collection; National Gallery of
Canada, 1982

51
Study for *The Death of Joseph*
About 1897-1899

Graphite on buff wove paper

14.1 x 12.3 cm

Ottawa, The National Gallery of Canada,
inv. 28108.17

PROVENANCE

Studio of the artist; Gabrielle Messier; Edward
Bourbeau; private collection; National Gallery of
Canada, 1982

52
Study for *Saint Luke*
About 1897-1899

Graphite on buff wove paper

12.1 x 13.4 cm

Ottawa, The National Gallery of Canada,
inv. 28108.23

PROVENANCE

Studio of the artist; Gabrielle Messier; Edward
Bourbeau; private collection; National Gallery of
Canada, 1982

53
Study for *Saint Matthew*
About 1897-1899

Graphite on buff wove paper

10.2 x 10.8 cm

Ottawa, The National Gallery of Canada,
inv. 28108.21

PROVENANCE

Studio of the artist; Gabrielle Messier; Edward
Bourbeau; private collection; National Gallery of
Canada, 1982

54
Study for *Saint Mark*
About 1897-1899

Graphite on buff wove paper

12.2 x 12.3 cm

Initialed lower left: *OL*

Ottawa, The National Gallery of Canada,
inv. 28108.22

INSCRIPTIONS

Verso: Study for *Saint Mark*

PROVENANCE

Studio of the artist; Gabrielle Messier; Edward
Bourbeau; private collection; National Gallery of
Canada, 1982

55
Study for *Saint John*
About 1897-1899

Graphite on buff wove paper

10.2 x 11.1 cm

Ottawa, The National Gallery of Canada,
inv. 28108.24

PROVENANCE

Studio of the artist; Gabrielle Messier; Edward
Bourbeau; private collection; National Gallery of
Canada, 1982

52

53

54

55

56
Study for *Saint John*
About 1897-1899

Graphite on blue wove paper

10.4 x 11.4 cm

Ottawa, The National Gallery of Canada,
inv. 28108.25

PROVENANCE

Studio of the artist; Gabrielle Messier; Edward
Bourbeau; private collection; National Gallery of
Canada, 1982

56

CRAIG STIRLING's study has shown the importance and complexity of the interior renovation of the Church of Saint-Hilaire, a turning point in Leduc's career.[1] This, the first overall scheme of decoration with original artwork, introduced a theme hitherto unused in Quebec, the Seven Sacraments. The project, carried out after a seven-month trip to London and Paris, was hailed as a triumph and was to obtain for Leduc other commissions of the same sort.[2] Since the church in question was that of the village where he had been born, it constituted an even greater challenge, in that the artist had to succeed in this task in order to prove himself to his fellow parishioners.[3]

In carrying out this commission, Leduc could rely on unstinting help from Father Joseph-Magloire Laflamme (1848-1926) (cat. 165), who on his arrival at Saint-Hilaire in September 1894 had immediately started on renovating and embellishing the church. The project continued until his departure for the parish of Saint-Romuald, in Farnham, in 1900 (cat. 135).[4] The church decoration fund, built up by raffles, bazaars, festivals and special collections, brought in the seven thousand dollars necessary for the task.[5]

The recent discovery of the contract for the execution of the paintings provides the exact dates on which the job was commissioned and completed. The contract was signed on April 22, 1897, and ended on April 20, 1900.[6] It is typical of contracts for this type of commission, stating the programme of decoration, the deadlines for execution, the quality standards and the parties and sums of money involved:

I, the undersigned, undertake to make and execute to the best of my ability fifteen oil paintings and the fourteen Stations of the Cross designed as follows, and to be placed in the Church of Saint-Hilaire; two large paintings, one on each side of the choir – one showing the Adoration of the Magi and the other the Ascension of Our Lord; two paintings over the side altars, one of Saint Hilary and the other showing the Assumption of the Blessed Virgin. One painting on the wall fac-ing the pulpit. The Magdalene at the feet of Our Lord in Simon's house. Four paintings on the left wall, two at each side in the places prepared for them, showing the Baptism of Our Lord. The institution of the Eucharist. The keys of the kingdom given to Saint Peter by Our Lord, and the Marriage of the Blessed Virgin and Saint Joseph; two paintings on the wall above the staircases complete the Seven Sacraments with allegories of Confirmation and Extreme Unction. Lastly, under the galleries, on the walls four paintings of the four Evangelists. The Way of the Cross of the size already prepared for on the walls, must be a copy of a Way of the Cross admired by artists or of similar artistic and real value.

These paintings must be installed in the course of the year eighteen hundred and ninety-eight, and judged worthy to stand alongside the present decoration of the church.

In return for said aforementioned paintings and Way of the Cross, the Reverend Father J. M. Laflamme, priest of the said parish of Saint-Hilaire, engages to pay the said Ozias Leduc, also a signatory hereto, the sum of nine hundred and fifteen dollars at the current rate within the time allotted for the installation of the said paintings and Way of the Cross, and acknowledges receipt this day the sum of two hundred dollars in quittance of the same in duplicate – personal commitment.

St-Hilaire this twenty-second day of April eighteen hundred and ninety-seven.

O. Leduc / J. M. Laflamme, priest

We the undersigned declare that we have received mutual quittance for the said aforementioned agreement, and declare it terminated as of the date here below. St. Hilaire 20 April 1900. O. Leduc J. M. Laflamme, priest

[in the left margin of the first page]

settled April 20 1900 / 2 large paintings for the choir $125.00 each / 2 paintings for the altars $75.00 each / wall facing pulpit $75.00 / the 4 others in the nave $50.00 each / The 4 Evangelists $25.00 each / The two [paintings] on the staircase walls $25.00 each / The Way of the Cross $90.00.[7]

This important document is, however, vague about how far the work had progressed by April 1897 and fails to mention who was responsible for the choice of the iconographic programme. The contact specifies that the paintings are to be installed "in the places prepared for them", just as the Way of the Cross is to be "of the size already prepared for on the walls",[8] and that these paintings should be "judged worthy to stand alongside the present decoration of the church". In April 1897, Leduc had already painted all of the decorative patterns that were to link the neo-Gothic style of the church and the projected paintings, and had thus settled on the placing and size of the latter. The vine tendrils around the vault of the choir, the fleur-de-lys motif that covered the whole surface of the dome, the ornamental borders around the ribbed vault of the nave, the Gothic arches surrounding the paintings, the imitation mosaic and the plants in painted pots at the bottom of the walls of the nave were all part of the preliminary programme.[9]

The completion of a first painting for the church (cats. 25-26), together with the historical and iconographic research Leduc had carried out in his own library (fig. 50), suggest that the artist was a valuable colleague for Father Laflamme. The overall design, undoubtedly largely due to Leduc, deals mainly with the Sacraments (figs. 16-22) and the Evangelists (figs. 23-26), which occupy the walls of the nave. In the choir and the side altars are an *Adoration of the Magi* (fig. 27), an *Ascension* (fig. 28), an *Assumption* (fig. 29) and a *Saint Hilary Writing His Treatise* (fig. 30).[10]

To do further research on this project, Leduc went to study in Europe in 1897. The only known letter of his from Paris, addressed to Father Laflamme and dated June 24, 1897, suggests that work is proceeding more slowly than expected.

In between my visits to museums I carry on painting your pictures, trying to make use of the things I have seen but not yet practised too often ... As my means are slender, I have been considering not executing the Stations of the Cross here but rather using all the time at my disposal – which will be too short for me to complete the programme – in studying the principal work, collecting the largest possible

Fig. 16 Fig. 17 Fig. 18 Fig. 19

Fig. 20 Fig. 21 Fig. 22

amount of material and information; and it will be on this basis that I shall build my work, which I hope may come close to realizing the pure ideal that each of us carries within.[11]

The forty drawing for the church shown in the exhibition (cats. 27-56, 57-66) enable us to reconstruct in part how the project developed and how Leduc approached it. The variety of mediums and supports, as well as the numerous studies for each work, show the care that went into their execution. Each painting was prepared for with studies of anatomy, hands and facial expressions, then individual nude figures drawn from lay figures, ultimately arranged in groups, with drawings of drapery, colour studies and the layout of the work as a whole squared off. Leduc does not seem to have produced a cartoon as such, but rather a model or drawing to scale then squared for transfer to canvas. The paintings executed in the studio were later mounted on the church walls.

A sketchbook begun in Paris contains twenty-seven drawings, including ten pages of studies of heads and hands to be used in Saint-Hilaire (cats. 57-66) and to serve as a stockpile of images. The same female model appears to have been used for two angels' heads in the *Assumption*

Fig. 16-30 Ozias Leduc, about 1897-1899, oil on canvas, glued in place (Church of Saint-Hilaire).

Fig. 16 *The Baptism of Christ*, 304 x 147 cm.

Fig. 17 *Christ in the House of Simon*, 304 x 175 cm.

Fig. 18 *The Supper at Emmaus*, 304 x 104 cm.

Fig. 19 *Pentecost*, 168 x 153 cm.

Fig. 20 *The Marriage of the Virgin*, 304 x 147 cm.

Fig. 21 *Christ Giving the Keys to Saint Peter*, 304 x 104 cm.

Fig. 22 *The Death of Saint Joseph*, 168 x 153 cm.

Fig. 23 *Saint John*, about 1897-1899, 108 x 116 cm.

Fig. 24 *Saint Matthew*, 108 x 116 cm.

Fig. 25 *Saint Mark*, 137 x 156 cm.

Fig. 26 *Saint Luke*, 137 x 156 cm.

Fig. 23

Fig. 24

Fig. 25

Fig. 26

(fig. 29), for Mary Magdalene's face in the *Christ in the House of Simon* (fig. 17) and for the head of the Virgin in *The Death of Saint Joseph* (fig. 22). Similarly, certain detailed studies of hands were used in four paintings, the same study being used for two different figures. Thus, the hand in the centre of the first page (cat. 57) can be found again in the painting of Saint Hilary (fig. 30) and in the figure of Saint Joseph in *The Marriage of the Virgin* (fig. 20).

Each figure in the paintings is studied mainly through the use of a lay figure (cats. 28, 48).[12] Some sketches (cats. 34, 48) indicate how Leduc "dressed" the pose so as to create the character required by the setting, and how he translated the expressiveness of the physical gesture into a symbolic language of movement. Other sketches incorporate the background elements of landscape

(cats. 35-36, 54) and architecture (cats. 37, 40) in which the scenes are set.

Parts of the composition are often reworked (cats. 48-51), demonstrating the development from academic study to an imaginative transposition, the search for "a multiplicity of symbolic expression to nourish our Christian faith and our love of each other".[13]

The group studies incorporate the life studies into the main composition. They are invariably executed in a schema of the same shape and proportions as the eventual paintings, and are bordered by lancet or pointed arches as in the finished paintings. These group studies are partially or entirely squared off (cats. 33, 42, 46) to facilitate transfer of the composition.

The final stage in the conceptual process was the studies in colour (cat. 45), which pulled together the deco-

rative scheme as a whole and provided the light values in the composition of each work. These studies were begun in Paris and worked on at least into 1899, as is made clear from photographs of the works and of Correlieu (figs. 12, 105).[14]

In working on this project, Leduc succeeded in expanding the formal vocabulary of wall decoration. The murals are notable for a pronounced two-dimensionality. The sketches show how each composition is initially created with oblique lines to accentuate perspective (cats. 39, 43, 49). A frontal bias prevails, however, with the action and figures placed parallel to the plane of the composition. The figures are in fact outlined in a darker colour that makes them stand out against the background, further reducing the modelling effect.

Despite the fact that Leduc made many studies from life and researched

Fig. 27   Fig. 28   Fig. 29   Fig. 30

his compositions from many viewpoints, one can still identify a number of sources that show the breadth of his eclecticism and his way of adapting his sources.[15] Among the references that indicate the extent of his background and his knowledge of contemporary painting are *The Ascension* by John Lafarge (1835-1910), *The Disciples at Emmaus* by Luc-Olivier Merson (1846-1920), and the sculpture group *Apollo Reclining, Served by Nymphs* by François Girardon (1628-1715) in the gardens of Versailles.[16]

The initial studies generally include a background and props in the antique style. In the paintings, these elements are replaced by the vegetation, landscape and furnishings that give to each scene some local colouring. Examples of this are the chair in *The Supper at Emmaus* (fig. 18), the forest where the *Baptism of Christ* (fig. 16) takes place, and the mountain backgrounds in *The Ascension* (fig. 28) and *Christ Giving the Keys to Saint Peter* (fig. 21).

In 1900, once Leduc's decoration of the Church of Saint-Hilaire had been completed, it was immediately recognized as true art. The educational and religious role of these works took second place to their artistic merit.[17] During the 1940s, the Catholic press would attempt to reiterate the primary function of these works, emphasizing that their message is a spiritual one. Even the critic Maurice Gagnon, not a writer much inclined to religious lyricism, let down his guard.

The Assumption ... is an outpouring of prayer and celestial happiness. These figures have been released from the heavy load we bear on our souls. The eloquence of their gestures harmonizes with this glorification of Mary, this choir of angels strewing flowers and lulling us with music to conceal the fact that they are carrying away from the earth the Virgin who was a poem of all the virtues. She is to receive her reward at last. Already she is with God, and the ecstatic joy we see in her eyes has taken her far away from us.[18]

Despite much restoration,[19] the interior design of Saint-Hilaire retains some of the impact and glamour that so impressed the people of Saint-Hilaire as well as the young Paul-Émile Borduas, who stated that he owed his career and indeed the very basis of his art to his repeated encounters with the paintings of Saint-Hilaire.[20] This testimony alone would suffice to show that this monument was the single greatest influence on the history of painting in Quebec.

L. L.

Fig. 27   *The Adoration of the Magi*, 609 x 242 cm.

Fig. 28   *The Ascension*, about 1897-1899, approx. 609 x 242 cm.

Fig. 29   *The Assumption*, 304 x 195 cm.

Fig. 30   *Saint Hilary Writing His Treatise*, 304 x 195 cm.

Fig. 31 Ozias Leduc, Study for *Faith*, undated, graphite on grey paper, 27 x 11.4 cm (BNQ 327/9/38).

1 J. Craig Stirling, *Ozias Leduc et la décoration intérieure de l'église de Saint-Hilaire*, "Civilisation du Québec" series (Quebec City: Ministère des Affaires culturelles, 1985), which, with the omission of one Appendix, is a French translation of J. Craig Stirling "The St-Hilaire Church Interior Decorations (1896-1900) of Ozias Leduc", Master's thesis, Concordia University, 1981.

2 *The Assumption*, for example, became one of Leduc's best-known religious works through press coverage. An undated document in a collection of personal papers shows it was his own favourite of the Saint-Hilaire works.

The elegance of the composition was recognized during its inception in Paris. Rodolphe Brunet stated, "I've seen sketches by [Leduc] … for paintings that look very promising. The rendering is such that the subjects seem alive … The Blessed Virgin in his *Assumption* is so delicately painted, with such perfect artistry, that it would be hard to find its match anywhere in Canada." (Rodolphe Brunet, "Chronique européenne – Paris, samedi 25 décembre 1897", *Le Monde illustré* [Montreal], February 12, 1898, p. 659.)

This image was to be used again for the initial decoration at Rougemont (fig. 131) and in part for the Chapel of Notre-Dame-de-Bonsecours (fig. 137). Leduc in fact suggested making a copy of it for the Church of Notre-Dame-de-la-Présentation in Shawinigan-Sud (Agenda 1947-1952, September 1951, BNQ 327/3/11). The artist also made copies of the Saint-Hilaire Stations of the Cross for the churches in Antigonish and Farnham; Borduas was to use his designs for the church at Rougemont. As late as 1945, Leduc was offered a commission from the Trappist monastery in Mistassini on the strength of the reputation of the Saint-Hilaire decor (BNQ 327/7/17).

3 His friend and future collaborator Dr. Ernest Choquette (cat. 92) was enthusiastic as soon as the work of decoration began: "Yes, I am happy to compliment Leduc: not because he is my friend and fellow-parishioner … or rather yes, because he is my friend and fellow parishioner, and I am sad today to think that I was among the indifferent; I could have proclaimed his talent earlier, and I did not … And now he is in the process of transforming the church of my village into a true gallery of art, which is why the other day I followed the Stations of the Cross through his paintings, and I swear I did not miss a single Station." (Dr. [Ernest] Choquette, "Un artiste de mon pays", *La Patrie* [Montreal], December 3, 1898, p. 2.)

4 The preparations and implementation of the renovation and interior decoration programme are documented by correspondence between Father Laflamme and the Bishop of Saint-Hyacinthe, Msgr. Moreau (Archives de l'Évêché de Saint-Hyacinthe, XVII, c. 35). See Stirling 1985, Chapter 4.

5 The cost was estimated by Laflamme at $7,000, payable by the Parish Works and the Church Decoration Committee (letter from Laflamme to Msgr. Moreau, April 28, 1897, Archives de la Société d'Histoire de Belœil – Mont-Saint-Hilaire, P25/D10). See also articles announcing the festivals and bazaars organized to raise the funds: "La Paroisse de St-Hilaire, comté de Rouville", *La Presse* [Montreal], December 19, 1896, p. 1, and in *Le Courrier de Saint-Hyacinthe*, December 29, 1896, p. 3; December 31, 1896, p. 3; January 12, 1897, p. 3.

"There will be a grand bazaar at St-Hilaire … This will be an ideal opportunity to view these works, unanimously considered to be of the highest artistic standard; artworks deserve to be recognized here."

("Grand bazar à St-Hilaire", *Le Courrier de Saint-Hyacinthe*, February 20, 1900, p. 3, and March 10, 1900, p. 3.)

Father Laflamme felt personally responsible for the costs of the paintings. This seems to be the implication of the phrase "personal commitment" in the contract of April 22, 1897, given on p. 49. Laflamme uses this as his reason for refusing the pastorship at Sainte-Anne in Sorel: "I still have work to complete here – *the contracts are signed, they are for the paintings and* I am solely responsible" (letter from Laflamme to Msgr. Moreau, August 19, 1897, Archives de la Société d'Histoire de Belœil – Mont-Saint-Hilaire, P25/D10).

6 One article, however, suggests the work may have been completed by the fall of 1899: "We scarcely recognize the old Church of Saint-Hilaire in its splendid new guise. Both the exterior and the interior of the church have been entirely renovated. The superb paintings were executed by Mr. F. [*sic*] Leduc, a talented artist who has studied under the great teachers of Paris." ("La paroisse de St-Hilaire célèbre le centenaire de sa fondation", *Le Courrier de Saint-Hyacinthe*, October 26, 1899.)

7 "Engagement de M. Ozias Leduc, artiste décorateur et peintre en tableaux de la paroisse de St-Hilaire et du Rev. J. M. Laflamme ptre curé de la paroisse aussi de St-Hilaire", Service des archives de l'archidiocèse de Sherbrooke, Msgr. Desranleau papers, P2/7.4.1A. The quittance of the said contract written in Laflamme's hand and signed by Leduc in confirmation of the contract's termination is there also.

8 In May 1896, Leduc already had prints of Petrak's Way of the Cross after Furich, which he was to use in his designs for Saint-Hilaire (BNQ 327/11/2.1-2.14).

9 An article that appeared in *La Presse* on December 19, 1896 ("La Paroisse de St-Hilaire, comté de Rouville", p. 1) regarding the unveiling of the church renovations makes it clear that the work took from May to December 1896: "The work of decoration was undertaken by members of the parish, Mr. Leduc and Mr. Martin, who are already known to the public. The design was conceived by Mr. Ozias Leduc, a young artist from Saint-Hilaire whose work is appreciated not only in Montreal, where he has exhibited several paintings at the School of Fine Arts, but also in Chicago, where it was shown at the World's Fair. The artist is a modest person with a lively intelligence and energy. Mr. Philippe Martin, a gifted young painter of the parish, has been his assistant in carrying out the work … Last October the scaffolding was removed from the nave, and the sense of achievement was near, but there remained the unfinished choir, and one could not yet judge. It was truly a revelation to the parishioners when [on December 8] the project was seen in its entirety … The paintings have not yet been installed in the church, as Mr. Leduc is still working on them." On payment for the contract, see Stirling 1981, pp. 221-227.

An old photograph shows the original condition of the interior before the restoration work of 1928 (BNQ 327/11/1.2).

In subsequent undertakings of this kind, Leduc used the same method, that is, executing the decorative elements beforehand with a team of assistants. Thus he gained more time to arrive at definitive versions of his paintings.

10 A drawing of *Faith* (fig. 31) proposes a design based on the theological virtues (BNQ 327/9/38). The border presents various possibilities for ornamental bands.

The document "Voici une église. Entrons", transcribed by Gabrielle Messier (BNQ 327/2/38), reveals the circumstances and motivations that led Leduc to undertake this project:

"Even before it was built, we felt that this would be a living church, a reflection of our past and of our community's soul. It was built with love, and our hopes were fulfilled.

It was to be simple and well proportioned, like other churches in the neighbourhood. Its flesh and bones, its appearance and reality would be constructed from the beautiful stone of our fields and hills, rocks as softly tinted as frescoes. Rocks and stones we could pick up, one by one, in our hands, looking at them, seeing them, loving them …

The work was carried out by conscientious and honourable workmen; the whole interior of the church expresses their commitment to perfection. The church's decoration, the precious garment it wears, has been created by an artist of sensitivity, a convinced idealist who has spared no pains to make a success of the project entrusted to him. In 1897, at the age of thirty-three, already a fully trained artist of some standing, he decided to travel to Europe to see not only the monuments of the past but also what the present age could offer.

In short, this was a research trip funded out of limited means. On his return, the artist set to work with a passion, because it was work he loved as he loved our church.

He made it comforting first for himself and perhaps also for others who would come and pray for a little happiness.

The beauty we see is the result of exact proportions, of rules governed by that order which seems to be, must be, the pivot around which the human soul circles, trembling and in fear, with its unappeasable thirst for happiness.

We see how the church embodies on a human scale a combination of natural elements and a moral and artistic vision".

Much of the above text appears also in a late autobiographical piece entitled "Pourquoi nous aimons notre église" (BNQ 327/2/38), where Leduc adds, "We love our church inexpressibly, passionate in our faith, for we see that the two resemble each other. So much care has gone into beautifying this dwelling that God in His eternity made of pure spirit for Himself, for His Holy Spirit, for His Word, built and made to contain the inconceivable Trinitarian mystery of His being, His existence, His neverendingness."

11 Service des archives de l'Archidiocèse de Sherbrooke, Msgr. Desranleau papers, P2/7.4.1A.

12 Such a lay figure is a main element in several of Leduc's still-lifes (cat. 90, fig. 5). A sketchbook from Paris (cat. 63) seen in the *Still Life (with Lay Figure)* (cat. 90) tends to confirm that the artist often used this piece for studies as if it were a live model. That he also owned an *écorché* is evident from a photograph (National Gallery of Canada, Jean-René Ostiguy papers).

13 Leduc's text on the Church of Saint-Hilaire, "Pourquoi nous aimons notre église", BNQ 327/2/38.

14 A photograph of *Saint Hilary Writing His Treatise* is dated November 25, 1898 (BNQ 327/11/1.4); four photographs of *The Ascension* are extant (private collection and BNQ 327/11/1.9); another dated August 20, 1898, shows a large scale drawing of the composition (BNQ 327/11/1.10). Another bears dates that probably refer to the period in which the painting was executed: August 20 and October 12, 1898 (BNQ 327/11/1.2). Other undated photographs of Leduc's studio show unfinished paintings (e.g. fig. 105). In a photograph of Leduc painting *The Death of Saint Joseph*, the frame for the 1898 *Pigeons* (cat. 103) sits proudly on an easel (National Gallery of Canada, Jean-René Ostiguy papers). See also the photographs: BNQ 327/13/1.11-1.13; 2.14; 4.5e; 5.8; 7.1; 7.2; 7.6.

15 Comparisons were often made between the French mural artists and the Synthetist movement: "In the Church of Saint-Hilaire, in the story of Mary Magdalene, a maidservant in the background is rendered with a simplicity very akin to that of Puvis de Chavannes's figures. The landscape behind Saint Matthew, although ordered as an element of the composition, has the truth and sincerity of a private vision, a synthesis of musings on nature." (André Lecoutey, "Les décorations religieuses d'Ozias Leduc", *Arts et pensée*, vol. 3, no. 18 [July-August 1954], p. 186.)

16 This work by Lafarge in the Church of the Ascension, New York City, was reproduced in *The Century Magazine*. A copy of this issue and a print of the work can be found among Ozias Leduc's papers, BNQ 327/14/14; 327/14/4. Merson's stained glass window *The Disciples at Emmaus* was reproduced in *Art et Décoration*, vol. 1 (January-June 1897), before p. 1. Leduc may have seen the actual Girardon group that inspired his *Christ in the House of Simon* (fig. 17). See also Stirling 1985, Chapter 7.

17 See note 5. In "Saint-Hilaire-sur-Richelieu – Un des coins pittoresques de la province de Québec", *La Presse* [Montreal], June 23, 1921, p. 19, the church is compared to and becomes part of the region's natural beauties.

18 Maurice Gagnon, "La Peinture moderne – Peinture religieuse", *Technique*, vol. 15, no. 4 (April 1940), p. 252.

19 A series of restorations has gradually changed the interior decoration of the Church of Saint-Hilaire. In late 1920, Father Laflamme informed Leduc of his wish to have the church cleaned and restored (BNQ 327/6/5; 327/8/27; 327/6/6). The cleaning was carried out in 1925 under the direction of Jean-Baptiste Allaire (time sheets and invoices of J.-B. Allaire, Archives de la Société d'Histoire de Belœil – Mont-Saint-Hilaire, Armand-Cardinal papers). Major restoration work was undertaken under Leduc's supervision between July and December 1928 (BNQ 327/2/38-41, 327/9/39; National Gallery of Canada, Jean-René Ostiguy papers; ASHBMSH, Armand-Cardinal papers). In later years, the lighting was changed and the choir altered by building a screen above the high altar to incorporate a gallery; in 1929, statues were exchanged with the Carli company, and in 1931, two stained glass windows by Pellus after designs by Leduc were installed, a *Pietà* and a *Christ the King* (BNQ 327/8/37; ASHBMSH, Armand-Cardinal papers, correspondence files). See also Stirling 1985, Chapter 8. A further intensive cleaning was done in 1953-1954, and the most recent restoration in 1983.

In 1948, Leduc launched a campaign to have the church classified as a historical monument (BNQ 327/9/11). The building was declared classified in 1965 and the paintings in 1976.

20 "From my birth until the age of fifteen, these were the only pictures I ever saw. You cannot imagine my pride in having experienced this unique source of pictorial poetry at a time when the smallest impressions leave their mark and decide the direction our critical sense will take, without our knowing it." (Paul-Émile Borduas, "Quelques pensées sur l'œuvre d'amour et de rêve de M. Ozias Leduc", *Canadian Art*, vol. 10, no. 4 [Summer 1953], p. 158; quoted in English from Paul-Émile Borduas, *Writings: 1942-1958*, trans. François-Marc Gagnon and Dennis Young [Halifax: Press of the Nova Scotia College of Art and Design, and New York: New York University Press, 1978], p. 131.)

SHEETS FROM A SKETCHBOOK

(Cats. 57-83)

57

Study of Three Hands

1897

Graphite on cream wove paper

13.2 x 17.7 cm

Initialed and dated upper right: *OL Paris 189[7]*

Renée Bergeron collection

PROVENANCE

Studio of the artist; René Bergeron,
Chicoutimi, 1955; Renée Bergeron

58

Study of Three Hands

1897

Graphite on cream wove paper

13.3 x 18 cm

Dated lower right: *1897*

Renée Bergeron collection

PROVENANCE

Studio of the artist; René Bergeron,
Chicoutimi, 1955; Renée Bergeron

59

Study of Four Hands

1897

Graphite on cream wove paper

13.3 x 17.9 cm

Dated upper left: *1897*

Renée Bergeron collection

PROVENANCE

Studio of the artist; René Bergeron,
Chicoutimi, 1955; Renée Bergeron

57

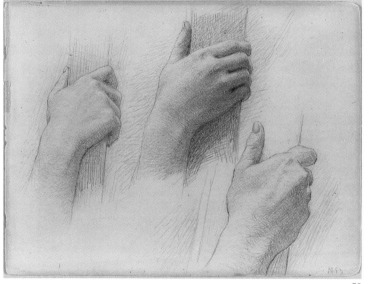

58

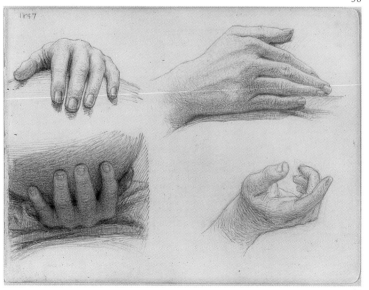

59

60

61

62

60

Study of Three Hands, Two with Fingers Laced

1897

Graphite on cream wove paper

13.3 x 18 cm

Initialed and dated lower right: *OL 1897*

Renée Bergeron collection

PROVENANCE

Studio of the artist; René Bergeron, Chicoutimi, 1955; Renée Bergeron

61

Two Studies of a Woman's Head

1897

Graphite on cream wove paper

13.3 x 17.8 cm

Monogrammed and dated upper right: *OL Paris 1897*

Renée Bergeron collection

PROVENANCE

Studio of the artist; René Bergeron, Chicoutimi, 1955; Renée Bergeron

62

Study of a Head and Joined Hands

1897

Graphite on cream wove paper

13.3 x 17.9 cm

Monogrammed and dated lower left: *OL Paris 1897*

Renée Bergeron collection

PROVENANCE

Studio of the artist; René Bergeron, Chicoutimi, 1955; Renée Bergeron

63

Study of a Young Woman in Profile and Two Hands

Graphite on cream wove paper

13.3 x 17.8 cm

Renée Bergeron collection

PROVENANCE

Studio of the artist; René Bergeron, Chicoutimi, 1955; Renée Bergeron

63

64

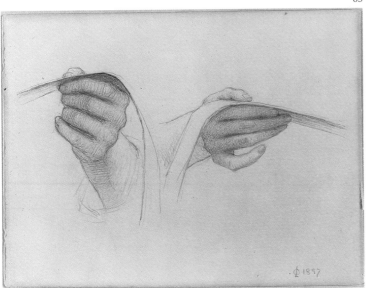

65

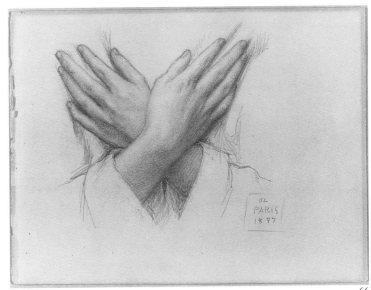

66

64
Study of a Reclining Young Woman and a Foot

1897

Graphite on cream wove paper

13.3 x 17.9 cm

Initialed and dated lower right: *OL 1897 Paris*

Renée Bergeron collection

PROVENANCE

Studio of the artist; René Bergeron, Chicoutimi, 1955; Renée Bergeron

65
Study of Two Hands Holding Phylacteries

1897

Graphite on cream wove paper

13.3 x 18 cm

Monogrammed and dated lower right: *OL 1897*

Renée Bergeron collection

PROVENANCE

Studio of the artist; René Bergeron, Chicoutimi, 1955; Renée Bergeron

66
Study of Crossed Hands

1897

Graphite on cream wove paper

13.3 x 17.9 cm

Initialed and dated lower right: *OL PARIS 1897*

Renée Bergeron collection

PROVENANCE

Studio of the artist; René Bergeron, Chicoutimi, 1955; Renée Bergeron

67

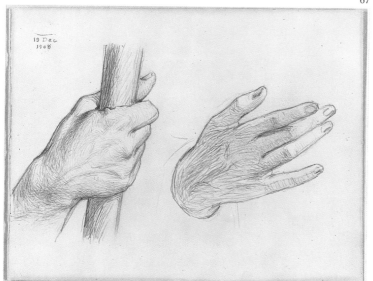

68

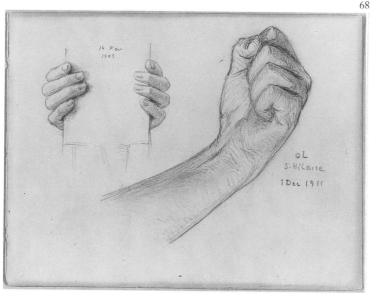

69

67

Study of Two Hands

1909

Graphite on cream wove paper

13.4 x 18 cm

Dated centre right: *8 Jan 09*; dated lower right: *S. Hilaire 09*

Renée Bergeron collection

68

Study of Two Hands, One Holding a Pole

1908

Graphite on cream wove paper

13.4 x 17.9 cm

Dated upper left: *19 Dec 1908*

Renée Bergeron collection

69

Study of Three Hands

1909 and 1911

Graphite on cream wove paper

13.3 x 18 cm

Dated upper left: *14 Fev 1909*; initialed and dated lower right: *OL S. Hilaire 1 Dec 1911*

Renée Bergeron collection

70

Study of Two Outstretched Arms

1912

Graphite on cream wove paper

13.3 x 18 cm

Dated upper left: *28 Jan 1912*

Renée Bergeron collection

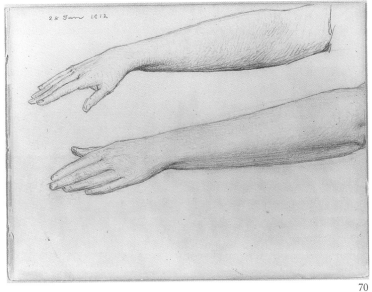

70

71

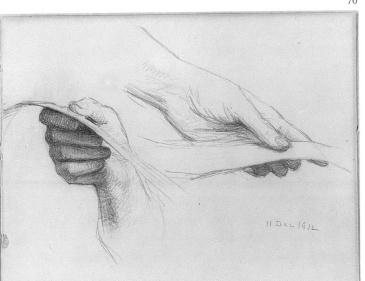

72

73

71
Study of Two Closed Hands

1912

Graphite on cream wove paper

13.4 x 17.9 cm

Monogrammed and dated centre left:
OL 17 fev 1912; dated centre right: *26 Fev*

Renée Bergeron collection

PROVENANCE

Studio of the artist; René Bergeron,
Chicoutimi, 1955; Renée Bergeron

72
Study of Two Hands Holding Phylacteries

1912

Graphite on cream wove paper

13.3 x 17.9 cm

Dated lower right: *11 Dec 1912*

Renée Bergeron collection

PROVENANCE

Studio of the artist; René Bergeron,
Chicoutimi, 1955; Renée Bergeron

73
Study of Two Hands, One Resting on the Other

About 1915

Graphite on cream wove paper

13.4 x 17.8 cm

Renée Bergeron collection

PROVENANCE

Studio of the artist; René Bergeron,
Chicoutimi, 1955; Renée Bergeron

74

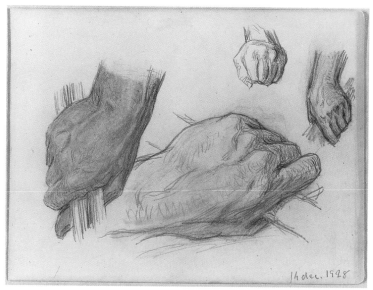

75

74

Study for the *Portrait of the Honourable Joseph-Napoléon Francœur*

About 1920

Graphite on cream wove paper

18 x 13.3 cm

Renée Bergeron collection

PROVENANCE

Studio of the artist; René Bergeron, Chicoutimi, 1955; Renée Bergeron

75

Study of Four Closed Hands

1928

Graphite on cream wove paper

13.3 x 17.8 cm

Dated lower right: *14 dec. 1928*

Renée Bergeron collection

PROVENANCE

Studio of the artist; René Bergeron, Chicoutimi, 1955; Renée Bergeron

76

77

78

78

Study of Drapery

1941

Graphite on cream wove paper

17.9 x 13.3 cm

Initialed and dated lower right: *O.L. 1941*

Private collection

INSCRIPTIONS

Verso: label of a certificate of authenticity signed by Gabrielle Messier and J. M. Gagnon

PROVENANCE

Galerie Place Royale; Pierre Gadbois; private collection, 1971

79

Study of an Arm, with Closed Fan

1941

Graphite on cream wove paper

17.7 x 13.3 cm

Dated upper right: *23 mars 1941*

Renée Bergeron collection

PROVENANCE

Studio of the artist; René Bergeron, Chicoutimi, 1955; Renée Bergeron

76

Study for the *Portrait of Madame St-Cyr*

About 1938-1939

Graphite on cream wove paper

17.8 x 13.3 cm

Renée Bergeron collection

PROVENANCE

Studio of the artist; René Bergeron, Chicoutimi, 1955; Renée Bergeron

80

Study of an Arm

About 1941

Graphite on cream wove paper

13.4 x 18 cm

Renée Bergeron collection

PROVENANCE

Studio of the artist; René Bergeron, Chicoutimi, 1955; Renée Bergeron

77

Self-portrait

1934

Graphite on cream wove paper

13.3 x 17.8 cm

Monogrammed and dated centre left: *OL II AVRIL MCMXXXIV*

Renée Bergeron collection

INSCRIPTIONS

Recto, upper left: *OZIAS LEDUC / PORTRAIT FAIT VERS L'AGE DE / QUARANTE V / ANS / REDESSINÉ D'A-/ PRÈS UN CRO-/ QUIS PEINT A l'HUILE*

PROVENANCE

Studio of the artist; René Bergeron, Chicoutimi, 1955; Renée Bergeron

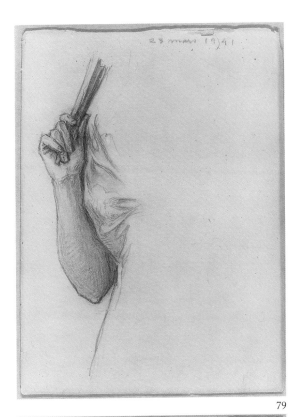

79

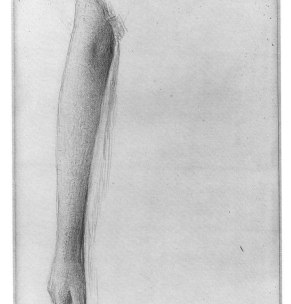

80

81

82

83

81
Study of an Arm, with Open Fan
 About 1941
 Graphite on cream wove paper
 17.7 x 13.3 cm
Renée Bergeron collection
PROVENANCE
Studio of the artist; René Bergeron,
Chicoutimi, 1955; Renée Bergeron

82
Study for the *Portrait of Thérèse Brouillette*
 1940
 Graphite on cream wove paper
 13.4 x 18 cm
Dated lower left: *29 JANV. 1940*; dated lower right: *3 mars 1940*
Renée Bergeron collection
PROVENANCE
Studio of the artist; René Bergeron,
Chicoutimi, 1955; Renée Bergeron

83
Study of Two Hands, One Resting on the Other
 About 1940
 Graphite on cream wove paper
 13.3 x 18.9 cm
Renée Bergeron collection
PROVENANCE
Studio of the artist; René Bergeron,
Chicoutimi, 1955; Renée Bergeron

THIS sketchbook is the only one of Leduc's to be found almost complete; twenty-seven sketches from it (cats. 57-83), executed between 1897 and 1941, are known. All are studies from life. The earliest drawings date from Leduc's stay in Paris; the last ones were done in his studio in Saint-Hilaire. They were used by the artist as reference material for portraits and religious paintings. This notebook demonstrates both Leduc's working methods and the development of his graphic technique over more than forty years.[1]

For every completed work, Leduc usually made many preliminary studies, some just a few rapid lines and others more finished and then squared off. Some are studies for details, while in others the whole composition of the painting-to-be is sketched out. According to Leduc, "Drawing is the most intellectual aspect of a picture."[2] In these preparatory drawings, the whole work is already present: the lines, light and shade, modelling and composition. Some sketches have Leduc's marginal notations of the colours to be used in the final painting, the symbolism aimed at and even the placing of the work and its frame on the wall in the case of religious decoration. The artist's scrupulous and disciplined draftsmanship has often been remarked on by critics. Shortly after Leduc's death, Noël Lajoie wrote, "The drawings by Leduc are not to be missed. They are exquisite, executed with incredible skill and finesse, supremely poetic. And some are just sketches: heads, hands, the folds of a robe, drawn on a piece of paper – 'studies' to which the artist himself attached no importance. And yet they are as lovingly drawn as any of his finished paintings."[3]

The sketchbook also shows how Leduc's graphic style evolved. In the drawings made in Paris (cats. 57-66), shapes are clearly outlined, with the modelling and shadows done in very fine hatching or cross-hatching, and the reserve white of the support supplying the areas of brighter light. Thereafter, the linear drawing becomes bolder, with outlines reworked several times; circular

Fig. 32   Ozias Leduc with the *Portrait of Florence Ducharme*, about 1942-1943 (photo by Albert Tessier; Archives du Séminaire de Trois-Rivières, Albert Tessier papers, FN-0014-P2-34a-45).

strokes (cats. 67, 82) and zigzags (cats. 67, 75) herald a new freedom of handling. Around 1910, broader, looser hatching surrounds shapes in which the white areas are more frequent (cats. 72, 73). As the drawing becomes freer, the figures grow simpler (cat. 75). In some sketches (cats. 76, 79), long parallel hatching is crossed on the vertical by short strokes – a style of drawing the artist brought to perfection in his portraits just preceding 1920, notably of Léo-Pol Morin (cat. 160) and Olivier Maurault (cat. 161).

The individual drawings in the sketchbook are referred to in the entries on the works they are related to: studies for the Church of Saint-Hilaire (cats. 57-66); *Endymion and Selene* (cat. 61, see cat. 129); *Self-portrait* (cat. 77, see cat. 108); *Portrait of Guy Delahaye* (cats. 70-71, see cat. 139); *Portrait of Josée LaRoque de Roquebrune* (cat. 73, see cat. 156); *Portrait of Joseph-Napoléon Francœur* (cat. 74, see cat. 171); *Portrait of Madame St-Cyr (The Lady in Red)* (cat. 76, see cat. 227); *Portrait of Thérèse Brouillette* (cats. 82-83, see cat. 231). Four sheets (cats. 78-81) are devoted to the

Portrait of Florence Ducharme, a painting known from a photograph of Leduc's studio (fig. 32). Lastly, there are three drawings (cats. 67-69) dated between 1908-1909 and 1911, still unidentified at present, which may have been sketches related to church decoration.

M. L.

1   Leduc kept the sketchbook all his life: it was not until 1955, after his death, that it was sold to René Bergeron. It probably originally held thirty-two leaves. Bergeron brought together twenty-six pages of sketches, one endpaper and a page with an inscription in the artist's hand. He then mounted each sheet in a single frame, somewhat altering the order of the pages "to improve the general arrangement". For a better understanding of Leduc's working methods, we have put the sketchbook back into its original order, adding a page found in a private collection (cat. 78).

2   Quoted in Laurier Lacroix *et al.*, *Ozias Leduc the Draughtsman*, exhib. cat. (Montreal: Concordia University, 1978), p. 104.

3   Noël Lajoie, "Un hommage au peintre Ozias Leduc, 1864-1955", *Le Devoir* [Montreal], January 14, 1956, p. 8.

84

Portrait of Eugénie Goulet

1897

Oil on canvas

55.5 x 48.4 cm

Monogrammed and dated upper left: *18 OL 97*

Farley family collection

PROVENANCE

Studio of the artist; Eugénie Goulet; Arthur and Élisa Goulet, Saint-Hilaire; Marguerite Phaneuf, Astoria, New York; Pauline Morin Farley, Montreal; Farley family

THE sitter was a neighbour of the Leduc family in Saint-Hilaire. Eugénie, the eldest daughter of Arthur Goulet and Élisa Auclair, was born on August 14, 1874, and on October 16, 1894,[1] married Joseph Anaclet Chagnon, an employee of the Montreal transport commission. Although done in 1897, the painting may well have been a wedding present from the artist, completed just before his departure for Paris. Eugénie Goulet died a year later, on February 24, 1898, at the age of twenty-three.

The subject is shown full face, her head very slightly tilted, gazing dreamily into space and completely caught up in the moment. The moiré taffeta dress is rendered with meticulous care, as are the folds in the jabot and sleeves and the lace covering the bodice. The pleated high shoulders give the delicate-looking sitter a more commanding presence. Vivid contrasts are obtained between the dark clothing and the gleaming flower-shaped brooch placed almost at the centre of the composition, and between the background and the luminosity of the face. The features are rendered in a light sfumato that creates a warm sense of peace, serenity, almost resignation. Was the sitter already suffering from the illness that was to prove mortal the following year? This painting is one of many portraits of relations and friends undertaken by Leduc of his own accord over the years. Since these works were not commissioned, he felt able to paint with greater freedom.

M. L.

---

1   This biographical information was kindly provided by Pauline Morin Farley, the sitter's niece.

84

85

Portrait of Rodolphe Brunet

1897

Oil on panel

27.2 x 21.9 cm

Monogrammed and dated centre right: *18 Leduc 97*, encircled with an *O*

Montreal, Jean-Pierre Valentin collection

INSCRIPTIONS

Verso: *Paysage: 2,7 x 4,8 cm*

PROVENANCE

Studio of the artist; Rodolphe Brunet, 1897; Rolande Brunet-Raymond, 1949; Galerie l'Art français, Montreal, 1988; Jean-Pierre Valentin

IN composition and technique this work closely resembles the *Portrait of Eugénie Goulet* (cat. 84), painted in the same year of 1897. However, although Leduc was in a hurry to complete the young woman's portrait before he left Saint-Hilaire for France, he painted Brunet's picture in Paris. Rodolphe Brunet (1869-1949) had published as a poet and journalist before spending seven years in Paris around the turn of the century. It was doubtless in his capacity as chairman of the Société canadienne de Paris that he met Leduc.[1]

After studying law at Laval University in Montreal, Brunet worked for several newspapers, including *Le Monde illustré, La Patrie, La Minerve* and *La Presse*, publishing poems and articles on a variety of subjects, from

literature, music and the visual arts to history and politics.[2] In 1890, he became vice chairman of the Cercle Dollard, a Montreal literary society. Around 1893-1894, he left for France, where he became friendly with a number of Canadian writers and artists, and collected their work. They included Raoul Barré, Henri Beau, Joseph-Charles Franchère, Charles Gill, Murray Prendergast, Joseph Saint-Charles and Suzor-Coté.[3] In 1896, he was elected the first chairman of the Société canadienne de Paris, of which he was a founding member, and the following year sat on the organizing committee for a reception given on July 22 in honour of Sir Wilfrid Laurier and his wife. During his time in Paris, Brunet wrote the "Chronique européenne" column for *Le Monde illustré*, in which he chronicled the professional and leisure activities of French Canadians in Paris. He also worked for the newspaper *Le Gaulois*, offering information services to Canadian and American visitors to Paris.

As in the *Portrait of Eugénie Goulet*, Leduc freezes a moment of time, in a sfumato effect, with no hint as to place or period save for the clues given by clothes. Meticulous attention is paid to the details – the black suit, the stiff collar, the loosely tied tie with its tiepin – that give the sitter his dandified air. Much struck by Leduc's meticulous technique, Brunet himself wrote, "I have seen a very well done portrait of his and sketches for paintings that look extremely promising. The rendering is such that the subjects seem alive", and compared him to the Italian old masters rather than his contemporaries: "Mr. Leduc is no admirer of the Impressionist style or of the gallery devoted to the leaders of this new school at the Musée du Luxembourg. He is among those who believe that this gallery might aptly be renamed the Chamber of Horrors. And he is right. His own style is very different."[4]

Brunet's opinion was doubtless based on a comparison of the portrait's highly finished look, the result of innumerable brush strokes, with the looser Impressionist handling, and of his muted palette with their brighter colours. What is more, this was one of the few times that Leduc chose a permanent and sturdy support: a finely finished wood panel

Fig. 33   Ozias Leduc, *Landscape* (on the back of the *Portrait of Rodolphe Brunet*), 1897, oil on panel, 2.7 x 4.8 (Montreal, Jean-Pierre Valentin collection).

like those used by Renaissance painters. For the first time, he signed with a monogram where the initial letter of his first name becomes a circle containing his name and the date the work was executed. Two thirds of the back of the panel is covered with brown on which Leduc painted a miniature landscape (fig. 33) in the thickly pigmented manner of his pochades of the 1900s (cats. 110-116).[5] Lit by twilight colours, a path crosses a field diagonally and disappears into the distance. This tiny landscape is an enigma: is it a reminiscence of a French landscape seen during an outing to the Paris suburbs, or a nostalgic memory of the Richelieu Valley?

M. L.

1   In 1890, Brunet was writing regularly for *Le Monde illustré*; in the fall of that year, this paper was the first to draw attention to Leduc's works on exhibition at the Salle Cavallo and to predict that "this artist has a great future" (G. A. Dumont, "L'Exposition des beaux-arts III", *Le Monde illustré* [Montreal], October 11, 1890, p. 374). Following the publication of this article, the newspaper printed a letter from Leduc, dated October 16, 1890, gratefully acknowledging this "first encouragement" ("À propos de l'exposition des beaux-arts", December 13, 1890, p. 511). It is unlikely that Brunet and Leduc were acquainted at this point, since Leduc's letter was written from Bécancour, where he was working with Adolphe Rho. Although Leduc himself was not very active in the Société canadienne in Paris, it is in all probability there that he met Brunet.

2   Biographical notes on Rodolphe Brunet were kindly provided by his daughter Rolande Raymond.

3   In 1934, Brunet offered to sell twenty paintings from his collection to the Musée du Québec. After favourable recommendations from Paul Rainville and Charles Maillard, the museum acquired eight of these paintings (Musée du Québec, Rodolphe Brunet file).

4   Rodolphe Brunet, "Chronique européenne – Paris, samedi 25 décembre 1897", *Le Monde illustré* [Montreal], February 12, 1898, p. 659.

5   Gabrielle Messier relates how Leduc loved to surprise his friends by hiding a second work in the wrapping around a painting, or even, as here, painting a second one on the back, which would be unseen by the viewer.

86

86
Bending Head
1897

Oil on paper mounted on laminated panel

18.4 x 28 cm

Signed upper right: *OZIAS LEDUC*; signed lower left: *–OZIAS LEDUC–*; dated lower right: *–PARIS 1897–*

Private collection

INSCRIPTIONS

Verso: *Musée de la Province de Québec cat. no 42 Propriété de M. et Mme Edouard Clerk, Trente-de-Saint-Hilaire, Qué.; Une flamme ? C'est toi Petite image à l'âme immobile Parcelle du vaste Univers De mon désir. On te reconnaît dans la Maison hospitalière Ou déjà, Brulent les cœurs Pour l'Art. Le divin Art!; Mons Madame Edouard Clerk Saint-Hilaire 27 Dec. 1943 Ozias Leduc; A M. Edouard Clerk Exposition de Québec; from M. E. Clerk ro 69-3-69 St-Hilaire sur Richelieu; Étude - Tête penchée - Leduc; h.p. 11" x 7 1/2"; from S. Clerk, Mont St-Hilaire Ro 139-2-73; Temporary Label Art Gallery of Ontario; Consideration Purchase (CH) Leduc, O., Etude, Tête penchée M. Stephen Clerk, Quebec; vendu à Stephen & Thérèse Edouard Clerk*

PROVENANCE

Studio of the artist; Mr. and Mrs. Édouard Clerk, Saint-Hilaire, 1947; private collection, 1982

87

87
Study for *Erato (Sleeping Muse)*
1897

Graphite on paper

15.3 x 13.8 cm

Signed and dated lower left: *18 LEDUC 97*

Private collection

INSCRIPTIONS

Recto, upper left: *Paris 1897*

Verso: *Ozias Leduc (St-Hilaire, Qué. 1864-1955 St-Hyacinthe, Qué.) Nu couché 1897 graphite sur papier; prêt; Temporary Label Art Gallery of Ontario Consideration Purchase Leduc Ozias La nue penchée ou Muse endormie 1897 crayon on paper coll. Mr. & Mrs. Edouard Clerk - Mont St-Hilaire, P.Q. c/o Monette, Clerk Michaud, Barakett & Levesque, Montréal, P.Q. 8358*

PROVENANCE

Studio of the artist; Mr. and Mrs. Édouard Clerk, Saint-Hilaire; private collection, 1982

IT was in Paris in 1897 that for the first time Leduc had access to a live model and produced a number of studies of the head, hands, feet and torso (cats. 57-66). His aim was to study expressiveness in gesture, seeking poses for the biblical characters in his designs for the Church of Saint-Hilaire. He also had in mind another painting on a secular subject. During these sittings, he produced a reclining nude in graphite (cat. 87) and a small-sized study of the same model in oils (cat. 86). After his return to Saint-Hilaire, these two studies provided the inspiration for a more ambitious project, a large charcoal drawing (cat. 88) followed by an oil painting (cat. 89).

The small study of the reclining nude, in which the model occupies the centre of the composition, is most carefully rendered. The figure is outlined by a contour line, while a tight network of parallel hatching over a stumped background brings out the skin values; diagonal hatching obscures the background and brings the composition to life, though there is no indication as to the setting or even what the model is lying on.

In the small oil, also executed from life in Paris, the model's head and arms provide the focus. The smooth handling, save for thicker pigment on the left arm, and the pearly colours heighten the peaceful atmosphere of the work. Leduc was very fond of this little canvas. He considered it one of his ten best paintings[1] and sometimes subtitled it *The Sad Muse*.[2]

The large charcoal on canvas shows the same pose, with the nude figure here reclining on a rock in the midst of a landscape. The light, the placing of the figure and the formal relationships focus attention on the model, while a piece of cloth at the feet describes an ellipse that unifies the composition. Jean-René Ostiguy suggests that "the artist had at first conceived his Parisian model as a 'sleeping bather,' a standard theme for Academic painters".[3] The emphasis on the model and on the drapery lying at her feet seems to confirm this reading. For nineteenth-century artists, the theme of the bather was a pretext for painting female nudes.[4] It is not by chance that this nude is sleeping. The observer-voyeur is offered the pleasure of seeing together with that of transgressing, just as for the artist, idealism is perhaps mingled with a delight in disobeying the laws of Catholicism. But at the bottom right corner of the work, partly cut off by the frame, a lyre is visible under the cloth, and this transforms the theme: the girl's young body, highlighted against the dark background of undergrowth, is in fact Erato, the muse of lyric poetry.

In the oil painting, the composition is somewhat different. The model is moved away from the centre, creating two independent areas, one reserved for the figure and the other for the deep undergrowth, while in the foreground, a branch, a piece of drapery and the lyre offer a strong counterpoint. Two masses – the figure and the drapery – are strongly lit. The brushwork is apparent, the thick pigment having been applied with a palette knife in some areas, as in the rock the figure is lying on, and the undergrowth beside her legs. The skin colouring reflects the colours of the vegetation – ochres and greens. The pine branch echoes the model's angular pose and draws the eye towards it.

In turning the nude into Erato, Leduc enters the realm of abstract allegory, abandoning the academic theme for a Symbolist approach, as though modesty obliged that his nude be offered the support of Antiquity. During his time in Paris, Leduc was still quite conservative in his technique and compositions. This is apparent in a letter he sent to Father Joseph-Magloire Laflamme (cat. 165), dated June 24, 1897. He had been very surprised on visiting museums and galleries to see original paintings he knew only from black-and-white reproductions, and also by the audacity of the avant-garde artists.

Most artists today do astonishing things, seeking above all to be different. You feel that their main concern is to attract attention, to shock people. This is understandable up to a point, given the enormous number of paintings to be seen merely in the only two exhibitions I have visited, on the Champs-Élysées and the Champ-de-Mars, and there are many other private galleries. You will not be surprised to learn that this general tendency somewhat spoils my pleasure.[5]

At the end of this letter, Leduc states that he is preparing himself mentally for the task of decorating the Church of Saint-Hilaire, so that it may reflect "the purest ideal that each of us carries within". In *Erato (Sleeping Muse)*, he transcends his model, projecting onto her a divine ideal of beauty. According to Michèle Haddad, "The painter who, plunging into irreality, places his nude in a landscape, has found the simplest way of expressing the archaic concept of the cosmic fusion of being and nature,"[6] and Frédérik Tristan has remarked, "Woman not only *represents* nature, but she *is* both nature and the soul of that nature."[7] Leduc respected the "Platonic idea of beauty according to which the beauties of the flesh express the beauties of the soul".[8] On the back of *Bending Head* (cat. 86), he later wrote:

A flame?
It is you
Little image with the motionless soul
Fragment of the vast Universe
Of my desire.
You are recognized
In the hospitable house,
Where hearts
Already burn for Art.
Divine Art!

The female nude modestly turned in on herself already represented for the painter an object of desire, which he appropriates to himself by idealizing her and placing her in close harmony with nature. Like Pygmalion, he fell in love with his own creation. Erato's passivity is only an illusion: this is the stage of meditation, of contemplative withdrawal, necessary to creation. Erato symbolizes the potential power of the imagination as opposed to nature (the right-hand side of the painting), the source of inspiration. For Leduc, the creative process is both ideation – the transmission of an idea – and idealism – the longing to attain an ideal. This painting eloquently conveys Leduc's own personal symbolism.

M. L.

1   Draft of a letter from Ozias Leduc to Mackenzie Waters, chairman of the Fine Arts Committee for the Canadian National Exhibition [July 9, 1948], BNQ 327/9/11.

2   See Leduc's Diary for May 22 and June 15, 1947, BNQ 327/3/11.

3   Jean-René Ostiguy, *Ozias Leduc: Symbolist and Religious Painting*, exhib. cat. (Ottawa: National Gallery of Canada, 1974), p. 126.

4   This subject had certainly attracted Leduc's attention in Paris. Some years later, on September 18, 1906, in reply to a letter from H. D. Bates, chairman of the Boston printers Bates & Guild Company, inviting subscribers to the periodical *Masters in Art* to suggest the names of ten masterworks of painting, Leduc proposed *The Source* by Ingres (1780-1867), which he had doubtless seen in the Louvre (BNQ 327/5/16). What is more, the rendering in oils of the rock in *Erato (Sleeping Muse)* recalls the technique in another French painting called *The Source*, by Gustave Courbet (1819-1877).

5   Service des archives de l'Archidiocèse de Sherbrooke, P25/D10.

6   Michèle Haddad, *La Divine et l'Impure – Le Nu au XIXe siècle* (Paris: Éditions du Jaguar, 1990), pp. 63-64.

7   Quoted in *ibid.*

8   *Ibid.*, p. 85.

88
Study for *Erato (Sleeping Muse)*

About 1898

Charcoal on canvas

61 x 91.2 cm

Quebec City, Musée du Québec, inv. 94.10

INSCRIPTIONS

Verso: *Ozias Leduc Nu endormie sur un rocher Sleeping female nude in a landscape 1898 fusain sur toile charcoal on canvas 60 x 90,5 cm collection privée private collection*

PROVENANCE

Studio of the artist; Claude Rousseau, Montmagny, 1955; Musée du Québec, 1994

89

Erato (Sleeping Muse)

1898

Oil and graphite on canvas

58.8 x 93.8 cm

Signed and dated lower right: *1898 OZIAS LEDUC*

Private collection

INSCRIPTIONS

Verso: *Muse endormie – Leduc h.t. 25" x 38"; artist:*
Leduc title: Muse endormie; from M.E. Clerk Ro
69-3-69 St-Hilaire-sur-Richelieu; from S. Clerk,
Mont Saint-Hilaire Ro 139-2-73

PROVENANCE

Studio of the artist; Mr. and Mrs. Édouard Clerk,
Saint-Hilaire; private collection, 1982

90
Still Life (with Lay Figure)
1898

Oil on cardboard

28 x 24 cm

Monogrammed and dated upper left: *18 LEDUC 98*, encircled with an *O*

The Montreal Museum of Fine Arts, gift of the Succession J.A. DeSève, inv. 1984.40

INSCRIPTIONS

Along the border of the composition: *OSIAS LEDUC A PEINT CE TABLEAU en FEVRIER et MARS 1898 à S^T HENRI de MONTREAL / DESSIN// COULEUR // COMPOSITION // LA // TRINITE//DU//PEINTRE*

Verso (torn label, Art Association of Montreal?): *Still-Life O. Leduc St-Hilaire $40.00*

PROVENANCE

Marius Dufresne, Montreal; Société historique du Lac Saint-Louis; Montreal Museum of Fine Arts, 1984

S TILL-LIFE work is not a very distinguished form of art; but the public desires it, and is willing to pay for it, and the artist who has the necessary skills uses it to provide bread and butter until recognition in more elevated walks of art comes to him.[1]

Although offered for sale for $40 when exhibited at the Art Association of Montreal in 1898, this *Still Life* is hardly the sort of potboiler the commentator just quoted considered works in this genre to be. It is a highly complex painting, the most intricate investigation of the creative process Leduc had yet made. Done soon after he returned to Montreal from a seven-month stay in Paris (see cats. 57-66), fresh from his artistic coming of age and undoubtedly feeling the power of his emerging talent, this *Still Life* is both an aesthetic manifesto and, in its essence, a self-portrait.

The overlapping objects it depicts – sketchbook, preparatory drawings, mirror, art periodicals and lay figure – are arranged from foreground to background in a narrow, stepped sequence that culminates in a painting of a man with eyes closed, propped against a curtain. Some of these objects may be precisely identified. The female figure in the open sketchbook was used for Mary Magdalene in *Christ in the House of Simon* for the Church of Saint-Hilaire

Fig. 34 Philippe-Guillaume Curtius, *Dying Voltaire*, undated, wax (Philadelphia Museum of Art, inv. 43-95-105).

(fig. 17); the sheet showing an arched frame, leaning against the mirror, is a preparatory drawing for the panel of Saint Matthew, also for the Church of Saint-Hilaire (fig. 24); the figure with closed eyes is based on a wax sculpture, *Dying Voltaire* (fig. 34), attributed to Curtius (1737-1794), that Leduc had inherited from his teacher Luigi Capello. On the other hand, the magazines are perhaps – but only perhaps – issues of *The Studio*, the object atop them the carved handle of an ornate letter opener, and the lay figure's gesture one of dance. These products and tools of the artistic endeavour, then, symbolize the artistic process.

The round mirror, at the physical centre of the composition, is also the work's metaphysical pivot, functioning as a metaphor of the authority of the artist. The fact that part of its surface is obscured by sheets of paper points to the veiled nature of ultimate truth. And the image reflected is a complex one, for in it converge the lay figure set against the backdrop painting of a man with closed eyes and, apparently hanging on the wall behind the actual set-up of objects, an unidentified *Angelus*, where two figures can be discerned standing in a field, their heads bowed and hands clasped in prayer as the bell of a distant steeple tolls. Thus juxtaposed in the mirror, the *Angelus*, the

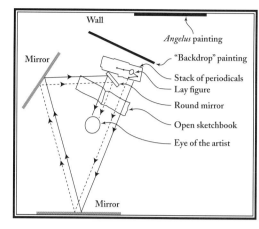

Fig. 35 Diagram showing the position of the three mirrors.

lay figure and the figure with closed eyes supersede their basic identity as artist's materials and products to symbolize states of perfection: the uplifted face and closed eyes of the male figure suggest a transcendent spiritual harmony; the lay figure is a model of the ideal proportions of the human figure; and the Angelus, the Prayer of the Incarnation, refers to the Word made flesh as the living Christ.

Absent from the mirror reflection, however, is the image of the artist himself at work on his creation. In the spot where one might expect the artist to appear is instead the figure with closed eyes. In a traditional self-portrait, one sees the artist and not the mirror; in this self-portrait, one sees the mirror and not the artist. But Leduc is there. Exclusion of his head from this reflection would have required the deployment of two other large mirrors: one facing the wall the *Angelus* hangs on and another positioned at an angle so as to reflect an image of the ensemble from the first additional mirror onto the small round mirror and, finally, to the artist's eye.[2]

A reconstruction of the set-up reveals that to paint this scene, Leduc would have had to place himself within the triangle defined by the three mirrors (fig. 35); but the artist, like God in Creation, stands unseen amid his created universe. The right-hand side of the inscription around the work's perimeter (destined to be hidden by the frame)

reads, "drawing, colour, composition: the painter's trinity", a further hint of the godlike nature of the artistic creator. Thus, this work explores the role of the artist as an authority independent of nature by implying an analogy between artistic and divine creation.

Indeed, as tools and products of the artistic process, the objects represented are one step removed from simple objects. Leduc is in a philosophical dialogue, not with unadulterated nature, but with the history and tradition of art itself. Through intellectual artifice and painterly virtuosity, Leduc has transformed a "bread and butter" genre into a highly complex work that amply demonstrates he had already travelled far along the "elevated walks of art".

A. G.

1 "Spring Exhibition: Second Notice", *The Montreal Daily Witness*, March 22, 1900, p. 4.

2 The reversed image of the lay figure in the round mirror also indicates the use of two additional mirrors.

91

The Ribauds

1898

Oil on cardboard

31.5 x 22.7 cm

Signed and dated lower right: *O. Leduc Nov. 1898*

Luc Choquette collection

INSCRIPTIONS

Recto, lower left: *Au Dr Choquette*

PROVENANCE

Studio of the artist; Dr. Ernest Choquette, Saint-Hilaire, 1898; Luc Choquette, Montreal

91

IN the summer of 1898, Dr. Ernest Choquette (cat. 92) published his first novel, *Les Ribaud*. In December of that year, Leduc dedicated to the writer a small painting inspired by a scene from the book. This work, then, was not conceived as an illustration to the book, but rather as a tribute to the writer, a visualization of a key passage in the novel.

Les Ribaud is a love story set during the Patriote Rebellions between 1834 and 1837. Madeleine is seduced by Percival Smith, an English officer stationed at Fort Chambly. Her father, Dr. Ribaud, is both grieved and insulted, for his patriotic pride cannot accept a marriage with the oppressor, nor can he forget that his own son has been killed in a duel in which Smith was implicated. He feels that loyalty, honour, pride and patriotism all dictate that he should kill the Englishman as he leaves for Saint-Charles to put down the Rebellion. Smith, however, out of love for Madeleine has vowed not to fight against the Patriotes. He passes his duties of commander to the flag-bearer and consequently escapes death to marry Madeleine at last.

Leduc was inspired by the most dramatic moment in the book: Dr. Ribaud, torn between his personal honour and his love of his daughter, is preparing to fire on Smith, with his servant François by his side. The artist depicts the rebels hidden by a row of trees, their ammunition at their feet, watching for the redcoats to come into view on the path along the Richelieu River. In the foreground, the dramatic intensity of the atmosphere is captured solely through the use of a monochrome brown that

also accentuates the autumnal bleakness of the scene. The background, where the action takes place, is done in a lighter range of colours, with grey-blue shades for the sky and the mountain of Saint-Hilaire. Dr. Ribaud seems to be very much the character described in the novel: strong, courageous and proud, he looks as sturdy as the oaks that screen him.[1]

Dr. Choquette was pleased with the painting. As he wrote,

It's all there, the picture sums up the book … a corner of my mountain, a bend in the Richelieu, the tall trees stripped by the November winds, the Saint-Charles road, and in the background the winding path taken by the detachment of English troops as far as the place where the captain fell to the Patriotes' bullets. And standing out in full light against the grey maple trunks, Dr. Ribaud, immense and impressive, ennobled by the magic touch of the artist, who has given him a strikingly memorable head.

Everything in the painting lives, breathes and floats in an autumnal landscape with its details of a few last leaves still dangling from the branches and the misty look of the bluish grey sky.

Dr. Choquette's enthusiastic account ends:

When painting does this, when it renders visible our dreams, the things we have imagined, that is when we truly learn to love it. I would say that this small painting was what began to teach me how supremely beautiful and real the art of painting can be.[2]

M. L.

---

1 For this painting, Leduc made a preparatory nude study (graphite on cream laid paper, 21.4 - 22 x 25.7 cm, private collection).

2 Dr. [Ernest] Choquette, "Un artiste de mon pays", *La Patrie* [Montreal], December 3, 1898, p. 2.

93

92

Portrait of Dr. Ernest Choquette

1899

Charcoal on paper, 43.4 x 35.5 cm (oval)
Monogrammed and dated lower right: *18 LEDUC
99*, encircled with an *O*

Private collection

INSCRIPTIONS

Verso: *Docteur Ernest Choquette; Portrait oval - Dr
Ernest Choquette fusain 17" x 13 1/2"; from S. Clerk,
Mont Saint-Hilaire RO 139-2-73; Temporary Label
Art Gallery of Ontario Extended Loan Leduc, Ozias:
Portrait of Dr Ernest Choquette Charcoal on paper
collection of Mr and Mrs Edouard Clerk, Mont Saint-
Hilaire, Quebec, C/o Monette, Clerk, Michaud,
Barakett, and Levesque, Montreal, P.Q.; From M. E.
Clerk ro 69-3-69 St-Hilaire-sur-Richelieu*

PROVENANCE

Studio of the artist; Dr. Ernest Choquette, Saint-
Hilaire; Mr. and Mrs. Édouard Clerk,
Saint-Hilaire; private collection

93

Claude Paysan

1899

Charcoal with whitish grey gouache highlights, traces of graphite on laid paper

50.4 x 31.2 cm

Monogrammed and dated lower left: *18 LEDUC
99*, encircled with an *O*

Private collection

INSCRIPTIONS

Verso: *Couverture du livre Claude Paysan - Dr
Choquette; Couverture du livre Claude Paysan -
Leduc; fusain 12" x 19" from S. Clerk, Mont St-Hilaire
Ro 139-2-73*

PROVENANCE

Studio of the artist; Mr. and Mrs. Édouard Clerk,
Saint-Hilaire, 1953; private collection

94

96

97

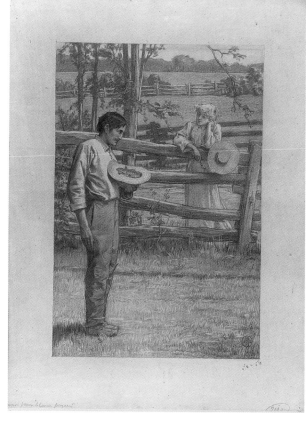

94

"Les autres s'étaient mis à genoux…"

1899

Charcoal on paper

36.2 x 51.8 cm

Monogrammed and dated lower left: *18 OL 99*

Luc Choquette collection

INSCRIPTIONS

Verso: *La prière Luc Choquette*

PROVENANCE

Studio of the artist; Mr. and Mrs. Luc Choquette, Montreal, 1943

95

"Mais elle, ceci l'amusait ce grand garçon si brun…"

1899

Charcoal on paper

60.5 x 45.5 cm

Monogrammed and dated lower right: *18 LEDUC 99*, encircled with an *O*

Luc Choquette collection

PROVENANCE

Studio of the artist; Mr. and Mrs. Luc Choquette, Montreal, 1943

96

"Du train qu'ils y allaient…"

1899

Charcoal with white gouache highlights
on laid paper

33.5 x 47.8 cm

Monogrammed and dated lower right: *18 OL 99*

Private collection

97

"Dès ce moment… ce fut un entrain général."

1899

Charcoal with white highlights on wove
paper

32.8 x 47.2 cm

Monogrammed and dated lower left: *18 OL 99*

Ottawa, The National Gallery of Canada,
inv. 16728

98

99

98

"En passant, après son boniment…"

1899

Charcoal on paper

35.7 x 49.1 cm

Monogrammed and dated lower right: *18 OL 99*

Luc Choquette collection

99

"… Claude qui l'observait en silence …"

1899

Charcoal with white gouache highlights
and grey, blue and yellow watercolour on
paper

34.7 x 49.2 cm

Monogrammed and dated lower left: *18 OL 99*

Private collection

100

101

102

100

"Ils étaient venus de loin, ..."

1899

Charcoal with white highlights on laid paper

34.6 x 48.5 cm

Monogrammed and dated lower left: *18 OL 99*

Ottawa, The National Gallery of Canada, inv. 16729

PROVENANCE

Studio of the artist; Mr. and Mrs. Luc Choquette, Montreal, 1943; National Gallery of Canada, 1971

101

"Alors, auprès, tout de suite, ce fut un cri égorgé de louve..."

1899

Charcoal on laid paper

46 x 32 cm

Monogrammed and dated lower left: *18 OL 99*

Private collection

INSCRIPTIONS

Verso: *Claude retrouve son frère effet de nuit - fanal - chien hurlant - Justement Jacques Jean-Louis fut retrouvé en chaloupe*

PROVENANCE

Studio of the artist; Mr. and Mrs. Édouard Clerk, Saint-Hilaire; private collection, 1970

102

"Ils s'en vont... s'agenouiller devant deux croix de bois semblables."

1899

Charcoal on paper

30.6 x 45.3 cm

Monogrammed and dated lower left: *18 OL 99*

Kingston, Ontario, Agnes Etherington Art Centre, Queen's University, inv. 36-027

INSCRIPTIONS

Verso: *Ozias Leduc Exh. Agenouillés au cimetière From L. Choquette, Mtrl R0 647-12-73; The National Gallery of Canada Titre de l'exp.: O. Leduc Cat. no 17 Boite no 6*

PROVENANCE

Studio of the artist; Mr. and Mrs. Luc Choquette, Montreal, 1943; Agnes Etherington Art Centre, 1993

On December 3, 1898, Dr. Ernest Choquette had an article published in *La Patrie* in which he paid tribute to his friend Ozias Leduc, who had just given him a small painting (cat. 91) inspired by Choquette's first novel, *Les Ribaud*. In it, he announced to the readers:

Leduc and I have a project, an insane project: this winter we are going to produce something new – an illustrated book ...

Has this ever been done here before? If it has, we renounce our project, for we want to do something new – two Canajuns from Saint-Hilaire have a notion to astound people.[1]

Author and artist kept their promise, and the novel was published on August 30 of the following year. It was an ambitious project: Leduc executed fifteen large charcoal drawings and the cover page in gouache, as well as a charcoal portrait of the author for the frontispiece. A collaborative venture on this scale was unparalleled in the publishing history of French Canada.[2] On April 29, 1899, *La Patrie* announced the forthcoming publication of excerpts from *Claude Paysan* in serial form and printed two of Leduc's illustrations: the *Portrait of Dr. Ernest Choquette* (cat. 92) and the scene of *The Sower*.[3] The instalments were to be published daily from July 1 to August 4.

As the subheading in *La Patrie* put it, the novel tells "An Idyll of Country Life on the Banks of the Richelieu". After his father's death, Claude Drioux, the chief protagonist, takes over the family lands and supports his bereaved mother. His comrade Jacques arrives to share his labours and stand by his friend. Claude soon falls in love with Fernande Tissot, a city girl from a prosperous family who spends her summers by the Richelieu. Although she is fond of Claude, Fernande is not in love with him, and furthermore knows that she has a fatal lung disease. Claude suffers in silence, for his feelings of social inferiority make it impossible for him to declare his love. On the day of Fernande's death, he is drowned in a storm on the Richelieu River. His loyal friend Jacques keeps his promise to take Claude's place in caring for his mother.

Dr. Choquette's novel has been categorized by Maurice Lemire as a rural novel, that is, a story "set in the countryside with country people as the main protagonists".[4] Here the love story and the insight into male psychology are more important than the insistence on rural values so common in the regionalist novels of the 1920s. In 1928, after another commission for illustrations, this time for the novel *La Campagne canadienne* by Adélard Dugré, s.j.,[5] Leduc began to be known as "a painter of the soil".[6] And yet his main concern was to carry out his commissions faithfully, without taking a stance.

Dr. Choquette suggested twenty subjects for illustrations. Leduc selected fourteen of them and chose two others of his own.[7] The illustrations depict the key moments of the plot and may be divided into three main groups: the activities of farm life and the customs of country folk, such as the tasks of fall (cat. 93), sowing (whereabouts unknown), threshing (cat. 96) the yearly Beggars' Visit (cat. 98), the observance of the Month of Mary (cat. 100) and the Shrove Tuesday dance (cat. 97); the events in Claude's emotional life, such as the arrival of his friend Jacques (whereabouts unknown),[8] his loneliness after Jacques's departure for the United States (whereabouts unknown), Claude reading a letter from Jacques announcing his imminent return (private collection), Claude and Fernande meeting (cat. 95), and Claude spying on Fernande (cat. 99); and finally, scenes evoking life's end, such as Claude's father receiving Holy Communion on his sickbed (cat. 94), the loneliness of the widow Julienne (whereabouts unknown), Fernande's illness (Musée du Québec),[9] Claude's drowning (cat. 101) and the prayers at the graveside (cat. 102).

Leduc rendered these events in the same mood as his portraits of the period – they breathe an air of calm and serenity. Each illustration is a completed drawing and the occasion for a study in lighting effects. The cover illustration (cat. 93) conveys the tone of the book and its setting: the young farmer at his fall tasks is daydreaming, leaning against the fence with the Richelieu Valley stretching before him, the river and Mount Saint-Bruno in the distance. The sun's rays penetrate the clouds, and the picture is framed by a mosaic Gothic arch reminiscent of the frames of the paintings in the nave of the church at Saint-Hilaire, which Leduc was decorating at the time. A scroll-like cartouche at the lower right bears the words of a song that sum up the plot. The *Portrait of Dr. Ernest Choquette*, executed from a photograph,[10] renders the face in minute detail, the clothes more sketchily.

Leduc's illustrations, incorporated into the novel, follow Dr. Choquette's story closely, evoking the setting, the people, the happenings and the atmosphere. In the scene where the elder Claude is receiving Extreme Unction (cat. 94), time stands still in a moment of reflection symbolized by the three ages of man. In the meeting of Claude and Fernande (cat. 95), the fence plays a symbolic role, stressing the isolation of each of the two, with shyness on the one side and incomprehension on the other. The threshing (cat. 96) is handled in a vivid manner with back lighting and movement rendered through the diagonals of the flails and the bold cross-hatching representing the accumulating heaps of straw on the ground. The Shrove Tuesday dance (cat. 97), depicted with an almost pointillist technique, shows a lively scene, illuminated by lamplight and firelight. The composition of the picture of the yearly Beggars' Visit (cat. 98) is structured by the trees in the foreground and the shade they offer for private talk. Fernande and Claude's meeting by the river (cat. 99) is richly lyrical; we can feel the silence. The Month of Mary picture (cat. 100) is composed of curved lines (the path, the fences, the road) leading the eye up to the village crowned by the spires of church and convent and beyond to Mount Saint-Hilaire. At the climax of the story, nature itself becomes part of the drama: the wild waves that overturn the canoe, the shattered tree trunk, the gale in the branches and the stormy sky compose the setting in which Claude's body is found (cat. 101). The final illustration (cat. 102) to a book dominated by the deaths of three of its characters – the elder Drioux, his son Claude and Fernande – shows two silhouettes praying in a graveyard. They are Julienne the mother, and Jacques, seen at sunset, just before a dusk that suggests the extinction of this earthly life.

The pictures inspired by *Les Ribaud* and *Claude Paysan* are among the first indications of Leduc's interest in the landscape around him: the Richelieu River and Valley and Mount Saint-Hilaire. Initially, he rendered the landscape in a naturalist style. Three landscapes commissioned by the Honourable Philippe-Auguste Choquette (cats. 120-122) in 1900-1901 were directly inspired by these illustrations.

M. L.

---

1 Dr. [Ernest] Choquette, "Un artiste de mon pays", *La Patrie* [Montreal], December 3, 1898, p. 2.

2 See introduction to Section II, especially notes 11-13.

3 "Claude Paysan – Une idylle de la Vie Rurale sur les Bords du Richelieu", *La Patrie* [Montreal], April 29, 1899, pp. 1, 10.

4 Maurice Lemire, *Dictionnaire des œuvres littéraires du Québec*, vol. 2: *1900-1939* (Montreal: Fides, 1987), pp. XXIV-XXV. For a summary of the novel *Claude Paysan*, see vol. 1: *Des origines à 1900* (1980), pp. 128-129.

5 It has proved impossible to date to find the original illustrations for this novel. For a summary of the plot, see Lemire 1987, pp. 173-174.

6 Arthur Lemay, "Un artiste du terroir à St-Hilaire de Rouville: l'œuvre du peintre Osias Leduc", *Le Terroir*, vol. 3, no. 11/12 (March-April 1928), cover and pp. 186-187.

7 Handwritten list of Dr. Choquette, BNQ 327/3/5. The portrait of the author was not commissioned by Dr. Choquette. Was it ordered by the publisher?

8 This illustration was one of Leduc's own ideas; he wanted to include a winter scene, having already depicted the three other seasons.

9 Dr. Choquette had suggested illustrating the visit by Claude and Julienne to Fernande's sickbed. Leduc chose instead to depict Fernande alone in her room and even executed two drawings of the scene (see the photograph of the rejected drawing, BNQ 327/12/6.10).

10 BNQ 327/13/4.6.

103
Pigeons
1898

Oil on canvas

39.6 x 32.4 cm

Monogrammed and dated upper left: *18 OL 98*

Saskatoon, Mendel Art Gallery, inv. 90.2

PROVENANCE

Studio of the artist; Louis-Philippe Brodeur, on loan(?), 1899; studio of the artist, 1900; Dufresne(?), 1916; Mendel Art Gallery, 1990

104
The Woodcock
1899

Oil on canvas

39.7 x 30.5 cm

Inscribed, initialed and dated lower right: *PARTIE D'APRES SUZOR COTÉ O.L. 1899.*

Private collection

PROVENANCE

Commissioned by Louis A. Boyer, Montreal, 1899; Galerie l'Art français, Montreal; private collection, 1985

T HE only still lifes of dead game Leduc painted are *The Woodcock* and *Pigeons* (presented here in its original frame, which was designed by Leduc and is now in the collection of the Musée du Québec; see fig. 48). The two birds in *Pigeons*, suspended by their claws from a string hanging from a nail in the wall, occupy virtually the entire picture area. Their subdued brown and slate grey-blue tones complement the more luminous gold of the backdrop. Birds and ground have both been loosely painted. If *The Woodcock* is more tightly modelled, it is perhaps because it is based on a work by another artist, whose rendition was much more academic (fig. 36).

In the context of still-life painting in Canada, neither of these works by Leduc is unusual. Many contemporaries employed such imagery, which, since the third quarter of the century, had become part of a trend to document the spoils of the sporting activities of the bourgeoisie.[1] As surrogate hunting trophies, such paintings were class symbols, even for collectors who were not sportsmen themselves.

Although the circumstances of Leduc's decision to execute *Pigeons* are not known,[2] correspondence detailing

---

the commissioning of *The Woodcock* suggests that he was targeting just such a clientele. The particulars are revealed in a series of letters Leduc received from the lawyer Louis A. Boyer, a self-styled collector and promoter of Canadian art whose contact with the artist was effected through Louis-Philippe Brodeur (cat. 123), their mutual friend and Boyer's partner in the Montreal law firm Dandurand, Brodeur and Boyer.

From the first letter, one can infer that Boyer, in the market for a picture of dead game painted after nature, was shown *Pigeons*.[3] Conscious of the preferences of his collector-friends and not partial to pigeons himself, he asked Leduc about painting a pair of woodcocks, a subject much more popular with the circles within which Boyer proposed to promote Leduc's work.[4]

After unsuccessful attempts to obtain satisfactory specimens of birds and after bandying about the possibility of a still life of fruit or a bouquet of carnations instead,[5] the client eventually proposed that Leduc copy a still life of a woodcock by Suzor-Coté, then one of French Canada's premier artists – Boyer had recently encountered the painting and greatly admired it.[6] Clearly attempting not to ruffle the artist, the lawyer magnanimously allowed him to choose the painting's background colour.[7]

Boyer's verdict? Leduc's effort was "superb"; one would be hard pressed to

Fig. 36   Marc-Aurèle de Foy Suzor-Coté, (1869-1937) *The Woodcock*, oil on canvas, 40.1 x 29.9 cm (private collection).

103

104

tell which of the two works was the original.[8] While Leduc's painting is in fact close to its model, variations in lighting, background colour and such details as the articulation of the feathers – not to mention the pointed inscription, "starting from Suzor-Coté" – indicate that Leduc attempted to make *The Woodcock* his own.

It is not known how Leduc felt about being relegated, in this first private commission, to the role of copyist in a genre in which he had achieved a certain reputation,[9] but he seems to have appreciated Boyer as a "contact".[10] His subsequent willingness to meet with a friend of the lawyer-collector's about a potential commission for a portrait of a horse[11] indicates that Leduc accepted the woodcock project as a necessary aspect of earning a living from art. It is possible that the commission of *The Woodcock*, and the ensuing opportunities for dissemination of work in this genre through private avenues, encouraged Leduc to

submit the earlier, original *Pigeons* for public exhibition more than a year after it was completed.

A. G.

1 See Daniel Fowler (1810-1894), *Crane* (1869; Toronto, Royal Ontario Museum, inv. 976.384.2); Cornelius Krieghoff (1815-1872), *Still Life with Bufflehead and Shorebird* (1871) and *Still Life with Spruce Grouse and Quail* (undated; Sotheby's, Toronto, May 31, 1990, lot nos. 247-248); T. Mower Martin (1838-1934), *Ducks* (exhibited in 1893 at the RCA in Montreal; reproduced as line drawing in *Montreal Daily Star*, March 8, 1893, p. 3); Charles Gill, *Still Life with Fish* (1895; reproduced in J. Russell Harper, *Painting in Canada: A History*, 2nd edition [Toronto and Buffalo: University of Toronto Press, 1977] p. 256, fig. 99); Marc-Aurèle de Foy Suzor-Coté, *Still Life, Duck* (1897; Musée du Québec, inv. 46.115); Zotique Fabien, *Study of Fish* (exhibited 1899 at the RCA in Montreal, no. 48; reproduced as line drawing in "Opening Night", *The Montreal Daily Witness*, April 8, 1899, p. 14); Charles Huot, *Still Life, Ducks* (Musée du Québec, inv. G 55 106 P).

2 Jean-René Ostiguy, *Ozias Leduc: Symbolist and Religious Painting*, exhib. cat. (Ottawa: National Gallery of Canada, 1974), p. 198, asserts that *Pigeons* was commissioned by a client who refused the work on the grounds that it was "too personal" and who then requested a still life in the manner of Suzor-Coté. This interpretation is

based on a misreading of the correspondence from L. A. Boyer (BNQ 327/5/9).

3 Letter from Boyer to Ozias Leduc, January 18, 1899, BNQ 327/5/9. It is unclear whether the painting had already been showcased in Brodeur's office, or if it had been brought in specifically to show Boyer an example of Leduc's work in this genre.

4 *Ibid.* Boyer mentions that he had already commissioned Charles Huot to paint a still life of a salmon and trout.

5 Letter from Boyer to Ozias Leduc, January 27, 1899, BNQ 327/5/9.

6 Boyer to O. L., February 7, 1899, BNQ 327/5/9.

7 Boyer to O. L., February 11, 1899, BNQ 327/5/9.

8 Boyer to O. L., March 21, 1899, BNQ 327/5/9.

9 The *Montreal Gazette* promised its readers in 1895 that "O. Leduc will have on exhibition one of his matchless pieces of still life" ("The Spring Exhibition", February 28, 1895, p. 2).

10 Boyer several times indicates that a Leduc "original" of woodcocks was still in his plans (Boyer to O. L., March 21, 1899, BNQ 327/5/9; October 28, 1901, BNQ 327/5/11).

11 Boyer to O. L., March 6, 1900, and March 20, 1900, BNQ 327/5/10. It is not known if this particular project came to fruition.

105

106

105
My Portrait
About 1899

Charcoal and graphite on paper

35.9 x 29.1 cm

Signed lower right: *Ozs Leduc*

Luc Choquette collection

INSCRIPTIONS

Recto, lower left: *Mon Portrait*

PROVENANCE

Studio of the artist; Mr. and Mrs. Luc Choquette, Montreal, about 1943

106
Self-portrait
About 1899

Charcoal on laid paper (watermark: *Ingres*)

36.5 x 26.5 cm

Initialed lower right: *O.L.*

Ottawa, The National Gallery of Canada, inv. 16730

PROVENANCE

Studio of the artist; Dr. Ernest Choquette, Saint-Hilaire; Mr. and Mrs. Luc Choquette, Montreal; National Gallery of Canada, 1971

107
My Portrait
1899

Oil on paper glued to wood

33 x 26.9 cm

Monogrammed and dated upper left: *18 LEDUC 99*, encircled with an *O*

Ottawa, The National Gallery of Canada, inv. 16996

INSCRIPTIONS

Verso: *1899 MON PORTRAIT À 35 ANS; 1899; OZIAS LEDUC; Ce portrait appartient à Mlle. Gabrielle Messier Ozias Leduc le 6 Déc 1942*

PROVENANCE

Studio of the artist; Gabrielle Messier, Saint-Hilaire, 1942; National Gallery of Canada, 1972

108

Self-portrait

About 1909

Oil on cardboard

19 x 25.5 cm

Signed lower right: *OZIAS LEDUC*

Quebec City, Musée du Québec, inv. 86.38

INSCRIPTIONS

Verso: *Ozias Leduc vers l'âge
de 45 ans; 16 oct. 1901 (?); D48334', recouper et
fournir 1 1/2 F HLL - 800 - VU - 7 X 9 1/2;
D-48334; 1 - Vu 7 x 9 1/2 + 1/2 F F LL - 800; D-48 -
334; 1 - Vu 7 x 9 1/2; 1 1/2 F H LL - 800*

PROVENANCE

Studio of the artist; Mr. and Mrs. Édouard Clerk,
Saint-Hilaire; Sotheby's sale, lot 722, Toronto, 1985;
Galerie Claude Lafitte, Montreal; Musée du
Québec, 1986

THE 1983 exhibition *The Hand Holding the Brush*, which brought together self-portraits of many Canadian artists, made it possible to formulate some general statements about the genre. The exhibition's curator Robert Stacey suggested that the self-portrait reflects "the process of artmaking and the self-image of the artist in our society".[1] In a self-portrait, the artist plays three parts: he is at once model, spectator and creator of the work, the being pondering his technique and his creation, what France Borel calls "fusional autarky".[2] As Michel Tournier explains,

When the Bible tells us that God made man in His own image, what can it mean but that man is Jehovah's self-portrait? Man, the image of God. Of what God? Of God making His own image out of clay, that is, a creator in the process of creating. This is the essence of the self-portrait; it is the only portrait that reflects the creator at the very moment of creation.[3]

The self-portrait, according to Tournier, corresponds to the *natura naturans* defined by the philosopher Spinoza (1632-1677), that is, "a nature that is an active outpouring of divinity".

The first known self-portraits by Leduc, an oil entitled *My Portrait* (cat. 107)[4] and a preparatory sketch for this in charcoal with the image reversed (cat. 106), date from 1899, when the artist was thirty-five. In the same period, he made a drawing also called *My Portrait* (cat. 105). About ten years later, he painted his own head again in oils (cat. 108); in 1934, he copied this work in pencil in a sketchbook (cat. 77).[5] Throughout this period, he made little pencil sketches of himself in a humorous, even caricatured, style.[6] The artist also depicted himself surreptitiously in some of his religious paintings, as a way of signing his work: in the Cathedral of Saint-Charles-Borromée in Joliette (fig. 6), one of the disciples in the scene of *Christ Calming the Waves*[7] has his features, as does an apostle in the *Pentecost* (fig. 19) in the Church of Saint-Hilaire. Finally, there is a photographic self-portrait probably made at the turn of the century (fig. 15). The reasons why an artist chooses to depict himself or herself are various: vanity or an exercise in narcissism, a wish to be remembered, an essay in style or a piece of self-promotion by a painter wishing to display his skill and success. Leduc's motivation seems rather to have been a search for his own identity and an inquiry into the artist's role in society.

My Portrait (cat. 107) is a head-and-shoulders portrait in a three-quarters pose with the head turned squarely on to the spectator. The features are captured in smooth brush strokes with no underlying line drawing. The thickness of the pigment suggests that the artist struggled with his medium for a while. The formal relationships, the limited range of colours and the violent chiaroscuro focus the viewer's attention on the intensity of expression in the upper part of the sitter's face. The eyes and forehead are brightly lit, while the lower part of the face is in shadow. The tenseness of the pose, apparent also in the charcoal sketch (cat. 106), shows the artist deep in thought; this self-portrait invites the observer to ponder on the concentration required by the creative process. As Stacey remarks, "The self-portrait is more than a confession or a gasconade, a self-grilling or a self-commendation: it is, or should be, an earnest of all that an artist hopes to achieve through, and for, art."[8]

Leduc uses the self-portrait as a way of expressing his notion of the artist as "a herald of ideas".[9] This approach is similar to that of the Northern European artists of the Romantic school for whom art was a way of communicating with the spiritual mysteries it is the artist's duty to reveal.[10] The Symbolist artists inherited this concept of art. Opposed to realist and naturalist credos, they found inspiration in idealist and mystical traditions. Leduc's intensely questioning gaze in *My Portrait* affirms the subjective, intellectual and spiritual values he held dear.

The self-portrait in the Choquette collection (cat. 105) is executed with broad, swift hatching. The body, seen in profile, appears as if in movement because of the angle of the head. With this gesture, the artist-sitter establishes contact with the spectator. Could this sketch have been a study abandoned by Leduc because the dreamy look in the eyes did not have the intensity of expression he wanted for the oil self-portrait?

The *Self-portrait* in the Musée du Québec (cat. 108) conforms more to the definition of a realist portrait: shapes are outlined, modelling is obtained through the interplay of light and shade, and the source of light is very specific. The artist is plainly dressed in a shirt and bow tie, a style more middle class than bohemian. A studio setting is sketchily suggested by a picture rail with four small frames resting on it. It is the psychological approach, conveyed by the intense gaze, that prevails here.

In his self-portraits, Leduc never depicted himself at work or even with the tools of his art, though these were often the subject of his still lifes. The still lifes of objects in his studio, however, may be interpreted as allegorical self-portraits (cats. 12, 90). Leduc was primarily concerned to demonstrate that in the act of creation, intellectual effort is more important than technical skill. His self-portrait photograph (fig. 15) is the only one that shows him with a prop – a camera, as a way of indicating that he does possess another craft. The restraint apparent in *My Portrait* has changed to a slightly mocking attitude, accentuated by the angle of the artist's battered hat. Leduc is not taking himself seriously here. He is perhaps interested in observing himself by means of a technical procedure that he considers useful in his painting, but he is not yet ready to grant it the status of art.[11]

M. L.

1 Robert H. Stacey, *The Hand Holding the Brush: Self Portraits by Canadian Artists*, exhib. cat. (London, Ontario: London Regional Art Gallery, 1983), p. 11.

2 France Borel, *Le modèle ou l'artiste séduit* (Geneva: Skira, 1990), p. 41.

3 Michel Tournier, *Des clefs et des serrures; images et proses* (Paris: Éditions du Chêne/Hachette, 1979), quoted in *La famille des portraits*, exhib. cat. (Paris: Musée des arts décoratifs, 1979), p. 36.

4 Leduc considered this one of his ten best paintings (draft of a letter from Ozias Leduc to Mackenzie Waters, chairman of the Fine Arts Committee for the Canadian National Exhibition [July 9, 1948], BNQ 327/9/11).

5 In 1947, he made a copy of this sketch on a loose sheet that he gave to Jeannette Bergeron, René Bergeron's wife (private collection).

6 Self-portraits in graphite, 10.5 x 8.5 cm (private collection); 15.3 x 12 cm (private collection); 23 x 15.5 cm (whereabouts unknown); also two self-portraits dashed off on the back of engravings for the eighth and eleventh Stations of the Cross that he would use in the Church of Saint-Hilaire (BNQ 327/14/5), and several portrait photographs.

7 Draft of a letter from Ozias Leduc to Abbé Eugène Martin, dated September 3, 1932, BNQ 327/8/38.

8 Stacey 1983, p. 21.

9 Definition of the artist given by Ozias Leduc in a speech to members of the Union catholique des cultivateurs in 1928, BNQ 327/4/3.

10 See Robert Rosenblum, *Modern Painting and the Northern Romantic Tradition: Friedrich to Rothko* (New York: Harper & Row, 1975), pp. 62-64.

11 It was only in 1934 that Leduc admitted to Paul Gagné, his photographer friend from Sherbrooke, that he was "more and more convinced that photography is an art" (draft of a letter dated April 18, 1934, BNQ 327/8/40).

109

Portrait of a Woman, also called
Portrait of Madame Lebrun
1899

Oil on canvas
42.8 x 32.5 cm
Monogrammed and dated upper right:
18 LEDUC 99, encircled with an *O*

Paul Gouin collection

PROVENANCE

Studio of the artist; Paul Gouin, Montreal, 1943;
Paul Gouin estate

IT is fitting that the same year Leduc executed the self-portrait entitled *My Portrait* (cat. 107), he should have portrayed his beloved sister Adélia (1870-1946) in this *Portrait of a Woman*,[1] for they were kindred spirits, both dedicated to the pursuit of perfection in their respective crafts.

Adélia, who was an accomplished seamstress, is depicted with needle and thread in lap. The needle, resting between her fingers, is set against a piece of intricate lacework that echoes the lace on the cuffs, collar and bodice of her blouse, whose singular brilliance within the picture draws attention to itself as a fine specimen of her handiwork.

On the basis of these attributes, it is tempting to place this portrait with numerous other Edwardian images of women engaged in women's work. But Leduc's painting transcends this genre. In examples like *Crazy Patchwork* by William Brymner (1855-1925),[2] *Sewing Lesson* by Frederick Challener (1869-1959),[3] *The Knitter* by Charles Huot[4] and *Anne Cruikshank* by William Cruikshank (1849-1922),[5] a single figure, set in a cozy – or decidedly feminine – domestic space, is deeply absorbed in her activity. Leduc's Adélia, on the other hand, is placed in an austere, gender-neutral room and, like the artist himself in his self-portrait, gazes intensely past the viewer. Straightbacked and prim, she conveys an aura of saintliness that corresponds to Leduc's assessment of her as "charity personified", with a devotion to others that "cannot be too highly praised".[6] Indeed, *Portrait of a Woman* has more in common with the portraits of nuns – prayer books and crucifixes in hand – that had occupied such a prominent place in the portraiture tradition in French Canada than with scenes of blissful domestic activity. It is a measure both of Leduc's respect for his sister's artistic professionalism and moral character, and of his personal affection for her that this painting can be considered as much an idealized portrait of an independent woman as the intimate portrayal of a family member.

Although *Portrait of a Woman* was exhibited twice by Leduc while still in his possession, it seems not to have elicited any response whatsoever from the press. Only in 1943, after a tug-of-war among three interested buyers led to its finally entering the collection of Paul Gouin,[7] did the *Portrait of Madame Lebrun* (as it then came to be called), begin to be exhibited frequently and referred to regularly as one of Leduc's most accomplished paintings.

A. G.

---

1 Adélia was married to her cousin Ernest Lebrun, brother of Leduc's future wife Marie-Louise. A man of diverse talents (he was a mechanic, electrician, journalist, filmmaker and photographer), Lebrun on occasion was involved in Leduc's artistic projects, such shared interests helping establish a life-long close friendship. See "M. Ernest-Léopold Lebrun…", *Le Petit Journal*, November 4, 1944.

2 1886 (National Gallery of Canada, inv. 309).

3 1896 (National Gallery of Canada, inv. 23154).

4 Undated (Musée du Québec, inv. A 34 191 P).

5 Undated (Art Gallery of Ontario, inv. 58/14).

6 Draft of an obituary to be submitted to *Le Courrier de Saint-Hyacinthe* [after April 27, 1946], BNQ 327/9/9.

7 See the letter from Maurice Gagnon to Ozias Leduc, January 20, 1943, BNQ 327/7/15; the draft of a letter from Leduc to Gagnon [after January 20, 1943], BNQ 327/9/6; the letter from Leduc to Paul Gouin, February 4, 1943, NAC, Paul Gouin papers, MG 27 III D 1, vol. 5; the letter from Luc Choquette to Leduc, February 24, 1943, BNQ 327/7/15; the draft of a letter from Leduc to Choquette, March 7, 1943, BNQ 327/9/6; the letter from Gouin to Leduc, March 25, 1943, BNQ 327/7/15; and the draft of the letter from Leduc to Gérard Langevin [after September 22, 1946], BNQ 327/9/9.

110

110

Landscape beside a River

1899

Oil on layered cardboard

9.5 x 13.4 cm

Monogrammed and dated upper left: *18 OL 99*

Pierrette Filion-Véronneau collection

PROVENANCE

Studio of the artist; René Bergeron, Chicoutimi;
Pierrette Filion-Véronneau, 1957

11

111

111

Landscape with Mountain

1900

Oil on paper glued to cardboard

12.2 x 15.9 cm

Monogrammed and dated upper left: *19 OL 00*

Private collection

INSCRIPTIONS

Verso: *6 chemises 46 DR 18 OL 92 10550 10807*

PROVENANCE

Studio of the artist; René Bergeron, Chicoutimi;
Jules Landry; private collection

112

Landscape with Trees

About 1900

Oil on heavy cardboard

18.3 x 12.8 cm

Signed lower right: *OZIAS LEDUC*

Private collection

INSCRIPTIONS

Verso: *900*

PROVENANCE

Studio of the artist; René Bergeron, Chicoutimi;
Jules Landry; private collection

113

Landscape

About 1900

Oil on wood

17.5 x 22.8 cm

Musée d'art de Joliette, gift of Paul Ivanier,
inv. 1985.060

INSCRIPTIONS

Verso: labels of Galerie Morency and Walter
Klinkhoff Gallery; certificate of authenticity signed
by Gabrielle Messier and Lucie Vary

PROVENANCE

Paul Ivanier; Musée d'art de Joliette, 1985

114

Landscape (near Antigonish, Nova Scotia)

About 1902

Oil and graphite on cardboard

12.7 x 17.2 cm

Private collection

INSCRIPTIONS

Verso: *Vue près Antigonish, N.E. Ozias Leduc; 138*

PROVENANCE

Studio of the artist; Gabrielle Messier, Saint-
Hilaire; private collection, 1955

113

114

115

115
Summer Landscape
About 1900

Oil on cardboard mounted on corrugated cardboard

10.6 x 19 cm

Signed lower right: *OZIAS LEDUC*

Cordier-McAllister collection

INSCRIPTIONS

Verso: *Provenance: L'Art canadien*; *Yvon Rousseau*; labels of Galerie d'art Michel Bigué and Encadrements Marcel

PROVENANCE

Studio of the artist; Galerie l'Art canadien, Chicoutimi; Claude Rousseau, Montmagny; Yvon Rousseau; Galerie d'art Michel Bigué; Fernand Cordier, June 1989

116

116
Setting Sun
About 1900

Oil on cardboard

18.5 x 25.3 cm

Signed lower left: *OZIAS LEDUC*

Private collection

INSCRIPTIONS

Verso: label of Galerie l'Art français

PROVENANCE

Studio of the artist; private collection, after 1940

117
View of Manchester, New Hampshire

About 1906

Oil and graphite on cardboard

13 x 20.5 cm

Signed lower left: *Ozias Leduc*

Gérard and Gisèle Lortie collection

PROVENANCE

Studio of the artist; Mr. and Mrs. Gérard Lortie, Montreal, about 1950

117

THE predominance of religious subjects, allegories and still lifes in Leduc's output might seem to indicate that landscape was only a secondary interest for the artist prior to the great Symbolist landscapes of the period 1912-1921. But although he was not executing landscapes as such, his interest in the genre is apparent in his illustrations for *Claude Paysan* (cats. 93-102), in the three narrative scenes commissioned by Philippe-Auguste Choquette (cats. 120-122) and in his allegories (cats. 89, 130).

This interest in nature is also visible in various sketches, none of which seems to have been developed into a finished work, and in the landscapes found in his religious and allegorical paintings using other sources. Only *Setting Sun* was deemed worthy of exhibition, at the Bibliothèque Saint-Sulpice in 1916. The sketches remained in Leduc's studio until the end of his career, when they were put on the market.

Leduc's several ways of approaching landscape can be seen in these eight colour pochades executed between 1899 and 1906, which range from nature studies to imaginary landscapes.

The variety of scenes depicted suggests that these sketches were made in leisure moments, such as when Leduc was away from home working on commissions for church decoration. The view of George Bay, near Antigonish, Nova Scotia, is topographically accurate, while both it and the landscape near Manchester, New Hampshire, demonstrate unusual effects of light.

Once again, it is the light and the atmosphere that seem to dictate the choice of view in *Summer Landscape* and *Setting Sun*. The slanting late-afternoon light and the red of the setting sun help create a vision of nature that is calm and peaceful despite being subject to the vicissitudes of time and natural forces.

Landscape beside a River, *Landscape with Trees* and the *Landscape* from the Musée d'art de Joliette, as well as the small landscape hidden on the back of the *Portrait of Rodolphe Brunet* (fig. 33), show the freedom of approach of these sketches. Their pictorial quality is enhanced by the transparency of some colours, which blend in with the support, the more thickly applied colour elsewhere and the reworking with the hard tip of the brush.

The small size of these panels actually transmits a greater sense of awe than a vast panorama. The *Landscape with Mountain* is based on an imaginative vision of nature, reflecting Leduc's credo that any depiction of nature is not solely a matter of how the material is handled but first and foremost a matter of how the artist views what he sees: "Every artist compiles his own version of a dictionary of nature, tools in hand. It is therefore in the work of artists who depict a humanized nature that one finds the symbols, always somewhat veiled, that can shed light on the way of him who wishes to enter the kingdom of nature by the path of art."[1]

L. L.

---

1   Ozias Leduc, "Art. La source des arts plastiques", undated manuscript, BNQ 327/4/10.

118
Open Window

About 1900(?)

Oil on cardboard

30.5 x 22.7 cm

Montreal, Jean-Pierre Valentin collection
INSCRIPTIONS
Verso: label of Galerie l'Art français
PROVENANCE
Studio of the artist; Galerie l'Art français,
Montreal, about 1956; Jean-Pierre Valentin

I N 1956, during an exhibition of works by Leduc at the Galerie l'Art français, this painting was reproduced in *La Presse* with the following commentary by Rodolphe de Repentigny:

Since it is fashionable to find in Leduc's work the glimmerings of various schools of contemporary painting, it could be said that we have a forecast of geometric painting in this picture: the clearly delineated and tightly interwoven planes produce a composition whose perspective changes as the observer moves. The browns, greys and silver tones give an impression of palpable luminosity. The painter signed this work in the centre, as if it were a graffito on a wall.[1]

This painting is indeed made up of geometric shapes with bold dark outlines. The walls and ceiling are painted in monochrome browns, while the landscape glimpsed through the window is composed of green, blue and blue-grey. Leduc was almost certainly inspired by a photograph of a young woman in a similar upper-storey room (fig. 37). In the painting, the human presence has apparently vanished, but as José Pierre says of certain Symbolist pictures, "These indoor scenes … are objects to contemplate, and as such, something like the mirror of the observer's soul."[2] And it could be added, of the creator's soul. As Jean Clair has pointed out, "Never before has the 'interior', that metaphor we use in speaking about houses, appeared a more appropriate evocation of the places so dear to Symbolist painters. The world of the home, of domesticity and the hearth, is first and foremost the world of the interior, of the *Innenwelt*, of quiet repose and inwardness."[3]

In Leduc's painting, the impasto in the window embrasure and on the right-hand wall that reflects the light from outside suggests a presence, that of the painter. The very brushwork itself carries significance: it refers to the process of creation and identifies both the artist and his style. The enigma of the missing graffito seen by de Repentigny is, if true, quite telling in regard to the importance of the brushwork: what need is there of the artist's signature when his painting is

Fig. 37   Young girl (Ozéma Leduc?) in an upper-storey room, about 1900 (photo by Ozias Leduc, printed from glass negative No. 55, BNQ_327/13/2.16).

powerful enough to identify him? The window is open not on a *veduta*, but on material for painting.

M. L.

1   [Rodolphe de Repentigny], "Un petit Leduc de haute époque", *La Presse* [Montreal], February 11, 1956, p. 74.

2   José Pierre, *L'Univers symboliste – Décadence, symbolisme et Art nouveau* (Paris: Somogy, 1991), p. 208.

3   Jean Clair, "The Self beyond Recovery", in *Lost Paradise: Symbolist Europe*, exhib. cat. (Montreal: Montreal Museum of Fine Arts, 1995), p. 130. The theme of interiors appears frequently in Symbolist painting. It was the German artist Caspar David Friedrich (1774-1840) who introduced this hint of mystical content in his paintings around the turn of the nineteenth century; see the reproduction of his *Woman at a Window* in Robert Rosenblum, *Modern Painting and the Northern Romantic Tradition: Friedrich to Rothko* (New York: Harper & Row, 1975), p. 32. This painting by Leduc also recalls a chalk and pastel drawing by James McNeill Whistler (1834-1903), *The Palace in Rags* (1879-1880), reproduced in *Whistler 1834-1903*, exhib. cat. (Paris: Réunion des Musées nationaux, 1995), p. 185.

119

Study for *Fall Plowing*

1900

Charcoal heightened with white chalk on laid paper

31.5 x 47.7 cm

Monogrammed and dated lower right: *19 OL 00*

Private collection

INSCRIPTIONS

Recto, lower left: *« Labour d'automne » Dessin pour un tableau (au juge A. Choquette, Québec)*
Verso, labels from National Gallery of Canada: *O. Leduc cat. no 21 boite 6 Leduc: Les labours d'automne à Saint-Hilaire - from L. Germain, Ottawa Ro 467-9-73 Leduc Exh.*

PROVENANCE

Studio of the artist; Charles-Lucien Germain, Toronto (bequest of the artist), 1955; private collection, 1978

119

JEAN-RENÉ OSTIGUY has noted that "landscape has meaning only inasmuch as it portrays an emotion or an idea".[1] This statement, a definition of the Symbolist approach to painting, is eminently applicable to the work of Ozias Leduc. *Fall Plowing*, *The Choquette Farm, Belœil* and *The Hayfield* all display his characteristic intimist vision, even though at first sight, it is the narrative element of the compositions that engages the eye.

The relevance of dealing with these landscapes under one heading lies in the fact that they can be thought of as a kind of triptych illustrating three striking moments in the passage of the seasons (the cycle was never completed with a fourth scene). Furthermore, all three were painted at the request of the Honourable Philippe-Auguste Choquette (1854-1948). The artist was friendly at this time with the Choquette family of Belœil, not only Abbé Charles-Philippe Choquette (fig. 104), but also his brother Ernest, whose first novel, *Claude Paysan*, had just been published with illustrations by Leduc (cats. 92-102).

As regards the exact date of execution, we know that all three of these works, recently completed, were still in the artist's studio on April 8, 1901.[2] Framed by Louis Morency, they were shown in his new gallery at 183 Saint-Jean Street, Quebec City, in June of that year.[3] Given the date that appears on the study for *Fall Plowing* (cat. 119), it seems likely that the landscapes were largely painted in the year 1900.

In the study the subject is handled in a more descriptive manner, with its cloudscape and the greater emphasis on the labourer. The composition of the final canvas is quite different. Between one treatment and the next, the creative process has transformed a rural topic into a theme for meditation.[4] The recently restored painting, far from being more austere than the preparatory study, evokes all the gentle poetry of late fall in the countryside. The solitary farmer in his field pursuing his age-old avocation embodies a sense of winter quiet. The work breathes an atmosphere of meditative peace, an effect largely due to the subtle painterly quality of the brush stroke and the definition of the space.

One of the first things one notices about *Fall Plowing* is that here Leduc is once again, as in *The Choquette Farm, Belœil* and *The Hayfield*, using the trees and the pole fence to establish spatial parameters. In all three works, the fence appears in the foreground, enabling the observer to become part of the landscape while isolating the scene beyond. In *Fall Plowing*, the interweaving of the fence poles, balanced by the harmonious fili-gree of the tree on the left, its branches reaching into the sky, heralds the interlaced plant forms of the great landscapes, such as *Blue Cumulus* of 1913 (cat. 143) and above all *Mauve Twilight* of 1921 (cat. 173). But the fence itself has a utilitarian function: it gives stability to the composition. As in *The Choquette Farm, Belœil*, it serves as a demarcation line beyond which the other elements of the scene unfold. Like the lines of a musical staff, the fence introduces a visal motif repeated in the furrows running parallel to it and linked to the grassy meadow, the horses and the farmer, as well as to the tree at the left. The outline of the tree, which Leduc moved somewhat in the final work, has a special role, which is to isolate from the rest of the picture something that could be called a second subject. The painted surface within the arc described by the trunk and branches of the tree is in fact a second landscape, with a winding rivulet and vegetation in the distance. Thus, *Fall Plowing* becomes for the artist an opportunity to express his feelings about the spoliation of nature, above and beyond the main theme of the work. In terms of this concept of landscape, it is interesting to note that the draft horses are placed farther off in the painting than in the sketch and, thus, given less importance. The

120
Fall Plowing

1901

Oil on canvas

62.2 x 91.4 cm

Signed and dated lower left: *O. Leduc 1901*

Quebec City, Musée du Québec, inv. 42.57

PROVENANCE

Studio of the artist; the Honourable Philippe-Auguste Choquette, Quebec City; Musée du Québec, 1942

same use of a sub-theme alongside the main one is also found in *The Choquette Farm, Belœil*, where the fence together with the birds in the snow in the foreground to the right create an independent subsidiary scene. This also has the effect of counterbalancing the two trees to the left, which Leduc altered and moved from their original position in the photograph he used as a source (fig. 38).

Although Leduc made use of photographs in painting *The Choquette Farm, Belœil* and *The Hayfield*, his vision of these landscapes nonetheless goes beyond the representational to achieve what might be called reality. In this regard, his friend Gustave Ouimet remarked that he found the horses in *Fall Plowing* insufficiently animated (he even suggested that Leduc paint them

different colours, advice Leduc failed to follow, being more concerned with suggestion than description).[5]

In terms of aesthetic values, the subtle light effects and the restricted range of colours, particularly in *Fall Plowing* and *The Choquette Farm, Belœil*, show Leduc aiming at conveying a sense of tranquillity as simply as possible, choosing to concentrate on effects of texture. The skyscapes in these works are also rendered in harmony with the subtle grey and beige tones that predominate. Between the study for *Fall Plowing* and the finished work, the configuration of the clouds changes from rounded shapes to more sweeping ones, creating a more restful atmosphere.

Unlike the other two paintings, *The Hayfield* is more straightforwardly descriptive and uses greater contrasts of

121

colour. In this regard, it is closer to the illustrations for *Claude Paysan* (cats. 93-102), where the motifs of fence and trees serve as settings for the figures. In *The Hayfield*, the actions and gestures of the farmworkers are clearly identifiable,

whereas in the other two canvases, the human figures are absorbed into the landscape as a whole, as with the plowman and his team in *Fall Plowing* and the small figure drawing water to the right of the conifer in *The Choquette Farm, Belœil. The Hayfield* thus represents a counterpoint to its two companion pieces. It is a painting that glorifies the abundance of nature through a range of glowing colours. The textural effects are rendered so as to create a pictorial surface where every stroke of colour enriches the work as a whole.

These three paintings are eloquent testimony to Leduc's poetically inclined temperament, his intimist approach, and the complexity and subtlety of his painting.

P. L'A.

121

The Choquette Farm, Belœil
1901
Oil on canvas
61.2 x 91.6 cm
Signed and dated lower left: *O. Leduc 1901*
Quebec City, Musée du Québec, inv. 78.93
INSCRIPTIONS
Verso: label of Walter Klinkhoff Gallery Inc.
PROVENANCE
Studio of the artist; the Honourable Philippe-Auguste Choquette, Quebec City; Walter Klinkhoff Gallery, Montreal; Musée du Québec, 1978

Fig. 38　The Choquette house, Belœil, about 1900 (photo by Ozias Leduc, printed from glass negative No. 171, BNQ 327/12/13.25).

122
The Hayfield
1901

Oil on canvas

61 x 91.5 cm

Signed and dated lower right: *O. LEDUC 1901*

Private collection

PROVENANCE

Studio of the artist; Dr. Ernest Choquette, Saint-
Hilaire; Choquette estate; Walter Klinkhoff
Gallery, Montreal; private collection, 1975

1   Jean-René Ostiguy, *Marc-Aurèle de Foy Suzor-Coté:
    "Winter Landscape"*, "Masterpieces in the National
    Gallery of Canada" series, no. 12 (Ottawa: National
    Gallery of Canada, 1978), p. 5.

2   Jean Remuna [pseudonym of Arsène Bessette], "M.
    Osias Leduc", *Le Canada-Français* [Saint-Jean],
    May 3, 1901, p. 2.

3   "Belle peintures", *L'Union des Cantons de l'Est*
    [Arthabaska], June 14, 1901, p. 2.

4   Leduc seems to have been absorbed by a passage from
    Ernest Choquette's novel *Claude Paysan*, which he had
    just illustrated:
    Gone are the leaves from the trees and the green clover
    from the fields; gone are the balmy, scented breezes.
    Everywhere, their place has been taken by dead suns,
    icy blasts and seared sap.
        But hope lingers for the days ahead, for the abun-
    dance of harvests to come. Amid the November
    desolation, a man traverses his field, matching the
    steady pace of his horses.
        It is plowing time – the violent harrowing that
    readies the soil for sowing in spring, stimulating in
    advance its fertility and liberality.
        Being of the school and race of true country folk,
    Claude is there, cleaving the entire field into even fur-
    rows with his plowshare. The steaming earth he turns

with each monotonous back-and-forth of the horses
settles in undulating waves like the waters of the
Richelieu scurrying before westerly winds.
    The stubble crunches under the iron; resisting, the
earth moans before being gashed mercilessly open in
these salutary wounds. (Ernest Choquette, *Claude
Paysan* [Montreal: La Cie d'Imprimerie et de Gravures
Bishop, 1899], p. 27.)

5   Letter from Gustave Ouimet to Ozias Leduc, undated,
    BNQ 327/5/11.

123

Portrait of the Honourable
Louis-Philippe Brodeur

1901-1904

Oil on canvas

99 x 126 cm

Monogrammed and dated upper left: *19 LEDUC 04*, encircled with an *O*

Ottawa, House of Commons, inv. 0-457.1

PROVENANCE

Studio of the artist; House of Commons

Fig. 39　Ozias Leduc, Study for the *Portrait of the Honourable Louis-Philippe Brodeur*, about 1901, graphite on scrap paper, 19.5 x 16.3 cm (private collection).

Fig. 40　Louis-Philippe Brodeur, 1901 (photo by Ozias Leduc, printed from glass negative No. 293, BNQ 327/13/3.4f).

THE Liberal member for the riding of Rouville, lawyer Louis-Philippe Brodeur (1862-1924) commissioned his portrait from Leduc on being appointed Speaker of the House of Commons in February 1901. This was the thirty-seven-year-old artist's first commission for an official portrait. Brodeur, a native of Belœil, lived in Saint-Hilaire when parliament was not in session. By choosing Leduc to paint his portrait, he was helping a neighbour whom he had met some years earlier through his boyhood friend Dr. Ernest Choquette (cat. 92).[1]

For the execution of Brodeur's portrait, Leduc combined sittings with photographs. This method was a useful one, since the Speaker was rarely in Saint-Hilaire and Leduc himself was very busy with church decoration in Rougemont, Antigonish and Halifax. Initially, Brodeur showed the artist photographs of himself taken by the Notman studio in Montreal;[2] Leduc rejected these, however, preferring to use photographs he had taken himself.[3] The number of photographs – eleven – and the range of poses show the artist looking for the most appropriate approach. He hesitated between the formal, solemn pose traditional for parliamentary portraits and one more suited to the sitter's

personality and to the two men's acquaintanceship. The only known preparatory sketch shows Brodeur in the Speaker's chair with a document in his hand in the tradition of official portraits (fig. 39). The final portrait is far different from the sketch. Its originality lies in the horizontal format of the canvas and the relaxed pose inspired by one of Leduc's photographs (fig. 40).[4] The head and hands are meticulously rendered; the three-quarters pose is that of a man at ease absorbed in thought. It is not the sitter's rank or social status that impress, but rather the vivid intensity of his gaze. As Leduc said of his portraits to Msgr. Olivier Maurault (cat. 163), "What I am aiming at is certainly a likeness, which I consider necessary up to a certain point; but it is primarily the subject's character and habitual manner that I try to capture."[5] In the *Portrait of the Honourable Louis-Philippe Brodeur*, the pose selected by the artist seems a true reflection of the model's personality – a man who knows how to listen, perhaps an authoritarian character, but also just and well intentioned. These were qualities demonstrated by Brodeur during his term as Minister of Internal Revenue (1906-1911) and Judge of the Supreme Court of Canada (1911-1923).

Leduc handles the foreground and background of this painting separately. To achieve a likeness, he uses a linear drawing, a soft brush stroke and a limited, rather dark palette for the figure. The interplay of light and shade draws the viewer's eyes to the face and hands, the most expressive parts of the body. The background consists of a wall and a curtain on which the artist makes the light play in small strokes of colour. This area appears to produce its own light through the contrast of the complementary colours yellow and violet, which gives a strong chiaroscuro effect; the interplay of light and shadow creates a halo around the sitter and throws the curtain into relief. These glowing colours recall the twilight shades so often used by Leduc in both his landscapes and religious art; they are also reminiscent of the luminous background of the *Still Life (with Lay Figure)* (cat. 90). The drapery, strictly functional, creates space and dynamic tension within the composition. It cuts the background into two geometric shapes, a square and a rectangle, producing the illusion of off-centering the pyramidal mass of the foreground. The difference in the handling of the fore-

and background creates the impression that the artist was looking at his sitter from two distinct psychological viewpoints. In the foreground, he tries to create a likeness as a courtesy to the sitter, producing a portrait testimonial that keeps alive the memory of Louis-Philippe Brodeur. The familiar and intimist mood of the work expresses the relationship between sitter and artist; it conveys a mutual understanding and trust. In the background, Leduc has enjoyed executing a "tableau": a radiant harmony of colours on a flat surface.

M. L.

1   Seven letters dated between February 1901 and June 1904 document the progress of this commission, BNQ 327 15/11, 13, 14.

2   A photograph of Brodeur taken by the Notman studio is in the Notman Archives of the McCord Museum of Canadian History, no. 139878.

3   The glass negatives of these prints are nos. 287-290, 292-297, 301 (BNQ 327/13/3.4a-k). Three prints are reproduced in Laurier Lacroix *et al.*, *Ozias Leduc the Draughtsman*, exhib. cat. (Montreal: Concordia University, 1978), p. 40.

4   Print of no. 293, with squaring directly on it, BNQ 327/13/3.4F.

5   Msgr. Maurault reports on a conversation held with Leduc twenty years earlier in Olivier Maurault, [pseudonym Louis Deligny], "Ozias Leduc peintre mystique", *Le Mauricien* [Trois-Rivières], vol. 2, no. 2 (February 1938), p. 29.

124
Study for *The Repentant Magdalene*

About 1902

Graphite on paper

12.3 x 12.1 cm

Signed lower right: *O LEDUC*

Private collection

INSCRIPTIONS

Verso: *Marie Magdeleine*; *Ozs L.*; and label of Rolland Picture Frame

PROVENANCE

Studio of the artist; Mr. and Mrs. Jean Lanctôt, Belœil, 1952; private collection, 1994

125
The Repentant Magdalene

1898-1902

Oil on canvas

31.7 x 31.6 cm

Signed lower left: *OZIAS LEDUC*

Quebec City, Musée du Québec, inv. 80.45

INSCRIPTIONS

Verso: *collection Mademoiselle Gabrielle Messier, 40 rue Messier, Saint-Hilaire-sur-le-Richelieu, Province de Québec, Canada "Marie Madeleine repentante par Ozias Leduc $3,000. Gabrielle Messier*

PROVENANCE

Studio of the artist; Gabrielle Messier, Saint-Hilaire; Musée du Québec, 1980

[Photographed before restoration]

MARY MAGDALENE had been previously depicted by Leduc, in his decoration programme for the Church of Saint-Hilaire. Based on an episode from the Gospel of Saint Luke, she is represented as the sinner (cat. 17), kneeling at Christ's feet with eyes downcast in the moment just before she receives his forgiveness. She is the picture of piety.

In the easel painting *The Repentant Magdalene*, conceived shortly after, Leduc portrays a later period in her life as described in the apocryphal *Golden Legend*. The Magdalene has renounced all worldly goods and material nourishment and lives in a wilderness grotto. Sustained by her inward meditations alone, she attains enlightenment and oneness with God. Leduc's Mary, wearing nothing but a sackcloth slung loosely around her hips, is seated before a rock upon which are set a Bible and skull. Diverting her attention from these

124

objects, she buries her head in her arm in deep contemplation. A stream of light, conceivably that of "enlightenment", enters the grotto, striking her back and the top corner of the Bible.[1]

This repentant Magdalene, too, is the picture of piety. Yet, far from ascetic, she is voluptuous; and to all intents and purposes, she is treated as a nude. A warm, sensual light plays upon the curves of her exposed, elongated back, decreasing in brightness down her spine only to glow once again on her hip, just above the drapery. In the tradition of the eighteenth and nineteenth centuries, Leduc's treatment of the theme exhibits a tension between the ostensibly religious subject matter and its secular eroticism.[2]

Leduc's male friends certainly responded to this subtle eroticism. Arsène Bessette, in a personal letter to the artist, referred provocatively to "the dear little Magdalene, who awaits only the strength of your will for her flesh – the pink flesh of a sinner – to glow in all its freshness and brilliance".[3] And in an article in 1898, Ernest Choquette (cat. 92), if less blatant about the Magdalene's sexuality, referred

to the work as a nude and focussed on the fleshly aspects of the figure, "where never has truer flesh breathed from every pore".[4]

Choquette, interpreting Leduc's *Magdalene* as a secular work, expected it would represent the artist at the 1900 Paris Exposition universelle, bringing him great critical recognition. However, this was to be virtually the only public reference to *The Repentant Magdalene* during Leduc's lifetime.[5] Like the artist's other nudes (cats. 19, 89, 130), considered too risqué for the morals of his society, it was relegated to the backroom of his studio.

A. G.

125

1   The light effect on the figure's back is similar to that in *Atala* by Andrea Gastaldi (1810-1889), the teacher of Luigi Capello, with whom Leduc apprenticed. (Reproduced in Alexandra Shtychno, "Luigi Giovanni Vitale Capello, a.k.a. Cappello (1843-1902), Itinerant Piedmontese Artist of Late Nineteenth-century Quebec", Master's thesis, Concordia University, Montreal, March 1991, fig. 26). Athough little is known about Capello's easel painting, it is conceivable that this compositional effect was passed on to Leduc through his teacher.

2   For the changing perceptions of the Magdalene, see Marjorie Malvern, *Venus in Sackcloth: The Magdalen's Origins and Metamorphoses* (Carbondale and Edwardsville, Illinois: Southern Illinois University Press, 1975); Colette Melnotte, "La Madeleine au XIXᵉ siècle: tradition et modernité", in *Marie Madeleine dans la mystique, les arts, et les lettres* (Paris: Beauchesne, 1988), pp. 225-243; and Susan Haskins, *Mary Magdalen: Myth and Metaphor* (London: HarperCollins, 1993). The implicitly contradictory nature of Magdalene imagery in the eighteenth century is revealed by Diderot who, commenting on Carle van Loo's (1705-1765) *Madeleine dans le désert* (Salon 1761), took issue with the lusciousness of the setting, maintaining that it was more appropriate for a pair of lovers than for a woman with a burdened soul. See Denis Diderot, *Salons*, ed. Jean Seznec and Jean Adhémar, vol. 1 (1759, 1761, 1763) (Oxford: Clarendon Press, 1957), p. 110. Similarly ambiguous treatments of the theme in the nineteenth century are Paul Baudry (1828-1886), *Sainte Madeleine couchée* (Salon 1859; Nantes, Musée des Beaux-Arts; reproduced in Melnotte, p. 231); *The Penitent Magdalene Reading in Her Grotto* (nineteenth-century chromolithograph after a painting from about 1742 by Pompeo Batoni [1708-1787]; reproduced in Haskins, p. 309); Jean-Jacques Henner (1829-1905), *La Madeleine* (1885; reproduced in Frederic Lees, "The Work of Jean-Jacques Henner", *The Studio* [London], vol. 18, no. 80 [November 1899], p. 83). Leduc would have known Henner's work, if not first-hand from his time in Paris, then through such reproductions.

3   Letter from Bessette to Ozias Leduc, February 24, 1902, BNQ 327/5/12.

4   Dr. [Ernest] Choquette, "Un artiste de mon pays", *La Patrie* [Montreal], December 3, 1898, p. 2

5   When *The Repentant Magdalene* finally made its public debut in the Leduc exhibition at the Lycée Pierre-Corneille, Montreal, on June 19, 1954, it received no comment in any review.

126

Study for the *Portrait of Msgr. John Cameron*

1903

Oil on paper glued to wood

23.1 x 16.5 cm

Signed lower right: *OZIAS LEDUC*

The Montreal Museum of Fine Arts, purchase, Horsley and Annie Townsend Bequest, inv. 1964.1448

INSCRIPTIONS

Verso: *O. Leduc Exh. Portrait of Mon. O'Connor; From: M.M.F.A. RO 389-7-73; Walter Klinkhoff Gallery, Montreal. Monsignor O'Connor. Panel Size: 9 1/4 x 6 1/2". Ozias Leduc. A Guaranteed original work by the master; The National Gallery of Canada. Title of Exh.: O. Leduc. Cat. No.: 24. Box no.: 8; M.B.A.M.; 3886; "6575", "23667" deux fois; "3118"; "He fugitis"; "1/2"; 3015 gu ?; Mons. O'Connell; "C-L-22-JJC+C; Mgr O'Connell"; "Mgr. O'Donnell Antigonish"; "JCC+C";"C-L-22-"; "#23667-".*

PROVENANCE

Walter Klinkhoff Gallery, Montreal; Montreal Museum of Fine Arts, 1964

This small oil study was the basis for Leduc's imposing formal portrait of John Cameron, Bishop of Antigonish, Nova Scotia (fig. 41). The Sisters of Mount Saint Bernard College, of which Cameron was the founder, commissioned the portrait to commemorate the fiftieth anniversary of his ordination to the priesthood. In 1903, Leduc decorated the Sisters' chapel,[1] a contract he no doubt received on the strength of his decoration of Saint Ninian's Cathedral, Antigonish, undertaken the previous September (fig. 132).

The oil study, an intermediary stage between a photograph (fig. 42) and the finished portrait, allowed Leduc to work out the composition and the light and colour relationships. From the photograph, Leduc took only the figure of Cameron and the table with three books, one of which the Bishop grasps in his left hand. In the study, Leduc has added two more books and, at the extreme right, a religious statue, identifying the model as priest and scholar as well. The painted backdrop of the studio photograph has been discarded in favour of an indeterminate "screen" of striated diagonal brush strokes. Those in the centre cut a vertical swath of light, effectively setting off the full-length figure. The study depicts Cameron as an aged man with a lined face but celebrates his half-century of dedication to the Church first and foremost. Accordingly, the pectoral cross is emphasized, through its heightened gold colour and central placement.

The changes in the finished work are significant: the statue is omitted, while the books, which are incidental props in the study, assume greater importance through their articulation. The dramatic increase in size further contributes to a stunning transformation in the characterization of the subject. In the immense finished painting – 251 x 180 cm – Cameron, no longer just a hard-working priest, becomes a truly elegant and magnificent figure. His face made more youthful and his body subtly elongated, he exudes strength and dignity. The pectoral cross is now barely discernible against the majestic magenta and rose of

Fig. 41 Ozias Leduc, *Portrait of Msgr. John Cameron*, 1903, oil on canvas, 251 x 180 cm (Antigonish, Nova Scotia, Saint Francis Xavier University).

Fig. 42 Msgr. John Cameron

his vestments, and the greater focus on the books conveys his seminal role in the development of higher Catholic education in the Maritimes. The statelier final rendering of Cameron serves to emphasize his reputation as a respected administrator, scholar and educational visionary for the Catholic Church in Canada.[2]

A. G.

1 The decoration of the chapel was finished in July. The portrait of Cameron was installed on the 27th, three days after the arrival of the gilt frame and ten days after the date being commemorated. (Information from the College's "entries" provided to Laurier Lacroix by Sister Catherine MacNeil, November 16, 1970.) Leduc's cousin Ernest Lebrun was to have made touch-ups to the portrait in late 1904, but for reasons unknown these were not carried out. See the letter from Sister Saint Joseph le Juste to Leduc, November 27, 1904, BNQ 327/5/14.

2 See Raymond Angus MacLean, *Bishop John Cameron: Piety and Politics* (Antigonish, Nova Scotia: The Casket, 1991).

127

The Réveillon

1906

Charcoal and chalk on paper

46.6 x 32.7 cm

Signed vertically and dated lower left: *O LEDUC 1906*

Quebec City, Musée du Québec, inv. 54.101

INSCRIPTIONS

Recto, lower right: *A Edmond J. Massicotte / O. Leduc*

PROVENANCE

Studio of the artist; Edmond-J. Massicotte; Galerie l'Art français, Montreal; Musée du Québec, 1954

IN 1906, Leduc provided an illustration for "Le Réveillon", one of the *Contes vrais* by Pamphile Lemay (1837-1918) published by the Librairie Beauchemin. The first edition appeared in 1899, the same year as Ernest Choquette's *Claude Paysan* (cats. 92-102). Other illustrations were commissioned by J. Y. Saint-Jarre, editor of the illustrated edition, from Edmond-Joseph Massicotte, Jean-Baptiste Lagacé, Georges Delfosse, Albert-Samuel Brodeur, Raoul Barré, Joseph-Arthur-Pierre Labelle, Ulric Lamarche, Henri Julien, Georges Latour, Charles Huot and Jobson Paradis. Correspondence between Saint-Jarre and Leduc indicates that in March 1906, it was suggested the artist illustrate a second story. Saint-Jarre therefore sent him two, "Patriotisme" and "Le Marteau du jongleur".[1] However, doubtless because he was overloaded with church decoration work in Farnham, Quebec (cat. 135, fig. 132), and Manchester, New Hampshire (fig. 133), Leduc never submitted more than the one illustration.

"Le Réveillon" is a fantasy tale with a plot halfway between dream and reality. The narrator falls asleep during a celebration on Christmas Eve, after midnight Mass. In his dream, he hears old Gaspard Le Mage telling how one Christmas night he found his way again after getting lost. Leduc decided to depict the moment when Le Mage, a young man at the time he tells of, is guided by the star of the Magi: "The star slipped through the clouds, and its rays showed me the road to the church." And the old storyteller adds, "It came down like a lightning flash from the heights of heaven and came to rest, like a glorious lamp on the holy pinnacle."[2]

In the foreground of Leduc's illustration, a young man is watching the star blazing in the night. He is at the edge of a clearing, his body seeming almost part of the evergreens and shrubs around him. These elements combine to form a capital L, like a sort of frame to the image. Leduc used the same L-shape in writing his name and the date 1906 at the bottom left corner. The method of executing the foreground in shadow with emphatic dark areas creates an effect of backlighting, setting off the luminous scene beyond the figure. This repoussoir arrangement serves to accentuate the main composition, and the artist thus establishes a demarcation line between the real and the supernatural. The rest of the image is delicately drawn in pencil, bringing out the grain of the paper. Still basing himself on the story, Leduc places fences in the midground, parallel to the one in the foreground, together with fir stumps and guideposts protruding from the snow. These elements help to lead the spectator's eye towards the church.

It is a charming thought that for the figure in profile in the foreground, Leduc may have used the features of his young friend Guillaume Lahaise, born in 1888 (cat. 138). The profile, especially the shape of the nose and the upper jaw, strongly suggests this. The young man in question lived near the Church of Saint-Hilaire and had known Leduc since the age of ten.[3]

This drawing, which belonged to Edmond-J. Massicotte as the inscription shows, is evidence of the respect Leduc felt for his fellow illustrator.[4]

P. L'A.

1   Letter from J.-Y. Saint-Jarre to Ozias Leduc, March 19, 1906, BNQ 327/5/16. There is in a private collection a preparatory drawing for "Le Marteau du jongleur".

2   Pamphile Lemay, "Le Réveillon", in *Contes vrais* (Montreal: Librairie Beauchemin, 1907), pp. 390-391.

3   Robert Lahaise, *Guy Delahaye et la modernité littéraire*, "Cahiers du Québec/Littérature" series (Montreal: Hurtubise/HMH, 1987), p. 27. A photograph of the poet as a child, is reproduced on p. 95.

4   Laurier Lacroix *et al.*, *Ozias Leduc the Draughtsman*, exhib. cat. (Montreal: Concordia University, 1978), p. 43.

128

Study for *Endymion and Selene*

About 1906

Charcoal on cream laid paper,
graphite border

30.7 x 35.1 cm

Initialed lower right: *O L*

Private collection

PROVENANCE

Studio of the artist; private collection, gift of the
artist, about 1940

129

Endymion and Selene

About 1906

Oil on canvas

23.8 x 27.5 cm

Signed lower left: *OZIAS LEDUC*

Ottawa, The National Gallery of Canada, inv. 6401

PROVENANCE

Studio of the artist; Gabrielle Messier, Saint-
Hilaire, gift of the artist, 1954; National Gallery of
Canada, 1955

THE critics of the 1950s were dismissive of this painting on a mythological subject: "purely literary interest",[1] "sentimental and unconvincing",[2] "insipid",[3] "use of glazes rather than superimposed brush strokes, thin cold colours, a stiffness of line".[4] Such comments show how hard it was for critics at the time to accept a work of a Symbolist kind. At first sight, of course, it is the narrative element that dominates – the story of Selene, goddess of the Moon, and Endymion, the beautiful shepherd boy with whom she falls in love. Zeus has promised Endymion he will grant him a wish, and Endymion asks to sleep eternally. Every night Selene (often portrayed as the goddess Diana) enters the cave on Mount Latmus to gaze at her beloved. Motionless and unconscious, Endymion still seems alive and young.

With infinite gentleness, she (Diana) kisses that eternally youthful brow and returns to Olympus, but proud Endymion does not suspect that for an instant Happiness has bent near his slumbers and that, like so many others, he has been unable to seize it.[5]

Leduc sets the scene in the required grotto lit by the torch Selene holds; the setting, with two openings in the background, one of which looks onto a forest, is not unlike the legendary Fairy Grotto of Mount Saint-Hilaire. The two figures, placed in the near foreground, are depicted in minute detail.[6] Both were inspired by drawings from life: a reclining female nude, whose features resemble those of the artist's wife Marie-Louise Lebrun, is oddly enough the model for Endymion,[7] while Selene has the reversed features of a female model drawn in Paris (cat. 61). The artist also made a study for a composition in the nude (cat. 128) that establishes the pose of Endymion and Selene without a setting. The atmosphere of gentleness and tenderness in the final painting is due to both the pose of the two figures and the pastel tones used. Leduc is experimenting here with sexual ambiguity: Endymion still has the feminine features of the original model, while Selene's left arm and hand look somewhat masculine. The myth of androgyny was much used by Pre-Raphaelite and Symbolist artists who saw in it humanity's aspiration

towards an ideal of perfection.[8] Leduc also has recourse to other symbols. The moon, personified by Selene, whose symbols are the crescent and the torch, represents the imagination, dreams, the subconscious and instinctive impulses, as well as being associated with rites of passage, from waking to sleeping and from life to death. The laurel leaves above Selene's head stand for immortality, the ivy around Endymion represents "the eternal cycle of death and rebirth, the myth of the endless return",[9] as well as the "persistence of desire". The rose represents "perfection achieved, faultless accomplishment ... It symbolizes the cup of life, the soul, the heart, love."[10] The circular movement of the composition, the grotto and the narrow opening on the right all refer to female sexual symbols. Could this painting, with its eloquent imagery, be a pendant to *Erato (Muse in the Forest)* (cat. 130)? While the latter work evokes the Muse as inspiration, *Endymion and Selene* could be an allegory of desire: desire for perfection, for immortality, but also erotic desire.

M. L.

129

1 Paul Gladu, "Ozias Leduc ou pourquoi il se fit ermite…", *Notre temps* [Montreal], January 16, 1956, p. 4.

2 Claude Picher, "Chronique – *Québec* – Ozias Leduc", *Culture*, vol. 17, no. 1 (March 1956), p. 81.

3 R[odolphe] de Repentigny, "Images et plastiques – Il faut connaître Ozias Leduc", *La Presse* [Montreal], January 14, 1956, p. 66.

4 R[odolphe] de Repentigny, "À l'Art Français – une exposition qui révèle le travail le plus intime d'Ozias Leduc", *La Presse* [Montreal], February 14, 1956, p. 24.

5 Odette Montausier, "Diane vs Endymion", cutting from an unidentified newspaper in Leduc's possession (possibly *Le Canada*, April 1927, p. 6), BNQ 327/17/4.

6 The composition resembles that in a painting by Gustave Courbet (1819-1877) entitled *The Awakening*, or *Venus and Psyche*. This shows two female figures, one trying to waken the other by tickling her face with rosebuds (reproduced in Michèle Haddad, *La Divine et l'Impure – Le Nu au XIXᵉ siècle* [Paris: Éditions du Jaguar, 1990], p. 98).

7 Reproduced in Laurier Lacroix *et al.*, *Ozias Leduc the Draughtsman*, exhib. cat. (Montreal: Concordia University, 1978), p. 24.

8 On this myth, see Guy Cogeval, "Adolescent Awakenings", in *Lost Paradise: Symbolist Europe*, exhib. cat. (Montreal: Montreal Museum of Fine Arts, 1995), pp. 308-310.

9 Jean Chevalier and Alain Gheerbrant, *Dictionnaire des symboles* (Paris: Robert Laffont, 1982), p. 571.

10 *Ibid.*, p. 822.

130
Erato (Muse in the Forest)
About 1906
Oil on cardboard
27.9 x 22.9 cm
Signed lower right and lower left: *OZIAS LEDUC*
Ottawa, The National Gallery of Canada,
inv. 17652
PROVENANCE
Studio of the artist; Mr. and Mrs. Édouard Clerk,
Saint-Hilaire; Fernande Choquette-Clerk estate;
National Gallery of Canada, 1974

IN 1906, Leduc married his cousin Marie-Louise (fig. 107), née Lebrun, the widow of his former teacher Luigi Capello.[1] In a reminiscence of his wife, the artist, praising her musical talent and interest in all things artistic, referred to her as his "invaluable collaborator".[2] Erato is the muse of love poetry; her attribute is a musical instrument, the lyre. It is conceivable that Leduc painted *Erato (Muse in the Forest)* as a tribute to his own "muse" Marie-Louise, in celebration of their recent marriage. He seemed loath to part with the painting, keeping it in his possession until it entered the collection of his friends Fernande and Édouard Clerk, who were the trusted keepers of his other nudes (cats. 19, 87, 89). The painting was not exhibited publicly during Leduc's lifetime, having first been shown in the National Gallery of Canada's 1955 Leduc retrospective.

The painting belongs to the series of mythological-allegorical female nudes that had become part of the artist's repertoire towards the end of the 1890s (cats. 19, 89). Among these earlier works, *Erato (Sleeping Muse)* (cat. 89) is closely related to *Erato (Muse in the Forest)* thematically. In both, the muse assumes her traditional role as an allegory of inspirational beauty, echoing the magical figures that, legend had it, inhabited the nooks and crannies of Leduc's own mountain.[3] Yet, although Leduc set the two works side by side in a photograph (fig. 43), the later one is more intimate and shows a significant reconceptualization of the Erato theme.

Though passive, reflective and isolated like the sleeping muse, the forest muse is presented more iconically. Here, Erato stands deep within the nocturnal forest; one hand rests on the boulder where she has laid her lyre. Eyes closed, she lifts her face heavenward as if in spiritual rapture. Behind her, the slope of the mountain rises sharply, densely populated with the thin, rhythmically spaced verticals of the tree trunks. An intensely glowing light illuminates a clearing, penetrating the dark woods behind and – despite her position in shadow – bathing the nude Erato in sensual golden rays. Thus inscribed in a halo of light, the figure becomes an icon. The symmetrical composition, collapsed perspective and mystical lighting transcend the relative naturalism of the earlier *Erato* to create a Symbolist work. A product of images and ideas Leduc may have first encountered during his stay in Paris in 1897 and subsequently would have gleaned from his reading,[4] *Erato (Muse in the Forest)* marks new aesthetic tendencies that were to manifest themselves with heightened effect in the artist's landscapes of the next decade.

A. G.

1 Capello and Marie-Louise, for reasons unknown, had parted ways in the late 1880s. His last years were spent at the Salesian Orphanage in Paris, where he died in 1902. (Alexandra Shtychno, "Luigi Giovanni Vitale Capello, a.k.a. Cappello (1843-1902), Itinerant Piedmontese Artist of Late Nineteenth-century Quebec", Master's thesis, Concordia University, March 1991, pp. 25-29.)

2 René Bonin, "À 90 ans, le peintre Leduc entreprend une Assomption", *La Patrie* [Montreal], October 18, 1953, p. 76.

3 See Laurier Lacroix, "The Dream Mountain of Ozias Leduc", *ArtsCanada*, vol. 35, no. 3 (October-November 1978), p. 10.

4 *Art et Décoration*, to which Leduc subscribed from its inception in 1897, is only one possible source for his developing Symbolist tendencies. Another is *International Studio*, to which he may also have subscribed. The form and content of *Erato (Muse in the Forest)* place it alongside a number of contemporary European Symbolist renditions of allegorized women – muses or femmes fatales – in nature. The *Monument for the Grave of Segantini*, from about 1906, of Leonardo Bistolfi (1859-1933) seems particulary close in conception. The sculpture was allotted a full-page reproduction in both *Art et Décoration* (Fierens-Gevaert, "Le Monument Segantini par Leonardo Bistolfi", vol. 20 [July-December 1906], p. 19) and

Fig. 43　Interior of Leduc's studio, showing a reproduction of Frost's *Sabrina* and, visible in the mirror, *Erato (Muse in the Forest)*, *Erato (Sleeping Muse)* and a biscuit-ware *Crouching Nude* (photo by Ozias Leduc, printed from glass negative No. 311, BNQ 327/12/13.20).

International Studio (Alfredo Melani, "Italian Art at the Milan Exhibition", vol. 29, no. 113 [July 1906], p. 149). Other comparable works are: Henri Martin, *Beauté*, which was reproduced in Léonce Bénédite, "La lyre et les Muses par Henri Martin", *Art et Décoration*, vol. 7 (January-June 1900), p. 2; G. Segantini (1858-1899), *Edelweiss* (1895; private collection), reproduced in Vittorio Pica, "The Last Work of Giovanni Segantini", *International Studio*, vol. 21, no. 84 (September 1904); Fritz Erler's (1868-1940) depiction of a female nude, reproduced in *Jugend*, vol. 5 (1898), p. 74 (as noted in Pierre Landry, "L'Apport de l'Art nouveau aux arts graphiques au Québec de 1898 à 1910", Master's thesis, Laval University, 1983, p. 106). The figure of Erato as it appears in *Erato (Muse in the Forest)* was used by Leduc on at least one other occasion, in the artist's design for a poster for *Art et Décoration*, about 1907 (ill. A, p. 190). See Jean-René Ostiguy, *Ozias Leduc: Symbolist and Religious Painting*, exhib. cat. (Ottawa: National Gallery of Canada, 1974), p. 201. The painting *Erato (Muse in the Forest)* itself is seen in a still life of 1907 (reproduced in *ibid.*, p. 190), where it assumes a central position among other images of women in states of spiritual transfiguration.

Fig. 44   Abbé Olivier Leduc, priest of the parish of Saint-Aimé (negative No. 59, BNQ 327/13/5.5).

131
Portrait of Abbé Olivier Leduc
1906

Oil on canvas

92.3 x 76.4 cm

Signed and dated lower left: *O Leduc 1906*

Private collection

PROVENANCE

Studio of the artist; estate of the artist; Louis Perron; Dr. Gilles Maille; Gerard Gorce Beaux-Arts Inc; private collection, 1978

THE client asked the artist to redo the priest's hands – "You've given him a bricklayer's hands!" – but Ozias Leduc refused, preferring to keep his painting rather than flatter anyone, whoever it might be.

This canvas is still in his studio …

The whole composition is remarkable for its simple perfection. The hands are particularly successful. They seemed to me real, and very eloquent, harmonizing well with the rest of the portrait.

This proves that Ozias Leduc is not a worldly artist, and that he pays court to no one. If you want an improvement on nature's gifts, don't go and see Ozias Leduc. He is a sincere man and a thorough master of his art.

What matters to him is truth.[1]

Paul Gladu, who admired Leduc's attitude as well as the painting's style, thus describes what happened to the *Portrait of Abbé Olivier Leduc.* That same year, Father J.-Z. Vincent (cat. 132), had also turned down a portrait painted by the artist, and both priests had the same complaint: they could not accept the way their hands were painted, objecting that they looked like those of manual labourers. Yet, in each case Leduc worked from photographs provided by the sitter himself, and a comparison of the portraits and the photographs shows that he was careful about capturing physical likeness. These two similar situations show how hard the job of the portrait artist is. As Max Friedländer emphasizes,

The job of painting a portrait entails something akin to obsequiousness, against which creative power puts up a fight …

The portraitist is quite specifically in a subservient position to the patron – who, even if he does not consider himself knowledgeable in matters of art, still thinks he knows himself better than the artist and therefore feels entitled to pronounce judgment on the portraitist's performance. From the degrading pressure exerted by the pretensions, wishes, vanity of the patron no successful portraitist … could escape.[2]

As he had already indicated to Olivier Maurault, Leduc sought to make a portrait both a physical and a psychological likeness of the sitter.[3] Abbé Olivier Leduc (1846-1909), parish priest of Saint-Aimé in the county of Saint-Hyacinthe, was sixty when Leduc painted his portrait. He was known as a builder: it is to him that we owe churches and presbyteries in Sweetsburg, Frelighsburg and Rougemont, as well as the presbyteries of Saint-Robert and Sainte-Aimé.[4] He was also said to be "frugal", "modest", full of "great good sense" and "unbounded piety", although of a somewhat contentious character.[5]

Abbé Leduc's pose here is the same as in the photograph (fig. 44): he is sitting in a comfortable armchair, slightly off-centre in a three-quarter pose. With the palette knife, Leduc has created an abstract background saturated with pigment but bringing out the weave of the canvas. The sitter stands out clearly against this background, which is painted mainly in tones of yellow, green and brown.

M. L.

1   Paul Gladu, "L'Ermite de Saint-Hilaire: le peintre Ozias Leduc", *Le Petit Journal* [Montreal], November 29, 1953, p. 61.

2   Max J. Friedländer, *Landscape, Portrait, Still-life: Their Origin and Development*, trans. R.F.C. Hull (New York: Schocken Books, 1963), pp. 232-233.

3   See the interview with Leduc quoted in the entry on the *Portrait of the Honourable Louis-Philippe Brodeur* (cat. 123), and cited there in note 5.

4   "Mort du curé de Saint-Aimé", *La Patrie* [Montreal], November 15, 1909.

5   "Nécrologie", *Séminaire de Saint-Hyacinthe. Année scolaire 1909-1910*, no. 32 (Saint-Hyacinthe: Imp. du Courrier, 1910), pp. 37-42.

132
Portrait of Abbé Joseph-Zéphirin Vincent

About 1906

Oil on canvas mounted on cardboard

55.8 x 45.7 cm

Signed lower left: *OZIAS LEDUC*

Montreal, McCord Museum of Canadian History, inv. M.963.14.2

INSCRIPTIONS

Verso: *Ozias Leduc Exh. Portrait du curé Vincent From Mc Cord Mus. Mtrl Ro 700-12-73; The National Gallery of Canada cat no 28 box no 4*

PROVENANCE

A. Sidney Dawes; McCord Museum of Canadian History, 1963

MANY of Leduc's works, especially his murals, have suffered the ravages of time and accident as well as disfiguration as a result of hasty "restorations".[1] The case of this painting is, however, different, for it was the artist himself who mutilated it. We have here a clear example of the problems of the portrait artist: not only must he achieve a good likeness, but he must also convey the image the sitter has of himself.[2]

Leduc accepted a commission to paint the portrait of the parish priest of Saint-Grégoire in Iberville, Joseph-Zéphirin Vincent (1852-1910) in late 1906.[3] The painting, based on a photograph,[4] shows the sitter ensconced in a wicker armchair that casts a mellow light

133

Hand of Abbé Joseph-Zéphirin Vincent

About 1906

Oil on canvas mounted on cardboard

24.5 x 29 cm

Signed lower right: *O. Leduc*

Métabetchouan, Béatrice Coulombe collection

PROVENANCE

Studio of the artist; René Bergeron, Chicoutimi; Béatrice Coulombe

on the wall in the background. The composition is closed off by two strong elements: the edge of a door frame and the lower corner of a picture frame.

This portrait was rejected; Leduc kept it (fig. 45) and eventually cut it into three parts. Gilles Corbeil, to whom Leduc confided the reasons for this gesture, explains:

I could also mention the story of the portrait of some priest or other who was dissatisfied with the hands Leduc had given him and refused categorically to accept the painting. "And yet," said Leduc, "they *were* his hands

Fig. 45   Ozias Leduc in his studio with the *Portrait of Joseph-Zéphirin Vincent*, August 15, 1936 (BNQ 327/13/1.17).

… They were red and calloused like a peasant's, but he would have liked them white and soft like the hands of a canon." And he added with the most enchanting honesty, "I couldn't paint what I couldn't see." A year before his death, fed up with seeing the painting still there, he decided to cut it up: "So," he said to me one day, "that will make three little paintings, one of the right hand, one of the left hand and the last of the face." And the curious thing is that he sold all three of them.[5]

What the priest saw, according to Leduc, as an excessive realism could perhaps be simply painter's licence, which the sitter found hard to accept. The hands, shown foreshortened, are rendered in brush strokes and effects of light and pigment that, while anatomically correct, reveal as much of the painter's technique as they do of the priest's country origins.

L. L.

1   The Chronology shows some sixteen religious works by Leduc that have been destroyed or mutilated.

2   See also the preceding entry, as well as those on the portraits of *Joseph-Napoléon Francœur* (cat. 171), *Madame St-Cyr* (cat. 227) and *Madame Labonté* (cat. 235).

3   Vincent wrote in a letter to Leduc dated November 15, 1906, "As I imagine that the preliminary studies for the portrait will not take long, I expect you will have ample time to make them then", that is during Vincent's next visit to Saint-Hilaire (BNQ 327/5/16).

There exists a study for this portrait (oil, pastel and charcoal on cardboard, 20.3 x 12.8 cm, private collection; photo BNQ 327/12/1.5), which Leduc turned into Saint Francis Xavier at the request of the purchaser.

Vincent was priest of the parish of Saint-Grégoire from 1896 to 1908, and then of Saint-Hugues from 1908 to 1910. He was best known for his temperance crusade. In 1906 he began on the project of decorating the church. Having asked Leduc to submit designs, he told him on February 22, 1907, that he could not give him the contract (BNQ 327/5/17).

4   A print is in BNQ 327/13/6.9.

5   Gilles Corbeil, "Un hommage au peintre Ozias Leduc, 1864-1955. Rencontres avec Ozias Leduc", *Le Devoir* [Montreal], January 14, 1956, p. 8.

134
Profile in Cloud
1908

Charcoal on paper

18 x 11 cm

Signed and dated lower right: *1908 O LEDUC*

Jean-Paul Riopelle collection

PROVENANCE
Studio of the artist; Gilles Corbeil, 1954;
Jean-Paul Riopelle

I N this charcoal drawing Leduc was experimenting with textural effects, combining scumble with accumulated fine lines and heavier ones to create space and the interplay of light and shade. The upper section of the work is the more detailed and, except for the horizon line, it is the sky that contains the most clearly defined shapes. This demarcation is very apparent on the left between the light and dark areas of sky, emphasized by the clearest lines. It was no doubt the sinuosity of these lines that inspired the title *Profile in Cloud* given to this work on paper.[1]

This landscape, like most of Leduc's landscapes, brings us back to the problem with works in the Symbolist tradition. Symbolism, as defined by many of its theoreticians, claimed that creative subjectivity came first, to such an extent that, paraphrasing Moréas (1856-1910), one might say that the idea behind the work should never be revealed just as it is, or stripped of its richly formal robes.[2] The interpretation of motifs in the work can never be reduced to the mechanical decoding of symbols (which it might often be more correct to call allegories).

Although by its very nature Leduc's religious output cannot avoid references to codified symbols, it nonetheless seems risky to try and "read" his landscapes, confusing the Symbolist creed with the symbolism of images. Avoiding this trap, we may well fall into another, that of projecting our own fantasies. Symbolist works reject conventional codes of reference and encourage an inward and subjective interpretation, thus opening the door to this kind of reading. The landscape painter Caspar David Friedrich, for example, gave this advice to artists: "Close your bodily eye, so that you may see your picture first with the spiritual eye. Then bring to the light of day that which you have seen in the darkness so that it may react upon others from the outside inwards."[3] With this argument, he was in a way authorizing a multiplicity of individual interpretations, recognizing that in the end, anyone can see in a work what they want to see.[4]

In 1974, Jean-René Ostiguy pointed out that the Surrealist look of the profile in the cloud had occurred to Jean-Paul Riopelle, the drawing's owner. It is true that Symbolism (or at least the Symbolism that avoided the tawdry mysticism of many of the Salon de la Rose+Croix exhibitors and the delicate affectation of some strains of the movement) must be considered the precursor of Surrealism. But is it not the case that the individual projection of the viewer looking at these works may influence the reading? Is there any better "paranoiac screen" than a cloudy sky? The landscape entitled *Profile in Cloud* is an example of this, especially as it is just as possible to see two profiles in the sky, one negative and the other positive. But however it is interpreted, this drawing is neither narrative nor anecdotal; in its formal characteristics, it heralds the individual approach to landscape formulated by Leduc in his work from the 1910s.

E. T.

1 This is how we interpret the entry in Leduc's Diary for February 7, 1954: "To Mr. Gilles Corbeil, two small drawings including the profile in cloud…" (BNQ 327/3/12).

2 Jean Moréas, "Un manifeste littéraire: Le Symbolisme", *Le Figaro* [Paris], Saturday, September 18, 1886.

3 Quoted in William Vaughan, *Romantic Art* (London: Thames and Hudson, 1978), p. 147.

4 See Charles Rosen and Henri Zerner, *Romanticism and Realism: The Mythology of Nineteenth-century Art* (New York: Viking Press, 1984), pp. 67-70.

5 Jean-René Ostiguy, *Ozias Leduc: Symbolist and Religious Painting*, exhib. cat. (Ottawa: National Gallery of Canada, 1974), no. 29, p. 139.

135

Study for *The Coronation of the Virgin*

About 1910

Oil on cardboard mounted on cardboard

25.5 x 43 cm

Signed lower left: *OZIAS LEDUC*

The Montreal Museum of Fine Arts, gift of
Maurice Corbeil, inv. 1986.35

PROVENANCE
Studio of the artist; Mr. and Mrs. Maurice Corbeil,
Montreal, 1952; Montreal Museum of Fine Arts,
1986

THE present church of Saint-Romuald in Farnham, county of Mississquoi, was consecrated on December 8, 1904.[1] The following year, when Joseph-Magloire Laflamme (cat. 165), parish priest since 1900, decided to have the interior of his new church suitably decorated, he turned to Ozias Leduc, whom he had commissioned to decorate the Church of Saint-Hilaire some years earlier (cats. 27-56).

Letters exchanged between Leduc and Father Laflamme enable us to follow the progress of this big project. The two men began to work together in the summer of 1905, when Laflamme mentions in a letter of August 1 a plan for a painting "surrounding the altar".[2] Leduc worked for Farnham from then on, as we learn from a bill totalling $2,965 he sent Father Laflamme on February 18, 1907.[3] In addition to the "large painting of the *Sermon on the Mount* (fig. 134) in the chancel, and the screen behind the high altar showing the *Glorification of the Cross*", Leduc had by this time completed the Stations of the Cross as well as the four paintings for the ceiling – *The Nativity* [Adoration of the Magi], *Jesus Raising the Son of the Widow of Nain, Christ Giving the Keys to Saint Peter* and *The Holy Spirit Comes Down upon the Apostles* – and the paintings of the four Evangelists in the choir.

The interior decor of the Farnham church was completed over the next four years with the addition of six other paintings by Leduc: two above the side altars probably painted in 1910,[4] a *Holy Family in the Carpenter's Shop* and a *Coronation of the Virgin*, and four others

in the aisles above the confessionals, dating from 1911-1912.[5] Following some unfortunate restoration work carried out in the mid-1960s, it is difficult today to judge Leduc's achievement at Saint-Romuald. Only three of the paintings hung above the confessionals have escaped the clumsy efforts of the "restorers" – *The Presentation of the Virgin in the Temple, Saint Francis of Assisi Receiving the Stigmata* and *Saint Aloysius of Gonzaga Receiving Holy Communion*.[6]

This explains the difference between the style of the modello (cat. 135) and that of the oil painting of *The Coronation of the Virgin* in its present condition (fig. 46). And yet, Leduc considered the latter the best of his Farnham paintings (fig. 47).[7] The scene shows Christ enthroning His mother in heaven and placing a crown on her head. Both figures are seated upon a mass of clouds in the shape of a throne. In the background, a rainbow crosses the sky, linking the groups of cherubim in the lower corners of the triangular composition. The apex is occupied by the symbol of the Holy Trinity. As Leduc was to note later, "the source of radiance" comes from this symbol. He wanted "the whole scene to be bathed in a warm and colourful light with orange tones predominant".[8] The hatchlike brush stroke employed here helps this effect. It is not surprising, therefore, that the model for *The Coronation of the Virgin* is one of Leduc's most luminous works.

According to Philippe Verdier, "The coronation of the Virgin is the apotheosis of redeemed humankind from an eschatological point of view."[9] The subject, which comes from the apocryphal tradition, seems to have been a favourite of Leduc's, since he painted it at least three more times: in Saint-Charles-Borromée in Joliette in 1893; in Notre-Dame-de-Bonsecours (fig. 137) in Montreal in 1908; and at the end of his career in Notre-Dame-de-la-Présentation in Shawinigan-Sud (completed by Gabrielle Messier; fig. 92).

Y. L.

1   "L'inauguration d'un temple", *La Presse* [Montreal], December 12, 1904, p. 8.

2   BNQ 327/5/15.

3   Parish records of Saint-Romuald, Farnham.

4   As is clear from a letter by Laflamme to Leduc dated March 26, 1910, the painter was working at the time on the modello of the painting *The Holy Family in the Carpenter's Shop* (BNQ 327/5/20). There is every reason to believe that its companion piece, *The Coronation of the Virgin*, dates from the same period.

5   It seems very likely that Father Laflamme had these paintings in mind when he asked Leduc on January 14, 1911, to "be sure to finish the 4 other little paintings for the transepts" (BNQ 327/5/21). The scaffolding ready to instal the works in question was still in place the following spring, as we learn from another letter from Laflamme to Leduc dated April 22, 1912 (BNQ 327/5/22).

6   The fourth painting is of *Saint Anthony of Padua*.

7   In the list Leduc made of his "Mural paintings and decoration", kept in a collection of private papers, he states that the "Paintings preferred by the artist" at Farnham were *The Coronation of the Virgin* and *Saint Francis Receiving the Stigmata*.

8   Letter from Ozias Leduc to Abbé Aimé Joyal [after October 14 and before November 5, 1946], BNQ 327/9/9.

9   Philippe Verdier, *Le Couronnement de la Vierge. Les origines et les premiers développements d'un thème iconographique* (Montreal: Institut d'études mediévales Albert-le-Grand, 1980), p. 9.

Fig. 46   Ozias Leduc, *The Coronation of the Virgin*, after restoration carried out in 1965 (Farnham, Church of Saint-Romuald).

Fig. 47   Ozias Leduc, *The Coronation of the Virgin*, about 1910, oil on canvas (Farnham, Church of Saint-Romuald; BNQ_327/11/3.28).

136

136

Study for *The Martyrdom of Saint Barnabas*

About 1911

Charcoal on paper

61 x 38.3 cm

Signed lower right: *Ozias Leduc*; signed lower left: *O. LEDUC*

Quebec City, Musée du Québec, inv. 53.111

137

The Martyrdom of Saint Barnabas

1911

Charcoal on canvas, heightened with oil

610 x 305 cm

Initialed and dated lower left: *19 O.L. 11*

Quebec City, Musée du Québec, inv. 66.88
Photo by Ozias Leduc

137

THE commission for this religious work, the style of which is unique in Leduc's output, was due to the parish priest of Saint-Barnabé-Sud. Father Joseph-Urgèle Charbonneau, formerly the incumbent at Saint-Hilaire from 1900 to 1904, wanted his church decoration completed and addressed himself to Leduc, whom he admired.[1] In January 1910, he got in touch with the artist to offer him the contract. The most vital question was how to depict Saint Barnabas. In the lives of the saints, he is described as the assistant of Saint Paul and as having spread the Gospel of Saint Matthew through his native island of Cyprus, where he died about 62 A.D.

Since Saint Barnabas is rarely represented in religious imagery,[2] Father Charbonneau and Leduc consulted the Bishop of Saint-Hyacinthe, Msgr. Alexis-Xyste Bernard, who in turn consulted the Bollandists[3] before agreeing to the artist's proposal: "Should I allow your artist to paint Saint Barnabas being stoned on the steps of the Synagogue?" he wrote. "I am inclined to grant him permission. The Saint's martyrdom must in fact have begun on the Synagogue steps even if it did not end there. Besides, the Synagogue would make a very impressive background to the painting. That is my humble opinion."[4] Leduc combined stoning and immolation, a double torment allying the weight of earth to the evanescence of air.

In addition to the choice of subject, the commission posed a second problem in terms of the size the picture was to be. The space reserved for it was twice as high as it was wide. Furthermore, it would not be possible to fix the canvas in place by the process of marouflage, as the wall was prone to water seepage.[5]

The painting, which cost $200, was blessed on April 28, 1912.[6] It is a huge drawing in charcoal on primed canvas, like a few others Leduc executed in the course of his career (cat. 88).[7] He seems to have liked the technique because of the ease with which the pigment gives an effect of semi-gloom to material and texture. Hatching is used in various expressive ways, modelling draperies, bark and smoke. Highlights in oil light up the fire in the foreground and illuminate the faces of the torturers. The composition is structured by long diagonals describing the cliff and the outline of the town framed by the undulating lines of the smoke and the trees. In the centre of the composition, the saint seems almost to levitate, caught up by gravity that pulls him to the fire and yet suspended in space, ready to rise to heaven to claim his martyr's palm.[8]

The painting has undergone many vicissitudes. The church, built in 1898, was partly destroyed by a hurricane in 1950 and had to be demolished.[9] Since there was not room in the new building for this work, it was given back to Leduc in 1952.[10] According to Guy Viau, it was Leduc himself who suggested that the enormous original canvas should be cut into six pieces to be sold separately.[11] It was in this state when acquired by the Musée du Québec in 1966, before being specially reassembled for this exhibition through the efforts of the staff of the Centre de conservation du Québec.

L. L.

1 Despite enquiring about the progress of the work, Abbé Charbonneau wrote to Leduc on August 24, 1910, "I prefer to give you all the time you need in order to have better finished work worthy of your reputation" (BNQ 327/5/20).

2 Louis Réau, *Iconographie de l'art chrétien*, vol. 3 (Paris: Presses universitaires de France, 1958), pp. 178-181, states that in Christian art only three scenes from Barnabas's life are depicted: his preaching, the sacrifice at Lystra and his curing the sick. Leduc wrote to Father Charbonneau on September 12, 1910, about the difficulty he was finding in researching the Saint's life: "I have done a lot of research in the hope of finding reproductions of good paintings on the subject, without finding anything, so I have set to work on the composition I submitted to you – it will make the task a little longer but I hope you will like it" (BNQ 327/8/17).

3 The Bollandists, a society made up largely of Jesuits, continued the work of publishing the lives of the saints begun in 1643 by Jean Bolland. Father Charbonneau, rather uneasy about how Leduc might interpret the subject, asked his Bishop's permission before accepting the proposal (letter from Father J.-U. Charbonneau to Msgr. Bernard, January 14, 1910, Archives de l'Évêché de Saint-Hyacinthe, XVII, c. 13, Saint-Barnabé file).

4 Letter from Msgr. Bernard to Father Charbonneau, January 17, 1910, parish archives of Saint-Barnabé-Sud. Leduc kept a transcript of this letter (BNQ 327/5/20). Msgr. Bernard seems to have been particularly sensitive about the orthodoxy of works found in the churches of his diocese. Charbonneau wrote to Leduc on January 21, 1910, "Monseigneur is sure to pay scrupulous attention to work by a French Canadian" (BNQ 327/5/20).

5 Letter from Father Charbonneau to Leduc, August 24, 1910, BNQ 327/5/20. This factor enabled the painting to be removed prior to the church's demolition in 1950.

6 Parish archives of Saint-Barnabé-Sud, livre des délibérations, April 28, 1912.

7 *Stormy Landscape with Rainbow* (1914) is another fine example (reproduced in Laurier Lacroix *et al.*, *Ozias Leduc the Draughtsman*, exhib. cat. [Montreal: Concordia University, 1978], p. 48). Among the many preparatory drawings for the *Martyrdom*, besides the squared modello exhibited here, is a page dated December 1911 that focusses on the figure of the Saint (reproduced in Jean-René Ostiguy, *Ozias Leduc: Symbolist and Religious Painting*, exhib. cat. [Ottawa: National Gallery of Canada, 1974], p. 142).

8 The critic Maurice Gagnon felt that this was one of Leduc's finest works. He wrote, "Leduc the painter is too great to have been just a philosopher. The most remarkable achievements of his career – *Golden Snow*, *Green Apples*, *The Concrete Bridge*, *Mauve Twilight*, *Portrait of Madame Lebrun*, *Joan of Arc* and *Saint Barnabas* – bear witness to intelligence and artistry perfectly blended with taste" (Maurice Gagnon, *Peinture moderne* [Montreal: Éd. B. Valiquette, 1940], p. 200).

9 Bernard Blouin and Jean-Noël Dion, *Histoire de Saint-Barnabé-Sud 1840-1990* (Sherbrooke: Louis Bilodeau & fils, 1989), pp. 25-27.

10 On this subject, see the correspondence between Leduc and Father Louis Forest of Saint-Hilaire, who acted as a go-between: O.L. to Louis Forest, December 31, 1951, BNQ 327/7/14; Forest to O.L., December 31, 1951, BNQ 327/8/5; O.L. to Forest, February 8, 1952; and O.L. to Father Beauregard, [mid-February 1952] BNQ 327/9/15. On May 6, 1952, Leduc noted in his diary that he was taking back his painting, which had been brought to him by Roger Laflamme (BNQ 327/3/11).

11 The mural "was cut in pieces by order of Ozias Leduc himself, who hoped to sell the more interesting details in order to pay his bill at the hospital where he spent the final weeks of his life" (letter from Guy Viau to André Giroux, September 13, 1966, Musée du Québec, work file).

The Struggle between the Material and the Intellectual

THE selection of Ozias Leduc's work (fig. 48) to inaugurate the exhibition galleries of the new Bibliothèque Saint-Sulpice in February 1916 served to confirm the artist's growing stature in the French-Canadian art world.[1] Leduc's reputation as an ecclesiastical painter would certainly have appealed to the library's director, the Sulpician Olivier Maurault (cat. 163). Although this exhibition in the library's galleries on Saint-Denis Street included a retrospective section, it also provided the painter with an opportunity to show his most recent work, which represented the culmination of his artistic output.

The period between 1912 and 1921 is the central point of Leduc's career, and the quality of the works produced during these years resulted in a series of successes that were the outward signs of the esteem his peers and the public alike accorded him. His election as an Associate Member of the Royal Canadian Academy in 1916, together with the National Gallery of Canada's purchase of *Green Apples* (cat. 148) and *Golden Snow* (cat. 152), consolidated his pre-eminence.[2] Landscapes and portraits of friends recur frequently in the work from this period, which includes some of his best-known paintings: *Blue Cumulus* (cat. 143), *Day's End* (cat. 144), *Grey Effect (Snow)* (cat. 146), *Green Apples*, *The Concrete Bridge* (cat. 149), *Golden Snow*, *Afterglow* (fig. 52) and *Mauve Twilight* (cat. 52).

Although somewhat older than the other participants, Leduc was active in the movements that were then galvanizing Montreal's young intellectuals. On the one hand, his religious commissions, traditionalism and attachment to national, local and rural values aligned him with the group behind *L'Action française* – a magazine founded in 1917 whose position, under the influence of Abbé Lionel Groulx (1878-1967),

1   Suzor-Coté was better known at the time, but he probably had no need of this promotional outlet since he inundated the annual exhibitions of the Art Association of Montreal and the Royal Canadian Academy with his works and was a member of the Montreal Arts Club, as well as exhibiting regularly in Toronto.

For the series of exhibitions held at the Bibliothèque Saint-Sulpice, Maurault generally chose younger artists, at the start of their career.

2   This period was marked by several significant events in the artist's private life: the start of construction of the large house he had been planning since 1913, and the death of his parents – his mother on April 25, 1918, and his father on August 29, 1921.

3   On this movement, see especially Susan Mann Trofimenkoff, *Action française: French Canadian Nationalism in the Twenties* (Toronto: University of Toronto Press, 1975).

became after 1918 increasingly nationalistic.[3] This outlook was shared by a number of Leduc's close acquaintances and friends, including Édouard Montpetit, Olivier Maurault, Henri d'Arles, Adélard Dugré and Philippe Perrier. On the other hand, personal sympathy and his own intellectual curiosity prompted Leduc to frequent young people who saw themselves as proponents of the avant-garde. He became associated with a literary circle whose members, also art enthusiasts, made him part of a network that held sway in Montreal during the 1914-1918 war.[4] His collaboration with Guy Delahaye on the 1912 publication of *"Mignonne, allons voir si la rose…" est sans épines* (cats. 140-142)[5] was undoubtedly a decisive factor in his inclusion in this group of intellectuals conversant with the latest works from France. A number of young writers, musicians and artists recently returned to Montreal from Paris – some because their studies were complete, some because of the outbreak of war – including Robert LaRoque de Roquebrune (cat. 155), Léo-Pol Morin (cat. 160), Paul Morin, Fernand Préfontaine, the brothers Henri (1884-1950) and Adrien Hébert (1890-1967), and Marcel Dugas, joined forces to produce the magazine *Le Nigog*, which was published throughout 1918 with a cover designed by Leduc (fig. 111).[6] All were keen advocates of Symbolism and familiar with the new aesthetic approaches that gave precedence to form over literal representation of the subject.[7]

While Leduc was hardly a lead player on the cultural scene, his moderate and conciliatory nature and the ties that bound him to the writers and musicians comprising the group known as the *parisianistes* made his role a nonetheless significant one. Encouraged by all these contacts, Leduc spent the decade leading up to 1920 pursuing his preoccupation with the formal aspects of painting while continuing to focus on the personal subjects that reflected his taste for a painting of "ideas".

Leduc's growing interest in Symbolism became manifest in his religious works[8] and signalled a change in his ecclesiastical style. The three major ensembles produced during these years embody theological and mystical explorations that resulted in a more personal approach, from both the formal and iconographical points of view: the Church of Saint-Enfant-Jésus in the Mile-End district of Montreal (cats. 166-167), the designs for the stained glass windows of the Pauline Chapel in the cathedral of Sherbrooke (cats. 168-169) and the painting entitled *The Apotheosis of Saint Joan of Arc*, made for the Church of Saint-Raphaël, Île-Bizard (1919).

4 Among acquaintances and friends of Leduc's who published works during these years were Henri d'Arles, *Poètes français contemporains, eaux-fortes et tailles-douces* (1913); Arsène Bessette, *Le Débutant* (1914); Marcel Dugas, *Feux de Bengale* (1915); and Albert Laberge, *La Scouine* (1918). Leduc's relationships with this group of art-lovers and collectors also resulted in his designing bookplates in the early 1920s for Olivier Maurault (fig. 55), Joseph Barcelo, Yves Tessier-Lavigne and Paul Lavoie. (Laurier Lacroix et al., *Ozias Leduc the Draughtsman*, exhib. cat. (Montreal: Concordia University, 1978), pp. 61, 63-65, 73-74.

5 See Robert Lahaise, *Guy Delahaye et la modernité littéraire*, "Cahiers du Québec/Littérature" series (Montreal: Hurtubise/HMH, 1987), pp. 127-224.

6 For a contemporary evaluation of *Le Nigog*'s role within the ideological context of the period, see Léo-Paul Desrosiers, "L'École du Nigog", *Le Nationaliste* [Montreal], August 10, 1919, p. 2.

7 On this group of intellectuals, see "La Genèse et l'expression d'une pensée", in *Le Nigog* (Montreal: Fides, 1987), "Archives des lettres canadiennes", vol. 7, pp. 9-82.

In 1913, the Art Association of Montreal's Spring Exhibition included works by John Lyman, A. Y. Jackson and Randolph Hewton, all described as Post-Impressionist. Over the next decade, Montreal painting focussed largely on explorations into colour and the treatment of urban themes. A major exhibition held at the AAM in January 1909 introduced the Montreal public to certain aspects of contemporary French painting.

8 In a letter to Maurault dated April 27, 1917 (Archives du Séminaire de Saint-Sulpice, Olivier Maurault papers), Leduc made particular mention of the research done by Émile Mâle (1862-1954). The artist also met Maurice Denis (1870-1943), whose writings he was already familiar with when Denis visited Montreal in 1927 (fig. 116). In 1921, Maurault, encouraged by the revival of religious art in France, published a leaflet (under the pseudonym of Louis Deligny) on Leduc's interior for the baptistry of the Church of Saint-Enfant-Jésus in Mile-End.

Leduc's easel paintings show evidence of a similar desire to explore the notion of correspondence between the material world and the subject being portrayed, and their pictorial equivalent.

Art does not strive to copy the appearances of nature or to depict the ideal, but only to make a beautiful object by manifesting a *form* using perceptible signs. To achieve this single goal [the artist] will invent them, and they will thus lend themselves to the transfiguration of the material appearances of nature.[9]

This search for visual equivalents to the message being conveyed often took the form of a battle metaphor, representing the long struggle to attain Beauty.

The beauty thatx we seek and find. The beauty we are given has its source in the very depths of the acknowledged resemblance between Creator and created. Beauty is a concrete fact, it exists resplendent as part of the order that governs the relations between matter and spirit.

The order desired by Him who can make worlds, who brings by stages the being evolving towards its ideal form, towards its perfection. The same is true of things, which are thus beautiful.[10]

At a time when the First World War was propelling Quebec and Canada – on the political, economic and industrial fronts, and in the expanding realm of communications – into a modern era marked by outbursts of nationalist feeling, Leduc was pursuing his quest to better define and understand the sublime role of the artist within society – the role filled so ideally by Verlaine: "This god, this faun, this poet, this Ariel fallen and reborn, [who] has perfected the miracle of the Christian superman and of a being subject to all earthly infirmities."[11]

L. L.

9   Ozias Leduc, "Notes sur l'art", BNQ 327/3/17. Elsewhere, Leduc adds, "From the order whose foundation rests on the possibilities of matter alone – dimensions, form, colour, position, distance, sound and movement will result in a spectacle of great beauty" (BNQ 327/3/18).

10   Ozias Leduc, "Textes poétiques", BNQ 327/3/17.

11   During a lecture given in about 1928 to the Saint-Hilaire branch of the Union catholique des cultivateurs, Leduc quoted this passage from the poet Marcel Dugas's 1928 study of Verlaine.

138

Portrait of Guy Delahaye

1911

Oil on canvas

39 x 39 cm

Signed, dated and dedicated upper left: *A M^oN*
AMI GUY DELAHAYE O LEDUC 1911

Quebec City, Musée du Québec, inv. 77.24

PROVENANCE

Studio of the artist; Mr. and Mrs. Maurice Corbeil,
Montreal, 1952; Musée du Québec, 1977

139

Study for a *Portrait of Guy*
Delahaye

1912

Charcoal on brown wove paper

65.1 x 31.7 cm

Signed lower left: *O LEDUC* ; dated lower right:
1912

Private collection

INSCRIPTIONS

Verso: labels of Musée de la Province de Québec;
Royal Canadian Academy of Arts; Galerie l'Art
français

PROVENANCE

Studio of the artist; Ozias Leduc estate;
Dr. Guillaume and Mrs. Marie Lahaise;
private collection

138

L EDUC's friendship with François-Guillaume Lahaise (1888-1969) dated from 1898, when Lahaise began watching the artist at work in the Church of Saint-Hilaire. Subsequently, the young student often spent his "Sunday afternoons conversing on art, philosophy and science" in Leduc's studio, or accompanying him on "walks through the woods, and along the Chemin des Trente, and the little garden and the large orchard, and the headland where we go to watch the sun set, and to search for fossils".[1] In 1907, while studying medicine, Lahaise began publishing poems in the newspaper *La Patrie*, under the pseudonym of Guy Delahaye.[2] After the appearance in 1911 of a collection of poems entitled *Les Phases*, which aroused harsh criticism, Leduc undertook a first portrait of the author (cat. 138). The following year, the poet issued an ironic and disdainful reply to his detractors by publishing "*Mignonne, allons voir si*

la rose ..." *est sans épines*, and Leduc executed two more likenesses of Lahaise – a charcoal study (cat. 139) and an oil (fig. 49).

In the 1911 *Portrait of Guy Delahaye* belonging to the Musée du Québec, the model is shown in profile, seated in the midground. The figure is set against an abstract background. Chromatic contrasts have been employed to model the head, while the clothes and the right hand have been rendered only summarily. According to art historian Max Friedländer, the profile pose makes the model seem distant and solitary, almost like an inhabitant of another world. He adds that the profile view, while creating a sense of permanence, presents the subject in fragmentary form: "We feel less the presence of a living person than that

Fig. 49   Ozias Leduc, *Portrait of Guy Delahaye*, 1912, oil on canvas, 64.8 x 31.1 cm (private collection; photo by Ozias Leduc, printed from glass negative No. 22, BNQ 327/12/3.25).

139

the memory is conjured up of some immortalized personality – a memory that has preserved only the essential features, but these with concentrated sharpness."[3] Guy Delahaye himself decided that the portrait should be a profile view, and he was perfectly aware of the resulting "restriction ... placed on the artist's inspiration".[4] Perhaps, in choosing to be immortalized thus, remote and cut off from the spectator, the poet was distancing himself from the public and critics who had failed to understand him in *Les Phases*.

The work's strict two-dimensionality, the pictorial quality of the drawing and the artificial lighting combine to make this a Symbolist painting. Leduc has employed two very unusual attributes to represent his model: a garland of laurel leaves and a circle divided by three radii, which appear on the wall at the level of the poet's shoulder. The laurel leaf symbolizes inspiration and moral value, and also recalls the immortal glory accorded to the poets of Antiquity.[5] The circle with three radii is a symbol dear to both poets and painters. The circle is a perfect form with no beginning and no end, suggesting eternity. The number three has several connotations: the Trinity (the Father, the Son and the Holy Ghost), Art (the True, the Beautiful and the Good), Time (past, present and future) and Space (height, width and depth).[6] The poems in *Les Phases* are also structured in tripartite fashion: nine-foot verses arranged in three triplets with three rhymes. Moreover, Leduc himself based his whole art on three formal components: "drawing, colour, composition: the painter's trinity".[7] The sketchy rendering of the hand is surprising, for Leduc was particularly adept at portraying this part of the anatomy (see cats. 57-60). Here, the deliberately unfinished hand concentrates the spectator's full attention on the model's head and, consequently, on his intellectual qualities. Perhaps, too, the artist was foreshadowing the end of his friend's literary career, for Delahaye published little after the appearance of *Mignonne* – a few signed articles and an anonymous book, *L'Unique Voie à l'unique But*. In 1919, he even abandoned his pseudonym, returning to "the only name my mother ever gave me"[8] and devoting himself from then on, after twelve years of wandering and medical studies, almost exclusively to psychiatry.

The charcoal preparatory drawing for the 1912 *Portrait of Guy Delahaye* shows the same hieratic pose, but the model is standing, within an oblong format. Here, the attribute accompanying the poet is even more evocative than in the 1911 work. Behind Delahaye, the artist has depicted a female figure, head hidden by a veil:[9] it is Erato, the Muse of lyric poetry, stretching her arms towards a whirling form. As Ostiguy has perceptively suggested, this form may be the "nebula Andromeda in the vicinity of the Square of Pegasus",[10] for Andromeda is a spiral-shaped galaxy, and Pegasus, the winged horse of Greek mythology, is often associated with poetic inspiration.[11] In addition, "the spiral conjures up the evolution of a force; with its double significance of involution and evolution, it is linked to the symbolism of the wheel".[12] The circle that appears in the 1911 painting therefore has a similar meaning to the whirling shape in the portrait of 1912 – a shape that also symbolizes movement guided by the superior forces that trigger the creative process.[13] Leduc actually explained the aim of the portrait very clearly: he wished "to symbolize the influence of a dream, through the deliberate, calculated pose of the figure and also through the accessories, the mood".[14]

In his use of François-Guillaume Lahaise's pseudonym in the dedication that appears in the upper left-hand corner of the 1911 portrait and his employment in both works of emblems associated with the art of poetry, Leduc was addressing the poet rather than the twenty-two-year-old doctor. Clearly, it was the artist's desire that these portraits be seen as an expression of his admiration for Guy Delahaye and of his confidence in the survival of the poet's work.

M. L.

1   Letter from Lahaise to Ozias Leduc, June 15, 1916, BNQ 327/6/1.

2   On Guy Delahaye, see Robert Lahaise, *Guy Delahaye et la modernité littéraire*, "Cahiers du Québec /Littérature" series (Montreal: Hurtubise/HMH, 1987) and for a newly annotated edition of his works, see Robert Lahaise, *Guy Delahaye: œuvres parues et inédites* (Montreal: Hurtubise/HMH, 1988). For an analysis of the avant-garde character of his poetry, see André-G. Bourassa, *Surréalisme et littérature québécoise* (Montreal: L'Étincelle, 1977), pp. 23-29.

3   Max J. Friedländer, *Landscape, Portrait, Still-life: Their Origin and Development*, trans. R.F.C. Hull (New York: Schocken Books, 1963), pp. 235-237.

4   Letter from Delahaye to Ozias Leduc, June 15, 1916, BNQ 327/6/1. The composition of this portrait is very like that of a painting by Victor Scharf (1872-?), entitled *Portrait*, which Leduc may have known from a reproduction that appeared in *The Studio*, vol. 41, no. 172 (July 1907), p. 153.

5   Jean Chevalier and Alain Gheerbrant, *Dictionnaire des symboles*, "Bouquins" series (Paris: Robert Laffont/Jupiter, 1982), p. 563.

6 Marcel Dugas, quoting from an interview with Guy Delahaye, refers to the connotations associated with the figure three and to Delahaye's explanation: "My poetic form is based on a fact older than the world itself, eternal like God, which existed long before Solomon ... It rests on the necessary link between one and three, between unity and trinity" ("Les 'Phases' et M. Albert Lozeau", *Le Nationaliste* [Montreal], May 1, 1910, p. 2).

7 Inscription by Ozias Leduc around his *Still Life (with Lay Figure)* (1898; cat. 90).

8 Letter from Delahaye to Leduc, November 5, 1919, BNQ 327/6/4.

9 This head can be related to the one that appears, surrounded by several circles, on Leduc's business card (fig. 4). This idea of representing a floating muse behind a poet had been employed by the painter Raphaël Collin (1850-1916) in his picture *Les Harmonies de la Nature inspirent le compositeur* (The Harmonies of Nature Inspire the Composer), of which Leduc may have seen a reproduction in the magazine *Art and Décoration*, vol. 3 (January-June 1893), p. 132.

10 Jean-René Ostiguy, *Ozias Leduc: Symbolist and Religious Painting*, exhib. cat. (Ottawa: National Gallery of Canada, 1974), p. 144.

11 Chevalier and Gheerbrant 1982, p. 736.

12 *Ibid.*, pp. 906, 909.

13 *Ibid.*, p. 960.

14 Letter from O. L. to Delahaye, July 4, 1916, quoted in Lahaise 1987, p. 184. The original of this letter has not been found.

140

Clowns

1912

Brown ink and graphite on beige wove paper

26.2 x 20.4 cm

Monogrammed and dated centre right: *19 OL 12*

Private collection

INSCRIPTIONS

Verso: *9 octobre 1988 A notre petit Maxou qui aime les clowns ... un peu clown lui-même Mami Papi*

PROVENANCE

Studio of the artist; René Bergeron, Chicoutimi; Dr. Otto Bengle, Outremont, about 1950; private collection, 1988

141

Horror, Horror, Horror

1912

Ink and graphite on paper

26.2 x 20.4 cm

Initialed centre right: *OL*

Quebec City, Musée du Québec, inv. 86.40

INSCRIPTIONS

Recto (in a circle): *HORREUR HORREUR HORREUR*

PROVENANCE

Roger Chaput, Montreal; Galerie Claude Lafitte, Montreal; Musée du Québec, 1986

142

Open Book

1912

Ink on beige paper

22.5 x 18.6 cm

Initialed and dated in centre: *OL 1912*

F.-M. Gagnon collection

INSCRIPTIONS

Recto: *A Maurice Gagnon / Cette vieille et symbolique image déja / évocatrice par anticipation et cependant / toute actuelle du rayonnement ardent de votre livre "Peinture moderne" / 20 nov. 1940 Ozias Leduc / de tout cœur*

PROVENANCE

Studio of the artist; Maurice Gagnon, Montreal, 1940; F.-M. Gagnon

14

IN agreeing to execute the nine tailpieces for *"Mignonne, allons voir si la rose..." est sans épines*, Leduc was going out on a limb, for the book of poetry written by his friend Guy Delahaye (cats. 138-139),[1] was guaranteed to raise controversy if not vitriolic criticism. A pointed rejoinder to the critics who had savaged *Les Phases* (1910), Delahaye's first collection of poems, *Mignonne* is a cunningly satirical piece of work – "deliberately provocative foolery raised to the third power",[2] – driven by *la blague* and even less accessible than its predecessor.[3] Leduc's tailpieces, conceived in close collaboration with the poet,[4] are the perfect companions to the text in the esoteric and arcane implications of their iconography.

With the inscription "By the invocation of Janus" emblazoned on the first page, Delahaye sounds the note of warning. The duality and irony implied by Janus, the god with two faces, are equally manifest in Leduc's drawings and the poet's text. In *Clowns*, for example, which comes after the Preface, a jester performs a handstand on a ball balanced

141

142

on a tightrope – of barbed wire no less! – a tour de force of flexibility and control.[5] A Pierrot figure, flabbergasted by this feat, makes as if to regain his balance. These two figures can be seen to represent Delahaye and his critics, but which is which? Is Delahaye the jester whose poetic tricks have thrown off balance those critics who would cling naïvely to the safety of a literature that exalted the traditions, customs and values of French Canada in a conventionally narrative mode? Or is Delahaye rather the unbalanced Pierrot, the "neurasthenic pariah" that this figure had come to represent in the late nineteenth century?[6] After all, one critic had dismissed Delahaye's poetry as symptomatic of a descent into mental instability.[7] In this context, does the jester, in a stance of absolute rigidity, embody the inflexibility (or rectitude, depending on one's perspective) of those critics who toed the traditionalist line? The question mark that punctuates the vignette is not just a visual echo of the Pierrot's disbelief,[8] but a pictorial articulation of the ambiguity of the image.

This cryptic introductory illustration sets the tone for the rest of the tailpieces. At the close of the Bibliography, for example (which comes not at the end of the book, but just before Delahaye's text proper), is *Open Book*, complete with celestial rays, swirling clouds and stars emanating from its hallowed pages. Like the parodic Bibliography, Leduc's illustration is intentionally overblown. While it may suggest the author's deference to the authority of literary tradition in response to the critics' earlier accusations of unoriginality,[9] it is made ironic through Delahaye's tongue-in-cheek citations of tomes both weighty and insubstantial. An alternative reading, however, is that the book represents a work by the poet himself. With swirling masses of air that signify creative energy, much as in Leduc's *Portrait of Guy Delahaye* (fig. 49),[10] the open book – contents derived from the poet's own inspiration without recourse to "sources" – is a stamp that legitimizes his own collection *Mignonne* as a work of pure originality.[11]

Horror, Horror, Horror is the tailpiece for "Méduse", a song trilogy. The saintliness of the "very beautiful"[12] muse, suggested by her subdued demeanour and draped head slightly inclined within a halo, is subverted by the writhing serpents escaping from beneath her headdress, as well as by the word "horror" inscribed three times in a curve that constitutes a halo. In their respective paradoxical renderings of the Muse who, as revealed in the three "chants", both "amuses" and "abuses" not only the author but the critic and his minion,[13] Delahaye and Leduc contend that nothing is absolute. Just as the cruel Medusa lurks behind her guise of saintliness, so does a traditional Delahaye hide behind his mask of incomprehensibility. By quoting the closing line of the *Chanson de Roland* (the famous French epic poem that exalts the combined virtues of Christianity and patriotism) as the last line of his own poem (which appears just before the illustration of the Medusa),[14] Delahaye the modernist mockingly claims that his poetry is no less worthy of a place in history. Once again, text and image engage in an interplay that enriches the equivocal nature of Delahaye and Leduc's collaboration.

In a tribute that reveals Leduc's continued acceptance and admiration of the publicly maligned poetry of Delahaye, the artist dedicated the original drawing *Open Book* to Maurice Gagnon on the occasion of the publication of that art historian's book *Peinture moderne* (1940). The inscription makes it clear that the enlightened stance of this later defender of modernism, to Leduc, was already inherent in Delahaye's *Mignonne*.

A. G.

1 Leduc's exhibition of a *Portrait of Guy Delahaye* in 1912 at the Art Association of Montreal and the Royal Canadian Academy in Ottawa may be seen as a gesture in support of the poet. *Mignonne* appeared November 30, 1912. See Robert Lahaise, *Guy Delahaye et la modernité littéraire*, "Cahiers du Québec/Littérature" series (Montreal: Hurtubise/HMH, 1987) p. 211. See also Robert Lahaise, *Guy Delahaye: œuvres parues et inédites* (Montreal: Hurtubise/HMH, 1988), p. 19. Recent discussions of *Mignonne* are included in Lahaise 1987, pp. 199-224; in Renald Berubé "Guy Delayahe: transtextualité, blague, silence (Petit Inventaire)", *Protée*, vol. 15, no. 1, winter 1987, pp. 44-55, and Renald Berubé, in Maurice Lemire, ed., *Dictionnaire des œuvres littéraires du Québec* (Montreal: Fides, 1980), vol. 2: *1900-1939*, pp. 710-712.

2 Olivar Asselin, "Préface", *Mignonne*, p. XVI.

3 For a consideration of *blague* as an avant-garde ironic and parodic device for disorientation in the late nineteenth and early twentieth centuries, see Jeffrey Weiss, "'Marcel Duchamp Qui Est Inquiétant': Avantgardism and the Culture of Mystification and *Blague*," in *The Popular Culture of Modern Art: Picasso, Duchamp, and Avant-gardism* (New Haven: Yale University Press, 1994), especially pp. 109-112.

4 This is evidenced by Delahaye's explanation of the illustration's iconography on what appears to be a proof of Leduc's tailpiece for the poem "Amour et Amour": "intertwined eye – triangle (God) and the serpentheart (devil)." See Lahaise 1987, p. 207, ill. 61.

5 The acrobat's flexibility was seen to reflect the malleability of "the joke", as discussed in the Preface. See Marcel Henry [pseudonym of Marcel Dugas], "Tentative d'interview", *L'Action*, February 22, 1913, p. 3 ("The acrobats, whose anatomy, we may conclude, is supple, sum up the Preface by Asselin"). Barbara Ann Winters, "The Work and Thought of Ozias Leduc in the Intellectual and Social Context of His Time", Master's thesis, University of Victoria, May 1990, p. 186, sees the equilibrium of the acrobat's performance as linked to Delahaye's own references to the equilibrium of *Mignonne* (p. XXVII).

6 See Robert Storey, *Pierrot: A Critical History of a Mask* (Princeton, New Jersey: Princeton University Press, 1978).

7 Referring to *Les Phases*, the poet Albert Lozeau ("'Les Phases', ou le danger des mauvaises fréquentations," *Le Devoir* [Montreal] , April 19, 1910, p. 1) wrote, "It is bizarre, like the onset of insanity." Delahaye quoted this very sentence in *Mignonne*'s "Notes sérieuses" (p. XXVII).

8 Winters 1990, p. 186.

9 See Lozeau 1910.

10 Leduc also used the "whirlwind" motif to signify the same idea in his decoration of the Bishop's Chapel, Sherbrooke.

11 As noted in Henry 1913, "the book in which life is submerged to re-emerge in all its truth".

12 *Ibid.*

13 Delahaye calls him Panurge, after the character in Rabelais's *Pantagruel*. Given the poet's homophonic play between French and English in his title "Notes sérieuses. Not serious", a similar punning on "Mignonne/minion" is no doubt to be understood.

14 "Ci finit la geste que Téroulde déclamait." ("Here end the deeds declaimed by Turoldus"; *Mignonne*, p. 14.)

143
Blue Cumulus
1913
Oil on canvas
92.1 x 61.6 cm
Signed and dated lower right: *19 O 13 LE DUC*

Fredericton, New Brunswick, The Beaverbrook Art Gallery, purchased with funds from Friends of The Beaverbrook Art Gallery

PROVENANCE
Studio of the artist; Oscar Dufresne, Montreal; Dominion Gallery, Montreal, 1962; Beaverbrook Art Gallery, 1962

IN the foreground of this painting is a large tree struck down by a storm. Its trunk broken off from the stump at some height is like it, shattered into splinters. In the sky a large blue cloud with a coloured crest lit from behind by an imagined ray of sun quite low on the horizon.

It was in these telegraphic but suggestive terms that, in 1944, Leduc described *Blue Cumulus*.[1]

Blue Cumulus actually summarizes the principal project that was to preoccupy Leduc for the remainder of his career: the reconciliation of the forces of good and evil through the enlightenment of knowledge. The choice and arrangement of the elements that compose the landscape form an allegory on the desire of man, in his quest for the ideal, to tame matter and thus be restored through his own intellectual and spiritual elevation to humanity's original state.

In the foreground, the "large tree struck down by a storm" occupies two thirds of the composition. The land is divided into two areas by wooden fences, with the tree stump located in front of the first barrier. The ivy-covered stump, in the right foreground, bears the artist's monogram and the date of the work.[2] The tree's branches have fallen onto the sloping field bounded by the two fences, as if striving to reach and mingle with the cloud.[3]

In his description of the shattered tree, Leduc gives a new sense to the word *aiguillette* – literally "small needle" – using it to refer not to the instruments used by his sister to work her embroidery (cat. 109), but to the rocky points and peaks that create the jagged profile of a mountain's summit.[4] In the painting, a similarly rough and craggy landscape contained within the tree has been laid bare by the power of the wind and lightning. A few peaks pierce the sky, apparently yearning towards the "large blue cloud" that fills the upper part of the painting. Beams reach from the low setting sun to the very top of the cloud and set the whole sky aflame.

The choice and combination of the formal and iconographical elements that make up *Blue Cumulus* result in what the painter and poet Émile Vézina called "analogical harmonies of profound richness and delightful lustre".[5] The painting is the first in a series of nine Symbolist landscapes on which the artist worked between 1913 and 1921.

L. L.

1 This description was provided by Leduc when he was requesting the loan of the painting for the exhibition of his works held at the Musée de la province de Québec (Ozias Leduc to Candide Dufresne [mid-March 1944], BNQ 327/9/7).

2 His name is inscribed inside a triangle whose apex divides the date. This is apparently the only occasion on which Leduc employed this monogram, so revealing of his view of painting as the temporal manifestation of Creation. See the entry for *Still Life (with Lay Figure)* (cat. 90).

3 The extraordinary evocative power of the cloud, grounded in its constant transformations and its association with dreams and ever-changing nature, made it one of the natural images most frequently employed by Symbolist artists. See especially George Frederick Watts (1817-1904), *Green Summer* (reproduced in *The Studio*, vol. 38, no. 161 [August 1906], p. 193); Albert Pinkham Ryder (1847-1917), *The Forest of Arden* (Metropolitan Museum of Art, New York); and Prince Eugen (1865-1947), *The Cloud* (1896, Prins Eugen Waldermarsudde, Stockholm).

4 The original reads: "Son tronc brisé séparé de sa souche à une certain hauteur est comme elle déchiquetté en aiguillettes." This kind of craggy-mountained landscape, symbol of the bleak surroundings of fallen humanity, appears in a number of other drawings and paintings by Leduc (cats. 111, 154, 186, 250).

5 Émile Vézina, "Notes d'art – L'exposition Leduc", *Le Devoir* [Montreal], February 21, 1916, p. 1.

144
Day's End

1913

Oil on canvas

50.8 x 34.3 cm

Signed lower left: *O LEDUC*; dated lower right: *1913*

The Montreal Museum of Fine Arts, purchase, Horsley and Annie Townsend Bequest, inv. 1960.1271

INSCRIPTIONS

Verso, labels: *Lycee Pierre Corneille, Exposition Ozias Leduc, 12-15 juin, 1954; Frame by W. Scott & Sons, 225 Notre Dame St. W., no. 405. 1929; MMFA. 38. From: Gerard O. Beaulieu, "Fin du Jour" by Leduc; Canadian National Exh. Toronto. Fine Arts Department Title: Fin du Jour. Artist: O. Leduc. Address: Saint-Hilaire, Que.; Royal Canadian Academy. Montreal Exhibition. 1913. Title: Fin du Jour. Artist: O. Leduc; MMFA. Le Musee des beaux-arts de Montreal. no.: 60.1271. Artist: Leduc, Ozias. Canadian. Title: Fin du Jour. How acquired: Horsley & Annie Townsend Bequest, 1960. Beaulieu, Gérard O. (1955-1960)*

PROVENANCE

Studio of the artist; Louis-Joseph Barcelo, Montreal; Gérard O. Beaulieu, 1955; Montreal Museum of Fine Arts, 1960

THE draft of a letter written to the historian Gustave Lanctôt, dated December 1, 1927, facilitates the task of analyzing this painting. A few days earlier, Lanctôt had expressed interest in acquiring a work by Leduc "if my modest means permit".[1] Leduc replied:

I have no other paintings than those presently in my Saint-Hilaire studio. I would draw your attention to one of these paintings, entitled "Day's End", which represents a huge, brownish-coloured cliff, getting darker towards the bottom, that people no longer visible, miners or geologists, have reached using a long rope ladder still suspended across the rock face. At the bottom of the ladder on the right lie some tools, and more towards the centre there is a dying fire. A trail of slow, bluish smoke rises up, curling randomly against the damp, absorbent rock.[2]

Admittedly, Leduc does not specify the exact location of his picture. Its first owner, the lawyer Joseph Barcelo (Lanctôt apparently failed to follow up on his proposition) referred familiarly to the work as the *Portes de fer* – Iron Gates. (In fact, in an unconscious tribute

to Rodin, it seems the work has even occasionally been called *Les Portes de l'Enfer* – The Gates of Hell!)[3] Leduc caught wind of this interpretation and was seemingly much irritated by it, for there are no fewer than five notes among his papers where he reiterates that his painting "has nothing to do with the Iron Gates described in the legendary history of Saint-Hilaire".[4] This statement is an allusion to a passage in his article "L'histoire de S.-Hilaire – On l'entend, on la voit", where he describes the famous "iron gates".

The imagination, confronted with the vertical spread of two almost-touching segments of rock that rise up at the base of the mountain, sees them as immobile gates, coloured by time and iron-rich infiltrations. Legend has labelled them "the iron gates". Today, these once-opening gates are closed and forever still.[5]

It is true that this description might mislead those who have never seen the two large rocks known as "the iron gates", which flank a trail leading from the foot of the mountain, not far from the Collège Saint-Hilaire; in days gone by, horse-drawn carts carried their loads of wood between them. Moreover, the rest of the passage stresses the fact that behind these gates there lies, today, a "mystery".

But Leduc's painting has nothing to do with these "iron gates", as Louise Beaudry, with the assistance of the late Armand Cardinal, has clearly and convincingly shown.[6] Cardinal believed the site represented by Leduc to be located in another direction entirely, on the south-eastern side of the mountain, near the village of Sainte-Marie-Madeleine. At this spot there is, indeed, at the end of a long and winding forest track, a crag rising at least twenty metres high. With each spring thaw, the waters of the Sainte-Marie-Madeleine Falls stream down the rock. However, the visual evidence linking the picture with this new site is far from conclusive.

Might we make more headway if we concentrated on the idea that the painting's principal subject is a geological

Fig. 50   Ozias Leduc, *Brown Quarry* (study for *Day's End*), about 1913, graphite on grey-blue paper, 17.7 x 12.8 (Montreal Museum of Fine Arts, inv. Dr.936.165).

expedition to Saint-Hilaire? This, after all, is what is indicated by the tools, the rope ladder and the remains of a camp. In fact, there was a very famous expedition to Mount Saint-Hilaire about which Ozias Leduc must have known, since it involved his friend Abbé Charles-Philippe Choquette (fig. 104), who had recorded the details of the adventure in a typewritten manuscript entitled *La Montagne de Belœil. Description géologique et pittoresque.*[7] The main goal of the 1881 expedition, however, was to penetrate the mystery of the Fairy Grotto,[8] which leads us to a site even less like the one portrayed in the painting: the opening of the grotto takes the form of an upside-down triangle and is located on the western flank of the mountain, above the main slope.

But there exists a preparatory drawing for *Day's End* (fig. 50) that may provide the key to the puzzle; it bears the inscription *Brown Quarry*. This can only refer to the De-Mix et Poudrette quarries, a little to the north of the Saint-Marie-Madeleine Falls cliff, where there are deposits of pegmatite covered with a dark stratum ranging from black to brown, that is rich in iron and manganese.[9] This means, of course, that there is little hope of finding the exact rock face depicted in Leduc's painting, for an operating quarry is by definition constantly changing. This interpretation is confirmed by the earliest letter mentioning the painting, written by Msgr. Olivier Maurault to the artist, where the author refers to *Day's End* as "your 'quarry bed' with the rope ladder and blue smoke".[10]

Apparently, then, the subject of the painting is a descent into the bowels of the mountain (the ladder is not, here, a symbol of ascension) aimed at discovering its secret. Possibly, the bluish smoke arises from incense burning on the altar of science, but it is also a line "curling randomly against the damp, absorbent rock" and, as such, an artistic tribute to the achievements of researchers.

F.-M. G.

1 Letter from G. Lanctôt to Ozias Leduc, November 28, 1927, BNQ 327/6/9.

2 Draft of a letter from Ozias Leduc to Gustave Lanctôt, December 1, 1927, BNQ 327/8/33.

3 For example, R[odolphe] de R[epentigny], "Propos et impressions de Riopelle", *La Presse* [Montreal], May 28, 1955, p. 74, reporting comments by Riopelle.

4 BNQ 327/3/3.

5 Ozias Leduc, "L'histoire de S.-Hilaire – On l'entend, on la voit", *Arts et pensée*, vol. 3, no. 18 (July-August, 1954), p. 167.

6 Louise Beaudry, *Contemplative Scenes: The Landscapes of Ozias Leduc*, exhib. cat. (Montreal: Montreal Museum of Fine Arts, 1986), pp. 26-31.

7 Undated eleven-page manuscript, Archives du Séminaire de Saint-Hyacinthe.

8 Dr. L. D. Mignault, "La Grotte des Fées", *The Canadian Antiquarian and Numismatic Journal*, vol. 10, no. 2 (October 1881), pp. 58-60.

9 Guy Perrault and J. A. Mandarino, "The Monteregian Hills: Mineralogy of Mount St. Hilaire", *International Geological Congress*, Twenty-fourth Session, Ottawa, 1972, pp. 1-12.

10 Olivier Maurault to Ozias Leduc, December 13, 1920, BNQ 327/6/5.

145

Study for *Grey Effect (Snow)*

1914

Charcoal on paper

48.5 x 37.2 cm

Signed lower right: *Ozias Leduc*

Quebec City, Musée du Québec, inv. 86.39

PROVENANCE

Studio of the artist; Mr. Hudon, 1953; Galerie l'Art canadien, Chicoutimi, 1959; Réal d'Anjou, Sillery; Musée du Québec, 1986

146

Grey Effect (Snow)

1914

Oil on canvas

47.2 x 36.6 cm

Signed and dated lower right: *O LEDUC 1914*

Quebec City, Musée de la civilisation, on deposit from the Séminaire de Québec, inv. 1991.177

INSCRIPTIONS

Verso: *effet gris (neige); from Musée du Séminaire de Qué RO. 695-12-73; The National Gallery of Canada Galerie Nationale du Canada Title of Exhibition Titre de l'exposition: O. Leduc Catalogue no. N. de catalogue: 34 Bos no. N. de la caisse: 10; Art Association of Montreal ?; "68"; tue effel jus xrey; Canadian...... fine arts department*; labels: *Exhibition of Picture given by Canadian Artist ... in aid of the Patriotic Fund under the auspices of the Royal Canadian A.; 7 5* (in a circle); *"2"; Canadian Artists Patriotic Fund exhibition -1915; 725 SME; Ozias Leduc exh Leduc: Poudrerie (St-Hilaire) Paysage d'hiver*

PROVENANCE

Ceded by the artist to the Comité de secours national de France at the request of the Royal Canadian Academy of Arts; Msgr. Walter Cannon, Quebec City, 1914; Séminaire de Québec, Quebec City, 1960; Musée de l'Amérique française, Quebec City, 1991; Musée de la civilisation, 1995

"BY giving the commonplace higher meaning – the familiar an enigmatic look, the known the prestige of the unknown, the finite the appearance of the infinite – I make it Romantic."[1] It was through words that the poet Novalis (1772-1801) effected the transmutation of the familiar into the romantic; Leduc, for his part, used the materials of pictorial representation to invest the landscapes of his surroundings with a symbolic dimension. The intimism of *Grey Effect (Snow)* has its source in the continuation of the fir trees outside the pictorial frame and in the breadth of the rising curve of the trees and the small hill, which creates an effect of monumentality. This structure is countered by the work's relatively small size, by the simultaneous impressions of concavity and convexity that mould the snowy surface in the centre, by the subtle modulations of grey and by the varied brushwork, which, clearly yet subtly, distinguishes the different areas and features and produces the delicate physical charm that can only be felt in the presence of the painting itself. *Grey Effect (Snow)* is a fine example of the subjective, Symbolist approach typical of Leduc's landscapes.

The charcoal preparatory sketch and the oil painting are remarkably similar. Aside from using the same composition and format (give or take a centimetre), Leduc has in both cases employed a different treatment for the three areas forming the sky, trees and snow. In the painting, the sky is rendered by small strokes of a slightly greenish blue-grey colour, between which we catch glimpses of the brownish sizing. The snowy area is created by longer, more flowing strokes in a slightly yellower grey than the sky. Here, the paint layer completely covers the ground except near the horizon line and around the branches. The trees themselves are built up in even longer brush strokes of brown, green and blue-grey, with heavier impasto in the lighter areas. The subtlety of the greys, tinged as they are with blues, yellows and greens, is quite extraordinary and translates Leduc's ideas to perfection. As he said, "Colour is everything in the painter's work. This colour is not light but changes with the light ... For the painter, daylight means colour, like the seasons or climates."[2]

The charcoal drawing is also the result of three different treatments. The sky is a combination of scumbling and lines that creates a quite pronounced texture, like that of the same section in the oil painting. The snow is rendered for the most part by a light scumble whose darkness is varied to represent the areas of light and shadow, although towards the base of the drawing a few lines overlay the rubbed charcoal. In the very dark trees, composed of heavily smudged charcoal strokes with more definite lines here and there, there is considerable accumulation of the medium – except, naturally, in the lighter areas – which is opposite to the painting, where the paint layer gets thicker as the colour gets paler. In spite of these similarities of format, composition and treatment, however, the overall feeling created by the two works is not exactly the same. The effects of concavity and convexity produced by the paint layer in the oil are absent from the charcoal. In the drawing, the horizon and contours are rendered by a line, although a smudged one. The various areas of the composition are thus more clearly defined than in the painting, where the visibility of the primed surface of the canvas in both the sky and the transition areas between the elements results in a less marked separation between the different planes.

At the start of the First World War, Leduc submitted *Grey Effect (Snow)* to an exhibition organized by the Patriotic Fund. Several contemporary critics remarked on the large number of winter landscapes among the works presented, including those by Maurice Cullen, Suzor-Coté, Tom Thomson (1877-1917), A. Y. Jackson (1882-1974), Clarence Gagnon and Lawren Harris (1885-1970). The reviewer for *La Presse* made particular mention of the painting entitled *Grey Effect (Snow)*, "one of the most interesting in the exhibition", in which he saw signs of "a highly original talent, a new and very keen vision, a great artistic sense".[3] And he went on to make an extremely revealing remark, sociologically speaking, about the significant part played by an artist's strategic and geographical position in his recognition by the art world: "There is no doubt that if this artist was working in a major centre and had the society of other talented artists to stimulate and encourage him, he would soon take his place among the great painters of Canada."

This anonymous journalist, probably Albert Laberge,[4] continued his defence of Leduc again a week or so later, writing, again in *La Presse*, about the opening of the Art Association's Spring

145

146

Exhibition. He referred to Ozias Leduc's contribution, *Green Apples* (cat. 148), as being "the most beautiful" and "one of the most remarkable" in the show, placing Leduc "in the very first rank of Canadian painters".[5] It seems, then, that while Leduc was already well known for his religious works, portraits and still lifes, his new landscapes, more Symbolist in nature, were attracting a different set of enthusiasts. The journalist with *La Presse* went on to recommend the inclusion of *Green Apples* in "the national collection in Ottawa", and this actually occurred a few months later. This was the first of Leduc's works to be acquired by the National Gallery.

E. T.

1 Novalis, "Logologische Fragmente II", in *Das Philosophische Werk I* (1798).

2 Ozias Leduc, "Dires sur le symbolisme", quoted in Janice Seline, "The Real and the Ideal: Progress in the Landscapes of Ozias Leduc", in Laurier Lacroix *et al.*, *Ozias Leduc the Draughtsman*, exhib. cat. (Montreal: Concordia University, 1978), p. 113. In discussing *Grey Effect (Snow)*, Laurier Lacroix has also pointed out, "Snow is not white in Leduc's work, it is golden (1916), mauve (1921) or grey" (*ibid.*, p. 47).

3 "Remarquable exposition de tableaux", *La Presse* [Montreal], March 16, 1915, p. 3. Leduc was also briefly mentioned in *Le Devoir*, sandwiched between Gagnon and Jackson: "from Clarence A. Gagnon a pretty snow scene, a beautiful morning sun, and then a subtly grey snowscape from O. Leduc, and another highly colourful and energetically painted one by A. Y. Jackson" (Henri Fabien, "À la galerie des beaux-arts – L'exposition d'œuvres canadiennes données au profit du fonds patriotique", *Le Devoir* [Montreal], April 3, 1915, p. 5).

4 Starting in 1907, Albert Laberge, a sports writer with *La Presse* from 1896 until his retirement in 1932, began to occasionally serve as the paper's art and literature critic. See Paul Wyczynski's critical edition of Albert Laberge, *La Scouine* (Montreal: Les presses de l'Université de Montréal, 1986), p. 17.

    Although the articles quoted here are not signed, the style and the generous use of superlatives indicate that they were probably by Laberge. See Esther Trépanier, "Deux portraits de la critique d'art des années vingt. Albert Laberge et Jean Chauvin", *The Journal of Canadian Art History*, vol. 12, no. 2 (1989), pp. 141-173.

5 "Ouverture de l'exposition de peintures et de sculptures", *La Presse* [Montreal], March 27, 1915, p. 30.

147
Judith

About 1914

Oil on cardboard

21.2 x 27.4 cm

Signed lower left: *Ozias Leduc*

Quebec City, Musée du Québec, inv. 78.49

PROVENANCE

Studio of the artist; Gilles Corbeil, Montreal, 1951;
Paul Audette, Chicoutimi; Galerie d'art Charles-
Huot, Quebec City; Musée du Québec, 1978

As an interpretation of the theme of Judith, this painting breaks sharply with tradition. Here are none of the attributes normally employed to distinguish the central character from Salome – no bloodied head, maidservant or sack. Instead, an almost androgynous figure with closed eyes, completely enveloped in a cloak, seems to be meditating on a sword held with the point turned towards her. Nevertheless, it is an interpretation that succeeds in being both extremely faithful to the spirit of the Bible story and entirely in tune with the modern Symbolist formulation of a religious theme as understood by Maurice Denis.

In retelling the story of Judith, tradition has generally concentrated on its most violent episode, the one most likely to stir the imagination: the decapitation of Holofernes, general of the army of Nebuchadnezzar, an Assyrian king who had resolved to "cover all the face of the earth" and force all nations and tribes to "call upon him as god" (Judith 2:19, 3:8). In spite of the heroine's chastity,[1] the general's beheading was the part of the story most likely to trouble the masculine imagination, for it recounts the ruthless vanquishing of male military power by feminine seduction. Although

sanctioned by divine will, this threat from Woman is invariably emphasized by the presence of the severed head, which appears even more often than the sword. Some artists have gone so far as to portray the moment of decapitation itself – Johan Liss (1570-1629) (about 1629-1630, National Gallery, London), for example, and Artemisia Gentileschi (1597-1651) (about 1620, Uffizi Gallery).

During the nineteenth century, the Symbolist sensibility gave rise to a number of representations of Judith and Salome that deviate from the biblical accounts and offer a series of fantasy-based visions that fall into the category of the femme fatale – that threat to a man's psychological and physical well-being.[2] Notable among these is Gustave Moreau's (1826-1898) version of Salome, whose erotic perversity served as the basis for later literary renderings by J.-K. Huysmans (1848-1907) and Oscar Wilde (1854-1900). The Judith theme, too, has often been associated with the evils of female sexuality, and this has occasionally led to confusion between the two characters; for example, Gustave Klimt's (1862-1918) painting *Judith I* (1901, Österreichische Galerie, Vienna) is often referred to and catalogued as a Salome,

despite the inscription of its title, *Judith und Holofernes*, on the original frame.[3]

Ozias Leduc's painting breaks entirely with Symbolism's literary and erotic version. The figure of Judith is shown in profile, without any of the attributes of seduction, and both the body and hands are entirely covered by a cloak or coat that allows no glimpse of the great beauty referred to in the Book of Judith. The picture's seductiveness resides in the paint itself and in the luminosity of the reds and yellows of the coat, which are reflected in the face and provide a contrast with the blues, greens and coppery browns of the background landscape. Apart from the sword, there is not a single anecdotal detail to distract our attention from the central figure, which, in a close-up, intimist composition, virtually fills the pictorial space. Though the painting contains none of the elements usually found in traditional accounts, this Judith still strikes us as an extremely faithful reflection of the heroine described in the Apocrypha. In the original story, Judith's beauty is simply a tool that enables her to mete out divine vengeance. This blameless widow's predominant qualities, those for which she is known and respected within her community, are wisdom and piety.[4] It is these virtues that give her the right to reprimand Ozias and the governors of the city of Bethulia. They, under pressure from a population starving under the siege imposed by Holofernes' army, have decided to call upon God to come to their aid within five days; if he fails to comply, they will surrender the city and thus allow the enemy to pillage the sanctuary. Judith reproaches them for provoking God and for attempting to "comprehend his purpose", for, she says, "God is not as a man, that he may be threatened" (Judith 8:14, 16). She offers to intervene and, having won the consent of the governors, prays to God at some length.

Behold their pride, and send thy wrath upon their heads; give into mine hand, which am a widow, the power that I have conceived. Smite by the deceit of my lips the servant with the prince, and the prince with the servant: break down their stateliness by the hand of a woman. For thy power standeth not in multitude, nor thy might in strong men: for thou art a God of the afflicted, an helper of the oppressed, an upholder of the weak, a protector of the forlorn, a saviour of them that are without hope. (Judith 9:9-11.)

After her prayer, Judith "rose where she had fallen down", "put off the garments of her widowhood", "washed her body all over", "anointed herself with precious ointment" and "decked herself bravely, to allure the eyes of all men that should see her" (Judith 10:2-4) and thus succeed in infiltrating the enemy camp.

While pictorial tradition has focussed on subsequent events recounted in the Book of Judith, Leduc has set his image during her prayer, before her transformation into a figure of seduction, at the moment when she expresses her profound faith in God but is simultaneously filled with the conviction that God's help must be made manifest in human action. Here is proof of Judith's great wisdom: she does not tempt God but conceives the plan that will allow his name to triumph.

Leduc, then, turns back to the fundamental, religious nature of the Judith character. From the formal point of view, his interpretation digresses slightly from the letter of the text, but only in order to express his profound understanding of the role of Symbolism in modern religious art, as outlined in the theories of Maurice Denis. In the Apocrypha, the passage concerning Judith's prayer relates that she "fell upon her face, and put ashes upon her head … and cried with a loud voice" to the Lord (Judith 9:1). Deliberately avoiding theatricality, Leduc has translated the act of prayer in a more meditative, introspective pose. Although the sword does appear as an allegorical element, it will be observed that it has been placed (frontally and shortened) so that it can also be read as a cross, thus transcending the religious framework of the Old Testament. Leduc takes us beyond the kind of allegorical painting denounced by Denis, who believed that Symbolist art should employ visual equivalents to suggest and represent, rather than reproduce.[5] Here, it is through the light, the close-up composition that encloses the figure within the total surface and the sword within the space created by the figure, the harmony of the lines, the diagonals of the head and the sword – in short, through the visual elements – that Leduc has created the intimate, spiritual atmosphere of the heroine's invocation. The artist offers a personal interpretation of the story of Judith that embodies a view of prayer as subjective and personal, but also an understanding of the process as leading necessarily to action. Leduc's *Judith* thus meets the criteria of Denis, who believed that the modern Symbolist artist who was also a Christian should work on our "most intimate core, and release from the mysteries of the inner life the unclouded figure of our faith. Thus, out of the religious experience of the artist, his personal experience, springs the work of art."[6]

E. T.

1　Judith's virtue is saved by Holofernes' drunkenness. She declares, "As the Lord liveth, who hath kept me in my way that I went, my countenance hath deceived him to his destruction, and yet hath he not committed sin with me, to defile and shame me" (Judith 13:16).

2　In certain cases, decapitation (of which representations featuring John the Baptist, Holofernes and Orpheus abound in Symbolism) is openly associated with castration. In Julius Klinger's *Salome*, for example, she holds not a head, but a bloodied penis (1909, coloured zincograph, Galerie Michel Pabst, Munich).

3　This is also true of Klimt's *Judith II* (1909, Venice, Galleria d'Arte Moderna), which is frequently presented under the title *Salome*. See Gottfried Fliedl, *Gustave Klimt* (Cologne: Benedikt Taschen, 1990), p. 140. The association of the character of Judith with female cruelty also appears in Goya (1746-1828), who exhibited a *Judith* (1821-1822, Prado Museum) on the ground floor of the Quinta del Sordo as a pendant to *Saturn Devouring His Sons*. See William Vaughan, *Romantic Art* (London: Thames and Hudson, 1978), p. 98.

4　Ozias says to Judith: "For this is not the first day wherein thy wisdom is manifested; but from the beginning of thy days all the people have known thy understanding, because the disposition of thine heart is good" (Judith 8:29.)

5　Maurice Denis, "Le symbolisme et l'art religieux moderne", in *Nouvelles théories sur l'art moderne, sur l'art sacré 1914-1921* (Paris: L. Rouart et J. Watelin, 1922), pp. 175-176.

6　*Ibid.*, p. 190.

148
Green Apples
1914-1915

Oil on canvas

63.3 x 94.4 cm

Signed and dated lower left: O LEDUC 1914-15

Ottawa, The National Gallery of Canada, inv. 1154

PROVENANCE

Studio of the artist; National Gallery of Canada, purchased from Canadian National Exhibition, 1915

No. 219, "Green Apples", by O. Leduc, is probably the most beautiful painting in the Salon. It is a poem of beauty, harmony, grace and colour. The laden branches bend under the weight of the fruit to form garlands. Between the branches, the sun casts lovely tones of light and shadow. It is as charming a canvas as could possibly be. The visitor pauses in admiration and moves on reluctantly, only to return again. It is one of the most remarkable paintings hanging in the galleries of the Art Association and puts Mr. Leduc in the very first rank of Canadian painters. This canvas is worthy of the national collection in Ottawa, and the government should acquire it without delay.[1]

An anonymous critic, most likely Albert Laberge, wrote this assessment of Leduc's painting upon having viewed it at the Art Association of Montreal's Annual Spring Exhibition in 1915. This was the first time a painting by Leduc had received such extended public appreciation. It elicited praise in private as well. A. Y. Jackson, whom Laberge considered one of the best artists in Canada, responded to Green Apples with admiration. "If that man were part of a group of painters that could stimulate him and force him to produce", Jackson said enthusiastically, "he would be the foremost among us, for he has originality and is a marvellous colourist."[2] To another individual, he asserted that Green Apples was "the most interesting thing in the show".[3] Laberge's suggestion that the National Gallery of Canada purchase the work did not go unheeded: Green Apples entered that institution's collection that same year (but only after being exhibited a second time, at the Canadian National Exhibition in Toronto).[4] It was the National Gallery's first acquisition of a painting by Leduc.

Green Apples has met with a variety of responses throughout its long history of public exposure. Most recent commentary has focussed on its iconography, interpreting it in terms of specifically Christian connotations, be it the idea of "Man's progress towards God",[5] the Gates of Paradise[6] or the Temptation in the Garden of Eden.[7] However, the work exerted a subtler attraction on the critics who first wrote about it. According to Laberge, the viewer is lured not by the "gate" of apple branches per se, but by the work's beauty as effected through its gentle tones and graceful forms. For Robert de Roquebrune (cat. 155), Green Apples demonstrated Leduc's "decorative mastery", and was the product of a desire not for religious exposition but to idealize nature in keeping with a "dream."[8] Like Jackson, he signalled it as an "original", a sentiment shared by painter-critic Wyly Grier (1862-1957), who praised the painting's "distinctive and almost unique character".[9]

But whatever the response it elicits, the painting has a stunning effect. A pink-orange field is framed by a rhythmically lyrical arrangement of lines and forms. Viewed in close-up as if from beneath an apple tree, the branches laden with leaves and fruit are set against the dusky sky suffused with the expiring rays of daylight. The boughs extend in a gentle arch across the top of the picture, then cascade in three streams down the surface left, centre and right, curving in graceful counterpoint. The repetition of the apples' circular forms is enhanced through the black lines that insistently circumscribe them. Far beyond, the sky is softly modulated through the spectrum, the luminous yellow descending into orange, then pink, then violet and finally blue as it enshrouds the distant, barely perceptible orchard in darkness.

This painting, which introduced Leduc to the larger Canadian public, has continued to fascinate a wide range of viewers. So, notwithstanding Grier's 1915 quip that Green Apples would not "arrest for a moment the peregrinating philistine",[10] time has indicated that all who wander by are captivated by this image.

A. G.

1 "Ouverture de l'exposition de peintures et de sculptures", La Presse [Montreal], March 27, 1915, p. 30.

2 Jackson's commentary was related by Laberge to Leduc in a letter [after 23 March 1916], BNQ 327/6/1.

3 Letter from Jackson to Dr. MacCallum [postmarked July 1, 1915], National Gallery of Canada, MacCallum Papers/1.71 -MacCallum.

4 According to Gabrielle Messier, Leduc often voiced his wonderment at why the National Gallery waited until the painting's second exhibition before they committed themselves to buying it (Inventory of Leduc's Works Compiled by Messier, BNQ 327/9/29).

5 Louise Beaudry, Contemplative Scenes: The Landscapes of Ozias Leduc, exhib. cat. (Montreal: Montreal Museum of Fine Arts, 1986), p. 34. Beaudry's interpretation in part was based on the unusual viewpoint whereby the spectator, positioned under a tree as it were, is confronted with a "barrier" of branches.

6 Henry Lehmann, "Contrast in Values: Ozias Leduc and Freda Bain at McCord", The Montreal Star, October 5, 1974, p. D-9: "Now the guiding light of his earlier paintings bursts forth with hallucinatory force. Green Apples could just as well be the gates of St. Peter."

7 See Hervé Biron, "Le chant du cygne d'Ozias Leduc", Le Mauricien médical, vol. 4, no. 2 (1964), pp. 49-64, who notes that the apples in the scene of the Temptation (fig. 82) in the decoration of Notre-Dame-de-la-Présentation, Shawinigan-Sud, recall those of Green Apples.

8 Robert de Roquebrune, "L'exposition Leduc", L'Action [Montreal], February 19, 1916, p. 1.

9 E. Wyly Grier, "Canada National Gallery and Its Recent Purchases", Christian Science Monitor [Boston], November 17, 1915.

10 Ibid.

149

The Concrete Bridge

1915

Oil on canvas

50.8 x 34.8 cm

Signed and dated lower right: *O LEDUC 1915*

The Montreal Museum of Fine Arts, gift of
Mr. and Mrs. Maurice Corbeil, inv. 1991.10

INSCRIPTIONS

Verso, labels: *1915 Royal Canadian Academy
Montreal Exhibition Title: The … Bridge; Le pont de
béton Collection particulière Bibliothèque S. Sulpice,
Montréal fév-mars 1916; La Société des artistes de
Québec 1916 Exposition Annuelle Annual Exhibition;
Title: Le pont de béton; no 382 1916 Canadian
National Exhibition Toronto Fine Arts Department*

PROVENANCE

Studio of the artist; Édouard Barcelo, Saint-
Hilaire; Louis-Joseph Barcelo, Montreal, 1954;
Mr. and Mrs. Maurice Corbeil, Montreal, about
1960; Montreal Museum of Fine Arts, 1991

AN imposing bridge, looming
through the deep shadows of the
departing night, arches across a creek.
The pervasive blue tonalities, ponder-
ously dark at the bottom, become lighter
as the bridge soars to almost touch the
top of the picture. The arch, one of its
edges streaked with the light of dawn,
allows a view to a distant landscape and
clouded sky.

The Concrete Bridge, with a man-made
structure as its primary focus, is somewhat of an anomaly among the artist's
painted landscapes of this period in
which he generally preferred an idealized
vision of transient nature. There is no
commentary from the artist himself as to
the intended meaning of the painting,
but the monumentality of the bridge relative to the disproportionately small
stream it spans, combined with its construction of concrete – material of
modern technology – suggests that
Leduc has treated it as a symbol of the
advent of modernity. Yet, his ambiva-
lence towards change is evident in his
decision to depict a conventional arch
bridge.

By portraying this subject matter,
Leduc tentatively tested the waters of
modernism. And it is perhaps this aspect
in part that caught the attention of
Roquebrune (cat. 155) who, in his critique of the painting, tried to promote
the work – and its
appreciation by the
Montreal public – as an
impetus for what he
understood to be cul-
tural progress.[1] "The
small canvas from the
most recent Salon
represents nothing,
pictorially, but a viaduct
in the gathering night,"
he proposed. "But a
night charged with
mystery, shimmering
and rustling, where the
great span of a bridge
assumes the appearance
of a triumphal arch
awaiting the sun's
rays."[2] Leduc's massive
bridge, it seems, points
but to the future.

Ironically, the tonal,
atmospheric treatment
that served to idealize
the bridge and, by
extension, helped to
underline the romanti-
cism of the notion of a
triumphal arch and its
connotations of "prog-
ress", is of an aesthetic
planted on the firm
ground of tradition. It
is no doubt for this
reason that some con-
temporary commentators recognized
Leduc as a traditionalist.[3] Indeed, the
painter, while looking through the arch
of the bridge to the future, still stands on
the banks of the past.

A. G.

---

1 The notion of cultural progress as it relates to issues of
modernism and nationalism, particulary in the context
of Roquebrune's critique (Robert de Roquebrune,
"L'exposition Leduc", *L'Action* [Montreal], February 19,
1916, p. 1) is discussed in depth in Arlene Gehmacher,
"The Mythologization of Ozias Leduc", Ph.D. dissertation, University of Toronto, April 1995, pp. 79-122.

2 Roquebrune 1916. Roquebrune had lauded the work
earlier, on the occasion of the Royal Canadian
Academy exhibition in 1915, referring to it as a "marvellous canvas" and expressing his dismay that it could be
surrounded by such "miserable attempts". (Letter from
Roquebrune to Ozias Leduc, November 29, 1915,
BNQ 327/5/25.)

3 See Émile Vézina, "Notes d'art – L'exposition Leduc",
Le Devoir [Montreal], February 21, 1916, p. 1, whose
assessment was to the point: "He is a traditionalist."
The comments that artist John Johnstone made on the
occasion of the 1915 RCA exhibition, related to Leduc
by J. E. Wilfrid Lecours (cat. 158), do not allow for such
a straightforward interpretation: "It is one of the exhibition's gems, by a fellow named Leduc, who last year
exhibited a remarkable canvas – 'Apples' [cat. 148],
which was purchased by the government. The Jury
member whom I know would also have bought the
'Bridge', but they like to spread their patronage around.
He also added this: I am surprised no one has yet
bought Mr. Leduc's canvas." (Letter from Lecours to
O.L., December 14, 1915, BNQ 327/5/25.)

150

Autumn Landscape

1915

Oil on canvas

50.8 x 66.7 cm

Signed and dated lower left: *O LEDUC 1915*

Private collection

PROVENANCE

Studio of the artist; Louis-Joseph Barcelo, Montreal; private collection

151

Autumn Landscape

About 1915

Oil on cardboard

12.8 x 20.4 cm

Signed lower left: *OZIAS LEDUC*

Dr. and Mrs. Byrne Harper collection

INSCRIPTIONS

Verso: *Automn scene; 2055; 45887*

PROVENANCE

Studio of the artist; [Olivier Maurault?]; Jean Désy, Boucherville; Dominion Gallery, Montreal; Atara and Murray Marmor, Montreal; Waddington & Gorce Gallery, Montreal; Dr. and Mrs. Byrne Harper

150

151

THE larger of these two autumn landscapes portraying Hertel Lake was exhibited for the first time at the Bibliothèque Saint-Sulpice in 1916. Albert Laberge included it in a list of landscapes that are, according to him, veritable "poems". "They are the impressions of a poet," he wrote, "a great poet."[1] Émile Vézina, for his part, saw in these works "analogical harmonies of profound richness and delightful lustre".[2]

The smaller of the two autumn scenes was acquired by Ambassador Jean Désy, a fact he mentioned in a letter to Jean Chauvin, which the latter quoted on October 18, 1955, to Alan Jarvis, director of the National Gallery of Canada: "As you probably know, I have two [paintings] at the Embassy. One is an autumn landscape of Belœil, and the other represents Saint-Isidore, in the painter's garden."[3] But Msgr. Maurault apparently had the work in his possession long before this. In a letter to the artist dated January 5, 1921, he accused himself of "having done a bad thing" in depriving Leduc of his small pictures, especially his sketch of Hertel Lake".[4] Since he calls

the work a sketch, it is probable that Maurault was referring to the small painting belonging to Désy. In 1938, Maurault knew that "the Saint-Hilaire Lake" was already "in the hands of Mr. Jean Désy". Perhaps he served as intermediary between the painter and the ambassador?

As Maurault had accurately divined, the real subject of these autumn landscapes is Hertel Lake, which is mentioned in Leduc's famous essay, "L'histoire de S.-Hilaire – On l'entend, on la voit". The artist describes it as a

large reservoir of crystalline water, a dazzling mirror beneath the sky's sun, but fathomless in the dark of night ... We are still in the area levelled by the thrust of the Mountain through the sediments that formed at the bottom of the great sea of bygone days.

Here is the road leading up to the lake, which takes us in and out of the region. Here is Sugarloaf Trail, Cedar Wood Road and Lime Kilns Road, and the lakeside track all blooming with red and yellow.[5]

Leduc defines Hertel Lake as a "mirror" and a "fathomless" pool, depending on whether it is seen during the day or at night. Both these paintings are day views, and as a result the reflection in the water plays an important role. It reproduces the sinuous line of the treetops and some of the mountain's magnitude. But, like the cooking pot in *Still Life, Onions* (cat. 16), the lake is a mirror that distorts, allowing the painter even greater freedom in his treatment of the foliage. This was what Laberge had sensed in speaking of "impressions", if not impressionism, in these paintings, with their highly evident brush stroke. Leduc's brush actually follows the light's track from left to right, recording the least projection of leaves and the least undulation of terrain.

The depth of the lake is suggested by the verticality of the image in the water. This is particularly noticeable in the larger work, where the curve of the bank is lost in the reflection of the trees, which descends like a curtain.

F.-M. G.

---

1 A[lbert] Laberge, "L'œuvre d'un artiste", *L'Autorité* [Montreal], March 11, 1916, p. 2.

2 Émile Vézina, "Notes d'art – L'exposition Leduc", *Le Devoir* [Montreal], February 21, 1916, p. 1.

3 National Gallery of Canada, J.-R. Ostiguy papers.

4 Letter from Olivier Maurault to Ozias Leduc, January 5, 1921, BNQ 327/6/6.

5 Ozias Leduc, "L'histoire de S.-Hilaire – On l'entend, on la voit", *Arts et pensée*, vol. 3, no. 18 (July-August, 1954), p. 166.

152

Golden Snow

1916

Oil on canvas

137.8 x 77.2 cm

Signed and dated lower right: *O. LEDUC 1916*

Ottawa, The National Gallery of Canada, inv. 1368

PROVENANCE

Studio of the artist; National Gallery of Canada, purchased from Royal Canadian Academy exhibition, 1916

THE sweeping southwest slope of Mount Saint-Hilaire, culminating in a rocky summit, provided a magnificent natural backdrop to Leduc's home and studio. Between 1915 and the end of the decade, Leduc made at least three renditions of the motif: the charcoal drawing *Sugarloaf* (fig. 51),[1] a bookplate design (cat. 172) and *Golden Snow*.

Although the melting snow depicted would seem to indicate a winter or spring thaw, the painting's essence is more evocative than temporal. In fact, Leduc actually painted it in his studio in September,[2] and there are various accounts describing the scene's evolution from a mountainside in autumn splendour to a slope awash in a snowy river of gold.[3]

Golden Snow gives a full view of the wooded mountainside, with the crowning sugarloaf threatening to push beyond the top of the canvas. The painting's two focuses – the lower flank of the mountain and the rocky summit – resolve into one image through a kind of dual perspective. The immediate foreground is

Fig. 51   Ozias Leduc, *Sugarloaf*, 1915, charcoal on paper, 18.4 x 11.7 (private collection).

seen from an angle close to the ground, while in contrast, the gold-suffused middle area is seen from a higher vantage point. This double viewpoint tends to flatten the picture plane, and the rapid and disjunct visual transition from one area to the other pulls the viewer's attention towards both focuses at once.

The gilded winding patterns of the snow imbue this image with an inner pulsation driven by the force implicit in the landscape's perpetual evolutionary transformation,[4] thus creating a tension with the stillness conveyed by the flattened perspective. As Leduc portrays the mountain, it is both an imposing, static monolith and, paradoxically, a surging source of energy.

This dualism corresponds to the mountain's dual significance – religious as well as geological – in the region. During the nineteenth century, the mountain was a pilgrimage site: fourteen Stations of the Cross led to the summit, where a chapel stood surmounted by a thirty-metre cross.[5] In light of this, *Golden Snow* may perhaps be interpreted as a conceptual pilgrimage, a spiritual ascent to the sacred summit of the holy mountain, with any need for man-made shrines having been subsumed by the mountain itself.

Golden Snow held an important place in Leduc's career. Purchased by the National Gallery of Canada from the Royal Canadian Academy exhibition of 1916, after the artist had been voted an Associate Member, it thereafter received broad public exposure across Canada and internationally.[6] The painting came to represent Leduc's art and Canadian art in general, and its influence on his stature in the Canadian artistic community perhaps led Leduc to place *Golden Snow* at the top of his list of his best works.[7]

A. G.

---

1 The posthumously titled *Sugarloaf* is dated September 3, 1915. While its medium and dimensions might lead one to view it as a study for *Golden Snow*, a comparison of the two compositions reveals the drawing to be an independent work in the development of Leduc's sustained conceptualization of the local mountain as a spiritual and organic entity that came to fruition in *Golden Snow*.

2 Letter from Ozias Leduc to Eric Brown, Director of the National Gallery of Canada, April 25, 1917 (NGC Curatorial files).

3 See Jean Chauvin, *Ateliers: études sur vingt-deux peintres et sculpteurs canadiens* (Montreal and New York: Louis Carrier and Co., 1928), pp. 125-126, and Gilles Corbeil, "Ozias Leduc, peintre de natures mortes", *Arts et pensée*, vol. 3, no. 18 (July-August 1954), p. 171.

4 Leduc would play up this aspect in his written history of the region, "L'histoire de S.-Hilaire – On l'entend, on la voit", which he prepared for *Arts et pensée*, vol. 3, no. 18 (July-August 1954). And the illustration of *Golden Snow* adjacent to a passage in the text that refers to the mountain in such organic terms is perhaps not merely fortuitous.

5 See the engraving *Vue du Monument National et religieux érigé sur la montagne de St-Hilaire de Rouville, (Canada)* (1841), reproduced in Mary Allodi, *Printmaking in Canada: The Earliest Views and Portraits*, exhib. cat. (Toronto: Royal Ontario Museum, 1980), p. 150. The cross was erected in the autumn of 1841 on the initiative of Msgr. Forbin-Janson, Bishop of Nancy, whom the French-Canadian clerical elite esteemed for his role in renewing religious fervour in French Canada. The cross toppled in 1846, but the chapel remained until 1877, when it was destroyed by fire. See N.-E. Dionne, *Mgr de Forbin-Janson. Sa vie – son œuvre en Canada* (Quebec City: Léger Brousseau, 1895), and Frs-X. Coté, "Mgr de Forbin-Janson, évêque de Nancy et de Toul, et le mouvement religieux du Québec vers 1840", in *Documents maskoutains*, No. 16 (Saint-Hyacinthe: Société d'histoire régionale de Saint-Hyacinthe, 1943), pp. 25-48. The local citizenry perpetuated the history of the cross and chapel well into the twentieth century. See the letter from Guillaume Lahaise to Ozias Leduc, October 1, 1916, BNQ 327/6/1; É.-Z. Massicotte, "La Croix du mont St-Hilaire", *La Vérité* [Montreal], July 26, 1928; and the letter from Ozias Leduc to Armand Cardinal, March 19, 1951, Centre d'archives du Séminaire de Saint-Hyacinthe, Fp 12, Doss. 39.

6 Also, a reproduction of *Golden Snow* was featured in an article on the RCA's 1916 exhibition: H. Mortimer-Lamb, "The Thirty-eighth Exhibition of the Royal Canadian Academy of Arts", *International Studio*, vol. 61 (June 1917), p. 31. One reader in New York was prompted to write to Leduc to inquire whether any of his works were on exhibition in the city ([signature illegible] to Ozias Leduc, March 22, 1917, BNQ 327/6/2).

7 The list was drawn up by Leduc at the request of Mackenzie Waters, Chairman of the Fine Arts Committee for the Canadian National Exhibition (letter from Ozias Leduc to Mackenzie Waters, [July 9, 1948], BNQ 327/9/11).

153

Afterglow

1916

Graphite on white wove paper

13.7 x 12.1 cm

Signed and dated lower right: *O LEDUC 27 FEV. 1916*

Private collection

INSCRIPTIONS

Recto lower left: *LUEURS DU SOIR*

PROVENANCE

Studio of the artist; Guillaume Lahaise, 1916; private collection

THE aesthetic empathy between Leduc and his friend the Symbolist poet Guy Delahaye (pseudonym of Guillaume Lahaise), to whom the artist had paid tribute in two portraits (cats. 138-139, fig. 49), is demonstrated by the content and history of this drawing and the related oil of the same title (fig. 52). Both versions present a shimmering vision of a snowbank viewed up close, its lower area veiled in shadow, its crest aglow with a bright, warm light. The structure is ambiguous; despite bulrushes that offer a spatial anchor and the crevice in the centre that suggests a route for visual progression into depth, the eye remains drawn to the surface. This planar effect is sustained through the rhythmic striations of graphite or paint, applied evenly and consistently in repetition, creating in the lower centre a swirling arabesque that is suspended in time and space. The pale glow of the dying midwinter day, along with the semicircle of dried bulrushes (hardy and ancient perennials that they are), point to a new day and a new season in the endless cycles of life.

The meaning of such an ethereal painting was lost on the uninitiated. As one baffled critic was driven to confess, "I could not, even with the best of intentions, understand *Afterglow*. A longer legend at the bottom of this painting is needed in order to know what the artist was attempting to portray. It is all rather mysterious impressionism."[1] Friends and acquaintances like Robert de Roquebrune (cat. 155) and Albert Laberge, on the other hand, gave their private assent to the work, lauding its beauty without feeling the need to assert a critical justification.[2]

Perhaps Leduc realized that only a fellow Symbolist could appreciate the work at that time. Thus, it was to his kindred spirit Delahaye, then on an extended stay in California and with whom he had been exchanging correspondence about their artistic ventures, that Leduc sent the completed drawing of his latest Symbolist landscape.[3]

A. G.

Fig. 52   Ozias Leduc, *Afterglow*, 1916, oil on cardboard, 40 x 32.4 (whereabouts unknown).

1   Quoted in English in Jean-René Ostiguy, "The Paris Influence on Quebec Painters", *Canadian Collector*, vol. 13, no. 1 (January-February 1978), p. 53. Ostiguy cites as his source Samuel Kébek [pseudonym of Alonzo Cinq-Mars], "La culture de l'art: une très belle exposition de peintures a lieu actuellement à Québec sous les auspices de nos hommes d'État", *Bulletin des agriculteurs*, June 9, 1916. The periodical citation is incorrect; the article's actual place of publication at this point remains unknown. The title of the article indicates that Cinq-Mars made his acquaintance with *Afterglow* when it was exhibited at the Société des artistes de Québec, June 10-24, 1916, in Quebec City.

2   In a letter to Leduc, Roquebrune commented, "How can I express to you my enchantment? It is but light and atmosphere. It is almost immaterial. I am delighted with it, but many people do not understand it." ([April 1916] BNQ 327/6/1.) Laberge, after offering Leduc his "heartiest congratulations", judged it to be "truly a very beautiful thing" (letter from Laberge to Ozias Leduc [after March 23, 1916] BNQ 327/6/1).

3   Laurier Lacroix *et al.*, *Ozias Leduc the Draughtsman*, exhib. cat. (Montreal: Concordia University, 1978), p. 49. From the extant correspondence, one can deduce that Delahaye received the drawing between the time of his letter to Leduc dated June 15, 1916, and another dated October 1, 1916, in which he belatedly thanks the artist for the work, which he deems "very beautiful" (BNQ 327/6/1). One might assume that Leduc included his drawing with his letter dated July 4, 1916, which is cited in Robert Lahaise, *Guy Delahaye et la modernité littéraire*, (Montreal: Hurtubise/HMH, 1987) "Cahiers du Québec/Littérature" series, p. 184. The original of this letter has not been found.

154
Landscape (Mountain Road)

1916

Graphite and traces of charcoal on paper

14.3 x 16.5 cm

Signed lower right: *O. LEDUC*; dated lower left:
12 DEC 1916

Private collection

INSCRIPTIONS

Verso, label: Galerie l'Art français

PROVENANCE

Atara and Murray Marmor, Montreal; Waddington
& Gorce Gallery, Montreal; Galerie Jean-Pierre
Valentin, Montreal, 1994; private collection

I mean by a picture a beautiful, romantic dream of something that never was, never will be, in a light better than any that ever shone, in a land no one can define or remember – only desire." On the occasion of his election to the Royal Canadian Academy of Arts as Associate Member in November 1916, Leduc offered this quotation from the British Symbolist artist Edward Burne-Jones (1833-1898) as a reflection of his own aesthetic sensibility.[1] It is a statement that captures the essence of the drawing *Landscape* and, for that matter, any of Leduc's painted landscapes from the same period (cats. 143-144, 146, 148-149).

Although Leduc dated this *Landscape* specifically December 12, 1916, it indicates particularity of neither season nor place. An empty road meanders in front of a hillock and across the foreground, curving down into an area of spatial ambiguity, a neverland cloaked in semi-darkness yet graced by softly twinkling specks of light. A brighter, celestial light, cradled in the valley on the distant horizon, awaits the eye at the end of its journey.

Leduc's choice of medium has helped conjure up this ethereal dreamscape. The soft graphite provides a velvety texture enriched by gentle highlights created by erasure and white pencil. Several areas are lightly articulated with hatchings or outlines, but only enough to offer a sense of spatial progression without sacrificing the aura of timelessness achieved by the ambiguity of light and space.

Such imaginary landscapes are more typical of Leduc's later years. Yet, already by 1916, the artist was expressing his preference for the mystical seduction of a land of dreams.

A. G.

1   The statement was made to Margaret L. A. Fairbairn, art critic for the *Toronto Star*, who had requested from the artist biographical notes and a photograph of himself for inclusion in an article on recently elected RCA members. See the letter from Fairbairn to Ozias Leduc, November 28, 1916, BNQ 327/6/1, and M.L.A. F[airbairn], "Royal Canadian Academy Has Two New Associates", *Toronto Star Weekly*, December 30, 1916.

155

Portrait of Robert LaRoque de Roquebrune

About 1915-1916

Charcoal on paper

61 x 47.5 cm

Signed upper left: *OZS LEDUC*

Quebec City, Musée du Québec, inv. 53.112

INSCRIPTIONS

Verso: "*ROBERT LAROQUE DE ROQUE-BRUNE OZIAS LEDUC*"

PROVENANCE

Studio of the artist; Musée du Québec, 1953

156

Study for the *Portrait of Josée LaRoque de Roquebrune*

About 1915-1916

Charcoal on paper

64.3 x 43 cm

Signed lower right: *OZS. LEDUC*

Quebec City, Musée du Québec, inv. 56.36

PROVENANCE

Studio of the artist; Ozias Leduc estate; Galerie l'Art français, Montreal, 1956; Musée du Québec, 1956

I N the third volume of his autobiography, *Cherchant mes souvenirs (1911-1940)*,[1] Robert de Roquebrune tells of his many visits to Leduc's studio during the period between 1912 and 1918, when he and his wife Josée (née Angers) were living in Belœil. Roquebrune was often accompanied on these visits by people anxious to meet the artist; thus began Leduc's friendships with the Sulpician Abbé Olivier Maurault, director of the new Bibliothèque Saint-Sulpice (cats. 161-163), the pianist and music critic Léo-Pol Morin (cat. 160), the pharmacist J. E. Wilfrid Lecours (cat. 158) and his wife Louise (née Higgins) (cat. 157), the architect Fernand Préfontaine, the author Marcel Dugas, and Adrien and Henri Hébert, respectively painter and sculptor.[2] In fact, during this period Leduc's studio became for a time a meeting and discussion centre for a certain segment of Montreal's elite. In 1918, this same group of friends launched the art magazine *Le Nigog* (fig. 111) – for which Leduc designed the cover illustration – and the Roquebrunes and Léo-Pol

Morin even spent the summer of 1918 living in an outbuilding in Leduc's orchard.[3]

Leduc executed portraits of several members of this circle, and, as was usually the case, it was at his suggestion that the young Roquebrune couple sat for him; he decided to work in charcoal, so as to spare his models protracted posing sessions. Exceptionally, the artist does not seem to have used photographs in executing these portraits, the models being apparently free to come and pose in his studio.[4] The portrait of Josée was finished first and was exhibited in 1916 at the Royal Canadian Academy's annual exhibition in Montreal. The couple took the drawing to Paris, where it was stolen from their Auteuil apartment during the Second World War. The Musée du Québec possesses an undated charcoal (cat. 156) for which the model, although unidentified, was definitely Robert de Roquebrune's wife.[5] This is confirmed by a study of arms that appears in a sketchbook (cat. 73), executed in about 1915, and a photograph of the model taken around the same time.[6] This drawing, undoubtedly a preparatory sketch, gives an idea of the lost portrait of Josée, which Roquebrune liked enormously and of which he left this enthusiastic description:

> Leduc had succeeded admirably in capturing the charm of that little head, those pensive, smiling eyes, the high forehead framed by silky hair. It was the youth and intelligence of this exquisite woman, whom he had contemplated so attentively for hours, that were set down on the paper, in black and white. Behind, he had placed her piano, flowers and books. The aim of this was symbolic. The painter admired the wit and poetry that were Josée's very essence.[7]

According to Roquebrune, Leduc's lengthy concentration on Josée's features awoke in the artist a definite attraction towards his model.[8] But for a portrait executed from life to be successful, does the painter not have to be in some sense seduced by his model? And does the latter not have to submit confidently to the artist's gaze? Certainly, the pose adopted

by Josée is relaxed, calm and entirely tension-free. Leduc has rendered the face, arms, bodice and skirt in considerable detail, although he has left out the background decor Roquebrune describes in the final work. This lost portrait was considered by the journalist Albert Laberge to be the "jewel" of the Royal Academy exhibition.[9]

The portrait of Robert was begun at the same period, that is around 1915-1916, but when the Roquebrunes left for France in 1919, it was still not finished,[10] and it remained in the artist's possession until its purchase by the Musée du Québec in 1953. The model posed in the artist's studio; seated in the visitor's chair, he holds his walking stick up in front of him. A few books are sketched in behind his left arm – an allusion to his passion for literature. He is shown in three-quarter profile, in a three-quarter-length view. The combination of the linearity of the style and the impression of depth created by the armchair and the strong foreground element of the cane, together with the suggestion of a light source in the upper left-hand corner, make it a portrait of some realism.

In his Diary, Leduc indicated that this portrait is "in the pose of Boldini's *Montesquiou*",[11] and thus it embodies a reference to the French Symbolist movement. In fact, Leduc based his composition on the *Portrait of Robert de Montesquiou* painted in 1897 by Giovanni Boldini (1842-1931). This portrait was reproduced in the November 1905 issue of *Art et Décoration*, to which Leduc was a subscriber (fig. 53). The well-known dandy and eccentric Count Robert de Montesquiou-Fezensac (1855-1921) took part in the gatherings of Symbolist poets and artists. This atypical aristocrat, much admired as a poet among Parisian salons of the Belle Époque, served as inspiration to J.-K. Huysmans for the character of the noble Des Esseintes, the central figure of his novel *À rebours* (1884), and to Marcel Proust (1871-1922) for the Baron de Charlus, in *À la recherche du temps perdu* (1913-1927). Robert de Roquebrune no doubt identified with the flamboyant Montesquiou, for he enjoyed playing the

Fig. 53   Giovanni Boldini, *Portrait of Robert de Montesquiou*, 1897, oil on canvas, 116 x 82.5 cm (Paris, Musée d'Orsay).

aristocratic dandy. Indeed, in his autobiographical novels, he attempted to embroider his background, and it was for the same reason that, around the time he was paying regular visits to Leduc's studio, he added the name of the district of his Armagnac ancestors, Roquebrune, to his family name of LaRoque.[12] During his time in Belœil, Roquebrune was an avid reader, and he was familiar with Robert de Montesquiou's better-known works.[13] Is it possible that the pose of the portrait was the sitter's idea? It is easy to imagine that the aesthetic theories of the French Symbolist movement were a hot topic of conversation at the encounters in Leduc's studio among those recently back from Europe, as they must have been during meetings of *Le Nigog*'s publishers. This latter group, who described themselves as "specialists" addressing an "elite", were attempting to formulate a new aesthetic approach to French-Canadian art and literature and at the same time combat the prevailing regionalism.[14] In his writings, Roquebrune adopted a lofty tone reminiscent of the character of Des Esseintes, "dropping" the names of well-known and obscure writers alike, as if he were conducting a conversation in high society. In the same vein, he condemned a number of authors and artists out of hand, winning bitter reproach from the defenders of regionalism. In 1919, in Paris, Roquebrune actually met Robert de Montesquiou, by then old, poor and virtually forgotten; still, he remained for the Quebec writer the quintessential example of the decadent aesthete.

Without being a direct copy of its inspirational source, the pose adopted by Robert de Roquebrune is as stiff and unnatural as that of Robert de Montesquiou. His gaze is lost in the far distance, precluding all contact with the spectator. Moreover, the diagonal of the walking stick cutting across the drawing creates a physical and psychological barrier that isolates the model in a world of fiction.

M. L.

1 Robert de Roquebrune, *Cherchant mes souvenirs (1911-1940)* (Montreal: Fides, 1968).

2 The correspondence between Ozias Leduc and Robert de Roquebrune, in the Leduc Archive at the BNQ (327), tells us a good deal about their friendship and their various projects between 1915 and 1938.

3 Letter from Josée LaRoque de Roquebrune to Ozias Leduc [May 9, 1918], BNQ 327/6/3.

4 The story of the two portraits is recounted in Roquebrune 1968, pp. 77-78.

5 However, there is no mention of this drawing in Roquebrune 1968.

6 Reproduced in *Le Nigog* (Montreal: Fides, 1987), "Archives des lettres canadiennes", vol. 7, p. 45.

7 Roquebrune 1968, pp. 77-78.

8 *Ibid.*, pp. 78-81.

9 [Albert Laberge], "De remarquables toiles au Salon de nos peintres", *La Presse* [Montreal], November 18, 1916, p. 17.

10 Card from Olivier Maurault to Ozias Leduc, Monday [August 4, 1919], BNQ 327/6/4.

11 Ozias Leduc's Diary, August 30, 1953, BNQ 327/3/12.

12 Jean-Guy Hudon, "Robert de Roquebrune", in *Le Nigog* 1987, p. 90.

13 Remarks made by Robert de Roquebrune during *Feu vert*, a programme about Robert de Montesquiou broadcast on Radio-Canada on November 29, 1973. The transcripts of this radio series (AM network) are in the NAC, MG 30/D 229.

14 See *Le Nigog* 1987.

157
Madame Louise Lecours, née Higgins
1916

Bronze medallion

22 cm (diam.); 2.4 cm

Signed and dated lower right: *19 O LEDUC 16*

The Montreal Museum of Fine Arts, purchase, Arthur Lismer Fund, inv. 1989.14

INSCRIPTIONS

Around the edge of the medallion: *Mme LOUISE LECOURS née HIGGINS*

PROVENANCE

Studio of the artist; Louise Higgins-Lecours, Belœil, 1916; Jeanne Lecours-Laferrière, Quebec City, 1947; Louise Laferrière-Morissette, Quebec City, 1975; Montreal Museum of Fine Arts, 1989

158
Portrait of J. E. Wilfrid Lecours
1916

Pastel and charcoal on paper glued to cardboard

61.2 x 46.8 cm

Signed and dated centre right: *19 LEDUC 16*

Private collection

PROVENANCE

Studio of the artist; J. E. Wilfrid Lecours, Belœil, 1916; Jeanne Lecours-Laferrière, Quebec City, 1947; private collection, 1975

158

THE pharmacist Joseph Édouard Wilfrid Lecours (1868-1927) and his wife Louise, née Higgins (1872-1947), were first introduced to Leduc in the early 1910s by Robert LaRoque de Roquebrune (cat. 155).[1] Between 1908 and 1922, the Lecours had their permanent residence in Belœil.[2] Wilfrid Lecours, joint owner of the Lecours & Lanctôt drugstore at the southeast corner of Sainte-Catherine and Saint-Denis Streets in Montreal,[3] was also a professor in the pharmacy faculty of Laval University at Montreal, of which he was

a founding member. Lecours is said to have been a great art enthusiast and particularly fond of Leduc's work.[4] In order to promote national art, he founded an association of businessmen and academics who all agreed to purchase one painting per year by a French-Canadian artist.[5] Leduc executed several portraits for the Lecours family, including the pastel of Mr. Lecours (cat. 158) and two portraits of his wife: one charcoal,[6] and a plaster medallion dating from 1916 (private collection) that Lecours took to Paris shortly after it was made to have

three bronze copies cast. The Montreal Museum of Fine Arts' work (cat. 157) is one of these.[7] Leduc also executed portraits of the Lecours' two young daughters – Marie-Thérèse (1896-1984) and Jeanne (1897-1975) – when, at age eighteen, they made their debuts at Villa-Maria College.[8]

Madame Louise Lecours, née Higgins is one of the very few sculptures by Leduc.[9] The model is shown in profile, head turned to the left. According to John Pope-Hennessy, the profile pose is the one most directly linked to the earliest

Fig. 54   J. E. Wilfrid Lecours (private collection; photo: Dupras & Colas).

portrait forms, such as the images of emperors that adorn Roman coins, the benefactors that appear in Gothic altarpieces and the many Renaissance bas-reliefs depicting artists.[10] It must be added, however, that the profile tradition was revived by numerous artists during the nineteenth century. In Pope-Hennessy's view, the decorative component of these portraits takes precedence over naturalistic representation. In the case of the Montreal Museum relief, the model's name, written in a semicircle, is an integral part of the composition. The artist's signature and three shamrocks (a reference to Louise Higgins's Irish roots) complete the medallion's border. The loose treatment of the hair and clothing creates a sense of movement that offsets the rigidity of the pose.[11] Leduc employed a similar profile pose in his portraits of Guy Delahaye (cats. 138-139). The journalist Émile Vézina, according to whom "The 'medal' profile of the poet Guy Delahaye is very fine,"[12] was quick to notice the decorative and commemorative aspects of this type of portrait.

Leduc stuck remarkably close to the photograph (fig. 54) he used in executing his *Portrait of J. E. Wilfrid Lecours*. The model is shown full face, against an abstract background. As Max Friedländer has pointed out, the frontal pose lends itself best to a naturalistic portrait: "The psycho-physical being manifests itself more openly, more in the instantaneity of mood" than in a profile.[13] The drawing style is typical of Leduc's production from the 1910s: long, swiftly applied diagonal hatch strokes in black charcoal and green and coral pink pastel, covering the whole of the very lively surface. The various planes are clearly defined by a contour line, and the modelling of the sitter's face is rendered by contrasts of light and shade. Leduc portrays Lecours as a man of sophistication and confidence, not afraid to proclaim his prosperity and status. When Lecours died, the artist wrote: "He was a friend … who was faithful to the end. His face will remain in my memory for a long time."[14]

M. L.

1   Letter from Ozias Leduc to Robert LaRoque de Roquebrune [early January 1927], BNQ 327/8/33. Information about the Lecours family has been kindly provided by Florence Bindoff, Pauline Lemonde, Louise Morrissette and Luc Choquette. In addition, the extremely lively descriptions of evenings spent with the Lecours household in Robert de Roquebrune, *Cherchant mes souvenirs (1911-1940)* (Montreal: Fides, 1968), pp. 86-90, are well worth reading.

2   The Lecours named their house "L'Abitation". For more on the history and architecture of this house, see the following articles by André Laberge in *Cahiers d'histoire de la Société d'histoire de Belœil – Mont-Saint-Hilaire*: "Histoire de la maison Coupal (L'Abitation de Wilfrid Lecours)", no. 40 (February 1993), pp. 3-15; "Wilfrid Lecours, un pharmacien à Belœil au début du siècle", no. 41 (June 1993), pp. 27-38 and cover; and "L'Abitation de Wilfrid Lecours et le mouvement *Arts and Crafts* au Québec", no. 46 (February 1995), pp. 24-39.

3   The Lecours & Lanctôt drugstore appears in a painting by Adrien Hébert entitled *Sainte-Catherine Street* (1926); see Pierre L'Allier, *Adrien Hébert*, exhib. cat. (Quebec City: Musée du Québec, 1993), p. 133, ill. p. 41.

4   Lecours was a member of the Cercle artistique et littéraire, which met at L'Arche during the twenties. In 1916, during Leduc's exhibition at the Bibliothèque Saint-Sulpice, he assumed the insurance costs arising from the loan of the painting *Green Apples* from the National Gallery of Canada (letter from Lecours to O.L., January 31, 1916, BNQ/327/6/1).

5   Philippe La Ferrière, "Du côté de chez Besner", *Amérique française*, vol. 12, no. 1 (April 1954), p. 57.

6   This drawing (whereabouts unknown), dated 1916, is mentioned in Laurier Lacroix *et al.*, *Ozias Leduc the Draughtsman*, exhib. cat. (Montreal: Concordia University, 1978), p. 51.

7   One copy disappeared in the fire that ravaged the Baie-Comeau Manor around 1950-1955. The remaining copy (whereabouts unknown) once belonged to Florence Bindoff (cat. 194), a friend of the Lecours family and of the artist. This is the version reproduced in Jean-René Ostiguy, *Ozias Leduc: Symbolist and Religious Painting*, exhib. cat. (Ottawa: National Gallery of Canada, 1974), p. 202.

8   The *Portrait of Marie-Thérèse*, a charcoal probably executed in 1913, also disappeared in the fire at the Baie-Comeau Manor. The *Portrait of Jeanne*, a charcoal dating from 1914, belongs to the Musée du Québec (reproduced in Lacroix *et al.* 1978, p. 51).

9   Only three other bas-reliefs by Leduc are known: *Portrait of Raoul Ducharme* (1911; whereabouts unknown); *Portrait of Fernande Choquette-Clerk* (1917; cat. 159); and *Loraine* (undated; whereabouts unknown). In executing these works, Leduc aligned himself with the various other early twentieth-century painters who tried their hand at sculpture, among whom were Suzor-Coté and Onésime-Aimé Léger (1881-1924).

10 John Pope-Hennessy, *The Portrait in the Renaissance* (Princeton University Press, 1979), pp. 35-36.

11 This work is reminiscent of the female portraits executed by Pre-Raphaelite artists like Edward Burne-Jones and Dante Gabriel Rossetti (1828-1882).

12 Émile Vézina, "Notes d'art – L'exposition Leduc", *Le Devoir* [Montreal], February 21, 1916, p. 1.

13 Max J. Friedländer, *Landscape, Portrait, Still-life: Their Origin and Development*, trans. R.F.C. Hull (New York: Schocken Books, 1963), p. 236.

14 Letter from Ozias Leduc to Robert LaRoque de Roquebrune [early January 1927], BNQ 327/8/33.

159

Portrait of Fernande Choquette-Clerk

1917
Plaster plaque with gilt finish
31.5 x 23.9 x 1 to 2 cm
Signed and dated centre right: *19 O LEDUC 17*

Private collection

PROVENANCE

Wedding gift from Ozias Leduc to Fernande Choquette and Édouard Clerk; private collection

THE model for this portrait, Fernande Choquette-Clerk (1890-1969), has given an extraordinarily sensitive and expressive account of her childhood visits to Leduc's studio in the company of her father, Dr. Ernest Choquette (cat. 92). During this period, Choquette was working on his novel *Claude Paysan*, for which Leduc was to provide the illustrations (cats. 93-102).

Before us stood the painter, wise, calm and pensive, like the sages of India … And then, there was a silence; the brief ritual pause – like a curtain drawn against the outside world – that in the studio invariably preceded the interminable conversations to come. Gay, witty, amusing and profound, punctuated by bursts of laughter and violent emotion, they were often excursions into the deepest reaches of the heart and soul, jugglings with words, endless discussions about a particular shade of green, the density of a shadow inside a barn or the depth of a fold in an angel's tunic …

From this voyage to the land of marvels, I would emerge … transformed, emptied of my usual essence and ready to cast new eyes upon the design created by the petals of a wild rose or the pendant clusters of a locust tree.[1]

Thus began the friendship between Fernande Choquette, nicknamed "Pompon", and Leduc, which would last until the artist's death. Under the pseudonym of Ruth Bohème, Fernande published a piece in *La Patrie* encouraging the public to visit Leduc's 1916 exhibition at the Bibliothèque Saint-Sulpice.[2] In her article, she laid some stress on the rural background of an artist "born, far from the city, in this remote landscape; child of the land and the mountain" and on the reverberations of this environment in his work, so full, she felt, of purity, power and freshness. Between 1917, when she married Édouard Clerk (1889-1982), and 1940, Fernande Choquette-Clerk lived first in the United States and later in Montreal. On her return to Saint-Hilaire in 1940, she began once again to make frequent visits to Leduc's studio. The mutual affection that linked the two undoubtedly brought much warmth to the painter's final years. On the death of his wife in 1939, Leduc thanked Fernande for her friendship with these words:

Your sympathy is infinitely precious to me. I feel it comes from a sensitive heart, without egoism, always ready to share the sorrows of those it encounters. The recollection, Madame, of the precious memory of your friendly visits to my studio touched me especially; thinking of them, the emptiness that now pervades it seems a little lessened.[3]

In 1943, as the result of his commission to decorate the interior of the Church of Notre-Dame-de-la-Présentation (cast. 237-253), Leduc began spending long periods in Shawinigan-Sud. In moments of homesickness, and particularly following various difficulties with his family, Fernande's friendship became even more important to him. She wrote, "Do not think on Saint-Hilaire with bitterness – it is a land 'of honey' that has inspired in you some of the most stirring things ever made in Canada."[4]

Leduc made this sculpted portrait of Fernande Choquette as a present on the occasion of her wedding, which took place on February 14, 1917.[5] The model, seen in profile, is flanked by vertical lines imitating the fluting of a column and surmounted by an Ionic capital. The

hairstyle is elaborate, with the upswept hair held by two bands, giving the profile a distinctly Roman look. It is, in fact, a highly decorative portrait: the dress and coiffure have been rendered in pronounced and very lively relief, and the whole image is enclosed by an architectural motif that contrasts sharply with the ground. The artist's use of the vocabulary of Art nouveau was possibly an allusion to the literary tastes of his model, who was an enthusiastic reader of the novels of Pierre Loti (1850-1923), so rich in descriptions of exotic climes.

M. L.

1   Fernande Choquette-Clerk, "À la mémoire d'Osias Leduc", *Le Clairon maskoutain* [Saint-Hyacinthe], June 15, 1956, p. 9.

2   Ruth Bohème [pseudonym of Fernande Choquette-Clerk], "Un peintre de « chez nous »", *La Patrie* [Montreal], March 11, 1916. p. 19.

3   Letter from Ozias Leduc to Fernande Clerk, May 2, 1939, in a private collection of personal papers.

4   Letter from Pompon Choquette-Clerk, Saturday [after May 22, 1944], BNQ 327/7/16.

5   There is another plaster version of this work without the decorative surround that appeared on the market in the late eighties (27.3 x 18.5 cm; whereabouts unknown).

160
Portrait of Léo-Pol Morin

About 1918

Charcoal on paper

50.2 x 33.1 cm

Signed and dedicated upper right: *A LÉO-POL MORIN O LEDUC*

Quebec City, Musée du Québec, inv. 82.34

PROVENANCE

Studio of the artist; Léo-Pol Morin, 1918; Morin estate; Robert P. Morin, Saint-Michel-de-Bellechasse; Musée du Québec, 1982

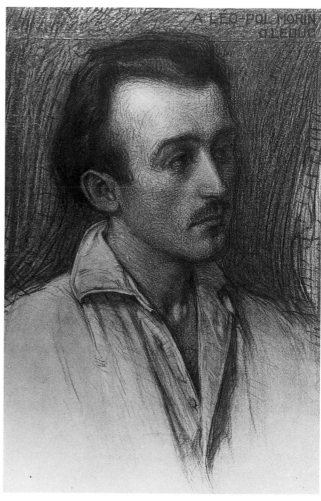

PIANIST and music critic Léo-Pol Morin (1892-1941) was introduced to Leduc by Robert de Roquebrune (cat. 155) on his return from Paris in the mid-1910s.[1] The musician seems to have fallen immediately under the spell of the painter's personality. In his very first letter, he does not stint on glowing epithets: "And you, 'silentiary' Leduc, prince of the superior smile, scorner of the raised voice, marvellous apologist of silence, artist".[2] The friendship was to last some ten years, although the two men met only occasionally, since Morin spent the years between 1919 and 1925 abroad.[3] During 1918, however, they saw each other often: both attended the meetings of *Le Nigog*, the magazine of which Morin was co-founder and co-director with Roquebrune and Fernand Préfontaine; and Morin and the Roquebrunes spent the few months before they left for Paris living in an outbuilding in Leduc's orchard.

Leduc's charcoal *Portrait of Léo-Pol Morin* bears a dedication but no date. Two pieces of evidence encourage us, though, to date it to 1918: in its drawing style, it is very similar to the *Portrait of Olivier Maurault, p.s.s* (cat. 161), dated 1918; and in the physical likeness and apparent age of the sitter, it is close to a photograph of Morin taken that year (private collection). Nevertheless, Leduc did not use this photograph in executing his portrait, for the poses are entirely different; since Morin was residing in Saint-Hilaire, he was evidently available for sittings. Morin presented the photograph to the artist with the following dedication: "To the silentiary Leduc, to Mrs. Leduc, with kindest regards. The Cave 7-XI-1918". "The Cave" was the name given by Morin and the Roquebrunes to the building they were occupying near Leduc's studio. This humorous reference to Plato's Myth of the Cave throws some light on the aesthetic theories of *Le Nigog*'s directors. Morin and Roquebrune were avid readers of the magazine *Le Mercure de France*, which broadcast the views of Symbolist writers and artists. It had published the manifesto by art critic Albert Aurier (1865-1892) explaining how Symbolist theories are based on the representation of the world of Ideas.[4]

The *Portrait of Léo-Pol Morin* is arguably the most intimate and sensual of all Leduc's portraits. It is a bust-length, three-quarter view, and the model's attitude is relaxed and meditative. The narrow, oblong face and the broad, prominent forehead are rendered in great detail, while the shirt is sketched in only rapidly. The background, covered with long vertical strokes broken by short horizontal lines, recalls that of the 1918 *Portrait of Olivier Maurault, p.s.s.*, but also, rather oddly, the rough rock face in *Day's End* (cat. 144). The informality of the model's clothing, quite unusual for the period, is proof of the closeness of the friendship between pianist and painter. Leduc has succeeded admirably in capturing the personality of his model, described by his friend Jean Désy as "physically delicate and frail", but also "unaffected", "trusting", "sensitive" and "strong-willed".[5]

M. L.

1 For a biography of Morin, see Bernadette Guilmette, "Léo-Pol Morin", in *Le Nigog* (Montreal: Fides, 1987), "Archives des lettres canadiennes", vol. 7, pp. 121-148.

2 Letter from Morin to Ozias Leduc, dated August 23, 1917, BNQ 327/6/2.

3 The correspondence between Leduc and Morin, held by the BNQ (327), began in 1917 and ended in 1927.

4 Albert Aurier, "Le Symbolisme en peinture: Paul Gauguin", *Le Mercure de France*, March 1891, pp. 155-165.

5 Jean Désy, "Éloge de Léo-Pol Morin", in Léo-Pol Morin, *Musique* (Montreal: Beauchemin), pp. 9-10. There are also two portraits of Morin by Adrien Hébert. Pierre L'Allier, *Adrien Hébert*, exhib. cat. (Québec City: Musée du Québec, 1993), cat. 14 and fig. 42, pp. 118-119.

161

Study for the *Portrait of Olivier Maurault, p.s.s.*

1918

Charcoal on cream laid paper (watermark: MICHALLET)

47.5 x 31.9 cm

Signed and dated centre right: *O LEDUC 1918*

Université de Montréal, inv. 76.10

INSCRIPTIONS

Verso, label: *Galerie l'Art français # 7937*

PROVENANCE

Studio of the artist; Ozias Leduc estate; Galerie l'Art français, Montreal; Université de Montréal

162

Study for the *Portrait of Olivier Maurault, p.s.s.*

About 1923

Charcoal on paper

62.1 x 47.5 cm

Signed lower right: *OZ Leduc*

Quebec City, Musée du Québec, inv. 71.83

INSCRIPTIONS

Verso: *No 45 ce dessin a servi à la peinture de Mgr Moreau*

PROVENANCE

Studio of the artist; Gabrielle Messier, Saint-Hilaire; Jean-René Ostiguy, Ottawa; Musée du Québec, 1971

163

Portrait of Olivier Maurault, p.s.s.

1916-1924

Oil on canvas

132.5 x 73.3 cm

Signed lower right: *OZIAS LEDUC*

Montreal, Comité du Patrimoine – Messieurs de Saint-Sulpice

INSCRIPTIONS

Verso, labels: *Leduc EXH. PORT. D'Olivier Maurault; From the college Andre Grasset Mtrl. Ro 737-1-74; Ozias Leduc cat no 55, boîte 3; peint entre 1920-25 Don de Mgr Maurault*

PROVENANCE

Studio of the artist; Olivier Maurault, p.s.s., Montreal, 1924; Collège André-Grasset, Montreal; Comité du Patrimoine – Messieurs de Saint-Sulpice

OLIVIER MAURAULT (1886-1968) expressed a wish to have his portrait painted by his friend Ozias Leduc,[1] suggesting in 1916 that the artist depict him as "the cathedral man".[2] The following year, Maurault learned that there existed a "flesh and blood caricature" of the projected portrait. "But I believed my idea to be original,"[3] he wrote to Leduc, after offering a description that rang a distant bell with the artist.[4] In 1918 and 1919, Leduc executed two charcoal portraits, one of them three-quarter length (cat. 161) and the other a semiprofile,[5] without the requested cathedral background. In 1923, Maurault broached the matter again: "If I seem somewhat obsessed with cathedrals, it is because I am writing the history of Notre-Dame."[6] Leduc then asked the priest to get him a photograph of the Montreal church, so as to "give this idea of a 'cathedralized' background a clear, definite, rational meaning. It would be good to show an evident link between the figure represented and these beautiful buildings. Notre-Dame is the ideal symbol."[7] In a progress report to Maurault, he concludes,

For the cathedralists (This word was seen in an article by Jean Rameau … at the time that Mr. Joris-Karl Huysmans made cathedrals fashionable. You know how.) and others we are likely to interest, we shall offer the following progression – Montreal, Rheims, Amiens, Paris.[8]

Maurault had to wait until May 9, 1924, for Leduc to send the portrait. The following day, he received a poem entitled "On the Sending of a Portrait", which ends with the following advice and dedication:

Examine it not from too far, nor too close
Either. Light will be its life
For light it was conceived. And by design
This sombre-hued painting is subdued
Do not laugh.
This portrait I have signed
Do not feel indignant
If now I follow at its heels
In a state of some emotion
even far from home.
So keep it

As a souvenir that speaks loud of
The sincerity and fullness of my heart,
And willingly
A reflection
Of my deep respect.[9]

Between sittings, Leduc used a photograph to remind himself of his model's countenance.[10] The 1918 charcoal sketch (cat. 161) offers an extremely detailed study of the features, and its delicate scumbling causes the light to glimmer on the face. Apart from the head, the image is rendered with long strokes, and the clothing and background are marked by strong vertical hatching that endows the study with considerable movement and spontaneity.

The 1923 sketch (cat. 162) is a three-quarter length view of the same pose as the earlier charcoal. The model wears a cape, secured at the neck by a ribbon tied in a bow. This sketch is principally a compositional study for the final painting, showing the pose in relation to a background depicting an arcade of pointed arches surmounted by the silhouettes of a number of cathedrals.[11]

In the final painting, Maurault is seen almost face on, and his features have lost some of the clarity notable in the preparatory sketches. Moreover, Leduc's "demolishing tool"[12] has obliterated the background cathedrals, although they can still be seen under X ray. The artist evidently had second thoughts about this element, preferring to replace it with another symbol: the garland of olive leaves[13] – an allusion to Abbé Maurault's first name – that he also employed in a bookplate made for the Sulpician around the same time (fig. 55).[14] The verticality

Fig. 55 Ozias Leduc, study for a bookplate for Olivier Maurault, about 1919, graphite on paper, 20.3 x 25.4 cm (BNQ 327/10/30).

161

162

of the decorative bands is reinforced by the main lines of the figure in the foreground; the left forearm is the only element forming a diagonal and thus creating a slight movement. The looseness of the drawing produces a feeling of confidentiality and intimacy. Only the eyes and nose are treated with any precision: the rest of the painting is slightly blurred. The execution of this portrait was slow and arduous, for Leduc's position was a delicate one. Maurault was his close friend, advisor and confidant. The artist was anxious not to disappoint him, particularly as he considered Maurault to be "a stern connoisseur",[15] one of those best able to understand his works.[16] On the very day he received the portrait, Olivier Maurault wrote in his journal,

The resemblance is adequate … But the treatment and tone are truly remarkable.

The green background, adorned with little yellow flames and olive leaves, was not the same when the portrait began. I had asked him to sketch in my favourite cathedrals, and the amenable painter had done so, in a highly original manner. But it must be admitted that these silhouettes attracted too much attention away from the head, especially the one of Rheims in the centre. Mr. Leduc ordered up a hurricane, and all the steeples disappeared under a layer of green.

For me, this work is priceless, for I know what it required of the artist in research and patience.[17]

The *Portrait of Olivier Maurault* is not a descriptive work but a symbolic one, emblematic of both the model's function and his personality. At the time the portrait was painted, Maurault, who was vicar of the Church of Saint-Jacques in Montreal, occupied the position of artistic director of the Bibliothèque Saint-Sulpice. It was in this capacity that, in February 1916, he mounted Leduc's first retrospective exhibition. Subsequently, Maurault held a number of prestigious appointments: parish priest of the Church of Notre-Dame in Montreal (1926-1929), principal of the Externat classique de Saint-Sulpice (1929-1934) and rector of the University of Montreal (1934-1955), where he oversaw, among other things, construction of the main pavilion on Mount Royal. While holding these various positions, Maurault offered Leduc commissions and recommended him for church decoration and illustration projects. In 1938, he even instigated the university's awarding to the artist of an honorary doctorate, in recognition of his career. In the dedication that accompanied the *Portrait of Olivier Maurault* when it was sent to its model, Leduc indicated his wish that it be seen as a tribute, a permanent testimony of his sincere affection and his "profound respect" for this "stern connoisseur" whose friendship and confidence were a support to him throughout his life.

M. L.

163

1 Letter from Maurault to Ozias Leduc, Tuesday evening [September 28, 1920], BNQ 327/6/5. The friendship between Leduc and Maurault, which lasted close to forty years, can be followed through their correspondence. The letters from Leduc to Maurault are with the Olivier Maurault papers of the Archives du Séminaire de Saint-Sulpice, while those from Maurault to Leduc are in the BNQ (327). For a more comprehensive study of this friendship and of Leduc's portraits of Maurault, see Monique Lanthier, "Portrait et Photographie chez Ozias Leduc", Master's thesis, University of Montreal, 1987, pp. 66-140.

2 This enthusiasm for cathedrals undoubtedly dated from his 1910-1913 stay in France, when he spent his Solitude (part of his religious training) at Issy-les-Moulineaux and pursued his literary studies at the Institut catholique de Paris.

3 Letter from Maurault to O. L., January 11, 1917, BNQ 327/6/2.

4 In a letter to Maurault dated January 16, 1917, Leduc wrote, "I vaguely remember having read the biography and seen the portrait" of this personage. Leduc had probably read the article by Félix Hautfort, "L'Homme des cathédrales – Mérovak évoquera l'Âme gothique...", *La Plume*, no. 242 (May 15, 1899), pp. 328-335. See also, Maurice Hamel, "Mérovak – L'homme des cathédrales", *Gazette des beaux-arts*, 6th period, vol. 59 (January 1962), pp. 53-60. Mérovak (pseudonym of Robuchon, 1874-1955) was an itinerant painter-sketcher who devoted himself mainly to illustrating Gothic architecture.

5 Reproduced in Laurier Lacroix *et al.*, *Ozias Leduc the Draughtsman*, exhib. cat. (Montreal: Concordia University, 1978), p. 60.

6 Letter from Maurault to O. L., Sunday [January 7, 1923], BNQ 327/6/8.

7 Letter from O. L. to Maurault, dated January 18, 1923. Leduc was probably drawing inspiration from the composition of Lévy-Dhurmer's (1865-1953) *Portrait of Georges Rodenbach*, which he had almost certainly seen reproduced in the January-June 1898 issue of *Art et Décoration*, p. 9.

8 *Ibid.*

9 BNQ 327/8/30.

10 According to Jean-René Lassonde, *La Bibliothèque Saint-Sulpice, 1910-1931* (Montreal: Ministère des Affaires culturelles, Bibliothèque nationale du Québec, 1986), ill. p. 47, this photo was probably taken in Paris between 1911 and 1913. It was likely a souvenir to commemorate the young priest's admission into the congregation of Saint-Sulpice in 1911. Leduc did not show the bands worn by Maurault in the photograph since this vestimentary feature was abolished in Montreal during the nineteenth century.

11 Although they are difficult to decipher, it is possible to identify the cathedrals depicted as follows: the profile on the extreme left resembles that of the cathedral of Strasbourg, with its single spire; the next two towers, behind Maurault's right shoulder, are like those of Montreal's Church of Notre-Dame; the two silhouettes on the right, whose towers are of different heights, do not appear to belong to the same façade; the first tower on the right is what remains of the Rheims cathedral after Leduc had decided to "obliterate the left part", as he said in his letter of January 18, 1923, cited above (note 7); the next tower, near Maurault's left arm, recalls the north tower of Notre-Dame in Paris. Most of the elements in the progression described by Leduc are there, but in a different order: Strasbourg, Montreal, Paris and Rheims.

12 Letter from O. L. to Maurault, January 18, 1923, cited above (note 7).

13 Within the Christian tradition, the olive branch is a symbol of peace.

14 Reproduced in Lacroix *et al.* 1978, p. 61. The bookplate also includes the spire of the Church of Saint-Jacques in Montreal, where Maurault was vicar from 1915 to 1926.

15 Letter from O. L. to Maurault, December 4, 1916.

16 Letter from O. L. to Maurault, April 12, 1920.

17 Maurault's Diary, pp. 58-59, Archives du Séminaire de Saint-Sulpice.

164
Head of a Man Shading His Eyes
1917

Charcoal on white laid paper

38.5 x 27.1 cm

Signed lower left: *O. LEDUC*; dated lower right: *FEV 1917*

Céline and Paul J. Audette collection

INSCRIPTIONS

Verso: *Ozias Leduc Tête d'homme se protégeant les yeux du soleil Head of a man shading his eyes 1917 fusain charcoal 38 x 27,5 cm Monsieur Paul Audette, Montréal*

PROVENANCE

Studio of the artist; Édouard Montpetit (?); René Bergeron, Chicoutimi; Céline and Paul J. Audette, 1968

Fig. 56   Ozias Leduc, *The Good Shepherd*, 1917, oil on cardboard, 23.5 x 27.3 (whereabouts unknown, BNQ 327/12/1.9).

TAKEN at face value, this charcoal drawing is but of a man staring into the space of the viewer while shielding his eyes from a bright light. Once it is recognized that this is Leduc himself, as comparison with a contemporary photograph reveals (fig. 48), both the shielding gesture (unusual for a self-portrait)[1] and the intensity of his gaze assume a more specific meaning, for they suggest a deep self-scrutiny.

In this sense, *Head of a Man Shading His Eyes* is a reprise of the romantic self-portrait Leduc had executed in 1899 (cat. 107), in which his face, highlighted to suggest a state of enlightenment, looms out of the darkness, his eyes reflecting upon himself with intense absorption. This earlier self-portrait of the painter, upon its exhibition at Leduc's first solo retrospective in 1916, prompted commentators to label the artist "priest", "poet", and "thinker".[2] It would seem that Leduc, by executing the self-portrait of 1917, was attempting to affirm such perceptions. He presents himself once again as the creator whose inspiration comes as much from within as from without. The hand shades the eyes from the blanching light, thus accentuating them to reveal a penetrating gaze that suggests the eyes of a seer, of one who is acutely aware of his role as an artist whose creations could provide the means for social redemption.[3]

With such connotations, it is perhaps not surprising that Leduc would consider the self-portrait an appropriate model for a particularly iconic rendition of *The Good Shepherd* (fig. 56),[4] also a figure of redemption.[5] While paintings of the Good Shepherd usually present a full-length figure of Christ carrying a sheep,[6] Leduc's model leads him to focus solely on the face of the Shepherd-Redeemer, who scans the fields searching for the wayward member of his flock.[7]

The widening of the format of *The Good Shepherd* to give a horizontal orientation allows for the inclusion of the attributes of halo and crook. A slight modification of facial features completes the transformation of Leduc to a Christ.[8]

A. G.

1 One example, however, is the *Self-portrait* from about 1747 by Sir Joshua Reynolds (1723-1792), in which the artist stands in front of his easel, brushes in hand. This work was reproduced in *The Studio* (London), vol. 10, no. 48 (March 1897), p. 92.

2 Ruth Bohème [pseudonym of Fernande Choquette-Clerk], "Un peintre de « chez nous »", *La Patrie* [Montreal], March 11, 1916. p. 19: "A gentle, peaceful head if ever there was one ... and the eyes, very serious eyes ... of a priest or poet ... one cannot say." A[lbert] Laberge, "L'œuvre d'un artiste", *L'Autorité* [Montreal], March 11, 1916, p. 2, reacts to the portrait in a similar vein: "Upon entering the gallery, the visitor is immediately drawn to a portrait of a man with a high forehead that seems to radiate light. The portrait of a poet and thinker. The face – fine, gentle and serious – is sympathetic, that of an intellectual."

3 Leduc articulated his ideas about the role of the artist in several of his later texts. See in particular the speech he gave to the Union des cultivateurs catholiques (BNQ 327/4/3) and the speech "Dires sur l'Art" (BNQ 327/4/2).

4 Olivier Maurault (cat. 163) knew of a "drawing in black" in the collection of Édouard Montpetit, a preparatory sketch for *The Good Shepherd*, which can almost certainly be related to *Head of a Man Shading His Eyes*. See Louis Deligny [pseudonym of Olivier Maurault], "Ozias Leduc peintre mystique", *Le Mauricien* [Trois-Rivières], vol. 2, no. 2 (February 1938).

5 Matthew 18:12-14; Luke 15:4-7; John 10:7-16.

6 Leduc himself had already executed such a version, in his copy (after Hofmann?) for the decorative programme of Saint Ninian's Cathedral, Antigonish, in 1903.

7 The interpretation of the gesture is based in part upon Leduc's good friend Olivier Maurault's comments that "the gesture of his right hand is a very expressive touch that further emphasizes the sorrowful anguish of the eyes" (Maurault to Ozias Leduc [after 27 March 1917], BNQ 327/6/2).

8 But not enough to fool Maurault who, upon seeing the painting exhibited at the Art Association of Montreal in 1917, was "pleased to recognize you somewhat in this Christ figure" (*ibid.*). It is not surprising that Leduc relinquished *The Good Shepherd* to his friend Maurault. As organizer of Leduc's first solo retrospective one year earlier, he was in a sense the artist's "saviour". The circumstances of Maurault's acquisition of the painting are revealed in three documents addressed to his mentor. All three are in the Archives du Séminaire de Saint-Sulpice, Ozias Leduc correspondence file: letters of April 27, 1917 (no. 8), and May 23, 1917 (no. 9), and a later poem "À Un Amateur…" (no. 35).

164

165

Portrait of Canon J.-M. Laflamme

About 1915-1917

Oil on canvas

90.5 x 76 cm

Signed lower right: *O. Leduc*

Centre d'archives du Séminaire de Saint-Hyacinthe

PROVENANCE

Studio of the artist; J.-M. Laflamme, 1920;
Séminaire de Saint-Hyacinthe
[Photographed during restoration]

BEFORE Olivier Maurault (cats. 161-163) and Father Arthur Jacob, Father Joseph-Magloire Laflamme (1848-1926) had played a vital role in the development of Leduc's career by offering him two commissions for church interiors – those of Saint-Hilaire (cats. 27-56) and Saint-Romuald, in Farnham (cat. 135, fig. 132).

According to remarks made by his contemporaries, Laflamme appears to have been a man of some arrogance, and much concerned with outward appearances. This is confirmed even by his obituary, in spite of the respectful tone dictated by the circumstances.

Mr. Laflamme was very fond of the external trappings of worship: he took pleasure in ceremonies and public events. He required his churches to be rich, ornate, splendid. If he had been a man of means, he would willingly have become a Patron of painters and architects, using them to the glory of God … He even believed that the Lord's ministers should have a share in this splendour, and he felt deeply that those honoured by the Church should not suppress their entitlements or hide the badges of their office … His charity made him free with praise and his habit of commending all around often led him to think a good deal upon himself.[1]

This combination of charity and vanity prompted Father Laflamme to take credit for Leduc's work and to lay considerable emphasis on the role he had played in furthering the career of the painter from Saint-Hilaire.[2] Hardly surprisingly, he expressed a repeated wish to have Leduc paint his portrait.

Who knows if the idea already broached may not be realized, to reproduce [a photograph of Laflamme] in painting, as a souvenir of all the projects we have executed together, a souvenir of the Church of Saint-Hilaire, which was the main starting point for the other undertakings elsewhere in New Brunswick … in the United States also … I am not begging. I am simply airing an idea that could be carried out with pleasure on one side and no less on the other at seeing it executed.[3]

Leduc selected the pose for this composition from several photographs (fig. 57), beginning the work in August 1915 and completing it in January 1917.[4] It was not until 1920, however, when Laflamme decided to present the portrait to the Seminary in Saint-Hyacinthe, that the model openly expressed certain reservations: "For my portrait, I would have liked it a little less close to the photograph, with the forms of the face a little softer, to give a less aged look, since it is to be placed in a gallery with others pictured at around sixty or even less."[5] In the face of the artist's refusal to make any alterations,[6]

Fig. 57   Canon J.-M. Laflamme
(private collection; photo: Homier Lavergne).

Laflamme accepted the portrait as it was.

The three-quarter pose borrowed from the photograph emphasizes Laflamme's domineering, theatrical personality. But Leduc went further in symbolizing the sitter's character, using a Mannerist style to render the gaunt face, and stressing the rather prominent eye sockets and the sharp contrast between the livid skin and the almost artificial red of the cheeks. These devices recall portraits by certain sixteenth-century Florentine artists, such as the one by Pontormo (1494-1556) of Prince Cosimo de' Medici (about 1518-1520, Uffizi Gallery).

L. L.

1   "M. le chanoine Laflamme", *Le Courrier de Saint-Hyacinthe*, March 5, 1926. Laflamme, son of a sexton, was born in Saint-Denis-sur-Richelieu. He was the parish priest in Saint-Éphrem d'Upton before working in Fall River, Massachusetts. From 1888 to 1894, he was chaplain at the Précieux-Sang monastery in Saint-Hyacinthe, subsequently becoming the parish priest in Saint-Hilaire and later, in Farnham. He was made canon in 1912, and he retired in 1915.
    An unpublished biography of Canon Laflamme by Abbé Pierre-Athanase Saint-Pierre offers a scathing portrait worthy of the French memorialist Saint-Simon (undated manuscript, Centre d'archives du Séminaire de Saint-Hyacinthe, A Fg41 D.1.15.1).

2   Laflamme was keen to associate himself with Leduc's career, which he considered highly successful: "the relations we have always maintained of *sincere appreciation* – whether near or far … if the works of one are admired, the two are not separate" (letter from Laflamme to Ozias Leduc, December 5, 1914, BNQ 327/5/24).

3   Letter from Laflamme to O. L., November 25, 1914, BNQ 327/5/24.

4   There are several letters that refer to the execution of this portrait. On November 25, 1914, Laflamme sent Leduc a first photograph (BNQ 327/5/24). In response to Leduc's hesitation regarding this choice, Laflamme wrote on December 5, 1914, defending his suggestion: "It would be difficult for me today to find a more acceptable reproduction. I would risk too much, I feel … The *man* possesses a certain air of natural mystery that suits him; knowing him as we do … one cares about oneself at any age, and this portrait suits me. It suits you too. I understand. And if I have to pose, we could correct a little." (BNQ 327/5/24.) In the first few days of August 1915, Laflamme sent Leduc two more snapshots (O. L. to Laflamme, August 1, 1915, Service des archives de l'Archidiocèse de Sherbrooke, Msgr. Desranleau papers, P2/7.4.1A II; Laflamme to O. L., August 3, 1915, BNQ 327/5/25). On August 12, Laflamme expressed delight that Leduc and Louis-Philippe Martin had both agreed to execute his portrait (BNQ 327/5/25). (Martin's is at the Seminary of Saint-Hyacinthe.) On April 29, 1916, the model enquired how the painting was progressing (BNQ 327/6/1), and on January 23, 1917, Leduc informed Laflamme that the portrait was finished (Service des archives de l'Archidiocèse de Sherbrooke, Msgr. Desranleau papers, P2/7.4.1A II). A letter from O. L. to Laflamme, January 29, 1917 (*ibid.*) provides some technical information about the work.

5   Letter from Laflamme to O. L., December 8, 1920, BNQ 327/6/5. The painting's whereabouts between January 1917 and December 1920 are not known. In 1917, Laflamme was retired and living in Montreal; later, he moved to Saint-Hyacinthe, where he lived simply and alone (*Le Courrier de Saint-Hyacinthe*, March 5, 1926). Did Leduc keep the portrait during these years? Whatever the case, the canon requested delivery of the painting on December 17, 1920, and Leduc responded on the 24th (BNQ 327/6/5; 327/8/26).

6   Letter from O. L. to Laflamme, December 16, 1920, BNQ 327/8/26. Laflamme's acceptance followed immediately (letter from Laflamme to O. L., December 17, 1920, BNQ 327/6/5).

166

Study for *The Holy Family in Nazareth*

About 1916

Graphite on paper

27.5 x 19.8 cm

Signed lower right: *OZIAS LEDUC*

Musée d'art de Joliette, gift of Michel and France
Aubriot, inv. 1982.011

PROVENANCE

Studio of the artist; Galerie l'Art français,
Montreal; Louis-Paul Perron, about 1967; Michel
and France Aubriot; Musée d'art de Joliette, 1982

167

Study for *The Sacred Heart of Jesus*

1917-1918

Graphite on beige paper

35.6 x 44.8 cm

Initialed centre right: *O.L.*

Montreal, Bibliothèque nationale du Québec –
Fonds Ozias-Leduc, MSS-327/10/24

PROVENANCE

Studio of the artist; Gabrielle Messier, Saint-
Hilaire; Bibliothèque nationale du Québec, 1972

I N the early 1930s, Leduc became anxious about plans to begin restorations in the Church of Saint-Enfant-Jésus in the Montreal district of Mile-End, where he had executed a number of works between 1916 and 1920. Accordingly, he wrote to the parish priest, J.-M. Thibodeau, "I am a creator who fears for his threatened creations, a creator who has received blows in the past. This [Sacred Heart] chapel is one of my most carefully studied works, one of those to whose execution I have devoted the most care. A work charged with an intense symbolism of the highest significance."[1] Leduc's misgivings unfortunately proved well founded: some of the paintings from this church were removed, mutilated and dispersed, while others were irretrievably altered by incompetent hands.

Leduc undertook this church interior in two distinct stages that show a clear shift in his style. In 1916, he was subcontracted by D.-Adolphe Beaulieu, a Montreal artist-decorator, to execute four paintings for the pendentives of the cupola, at the transept crossing.[2] Then, in 1917, following the church's renova-

tion and expansion, Leduc collaborated with the architect Louis-N. Audet on several other paintings – canvases that were to be fixed by marouflage to the panels of the pulpit and altars (fig. 138),[3] as well as the decoration of the baptistry, known as the Sacred Heart Chapel. These various projects were all completed by the spring of 1920, in time for the Easter festivities.

The four pendentive paintings, on the theme of Christ's childhood, were made according to Beaulieu's specifications and subject to the approval of Father Philippe Perrier. The four episodes depicted were *The Annunciation*,[4] *The Nativity*, *The Holy Family in Nazareth* and *Jesus among the Doctors*. Each composition featured the scene's main characters, portrayed in an imposing scale against an appropriate architectural or landscape background. In these narrative works, Leduc gave priority to the decorative dimension and to the accessibility of their iconography.

In undertaking the interior of the Sacred Heart Chapel, Leduc exercised considerably more freedom. He derived his theme from the chapel's function as a

Fig. 58   Ozias Leduc, *The Sacred Heart of Jesus*, 1917-1918 (Montreal, Church of Saint-Enfant-Jésus, Mile-End; photo retouched by Ozias Leduc, BNQ 327/111/5.4).

baptistry. He explained his aims in the following terms:

A composition inspired by a text from Saint Paul's epistle to the Romans – "Moreover the law entered, that the offence might abound. But where sin abounded, grace did much more abound."[5]

Theme of the decoration – The Redemption illustrated through four large compositions ... The Baptism of our Lord ... Jesus dying on the Cross ... the Sacred Heart at the foot of the Tree of Life, surrounded by eight angels carrying the Instruments of the Passion (This number, eight, being the figure of Regeneration, is repeated throughout the chapel) ... The Promise of a Redeemer showing at one end Adam and Eve cast out from the Garden of Eden and at the other the Immaculate Conception standing on the head of the Serpent.[6]

Besides the four compositions, Leduc designed all the other painted decorative elements, including those imitating draperies covering the lower part of the walls, the band framing each major scene, the emblems and the inscriptions.

For this project, Leduc employed the techniques and compositional forms favoured by nineteenth-century muralists, whose works he had certainly seen in many Parisian churches and public buildings. As in the Church of Saint-Hilaire, he used the technique of marouflage and the device of surrounding the principal paintings with frames painted directly on the canvas. The figures in *The Baptism of Christ* and *Christ on the Cross* are placed against a mosaic-like ground, while in *The Sacred Heart of Jesus* (fig. 58) they are arranged in a row in front of the Tree of Life, whose roots and branches overflow onto the painted frame – both compositions used frequently by such French artists as Hippolyte Flandrin (1809-1864), Eugène-Emmanuel Amaury-Duval (1808-1855) and Pierre Puvis de Chavannes (1824-1898).[7]

In his execution of this interior, however, Leduc was also influenced by the revival of sacred art in France, whose main proponents were Maurice Denis and Georges Desvallières (1861-1950). The choice of subject and the formal aspects of the work now came second, in fact, to religious considerations. *The Promise of a Redeemer* places the Virgin Mary at the heart of the mystery of the Redemption. Moreover, in *The Sacred Heart of Jesus*, Leduc innovatively introduces two secular scenes, on either side of the religious image. These two vistas, one showing a rural landscape, the other an urban one, are allusions to the notion of sanctification through work: on the one hand, we see a mother and child, sower and tiller; on the other, quarry workers and a partially constructed building with, in the background, the smokestacks of a factory and the dome of Montreal's cathedral. At the time, there actually was a quarry in the Mile-End area. The decorative motifs of the painted border, which include foliage and maple and apple products, are references to the local flora.

While Leduc was working at the Church of Saint-Enfant-Jésus, Abbé Lionel Groulx, defender of clerical nationalism and principal contributor to *L'Action française*, was living in the church's presbytery, for he was an associate of the parish priest, Father Perrier. Groulx's conservative ideology promoted rural life, seen as more likely to ensure the preservation of religion, language and traditional values. In the two secular scenes, Leduc does not opt in favour of one way of life over the other. His message is the essentially theological one that humanity can achieve redemption through labour. Once the work was complete, Leduc's friend Olivier Maurault (cats. 161-163) wasted no time in publishing a brochure on the interior of the Sacred Heart Chapel, in which, he claims, "Nothing has been spared: time, research, reflection. We are as a result indebted to Mr. Leduc for one of the two or three church interiors in our country of which we can be truly proud."[8]

M. L.

1   Undated draft of a letter from Ozias Leduc to M. Thibaudeau [*sic*], BNQ 327/9/18.

2   Leduc had worked for Beaulieu before. In 1906 and in 1909, he executed paintings for the Chapel of Notre-Dame-de-Bonsecours in Montreal (fig. 135), and in 1908, he designed a stained glass window for the Church of Saint John the Baptist, in New York (fig. 136); BNQ 327/5/16; 5/18; 5/19.

3   These paintings and their preparatory drawings are in the following collections: Musée du Québec, Musée d'art de Joliette, University of Montreal, Power Corporation and various private collections.

4   Reproduced in Jean-René Ostiguy, *Ozias Leduc: Symbolist and Religious Painting*, exhib. cat. (Ottawa: National Gallery of Canada, 1974), p. 153.

5   Handwritten document by Ozias Leduc, BNQ 327/2/1. The Bible verse is Romans 5:20.

6   Handwritten document by Ozias Leduc, in a private collection of personal papers.

7   On this subject, see Bruno Foucart, *Le Renouveau de la peinture religieuse en France (1800-1860)* (Paris: Arthéna, 1987).

8   Louis Deligny [pseudonym of Olivier Maurault], *La Chapelle du Sacré-Cœur, église du Saint-Enfant-Jésus, Montréal: une décoration du peintre Ozias Leduc* (Montreal: Imprimerie du Messager, 1921), p. 17.

168

Study for *The Conversion of Saint Paul*

1917

Gouache on cardboard, with traces of graphite, charcoal and coloured pencil

37.9 x 13.9 cm

Signed lower right: *OZIAS LEDUC*

La Corporation archiépiscopale C.R. du diocèse de Sherbrooke

INSCRIPTIONS

Recto, upper centre: *Saul Saul pourquoi me persé-cutez vous*

Verso: *21; COMA M.C. BCC*; labels of Galerie l'Art français; Lucien Encadrement Inc.

PROVENANCE

Galerie Jean-Pierre Valentin, Montreal; Corporation archiépiscopale C.R. du diocèse de Sherbrooke, 1988

169

The Martyrdom of Saint Paul

1919

Painted glass and lead

403 x 142.5 cm

Signed lower right: *Perdriau et O'Shea, Montreal*

La Corporation archiépiscopale C.R. du diocèse de Sherbrooke

INSCRIPTIONS

Recto, lower left: *Bonum certamen certavi cursum consummavi fidem servavi*; lower right: *in reliquo reposita est mihi corona justitiae*

PROVENANCE

Workshop of Perdriau & O'Shea; Pauline Chapel, Sherbrooke Cathedral; Corporation archiépiscopale C. R. du diocèse de Sherbrooke, on deposit to Musée du Québec, Quebec City, 1984-1995

ALTHOUGH well aware of the exigencies of designing a stained glass window,[1] Ozias Leduc agreed enthusiastically in March 1917 to execute a scale model for a *Conversion of Saint Paul* to fill one of the apse windows in the Pauline Chapel, now the crypt of Sherbrooke Cathedral.[2] For the chapel's two other windows, *The Martyrdom of Saint Paul* and *Saint Paul Preaching before the Areopagus*, the cathedral's architect, Louis-N. Audet, and the commissioner of the work, Msgr. Paul Larocque, had to be content with rough sketches and even cartoons.[3]

Since his mandate was to produce an original window in the medieval style,[4] Leduc skilfully combined diverse elements in the ogival space at his disposal. The mandorla, the quatrefoil, the broad border, the numerous fillets and the many small pieces of glass are all drawn from the vocabulary of the Middle Ages, while the plain volutes, more naturalistic plant motifs and opalescent glass chosen for the lower panel belong to an early twentieth-century repertoire.

Between the issuing of the commission and the work's completion in the spring of 1919, the model was altered radically, becoming more of a "painting in glass" than an antiquarian-style stained glass window.[5] In fact, it was as a result of remarks made by Audet concerning enlargement of the image, a reduction in decoration and the introduction of pale glass[6] that *The Conversion* (fig. 59) lost much of its dramatic intensity. Even *The Martyrdom of Saint Paul*, the subject finally selected for the central bay, underwent numerous modifications, including to its structure. However, both the division of the lower section into two panels, suggested by the glassmaker Henri Perdriau,[7] and the introduction of a wooden frame strengthened the composition.

Having a "strong dislike of insipid stained glass, lacking in consistency",[8] Leduc employed an emblematic border to link the windows' three sections; this border consists of squares intercut by the leaves of an oak tree, rooted near the base, that burgeons in the ogive. Aside from the opening panels adorned with phylacteries and the armorial bearings of various church leaders,[9] each carefully framed scene is surmounted by a half-length figure. The *Martyrdom* is completed by an *Apotheosis of Saint Paul*, the *Preaching before the Aeropagus* by a *Christ on the Cross*, and the *Conversion* by a *Good Shepherd*.

Leduc's *Conversion of Saint Paul* evidently drew inspiration from Raphael and Michelangelo,[10] the scenic disposition for the *Martyrdom* was taken from Rubens,[11] and the use of oak leaves and figure-revealing drapery show the influence of Burne-Jones;[12] yet, the visual effect of the Sherbrooke triptych, created by the overall design and the innovative border motifs, is clearly stamped with the artist's signature.

G. L.

1 Leduc had previously executed cartoons for the Church of Saint John the Baptist, in New York (fig. 136).

2 The correspondence between Audet and Leduc on the subject of these windows dates from March 7, 1917, to April 1, 1919. Audet's letters are in the BNQ 327/6/2-4, and the drafts of Leduc's replies are in BNQ 327/8/23-25.

3 Leduc's reply to the letter of February 17, 1919, BNQ 327/8/25. The sketch for *The Martyrdom of Saint Paul* is reproduced in Laurier Lacroix *et al.*, *Ozias Leduc the Draughtsman*, exhib. cat. (Montreal: Concordia University, 1978), p. 54. Given the scale model's painstaking detail (instead of just providing the main lines of the design and indicating the colours), it is understandable that Leduc was reluctant to produce more. The *Conversion* was commissioned on March 7, and the other two subjects were added on March 22 (letter from Audet to Leduc, BNQ 327/6/2).

4 Letter from Audet to Leduc, March 22, 1917, BNQ 327/6/2.

5 It is notable that in his letters of May 6 and June 11, 1918, the architect is still expressing a marked preference for the antiquarian style (BNQ 327/6/3).

6 Letter from Audet to O. L., May 4 and 6, 1918, BNQ 327/6/3.

7 Letter from Audet to O. L., June 11, 1918, BNQ 327/6/3. The introduction of a frame alters the dimensions of the window, necessitating adjustments of proportion. Henri Perdriau (1877-1950) was active as a glass stainer, under various company names, between 1910 and 1923.

8 Leduc's reply to Audet's letter of June 11, 1918, BNQ 327/8/24.

9 Depicted are the arms of Pope Benedict xv, Cardinal Bégin, Archbishop Paul Bruchési and Bishop Paul Larocque.

10 From Raphael (cartoons of the tapestries on the Acts of the Apostles) and Michelangelo (frescoes in the Pauline Chapel at the Vatican), Leduc borrowed the motif of a horse held by its bridle and possibly the image of the fallen Saul being raised by his assistants. Raphael's cartoons are reproduced in most of the monographs on this artist, including the one published by Hachette in 1909, *Raphaël, l'œuvre du maître*. For Michelangelo, see *The Complete Work of Michelangelo* (London: Macdonald, 1966), vol. 1, p. 265.

11 The idea of showing Saint Paul bound and on a stage probably comes from Rubens's *Beheading of Saint Paul*. This work is reproduced in *P.P. Rubens, l'œuvre du maître* (Paris: Hachette, 1912), p. 389.

12 For more on this, see Charles A. Sewter, *The Stained Glass of William Morris and His Circle* (New Haven and London: Yale University Press), 1974.

168

169

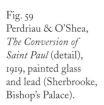

Fig. 59
Perdriau & O'Shea,
*The Conversion of
Saint Paul* (detail),
1919, painted glass
and lead (Sherbrooke,
Bishop's Palace).

170

Study for the *Portrait of the Honourable Joseph-Napoléon Francœur*

About 1920

Oil on cardboard

21.8 x 16 cm

The Montreal Museum of Fine Arts, gift of the Succession J.A. DeSève, inv. 1981.1

INSCRIPTIONS

Verso: *I Fabrique de Couleurs fines Maison Merlin Paul Denis, Suc.R Toiles et Articles de Dessin 19, rue de Médicis, 19 Paris; "26736-13"; labels: Galerie Bernard Desroches inc. 1194 ouest rue Sherbrooke Montreal H3A 1H6 TEL. 842-8648 Artiste: Ozias Leduc Titre: Portrait, Léo-Paul Morin Medium: Huile sur panneau Format: 9 3/4" x 6 5/8"; Encadrement Marcel*

PROVENANCE

Studio of the artist; Philippe-Darau Leduc, Saint-Hilaire; Galerie Bernard Desroches, Montreal, 1980; Montreal Museum of Fine Arts, 1981

171

Portrait of the Honourable Joseph-Napoléon Francœur

1920-1922

Oil on canvas

140 x 96 cm

Signed lower right: *OZIAS LEDUC*

Quebec City, Assemblée nationale

INSCRIPTIONS

Verso, label: CN MESSAGERIES Montréal

PROVENANCE

Studio of the artist; Assemblée nationale, 1922

170

IN February 1920, Dr. Ernest Choquette (cat. 92), then a member of Quebec's Legislative Assembly, informed Leduc that he had persuaded the new Speaker of the House, the Honorable Joseph-Napoléon Francœur (1880-1965), to commission the artist to paint his official portrait.[1] Choquette was evidently pleased for the artist, adding, "I am rather proud since I was keen to see a work from *my country* in parliament",[2] the "country" referred to being, of course, Saint-Hilaire. Leduc hastened to thank the Premier, Sir Lomer Gouin (1861-1929), for his support, promising that he would do everything in his power to prove himself "equal to the task".[3] In June, the artist travelled to Quebec City in order to execute the preliminary drawings from life.[4]

Subsequently, as was his habit, Leduc used photographs to remind himself of his model's features. Eighteen months later, in January 1922, the painting was still not finished, and Francœur became impatient.[5] Leduc replied, "It is an important work, and I should not like, by rushing the last stages, to jeopardize the effect I had hoped to achieve."[6] By March, the portrait was complete and had been framed, according to Leduc's specifications, by the owners of the gallery Morency Frères, in Montreal. At the artist's request, they hung the work in their window for several days before shipping it to Quebec City.[7]

On the arrival of the painting, the Honourable Speaker lost no time in making his reaction known: he was disappointed, and was not sure he would

accept the portrait.[8] Leduc immediately sent an explanation.

It was very painful for me to learn that this portrait has caused you such concern … However, this is not the first time that a work of art has been a matter of dispute. The one before you bears my name in full, and was therefore intended to be just as it is, not all superficial reality, but oriented towards a more inner life, which is another very interesting form of reality. Beneath appearances, there are generally many other layers of meaning.

In my works, I try to get to the essence, and it is not for me to say to what extent I succeed. That is the critic's job.

You are certainly free to refuse or accept your portrait, and I would like to reassure you by saying that I have absolutely no political influence, even in party politics. So feel free to follow the advice of your friends, who, I am sure, are both sincere and enlightened. For my part, I shall calmly await your decision.[9]

Leduc's reply was not sufficient to assuage the Speaker's uneasiness. On April 4, 1922, he wrote, "I do not want to enter into a debate about this painting. All those who have seen it, even specialists, while appreciating your work, have invariably said that it is the portrait of a man at least fifty-five years old. Is there a way to remedy this?"[10]

Towards the end of the month, Leduc travelled to Quebec City "with the aim of making the Honourable J.-N. Francœur younger".[11] After two sittings, the artist noted in his Diary that he had made "slight alterations to the portrait of the President of the House, who appears satisfied".[12]

Leduc seems to have used two photographs in executing this work. The first, from the Montminy studio in Quebec City, was almost certainly taken at the time of Francœur's appointment as Speaker, in December 1919, and probably served as his official photo (fig. 60). The second photograph is a frontal bust view of Francœur wearing an ordinary suit (fig. 61). In this latter image, the model looks noticeably older than in the first, although it was taken only six months later. This apparent aging is actually the result of numerous alterations made directly on the print by Leduc, who added pencil lines around the model's eyes, and on the cheeks and lips. Leduc executed a series of studies of Francœur's head, partly from life and partly based on these two photographs.

A first pencil drawing (cat. 74), executed around 1920-1921 and inspired by the full-length photo, served mainly to position the model's features and establish the tones of light and shade. The features are rendered in some detail, and the right side of the face is modelled and darkened by rapid hatching; the robe and the collar, with its turned-back points, are sketched in only summarily.

171

Fig. 60   Fig. 61   Fig. 62

Another sketch, inspired by the second photograph was executed in pencil on tracing paper (fig. 62). As in the photograph, the model appears considerably older than in the earlier study.

In the third preparatory study (cat. 170),[13] the model's apparent age does not coincide with either the photos or the final work. Leduc probably intended this sketch as a character study of his model that could act as an *aide-mémoire* for the official portrait. He nevertheless gave it the "look of an entirely finished portrait".[14] The interest of this modello lies in the strong impression of spontaneity and immediacy it creates. The extremely tight framing gives the work an intimism[15] that encourages contact between spectator and model. The artist's empathy for his model is manifested in the warm light that illuminates the upper part of the face and makes its owner seem far more affable than in the official portrait. Moreover, there are no clues to the location or the model's social status to distract attention away from the face. Leduc kept this work in his studio, although he never signed it.[16]

The three preparatory studies all offer clear indications of the pose that would be selected for the final portrait: a hieratic, frontal attitude, in which the model's head, as in the two photographs, is turned slightly away from the spectator. This classical pose is the one used in most official portraits of elected repre-sentatives, of both the National Assembly and the House of Commons. The image projected is that of a statesman highly conscious of his duties and responsibilities; the attitude bespeaks a firm authority, a vision directed towards the future and an absolute discretion regarding his own personal life. Leduc has shown enormous respect for his model. In fact, the premature ageing he imposed was designed to reinforce the impression of intellectual maturity he perceived as part of Francœur's character. Leduc also emphasized the power of the Speaker's personality by using a decorative element on either side of the figure to symbolize wisdom and strength – oak leaves,[17] an attribute of Zeus, the highest ranking of the gods of Greek mythology.

For this portrait, Leduc has employed a relatively two-dimensional space and a painterly treatment for both the figure and the ground. The gown is rendered in various tones of black with bluish highlights, while the background is in a range of greens. The extremely thick paint layer seems to indicate that the artist experienced some difficulty in the obtaining the effect he desired. The light, coming from the right foreground, illuminates and faintly enlivens the model's face and hands. In response to the Speaker's wish to appear younger, Leduc seems to have removed a few lines and shadows from the model's forehead and cheeks, resulting in a slight blurring

Fig. 60   Joseph-Napoléon Francœur (photo: Montminy; ANQQ GH 670-56).

Fig. 61   Joseph-Napoléon Francœur, photo with pencil retouches (BNQ 327/13/4.19).

Fig. 62   Ozias Leduc, *Portraits of Guy Delahaye and Joseph-Napoléon Francœur*, graphite on tracing paper, 23 x 18 cm (private collection).

of the facial features. The work is reminiscent of the *Portrait of Olivier Maurault* (cat. 161-163), which Leduc executed around the same time. In both cases, the model is accompanied by an attribute whose significance serves to reinforce the meaning of the painting, rather like the emblematic portraits of the Renaissance.[18] The symbolic element appears vertically in the predominant lines of the foreground.

In the *Portrait of the Honourable Joseph-Napoléon Francœur*, the physical and psychological representation of the model is subordinated to another aim: Leduc is attempting to express the high esteem in which he holds the parliamentarian, whose pivotal role in the National Assembly required both diplomacy and impartiality if the debates were to proceed smoothly.

M. L.

1 The various stages of this commission are recorded in twenty-nine letters, now at the BNQ (327), written between mid-February 1920 and June 9, 1922. For a short biography of the model, see Monique Lanthier, "Le Portrait d'homme d'Ozias Leduc au MBAM retrouve son identité", *The Journal of Canadian Art History*, vol. 9, no. 2, 1986, p. 168, and René Castonguay, "La Motion Francœur (1917-1918)", Master's thesis, University of Montreal, 1989, pp. 9-10, and Appendix 2, pp. XVI-XVIII.

2 Letter from Choquette to Ozias Leduc [February 13, 1920], BNQ 327/6/5.

3 Draft of a letter from Ozias Leduc to Sir Lomer Gouin, dated March 1, 1920, BNQ 327/8/26.

4 Draft of a letter from O. L. to Francœur [June 14, 1920] and draft of a letter to Alfred Nantel, parish priest of Saint-Raphaël, Île-Bizard, July 6, 1920, BNQ 327/8/26.

5 Letters from Francœur to O. L. dated January 23 and 28, 1922, BNQ 327/6/7.

6 Draft of a letter from O. L. to Francœur, January 25, 1922, BNQ 327/8/28.

7 Letters from O. L. to Morency, January 31, 1922, and Francœur, February 4 and [March 2], BNQ 327/8/28; letters from Morency to O. L., February 2 and 25, 1922; and letter from Francœur to O. L., February 7, BNQ 327/6/7.

8 Letter from Francœur to O.L., March 11, 1922, BNQ 327/6/7.

9 Draft of a letter from O.L. to Francœur, March 13, 1922, BNQ 327/8/28.

10 Letter from Francœur to O. L., April 4, 1922, BNQ 327/6/7.

11 Ozias Leduc's Diary, April 27, 1922, BNQ 327/3/9.

12 *Ibid.*, May 2, 1922.

13 For more on this study, see Lanthier 1986.

14 Draft of a letter from O. L. to Francœur, December 24, 1921, BNQ 327/8/27.

15 It was because of this intimism that the model of the study was initially identified (in an inscription on the verso of the work) as Léo-Paul [*sic*] Morin, whose portrait Leduc also painted.

16 Correspondence between Leduc and Francœur indicates the existence of another oil modello (whereabouts unknown), (letters from O. L. to Francœur, December 24, 1921, BNQ 327/8/27, and March 2, 1922, BNQ 327/8/28; letters from Francœur to O. L., January 28 and June 9, 1922, BNQ 327/6/7).

17 Jean Chevalier and Alain Gheerbrant, *Dictionnaire des symboles*, "Bouquins" series (Paris: Robert Laffont/Jupiter, 1982), p. 221.

18 See the chapter on emblematic portraits in John Pope-Hennessy, *The Portrait in the Renaissance* (Princeton University Press, 1979), pp. 205-257.

172

Study for a Bookplate for the School Board of the Parish of Saint-Hilaire

About 1918-1921

Graphite on scrap paper

16.2 x 10.1 cm

Montreal, Bibliothèque nationale du Québec - Fonds Ozias-Leduc, MSS-327/10/30

INSCRIPTIONS

Recto: *LIVRE APPARTENANT A LA COMMISSION SCOLAIRE DE LA PAROISSE DE SAINT-HILAIRE; PRENEZ SOINS DE MOI; JE VOUS INSTRUIRAI MON ENFANT*

PROVENANCE

Studio of the artist; Gabrielle Messier, Saint-Hilaire; Bibliothèque nationale du Québec, 1972

LEDUC's design for a plate for textbooks belonging to the Saint-Hilaire School Board was no doubt conceived during his tenure as school commissioner (1918-1921). Seemingly developed on his own initiative, the project attests to the artist's dedicated involvement in the social concerns of the local community.[1]

As with several other works from this period, Mount Saint-Hilaire figures prominently (cats. 144, 150-152). An emblem not only of the region's topography but also of the parish itself, its distinctive profile has been accentuated through outline so as to suggest the form of a mother's breast. The *petite patrie* is as much a nurturing force in a child's development as are the books for which the ex-libris was intended.[2] The bookplate's admonition, "Take good care of me," is leavened with the promise of intellectual guidance and spiritual sustenance – "And I will instruct you, my child."

While Leduc's bookplate is iconic in composition, it is nevertheless conceptually akin to the narrative images celebrating French-Canadian customs and traditions that were being produced around the same time and which Leduc himself, in his capacity as commissioner, awarded to students as academic prizes.[3] Like Edmond-J. Massicotte's *Le Retour de la messe de minuit* (1919)[4] and its ilk, the ex-libris design is didactic in intent and salutary in tone, meant to engender in the young scholars of Saint-Hilaire a healthy respect not just for their books, but also for their homeland.

A. G.

1 The bookplate appears never to have been adopted by the School Board. Leduc's contribution to the Board was recognized in 1972, when a local secondary school was named after him.

2 Laurier Lacroix *et al.*, *Ozias Leduc the Draughtsman*, exhib. cat. (Montreal: Concordia University, 1978), p. 59.

3 Letter from Ozias Leduc to E.-J. Massicotte [early June 1920], BNQ 327/8/26.

4 Reproduced in Casimir Hébert, Introduction to *Les Canadiens d'autrefois* (Montreal: Librairie Granger Frères, 1923).

173

Mauve Twilight

1921

Oil on paper mounted on canvas

92.4 x 76.8 cm

Signed and dated lower left: *OZIAS LEDUC 1921*

The Montreal Museum of Fine Arts, gift of Mrs. Samuel Bronfman in honour of the 70th birthday of her husband, inv. 1961.1320

INSCRIPTIONS

Verso, labels: *Art Association of Montreal. 38th Spring Exh. 1921. Title: L'heure mauve. $350. Artist: O. Leduc. Saint-Hilaire.; Lycee Pierre Corneille. Exposition Ozias Leduc 12-15 juin 1954.; Musee des beaux-arts de Montreal; From M.M.F.A. RO 384-7-73; O. Leduc Exhibition. L'heure mauve; The National Gallery. O. Leduc cat. no. 47 Box no.2; Framed by W. Scott & Sons. 225 Notre Dame St. West. Montreal. #564. 1950.; Musee de la province de Quebec, cat. #27. Propriete de M. Joseph Barcelo. 2105 est rue Sherbrooke, Montreal. L'heure mauve par Ozias Leduc.*

PROVENANCE

Studio of the artist; William Scott & Sons, Montreal, 1930; Louis-Joseph Barcelo, Montreal, 1954; Noël Lajoie, 1960; Montreal Museum of Fine Arts, 1961

An oak branch partially buried in the snow – thus could we summarize this painting from 1921. Yet, it is a far from ordinary work. As Rodolphe de Repentigny commented, "Texture, structure and tone have here reached their ultimate perfection."[1] Because it is an "abstract" composition that creates an ambiguous space and employs an original iconography, *Mauve Twilight* – painted eight years after *Blue Cumulus* (cat. 143) – is undoubtedly one of Leduc's most complex paintings. Light, form, texture and composition combine to create one of the great triumphs of his œuvre.

As the title indicates, the time of day depicted is the moment when day begins to turn into night.[2] This transitional interval, the time frame for most of Leduc's landscapes, was first portrayed allegorically by the artist in *Night* (cat. 19). The twilight hour is characterized by a veiled, coppery light in which objects no longer shine and shapes tend to fuse, blending into one another with diaphanous immateriality. Here, a "rose-like hue … conducive to extended reverie in the soft mildness of evening"[3]

makes the colours waxen and reduces the contrast between the brilliance of the snow, the vividness of the leaves and the glow of the bark, all of which are attenuated by the muted dullness of the hour.

The most unsettling aspects of the painting are certainly the scale and the viewpoint adopted by the artist. The image is actually a life-size detail presented parallel to the picture plane,[4] which means that apart from the light, there are virtually no references to the broader surroundings. However, the painterly effects are numerous: the chalky fresco-like texture, the multidirectional paint layer, the transparency and the uneven swathes of wash, and the hatch strokes of varying widths all serve to multiply the signs of the brush's presence.

The monumentality that has been conferred on this detail, which somehow links the macrocosmic and microcosmic realms, can be explained in part by the way the painting developed. Speaking of Leduc's work method, Olivier Maurault (cat. 163) wrote, "Some of his sketches became utterly transformed; for example his painting representing *Oak Leaves in the Snow* started out as a mountain pass leading into a sunset."[5] The realization that a panoramic view of a mountain gorge at dusk can become an image of a few leaves in the snow tells us a good deal about the synthetic qualities of *Mauve Twilight*.

The fleetingness of this instant is integrated into a temporality of another scale. In the heavy, already-melting snow, the end of a day is echoed in the end of a winter. The leaves' aerial cycle is over, and the fall of the oak leaves effectively prefigures their rebirth. The mass of branches in the upper part of the painting forms a kind of spout, out of which flows a veritable cascade of snow. But there are other images embedded in the branches: on the left we can decipher a crown and part of a ladder, while the right-hand side is closed off by a fence. The fence, the ladder and the crown are three images that recur repeatedly in Leduc's work, and their presence, however veiled, is of great significance.

The life cycle of the oak tree is a symbol of the continuity and everlastingness of nature; but it surely also represents humanity's place within the universe and our relation to our own destiny. Although here the image of the Fall predominates, cut off from the rest of the world, man is nonetheless offered moral tools (the love of God, knowledge) through which he can achieve the salvation he longs for.

L. L.

---

1 R[odolphe] de Repentigny, "Images et plastiques – Il faut connaître Ozias Leduc", *La Presse* [Montreal], January 14, 1956, p. 66

2 In *Les Ribaud* (1898, p. 49; see cat. 91), Ernest Choquette's heroine Madeleine describes this time of day as "that delicious hour when it is no longer day but not yet night", a time conducive to the exchange of confidences. Leduc chose to employ a similar dusky light for a number of works, including *The Choquette Farm, Belœil* (cat. 121).

   In a talk given to members of the Saint-Hilaire chapter of the Union catholiques des cultivateurs in 1928, Leduc contrasted the "grey and pink" colours of a dawn sky to the evening tones of "diaphanous gold and purple" (BNQ 327/4/3).

3 "Notes artistiques: exposition rétrospective", *Le Soleil* [Quebec City], January 12, 1946, p. 20.

4 According to Noël Lajoie, "Un hommage au peintre Ozias Leduc, 1864-1955, *Le Devoir* [Montreal], January 14, 1956, p. 8, "Like Degas, Leduc seems to have chosen a detail and removed it from a whole in order to make it more expressive." Lajoie, a painter and critic, was the owner of this work in 1960, the year before it was acquired by the Montreal Museum of Fine Arts. The Museum's director at the time, Evan Turner, had perceived the painting's importance and went to considerable lengths to ensure its purchase by his institution.

   As regards the choice of an "extremely amplified detail" as the painting's subject, Repentigny 1956 notes that with this painting, "Leduc embarks on a form of unrealism that is now the province of the best photographers."

5 Olivier Maurault, *Confidences* (Montreal: Fides, 1959) p. 135.

174

Mountainside in Cloud

1922

Charcoal on paper glued to cardboard

15.2 x 16.6 cm

Signed lower left: *O. LEDUC*; dated lower right: *24 JUIL 1922*

Quebec City, Musée du Québec, inv. 82.54

PROVENANCE

Studio of the artist; Mr. and Mrs. Lucien Thériault, Vaudreuil, gift of the artist, 1937; Claudia Atias, Laval; Musée du Québec, 1982

THIS beautiful drawing is another example of Leduc's interest in meteorological conditions (cats. 143, 146, 173). As Barbara Novak has remarked when speaking of similar preoccupations in Constable's work and that of the American landscapists of the Hudson River School: "The sky is a finely tuned paradigm of the alliance between art and science. In that mutable void, the land-scape artist's concerns – poetic, ideal and symbolic, empirical and scientific – were sharpened rather than blurred."[1] The detailed study of clouds, informed by L. Howard's *Essay on the Modifications of Clouds* (1802-1803), with its new dis-tinctions between nimbus, stratus, cumulus and cirrus, became one of the great challenges of nineteenth-century painting, not only for technical reasons, but also because of the theme's enor-mous symbolic potential. That his beloved mountain could be thus swal-lowed up by a cloud was bound to fascinate Leduc: "It is winter, the sky is grumbling, lost beneath masses of clouds. An astonishing orchestration of countless noises, ranging from the sharpest to the most subtle, music that is almost infernal, generated before our very eyes – but that would be no less haunting if it came from the enchanted bowels of the earth."[2]

F.-M. G.

---

1 Barbara Novak, "The Meteorological Vision: Clouds", *Art in America*, vol. 68, no. 2 (February 1980), p. 103.

2 Ozias Leduc, "L'histoire de S.-Hilaire – On l'entend, on la voit", *Arts et pensée*, vol. 3, no. 18 (July-August 1954), pp. 167-168.

IV. AFTER 1922

Between Symbolism and Nationalism

THE last thirty years of the career of Ozias Leduc (fig. 63) coincided with a particularly rich period in Quebec's history, of vital importance in its move towards modernity. Between 1922, when Leduc was working with Borduas's assistance on the decoration of the Bishop's Palace in Sherbrooke, and the artist's death in 1955, three years after Borduas had quit the province and the year the Plasticiens published their manifesto, Quebec underwent radical changes – changes in which the visual arts community played no small part. The ideological unanimity that, as Gérard Pelletier was to say, finally ended with the Quiet Revolution had, over the years, gradually been eroded under pressure from the new ideas that emerged from the Depression of the early thirties, the Second World War, international immigration and swift progress in communications and technology. Among the most important changes that accompanied the last part of the Saint-Hilaire painter's career were the opening of Montreal's École des Beaux-Arts in 1923, the development of a critical discourse in the visual arts and the proliferation of commercial art galleries, the founding in 1939 of the Contemporary Arts Society, the teachings of Pellan and Borduas, both of whom focussed on nonfigurative painting, and finally the publication of *Refus global*.

There is a sense in which Leduc himself embodied the forces and tensions that marked this crucial period in Quebec's history. The duality and distinctions that had first emerged in the 1910s between regionalism and conservatism on the one hand and internationalism and innovation on the other became more pronounced. Paradoxically, Leduc would eventually serve simultaneously as a model for the conservatism and clerico-nationalist values that dominated this period and as an example and reference point to the youthful avant-garde that revolved around

Fig. 63   Ozias Leduc, 1936
(photo: Albert Tessier; Archives du Séminaire de Trois-Rivières, Albert Tessier papers, inv. 0014-P2-34a-54).

Borduas.[1] In fact, Leduc became the object of a triple perception: by some he was seen as the quintessential religious painter; by others as the sage of Saint-Hilaire and an easel painter of unrivalled skill; and for a few, his principal impact was as master to an intellectual leader who would shake Quebec society to its very foundations – Paul-Émile Borduas.

Leduc seems to have assumed these three roles with some success and to have adapted to the different realities they reflected. At the local level, he fulfilled a number of public functions associated with his position as a person of note. He was elected to the Saint-Hilaire school board in 1918; in 1924, he became a municipal councillor and in 1934-1935 was deputy mayor (fig. 113); as of 1931, he also served as a churchwarden. He became deeply involved in his community, an authority who was consulted and enlisted for all sorts of projects – historical, civic (fig. 114), sporting, artistic and educational.[2]

This persona existed parallel to another, more wide-ranging one – that of "sage of the mountain", a kind of guru who was eagerly consulted and whose words were treasured for their laconic wit and wisdom.[3] The farming and church communities profited greatly from this wisdom, and Leduc produced numerous works specifically for them. He created devotional images (cats. 192, 232, 234) and illustrations for books (fig. 115) and periodicals,[4] and the reproductions of his church paintings won him the affection and respect of the clergy.[5] He addressed himself to farmers, with whom, as an apple grower, he felt a definite kinship.[6] At the period when his works were being capitalized on by the clerical and national press, Leduc produced several of his most symbolically complex religious interiors, including the chapel of the Bishop's Palace in Sherbrooke (cats. 175-182) and the baptistry in Montreal's Notre-Dame Church (fig. 140). His full artistic legacy, however, is embodied in Notre-Dame-de-la-Présentation, in Shawinigan-Sud (cats. 237-253). His ideas on the function of ecclesiastical decoration had become more rigorous, and he employed iconographical programmes that enabled him to adapt the most abstract theological messages to the requirements of the congregations that gathered in these houses of worship.

The demands imposed upon him meant that things were not always easy for the artist, and, as he confided to his friend Olivier Maurault, he experienced periods of doubt and insecurity in relation to his work.[7] The complex but stimulating situation in which he found himself probably encouraged him to deepen and refine his thinking in notes and more elaborate texts. His extensive writings from the 1930s and 1940s remain for the most part unpublished,[8] but some were presented as lectures.[9] His ideas on religious symbolism and the symbolism of colours

1   Jean-Paul Riopelle (b. 1923), Fernand Leduc (b. 1916), Françoise Sullivan (b. 1925), Ulysse Comtois (b. 1931) and Noël Lajoie (b. 1927) were among the young artists who visited Leduc at Correlieu.

2   His diverse activities included founding the commission for the beautification of Saint-Hilaire in 1924 and being in charge of the Saint Jean-Baptiste Day celebrations for 1925 (fig. 114), recreational organizer for the Chemin des Trente and a member of the Saint-Hilaire sports association.

3   The various stages in the construction of the Leduc myth are the subject of Arlene Gehmacher, "The Mythologization of Ozias Leduc (1890-1954)", Ph.D. dissertation, University of Toronto, April 1995.

4   La campagne canadienne, a novel by the Jesuit Adélard Dugré, which first appeared in 1925, was republished in 1927 in a deluxe edition illustrated with twenty drawings by Leduc (fig. 115). Dugré's book was an appeal against the emigration of French Canadians to the United States and "the moral disaster awaiting the man who, in a moment of confusion, denies his race and his religion". (Louis Laurent, "Au pays du roman", Le Quartier Latin [Montreal], October 15, 1925, p. 99.)

5   Leduc's religious works were reproduced in numerous periodicals, including La Revue franciscaine, July 1938; L'Action paroissiale, December 1942; Almanach de Saint-François, 1948; Prie avec l'église, July 18, 1948; Messager de Marie Reine des Coeurs, January, March and June 1949; Annales de la Bonne Saint-Anne-de-Beaupré, February and May 1950; Le Messager du Très Saint Sacrement, November 1950; Le Missionnaire oblat and Oblate Mission News, January 1954.

6   His lecture to the Union catholique des cultivateurs of Saint-Hilaire (BNQ 327/4/3) is a lengthy reflection on the place of art in society and the status of the artist. Leduc took pains to remind his audience how the aesthetic experience can be an everyday phenomenon that constantly renews the spectacle of nature.

7   The correspondence between Ozias Leduc and Maurault is in the Archives du Séminaire de Saint-Sulpice. Certain often veiled remarks indicate that Leduc needed his friend's support and encouragement. See, for example, the letters of January 16, 1917, and April 16, 1931. In the latter, speaking of his interior for the church in Lachine, Leduc wrote, "What you say is of great comfort to me. You know that I do not express myself fully in works of this kind, the fear of not pleasing, of being misunderstood really brings me down."

8   Some of his notes were published in Amérique française (July-August and December 1953, June, September and November-December 1954) and Arts et pensée (January-February, May-June and July-August 1954).

9   As well as the lecture given to the Saint-Hilaire chapter of the Union catholique des cultivateurs mentioned in note 6, there were the talk entitled "Remarques sur l'art", broadcast on August 21, 1936, during CKAC radio's programme L'Heure provinciale (BNQ 327/4/1) and the lecture "Dires sur l'art", given to the Société d'histoire régionale de Saint-Hyacinthe on December 11, 1939 (BNQ 327/4/2).

and numbers, together with his many philosophico-poetic texts, do much to enrich our understanding of his painted oeuvre. Leduc's writings clearly reveal his idealistic attitude to art, which is seen as an activity that contains and summarizes the character and essence of its author. He expresses a serene vision of an art that is the result of a process of osmosis between the artist and his work.

What is ART? Art is the sound of all that vibrates. It is the sound of a bell, a cymbal, a harp, a violin.

A sound that expresses emotion, a sound that is deep, abrupt, staccato, flowing, a sound that invades our whole being, our whole self.

A sound rooted in the sensibilities of the one who sets it going, but also in metals and their blending. Gold and silver, elements of the vibrating instrument.

An individual sound, a sound rooted in the personality of the artist.

A sound, also the effect of a tool.

ART is the sound of a soul.[10]

The last decades of Leduc's career were a time of public recognition. His reception in 1938 of an honorary doctorate from the University of Montreal (fig. 121) and the broadening of critical interest in his work, which attracted many new appraisals, are just two signs of the favour he enjoyed.[11] Following a number of events that included the exhibition of a selection of his paintings at the Musée de la Province in 1945-1946 (fig. 125), Leduc's work was the object of a more extensive commercial distribution than ever before. René Bergeron, in his Chicoutimi gallery L'Art canadien, and Gilles Corbeil, in Montreal, began to market Leduc's paintings. It was also Gilles Corbeil who edited the special 1954 issue of *Arts et pensée* devoted to Leduc and who mounted the exhibition held at the Lycée Pierre-Corneille in Montreal to coincide with the magazine's appearance. Close friends of the artist, including Maurault, Choquette and Bindoff, regularly purchased drawings and paintings that the artist had hitherto carefully preserved.

The artist's final months, spent at the hospital in Saint-Hyacinthe, unfolded at the same calm and measured pace as the rest of his life. It was a life whose central theme Leduc had defined thus: "I am haunted by a nostalgia for the perfect, and by a preoccupation with Beauty."[12] Conscious of the place he had attained in our history of art,[13] he must have gone to meet his Maker confident in the judgement of posterity. "I hope my efforts will be taken into account. Even if the finished work is not the sum of all knowledge or the brilliance of all possible beauty. Do not be alarmed − a work of visual art is only linked to time in one sense."[14]

L. L.

10 Ozias Leduc, "L'art qu'est-ce?", manuscript, BNQ 327/3/15. Elsewhere Leduc wrote, "The work of art dominates its creator, he is not its master, which he often regrets, and sometimes he himself sees in it a meaning he never intended" (draft of a letter from Leduc to Henri Guindon [January 1949], BNQ 327/9/12).

11 Notable among the new authors interested in Leduc and the major texts published on the painter and his work during this period are: Hormisdas Magnan, "Le coin des artistes", *Le Terroir* [Quebec City], vol. 2, no. 12 (April 1922), pp. 567-570; Jean Chauvin, *Ateliers: études sur vingt-deux peintres et sculpteurs canadiens* (Montreal and New York: Louis Carrier & Co., 1928), pp. 118-126; Arthur Lemay, "Un artiste du terroir à St-Hilaire de Rouville − l'œuvre du peintre Osias Leduc", *Le Terroir* [Quebec City], vol. 8, nos. 11-12 (March-April 1928), cover and pp. 186-187; Olivier Maurault, *Marges d'histoire*, vol. 1: *L'art au Canada* (Montreal: Librairie d'action canadienne-française, 1929), "Documents historiques" series no. 4, pp. 25, 36-39, 47-49, 51-60, 303; Maurice Gagnon, *Peinture moderne* (Montreal: Éd. B. Valiquette, 1940), pp. 185, 187, 189, 199-201, "Poèmes philosophiques du peintre Ozias Leduc", *Technique* [Montreal] vol. 16, no. 9 (November 1941), pp. 640-660, and *Peinture moderne* (Montreal: Éd. B. Valiquette, 1943), pp. 126-130; René Bergeron, *Art et Bolchévisme* (Montreal: Fides, 1946), pp. 90-96; Suzette Dorval, "Interview d'Osias Leduc", *Amérique française*, vol. 7, no. 3 (March-May 1949), pp. 21-23; Henri-M. Guindon, "À propos d'un dessin: Ozias Leduc, peintre marial", *Messager de Marie Reine des Coeurs*, vol. 46, no. 5 (January 1949), pp. 1-7, and "Une somme mariale − la peinture d'Ozias Leduc", *Messager de Marie Reine des Cœurs*, vol. 46, no. 7 (March 1949), pp. 77-82; Pierre de Ligny Boudreau, "Ozias Leduc of Saint-Hilaire", *Canadian Art*, vol. 10, no. 4 (Summer 1953), pp. 156-158; Paul-Émile Borduas, "Quelques pensées sur l'œuvre d'amour et de rêve de M. Ozias Leduc", *Canadian Art*, vol. 10, no. 4 (Summer 1953), pp. 158-168; Paul Gladu, "La vie et les arts − Ozias Leduc", *Notre Temps* [Montreal], September 19, 1953, p. 4, and "L'ermite de Saint-Hilaire: le peintre Ozias Leduc", *Le Petit Journal* [Montreal], November 29, 1952, p. 61; Rodolphe de Repentigny, "Le plus canadien et le plus universel de nos peintres", *La Presse* [Montreal], June 23, 1954, p. 48; and the special issue of *Arts et pensée*, "Hommage à Ozias Leduc", vol. 3, no. 18 (July-August 1954).

12 Draft of a letter from Ozias Leduc to Marie-Reine Laperrière, June 9, 1938, BNQ 327/9/1.

13 To René Bergeron, who had sent him an article he was planning to publish, the artist wrote, "Leduc claims to be in a class alone in the edifice of Canadian art. Attempting to explain this is quite a business, as is understanding it." (Draft of a letter from Leduc to René Bergeron, April 10, 1946, BNQ 327/9/9.)

14 Draft of a letter from Leduc to Louis-N. Audet, February 7, 1927, BNQ 327/8/33.

PREPARATORY DRAWINGS FOR THE BISHOP'S CHAPEL, SHERBROOKE (Cats. 175-182)

175

Study for *Mary Hailed as Co-redeemer*
About 1922
Graphite on wove paper
37.1 x 19.1 cm (irregular)
Ottawa, The National Gallery of Canada, gift of the artist, Saint-Hilaire, 1953, inv. 6233.1
INSCRIPTIONS
Recto: *2' 8" x 8 3/4"; EVA; ADAM; ARB[O]R VITA*
PROVENANCE
Studio of the artist; National Gallery of Canada, 1953

176

Study for *Mary Hailed as Co-redeemer*
About 1922
Oil and graphite on cardboard
43.3 x 26.8 cm
Signed lower right: *OZIAS LEDUC -*
Ottawa, The National Gallery of Canada, inv. 6233.2
PROVENANCE
Studio of the artist; National Gallery of Canada, 1953

177

Study for *The Annunciation*
About 1922
Graphite on wove paper
37.1 x 19.4 cm (irregular)
Ottawa, The National Gallery of Canada, gift of the artist, Saint-Hilaire, 1953, inv. 6232.1
INSCRIPTIONS
Recto: *TIGRIS; EUPHRATES; GION; FISON*
PROVENANCE
Studio of the artist; National Gallery of Canada, 1953

178

Study for *The Annunciation*
About 1922
Oil and graphite on cardboard
43.3 x 27.2 cm
Signed lower right: *OZIAS LEDUC*
Ottawa, The National Gallery of Canada, inv. 6232.2
PROVENANCE
Studio of the artist; National Gallery of Canada, 1953

175

176

177

178

179

180

181

182

179

Study for *Jesus Found in the Temple*
About 1922

Graphite on wove paper

37 x 19.7 cm (irregular)

Ottawa, The National Gallery of Canada, gift of the artist, Saint-Hilaire, Quebec, 1953, inv. 6234.1

INSCRIPTIONS

Recto: *A Ω; SAPIENTIA*

PROVENANCE

Studio of the artist; National Gallery of Canada, 1953

180

Study for *Jesus Found in the Temple*
1922

Oil, graphite and coloured pencil on cardboard

43.7 x 27 cm

Signed and dated lower left: *OZIAS LEDUC 1922*

Ottawa, The National Gallery of Canada, inv. 6234.2

PROVENANCE

Studio of the artist; National Gallery of Canada, 1953

181

Study for *The Crucifixion*
About 1922

Graphite on wove paper

37 x 19.4 cm (irregular)

Ottawa, The National Gallery of Canada, gift of the artist, Saint-Hilaire, Quebec, 1953, inv. 6235.1

PROVENANCE

Studio of the artist; National Gallery of Canada, 1953

182

Study for *The Crucifixion*
About 1922

Oil and graphite on cardboard

43.3 x 25.5 cm

Signed lower right: *OZIAS LEDUC*

Ottawa, The National Gallery of Canada, inv. 6235.2

PROVENANCE

Studio of the artist; National Gallery of Canada, 1953

183

Portrait of Msgr. Alphonse-Osias Gagnon

1928-1933

Oil on canvas

114.5 x 81.5 cm

Signed upper right: *OZIAS LEDUC*

La Corporation archiépiscopale C.R. du diocèse de Sherbrooke

INSCRIPTIONS

Recto, lower left: *S. EXC. R.MGR ALPHONSE OSIAS GAGNON 3me Évêque de SHERBROOKE 1927 1941*
Verso: *"année 1933"*

PROVENANCE

Studio of the artist; Archevêché de Sherbrooke, 1933

THE decoration of the Bishop of Sherbrooke's private chapel was described by the artist as a project that "I am all the more keen on, in that its position, in my career as an artist, which is starting to broaden out, is of critical importance."[1] Indeed, it was Leduc's most personal decoration project to date, for it was the first time he exercised practically complete iconographic and artistic control. The four drawings and corresponding oil sketches presented here are studies for the main panels of the decorative ensemble. Because of their closeness in iconography and colour to the final works, they faithfully represent the Bishop's Chapel programme as a whole.[2]

The chapel Leduc was engaged to decorate is neo-gothic in style, an intimate space about five by ten metres, rising two storeys in height. In 1921, when the artist was first approached about the project, the recently built chapel was bare of decoration save for the stained glass windows in the chancel depicting the Mysteries of the Rosary and six Litanies of the Virgin.[3] The dedication of the chapel to Mary dictated that Leduc's programme follow suit, but it appears to have been the artist's own decision to focus on Mary as Co-redeemer for the theme of his programme.[4]

The dogma of the co-redemption of humanity through the Virgin Mary is conveyed by a combination of figural and ornamental decoration, conceived to form a unified whole. The four principal figural panels – *Mary Hailed as Co-redeemer, The Annunciation, Jesus Found in the Temple* and *The Crucifixion* (figs. 64-67) – constitute the iconographical core of the programme.[5] Placed two on each side wall, they are what Leduc referred to as the "four stages of Redemption – four Annunciations."[6] All but the first of these "annunciations" of the co-redemptive acts of Mary are based on events from the Gospels, but as Leduc made clear, the panels were not to be intepreted as narrative depictions.[7] Rather, their effect is symbolic, achieved in part through their hieratic structure, formal qualities and basic iconological relationship to the first panel, the Old Testament-inspired *Mary Hailed as*

Fig. 64

Fig. 65

Fig. 66

Fig. 67

Co-redeemer, which provides the key to the whole ensemble.

In this painting, Mary, aureoled by a rainbow (symbol of hope) and standing on a crescent moon (symbol of her Immaculate Conception), hovers before the (apple) tree of life. Around the tree trunk slithers the serpent, and at the foot kneel the repentant Adam and Eve. Latin inscriptions in the banderoles that separate the main scene from the arch register reveal that Leduc is alluding to the Virgin Mary's state of grace[8] and to the prophecy of her role in the redemption of mankind.[9] At the apex of the arch, Leduc further reinforces the idea of redemption with symbols of justice (sword and scales), God's creative power (whirlwind) and eternity (circle), all interwoven into a single motif.[10]

The three other Annunciation-Redemption panels that follow this seminal painting in chronological sequence echo it in the use of emblems and inscriptions, and in composition, particularly the inclusion of symmetrical kneeling figures. The similarity in arrangement among all four, according to Leduc, "should confer a visual resemblance on these particular scenes, bringing them back, so to speak, to a single ideal decorative type that should contribute to the harmony desired for the decoration as a whole."[11] The four panels are complemented by a fifth that depicts *The Tree of Jesse*, representing the hallowed lineage of the Virgin. Spanning the width of the back wall, it provides

the visual connection between *Mary Hailed as Co-redeemer* and *The Crucifixion*, which face each other across the chapel, and serves to link the promise of the Old Testament with its fulfilment in the New. The five panels are connected by ribs and painted borders of repeated ornamental motifs and are embraced visually by the canopy of a rich Prussian blue vault with regularly spaced gold stars signifying the triumph of order.[12]

Leduc had been granted the commission for the decoration of the private chapel of the Bishop of Sherbrooke by Bishop Paul LaRocque (1846-1926) on the suggestion of the architect of the Bishop's Palace, Louis-N. Audet (1881-1971), with whom Leduc had collaborated on three previous decoration projects. The two most recent of these – the Pauline Chapel in the Cathedral of Saint-Michel, Sherbrooke (cats. 168-169), and the Sacred Heart Chapel in the Church of Saint-Enfant-Jésus, Mile-End, Montreal (cat. 167)[13] – were instrumental in garnering Leduc the contract. The stained glass windows of the Pauline Chapel would have provided the Bishop a first-hand encounter with Leduc's religious decoration. This presumably favourable initial impression was reinforced by the artist's decorative programme of the Sacred Heart Chapel at Saint-Enfant-Jésus, which had been the subject of a brief but detailed commentary by Olivier Maurault published in 1921, just prior to Msgr. LaRocque's decision to have his own chapel

Figs. 64-67 Ozias Leduc, oil on canvas, glued in place (Sherbrooke, chapel of the Bishop's Palace).

Fig. 64 *Mary Hailed as Co-redeemer*, about 1926-1927, approx. 445 x 229 cm.

Fig. 65 *The Annunciation*, about 1931-1932, approx. 445 x 232 cm.

Fig. 66 *Jesus Found in the Temple*, approx. 445 x 232 cm.

Fig. 67 *The Crucifixion*, about 1926-1927, approx. 445 x 232 cm.

decorated.[14] Featuring an explanation of the iconography of the chapel complemented with photographs of the paintings (fig. 58), Maurault's study provided the promotional tool with which Audet was able to secure the Bishop's Chapel commission for Leduc.[15]

Although the artist was given "complete freedom to act,"[16] Audet contributed considerably to the conceptualization of the programme, suggesting, aside from specific iconography, that Leduc take his inspiration from "tradition or the best of what has been done – I'm thinking above all of colouring – to create a work that would not be a skilful replica, but quite personal."[17] While Leduc did defer to tradition, using the colours of the famous Sainte-Chapelle in Paris[18] (without, however, creating a pastiche of the thirteenth-century chapel), he also took to heart the architect's proposal that the decoration be "quite personal." For, in choosing as his theme Mary Co-redeemer, Leduc focussed on a dogma that had been increasingly discussed in theological writings of the period but seldom articulated pictorially.[19] Ludger Larose's treatment of the theme in 1892 for the Sacred Heart Chapel at the Church of Notre-Dame in Montreal is a rare example.[20] But Leduc himself had already treated the theme twice, once in 1918 in the Sacred Heart Chapel at Saint-Enfant-Jésus and the following year as part of the proposed decoration programme for the Church of Sainte-Marie-de-Monnoir, Marieville (fig. 112).[21] But the "quite personal" aspect goes beyond basic iconography to more aesthetic concerns.

When Leduc stated in his notes that the paintings of the Bishop's Chapel are not historical narratives, he explained the difference between such a narrative interpretation and the more Symbolist approach he had taken in formal terms, using *Jesus Found in the Temple* as an example:

It is not the reunion of a family accidentally separated and now together again after numerous experiences mingled with anxiety that is represented, but something that does not have material form, that exists nonetheless, emanating elements, people and things that make up the image captured by our look – an exalted image, one would wish, the emotional idea uniting the viewer with the appearance produced by the colours and the drawn forms. In this something lies the infant Jesus, his words to which we do not possess the key, his mother with a sorrowful heart and the mission sent down to earth by the heavenly Father.[22]

For Leduc, the message – the divine wisdom of God as revealed to Mary – is embodied not simply in the narrative, but also in the form of the image. He notes that the Doctors of the Church are shrouded in shadow, thus signifying their relative ignorance, while the young Jesus, in contrast, stands in full light, suggesting the radiance of true wisdom.[23]

In ascribing the symbolic essence of these paintings to a concordance between the formal aspects of a work and the expression of an idea, Leduc shows his debt to the aesthetics of

Maurice Denis, who held a prominent place in the movement to renew religious decoration in France. The ideas expounded by Denis in his *Nouvelles théories*, a collection of essays and lectures published in 1922,[24] are the ideas fashioned early in his career, now applied specifically to sacred art. "Symbolism," he wrote,

is the art of conveying and inducing states of mind by means of relationships between colours and forms. These relationships, invented or derived from nature, become the signs or symbols of these states of mind: they have the ability to suggest them … It is the *means* of expression (line, form, volume, colour) and not the object represented that must be expressive. Such an idea implies the existence of correspondences between the lines, forms and colours and, on the other hand, our states of mind, between the visible and the invisible: a connection of ideas in relation to the connection of things.[25]

Leduc's admiration of Denis went beyond a humble embracement of the French artist's aesthetics. It becomes evident that Leduc perceived himself as the Canadian counterpart to Denis, invoking the Bishop's Chapel decoration in support of his claim as the prime agent for the renewal of religious decoration in Canada. By the time of his interview in 1927 with the critic Jean Chauvin, whose visit to the artist's studio was later to be recounted in *Ateliers*, the completed Sherbrooke *Crucifixion* was on display in his studio.[26] Leduc promoted himself to the critic as holding the same values as Maurice Denis; his role was to "renew Christian art".[27] It is a self-perception that was no doubt fuelled by the visit the French artist had made during his North American tour in 1927 to two of Leduc's religious decorations in Montreal (the baptistries at Saint-Enfant-Jésus and Notre-Dame),[28] and buttressed by Denis's lecture, which Leduc attended, on a modernist aesthetic for church decoration delivered on October 1 at the Cercle universitaire at the University of Montreal (fig. 116).[29] It is a self-image he presented at times unabashedly to the clergy.[30]

Although Leduc would conveniently cite the Bishop's Chapel as the work of the "Canadian Denis", the project was for many years the bane of his existence. The actual decoration of the chapel had begun in April 1922, but another ten years would elapse before Leduc managed to bring the project to completion. The ornamental decoration of the vault and borders was completed by May 1923,[31] but it took another year to determine the composition of the four principal panels. "You will see the sketches for my Sherbrooke paintings in poor colours," he wrote Maurault in June 1924. "I am about to launch into the large canvases."[32] Yet, the years intervening until the completion in 1932 of *The Tree of Jesse*, the last painting to be executed, saw Leduc increasingly distracted by community affairs, commissions and self-directed artistic projects. To his anxious patrons at the Bishop's Chapel, however, he explained that the delays in execution were due to extensive research into theology, symbolism, history and the dogmatic iconography of the Middle Ages.[33] "I hope my efforts will be taken into account," Leduc wrote, attempting to put Audet at ease. "Even if the finished work is not the sum of all knowledge or the brilliance of all possible beauty. Do not be alarmed – a work of visual art is only linked to time in one sense. When you see this completed decoration, you will forget the time spent working on it."[34] One cannot help wondering whether the "penitence" refered to in conjunction with his single-handed completion of *The Tree of Jesse*[35] was in atonement for his unnecessarily drawn-out execution of the Bishop's Chapel decoration.

In a letter to the art historian Gérard Morisset, written within one year of the completion of the Bishop's Chapel decoration, Leduc summed up the transcendent nature of the programme:

One must be convinced that there is greater profit in seeking in this work not ingenious interpretations but the will of the artist to tell us with his mind and wide-open heart what, as a man, he wants to communicate to his fellows. Divested of all complications, which any commentary could perhaps only magnify, these canvases become more accessible, they reach out to us with their human side. The analysis of a certain gesture or expression fully reveals this.[36]

Thus, the Symbolist conceptualization and treatment of the theme of Mary Co-redeemer allow for a profoundly direct but inexplicable communication between image and viewer. In his notes, Leduc explained that he wished, "in this chapel at the Bishop's Palace in Sherbrooke, a chapel dedicated to the Virgin Mary, to show, glorified by Art, the pre-eminent role played by the Mother of the Word made flesh, the Redeemer, in the redemption of Mankind from sin and shame."[37] So just as Mary, in partnership with her Son, redeems humanity through her deeds, so does the artist aid in the redemption of humanity through his art.

A. G.

1 Draft of a letter from Ozias Leduc to Msgr. Paul LaRocque, December 25, 1921, BNQ 327/8/27. The most thorough history of this commission and the most extensive formal and iconographic analysis of Leduc's decorative programme for it, is Laurier Lacroix, "La décoration religieuse d'Ozias Leduc à l'évêché de Sherbrooke", Master's thesis, University of Montreal, 1973. A detailed account of the conceptualization of the decorative programme is provided in Laurier Lacroix, "La chapelle de l'évêché de Sherbrooke: quelques dessins préparatoires d'Ozias Leduc", National Gallery of Canada Bulletin, no. 30 (1977), pp. 3-18 (summarized in English as "The Chapel of the Bishop's Palace in Sherbrooke: Some Preparatory Sketches by Ozias Leduc").

2 For a discussion of these works as studies, see Lacroix 1973 and Lacroix 1977. Their presentation together would have satisfied Leduc's desire that the two groups not be separated, for in his mind they offered "a greater understanding of my work" (draft of a letter from Ozias Leduc to H. O. McCurry, Director of the National Gallery of Canada, November 24, 1953, BNQ 327/9/16.) Leduc was writing in response to McCurry who in fact was the first to voice his concern that the sets remain together, suggesting that the artist include the pencil drawings for the sum ($260) he was receiving from the Gallery for the four oil studies (letter from McCurry to Ozias Leduc, November 24, 1953, BNQ 327/8/7). Leduc noted the purchase of the drawings by the National Gallery in his diary (November 24, 1953, BNQ 327/3/12) and repeated the notion that the two sets not be separated in the draft of a letter to Paul Gagné [after 18 December 1953], BNQ 327/9/16.

3 See the letter from Audet to Leduc, April 6, 1921, BNQ 327/6/6; and Lacroix 1973, p. 111.

4 Leduc explained the genesis of the basic iconography in a letter to Pierre de Ligny Boudreau, September 22, 1953: "This chapel is dedicated to the most Holy Virgin, who, in the artist's mind, should of necessity remain in the chapel. It was therefore decided to show the Mother of God participating in the mystery of mankind's Redemption from sin – Mary Co-redeemer was appropriate." (National Gallery of Canada Library, File "Ozias Leduc", Book 1 [photocopy]). For an introduction to the concept of Mary as Co-redeemer, see Mark I. Miravalle, Mary, Coredemptrix, Mediatrix, Advocate (Santa Barbara: Queenship Publishing, 1993).

5 As indicated in a manuscript by Leduc entitled "Décoration de la chapelle de l'évêché de Sherbrooke. Thème – Marie co-rédemptrice" (BNQ 327/2/27). Leduc sent this document to Maurault for the priest's critical input (letter from Ozias Leduc to Maurault [between July 3 and November 11, 1923], Archives du Séminaire de Saint-Sulpice, Maurault papers). Directly on the artist's outlined programme, Maurault inscribed a single comment regarding Leduc's text on the Third Sorrow of the Virgin: "This does not seem sufficiently theological to me."

6 Undated manuscript by Leduc, BNQ 327/2/27. (Lacroix 1973, p. 87.)

7 "In each painting … the subject was conceived to emphasize the concept of the dogma rather than the narrative aspect of the scene represented." The quotation has been culled from the artist's "notes précieuses", as indicated in Henri-M. Guindon, "Une somme mariale – la peinture d'Ozias Leduc", Messager de Marie Reine des Coeurs, vol. 46, no. 7 (March 1949), p. 78.

8 Proverbs 8:22: "The Lord possessed me in the beginning of his way, before his works of old."

9 Genesis 3:15: "And I will put enmity between thee and the woman, between thy seed and her seed; it shall bruise thy head …"

10 The idea of redemption is similarly reinforced by iconic motifs in the other three panels: for The Annunciation, a dove (Holy Spirit, thus purity, modesty, gentleness, humility) within a circle (eternity) superimposed on a cross (Redemption); for Jesus Found in the Temple, an equilateral triangle (Trinity) from which a cross emanates; for The Crucifixion, an elongated hand (God as Protector) within a wreath (Victory). See Leduc's manuscripts "1er tableau", "2ème tableau", "3ème tableau" and "4ème tableau", Archives de l'Archevêché de Sherbrooke, Box "Chapelle de Mgr L'Archevêque", Documents Ozias Leduc, VII-A-3.

11 Manuscript by Leduc, beginning "À propos des figures décoratives …" (ibid., p. 1).

12 Leduc explained his intention in the May 8-9, 1922, entry of his Sherbrooke Diary (BNQ 327/3/9): "Began searching for the ceiling decoration of my chapel. Meaning of this decor. Arrangement, drawing colour. Deep blue background strewn with gold stars and crescents. At certain points these stars and crescents of different sizes scattered on the blue, appearance of Milky Way. A chaos that little by little progresses and orders itself into a regularly disposed seed pan. To symbolize the state of confusion and disarray of Adam and Eve after the Fall. State of unhappiness and supreme contradiction to the saintly discipline that desired the advent of the Virgin Co-redeemer, where, in symmetrical order, all the merciful might of the Master and his Divine Justice gleam." As noted by Lacroix 1973, p. 96, note 4, Leduc decided against the "chaos" for the Bishop's Chapel decoration but later used the idea for the ceiling of the Baptistry at Notre-Dame, Montreal.

13 Leduc and Audet first collaborated in 1911 on the decoration of Saint-Edmond, Coaticook (fig. 137). See the correspondence from O. L. to Audet, Archives de la Société d'histoire de Sherbrooke, Louis-N. Audet papers, P44.

14 Louis Deligny [pseudonym of Olivier Maurault], La chapelle du Sacré-Coeur, église du Saint-Enfant-Jésus, Montréal – Une décoration du peintre Ozias Leduc (Montreal: Imprimerie du Messager, 1921).

15 After receiving a copy of the booklet from Leduc, Audet requested another to show the Bishop, who was intending to have his private chapel decorated (letter from Audet to Leduc, March 14, 1921, BNQ 327/6/6). It is a measure of Leduc's interest in the project that he took it upon himself to send three copies for Audet to distribute as he saw fit (draft of a letter from Leduc to Audet [after 14 March 1921], BNQ 327/8/27).

16 Letter from Leduc to Boudreau, September 22, 1953, National Gallery of Canada Library, File "Ozias Leduc," Book 1 (photocopy).

17 Letter from Audet to Leduc, June 13, 1921, BNQ 327/6/6. Lacroix 1977 includes illustrations of the various proposals made by Audet to Leduc.

18 Letter from Leduc to Maurault, July 22, 1921, Archives du Séminaire de Saint-Sulpice, Maurault papers: "I'm working on my Sherbrooke project. Colour of the Sainte-Chapelle."

19 Mary's role as Co-redeemer was legitimized in 1854 with the dogma of the Immaculate Conception.

20 The painting was lost in the fire that destroyed the chapel in 1978. Larose's work was a horizontal painting, partitioned visually into three sections, left to right: The Immaculate Conception, The Angel Expelling Adam and Eve, and Adam and Eve Expelled from the Garden of Eden.

21 Leduc, however, did not receive the commission; the submission form for the contract remained among the artist's papers (BNQ 327/2/23).

22 Letter from Leduc to Boudreau cited in note 16. The question of emotive communication between artist and painting is raised in a letter from Leduc to Gérard Morisset, August 24, 1933, ANQQ P597/5/110.

23 Leduc's manuscript "3ème tableau, 'Jésus retrouvé dans le temple'", cited in note 10.

24 Maurice Denis, Nouvelles théories sur l'art moderne, sur l'art sacré 1914-1921 (Paris: L. Rouart et J. Watelin, 1922). The information that Leduc owned a copy comes from Jean-René Ostiguy, Ozias Leduc: Symbolist and Religious Painting, exhib. cat. (Ottawa: National Gallery of Canada, 1974), p. 223. Leduc himself mentioned the book's full title and author in the draft of a letter to Charles-Émile Desautels [after 8 January 1932], in which he recommended art literature to the aspiring church decorator (BNQ 327/8/38). In 1925, Leduc received as a gift from Maurault a volume of Vingt-cinq sanguines, dessins rehaussés et dessins de Maurice Denis (letter from Ozias Leduc to Maurault, March 20, 1925, Archives du Séminaire de Saint-Sulpice, Maurault papers).

25 Denis 1922, "Pour l'art sacré", pp. 175-176.

26 Jean Chauvin, Ateliers: études sur vingt-deux peintres et sculpteurs canadiens (Montreal and New York: Louis Carrier & Co., 1928), p. 118.

27 Ibid., p. 121. The passage in full reads, "To renew Christian art, to take us to the sublime regions of mysticism, to instil in painters, sculptors and architects a better preparation for the building and decorating of our places of worship, to train young disciples, clergy and congregations in religious art, in a word to pursue in Canada the work done in France by Maurice Denis and Georges Desvallières, founders of the Ateliers d'Art Sacré – this is what has long been the mission Leduc has set for himself. He dreams that one day we will sing, as has been written, 'alleluia to the rebirth of Christian art'."

28 Leduc recorded the event in his Sherbrooke Diary, October 8, 1927, BNQ 327/3/9. Denis's indifference, noted by Leduc, seems not to have dulled his ardent desire to become the "Canadian Denis".

29 See "L'art chrétien en France", Le Devoir [Montreal], October 3, 1927, p. 2, and "Le maître Maurice Denis au Cercle universitaire", La Patrie [Montreal], October 3, 1927, p. 14.

30 "I am studying a church decoration project of high import to the renaissance of religious art that I am dedicated to. I have already had occasion to explain to you my thoughts on this renaissance, and during his recent trip to Montreal Maurice Denis, celebrated for the renewal of modern religious art in France, took some of the brief time at his disposal to look at some of my work in progress, especially the decorations of the baptistry at Saint-Enfant-Jésus. This kind visit further reinforced my determination, which is supported by the encouragement of several other personalities as well." (Draft of a letter from Leduc [to J. R. Granger], October 6, 1927, BNQ 327/8/33.)

31 Leduc was helped in this initial stage by Borduas, who arrived in Sherbrooke on June 19, 1922, and was immediately put to work "applying the green of the leaves on the Mystic Rosebush on the chancel ceiling" (Sherbrooke Diary, BNQ 327/3/9).

32 Letter from Leduc to Maurault, June 16, 1924, Archives du Séminaire de Saint-Sulpice, Maurault papers.

33 Draft of a letter from Leduc to Audet, February 7, 1927, BNQ 327/8/33.

34 Ibid. Bishop LaRocque, who had applied pressure to Leduc right from the start, died August 15, 1926. His fears at not living to see the completion of the decoration of "his" chapel were relayed several times to the artist. See, for example, the letters from Audet to O. L., October 15, 1921, BNQ 327/6/6; January 9, 1922, BNQ 327/6/7; April 22, 1924, BNQ 327/6/9. LaRocque may not have enjoyed the chapel during his lifetime, but Leduc, on the occasion of the National Gallery of Canada's purchase of the four oil and four pencil studies for the decoration, hoped that the late Bishop would, "in heaven, assess the official recognition of the artistic value of the work he had commissioned, at your suggestion" (draft of a letter from Leduc to Audet [January 1954], BNQ 327/9/17).

35 Draft of a letter from Leduc to Borduas, June 15, 1932, BNQ 327/8/38. Leduc was writing in response to Borduas's generous offer to help in the work's completion.

36 Letter from Leduc to G. Morisset, August 24, 1933, ANQQ, P597/5/110.

37 Guindon 1949, p. 78.

184

Enchanted Island
After 1922
Oil on canvas
76.2 x 137.2 cm
Signed lower right: *OZIAS LEDUC*
Private collection
PROVENANCE
Studio of the artist; Claude Rousseau, Montmagny, 1955; Galerie Michel Bigué, about 1988; private collection

AMONG the many comments inspired by *Enchanted Island* is one of particular interest made by Janice Seline: she speculates that the painting may represent a clearing on the summit of Mount Saint-Hilaire, which Leduc, in "L'histoire de S.-Hilaire", associated with the mountain's primitive beginnings as an island, as a landscape that is "the work of a lengthy past".[1] This analysis, together with the work's treatment, encourages us to see the painting as part of a Romantic and Symbolist tradition of which one of the driving forces – as the philosopher Jean-Marie Schaeffer has pointed out – is a sense of loss of Unity and a nostalgia for the harmonious and organic integration of all aspects of human existence, vanished since the advent of modernity.[2] To counter this feeling of loss, Romantic art aims to serve as mediator between the spiritual and material worlds and strives to embody in its creations the meaning and harmony of this lost Unity. In fact, Romantic and Symbolist painting is full of images of paradises lost, of gardens of the Golden Age, of cities submerged under water. While some of these – particularly in the work of Romantic artists like William Blake – portray the Garden of Eden in its biblical form, others draw upon nature, often that of the artist's immediate surroundings, to transmit the vision of spiritual harmony – as in the work of Caspar David Friedrich, for example.

Pictorial renderings of the theme of the Golden Age abound in Symbolist painting. When directly related to the theme of artistic creation, they often feature scenes of idyllic gardens inhabited by muses and female figures draped in

184

the classical style. All is bathed in an atmosphere of timelessness and a soft, almost crepuscular light. There are many such works in French painting, their authors including Puvis de Chavannes, Alphonse Osbert (1857-1939), Maurice Denis and a host of others.[3] In Canada, too, there was a definite interest in these themes during the first decade or so of the twentieth century. The creations of Franz Johnston (1888-1949) and Suzor-Coté and the various decorative and Symbolist works of Adrien Hébert come to mind, and there are others.[4]

Within the current of European Symbolism, we also find several examples of artists who depicted landscapes devoid of any human presence, often inspired by their own native region. Through their use of a nocturnal or evening light softened by climatic effects, compositional forms that accentuate the intimist and decorative character of the work and materials of peculiar expressiveness, these artists endowed their landscapes with subjective, Symbolist, sometimes mystical and

even nationalist dimensions. Worth mentioning here are the Scandinavian painters who so strongly influenced the Canadian artists of the Group of Seven. Leduc himself only knew these European artists' works through reproductions in *The Studio*. It is nevertheless notable that the paintings of some among them bear a definite resemblance to Leduc's, both in spirit and technique. This is particularly true of the Swedish artists Karl Nordström, Eugène Jansson (1862-1915), Helmer Osslund and Prince Eugen.[5] The same approach to landscape is also common in the work of a number of other Canadian artists, including Suzor-Coté (*Autumn Scene*, 1910, Musée du Québec).

Enchanted Island is, together with the vertical-format *Golden Snow* (cat. 152), one of the largest landscapes painted by Leduc. The treatment employed for the foreground of *Golden Snow* is similar to that used in the background of the present painting and prefigures the scroll forms that appear in many later religious works. A preparatory charcoal drawing

for this painting, entitled *The Enchanted Garden*,[6] shows the same generous style, wealth of curves and rendering of depth as in the oil version. However, the painting creates a stronger impression of horizontality by defining more clearly the linear arabesques that separate the various planes.

In its portrayal of a primitive natural paradise, *Enchanted Island* is very much a Symbolist work. In addition, several of its formal components show the influence of Art nouveau painting – the horizontal format, for example, and the prevalence of curved lines. Starting on the left and spreading across two-thirds of the space, the foreground is dominated by the arabesque formed by the pinks, yellows, browns and mauves of the flower clusters. This decorative garland serves as both a repoussoir and a frame for the picture space. Such use of a plant garland is a device found in European art, notably in the work of the Pre-Raphaelites, but also among Canada's Group of Seven, particularly in the painting of Tom Thomson, which was strongly influenced by Art nouveau (*Autumn's Garland*, about 1916, National Gallery of Canada; *Woodland Waterfall*, about 1916, McMichael Canadian Art Collection, Kleinburg, Ontario).

The predominantly pink arabesque in the foreground is echoed by the others, in darker tones of green, that link the middle and rear grounds. The tree carries these irregular scroll forms right to the upper edge of the painting, pulling the one on the left back towards itself in a circular movement that is powerfully reinforced by both the broad, directional brush stroke and the very pale pinks, yellows and mauves of the sky.

Aesthetically speaking, then, this *Enchanted Island* is clearly an heir to turn-of-the-century Symbolism. But it is interesting to compare it to a work rooted in another approach, an oil by Paul-Émile Borduas entitled *2.45*, or *The Enchanted Island* (fig. 68). It is true that Borduas initially titled his work *Devil's Island*, perhaps hesitating, as François-Marc Gagnon has suggested, to use a title already taken by his master.[7] Although the two works are very different, Borduas also employs a circular central form, which, owing to a network of blots in the foreground, can be read as a background plane. Moreover, the pink, green and black *taches* on the left seem to form the beginning of an arabesque. This compositional form could thus be seen as an abstract reference to the structure of Leduc's painting. As for the title *Devil's Island*, so different from Leduc's, it must surely be related to the existence of a specifically sexual element in the primal island space, translated by the presence of two nudes, notably a female figure with very obvious sexual characteristics. In Expressionism and Surrealism, human sexuality became a recognized component of creative – and destructive – energy. The dream of regaining the Unity lost through the decadence of civilization, of a return to "natural" harmony, had henceforth to encompass the reconciliation of man with his own sexuality. While the title *Devil's Island* may have said much about a Quebec in which attitudes towards

Fig. 68   Paul-Émile Borduas, *2.45*, or *The Enchanted Island*, 1945, oil on canvas, 45.1 x 52.4 (Montreal Museum of Fine Arts, inv. 1983.3).

sexuality remained ambivalent, Borduas's painting deserved to be renamed, albeit posthumously, *Enchanted Island*, for it is a twentieth-century interpretation of the dream of natural harmony, the reconciliation of man with himself and the magical order of nature – the very dream that was the focus of Leduc's essentially nineteenth-century version.

E. T.

1   Janice Seline, "The Real and the Ideal: Progress and the Landscapes of Ozias Leduc", in Laurier Lacroix *et al.*, *Ozias Leduc the Draughtsman*, exhib. cat. (Montreal: Concordia University), 1978, pp. 118-119.

2   Jean-Marie Schaeffer, *L'art de l'âge moderne: l'esthétique et la philosophie de l'art du XVIIIe siècle à nos jours* (Paris: Gallimard, 1992), NRF "Essais" series, pp. 88-89.

3   For example, Puvis de Chavannes, *The Sacred Grove Beloved of the Arts and of the Muses* (about 1884-1889, Art Institute of Chicago); Alphonse Osbert, *Soir antique* (Evening in Antiquity), (1908, Musée du Petit Palais, Paris), *La muse au lever du soleil* (1918, private collection); and Maurice Denis, *Les muses au bois sacré* (1893, Musée national d'art moderne – Centre Georges Pompidou, Paris), and *Soir trinitaire* (1891, Mrs. P. Déjean collection, Saint-Martin-de-Londres).

4   Franz Johnston, *The Magic Pool* (1917, NGC); Marc-Aurèle de Foy Suzor-Coté, *Evening Harmony* (1917, NGC), *Idyll* (MQ); Adrien Hébert, *"Setting Sun" Panel* (about 1914-1915, Irène Hébert collection, Joliette); *L'Idole brisée* (The Broken Idol) (1915, private collection, Calgary); *Une nuit un faune appelait* (One Night a Faun Called) (about 1918, Lucien Guyon collection, Richmond).

5   See Roald Nasgaard, *The Mystic North: Symbolist Landscape Painting in Northern Europe and North America, 1890-1940* (Toronto, Buffalo and London: Art Gallery of Ontario and University of Toronto Press, 1984).

6   Reproduced in Lacroix *et al.* 1978, p. 62.

7   François-Marc Gagnon, *Paul-Émile Borduas*, exhib. cat. (Montreal: Montreal Museum of Fine Arts, 1988), pp. 210-211.

185

Still Life (with Books and Magnifying Glass)
After 1924
Oil on fibreboard
22.6 x 31.8 cm

Signed lower right: *OZIAS LEDUC*

Ottawa, The National Gallery of Canada,
inv. 15802

INSCRIPTIONS

Verso: *(LES LIVRES ET LA LOUPE); # 7*

PROVENANCE

Studio of the artist; Mr. and Mrs. Luc Choquette,
Montreal; National Gallery of Canada, 1969

SPEAKING of Ozias Leduc's still lifes, Michel Dupuy wrote, "Faithful to the object, his canvases are essentially the inner landscape of a sensitive and meditative soul."[1] This *Still Life (with Books and Magnifying Glass)*, an apparently simple theme, can be analyzed on a number of levels. The artist's love of reading and books as a source of knowledge had already been illustrated early on in his career (cats. 11, 20-23). Here, the foreground contains an open book showing a black-and-white reproduction on the left, opposite a blank page. First enigma: Is the hard-to-decipher reproduction a landscape with shapes reflected in water, or a Vanitas featuring a centrally placed skull strongly lit from one side? Second enigma: Just behind the book and right in the middle of the composition is a postcard reproduction of a Cupid the Archer by the Italian artist Marcantonio Franceschini (1648-1729).[2] Then there are the twenty or so books, whose nine legible titles – *Jardin d'Épicure, Botanique, Profiles, L'Irréparable, L'Anneau d'or, Rebelle, Némésis, Oracle* and *Le Cid* – remind us of the omnipresence of words in painting[3] and fulfil a double role as titles and as words. "Jardin" and "botanique" evoke the study of nature; "rebelle", the rejection of tradition; "némésis", divine retribution for excess; "oracle", the revelation of hidden mysteries. As titles, the words reveal Leduc's literary, scientific and esoteric interests.[4] The artist's library was, in fact, a comprehensive one that included works on art, literature, history and sym-

bolism,[5] and his notes and inscriptions often focussed on these same subjects.[6]

Still Life (with Books and Magnifying Glass) is an allegory on artistic creation: art, as well as science, is a way of attaining knowledge. The table probably represents the artist's own work surface, while the art book is a source containing the art of the past and the reproductions symbolize the dissemination of art. The cupid symbolizes the love of work, of art, of creation. The books are a window onto knowledge. The magnifying glass permits the close examination and thus the analysis of objects. The drawing pen and the hinged ruler are the technical instruments used in creation. The work hanging on the wall, which seems to resemble the small oil sketches produced by Leduc early in the century (for example, cat. 111), is the fruit of the observations that lead to the creative act.

M. L.

1   Michel Dupuy, "Ozias Leduc, peintre et mystique", *Le Droit* [Ottawa], February 2, 1974, p. 21.

2   Reproduced in *Gli Uffizi – Catalogo Generale* (Florence: Centro Di, 1979), no. P 619.

3   There have been both a book and a recent exhibition devoted to this subject; see Michel Butor, *Les Mots dans la peinture* (Paris: Flammarion, "Les sentiers de la création – Champs", 1980); and *Poésure et Peintrie – "d'un art, l'autre"*, exhib. cat. (Musée de Marseille, Réunion des Musées nationaux, 1993).

4   From what is decipherable on the spines, the books can be identified as follows: Anatole France, *Le Jardin d'Épicure* (1894); Eugène Caustier, *Botanique à l'usage des élèves des classes de cinquième A et B* (1920); Paul Bourget, *L'Irréparable* (1884) and *Némésis* (1918); *L'Anneau d'or des grands mystiques, de Saint Augustin à Catherine Emmerich* (1924); Baron Régis de Trobriand, *Le Rebelle: histoire canadienne* (1842); *Petit zodiaque magique ou L'Oracle infaillible du beau sexe* [1891]; and Pierre Corneille, *Le Cid* (1636). Paul Bourget was not a favourite of Robert de Roquebrune (cat. 155), who published an article on this author in *Le Nigog*, August 1918, p. 275. The article sparked some indignation among readers. In the issue of the following October, Roquebrune published a letter from one of them, under the pseudonym of Julien Dorsenne, and attempted to defend himself using the sarcastic tone generally adopted by contributors to this publication.

5   For a partial list, see Jean-René Ostiguy, *Ozias Leduc: Symbolist and Religious Painting*, exhib. cat. (Ottawa: National Gallery of Canada, 1974), p. 223.

6   BNQ 327/4/8-14.

186

Landscape (Stream in a Gorge)
After 1927
Oil on cardboard
27.1 x 15.1 cm
Signed lower left: *O LEDUC*

Private collection
INSCRIPTIONS
Verso: *Jean Désy*
PROVENANCE
Studio of the artist; Jean Désy; Claire Bertrand; private collection, 1988

THIS landscape, like a number of others in Leduc's oeuvre, is somewhat perplexing. It was never exhibited during Leduc's lifetime or mentioned in the artist's correspondence; the first reference to the painting appeared only in 1938, in an article by Olivier Maurault (cats. 161-163), who, in characterizing Leduc's landscapes as seductive and in listing the various private and public collections in which they figured, pointed out that the artist still had in his studio "a sentimental landscape featuring a stream in a gorge, which will disappear one day, carried off by some impudent visitor".[1] It was no doubt shortly after this that Jean Désy, a friend of Maurault, purchased the painting for his country home in Boucherville.[2]

Owing to similarities in subject matter (cloud) and composition to *Blue Cumulus* (cat. 143), this *Landscape* has been dated to about 1913.[3] Although it is difficult to pinpoint the date, a reassessment of the work suggests that it was more likely executed sometime after 1927. In a letter to a collector interested in purchasing a work by Leduc, the artist refers to the availability of "some charcoal and black crayon drawings of small dimensions ... They are night effects, underbrush with snow, at twilight, etc."[4] The lack of any description approximating *Landscape* leads one to believe that the work had not yet been executed. Moreover, Leduc's delicate use of the palette knife, visible especially in the sky, is more characteristic of later works such as *Snowy Landscape* (1939-1945).[5] Also telling is the iconography. Désy described the painting as representing "a body of water in a narrow valley bathed in the light of dusk".[6] His interpretation of the image as being one of dusk does indeed correspond to the oppressive sense of desolation evoked by the barren rockscape that occupies half the picture area. *Landscape* is the sterile, unyielding earth that humanity must traverse.

The theme, in fact, is one that Leduc had addressed in his decoration programme for the Bishop of Sherbrooke's private chapel, which he had begun to conceptualize in the early twenties. In the panel *Mary Hailed as Co-redeemer* (cat. 176), Adam and Eve are situated in the garden after the Fall. The rock formation in the garden of the disgraced, particularly as it is rendered behind Adam, bears a similarity in its starkness to that in *Landscape*.[7] But not all is despair. Just as the Adam and Eve of the Sherbrooke panel have been given the promise of redemption by the presence of Mary, so too has the viewer of *Landscape*. With the upward sweep of the cliffs of the gorge echoing that of the cloud that ascends from a subdued blue-grey to an intense yellow, the viewer can only focus on the celestial promise of paradise regained.

A. G.

1 Louis Deligny [pseudonym of Olivier Maurault], "Ozias Leduc, peintre mystique", *Le Mauricien* [Trois-Rivières], vol. 2, no. 2 (February 1938), p. 5.

2 See the letter from Jean Chauvin to Alan Jarvis, Director of the National Gallery of Canada, October 18, 1955, regarding Désy's willingness to lend the painting to the National Gallery of Canada's 1955-1956 Leduc retrospective (National Gallery of Canada, file # 5.5, Leduc).

3 Louise Beaudry, *Contemplative Scenes: The Landscapes of Ozias Leduc*, exhib. cat. (Montreal: Montreal Museum of Fine Arts, 1986), p. 23.

4 Draft of letter from Ozias Leduc to Gustave Lanctôt, December 1, 1927, BNQ 327/8/33.

5 Oil on cardboard, 24.2 x 30.5 cm, Musée Pierre-Boucher du Séminaire de Trois-Rivières. Reproduced in Beaudry 1986, p. 58.

6 Letter from Jean Chauvin to Alan Jarvis, October 18, 1955, National Gallery of Canada, file #5.5, Leduc.

7 It is also similar to a landscape Leduc later included in the panel of *The Sower* in Shawinigan-Sud (fig. 85).

187

Soft Snow, also called *Snow Bank*
   After 1927
   Charcoal, coloured pencil and black ink
   on paper
   20 x 15.9 cm

Signed lower left: *OZIAS LEDUC*

Quebec City, Musée du Québec, inv. 53.114
   INSCRIPTIONS
Recto, lower centre: *Neige douce*
Verso: *Banc de neige OZ.L.*
   PROVENANCE
Studio of the artist; Musée du Québec, 1953

As suggested by Lacroix, *Soft Snow* may be dated to after 1927 on the basis of the use of coloured pencil, a medium Leduc had started employing in his drawings for the decoration of the baptistry at Notre-Dame Church.[1] In *Soft Snow,* he has taken advantage of the medium's waxy consistency. Its tendency to adhere only irregularly to the paper's surface effects the velvety texture suggested in the title.

Like many of Leduc's landscape drawings, which are neither sketches nor studies for other works (for example, cat. 154), *Soft Snow* is an autonomous work, a diversion from the larger projects the artist was immersed in. Its synthetic, almost japonist qualities indicate the work was conceived in the studio. The space consists of foreground and background alone, separated by a voluted line that defines the crest of a stylized wave of snow. Sculpted as much through the repeated curved strokes of blue, black and red crayon as by the winds that sweep across the mountain, this decorative wave provides a foil to the sugarloaf whose form, here simplified, is accentuated through the levelling of the upper slopes of Mount Saint-Hilaire.

Although the work's title is inscribed in the bottom centre of the drawing, *Soft Snow* has consistently been presented as *Snow Bank* ever since Leduc sold it to the Musée du Québec in 1953. Indeed, this is the title the artist himself recorded upon noting the transaction in his diary.[2] Leduc's retitling of the work may have been the result of a reassessment of the effect of the drawing. While the waxy substance does give a soft texture to the mountain snow, its insistent, striated application in the foreground crest that dominates the scene creates an almost impenetrable bank that, as Lacroix noted, has the effect of "visually and psychologically isolating the hillock that dominates Mont Saint-Hilaire".[3]

A. G.

1   Laurier Lacroix *et al., Ozias Leduc the Draughtsman,* exhib. cat. (Montreal: Concordia University, 1978), p. 81.

2   August 31, 1953, BNQ 327/3/12. Leduc received $25 for the drawing.

3   Lacroix *et al.* 1978, p. 81.

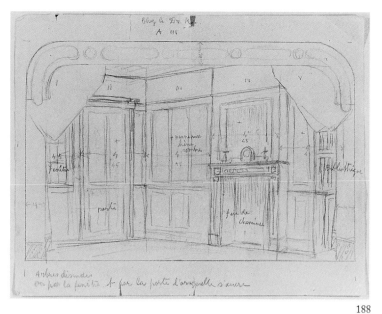

188

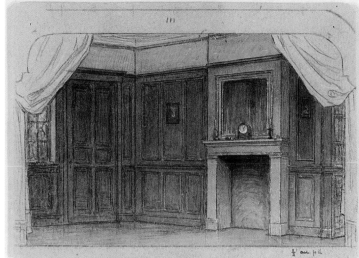

189

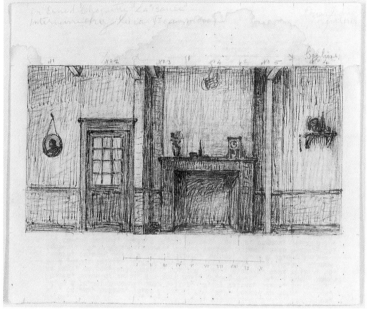

190

188

Scenery Study for *Madeleine*

1928

Graphite and blue pencil on green wove paper

20.7 x 27 cm

Private collection

INSCRIPTIONS

Recto, upper centre: *Chez le Dr R. / A III;* lower left: *Arbres dénudés / vu par la fenêtre et par la porte l'orsquelle s'ouvre;* centre: *Fenêtre / porte / panneaux / chêne / sombre feu de / cheminée / Bibliothèque*

PROVENANCE

Studio of the artist; Dr. Ernest Choquette, Saint-Hilaire; private collection

189

Scenery Study for *Madeleine*

1928

Graphite, blue, brown and grey ink, and gouache on grey-brown cardboard

17.4 x 24.2 cm

Private collection

INSCRIPTIONS

Recto, upper centre: *III;* lower right: *1/2 au pd*
Verso: *Étude pour le décor de Madeleine*

PROVENANCE

Studio of the artist; Dr. Ernest Choquette, Saint-Hilaire; private collection

190

Scenery Study for *La Bouée*

1929

Graphite and coloured pencil on white laid paper

17.9 x 21.5 cm

Signed and dated upper right: *Ozias Leduc 13 juil 1929*

Private collection

INSCRIPTIONS

Recto, upper left: *Dr Ernest Choquette "La Bouée" / Intérieur chez Lucas Beaumont; Coulisse*

PROVENANCE

Studio of the artist; Dr. Ernest Choquette, Saint-Hilaire; private collection

191

Scenery Study for *La Bouée*
1929

Graphite, coloured pencil and brown ink on white laid paper

17.8 x 24.1 cm

Signed and dated upper right: *Ozs Leduc 10 jui[l] 1929*

Private collection

INSCRIPTIONS

Recto, upper left: *Dr Ernest Choquette "La Bouée" Décor du 1ᵉʳ Acte Partie de Gauche*; lower left: *11'10" x 3'10" par panneau*

PROVENANCE

Studio of the artist; Dr. Ernest Choquette, Saint-Hilaire; private collection

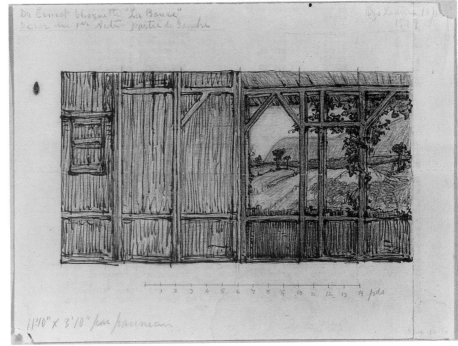

191

ROUND the turn of the century, the art of stage scenery was in an ambiguous position. Practised by artists with as much professionalism as was exercised in the decoration of churches, it was nonetheless taken far less seriously. And yet, the same names were often associated with the two art forms – François-Xavier Édouard Meloche and Toussaint-Xénophon Renaud (1860-1946), for example.[1] Of course, painted stage scenery, unlike canvases fixed to the walls of a house of worship, is by definition ephemeral; but whatever their reasons, critics of the period devoted far more attention to ecclesiastical art than they did to theatrical.

Leduc created several stage paintings – vertical cycloramas designed as backdrops – of which only sketches remain. The ones executed in 1896 (fig. 99) and probably 1899[2] show a relatively classical approach to scenography. Since the Renaissance, the rules governing this art, especially those concerning unity of place, allowed for three possible sets, for which Piero della Francesca (about 1420-1492)[3] and Sebastiano Serlio (1475-1554)[4] left famous models: a palace terrace for tragedy, a public square for comedy and a rural landscape for pastoral works. That Leduc was aware of these conventions is indicated by the first sketches, featuring terraces with monuments, and by descriptions of the three scenery paintings executed in 1924 and 1925 at the request of the Oblate Fathers of Collège Mathieu in Gravelbourg, Saskatchewan:

a street, a fortress and a forest.[5] He no doubt learned these elements of classical scenography from Luigi Capello, who created several such works in Quebec.[6] Moreover, the stage curtains that appear in Leduc's first backdrop sketches are in the Italian style: each of the curtain's two sections is designed to open by being lifted diagonally in the middle, and the artist planned that the attachment of the curtain to the frame of the stage would be concealed by a valance.

On his painted terraces, Leduc intended to instal monuments to Quebec heroes: Montcalm with Cap Diamant in the background in one case, and Cartier, Champlain and Maisonneuve in the other.[7] The artist's nationalism was again very evident in the sets he designed in 1928 and 1929 for the plays *Madeleine* and *La Bouée* by his friend Ernest Choquette (cat. 92), but his ideas about stage design seem to have changed considerably. Although he did use local images for the two backdrops – Fort Saint-Louis in Chambly and Mount Saint-Bruno for *Madeleine*, and Mount Saint-Hilaire for *La Bouée* – they were no longer the traditional general purpose scenes but corresponded to specific indications in Choquette's text.[8]

Furthermore, the backdrops were only visible through large openings in the realistic "built" sets that represented a drawing room, a doctor's consulting room, an outbuilding and the façade of a hotel. In 1897 and 1925, Leduc had been a scenery painter; he had now become a scenographer.

The same decorative approach can be employed in executing painted canvases for a theatre or for a church, since the requirements are fundamentally the same: to provide a background, create a sense of perspective, portray the themes appropriate to the surroundings. Even the process of using dramatic events of the text as a source in creating a scenic space of the stage is similar to the way in which a church decorator draws his subjects from the Bible and the lives of the saints. But transforming the empty space of a stage into a specific setting is a complex operation – one at which Leduc now excelled. He designed not only a backdrop with sliding side panels (as his friend J.-Auguste Rho [1867-1947] had done for a production of Racine's *Athalie*, presented at the Gesù theatre with Mendelssohn's incidental music in 1925),[9] but also built sets light enough to be used on tour. The set for *Madeleine*,[10] first used for the two performances in Saint-Hilaire on July 14 and August 18, 1928, was probably used at Montreal's Monument National on January 29 and 31, 1929; the director in both cases was Jeanne Maubourg Roberval (1875-1953), and the cast, with Thérèse Church in the title role, were mostly members of the Société canadienne d'opérette. The set for *La Bouée* was apparently not executed, and it was the comedies *L'Étincelle* and *Chut; voilà la bonne!* that Maubourg Roberval presented in Saint-Hilaire on July 4, 1929, with the same local star, Thérèse Church.

Set designers had developed ways of dealing with the stage directions for romantic and realist plays, especially those calling for set changes that were only possible in theatres where painted scenery could be lowered and raised at will. They began to opt for a single built set, or one that could be modified slightly from scene to scene. With his designs for *Madeleine* and *La Bouée*, Leduc was moving towards this solution. For Acts II, III and V of *Madeleine*, he conceived a single construction whose permanently visible central section – a veranda – could be moved stage right or stage left and still open onto a view of the fort at Chambly.[11] For *La Bouée*, the design was even more daring: for the Prologue and Scenes 2 and 4, which take place at the home of Dr. Duvert, and for Scenes 1 and 3, located in Lucas de Beaumont's farmhouse, Leduc planned only a single construction – the same one, in fact, used in the acts of *Madeleine* mentioned above – with a change of props and backdrop landscape being the only indications that the action occurs in a different place.[12] Moreover, in both plays, by manipulating the relationships between the background paintings and the lightweight modular set opening onto them, and a use of sliding panels on both sides, Leduc succeeded in minimizing the spatial restrictions of Saint-Hilaire's tiny stage.[13]

A. G. B.

1 Renaud was responsible for the ceiling of the Monument National. Meloche is mentioned in the 1899 and 1900 records of this same theatre in relation to the renting of a "painting cradle" (a scaffold fixed to a wall of the stage, used for painting scenery). See Renée Noiseaux-Gurick, "À la recherche des peintures scéniques du Monument-National", Les Cahiers d'histoire du théâtre du Québec, no. 1 (September 1990), pp. 9-12.

2 Reproduced in Laurier Lacroix et al., *Ozias Leduc the Draughtsman*, exhib. cat. (Montreal: Concordia University, 1978), pp. 21-22.

3 Pierre Francastel, *Peinture et société* (Paris: Gallimard), "Idées/Arts" series, no. 4, p. 83, ill.

4 Daniel Couty and Alain Rey, eds., *Le Théâtre* (Paris: Bordas, 1986), p. 42.

5 On this commission, see the correspondence between Georges Boileau, o.m.i., and Ozias Leduc, BNQ 327/6/9-10 and 327/8/30-31.

6 Gérard Morisset, *La peinture traditionnelle au Canada français* (Montreal: Cercle du livre de France, 1960), "L'Encyclopédie du Canada français" series, vol. 2, p. 135; Alexandra Shtychno, "Luigi Giovanni Vitale Capello, a.k.a. Cappello (1843-1902), Itinerant Piedmontese Artist of Late Nineteenth-century Quebec", Master's thesis, Concordia University, March 1991, pp. 22-24.

7 In 1825, the painter Louis-Hubert Triaud (about 1790-1836), assisted by the actor Schinotti, had built a terrace with a monument to Shakespeare, a London square and the gardens of Saint Helen's Island (Pierre-Georges Roy, "Le Cirque Royal ou Théâtre Royal", *Le Bulletin des recherches historiques*, vol. 42, no. 11 [November 1936], pp. 640, 650; see *La Gazette du Québec*, November 21, 1825, and *The Quebec Mercury*, February 16, 1832). At the opening of Montreal's Académie de Musique in 1875, the New York set decorator Seavy, assisted by J. W. Rough and E. Lewis, used a view of Mount Orford for a pastoral scene (*The Gazette* [Montreal], November 13, 1875, p. 2).

8 For example, for Act II of Madeleine, Choquette's directions are as follows: "In the foreground, on the left, a games table, two large armchairs. On the right, a rustic settee. Scattered seats. Flowers everywhere. On the left, a door opening into the doctor's consulting room, on the right, one leading to Madeleine's bedroom. Through a frame of Virginia creeper can be seen on the horizon, beyond the trees in the garden, the castellated walls of the fort, and the river on which motionless schooners laze in the peace of a summer evening" (Ernest Choquette, *Théâtre. Madeleine, pièce en cinq actes* [Épisode de 1837], followed by *La Bouée, pièce en quatre actes et un prologue* [Montreal: Déom, 1927], p. 25).

9 See the reproduction in André-G. Bourassa, "Scène québécoise et modernité", in *L'Avènement du Québec à la modernité culturelle*, Yvan Lamonde and Esther Trépanier, eds. (Quebec City: Institut québécois de recherche sur la culture, 1986), p. 167. Unlike Leduc's "practicable" sets, Rho's layered decors were designed exclusively for the stage of the Gesù.

10 For this set, Leduc was assisted by Dollard Church, who was also stage manager, and by two graduates of Montreal's École des Beaux-Arts who lived in Saint-Hilaire – Paul-Émile Borduas and Raoul Viens.

11 It is possible that this same decor was used for the first Jeunesses musicales event, as witness a photo kept in the Gesù archives and reproduced on the cover of *L'Annuaire théâtral*, no. 17 (Spring 1995). If so, it was a variation on a print by William Bartlett, dating from 1840. Leduc may have made use of Bartlett's print (simply replacing the boats by sailing ships, as requested by Choquette) because he had only ever seen the fort in an advanced state of decay; but it was also common for scene painters to draw inspiration from prints, especially those included in the *Practical Guide to Scene Painting and Painting in Distemper* by Frederick Lloyds (London, 1875).

12 Moreover, this was Choquette's intention: "Act I … Lucas de Beaumont's farmhouse … On the right: large room furnished in the Canadian habitant style: chairs, sofa, china cupboards; Norman fireplace, rag rug; calendar and prints hanging on the wall; work jackets and caps hanging in a corner. Door on the right. Bay window at the rear, with a view onto a vegetable garden, fruit trees, etc. On the left: lean-to structure communicating with the room, from which it is separated by a wall that does not reach right to the front of the stage. Rough wooden benches, farm implements, shovels, forks, harnesses, etc. … At the back are piles of straw and, in the distance, a barley field that reaches right to the foot of the mountain … As the curtain rises, Lucas is standing towards the back of the lean-to, sharpening his scythe. Sheaves of oats lie on the floor nearby" (Choquette 1927, p. 101). "Act II … At Dr. Duvert's house … Same set as in the first act – but with, on the left, a veranda with a view over the Richelieu, and leading on the right into a dispensary. Rustic chairs, hammocks, trees, greenery, etc." (*ibid.*, p. 119).

13 In those days, plays were performed in a room over the new school, near the church.

192

193

192

The Blessed André Grasset

　　1929

　　Gouache on white paper glued to
　　cardboard

　　37.4 x 27.3 cm

Monogrammed and dated lower centre: *19 OL 29*

Private collection

INSCRIPTIONS

Recto, below the main figure: *BIENHEUREUX /
ANDRÉ GRASSET / DE SAINT-SAUVEUR*; in
the panels of the triptych at left: *1758 /
MONTRÉAL; 1779 / SENS; at right: 1792 / PARIS;
1926 / ROME*
Verso: *Olivier Maurault pss 1265 St Denis 2900 Blvd
du Mt Royal*; label of Galerie Morency Frères

PROVENANCE

Studio of the artist; Olivier Maurault, p.s.s.,
Montreal, 1929; Collège André-Grasset, Montreal;
private collection

193

The Blessed André Grasset

　　About 1930

　　Stained glass, painted glass and lead

　　120 x 105 cm

Signed lower left: *G.E. PELLUS MONTREAL*

Private collection

INSCRIPTIONS

Recto, below the main figure: *BIENHEUREUX /
ANDRE GRASSET / DE SAINT-SAUVEUR*;
in the panels of the triptych at left: *1758 /
MONTREAL; 1779 / SENS; at right: 1792 / PARIS;
1926 / ROME*

PROVENANCE

Studio of G. E. Pellus; Collège André-Grasset,
about 1930; private collection

ANDRÉ GRASSET of Saint-Sauveur was born in Montreal on April 3, 1758, and baptised in Notre-Dame Church the following day. Very little is known about his life apart from these few facts: following the Conquest, at the age of six, he emigrated with his family to France; by 1779, he was a young priest serving on the staff of the cathedral at Sens; and, after being incarcerated in the Carmelite convent in Paris, Grasset – by then a canon – was among the 212 priests massacred in September 1792 for refusing to swear allegiance to the Civil Constitution.

Grasset was beatified with his fellow martyrs in October 1926. The painting executed for the occasion conveyed little about him.[1] To rectify this and pay tribute to the first native of Montreal to receive beatification, Olivier Maurault (cats. 161-163) commissioned Leduc to execute a monochrome gouache to serve as the basis for a devotional image.[2] The image, printed between April and June 1929,[3] was employed for the scale model of the window designed for Montreal's newly constructed Collège André-Grasset (cat. 193).[4]

In making the window, Guillaume-Ernest Pellus[5] added colour to the composition of Leduc's gouache. The beautiful red flashed glass, engraved with acid and highlighted with yellow, imbues the figure with remarkable liveliness; grisaille has been used to add depth to the buildings featured on the triptych's outer sections, which summarize Grasset's life.[6] Although Pellus stayed quite close to Leduc's image, he did make the hero's face somewhat thinner and adapt the original decorative elements: the mouldings have become fillets, and the Gothic triptych is set against a diamond-pane window rather than the Art Deco background that would have been virtually impossible to execute in glass.

Initially placed opposite the main entrance, the window subsequently spent over thirty years in the Sulpicians' Refectory (1962-1994). It is now in the college's oratory.

G. L.

1 Georges Delfosse made a copy of the beatification painting, which is reproduced in Olivier Maurault's pamphlet *La fête des Martyrs de 1792 à Notre-Dame de Montréal* (Montreal: Seminaire de Saint-Sulpice, January 1927). The painting makes direct reference only to the three bishops and the various religious communities to which the martyrs belonged.

2 Note by Ozias Leduc recording the commission, January 15, 1929, BNQ 327/3/10.

3 Note by Leduc, April 5, 1929, BNQ 327/3/10; letter from Leduc to Maurault, June 11, 1929 BNQ 327/8/35. Although Jean-René Ostiguy, Ozias Leduc: Symbolist and Religious Painting, exhib. cat. (Ottawa: National Gallery of Canada, 1974), p. 210, speaks of "success", all the copies traced date from 1929 (Laval University, Archives de Folklore, Larouche-Villeneuve papers, F. 716/142/54). It therefore seems likely that there was only a single edition printed.

4 The window was presented by René Labelle, who was then the Sulpicians' Provincial (A. M. Cimichella, *Le bienheureux André Grasset, martyr de la révolution française* [Montreal, 1987 (1947)], p. 17).

5 This master glazier was active in Montreal between 1920 and 1932. After a few years apparently spent working for the firm of O'Shea, Pellus is thought to have opened his own studio around 1929. There seems to be no mention of him after 1932, the year of his last advertisements. Later, it was his son Raymond-Émile who was listed in Montreal's Lovell directory. The latter, born in France in 1907, died in Montreal in 1965.

6 Leduc based his image of the old church of Notre-Dame on the painting by Georges Delfosse reproduced in O. Maurault, La Paroisse. Histoire de l'Église Notre-Dame de Montréal (New York and London: Louis Carrier, 1929), p. 55. A photograph of the cathedral in Sens also appeared in two works by Maurault published in 1927: *La fête des Martyrs...*(see note 1) and *Le bienheureux André Grasset de Saint-Sauveur et sa famille* (Montreal: Arbour et Dupont, 1927). Leduc apparently also obtained from Maurault an image of the Carmelite cloister where Grasset was martyred.

194

Portrait of Florence Bindoff
1931-1935
Oil on canvas
68.4 x 54.2 cm
Signed lower right: *OZIAS LEDUC*
Quebec City, Musée du Québec, inv. 77.463
PROVENANCE
Studio of the artist; Florence Bindoff, Montreal, 1935; Dominion Gallery, Montreal, about 1955; Walter Klinkhoff Gallery, Montreal, 1963; Sotheby's, Toronto, October 27-28, 1969, lot 131; Galerie Clarence Gagnon, Montreal; Musée du Québec, 1977

195

Portrait of Frederick Bindoff
1935
Oil on canvas
63.8 x 54.2 cm
Signed upper right: *OZIAS LEDUC*
Family collection
PROVENANCE
Studio of the artist; Frederick Bindoff, Montreal, 1935; Mr. and Mrs. Albert Edward Bindoff, about 1955-1956; Robert Bindoff, Victoria, British Columbia, 1972; Joan Bindoff, Ottawa, 1982; family collection, 1990

FLORENCE GORDON and Fred Bindoff were among Leduc's most cherished friends during the last thirty-five years of his life. The artist had made the couple's acquaintance by the time of their marriage in 1922.[1] Even after their move to Montreal in 1928, the couple remained in close contact with the artist. The group explorations of the mountain,[2] the picnic jaunts on its slopes (fig. 69), the exchange of gifts,[3] Mrs. Bindoff's regular visits to Leduc during his extended hospitalization before his death[4] and the introduction of Leduc to Paul Rainville, who in his capacity as curator of the Musée du Québec included Leduc in a retrospective of four Quebec artists,[5] reveal a relationship between couple and artist that was not only mutually beneficial, but also warm and caring. It is a measure of the congeniality of the friendship that the portraits of the Bindoffs were not commissioned by the couple but initiated by the artist himself.

Florence Bindoff (1897-1993) was noted for her elegance and graciousness,

194

qualities captured by Leduc in his almost full-length three-quarter profile portrait of her. Seated casually, she is nevertheless dignified; her relaxed pose serves to highlight her wealth as well as her refined sense of fashion. Her hands, resting gently in her lap, are carefully positioned to display the single-strand pearl bracelet and diamond rings whose brilliance is matched by the diamond pendant hanging around her neck. One leg is draped across the other so that the T-strap of her high-heeled shoe catches the light with a glint of amber that is echoed in the drop earring suspended from beneath her fashionable bob cut. This quiet elegance and understated wealth are particularly poignant in view of the Great Depression.

But Florence Bindoff is not portrayed merely as the epitome of fashion and wealth. The warm pervasive light that accentuates the sheen of the fine, delicate fabric of her simple dress is also used to imply her mental disengagement from the material things she wears with such style. Staring dreamily into space, she is set against a backdrop that pulsates with luminosity as if to signify a transcendence on the part of the sitter. A border of stylized leaves on the backdrop frames the composition.

Although the *Portrait of Frederick Bindoff* was taken up four years later, one can consider it a pendant to the portrait of his wife. The later painting is looser in execution and the background less articulated, but the two works are virtually identical in size; and more importantly, Frederick Bindoff (1889-1955), too, conveys the casual but dignified elegance seen in the earlier portrait. Leduc has presented Mr. Bindoff as the learned businessman, as was certainly befitting the sitter, who was a manager at C-I-L Industries. Straightbacked and frontal, in business attire with tie and handkerchief, his gaze engaging the viewer, he gives a sense of imposing formality nevertheless mitigated by the pose and ambient light. Seated, with legs crossed, Bindoff has seemingly been interrupted from reading a book, now resting in his lap with his thumb marking his place. The warm light that animates the space reveals the

195

strong but kind face of one who is self-assured in every aspect of his life.

Although Leduc often used photographs in creating a portrait (cats. 123, 171), he seems to have eschewed this approach with the Bindoffs' portraits.[6] It is as though their execution from life was to have helped him express the intimacy and familiarity of friendship, qualities that are largely suppressed by the reserve and dignity of both sitters.

A. G.

Fig. 69   Picnic in Leduc's orchard with (left to right) Florence Bindoff, Ozias Leduc, Marie-Louise Leduc, Fred Bindoff, Ernest Cormier, Françoise Rainville, June 1936 (BNQ 327/13/1.20).

1   Florence Bindoff in conversation with Monique Lanthier, April 20, 1988. Mrs. Bindoff recalls that she had been living in Beloeil since 1918 and first met Leduc around 1920-1921, through her friend Louise Higgins-Lecours (cat. 157).

2   Leduc's Diary, October 12, 1924 , BNQ_327/2/7, notes one such occasion: "With Sunday's pleasant weather a group of persons favourably inclined towards alpinism, comprising Mme Louise Higgins-Lecours, Mme Florence Gordon Bindoff, Mr. Wilfrid Lecours, Hercule Cantara and Ozias Leduc, visited the main grotto of the gorge on the south-east of the mountain of Saint-Hilaire and after long deliberation and animated discussion, decided to name it 'Grotto Louise', lots having been drawn fairly between the two names proposed, Mme Louise Higgins-Lecours and Mme Florence Gordon-Bindoff. All the excursionists present, being in agreement with this decision, signed their names." Mrs. Bindoff, in conversation with Laurier Lacroix and Monique Lanthier, July 24, 1992, also indicated that Leduc would lead them on guided tours of the mountain.

3   In the course of their friendship, Leduc gave the couple, among other items, two unidentified drawings (letter from the Bindoffs to Ozias Leduc, January 2, 1937, BNQ_327/7/9); a still life (fig. 123) and an Assumption (cat. 8) (letter from the Bindoffs to Leduc, May 13, 1940, BNQ_327/7/12); and two drawings from the series "Imaginations" (letter from the Bindoffs to Leduc, January 4, 1942, BNQ_327/7/14; Florence Bindoff, in conversation with Laurier Lacroix and Monique Lanthier, July 24, 1992). For the couple's gifts to Leduc, see, for example, the drafts of letters from Leduc [to the Bindoffs], December 21, 1941, BNQ_327/9/3; to the Bindoffs [January] 1946, BNQ_327/9/9; to the Bindoffs, January 13, 1949, BNQ_327/9/12.

4   Florence Bindoff, in conversation with Laurier Lacroix and Monique Lanthier, July 24, 1992.

5   The Rainvilles and the Bindoffs were neighbours in Montreal. (Florence Bindoff, in conversation with Laurier Lacroix and Monique Lanthier, July 24, 1992.)

6   According to Mrs. Bindoff, who visited the artist often in his studio, the portrait was executed over a period of five to seven sittings (Florence Bindoff in conversation with Monique Lanthier, April 20, 1988). Leduc did, however, make three graphite on paper preparatory studies for the *Portrait of Florence Bindoff*: about 1931, 27.3 x 18 cm (private collection); 1931, 22 x 15 cm (private collection); and 1931, 27.7 x 32.3 cm (private collection). A single study for the *Portrait of Frederick Bindoff* has been located: about 1935, graphite on paper, 21.5 x 17.7 cm (Galerie Jean-Pierre Valentin, Montreal).

196

196

The Ecstasy of Saint Theresa

1934

Oil and graphite on textured cardboard

19 x 26.1 cm

Signed and dated upper left: *OZIAS LEDUC 1934 INSPIRÉ DU BERNIN.*

Germain Lavallée collection

INSCRIPTIONS

Verso: *PEINT POUR MR L'ABBÉ E. ROUSSEAU VICAIRE A LA CATHÉDRALE SHERBROOKE P.Q.; OZIAS LEDUC 1934 A SAINT-HILAIRE P.Q.*

PROVENANCE

Studio of the artist; Euclide Rousseau, Sherbrooke; Marie-Anna Alexandre, Sherbrooke; Germain Lavallée

Her head thrown back, her eyes closed and her lips parted, Saint Theresa of Ávila, the great mystic, experiences the ecstatic love of her Creator. For the baroque sculptor Bernini (1598-1680), whose work inspired the painter in this instance,[1] divine love can show itself in the same passionate and carnal form as human love. Leduc pushes this interpretation even further by making the saint's halo into a crescent moon, thus associating her with the goddess Artemis, in Greek mythology the sister of Apollo, worshipped especially in Arcadia.[2]

The light in this erotic-religious scene is predominantly green, a colour associated with renewal and regeneration.[3] Leduc's choice of this colour is another manifestation of his belief that humanity is defined by the conflict of opposites, by the struggle between matter and spirit and the coexistence of the forces of good and evil. This theme is also apparent in the decoration of the chapel in the Bishop's Palace in Sherbrooke (cats. 175-182). Leduc's inscription on the back of *The Ecstasy of Saint Theresa* indicates that the work was painted at the request of Abbé Euclide Rousseau, curate of the cathedral of Sherbrooke.[4]

L. L.

1   The painting was inspired by a photograph of a detail of Bernini's sculpture, BNQ_327/14/6. *The Ecstasy of Saint Theresa*, still to be seen in the Church of Santa Maria della Vittoria in Rome, was completed in 1646.

At this point in his career as in the past, Leduc executed a number of paintings directly inspired by other works. These include the *Portrait of Sir John Coape Sherbrooke* (1937, Sherbrooke City Hall) from an engraving by Robert Field (about 1769-1819), and his *Duck-hunting on a Misty Morning* (undated, MQ) after G. de A. Ronchetti.

2   The artist had portrayed the moon goddess under a different name in *Endymion and Selene* (cat. 129).

3 Leduc's "Le Symbolisme des couleurs" (undated manuscript BNQ 327/4/8), begins with the words, "The choice of colours and of tones can change the overall impression given by a painting, giving to figures and even minor objects a language and philosophy of their own". Leduc's remarks about the colour green include the following: "Venus and Grecian Minerva were first and foremost green, chaste love and incorruptible virtue" (pp. 18-19).

4 In the spring of 1930, at the request of Father Bouhier of the Church of Notre-Dame in Montreal, Leduc had decorated the Chapel of Saint Theresa of Lisieux, near-by the baptistry he had just completed (Jean-René Ostiguy, "Étude des dessins préparatoires à la décoration du baptistère de l'église Notre-Dame de Montréal", National Gallery of Canada Bulletin, no. 15 [1970], summarized in English as "The Preparatory Drawings for the Decoration of the Baptistry of Notre-Dame Church in Montreal", p. 39; and letters from Father Bouhier to Ozias Leduc, BNQ 327/7/2, and from Ozias Leduc to Bouhier and Maurault, BNQ 327/8/36). This was a frustrating commission for the artist, who had only a few months to complete a Mystic Rosebush to set behind a statue of Saint Theresa by the sculptor Elzéar Soucy (1876-1970), as well as a painting of *The Death of Saint Theresa* for the altar stone.

197

197

Père Jacques Buteux, s.j.
1936-1937
Oil on panel
28.8 x 25.7 cm
Signed upper left: *OZIAS LEDUC*; dated upper right: *1936-37*
Private collection
INSCRIPTIONS
Verso: *LE PÈRE JACQUES BUTEUX*
PROVENANCE
Studio of the artist; Abbé Albert Tessier, Trois-Rivières, 1937; private collection

198

Père Jacques Buteux, s.j.
1936-1937
Oil on thin cardboard, mounted on laminated panel
39.8 x 35.3 cm
Signed and dated lower right: *OZIAS LEDUC 1936-37*
Musée Pierre-Boucher du Séminaire de Trois-Rivières, inv. L 77 29 P
PROVENANCE
Studio of the artist; Abbé Albert Tessier, Trois-Rivières, 1937; Musée Pierre-Boucher, 1977

THESE two paintings sprang from Leduc's friendship with Abbé Albert Tessier, who seems to have given the painter a manuscript on the life of the Jesuit missionary Père Buteux. Père Buteux was born in Abbeville, France, on April 9, 1599, and was put to death by the Iroquois on May 10, 1652. He came to Canada on June 24, 1634, to preach the Gospel in Trois-Rivières and the surrounding region, and became the apostle of the Attikamek, a band of the Montagnais people living in the upper Saint-Maurice, who traded with the French.[1]

On August 19, 1936, Leduc agreed to start working on a painting commissioned by Abbé Tessier after receiving the priest's manuscript.[2] As usual, the artist took longer to complete the project than his patron had expected. On November 18, 1936, he felt he ought to reassure the Abbé.

Here is how the adventure is faring. What is conveyed in the intensely poetic and yet restrained tone of your account of how the frail but determined Père Buteux came to evangelize your beloved Mauricie is an imaginative glimpse into a long-forgotten saga that, happily, you have rescued from oblivion. I doubt my ability to achieve the level of life-like intensity you succeed in conjuring up from the smallest detail in the most obscure chronicle, but I should like at the least to reproduce the feeling of serenity one senses throughout your account of that great-hearted priest – a serenity that indeed permeates your work as a whole.[3]

With this letter were enclosed "a few sketches" that, according to the artist, "represent various stages of the work in progress".

On April 16, 1937, Leduc finally sent not one but two paintings of the life of Père Buteux, expressing the hope that Father Tessier would "choose the one he preferred". "I was interested in the subject and could not resist making two goes at it, while attempting to depict in both canvases the character of the missionary in so far as we can imagine it."[4] Painting two pictures instead of one may not have been quite so spontaneous a gesture: Leduc did ask the priest if he could find "some art lover of his acquaintance" who might wish to purchase the other one. The artist's gamble paid off: a letter of April 28, 1937, confirms that the priest kept both canvases and that he had already shown them to "your talented young colleague from Nicolet", Rodolphe Duguay, who had been most enthusiastic about them.[5]

One of Leduc's last comments on his own work can be found in a letter to Abbé Tessier dated May 21, 1937.

In Père Buteux, I see a dedicated missionary, an idealist like Saint Francis of Assisi, alight with loving kindness and religious fervour, steeped in the splendour of nature. In this not implausible image, the "madwoman upstairs" (if that's who it is) recognizes a great resemblance to you, to your spiritual self and your goodness, which will not be forgotten by your fellow-countrymen.[6]

Statements such as this by the artist are of the greatest interest. We see that he is more concerned with portraying a character than with seeking a likeness,

198

which, at any rate would have been impossible in the case of this imaginary historical portrait. These works are even more impressive when compared with the painting of Père Buteux executed by another of the priest's protegés, Léo Arbour (b. 1912); this was based on a bust of the missionary by H. Angers (1870-1963), and it must be said that neither work is particularly inspired.

F.-M. G.

1 "Chronologie de la vie du P. Buteux", Archives du Séminaire de Trois-Rivières, Albert Tessier papers.

2 Letter from Ozias Leduc to Albert Tessier, August 19, 1936, *ibid.*

3 Letter from Leduc to Tessier, November 18, 1936, *ibid.* The Musée Pierre-Boucher has a number of preparatory drawings for this painting.

4 Letter from Leduc to Tessier, April 16, 1937, *ibid.*

5 Letter from Leduc to Tessier, April 28, 1937, *ibid.*

6 Letter from Leduc to Tessier, May 21, 1937, *ibid.*

"Imaginations" Series (Cats. 199-223)

199
Distant Mountain
1936
Graphite on cream wove paper
14 x 10 cm
Signed lower left: *OZIAS LEDUC*; dated lower right: *1936*
Private collection
INSCRIPTIONS
Verso: *No 2 - Montagne au loin*
PROVENANCE
Studio of the artist; Dr. Guillaume Lahaise; private collection

200
Evening, Dream House
1936
Charcoal and graphite on white laid paper
11.1 x 15.9 cm
Signed lower left: *OZIAS LEDUC*; dated lower right: *1936*
Private collection
PROVENANCE
Studio of the artist; Paul Gagné, Sherbrooke, 1936; private collection

199

201

201
Old Bonsecours Church, Montreal
1937
Graphite, red and yellow pencil on paper
16.2 x 11.5 cm
Signed lower left: *OZIAS LEDUC*; dated lower right: *- 1937 -*
Musée du Séminaire de Sherbrooke, inv. G-77-2882-P.S.
PROVENANCE
Studio of the artist; Abbé Hermini Dubuc, Sherbrooke; Musée du Séminaire de Sherbrooke

200

202

The Rainbow

1936

Graphite on wove paper

12.2 x 16.5 cm

Signed lower left: *OZIAS LEDUC*; dated lower right: *- 1936 -*

Ottawa, The National Gallery of Canada, gift of Mrs. Paul-Émile Borduas, Belœil, 1974, inv. 18308

PROVENANCE

Studio of the artist; Paul-Émile Borduas, Belœil; Mrs. Paul-Émile Borduas; National Gallery of Canada, 1974

203

204

205

203

Morning Mist

1936

Charcoal and graphite on paper

16.8 x 12.7 cm

Signed lower left: *OZIAS LEDUC*; dated lower right: *DEC. 1936*

Musée Pierre-Boucher du Séminaire de Trois-Rivières, inv. L 85 1294 D

INSCRIPTIONS

Verso: *BRUME MATINALE POUR MONS. L'ABBÉ ALBERT TESSIER AVEC MES SOUHAITS DE BONNE ANNÉE OZIAS LEDUC*

PROVENANCE

Studio of the artist; Abbé Albert Tessier, Trois-Rivières; Musée Pierre-Boucher

205

Veiled Moon

1937

Charcoal and graphite on white laid paper

16.9 x 12.7 cm

Signed lower left: *OZIAS LEDUC*; dated lower right: *1937*

Trois-Rivières, Musée des arts et traditions populaires du Québec, Robert-Lionel-Séguin collection, inv. 1983.6057

INSCRIPTIONS

Verso: *A LA BRUNANTE crayon noir estompe OZIAS LEDUC*; label of Galerie l'Art français (no 60873)

PROVENANCE

Studio of the artist; Gérard Malchelosse, 1942; Robert-Lionel Séguin, 1952; Musée des arts et traditions populaires du Québec, 1983

204

Serenity No. 2

1936

Graphite and charcoal on white wove paper

12.5 x 16.7 cm

Signed lower left: *OZIAS LEDUC*; dated lower right: *1936*

Université de Montréal, inv. 80.01

INSCRIPTIONS

Verso, label of Galerie Louis Morency enr.: *"Ce dessin d'Ozias Leduc appartient à Gérard Morisset 723, rue Saint-Cyrille Québec. mai 1940."*

PROVENANCE

Studio of the artist; Gérard Morisset, Quebec City, 1940; Université de Montréal, 1980

206

View of the Lake, Mount Saint-Hilaire

1937

Graphite and charcoal on white laid paper mounted on cardboard

13.1 x 16.7 cm

Signed lower left: *OZIAS LEDUC*; dated lower right: *1937*

Private collection

INSCRIPTIONS

Recto, lower centre: *"LE LAC - MONT ST. HILAIRE"*

PROVENANCE

Studio of the artist; private collection

206

207

Storm on Paper

1937

Graphite on beige wove paper
(back of an envelope)

17.9 x 12.8 cm

Signed lower left: *OZIAS LEDUC*; dated lower
right: *1937*

Private collection

INSCRIPTIONS

Verso: *La tempête (dans Menaud) 1937 Dessin de
Ozias Leduc; No 21 Tempête sur papier 3-4 JAN.
1937 OZIAS LEDUC*; label of Galerie Morency
Frères Ltée

PROVENANCE

Studio of the artist; Abbé Félix-Antoine Savard,
Clermont (Charlevoix county) 1937; private
collection

208

At the Twilight Hour

1937

Graphite and charcoal on cream laid
paper

16.5 x 13.1 cm

Signed lower left: *OZIAS LEDUC*; dated lower
right: *1937*

Madeleine Darche collection

INSCRIPTIONS

Verso: *8 janvier 1937; A L'HEURE BRUNE*

PROVENANCE

Studio of the artist; Mrs. Paul Gagné, Sherbrooke,
1937; Madeleine Darche (née Bédard), about 1943

207

208

"CLAIR DE LUNE LACTE"

209

211

209

Milky Moonlight

1937

Graphite and charcoal on
white laid paper

17 x 12.7 cm

Signed lower left: *OZIAS LEDUC*;
dated lower right: *1937*

Private collection

INSCRIPTIONS

Recto: *"CLAIR DE LUNE LACTE"*

PROVENANCE

Studio of the artist; Léonard
Préfontaine, Sherbrooke, about 1939;
private collection

210

Clouds in the Light

1937

Graphite and charcoal on wove
paper (back of an envelope)

17.4 x 9.3 cm

Signed lower left: *OZIAS LEDUC*;
dated lower right: *1937*

Ottawa, The National Gallery of
Canada, gift of the National Gallery
Association Docents, Ottawa, 1979,
inv. 23307

INSCRIPTIONS

Verso: *No 26 Nuages dans la lumière;
17 JANV – 1937*

PROVENANCE

Studio of the artist; Father Carmel
Brouillard, Montreal; Mrs. M.
Gordon; National Gallery of Canada,
1979

211

Landscape in Two Tones

1937

Charcoal and graphite on white wove
paper

15.2 x 9 cm

Signed lower left: *OZIAS LEDUC*; dated lower
right: *1937*

Jeanne L'Archevêque Duguay collection

INSCRIPTIONS

Verso: *"O. Leduc - La meule from Mde Rodolphe
Duguay Nicolet, Qué.*; two labels from National
Gallery of Canada: *cat. no 70 - boîte 9 - Leduc Exh.
La Meule From: Duguay, Nicolet-sud no 694-1-74*

PROVENANCE

Studio of the artist; Rodolphe Duguay, Nicolet,
1937; Jeanne L'Archevêque Duguay

210

212

214

213

212

Purity. Reflections, Sky, Trees and Water

1937

Graphite and charcoal on laid paper

13.1 x 16.7 cm

Signed lower left: *OZIAS LEDUC*; dated lower right: *1937*

Private collection

INSCRIPTIONS

Verso: *Le Richelieu à St-Hilaire O. Leduc Paul Gagné, Sherbrooke prop.*

PROVENANCE

Studio of the artist; Paul Gagné, Sherbrooke; private collection

213

Dead Wood

1937

Charcoal on cream laid paper

16.5 x 13.3 cm

Signed lower left: *OZIAS LEDUC*; dated lower right: *– 1937 –*

Private collection

PROVENANCE

Studio of the artist; Émile Filion, p.s.s., Montreal; Galerie S. Breitman; Louis V. Randall, Montreal, 1965; private collection

214

Shower at Dusk

1937

Charcoal on cream wove paper

12.7 x 15.5 cm

Signed lower left: *OZIAS LEDUC*; dated lower right: *1937*

Musée des beaux-arts de Sherbrooke, Sylvio Lacharité collection, inv. 90.8.6 G

INSCRIPTIONS

Verso: *"Ondée au crépuscule OZS L…" "A Mlle Gabrielle Messier, Très amicalement Ozs. Leduc"* No 35 1 AOUT 1937

PROVENANCE

Studio of the artist; Gabrielle Messier, Saint-Hilaire, 1937; Sylvio Lacharité, Sherbrooke; Luc Lacharité, Saint-Lambert, 1990; Musée des beaux-arts de Sherbrooke, gift of Luc Lacharité, 1990

215

216

217

215

Pine under Snow

1937

Charcoal and graphite on white wove paper

17.7 x 14.4 cm

Signed lower left: *OZIAS LEDUC*; dated lower right: *1937*

Private collection

INSCRIPTIONS

Verso: *No 36A PIN SOUS LA NEIGE 1937 OZIAS LEDUC*

PROVENANCE

Studio of the artist; private collection

216

Cold – Snow

1939

Graphite on white wove paper

10.5 x 13.8 cm

Signed lower left: *OZIAS LEDUC*; dated lower right: *– DEC. 1939 –*

The Montreal Museum of Fine Arts, gift of Luc Larochelle, inv. Dr.1992.10

INSCRIPTIONS

Verso: *Décédé en 1955 à 91 ans Mont St-Hilaire*; label of Les encadrements Michel enr.

PROVENANCE

Studio of the artist; Louis-N. Audet, Sherbrooke, 1939; Jean-Louis Audet, Sherbrooke; Ruth Larochelle, Sherbrooke, about 1980; Luc Larochelle, Montreal; Montreal Museum of Fine Arts, 1992

217

Northern Lights

1940

Graphite and charcoal on ivory wove paper

11.6 x 16.6 cm

Signed and dated lower right: *– OZIAS LEDUC FEV 1940 –*

Private collection

INSCRIPTIONS

Verso: *Clarté boréale*

PROVENANCE

Studio of the artist; Thérèse Brouillette, Saint-Hilaire, 1940; Bernard Cournoyer; private collection

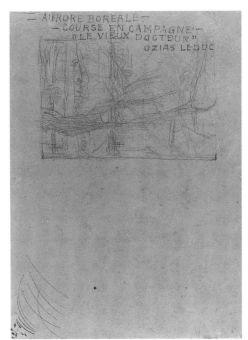

219 recto

219 verso

218

220

218

Solitude

1941

Charcoal on laid paper

16.1 x 10.3 cm

Signed lower left: *OZIAS LEDUC.*; dated lower right: *1941*

Private collection

INSCRIPTIONS

Verso: *No 43 Solitude 26 janvier 1941*

PROVENANCE

Studio of the artist; private collection

219

Aurora Borealis

1941

Charcoal and graphite on brown wove paper

16.9 x 12.5 cm

Signed lower left: *OZIAS LEDUC*

Private collection

INSCRIPTIONS

Verso: *– AURORE BORÉALE – / – COURSE EN CAMPAGNE – / « LE VIEUX DOCTEUR » / OZIAS LEDUC*

PROVENANCE

Studio of the artist; private collection

220

Approaching Winter

1941

Graphite, charcoal and black ink on paper

8.2 x 13.2 cm

Signed lower left: *OZIAS LEDUC;* dated lower right: *– 16 nov. 1941 –*

Private collection

INSCRIPTIONS

Verso: *"l'hiver qui vient" Nº 44 Ozias Leduc – 16 nov. 1941 –*

PROVENANCE

Studio of the artist; private collection

221

222

221

Radiance

1941

Charcoal on laid paper

13.2 x 16.6 cm

Signed lower left: *OZIAS LEDUC*; dated lower right: *1941*

Private collection

INSCRIPTIONS

Verso: *No 46 Rayonnement 23 Nov. 1941 Ozias Leduc*

PROVENANCE

Studio of the artist; Thomas Lahaise, Saint-Hilaire, about 1941; private collection, about 1970

222

Patterns (Melting Snow)

1941

Charcoal and graphite on cream white laid paper

16.5 x 9.9 cm

Signed lower left: *OZIAS LEDUC*; dated lower right: *1941*

Chrystian Beaudoin collection

INSCRIPTIONS

Verso: *No 47 "Méandres"*

PROVENANCE

Studio of the artist; Father Julien Déziel, o.f.m., Montreal; Chrystian Beaudoin

223

Snow on the Hill (Dusk)

1942

Charcoal and graphite on beige wove paper

16.1 x 11.5 cm

Signed lower left: *OZIAS LEDUC*; dated lower right: *1942 –*

Private collection

INSCRIPTIONS

Verso: *Nᵒ 49 Neige sur la colline (crépuscule) Ozias Leduc Oct. 1942; Nᵒ 49 Neige sur la colline (Crépuscule) Ozias Leduc Oct. 1942 A Madame Dr Gagner au Docteur et à Mireille Bonne et heu[reu]se année 1943*; labels: certificate of authenticity signed by Gabrielle Messier, Renée Bergeron Hamel and Galerie Renée Hamel

PROVENANCE

Studio of the artist; Dr. and Mrs. Roland Gagner, Saint-Hilaire, 1943; Galerie Renée Hamel, Sainte-Thérèse; private collection

223

224

Moonlit Twilight

About 1937
Oil on cardboard mounted on cardboard
32.7 x 23.2 cm

Signed lower left: *OZIAS LEDUC*

The Montreal Museum of Fine Arts, gift of the
International Mercantile Factors Ltd., inv. 1987.16

INSCRIPTIONS

Verso: label of Galerie l'Art français: *PAYSAGE
LUNAIRE*; exhibition label, *Contemplative Scenes:
The Landscapes of Ozias Leduc*; exhibition label,
Ozias Leduc: Symbolist and Religious Painting

PROVENANCE

Studio of the artist; received as a wedding gift, Mr.
and Mrs. Georges Doyle, Saint-Hilaire, 1941;
Galerie l'Art français, Montreal, about 1978;
International Mercantile Factors Ltd., about 1980;
Montreal Museum of Fine Arts, 1987

224

AWARE that artists always work with a certain core of ideas and subjects that give coherence to their work, contemporary painters have accustomed us to the notion of series. First the Impressionists and after them the American Abstract Expressionists ventured on this path, showing how an idea or a theme, handled in the same mediums, could be reworked with different nuances, and how the same approach or treatment could be made to illuminate differences and shades of perception.

In Leduc's output, we find a number of repetitions of secular and religious subjects. However, these were produced at random intervals and cannot properly be called series. It was not until the mid-1930s, a period when he received few commissions for paintings but wrote a great deal, that Leduc embarked on a succession of drawings that he thought of as a series, both in their formal and technical composition and in terms of the underlying inspiration and the people they were intended for.[1] These are landscapes "that spring from pure imagination. The author of these little squares of paper realizes they are of little value, but takes a sadistic pleasure in showering them on his friends."[2]

These drawings, executed on the spur of the moment and subject to no constraints other than the extent of the artist's inventiveness, represent in a way a return to his landscape period,[3] as well as an updating of his theory that a work of art is the visual result of an internal, subjective perception.

Paint what is imagined? Models? What I know to be, *what I see*. I can imagine an object, in the atmosphere created for it by my eyes, without any need for understanding what it is essentially. Imagining a World, lines, shapes and colours, means creating a World – a spiritualized World. Realizing this World means going beyond one's egoism. Awareness – Image: through these our fragile hearts escape from the round of day-to-day mediocrity and achieve a moment of eternity.[4]

The fifty-four works Leduc grouped under the title "Imaginations" are small-format pieces in charcoal and pencil, with the images outlined in black. They are usually titled and dated, as they were to be given as presents to family and friends on special occasions. Some of the drawings can be linked to paintings – *Moonlit Twilight* (cat. 224) was later done in oils in shades of green[5] – while many details refer back to completed compositions. These include the reworking of the rainbow theme (No. 6), the sugarloaf (No. 18), and the house brightly lit from the inside, a motif found in both *Evening, Dream House* (No. 4) and in the painting *The Ferryman's House* (cat. 226).

Most of the recipients of these drawings were close friends, some of long standing such as the Clerks (cat. 159) (No. 33), Guillaume Lahaise (cats. 138-139) (cat. 199), Thomas Lahaise (cat. 221), Mayor Bruce F. Campbell (No. 14), the photographer Paul Gagné and his wife (cats. 200, 208, No. 32), Msgr. Olivier Maurault (cats. 161-163) (No. 15), the painters Philippe Martin (No. 38) and Paul-Émile Borduas and his wife (cat. 202, fig. 70), the architect Louis-N. Audet (cat. 216, No. 8), the Bindoffs (cats. 194-195) (Nos. 13, 28, 45, 50), and others he had known not quite so long, such as Thérèse Brouillette (cats. 229-231), Gabrielle Messier (cat. 214), Claire Lavoie (cat. 218), Henriette Chivé (No. 37), Marie-Reine Lavallée (cats. 219-220), Reine Laperrière (No. 3) and her niece Gertrude Leduc (No. 1).

More recent acquaintances who received drawings as gifts included the painter Rodolphe Duguay (1891-1967) (cat. 211), members of religious communities such as the Franciscans Gonzalve Poulin (No. 31), Carmel Brouillard (cat. 210) and Julien Déziel (cat. 222), connoisseurs and collectors like Abbé Albert Tessier (cat. 203), Abbé Félix-Antoine Savard (cat. 207) and Abbé Émile Filion, p.s.s. (cat. 213), Lucien Thériault (Nos. 7, 22), Léonard Préfontaine (cats. 206, 209), and the glass worker Mathieu Martirano (No. 10), as well as people Leduc wished to thank, such as Gérard Morisset (cat. 204), Dr. Roland Gagner (cat. 223) and André Morency (No. 36). An impressive list drawn up systematically, to be found at the end of this entry, shows the titles and dates of the works together with the names of most of the recipients who visited Correlieu between 1936 and 1942.

The titles of the drawings are mostly very carefully chosen, and the repetition of the same subjects indicates the artist's wish to propose a reading or create an atmosphere. While some of the drawings are quite figurative, their titles illuminate a less concrete aspect of each work. Thus No. 24 (cat. 209), which depicts the house where Leduc was born, is entitled *Milky Moonlight*, while No. 32 (cat. 212), based on a view of Beloeil, is called *Purity. Reflections, Sky, Trees and Water*. With such titles the artist was stressing the imaginative nature of the series, the absence of reference to a specific object but rather an evocation of natural phenomena or atmospheres.

These titles evoke effects of dusk or nighttime light (Nos. 4, 7, 22, 26, 28, 35, 37, 52), the sky with its effects of clouds and rain, mist and smoke (Nos. 6, 9, 13, 15, 16, 26, 27, 31), the aurora borealis or northern lights (Nos. 10, 17, 41 and the Special No.) and the moon (Nos. 19, 24, 38, 39). Two of the four elements, earth and water, can be seen in drawings of Hertel Lake (Nos. 14, 20), reflections in water (Nos. 32, 38, 39) and the mountain (Nos. 1, 2, 33, 48). Other groups of subjects include winter (Nos. 8, 11, 30, 36a,

Fig. 70   Ozias Leduc, *Snow on Branches*, No. 11, 1936, graphite and charcoal 17 x 14.5 cm (private collection).

40, 44, 45, 47, 49, 50), and trees (Nos. 12, 34, 36), and there is one architectural scene (No. 5). Some titles stress a state of mind (Nos. 3, 18, 32, 43, 46) or the formal aspects of the drawing (Nos. 21, 29, 42, 51). It would be a mistake to confuse the title with the subject of any drawing, since they do not necessarily coincide. This is partly because poetic titles such as *At the Twilight Hour* (No. 23), *Sky in Turmoil* (No. 27) or *Approaching Winter* (No. 44) are too evocative to encapsulate a precise image, while even the drawings with titles that seem more specific – *Shower at Dusk* (No. 35), *Aurora Borealis* (Special No.) or *Morning Mist* (No. 16) – in fact have a quite different subject. And titles such as *Moonlit Twilight* (No. 22), *Landscape in Two Tones* (No. 29), *Serenity* (Nos. 3, 18) and *Solitude* (No. 43), for example, leave it to the viewer's imagination to identify a state of mind, a feeling or a pictorial experience.

The drawings of the "Imaginations" series represent the distillation of a private vision of nature characterized by reflected images, shimmering effects, ephemeral conditions created by shadows and the movement of clouds and light. They are an attempt to render the many-times-seen in a transcendent manner. These same emotions and atmospheres are what the artist also tried to capture in his poetry, as in the following extract from a poem entitled "The Sky Turns Blue":

The sun has fallen silent
A last moment of light,
A moment no one could describe,
Is lost in the now blue sky
Whose reflection in the water
Mingles with the inverted image of
the reeds.[6]

The formal language of the drawings combines curved lines and straight strokes with massed forms. The images thus created, shaded and blurred with highlights achieved with an eraser, are gentle and evocative. They aim above all to transfigure the "outward signs of nature"[7] and to draw the viewer into the dreamlike state induced by the contemplation of beauty.

L. L., M. L.

1 It was also in 1941 that Borduas began his celebrated series of gouaches that was exhibited in 1942 at the Ermitage (François-Marc Gagnon, *Paul-Émile Borduas*, exhib. cat. [Montreal: Montreal Museum of Fine Arts, 1988], pp. 117-137).

2 Letter from Ozias Leduc to Gonzalve Poulin, o.f.m., November 16, 1939, Archives des Franciscains.

3 Jean Chauvin, *Ateliers: études sur vingt-deux peintres et sculpteurs canadiens* (Montreal and New York: Louis Carrier & Co., 1928), p. 125, remarks, "What he brings home from a landscape he has seen is an impression, nothing more. He does not see his picture ready-made in nature, as if limited by its frame. His landscapes are deliberate rewritings, far from the direct emotion of his initial vision."

4 Ozias Leduc, "Peindre ce qui est penser", Textes poétiques, BNQ 327/3/17.

5 The drawing *Aurora Borealis* (Special No.) is a reprise of *On the Way to Midnight Mass,* which Leduc had done in 1919 to illustrate the story "La Noël à Saint-Hilaire", published by the Société Saint-Jean-Baptiste in the collection *Au pays de l'érable.*

6 Ozias Leduc, "Le ciel bleuit", Textes poétiques [before 1941], BNQ 327/3/15.

7 Ozias Leduc, Textes poétiques, BNQ 327/3/17.

"Imaginations" Series

Handwritten list drawn up by Ozias Leduc, transcribed and completed by Thérèse Brouillette (BNQ 327/3/4) and Gabrielle Messier (personal archive).

1936

1 *Rochers sur ciel* [Rocks against Sky] - 8 octobre 1937
Gertrude Leduc, Montréal

2 *Montagne au loin* [Distant Mountain]
Dr F.G. Lahaise, St-Jean-de-Dieu

3 *Sérénité n° 1* [Serenity No. 1] - 1er novembre
M. Reine Laperrière, Ottawa

4 *Soir, maison de rêve* [Evening, Dream House]
Paul Gagné, Sherbrooke

5 *Vieille église de Bonsecours, Montréal* [Old Bonsecours Church, Montreal] - 4 novembre 1936

6 *L'arc-en-ciel* [The Rainbow]
P.E. Borduas, Montréal

7 *Crépuscule* [Dusk] - 11 novembre 1936
M. L. Thériau, Montréal

8 *Neige tombante* [Falling Snow] - 11 novembre 1936
L.-N. Audet, Sherbrooke

9 *Fumée* [Smoke]

10 *Aurore boréale* [Aurora Borealis] - 2 juin 1939
Mathieu Martirano, Montréal

11 *Neige sur les branches* [Snow on Branches] -
29 novembre 1936
Mme Paul-Emile Borduas, Montréal

12 *Le vieux saule* [The Old Willow] - 7-8 décembre 1936
Raymond Desautels, Saint-Hyacinthe

13 *Rayons dans la brume* [Light Beams in the Mist]
M. et Mme Frederick Bindoff, Montréal

14 *Le lac. Montagne de St-Hilaire* [The Lake. Mountain of Saint-Hilaire]
Bruce F. Campbell, St-Hilaire

15 *Nuages dominants* [Threatening Clouds] - 1936
Abbé Olivier Maurault, Montréal

16 *Brume matinale* [Morning Mist]
Abbé Albert Tessier, Trois-Rivières

17 *Aurore boréale* [Aurora Borealis]
Léda Martel, Montréal

18 *Sérénité n° 2* [Serenity No. 2]
Gérard Morisset, Québec

1937

19 *Lune voilée* [Veiled Moon]

20 *Vue du Lac, mont St-Hilaire* [View of the Lake, Mount Saint-Hilaire]
Mme L. Préfontaine, Sherbrooke

21 *Tempête sur papier* [Storm on Paper] - 3-4 janvier 1937
Abbé F.A. Savard, Clermont, comté Charlevoix

22 *Crépuscule lunaire* [Moonlit Twilight] - 6 janvier 37
Mme Thériau, Montréal

23 *À l'heure brune* [At the Twilight Hour]
Mme Paul Gagné, Sherbrooke

24 *Clair de lune lacté* [Milky Moonlight]
Léonard Préfontaine, Sherbrooke

25 *La grande ourse sur l'horizon* [The Great Bear on the Horizon] - 14 janvier 1937
Jean Jolin, Saint-Hyacinthe

26 *Nuages dans la lumière* [Clouds in the Light] -
17 janvier 1937
Père Carmel Brouillard, Montréal

27 *Ciel en désordre* [Sky in Turmoil] - 21 janvier 1937

28 *Soir blanc* [White Evening]
M. et Mme Frederick Bindoff, Montréal

29 *Paysage deux tons* [Landscape in Two Tones] - 1er-2 février 1937
Rodolphe Duguay, Nicolet

30 *Neige sur la colline* [Snow on the Hill] - 9 février 1937
Louis-Philippe Robidoux, Sherbrooke

31 *Fumées industrielles* [The Smoke of Industry] - 12-13 février 1937
Père Gonsalve Poulin, o.f.m.

32 *Candeur. Reflets, ciel, arbres et eau* [Purity. Reflections, Sky, Trees and Water]
Paul Gagné, Sherbrooke

33 *Chemin montant* [Uphill Road] - 18 février 1937
M. et Mme Édouard Clerk, Saint-Hilaire

34 *Bois mort* [Dead Wood] - 23-24 juin 1937
M. l'abbé Filion, p.s.s.

35 *Ondée au crépuscule* [Shower at Dusk] - 1er août 1937
Gabrielle Messier, Saint-Hilaire

36 *Sous-bois* [Undergrowth] - 26 novembre 1937
André Morency, Montréal

36a *Pin sous la neige* [Pine under Snow]
Thérèse Brouillette, Saint-Hilaire

1938

37 *Paysage crépusculaire* [Landscape at Dusk] - 10 avril 1938 (ou 1940)
Henriette Chivé, Saint-Hilaire

38 *Clair de lune (reflets)* [Moonlight (Reflections)] -
24 décembre 1938
Philippe Martin, Saint-Hilaire

39 *Clair de lune (reflets)* [Moonlight (Reflections)] -
24 décembre 1938
Ferrier Chartier, Saint-Hyacinthe

1939

40 *Le froid - neige* [Cold – Snow]
L.-N. Audet, Sherbrooke

1940

41 *Lueurs boréales* [Northern Lights] - février 1940
Thérèse Brouillette, Saint-Hilaire

1941

42 *Contraste* [Contrast] - 12-13 octobre
Cécile Harris

43 *Solitude* [Solitude]
Claire Lavoie

Spécial *Aurore boréale* [Aurora Borealis]
Reine Lavallée

44 *L'hiver qui vient* [Approaching Winter] -
16 novembre 1941
Reine Lavallée

45 *Ombres du soir sur la neige* [Evening Shadows on the Snow] - 28 avril 1920 [1940]
M. et Mme Frederick Bindoff

46 *Rayonnement* [Radiance] - 23 novembre 1941
Thomas Lahaise

47 *Méandres (Neige fondante)* [Patterns (Melting Snow)] - 23 novembre 1941
Père Julien Déziel, o.f.m.

[1942]

48 *Le pic noir* [Black Peak] - 27 août 1942
Fernande Sabourin

49 *Neige sur la colline* (Crépuscule) [Snow on the Hill (Dusk)]
Dr Roland et Mme Gagner

50 *Neige au penchant du coteau (matin de brume)* [Snow on the Hillside (Misty Morning)] - octobre 1942
M. et Mme Frederick Bindoff

51 *Paysage (contre-jour)* [Landscape (backlit)]
M. et Mme Éd. Plourde, Beloeil

52 *Soir* [Evening]
Renée Plourde

225a

225b

225a

Study for *Old Man with Apples*

1938

Charcoal and graphite on brown cardboard

22.8 x 19.6 cm

Signed and dated upper right: *OZIAS LEDUC
1938*; initialed upper left: *OZ*

Private collection

PROVENANCE

Studio of the artist; private collection, 1941

225b

Old Man with Apples

1938

Oil on hardboard

22.8 x 19.5 cm

Signed and dated upper left: *OZIAS LEDUC 1938*

Private collection

PROVENANCE

Studio of the artist; Blanche Tétrault, 1942; Roger
Viau, Montreal, about 1956; private collection, 1978

THE subject of this small painting is the head of an old man seen between two baskets of apples, his impressive face lit by a golden light from the left. The colours – ochres, sienna and dark green enlivened by the red and yellow tones in the copper-coloured light – evoke autumnal afternoons and harvest time. The close-up view of the face and the tight framing, though reminiscent of photographic technique, suggest an allegory of fruitfulness and bounty. A transition from more straightforward portrait to allegory can be seen between the preparatory study and the finished work: in the study, which is reversed and squared off, attention is focussed entirely on the figure. The painting's bold brush strokes and areas of canvas left unpainted are characteristic of Leduc.

This genre portrait is in fact a posthumous one of the artist's father Antoine Leduc, whom Leduc had painted fifty years before (cat. 3). Painting from memory, Leduc created an image of his father as an archetype of the farmer. Calm and pensive, he proudly shows the fruits of his labour: splendid ripe apples. Leduc may well have identified with this portrait, for he always liked to be thought of as both a painter and an apple-grower.[1] This painting recalls the theme of redemption through work found in the two secular scenes at the Church of Saint-Enfant-Jésus, Mile-End (cat. 167), and in four paintings in the Church of Notre-Dame-de-la-Présentation in Shawinigan-Sud (cats. 250-253).

M. L.

---

1 The second owner of the painting believed it to be a self-portrait by Leduc, but the features bear a close resemblance to those in *Portrait of My Father* (interview of the painting's current owner by Monique Lanthier).

226

The Ferryman's House
1938-1939
Oil on hardboard
30.5 x 40.6 cm

Signed and dated lower left: *OZIAS LEDUC 1938-39*

Private collection
INSCRIPTIONS
Verso: *La maison du passeur 1938-39*
PROVENANCE
Studio of the artist; Léonard Préfontaine, Montreal, 1939; private collection

T HE *FERRYMAN'S HOUSE* was commissioned in early 1938 by Léonard Préfontaine to commemorate his marriage the previous year.[1] Originally from Sherbrooke, he had moved to Montreal upon his appointment as vice president of the Provincial Electric Works. The painting was to grace the walls of the Préfontaines' new Montreal home as part of their planned art collection devoted exclusively to renowned Canadian artists.[2] Its inclusion would fulfil their first and foremost desire of owning a Leduc.[3]

Although the artist had been given carte blanche[4] and had himself suggested a landscape,[5] he consulted with the photographer Paul Gagné, a mutual friend through whom he had made the Préfontaines' acquaintance, as to what his clients' preferences might be.[6] A slice of the mountain, a piece of sky, a bit of the Richelieu and, above all, the ferry that transported people across the river between Saint-Hilaire and Belœil were suggested by Gagné as the basis for a

landscape that would characterize the area and provide a visual document for "the whole land and for future generations".[7] Leduc used a photograph (fig. 71) by Louis-Philippe Martin (1872-1949), which contained all the pictorial elements proposed by Gagné and enabled him to reconstruct the scene in a historically accurate manner.

In the tranfer to canvas, Leduc has made some changes that effect an intimacy and timelessness that are lacking in the photograph and which imbue his painting with a Symbolist quality. He has cropped the right side and immediate foreground, thus positioning the boat much closer to the picture plane. The figures are eliminated and the boat cast in shadow, its bow just emerging into the heightened light that extends over to the far bank to rest with special brightness on the house; the viewer is thus invited to step aboard for the passage to the other side.

Leduc's landscape addresses both Gagné's historical concerns and his own

concerns as well. Suffused with nostalgia for the Saint-Hilaire of yore, the scene also provides a vision for a journey of spiritual enlightenment.

A. G.

Fig. 71   Saint-Hilaire seen from Belœil, about 1900 (photo: Louis-Philippe Martin; Société d'histoire de Belœil – Mont-Saint-Hilaire, Armand-Cardinal papers, inv. 4-63,3).

1 Fernande Préfontaine (wife of Léonard), in conversation with Monique Lanthier, August 2, 1994.

2 Letter from Préfontaine to Ozias Leduc, April 29, 1938, BNQ 327/7/10. See also the letter from Paul Gagné to Leduc, June 2, 1938, BNQ 327/7/10, in which he mentions that Préfontaine, for his "little collection is thinking of Clarence Gagnon, [Ivan] Jobin, [Suzor-] Coté." Gagné also indicates that Préfontaine's new position has allowed him the luxury of acquiring works by "our best painters". The price agreed upon for Leduc's commission was $40 (draft of a letter from Leduc to Préfontaine [1 May 1938], BNQ 327/9/1, and the letter from Préfontaine to O. L., May 16, 1939, BNQ 327/7/11).

3 Letter from Gagné to O. L., June 2, 1938, BNQ 327/7/10: "As to what subject he prefers, let me assure you that it is of no concern to him so long as your signature is at the bottom of the picture." Leduc's clients were no doubt pleased with the painting that boasted the artist's signature, which, boldly inscribed, affirmed the value of the acquisition and their place among judicious collectors.

4 Letter from Préfontaine to O. L., April 29, 1938, BNQ 327/7/10. The only restrictions were the work's dimensions, limited to about 12 x 16" [30.5 x 41 cm].

5 Draft of letter from O. L. to Préfontaine [May 1, 1938], BNQ 327/9/1.

6 Draft of letter from O. L. to Gagné, May 30, 1938, BNQ 327/9/11.

7 From the letter cited in note 3.

227

Portrait of Madame St-Cyr
1938-1939
Oil on canvas
182 x 112 cm
Signed lower right: *OZIAS LEDUC 1938-39*
Montreal, McCord Museum of Canadian History, inv. M 992.29.1

PROVENANCE

Studio of the artist; Mr. and Mrs. Alfred St-Cyr, Westmount, 1939; Gérald St-Cyr; Walter Klinkhoff Gallery, Montreal, 1981; Galerie Bernard Desroches, 1981; McCord Museum of Canadian History, 1992

IN 1930, when Leduc began to work on the Church of Les Saints-Anges-Gardiens in Lachine, the insurance broker he chose was Alfred St-Cyr, who some years later remembered the artist when seeking to commission a full-length portrait of his wife. The *Portrait of Madame St-Cyr* is one of the few commissioned portraits of a woman by Leduc. Unlike the other women he had painted, the sitter was not related to the artist, nor was she a friend prior to his receiving the commission. Since the painting was to hang at the head of the grand staircase of their Westmount residence, the St-Cyrs wanted an impressively large canvas. In its format and predominating colours, the *Portrait of Madame St-Cyr* has the look of an official state portrait, demonstrating the symbolic function of this kind of painting: to make apparent the sitter's social standing. The evening gown itself speaks volumes about her status. The sittings began in the spring of 1938, when Ethel-Loretta Leveque St-Cyr (1888-1964) was fifty years old. The portrait was finished in the spring of 1939, and the family was extremely pleased with it. Not only had Leduc produced a physical likeness, but he had also captured the sitter's generous, sensitive, dreamy, charming personality.[1]

The artist had no hesitation in choosing the pose, which was based on a photograph squared for enlargement (fig. 72). The pose is identically reproduced in one of the known studies for the portrait, a close-up of the head (cat. 76), and in the finished work. Leduc always focussed on the sitter's personality, and so here the viewer's eye is drawn to the head and right arm, the two most brightly lit areas of the canvas. A second preliminary drawing is extant, focussing on the right forearm.[2] On the back of this sketch, dated May 5, 1938, Leduc wrote, "Study of a glove for the Lady in Red (Madame St-Cyr)". The artist gave subtitles to a number of his portraits of women, depending on the dominating colour in the work. Like the American painter James McNeill Whistler, Leduc stressed the painterly qualities of these works – studies in shape and colour.

The Lady in Red stands in a theatrical pose, solemn and motionless, but the kind eyes and slight tilt of the head counterbalance the stiffness. The rich colours and the warm light around the model reinforce this impression of gentleness and dreaminess. At the sitter's insistence, Leduc gave her a smaller waist and a longer neck;[3] the slimming effect is also helped by the vertical effect of the folds of her gown. As in the *Portrait of Louis-Philippe Brodeur* (cat. 123) and the *Portrait of Florence Bindoff* (cat. 194), the artist renders the background in broad strokes of colour. This abstract painterly backdrop, slightly recessed, throws the figure in relief and focusses the viewer's attention on it.

M. L.

1 Information kindly provided by Gérald St-Cyr, son of the sitter.

2 This graphite sketch was in the collection of the late Gilles Corbeil. A photograph of it is held by the National Gallery of Canada.

3 See Gilles Corbeil, "Un hommage au peintre Ozias Leduc, 1864-1955 – Rencontres avec Ozias Leduc", *Le Devoir* [Montreal], January 14, 1956, p. 8.

Fig. 72   Ethel-Loretta St-Cyr, 1938 (photo by
Ozias Leduc, printed from glass negative No. 34,
BNQ 327/13/6.3).

228

Portrait of Aline Audet
1939
Oil on panel
27 x 21.7 cm
Signed and dated upper right: *OZIAS LEDUC 1939*
Private collection

INSCRIPTIONS
Verso: *"Fait par Ozias Leduc"*; label of Paul Gagné - Art & Photo

PROVENANCE
Studio of the artist; Mr. and Mrs. Louis-N. Audet, Sherbrooke, 1947; private collection, 1976

WHILE Leduc was finishing the decoration of the private chapel in the Bishop's Palace at Sherbrooke (cats. 175-182), he asked Sherbrooke architect Louis-N. Audet to find him a photograph of his daughter Aline, because he wanted to paint her.[1] Leduc made the portrait in 1939 and sent it to Audet in 1947.[2] This was probably the artist's way of expressing his thanks to Audet for having obtained for him this major commission from the diocese.[3] Leduc must also have guessed how sad Aline's parents were feeling after her departure for the community of the Congrégation de Notre-Dame in 1932.[4] Aline Audet, Sister Saint-Louis-des-Anges (1911-1986) "taught drawing for almost fifty years, thirty years at Mont Notre-Dame de Sherbrooke from 1944 to 1976".[5]

The sitter is shown slightly off-centre and fairly close-up in a three-quarter pose, her head turned towards the viewer and a dreaming look in her eyes.[6] The gleaming yellow of the dress against the green background creates a harmonious warmth of colour. The background with its dense vibrant shapes provides a contrast for the calm figure in the foreground, its colour and shapes evoking an imaginary landscape – foliage or bark covered with moss.

M. L.

1 Letter from Louis-N. Audet to Ozias Leduc, December 26, 1946, BNQ 327/7/18.

2 Letter from Louis-N. Audet to Ozias Leduc, January 14, 1947, BNQ 327/8/1.

3 The two had collaborated several times, as Audet recommended the artist as decorator for three of the churches he had built or renovated. Regarding these projects, see the entry for cats. 175-183. Leduc in turn recommended Audet for the rebuilding of the Church of Saint-Jacques in Montreal, which had burned down in 1933.

4 Biographical information was kindly provided by the sitter's sister, Jacqueline Audet-Délisle.

5 Andrée Désilets, "Sœur Aline Audet, une grande femme", *La Tribune* [Sherbrooke], April 18, 1986, p. B-2.

6 There exists a photograph of the sitter at the same age but in a slightly different pose. It is dated August 22, 1932, shortly before she entered the convent. The Musée d'art de Joliette has one of Leduc's preparatory sketches for the portrait, in graphite on tracing paper squared for enlargement, 17 x 12.5 cm.

230

229
Portrait of Thérèse Brouillette
1940
Charcoal on cream laid paper
41.9 x 33.3 cm
Signed lower right: *OZIAS LEDUC 1940*
Private collection
PROVENANCE
Studio of the artist; private collection

230
Portrait of Thérèse Brouillette
1940
Charcoal on bluish beige wove paper
21.5 x 16.4 cm
Signed and dated lower left: *OZIAS LEDUC 1940*
Private collection
PROVENANCE
Studio of the artist; private collection

231
Portrait of Miss B.
1940
Oil on canvas
24.1 x 27.5 cm
Signed and dated upper right: *OZIAS LEDUC 1940*
Private collection
INSCRIPTIONS
Verso, label of Musée de la Province de Québec: *cat. No. 39 -Propriété de Dr Jules Brahy, 361 est, Sherbrooke, Montréal. Portrait de Mlle B... 1940. par Ozias Leduc*
PROVENANCE
Studio of the artist; Thérèse Brouillette, Saint-Hilaire, 1940; Dr. Jules Brahy, Montreal, 1944; private collection

THÉRÈSE BROUILLETTE (b. 1914) taught in the Rang des Trente primary school from 1938 to 1941 and knew Ozias Leduc from her childhood. Her parents lived on the same road, and she remembers Leduc visiting the school as a commissioner in the 1920s while she was still a pupil.[1] She initially began coming to the painter's studio to escort two of her pupils who were taking private drawing lessons.[2] Thereafter Thérèse would occasionally act as secretary to Leduc, transcribing his texts and documents.[3] During the summer of 1940, at the artist's request, she posed in her free time for her portrait and also for *Mater Amabilis* (cat. 232).

Leduc made several preliminary drawings for Thérèse's portrait in addition to the two drawings in the sketchbook (cats. 82-83) and the two sheets shown here (the Musée du Québec owns another, less finished).

231

232

Mater Amabilis
1941
Oil on canvas
57.1 x 44.4 cm
Signed and dated lower left: *OZIAS LEDUC 1941*
Musée Pierre-Boucher du Séminaire de Trois-Rivières, inv. L 77 27 P
PROVENANCE
Studio of the artist; Abbé Albert Tessier, Trois-Rivières, 1941; Musée Pierre-Boucher, 1977

RENÉ BERGERON[1] stated that the critic Maurice Gagnon went so far as to describe Ozias Leduc as a "forerunner of the ultra-moderns".[2] This is a sweeping statement. Gagnon, in fact, was often critical of Leduc, who, he wrote, "oscillates between painterly talent and an idealism he has never cared to shed". The critic hails Leduc's oeuvre as "extraordinary" but also decries "a certain poverty of imagery, tied to the service of a religious hierarchy", which leads him to the surprising conclusion that Leduc "perhaps belongs more to the history of culture than to the history of painting".[3] Gagnon makes no reference to *Mater Amabilis*, although this work could justify such an opinion: the painting itself, as well as its dissemination and the reactions to it, speaks to us not only about the cultural history of Quebec but also, indirectly, about certain issues in the art world at the time.

Mater Amabilis is characteristic of Leduc's work in a number of ways, despite the constraints imposed by a commission. It was painted at the request of Abbé Albert Tessier, who wanted a religious picture that could be reproduced and used to propagate Catholic ideology.[4]

It is clear that the artist wished to create an image appropriate to a domestic setting. He wrote to Tessier that "*Mater Amabilis* is painted in light colours, which, when reproduced will, I hope, provide a pleasingly bright picture to harmonize with the white and pale tones usually found in Quebec homes."[5] Letters received by Leduc between 1941 and 1947 show how successful the image was with his friends and relatives in religious orders.[6]

There is also an oil sketch in a private collection. The drawings vary in mood; although the sitter remains recognizable, changes in composition, pose and hairstyle create different effects. Thus, the cameo view in grisaille presents the sitter in an idealized manner, while the background hatching, sometimes regular, sometimes less so, provides movement.

In the painting itself, the medallion on the wall indicates that the sitting took place in the artist's studio and associates the sitter with his earlier work.[4] Her delicate features are set off by the shimmering emerald and gold of the layers of pigment. Leduc was particularly proud of this portrait, and when he wanted to borrow it for an exhibition at the Musée de la Province de Québec, he recalled, "When I was painting this portrait in my studio, many people saw it and it has always been thought of as one of my most polished works."[5]

L. L.

1 Information obtained from an interview with Thérèse Brouillette Chabot, May 3, 1995.

2 Mrs. Chabot recalls that Leduc gave her advice on teaching drawing and provided her with geometric shapes to use as models. He had similarly encouraged Borduas when the latter began to teach art in 1930 (François-Marc Gagnon, *Paul-Émile Borduas (1905-1960): biographie critique et analyse de l'œuvre*, [Montreal: Fides, 1978], pp. 52-54).

3 The BNQ (327) holds some of her transcriptions of Leduc's poems as well as the list of works in the "Imaginations" series (cats. 199-224). From 1941 to 1943, Thérèse Brouillette was a novice in the convent of the Sisters of Les Saints Noms de Jésus et de Marie, teaching in Soulanges.

4 It is possible that this medallion, of which we see the lower part, is that of Louise Lecours, née Higgins (cat. 157). The circular frame and swirling movement echo the creation motif the artist had used in the *Portrait of Guy Delahaye* (cat. 139, fig. 49) and in the upper part of the *Mary Hailed as Co-redeemer* in the Bishop's Chapel, Sherbrooke (cat. 176).

5 Draft of a letter from Ozias Leduc to Alice Brouillette Comete, [1944] BNQ 327/9/20. Borduas was one of those who admired the quality of the work; after visiting Thérèse Brouillette's home, he wrote to Leduc, "I saw the portrait and was enchanted by the brilliance of its warm light" (letter from Borduas to Ozias Leduc, March 5, 1944, BNQ 327/7/16).

The intention of promoting the ideal of the French-Canadian Catholic family becomes even clearer on perusal of the prayer printed on the back of the missal-sized version of the picture. The Virgin is beseeched to watch over "our Christian homes ... the foundation of our Catholic, French-speaking nation". The prayer continues, "Keep our mothers faithful to their domestic duties; let them joyously embrace their responsibilities as Christian women and wives. And keep alive in the hearts of our young girls the love of virtue and devotion to their domestic tasks." Here, we see the bases of the clerical-nationalist ideology – religion, family, nation. The prayer conforms as well to the educational philosophy of the domestic science colleges advocated by Abbé Tessier. The economic and political situation in the early 1940s was a serious threat to this notion of the family. Not only had growing industrialization and urbanization already weakened the traditional family structure, but the advent of the Second World War took women into the factories and men to the front. In such a context, the devotion of young girls to Catholic virtues and family duties could no longer be taken for granted.

In terms of the arts in Quebec, the 1940s was a time when the fight to have modernism recognized was at its fiercest. With the rise of abstraction, the battle became savage. Those who clung to a traditional concept of art did not hesitate to extend their arguments to a wider socio-political context, linking the emergence of modernist art to the rise of Communism and to changes threatening Quebec society. One of the polemicists was René Bergeron, who in *Art et Bolchévisme* points to Leduc's painting as an ideal example of what art should be. Although Bergeron categorized *Mater Amabilis* as a "pretty picture",[7] Leduc himself considered the work important enough to be included in an exhibition of French-Canadian artists organized by the Musée de la Province de Québec in 1945.[8]

Mater Amabilis presents three psychologically distinct spaces: the traditional farmhouse; the landscape of the Saint-

232

Hilaire region (there are the Richelieu River, the village church and Mount Saint-Hilaire's sugarloaf); and the mystic space occupied by the Virgin, formally separated from the interior by the scrollwork surrounding the figure. Other formal elements establish links between these spaces: the shape of the scroll on which the Virgin stands is the same as that of the path outside.

Leduc's own description of this work is revealing: "In 'Mater Amabilis'," he wrote to Paul Gouin, "you have a Quebec farm kitchen, with a young woman quietly darning beside a cradle, while her menfolk work in the fields, and the presence of Our Lady and the Holy Child, a protective presence sensed by the young mother alone, watching her baby sleep."[9] It will be noticed that in referring to elements that do not actually appear in the final painting, this description provides the sort of edifying narrative function expected of such a picture. The commentary nevertheless ascribes to the work a broader connotation than that of clerical-nationalist ideology: "These imaginary scenes speak to the idealist in me, the man who, in looking at our Canadian earth still dreams, like Burne-Jones, of the 'Never-never Land', the land of dreams, if you will." This is an astonishing remark. It is true that in iconographic terms there is a reference to Burne-Jones: the handling of the figure of the Virgin, which differs from that of the other elements in the painting, recalls Pre-Raphaelite images. It is rather the reference to the "Never-never Land", "the land of dreams", that intrigues us. It would have been understandable as a description of Leduc's imaginary landscapes but cannot apply to the "Canadian earth" represented by this specific landscape, which, in his letter to Gouin, Leduc differentiates from the Never-never Land. Was the artist referring to a supernatural world evoked by the presence of the Virgin? If this was the case, it is surprising for a Catholic to associate such a world with a land of dreams. Although the notion of a Never-never Land was an essential component of the Symbolist aesthetic, it seems ill-suited as a description of this realistic landscape, so in keeping with conservative French-Canadian ideology.

In 1940, Maurice Gagnon wrote in *Peinture moderne* that Leduc's work represented a continual struggle between material and intelligence. The critic noted that sometimes the balance between the two broke down, that "reason in action" sacrificed "beauty in its own interests", and that "science, used by the Christian, banishes the painter to second place". Gagnon concluded that "Painting is not willingly ready to be sacrificed; it avenges itself on anyone who demands this."[10] Of Ozias Leduc's religious works, *Mater Amabilis* should perhaps be counted among such vengeances!

E. T.

1 René Bergeron was a collector and gallery owner. He was also known as an anti-Communist activist and pamphleteer on behalf of the École Sociale populaire, an organization founded in 1911 and led by the Jesuits to counter the influence, thought pernicious, of the "international" trade unions.

2 René Bergeron, *Art et Bolchévisme* (Montreal: Fides, 1946), p. 96.

3 Maurice Gagnon, *Sur un état actuel de la peinture canadienne* (Montreal: Société des Éditions Pascal, 1945), pp. 77-78.

4 It appeared in various formats, the first in the usual holy picture size of three inches by five (7.6 x 12.7 cm), entitled *Mater Amabilis, Sanctify Our Homes*, with a prayer on the back. There was also a larger reproduction suitable for framing, as was recommended by the secretary-treasurer of the school board of the village of Saint-Hilaire, J.E.M. Desrochers, who sent the teachers five copies donated by Leduc, to be distributed as school prizes. (Letter from J.E.M. Desrochers, secretary-treasurer, to the teachers of the parish of Saint-Hilaire, June 11, 1942, BNQ 327/9/21.)

5 Letter from Ozias Leduc to Abbé Albert Tessier, June 15, 1941, Archives du Séminaire de Trois-Rivières, Albert Tessier papers, F-N-0014.

6 Letter from Ozias Leduc to Tessier, February 19, 1942, ibid.; letters from Sister Marie-du-Bon-Conseil (Monastery of the Precious Blood, Ottawa) to Ozias Leduc, June 7, 1944, and April 5, 1947, BNQ 327/7/17 and 327/8/2; letter from Sylvio Ouellette to Ozias Leduc, September 9, 1945, BNQ 327/7/17; letter from Gérard Langevin to Ozias Leduc, February 9, 1947, BNQ 327/8/1. The Sisters of La Présentation de Marie asked his permission to enlarge the work "painted in appropriate colours" for the Marian Congress to be held in Ottawa in June 1947. (Letter from the Sisters of La Présentation de Marie to Ozias Leduc, March 3, 1947, BNQ 327/8/1, and reply from Leduc, March 5, 1947, BNQ 327/3/11.) The picture was also used to illustrate a number of Catholic publications.

7 Bergeron 1946, p. 94. In the 1940s, Bergeron was one of those opposed to the more open-minded Catholicism of people like Alain-Marie Couturier, o.p., and the Dominicans (Esther Trépanier, "Art moderne et catholicisme au Québec, 1930-1945: de quelques débats contradictoires", *Religion/Culture. Thèmes canadiens*, Association des études canadiennes, vol. 7, 1985, pp. 330-342). In the 1950s and 1960s, Bergeron changed his mind, as is apparent from his article "Le scandale de la nouveauté", *Arts et pensée*, no. 10 (July-August 1952), pp. 106-108, 110, the conclusions of which are repeated in his book *L'art et sa spiritualité* (Quebec City: Éditions du Pélican, 1961). In this book, Bergeron comes to terms with the "moderns", with Couturier and Maurice Denis. Although he continues to speak positively of Leduc's art, here, as in *Art et Bolchévisme*, he avoids the references to "pretty pictures" like *Mater Amabilis*, *The Holy Family* and *Ecce Corpus Meum* found earlier.

8 Letter from Ozias Leduc to Albert Tessier [mid-March, 1944], BNQ 327/9/7. In his letter to Tessier asking the priest to lend *Mater Amabilis* and *Père Buteux* (cat. 197) for the exhibition, Leduc describes his participation thus: "For me this should be a retrospective, featuring a choice of works executed over a half-century beginning in 1891."

9 Letter from Ozias Leduc to Paul Gouin, December 30, 1941, NAC, Paul Gouin papers, MG 27 III D1, vol. 5. Leduc was executing for Gouin a *Saint Isidore* (reproduced in Lacroix *et al.* 1978, p. 166) in a style comparable to that of *Mater Amabilis*.

10 Maurice Gagnon, *Peinture moderne* (Montreal: Éd. B. Valiquette, 1940), pp. 199-200.

233

Return from the Fields

1941

Oil on cardboard

25.5 x 18 cm

Signed and dated upper left: *OZIAS LEDUC 1941*

Musée Pierre-Boucher du Séminaire de Trois-Rivières, inv. L 82 180 P

INSCRIPTIONS

Verso: *"Mon père, Alphonse Tessier. Cadeau du peintre Ozias Leduc. Signé: Albert Tessier – 4 avril 1973. Moulure à la feuille d'or. Don des Filles de Jésus au Séminaire. 12 mai 1982."*

PROVENANCE

Studio of the artist; Abbé Albert Tessier, Trois-Rivières, 1941; Musée Pierre-Boucher, 1982.

T HIS painting was commissioned by Abbé Albert Tessier (1895-1976), vice principal of the seminary of Trois-Rivières and visiting examiner in the domestic science colleges.[1] Wishing to have a portrait of his father Alphonse Tessier (1861-1962), a farmer at Sainte-Anne-de-la-Pérade, he took a number of photographs and then asked various artists to create a work from one of them. Rodolphe Duguay made a charcoal drawing (fig. 73), Médard Bourgault (1897-1967) a sculpture in wood (fig. 74), and Ozias Leduc, this oil painting.

Fig. 73 Rodolphe Duguay, *Portrait of Alphonse Tessier*, 1930, charcoal heightened with white chalk on paper, 46.6 x 35 cm (Trois-Rivières, Musée Pierre-Boucher).

Fig. 74 Médard Bourgault, *Portrait of Alphonse Tessier*, 1940, wood, 35.5 cm (h.) (Trois-Rivières, Musée Pierre-Boucher).

Fig. 75 Alphonse Tessier (photo: TAVI [Albert Tessier and Avila Denoncourt] BNQ 327/13/6.4a).

Fig. 76 Alphonse Tessier (photo: TAVI [Albert Tessier and Avila Denoncourt] BNQ 327/13/6.4c).

233

Fig. 73

Fig. 74

Fig. 75

Fig. 76

Tessier greatly admired his father and believed him to be the ideal image for the clerical-nationalist ideology the priest wished to promulgate.[2]

Return from the Fields was drawn by Gabrielle Messier and finished by Ozias Leduc. This portrait of Alphonse Tessier with his scythe on his shoulder and his straw hat in his hand reproduces the pose in one of the photographs (figs. 75-76), but the landscape is the artist's own composition. The subject, in a three-quarter length pose, is seen from slightly below, gazing across his land.[3] His calm face is lit by a warm light from the left. This idealized image of the French-Canadian farmer not only expresses the nationalism of Albert Tessier but suggests the allegory of redemption through work proposed by Leduc some years earlier in a portrait of his own father (cat. 225b).

M. L.

1   Albert Tessier was appointed to this post in 1937 at the suggestion of Premier Maurice Duplessis. For more than twenty-eight years, he visited the domestic science colleges, which later became institutes of family education. A short biography can be found in *Albert Tessier: éducateur, collectionneur, cinéaste (1895-1976)*, exhib. cat. (Trois-Rivières: Musée Pierre-Boucher, 1994); his work with film is described in René Bouchard, *Filmographie d'Albert Tessier*, "Documents filmiques du Québec" series (Montreal: Fides, 1973).

2   Of his father, Tessier wrote, "As far back as my memories go, I see my father always with the same contemplative spirit, the same calm wisdom, the same steady way of doing his duty to the full, never impatient or disappointed because things were slow in coming … or never came at all." (*Rétrospective Albert Tessier* [Quebec City: Éditeur officiel du Québec, 1977], p. 11.)

3   This theme is found in works by painters of the Barbizon School like Jean-François Millet (1814-1875) and Jules Breton (1827-1905); in Quebec, Suzor-Coté also depicted the nobility of the tillers of the soil. This composition can also be compared with Edwin Holgate's (1892-1977) *The Lumberjack* from 1923 (reproduced in Jean-René Ostiguy, *Modernism in Quebec Art, 1916-1946*, exhib. cat. [Ottawa: National Gallery of Canada, 1982], p. 69.

234

234

Study for *The Holy Family*

1942

Gouache on the back of photographic paper glued to beige paper

16.8 x 11.8 cm

Signed lower left: *OZIAS LEDUC*; dated lower right: *1942*

Suzette Dorval-Cardinal collection

INSCRIPTIONS
Verso, label: *Croquis pour un tableau Une Sainte famille à mons. l'abbé Albert Tessier. Ozias Leduc*

PROVENANCE
Studio of the artist; Mr. and Mrs. Armand Cardinal, Saint-Hilaire; Suzette Dorval-Cardinal

ABBÉ Albert Tessier was pleased with the popularity of the image of *Mater Amabilis* (cat. 232) and, in 1942, suggested to Leduc that he do another religious subject, the Holy Family.[1] Leduc was interested. He had already made a preparatory drawing on the subject for a painting, never executed, for the Church of Saint-Romuald in Farnham (see cat. 135). He therefore wrote to Tessier describing the sketch, which he suggested using as a basis: the Holy Family was shown amidst everyday life, among tools in a carpentry shop like those his father and he knew well; the workshop to be bathed in the soft light of approaching dusk.[2] The priest, however, recalling that as a child he had said his prayers in front of a "traditional image of the sort found in every home", suggested a composition more expressive of the French-Canadian character, more likely to inspire devotion among Quebec families.

Can you create something on this theme that is more *canadien* in feeling? ... This would involve a composition on two levels ... The Holy Family above ... and below, a scene in the Quebec countryside, perhaps? I see a captivating picture in warm, light, lively colours. The French-Canadian element could be suggested by the background: fields, a wayside cross, houses, a church spire ... I am suggesting an outdoor scene, because I want something airy, full of light, that will captivate the imagination with an interplay of bright colours.3

In May 1942, Leduc sent Abbé Tessier a sketch in gouache he found "decorative", in which he follows the suggestion of a work on two levels: an earthly family, kneeling piously on the ground before the celestial Family, shown above on a cloud, "symbol of the link between heaven and our world", that is caught up in the branches of a "Canadian elm".[4] Above both groups stands the Holy Trinity, with God the Father symbolized by the hand that blesses and the Holy Spirit symbolized by the dove. This kind of composition in tiers is similar to that in paintings in the private chapel of the Bishop's Palace in Sherbrooke (cats. 175-

182). Abbé Tessier liked the general idea and the pastel colour scheme, but he asked for some changes: he wanted the Holy Family to dominate more and the cloud to be more transparent.[5] Leduc never painted this scene, despite his promise to Tessier to give it priority while he was working on the Church of Notre-Dame-de-la-Présentation in Shawinigan-Sud (cats. 237-253).[6]

M. L.

---

1 Letter from Albert Tessier to Ozias Leduc [early March 1942], BNQ 327/7/14.

2 Draft of a letter from Ozias Leduc to Albert Tessier, March 10, 1942, BNQ 327/9/5. The sketch is reproduced in Jean-René Ostiguy, *Ozias Leduc: Symbolist and Religious Painting*, exhib. cat. (Ottawa: National Gallery of Canada, 1974), p. 186.

3 Letter from Albert Tessier to Ozias Leduc, March 22, 1942, BNQ 327/7/14.

4 Letter from Ozias Leduc to Albert Tessier, May 23, 1942, BNQ 327/9/5. Gabrielle Messier confirms that there are three studies for the *Holy Family* extant: the one in the present exhibition; another very similar version, about 16.5 x 11 cm, in a private collection; and one in large format, on which she herself worked, an oil on pressboard, 75 x 51.5 cm, private collection.

5 Letter from Albert Tessier to Ozias Leduc, May 31, 1942, BNQ 327/7/14.

6 Letter from Ozias Leduc to Albert Tessier [early July 1946], BNQ 327/9/9.

235

Madame Labonté
1944
Oil on canvas
50.5 x 40.8 cm
Signed lower left: *OZIAS LEDUC*

Quebec City, Musée du Québec, restored in 1994 on the initiative of the Amis du Musée du Québec, with the support of Jean-Paul Étienne and Ariane Daoust as well as Louise Laferrière and Yvan Morrissette, inv. 53.113

INSCRIPTIONS
Verso: *"Madame Labonté Ozias Leduc 1944"*
PROVENANCE
Studio of the artist; Musée du Québec, 1953

MADAME LABONTÉ is a fictive title given by Leduc to this portrait, which was in fact that of a Mme Loranger. The portrait was commissioned by her grandson, a photographer with a studio in Shawinigan.[1] In 1944, while Leduc was working with his assistant Gabrielle Messier on decorating the Church of Notre-Dame-de-la-Présentation in Shawinigan-Sud, Loranger asked him to paint a portrait of his late grandmother and provided a photograph on which to base the painting (fig. 77). It was understood that Gabrielle Messier would work on it in her spare time. When the portrait was finished, Loranger turned it down, finding it "too artistic" and demanding a better likeness. Leduc retouched the painting, but Loranger was still not satisfied. On seeing the photographer's disappointment, Leduc apparently said to him, "If you wanted a photograph of your grandmother, you might have taken it yourself." He took the canvas back to Saint-Hilaire to work on at leisure in his own way. When it was finished, Leduc gave the painting its present title. In 1953, while visiting the artist's studio, Gérard Morisset purchased it for the Musée du Québec.

Since they had only a photograph to work from, Leduc and Messier could not change the position of the subject, who was seen in a three-quarter-length pose with the face looking at the viewer and the head slightly tilted to the left. And yet, the painting is not a carbon copy of the photograph. As in portraits by the Symbolist painter Eugène Carrière

(1849-1906), the sitter is shrouded in mystery, her features softened and blurred, her gaze lost in reverie. Although the portrait is of a recognizable, living being, the space around her lacks substance and any sense of place. These factors make it clear that *Madame Labonté* is a posthumous portrait. The chiaroscuro and limited colour range recall certain self-portraits by Rembrandt (1606-1669), especially the one painted in the year of his death, in which there is not the slightest concession made to the imminence of the Grim Reaper.

Madame Labonté also has much in common with Ozias Leduc's *My Portrait*, from 1899 (cat. 107). Forty-five years had elapsed between the execution of these two paintings, and yet how alike they are! Both go beyond simply representing an individual. In both works, Leduc respects two-dimensionality but places his subject in a weightless, timeless place; the forms are created with colour and without recourse to line drawing. Purely painterly elements – the tightness of the composition, the restricted palette and the intense chiaroscuro – heighten the expression of the two subjects. The piercing eyes in *My Portrait*, however, are replaced by the kind, calm gaze of *Madame Labonté*. Did Leduc bring something of himself to this posthumous portrait?[2] He was eighty

235

Fig. 77   Detail from a photograph of Madame Loranger (private collection).

years old when he finished it, almost as old as the subject herself, and indeed photographs taken of the artist at this time reflect qualities seen in *Madame Labonté*: kindness, tranquillity and resignation. Leduc makes of Mme Loranger an archetype, the personification of a moral virtue: goodness. *Madame Labonté* is a visionary portrait, of the kind the artist described: "This is the royal road to Beauty, to the crux of an art of glimpses, of evocation, not of appearance. An art built on the suppleness of an unfettered technique and the tools of leisure, the paintbrushes of time."[3]

M. L.

1   Gabrielle Messier kindly provided details about the commissioning of this painting.

2   As René Bouillot, *Le portrait photographique* (Paris: P. Montel, 1984), p. 7, states, "For the greatest portraitists, the model is just a mirror in which they see themselves."

3   Quoted in Guy Viau, *La peinture moderne au Canada français* (Quebec City: Ministère des Affaires culturelles, 1964), p. 12.

236
Still Life (with Book, Inkwell and Eyeglasses)
1948
Oil and graphite on canvas
28.5 x 37.9 cm
Signed and dated lower left: *OZIAS LEDUC 1948*

Noëlla Lagacé collection

INSCRIPTIONS
Verso, labels: certificate of authencity from Galerie
Bernard Desroches; Galerie Clarence Gagnon
(Gilles Brown); encadrement Marcel

PROVENANCE
Galerie d'art Clarence Gagnon (Gilles Brown);
Bernard Lagacé, 1988-1989; Noëlla Lagacé, 1990

By the 1940s, Leduc had for all intents and purposes discontinued the still-life genre. One of two exceptions, however, is this unfinished Still Life from 1948. The circumstances of its execution are unknown. It depicts an open book propped against a pile of curled-up drawings, one of whose corners is exposed. Neither the book nor the drawing has been developed enough to determine its contents. An inkwell and eyeglasses lie to either side. The grouping is set against a wall upon which, in the upper corners, two images with borders are faintly discernable.

Both the unfinished state and the less-than-ideal physical condition of this *Still Life*[1] preclude a full appreciation of Leduc's intention, either stylistic or iconographical. However, what seems to be a closely related painting, now lost (fig. 123), done in 1940 for the Bindoffs (cats. 194-195)[2] may provide evidence of the concerns Leduc was seeking to deal with and, by extrapolation, allow a glimpse of where the unfinished work presented here was headed. In the Bindoff still life, the books, drawings, reproductions and artist's tools in a stepped configuration within a narrow space are the objects and the arrangement seen in Leduc's earlier still lifes (cats. 11, 13, 20). But the inclusion of his drawing after Michelangelo's Medici Tomb sculpture *Dusk*, a book entitled *Destin* and a handbell points to a contemplation of the end of one's life.[3]

The unfinished 1948 *Still Life* is conceived in much the same way, and in fact, both it and the Bindoff work may be related to a single preparatory drawing,[4] different elements finding their way into each painting. Present in this *Still Life* are the drawing's inkwell and eyeglasses lying to either side of the book, along with the empty space on the back wall framed by the two corner sections so as to imply a cross. Though it is difficult to ascertain absolutely the meaning of this late canvas, its commonalities with the 1940 painting – as well as Leduc's trademark structuring of the space, the physical and iconological relationship of the objects to one another, and the diffuse blond light that animates the narrow space – hint at what this painting promised to be.

A. G.

1 According to the conservation report of the Montreal Museum of Fine Arts, September 22, 1995, there is retouching around the edges, and the upper corners evidence abrasion.

2 The painting was tailored to fit an existing frame in the possession of Leduc's friends. See the correspondence from Florence and Fred Bindoff to Ozias Leduc, December 27, 1939, BNQ 327/7/11, and May 23, 1940, BNQ 327/7/12. Upon Fred Bindoff's death in 1955, the painting was consigned to the Dominion Gallery, Montreal, from where it was purchased by G.H. Laframboise et Cie and offered to Maurice Duplessis in 1956 (see Jean-René Ostiguy, *Ozias Leduc: Symbolist and Religious Painting*, exhib. cat. [Ottawa: National Gallery of Canada, 1974], p. 192).

3 *Ibid.*

4 Reproduced in Laurier Lacroix *et al.*, *Ozias Leduc the Draughtsman*, exhib. cat. (Montreal: Concordia University, 1978), p. 92.

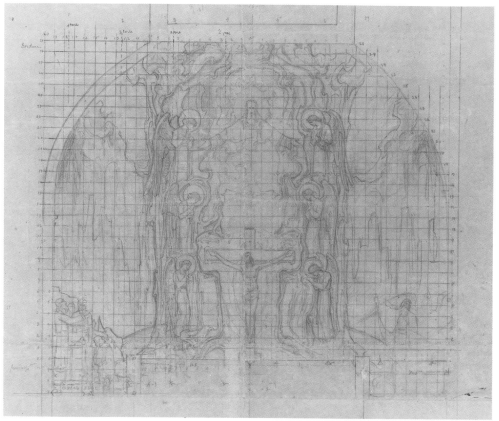

237

237

Study for *The Holy Trinity*
About 1942-1944
Graphite on brown paper
64.7 x 68.3 cm

Signed lower left: *OZIAS LEDUC*

Montreal, Bibliothèque nationale du Québec -
Fonds Ozias-Leduc, MSS-327/10/24

INSCRIPTIONS
Recto, upper left: *Bordure*; lower left: *Inscription*

PROVENANCE
Studio of the artist; Gabrielle Messier, Saint-
Hilaire; Bibliothèque nationale du Québec, 1972

238

238

Study for *The Holy Trinity*
About 1942-1944
Gouache, watercolour and ink on paper
25.6 x 26.2 cm

Art Gallery of Greater Victoria, British Columbia,
Harold and Vera Mortimer-Lamb Purchase Fund,
inv. 92.50

INSCRIPTIONS
Recto: *NOTRE PÈRE QUI ÈTES AUX CIEUX /* LUX
MUNDI; verso: *55341 Église de Shawinigan Ozias
Leduc pas à vendre*

PROVENANCE
Studio of the artist; Ozias Leduc estate; Galerie
l'Art français, Montreal, 1956; Galerie Jean-Pierre
Valentin, 1992; Art Gallery of Greater Victoria,
1992

239

240

239
Study for *The Offering of Melchizedek*
    About 1942-1944
    Ink and wash on cardboard
    29.3 x 20.3 cm

Quebec City, Musée du Québec, inv. 79.162.08
    INSCRIPTIONS
Verso: certificate of authenticity signed by
Gabrielle Messier and Monique di Cola
    PROVENANCE
Studio of the artist; parish of Notre-Dame-de-la-
Présentation, Shawinigan-Sud; Lévis Martin,
Trois-Rivières; Musée du Québec, 1979

240
Study for *The Sacrifice of Isaac*
    About 1942-1944
    Ink and gouache on cardboard
    29.2 x 20.5 cm

Quebec City, Musée du Québec, inv. 79.162.10
    INSCRIPTIONS
Verso: certificate of authenticity signed by
Gabrielle Messier and Monique di Cola
    PROVENANCE
Studio of the artist; parish of Notre-Dame-de-la-
Présentation, Shawinigan-Sud; Lévis Martin,
Trois-Rivières; Musée du Québec, 1979

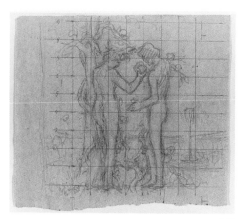

241

Study for *The Temptation of Adam and Eve*

About 1945
Graphite on paper
13.6 x 15.6 cm

Quebec City, Musée du Québec, inv. 79.165.03
INSCRIPTIONS
Verso: certificate of authenticity signed by Gabrielle Messier and Monique di Cola
PROVENANCE
Studio of the artist; parish of Notre-Dame-de-la-Présentation, Shawinigan-Sud; Lévis Martin, Trois-Rivières; Musée du Québec, 1979

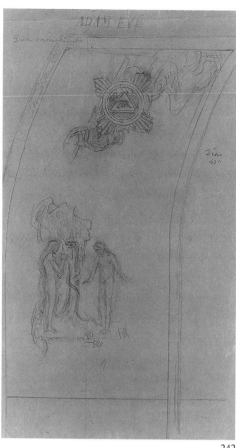

242

242

Study for *The Temptation of Adam and Eve*

About 1945
Graphite on paper
30.3 x 17.6 cm

Quebec City, Musée du Québec, inv. 79.165.02
INSCRIPTIONS
Recto: *ADAM-EVE; Dieu Omniscient; Dia 40"*
Verso: certificate of authenticity signed by Gabrielle Messier and Monique di Cola
PROVENANCE
Studio of the artist; parish of Notre-Dame-de-la-Présentation, Shawinigan-Sud; Lévis Martin, Trois-Rivières; Musée du Québec, 1979

243

Study for *The Temptation of Adam and Eve*

About 1945
Graphite on paper
20.2 x 14.1 cm

Quebec City, Musée du Québec, inv. 79.165.04
INSCRIPTIONS
Verso: certificate of authenticity signed by Gabrielle Messier and Monique di Cola
PROVENANCE
Studio of the artist; parish of Notre-Dame-de-la-Présentation, Shawinigan-Sud; Lévis Martin, Trois-Rivières; Musée du Québec, 1979

243

244

Study for *The Temptation of Adam and Eve*

About 1945

Graphite on paper

30.1 x 19.6 cm

Quebec City, Musée du Québec, inv. 79.165.01

INSCRIPTIONS

Recto: *TANTATION D'ADAM-D'EVE; Le contour de l'emblem = le meme blanc que celui accompagnant les bordures. Le blanc disposé en forme de brosse suggerant un rayonnement*

Verso: certificate of authenticity signed by Gabrielle Messier and Monique di Cola

PROVENANCE

Studio of the artist; parish of Notre-Dame-de-la-Présentation, Shawinigan-Sud; Lévis Martin, Trois-Rivières; Musée du Québec, 1979

245

Study for *The Temptation of Christ in the Wilderness*

About 1945

Graphite on paper

30.2 x 19.8 cm

Quebec City, Musée du Québec, inv. 79.166.01

INSCRIPTIONS

Recto: *TANTATION DE JESUS; N° 1*

Verso: certificate of authenticity signed by Gabrielle Messier and Monique di Cola

PROVENANCE

Studio of the artist; parish of Notre-Dame-de-la-Présentation, Shawinigan-Sud; Lévis Martin, Trois-Rivières; Musée du Québec, 1979

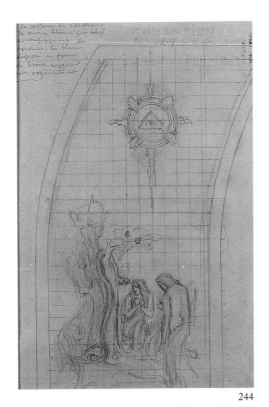

244

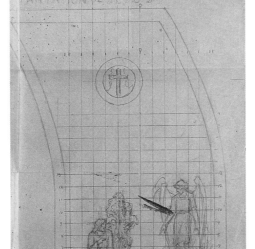

245

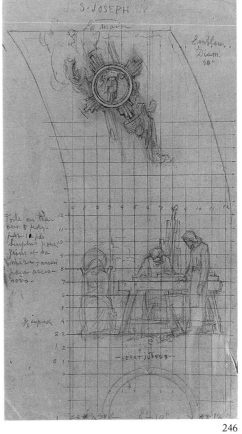

246

246

Study for *The Holy Family in the Carpenter's Shop*

About 1945

Graphite on paper

30.5 x 17.7 cm

Quebec City, Musée du Québec, inv. 79.164.02

INSCRIPTIONS

Recto: *S-JOSEPH; La main; Emblem Diam 40"; - ERAT JUSTUS-*; various notations on dimensions

Verso: certificate of authenticity signed by Gabrielle Messier and Monique di Cola

PROVENANCE

Studio of the artist; parish of Notre-Dame-de-la-Présentation, Shawinigan-Sud; Lévis Martin, Trois-Rivières; Musée du Québec, 1979

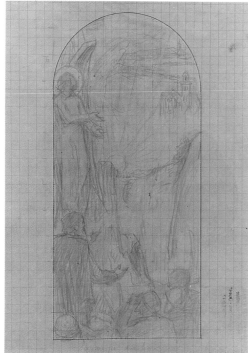

247

249

247

Study for *Père Jacques Buteux
at the Foot of Shawinigan Falls,
March 28, 1651*

About 1946

Graphite on paper

27.8 x 19.5 cm

Quebec City, Musée du Québec, inv. 79.167.10

INSCRIPTIONS

Recto: *La coupe[?] du bois*
Verso: certificate of authenticity signed by
Gabrielle Messier and Monique di Cola

PROVENANCE

Studio of the artist; parish of Notre-Dame-de-la-
Présentation, Shawinigan-Sud; Lévis Martin,
Trois-Rivières; Musée du Québec, 1979

248

Study for *Père Jacques Buteux
at the Foot of Shawinigan Falls,
March 28, 1651*

About 1946

Oil, charcoal and ink on plywood

42.5 x 24.2 cm

Signed lower left: *OZIAS LEDUC*

Quebec City, Musée du Québec, inv. 79.191

INSCRIPTIONS

Verso: *"Shawinigan-sud Paroisse Notre-Dame de la
Présentation croquis: Le père Jacques Buteux au pied
des chutes Shawinigan le 28 mars 1651 par Ozias Leduc
St-Hilaire (Rouville)."*

PROVENANCE

Nicole Blouin, Sainte-Foy; Musée du Québec, 1979

249

Study for *Père Jacques Buteux Put to
Death by the Iroquois, May 10, 1652*

About 1948

Oil, ink and charcoal on plywood

38.7 x 18.3 cm

Signed lower left: *OZIAS LEDUC*

Quebec City, Musée du Québec, inv. 79.158

INSCRIPTIONS

Verso: label: *"Croquis: le Père Jacques Buteux tombant
sous les coups des Iroquois le 10 mai 1652 par Ozias
Leduc St-Hilaire Rouville; Esquisse pour le tableau
"La mort du Père Buteux" dans l'église Notre-Dame de
la Présentation à Shawinigan-sud."*; certificate of
authenticity signed by Gabrielle Messier and
Mireille Gagner

PROVENANCE

Studio of the artist; parish of Notre-Dame-de-la-
Présentation, Shawinigan-Sud; Lévis Martin,
Trois-Rivières; Musée du Québec, 1979

248

250

251

252

250

Study for *Clearing the Land*

About 1950

Graphite and ink on paper

27.5 x 21.4 cm

Quebec City, Musée du Québec, inv. 79.169.01

INSCRIPTIONS

Recto: *Tablau N° 1; haut du chapi[t]au 9-7 1/4-; 6'-1/2" x 12'-5"*

Verso: certificate of authenticity signed by Gabrielle Messier and Monique di Cola

PROVENANCE

Studio of the artist; parish of Notre-Dame-de-la-Présentation, Shawinigan-Sud; Lévis Martin, Trois-Rivières; Musée du Québec, 1979

251

Study for *Clearing the Land*

About 1950

Oil, graphite and ink on plywood

42.6 x 24.2 cm

Signed lower right: *OZIAS LEDUC*

Quebec City, Musée du Québec, inv. 88.116

INSCRIPTIONS

Verso: *Le défrichement; le camp de bois; no 1; La buche (…)*

PROVENANCE

Marielle Fortin, Sainte-Foy, about 1966; Musée du Québec, 1988

252

Study for *The Paper Mill Workers*

About 1950

Oil and graphite on plywood

42.5 x 24.2 cm

Signed lower left: *OZIAS LEDUC*

Yves Gauthier collection / KPMG

PROVENANCE

Studio of the artist; parish of Notre-Dame-de-la-Présentation, Shawinigan-Sud; Jacques Laforest, about 1960; Galerie Michel-Ange, Montreal, 1995; Yves Gauthier, 1995

253

Study for *The Metal Foundry Workers*

About 1950

Oil, charcoal and graphite on plywood

38.5 x 18.3 cm

Signed lower left: *OZIAS LEDUC*

Quebec City, Musée du Québec, inv. 79.159

INSCRIPTIONS

Verso: certificate of authenticity signed by Gabrielle Messier and Mireille Gagner

PROVENANCE

Studio of the artist; parish of Notre-Dame-de-la-Présentation, Shawinigan-Sud; Lévis Martin, Trois-Rivières; Musée du Québec, 1979

253

I N 1932, when he was finishing decorating the private chapel of the Bishop's Palace in Sherbrooke (cats. 175-182), Leduc, exasperated by the way he felt people failed to understand his work as a muralist, confided to his friend Olivier Maurault (cats. 161-163),

Father, the interest you take in this decoration I am engaged on comforts me and distracts me somewhat from the dark wood I wander in here; aside from Audet the architect, no one seems to care at all about the painting. To be fair, they admit that it's good for protecting the walls, as is the canvas, especially in this case, when it is covered with thick layers of paint – I agree with them about this and feel a certain pride – that of the black man who whitewashes your ceiling – when I hear them say that everything is nice and clean, not a smudge anywhere – and that it will look fine when the scaffolding comes down![1]

A year later, in a letter to the same friend, he expressed his sense of discouragement: at the age of sixty-eight he still had to prove his "ability to design decoration" and to "execute it in situ".[2] This natural wish to have his work understood and appreciated was finally gratified by the last decoration project he undertook, for Abbé Arthur Jacob of the parish of Notre-Dame-de-la-Présentation in Shawinigan-Sud.[3] This priest's warm friendship for the artist who had come to complete the "great work" of decorating his church[4] was expressed with tact, admiration, and a consoling enthusiasm. In return, Leduc wrote to him, "Your dream, which the artist in me responds to, will be reality one day. Your will power and perseverance will make of it something real and beautiful that your parishioners will be proud to have helped create."[5] The artist often thanked Father Jacob for his support and his words of encouragement, but what he most admired in this patron was his understanding of "the mystique of Art".[6]

Priest and painter got to know each other in the summer of 1941.[7] On the recommendation of several churchmen, especially Msgr. Olivier Maurault, Jacob

visited Leduc in his studio and asked him to decorate his church.[8] The seventy-seven-year-old artist accepted the challenge, as he knew he could count on the help of Gabrielle Messier, who had been his studio pupil for a year. The agreement was signed on September 10, 1941, but the project was not accepted by the churchwardens and parishioners until the following April.[9] Leduc and Gabrielle Messier stayed in Shawinigan-Sud on several occasions, lodging at the presbytery and using a classroom in the Collège Notre-Dame as a studio. After 1945, Leduc preferred to work in his studio at Saint-Hilaire, as much for the light as for its other advantages: his collection of art books, privacy, economy and the opportunity to take a rest.[10] He travelled to Shawinigan for short periods while the canvases were being glued in place.

The general theme proposed by Father Jacob for the decoration was based on the Presentation of Mary in the Temple, for which the church itself was named.[11] The main painting behind the high altar would show *The Holy Trinity* (fig. 78) adored by angels; on either side of it would be two Old Testament scenes, the offering of Melchizedek and Abraham sacrificing his son. The *Christ on the Cross* was to have been sculpted in the round from a design by Leduc and set above the *Holy Trinity*, but in the end it was painted. Three paintings would be based on episodes in the life of the Virgin: *The Presentation of Mary in the Temple*, *The Annunciation* and *The Holy Family in the Carpenter's Shop* (figs. 79-81). The *Temptation of Adam and Eve* (fig. 82) was to be painted on the back wall of the church at the level of the organ loft, and its counterpart *The Temptation of Christ in the Wilderness* (fig. 83) on the opposite wall. Leduc had originally made alternative proposals for the nave: six paintings either on the life of the Virgin, or on historical subjects as suggested by Abbé Albert Tessier. The latter proposal was finally adopted: two paintings on the life and death of Père Jacques Buteux (figs. 88-89), the first missionary to the Mauricie region; four

paintings depicting contemporary life in Shawinigan through the most typical sorts of work in the area: *Clearing the Land*, *The Sower*, *The Paper Mill Workers* in the pulp-and-paper industry, and *The Metal Foundry Workers* of an aluminum plant (figs. 84-87). In the initial plan one last painting was to be executed, on the ceiling above the organ loft, a *Saint Cecilia* surrounded by Christian virgins, including the Amerindian Kateri Tekakwitha, but this was replaced by a *Coronation of the Virgin* (fig. 90).[12] The plan also called for groups of adoring angels for the choir and, for the upper part of the walls of the nave, angels with unfurled wings as caryatids to uphold the coffered ceiling. It also included a series of decorative motifs that would unify the components of the design.[13]

The first painting of the ensemble – first in its subject and also in its dominating position behind the high altar – is *The Holy Trinity*, or the *Divine Glory*, described by Leduc as a "great theological drama".[14] This ascensional composition shows the Son of God dying on the Cross for love of His Father, and the latter accepting the sacrifice of His Son, offered to humanity in the presence of the Holy Spirit and angels in adoration.[15] Leduc explained the symbolism of the Eternal Father as follows:

An old man, white not with age but in a subtle symbolism, white in the way that snow is white, or ice on the high peaks. The permanence of ice at these heights, and its unchanging colour, might suggest to mankind, struck with the idea of God without beginning or end, encompassing all duration, that the image that could be created of it could be inspired by the icy peaks and their shining whiteness. The eternal snows = symbol of immutability and perpetuity.[16]

On either side of the central panel are scenes from the Old Testament whose "symbolic link with the Sacrifice of the Cross is summed up in the Sacrament of the Eucharist which they prefigure":[17] on the left, *The Sacrifice of Isaac* – "Abraham sacrificing his son, as God the Father sacrifices His Son for love of us"[18] – and

Fig. 78

Fig. 79

ET INCARNATUS EST

Fig. 80

ERAT JUSTUS

Fig. 81

"SICUT DII ERITIS"

Fig. 82

NON IN SOLO PANE
VIVIT HOMO

Fig. 83

on the right *The Offering of Melchizedek* – "Melchizedek offering up bread and wine, prefiguring the Holy Sacrifice of the Mass".[19] The earliest preparatory studies for this huge mural date from the start of the project in 1942, but the painting itself was not completed until 1947.

The life of the Virgin was to be illustrated by four pictures. *The Presentation of Mary in the Temple*, unveiled in 1943, shows the first occasion on which the Virgin approaches the divine mystery. Leduc based his drawing on the traditional iconography of the subject, which was popularized in the Middle Ages through *The Golden Legend*[20] and which gave him the opportunity to create an elaborate architectural backdrop.

The Virgin Mary, a little girl approaching the doorway of the Temple which will be her home for a while, climbs the steps determinedly but stumbling a little because she is only small and is tired already. There are still ten steps to go. Her parents Anne and Joachim with their relations and friends are silent, holding their breath … The little preordained Virgin reaches her destination. The

maidens awaiting her at the top of the stairs are murmuring the words with which the Angel Gabriel will greet her: Hail Mary, full of strength and grace! Mary blessed among women.[21]

There followed in 1945-1947 *The Annunciation* and *The Holy Family in the Carpenter's Shop*, works based on suggestions by Father Jacob. In the former, the Angel Gabriel, bowing respectfully towards the Virgin, "holds his hands as if offering something. It is the gift of becoming the Mother of God."[22] The Virgin, awed by the apparition, gestures her consent. Both paintings illustrate the grace accepted by Mary that illuminates everyday family life. *The Holy Family in the Carpenter's Shop* illustrates redemption through work, a subject to be continued in the four secular paintings in the nave. The last painting, the *Coronation of the Virgin*, was begun in 1952 and completed from Leduc's sketches by Gabrielle Messier after his death. The work combines two episodes of the Glorification of the Virgin: the

Figs. 78-89 Ozias Leduc, oil on canvas, glued in place (Shawinigan-Sud, Church of Notre-Dame-de-la-Présentation).

Fig. 78   *The Holy Trinity*, 1944-1947, approx. 970 x 1280 cm.

Fig. 79   *The Presentation of Mary in the Temple*, 1943, 678 x 395 cm.

Fig. 80   *The Annunciation*, 1947, 335 x 325 cm.

Fig. 81   *The Holy Family in the Carpenter's Shop*, 1947, 300 x 356 cm.

Fig. 82   *The Temptation of Adam and Eve*, 1945-1947, 355 x 338 cm.

Fig. 83   *The Temptation of Christ in the Wilderness*, 1945-1946, 342 x 334 cm.

Fig. 84

Fig. 85

Fig. 86

Fig. 87

Fig. 88

Fig. 89

Fig. 90

Assumption and the Crowning in heaven by an angel under the throne of God in three Persons.

Two paintings near the organ loft treat of the Fall of Man and his redemption: *The Temptation of Adam and Eve* and *The Temptation of Christ in the Wilderness*. The former shows original sin, the moment when Adam gives in to temptation, with Eve holding out the forbidden fruit under the triumphant eyes of the Devil, who has a serpent's body and the head of a man. The Tree of the Knowledge of Good and Evil is an apple tree, as in the Latin tradition. Leduc places in the foreground a vine with abundant grapes, symbolizing redemption through the blood of Christ. Above the painting is the symbol of the eye of God. Our first parents fell, but Christ in the desert rejected sin; above the painting, the symbol of the Cross reminds us that Christ redeemed mankind from original sin through His death on the Cross.

Two paintings in the nave deal with the Christianization of the Mauricie region. *Père Jacques Buteux at the Foot of Shawinigan Falls, March 28, 1651* (fig. 88), painted between 1946 and 1948, shows the missionary and his companions, the first white men to sail up the Saint-Maurice. Father Jacob explained the narrative and symbolic aspects of the painting as follows:

The word "Shawinigan" means in the Native tongue: difficult passage. The waterfalls symbolize hardship, the difficulties of the voyage, but the missionary's commitment, symbolized by the angel of the Mauricie, is unshakeable. In his mind he sees down the centuries to the future development of Shawinigan-Almaville, symbolized by factory chimneys and church spires, even the front of our church in the mist from the falls. The artist has visualized the falls as a cosmic phenomenon represented by a cross of shining beams, intimating that although electricity

Fig. 91   Fig. 92   Fig. 93

Fig. 91   Eugène Nadeau, a founder at the Alcan plant in Shawinigan, 1950 (BNQ 327/13/5.11b).

Fig. 92   Gluing paintings in place at the Church of Notre-Dame-de-la-Présentation, Shawinigan-Sud (private collection).

Fig. 93   Gabrielle Messier, Ozias Leduc, Jean-Josaphat Gagnier and Arthur Jacob in front of the Church of Notre-Dame-de-la-Présentation, Shawinigan-Sud (BNQ 327/13/1.25).

was still unknown, there was in these waters a hidden force that would one day be harnessed to serve Christian civilization.[23]

For Leduc the painting could be summed up as "a vision of the religious and industrial development of the Shawinigan region".[24] *Père Jacques Buteux Put to Death by the Iroquois, May 10, 1652* (fig. 89), executed in 1948-1949, depicts the missionary's death at the hands of an Iroquois ambush during his second trip to the land of the Attikamek. "His companion Fontarabie has already fallen. Père Jacques has just received his death blow. He seems to be trying to bless his persecutors before dying … His guardian angel bears the martyr's merits before the Eternal Presence."[25]

The other principal theme in the decoration of the nave is that of redemption through work, a subject Leduc had tackled several times in the past, in easel paintings (cat. 233) and in murals (cat. 167). The four paintings on this theme shown here, *Clearing the Land*, *The Sower*, *The Paper Mill Workers* and *The Foundry Workers*, were painted between 1950 and 1952. They represent the main economic activities of this recently populated area: agriculture, the Belgo pulp and paper mill, and the

smelters of the Aluminium Company of Canada. The upper part of each painting contains emblems of each trade: a yoke, a mattock, a log driver's pickaxe, a plough and a triangular harrow for *Clearing the Land*; sprouting wheat, a ciborium, a Host and a bunch of grapes for *The Sower*; papyrus, a book and a printing press for *The Paper Mill Workers* and the anvil, oil lamp and crucible for *The Metal Foundry Workers*.

As was his wont, Leduc made many preliminary drawings and studies while designing and executing this series. Each painting was preceded by dozens of pencil sketches for working out details of figures and whole compositions.[26] The various studies for *The Temptation of Adam and Eve*, for example, show how complex was the research he undertook to determine the positioning of the figures and their size in relation to the scale of the building. In the drawings, we glimpse the monumental scope of scenes where movements are exaggerated to stress the symbolism of the gesture. For the scenes of industry, Leduc used photographs of men actually at work (fig. 91), so that he could re-create their habitual movements.[27]

The sketches are also rendered in monochrome heightened with a palette of muted tones like the blue and earth shades of the interior of Notre-Dame-de-la-Présentation, which are so conducive to meditation and tranquillity.[28] The interior is very stark, the nave being composed of a long rectangle with the corners cut off. The absence of ornamentation establishing a rhythm on the

surface of the walls obliged Leduc to find another way to incorporate his paintings. Instead of creating borders that would have no architectural basis, he chose to shape his compositions according to the surface of the wall. Thus, *The Holy Trinity* takes up the whole of the chevet wall; the angel caryatids are painted as prolongations of the transverse beams of the vault; the narrative scenes in the nave are inserted between the windows and have the same shape as the latter; and the four scenes in the corners are cut out around the figures and mounted directly on the wall. In this last case, the lack of any demarcation between the painting and the wall also made it easier to incorporate the painting, in monochrome earth colours, into the wall surface with its lighter colour.

As the paintings were executed on canvases about a metre and a half wide,[29] squaring off for enlargement was essential to transfer the compositions to the canvas without altering the relationships between the various elements. The canvas was then attached to the wall and held in place under pressure while drying by a wood framework. The mounting was done under the direction of Gabrielle Messier with the help of Father Jacob and of the curate Mieczyslaw Cieplak (fig. 92). Leduc's brother Honorius worked mainly on the stencilled patterns.

In 1948, the composer Jean-Josaphat Gagnier (1885-1949) (fig. 93) wrote a symphonic poem for organ, "L'Envolée mystique", inspired by the mural in the choir of Notre-Dame-de-la-

Présentation. Leduc heard the recording on the radio and wrote to Gagnier to congratulate him, adding,

Music is nothing but soul. Painting drags a body along with it. By your skill you bring them together, you create a song with words that are sounds, captive sounds, bound by an law whose echo in us reverberates with love and adoration, because we have the Faith, because we believe in Beauty … Please believe that I am deeply grateful for the consolation you have given me with your appreciation of my painting, which I wish could be both Poetry and Music in liberty![30]

M. L., L. L.

1 Letter from Ozias Leduc to Olivier Maurault, April 5, 1932, Archives du Séminaire de Saint-Sulpice.

2 Letter from Ozias Leduc to Olivier Maurault, January 25, 1933, *ibid.*

3 At the time, the village was called Almaville-en-Bas; it received its new name on August 4, 1948. Abbé Arthur Jacob was the parish priest of Notre-Dame-de-la-Présentation from July 1937 (Notes sur les paroisses, Archives du Séminaire de Trois-Rivières, F1-A3).

4 The long correspondence between Arthur Jacob and Ozias Leduc is in the BNQ (327).

5 Letter from O. L. to Arthur Jacob, December 24, 1941, BNQ 327/9/4.

6 Letter from O. L. to Arthur Jacob, May 19, 1943, BNQ 327/9/6.

7 Diary of Gabrielle Messier, June 24, 1941, personal archives of the writer.

8 Letter of recommendation by Olivier Maurault, January 29, 1942, BNQ 327/7/14: "This artist, whom I rank among the best in the land and who is undoubtedly the foremost painter of religious subjects in French Canada at this time … Mr. Leduc has a rare intellect, and he is also a Christian philosopher, a Catholic who has learned from the liturgy and the symbolism of the Middle Ages, the age of faith."

9 Letter from Jacob to O. L., April 4, 1942, BNQ 327/7/14.

10 Letter from O. L. to Jacob [after October 4, 1945], BNQ 327/9/8.

11 There is a copy of the specifications, dated September 10, 1941, BNQ 327/2/51.

12 In a letter to Olivier Maurault [after February 7, 1949], BNQ 327/8/3, Leduc mentions he is thinking of making a copy of his own *Assumption*, painted fifty years earlier for the Church of Saint-Hilaire, for one of the ceiling panels in the church in Shawinigan-Sud.

13 The estimated budget for the work as a whole was $4,625, to be paid to Leduc in several instalments, as he had to pay his assistants and buy all the materials needed, as well as pay for his lodging while in Shawinigan. In 1947, further amounts were paid him: $350 for the drawings for the six paintings for the nave and for a *Tree of Jesse* that was eventually replaced by the *Coronation of the Virgin*, and $3,100 for the paintings themselves (BNQ 327/2/55).

14 Letter from O. L. to Jacob, January 7, 1944, BNQ 327/9/7.

15 Ozias Leduc, "La Sainte Trinité" (manuscript), BNQ 327/2/55.

16 Ozias Leduc, "Almaville-en-Bas" (manuscript), BNQ 327/2/55.

17 Manuscript by Ozias Leduc beginning, "Les deux grisailles…", BNQ 327/2/55.

18 Arthur Jacob, *Légendes des tableaux de la décoration en l'église Notre-Dame de la Presentation d'Almaville, (aujourd'hui Shawinigan-Sud) comté de Saint-Maurice, P.Q.* (Trois-Rivières, Quebec: Imprimerie du Bien Public, 1960), p. 9.

19 *Ibid.*

20 Jacobus de Voragine, *Legenda Aurea*, based on apocryphal writings.

21 Letter from O. L. to Jean-Paul Jacob [after December 24, 1946] BNQ 327/9/9.

22 Letter from Arthur Jacob to O. L., June 18, 1945, BNQ 327/7/17.

23 Jacob 1960, p. 27.

24 Ozias Leduc's Diary for 1947-1952, July 5, 1949, BNQ 327/3/11.

25 Jacob 1960, p. 29. The pose of the dying Père Buteux is not unlike that of Saint Barnabas in *The Martyrdom of Saint Barnabas* (cats. 136-137).

26 Aside from the works shown here, the Musée Pierre-Boucher has a collection of drawings and sketches used for the figures of the caryatid angels and for the inscriptions, while several other drawings connected with the decoration of the Church of Notre-Dame-de-la-Présentation are in the BNQ 327/10/18-19.

27 Reproduced in Laurier Lacroix *et al.*, *Ozias Leduc the Draughtsman*, exhib. cat. (Montreal: Concordia University, 1978), p. 97.

28 On this subject, Leduc wrote, "As an idealist artist, I believe in the evocative power of colour, its tones and shades. Their eloquent interplay touches even the most insensitive – that is certain" (letter from O. L. to Jean-Paul Jacob [after December 24, 1946], BNQ 327/9/9). This goes along with a note jotted on the back of a sketch of The Annunciation and The Holy Family in the Carpenter's Shop for Notre-Dame-de-la-Présentation, BNQ 327/10/18: "The work of art touches before it instructs – it is altogether a presentiment."

29 Canvas imported from Mexico because of rationing of materials in wartime. This information was obtained from Gabrielle Messier.

30 Letter from O. L. to J.-J. Gagnier [after April 23, 1948], BNQ 327/9/11.

254

Twelfth Station of the Cross: Christ Dies upon the Cross

1949-1950

Oil, charcoal, graphite, gilt, gold leaf and wood on canvas

61.4 x 49.9 cm

Signed lower left: *OZS.L.*

Les Soeurs des Saints Noms de Jésus et de Marie du Québec

INSCRIPTIONS

Recto: *JÉSUS MEURT SUR LA [CR]OIX XIIÈME STATION*

PROVENANCE

Studio of the artist; Chapel of the Convent of Saint-Hilaire; Les Soeurs des Saints Noms de Jésus et de Marie du Québec, on deposit at the Musée du Québec, Quebec City, 1995

IN September 1949, the members of the Amicale du pensionnat of the Sisters of Les Saints Noms de Jésus et de Marie in Saint-Hilaire asked Leduc to paint for them the Stations of the Cross for the chapel of their alma mater.[1] The artist, with the help of three assistants, one of whom was Paul-Émile Borduas,[2] had already created the decoration for the half-dome of the apse in 1926.[3]

The contract Leduc signed stipulated that each Station should include only a few figures, shown head and shoulders. The work was to be finished by May of the following year without fail, in time for the celebration of the boarding school's centenary in June 1950.[4] The artist, now in his mid-eighties, painted all fourteen Stations in tightly framed compositions, with Christ and the background figures often shown half-length. The figures stand out against gold backgrounds patterned like mosaic. Each painting has a grey-blue gilt border with a small crucifix of cedar in relief at the top. A similar design can be found in the Stations of the Cross in the Church of Saint-Hilaire. Contrary to the expectations of the Amicale, the paintings were not attached to the walls but simply hung, as Leduc felt that the rough surface of the wall would not take priming.[5]

As a result of the artist's decision to show the figures close-up, the pictorial space is handled so as to make the maximum use of the surface available. The

Fig. 93a Ozias Leduc, *Eighth Station of the Cross: Jesus Speaks to the Women of Jerusalem*, 1949-1950, oil, charcoal, graphite, gold paint, gold leaf and wood on canvas, 61.4 x 49.9 cm (Chapel of the Convent Saint-Hilaire, on depost to the Musée du Québec, Quebec City).

Fig. 93b Ozias Leduc, *Second Station of the Cross: Jesus Receives His Cross*, 1949-1950, oil, charcoal, graphite, gold paint, gold leaf and wood on canvas, 61.4 x 49.9 cm (Chapel of the Convent of Saint-Hilaire, on deposit to the Musée du Québec, Quebec City).

clearest example of this is the eighth Station, *Jesus Speaks to the Women of Jerusalem* (fig. 93a), where Leduc uses the whole surface, placing the figures and the inscription all around the Cross. In this painting the composition is based on the diagonal lines of the cross, whereas in the twelfth Station, *Christ Dies upon the Cross*, the space is organized in a symmetrical manner. Sometimes, as in this Station and the fourteenth one, *Jesus Is Laid in the Sepulchre*, the work spills over beyond its own borders. In *Christ Dies upon the Cross*, the cross-piece of the Cross, partially obscuring the symbols of the sun and moon, extends beyond the gilt frame. In iconographic terms, the Virgin, Saint John and Mary Magdalene are shown simply as grieving faces at the bottom of the composition, thus fulfilling the terms of the commission.

The faces and gestures of the figures in the Convent of Saint-Hilaire's Stations of the Cross are by and large traditional, except in the case of the second Station, *Jesus Receives His Cross* (fig. 93b), where the artist has depicted the man behind Christ as a contemporary workman. This figure is reminiscent

of some of the labourers shown in the paintings in the nave of the Church of Notre-Dame-de-la-Présentation in Shawinigan-Sud, such as *Clearing the Land*, *The Paper Mill Workers* and *The Metal Foundry Workers* (cats. 251-253). The combination of these formal and iconographic elements produced a group of works which differ, if only subtly, from traditional images of the Way of the Cross, and which show Leduc as a painter involved with the renewal of religious art.

P. L'A.

1   Resolution of the board of the Amicale de Saint-Hilaire, dated September 14, 1949, Archives des Sœurs des Saints Noms de Jésus et de Marie, LO5, 11.3.

2   Excerpts from the records of the convent of Saint-Hilaire, August 2, 1926. This information was provided by François-Marc Gagnon.

3   Reproduced in François-Marc Gagnon, *Paul-Émile Borduas*, exhib. cat. (Montreal: Montreal Museum of Fine Arts, 1988), p. 29.

4   Record for June 17, 1950, Archives des Sœurs des Saints Noms de Jésus et de Marie, LO5/B, 4.3.

5   Letter from Ozias Leduc to the archivist of the Amicale du couvent de Saint-Hilaire, October 1, 1952, Archives des Sœurs des Saints Noms de Jésus et de Marie, LO5/E, 7.4.

Chronology

Works in the exhibition are identified by their catalogue numbers. A list of works by Leduc exhibited between 1890 and 1995 begins on page 305. Works not exhibited immediately following execution are listed in the Chronology (under the year they were made) as "other works". Further details of church decoration projects carried out by Leduc are given in a separate list, page 299.

Fig. 94

Fig. 95

Fig. 94   Adolphe Rho, Study for *Saint Alphege*, undated, gouache and graphite on paper, 24.4. x 93. cm (private collection).

Fig. 95   Adolphe Rho and Ozias Leduc, *The Baptism of Christ*, 1889, oil on canvas (Ein Karem, Israel, Church of Saint John).

Fig. 96   The Leduc family. Standing (left to right): Adélia, Honorius, unidentified, Ozéma, Ozias; in front: Ulric, Émilie (mother), unidentified (photo: Ernest Lebrun?, printed from glass negative No. 83, BNQ 327/13/1.33).

Fig. 96

1864
October 8: Born in Saint-Hilaire de Rouville to Antoine Leduc (cat. 3) and Émilie Brouillet (cat. 4). Baptized Joseph Azarie but called Osias (later Ozias), he is the second of ten children, four of whom died in infancy or childhood.

1880
Finishes Grade 6 at the Rang des Trente country school.
Autumn: Leduc enrols at the Model School, which he attends for the next three years. He is taught by Jean-Baptiste-Nectaire Galipeau (cat. 5).

1881
June 22: Marriage of Marie-Louise Lebrun (Leduc's first cousin and future wife) and Luigi Giovanni Capello, Italian immigrant artist, at the Cathedral of Saint-Jacques, Montreal.

1883
Works as a statue painter at Atelier T. Carli in Montreal (according to Gabrielle Messier).

1886
Becomes apprentice of Luigi Capello, with whom he executes *Interior of Saint Peter's Cathedral, Rome* (7' 9" x 10' 9" [236 x 328 cm]). The work is exhibited to raise funds for the construction of a wooden maquette of Saint Peter's, Rome, after which Montreal's cathedral (now called Marie-Reine-du-Monde) is modelled. (In 1952, Leduc donated the painting to the University of Montreal; whereabouts unknown.)
Decorates the Chapel of Saint Francis Xavier, Basilica of Sainte-Anne-de-Beaupré (fig. 127).

1887
First known still life (cat. 1) and landscape (cat. 2).

1888
Paints *Portrait of My Father*, about 1888 (cat. 3), and *Portrait of the Schoolmaster of Saint-Hilaire*, about 1888 (cat. 5).

1889
Working in the studio of Adolphe Rho, in Bécancour, for 20 cents an hour, paints *The Baptism of Christ* (fig. 95). (In February 1890, the painting, signed by Rho, was installed in the Church of Saint John, Ein Karem, a pilgrimage church near Jerusalem, as a gift from French Canadians.)

1890
Divides his time between Montreal and Saint-Hilaire (fig. 96), where, with the help of his father, he undertakes construction of his studio, Correlieu (fig. 108).
September: First participation in a public exhibition, the *Exposition des Beaux-Arts*, Montreal.

Other works executed in 1890: *My Mother in Mourning*, about 1890 (cat. 4); *The Assumption*, about 1890 (cat. 8).

1891
April: First participation in an Art Association of Montreal Annual Spring Exhibition; *Still Life, Violin* (whereabouts unknown) is purchased by the Montreal surgeon Dr. William Hingston.
June: Listed in *Lovell's Montreal Directory 1891-92* as living at 202 Saint-Martin Street, the same address as Marie-Louise Capello. She is listed as "widow of Louis", although Capello remained alive until 1902. (Leduc was also listed as a boarder at this address in the 1892-1893 edition.)

Other works executed in 1891: *The Enshrouding of Christ* (cat. 9); *Child with Helmet Guarding a Treasure* (cat. 10); *Saint Charles Borromeo*, after Charles Le Brun (originally in Church of Saint-Charles-Borromée, Lachenaie; church and painting destroyed).

1892

First church decoration commission, Church of Saint-Paul-L'Ermite (Joliette county).
April: Exhibits at the Art Association of Montreal, showing *Still Life, Books* (cat. 11), which wins a $100 first prize for a painting by a non-AAM member under the age of thirty.

Other works executed in 1892: *Phrenology* (cat. 12); *Still Life (Three Pennies)* (cat. 13); *Boy with Bread*, completed 1899 (cat. 15); *Still Life, Onions* (cat. 16).

1893

February-March: Exhibits with the Royal Canadian Academy, Montreal.
April: Publication of the first monographic article on Leduc, by Lucien de Riverolles. Exhibits at the Ontario Society of Artists, Toronto.
June: Listed in *Lovell's Montreal Directory 1893-94* as "painter", living at 195 Saint-Martin Street, the same address as Marie-Louise Capello. (The listing was also the same for Leduc and Mme Capello in 1894-1895 and 1895-1896, the last year that Leduc's name appeared. Thereafter, Mme Capello resided at 1132 Saint-Antoine Street in the suburb of Saint-Henri from 1897 to 1900, and at 1049 Saint James Street from then until 1906.)
Summer: First major decoration contract, for the Church of Saint-Charles-Borromée, Joliette (cat. 18).

Other works executed in 1893: *Night*, about 1893 (cat. 19); *Christ Blessing Little Children*, for the Chapel of Saint Joseph, Joliette (destroyed; fig. 97).

1894

March-April: Exhibits with the Royal Canadian Academy, Ottawa, the Art Association of Montreal, and the Ontario Society of Artists, Toronto.
December: Exhibits at the Ontario Society of Artists, Toronto.

Other works executed in 1894: *Reader* (Sotheby's Toronto, May 28, 1985, lot 864; whereabouts unknown; fig. 14); for the Church of Saint-Hilaire, *Saint Hilary Raising the Child Who Died without Baptism*, about 1894 (whereabouts unknown; see cats. 24-26).

1895

March: Exhibits at the Art Association of Montreal (fig. 98).
October: Exhibits at the Kermesse for Notre-Dame Hospital, Montreal.

Fig. 97

Fig. 98

Fig. 99

Fig. 100

Fig. 101

1896

Undertakes decoration of the Church of Saint-Hilaire. Executes two paintings for the Church of Saint-Charles-Borromée, Joliette. Designs sets for the Cercle Montcalm, a theatre company in Saint-Hyacinthe (fig. 99).

1897

March: Exhibits with the Royal Canadian Academy, Ottawa, and at the Art Association of Montreal.
May: Sponsored by the Church of Saint-Hilaire's Curé Laflamme (cat. 165), Leduc departs for Europe to gather ideas for the church decoration programme. In London May 19-25 and Paris until December 25. In July, rents studio space at 103 Rue de Vaugirard (fig. 100). While in Paris, meets other Canadian artists, such as Raoul Barré, Murray Prendergast and Joseph Saint-Charles, purchases books on ornamentation, and sketches in museums. Paints *Portrait of Rodolphe Brunet* (cat. 85).

Other works executed in 1897: *Portrait of Eugénie Goulet* (cat. 84); *Bending Head* (cat. 86).

1898

Biographical entry appears in three consecutive editions of the *American Art Annual* (New York).
January/February: Arrives in Montreal from Paris via New York. Resides in Saint-Henri, most likely at the home of Marie-Louise Capello, 1132 Saint-Antoine Street, and in Saint-Hilaire (fig. 101), where he executes paintings for the church (see cats. 27-56).
April: Exhibits at the Art Association of Montreal.
September: First evidence of friendship with Arsène Bessette, a journalist for *Le Canada français*, who requests commentary from Leduc on two of his short stories. (On August 13, 1899, Leduc attended a lecture by

Fig. 97   Ozias Leduc, *Christ Blessing Little Children*, 1893 (Joliette, Chapel of Saint Joseph; photo by Ozias Leduc, printed from glass negative No. 308, BNQ 327/11/7.31).

Fig. 98   Ozias Leduc, *Still Life (Books and Skull)*, 1895 (whereabouts unknown; photo: *Montreal Daily Star*, March 11, 1895, p. 5).

Fig. 99   Ozias Leduc, *Homage to Montcalm* (project for a scenery backdrop for the Cercle Montcalm, Saint-Hyacinthe), 1896, graphite, watercolour and gouache on brown paper, 32.5 x 45 cm (Montreal, McCord Museum of Canadian History, inv. M965.104).

Fig. 100   Artists' studios at 103 Rue de Vaugirard, Paris, where Leduc rented a studio from July to December, 1897.

Fig. 101   A festive dinner at Leduc's studio. Fourth and fifth from left: Ozias Leduc, Adélia Leduc (Yvon Handfield collection; photo: Ernest Lebrun?).

Fig. 102

Fig. 105

Fig. 103

Fig. 104

Fig. 106

Fig. 102   Ozias Leduc, *The Apotheosis of Saint Joseph* (model for the decoration project for Saint Joseph's Church, Biddeford, Maine), 1900, watercolour on paper, 45.5 x 60.5 cm (Musée régional de Vaudreuil-Soulanges, inv. X973.1104).

Fig. 103   Cover of Ernest Choquette's novel *Les Carabinades*, 1900, designed by Ozias Leduc (BNQ).

Fig. 104   Ozias leduc, *Portrait of Charles-Philippe Choquette*, about 1900, oil on canvas, 57.5 x 47.1 cm (private collection).

Fig. 105   Leduc playing checkers in his studio, about 1899-1900. Behind at left: *My Portrait* (cat. 105); *The Assumption* (cat. 8); *Christ on the Cross* (1890, private collection); studies for *Jesus Calming the Waves* and *The Resurrection* (1893, Joliette, Church of Saint-Charles-Borromée); a forest scene; reproduction of W. E. Frost's *Sabrina*; *Girl Reading* (cat. 21). Centre: *The Death of Saint Joseph* (about 1898-1899, Church of Saint-Hilaire). At right on the easel: *Les Carabinades* (1900, whereabouts unknown); *Mater Dolorosa* (cat. 6); *Portrait of Charles-Philippe Choquette* (1899, private collection). Behind easel: *Saint John* and *Saint Matthew* (about 1898-1899, Church of Saint-Hilaire) (photo printed from glass negative No. 359, BNQ 327/13/1.12).

Fig. 106   Advertisement for Leduc & Desautels (photo from a souvenir programme of the blessing of the bells of the Church of Sainte-Marie, Manchester, New Hampshire, 1906; Centre d'archives du Séminaire de Saint-Hyacinthe, Sec E série 2, dos 23, tir 41).

Bessette in Belœil. On May 3, 1901, an article by Bessette was published under the pseudonym Jean Rémuna in *Le Canada français*.)

Other works executed in 1898: *Erato (Sleeping Muse)* (cat. 89); *The Ribauds* (cat. 91); *Pigeons* (cat. 103).

1899

April: Exhibits with the Royal Canadian Academy, Montreal.
Summer: Gives drawing lessons to members of the Convent of Les Saints Noms de Jésus et de Marie, Saint-Hilaire. (Leduc served in this capacity again in 1901, 1902, 1907, 1912, 1914 and 1919, at the convents in Montreal, Outremont and Longueuil.)
June: Requested by Joséphine Dandurand to contribute a drawing to the Œuvre des Livres Gratuits, an organization that distributed free books, to send to the 1900 Exposition universelle in Paris. Mme Dandurand suggests depicting the arrival of books at a modest country home, in the presence of an invalid grandmother.

Other works executed in 1899: sixteen illustrations for Dr. Ernest Choquette's *Claude Paysan* and a portrait of its author (cats. 92-102); *The Woodcock*, after Suzor-Coté (cat. 104); *My Portrait* (cat. 107).

1900

Commissioned by the Honourable Philippe-Auguste Choquette, judge and Senator, to paint three works for $100: *Fall Plowing* (cat. 120), *The Choquette Farm, Belœil* (cat. 121) and *The Hayfield* (cat. 122).
February: Exhibits with the Royal Canadian Academy, Ottawa, and at the Art Association of Montreal.
May: Submits a proposal for the decoration of Saint Joseph's Church in Biddeford, Maine, for $4,600. Lists subjects for the nineteen paintings based on European works. Not known if project was executed (fig. 102).

Other works executed in 1900: *Les Carabinades* (whereabouts unknown; fig. 103); *Portrait of Charles-Philippe Choquette*, about 1900 (fig. 104); *Landscape with Mountain* (cat. 111).

1901

February: Leduc receives his first official public commission for the *Portrait of the Honourable Louis-Philippe Brodeur*, Speaker of the House of Commons (cat. 123).
March: Undertakes decoration of the Church of Saint-Michel, in Rougemont (fig. 129).

1902

February 16: Death at the Salesian Orphanage in Paris of Luigi Capello, Leduc's former master and the husband of Marie-Louise Lebrun, Leduc's future wife.
February: Exhibits at the Ontario Society of Artists, Toronto.
August 26: Enters into a partnership with his cousin Eugène L. Desautels, which lasts until 1907 (fig. 106).
September: Undertakes decoration of Saint Ninian's Cathedral, Antigonish, Nova Scotia (fig. 130).

Other works executed in 1902: *The Martyrdom of Saint Julia* (high altar of the Church of Sainte-Julie, Verchères; destroyed); *The Repentant Magdalene* (cat. 125).

1903

Drafts proposal for decoration of the Church of Saint-Mathias.
During his stay in Antigonish, accepts contracts for various decoration projects: residential (A. Kirk, March, August; Mr. MacIssak, Mr. Thomson, September), commercial (Halifax Banking Company, August) and public (Saint Francis Xavier College Assembly Room, August).
April: Undertakes decoration of the Chapel of Mount Saint Bernard Convent, Antigonish.
June: Invited to participate in an exhibition sponsored by the Société Saint-Jean-Baptiste at the Monument National, Montreal, October 13-18. Not known if Leduc participated.

August: Undertakes decoration of the Chapel of the Ladies of the Sacred Heart, Halifax (fig. 131).

September 3: An article by Leduc explaining the iconography of the decoration in Saint Ninian's Cathedral is published in the Antigonish *Casket*.

Requested by Gustave Ouimet to provide an illustration for the cover of his *Histoire de Saint-Hilaire de Rouville*.

Other works executed in 1903: *Portrait of Msgr. John Cameron* (fig. 41).

1904

Ill throughout much of the year. At various points in June, September and November, resides at 1049 Saint James Street, Montreal, the same address as Marie-Louise Capello.

September: Invited by Father Gerald Murphy to propose a decoration programme for Saint Patrick's Church, Halifax. Not known if project pursued.

1905

October: Undertakes decoration of the Church of Saint-Romuald, Farnham (fig. 132).

1906

January: Subcontracted by D.-A. Beaulieu, Montreal artist-decorator, to execute a circular painting (7' 6" [229 cm]); subject and destination unknown. Beaulieu requests two drawings, one of *Two Angels* and one of *Saint Agnes*.

April: Undertakes decoration of the Church of Sainte-Marie, Manchester, New Hampshire (fig. 133).

Invited by Sister Louise de Savoie, of the Saints Noms de Jésus et de Marie, Montreal, acting as intermediary for Curé A. Bourret of the Church of Sainte-Agathe, Winnipeg, to submit a bid for six paintings: *Saint Agatha Aged Thirteen at the Tribunal of the Prefect, Saint Agatha in Prison Receiving a Visit from Saint Peter, Annunciation* (10' x 12' 1/2" [304.8 x 367 cm]), *Assumption, Presentation of Jesus in the Temple* (4' x 8' [122 x 244 cm]), *The Holy Spirit*. Leduc's estimate (unknown) is considered too low by Sister Louise, who raises it to $1,000-$1,200. Unsuccessful(?).

August 31: Marriage of Leduc to his cousin Marie-Louise Lebrun at parish of Sainte-Cunégonde, Montreal (figs. 107-108).

September: At the request of Bates & Guild, publishers of the series "Masters in Art" to which Leduc subscribes, lists ten paintings he considers masterworks: Corot, *Dance of the Nymphs*; Whistler, *The Artist's Mother*; Millet, *The Gleaners*; Poussin, *Shepherds of Arcadia*; Ingres, *The Source*; Puvis de Chavannes, *Christian Inspiration;* Watts, *Love and Life*; Delacroix, *The Barque of Dante*; Claude

Fig. 107

Lorrain, *Embarkation of the Queen of Sheba*; Turner, *The "Fighting Téméraire"*.

October: Offers Joseph-Pierre Laberge, Curé of the Church of Sainte-Sabine, in Iberville, to decorate the church. Declined; contract already awarded.

November: Invited by Curé Joseph-Zéphirin Vincent of the Church of Saint-Grégoire, in Iberville, to submit proposal for the decoration of the church. (Leduc & Desautels were informed in February 1907 that their bid was unsuccessful.)

Other works executed in 1906: *View of Manchester, New Hampshire*, about 1906 (cat. 117); *The Réveillon* (cat. 127); *Endymion and Selene*, about 1906 (cat. 129); *Erato (Muse in the Forest)*, about 1906 (cat. 130); *Portrait of Abbé Olivier Leduc* (cat. 131); *Portrait of Abbé Joseph-Zéphirin Vincent*, about 1906 (cat. 132); *Portrait of Abbé Rodrigue Desnoyers* (destroyed 1963); *Portrait of Abbé Joseph-Delphis Meunier*, completed 1907 (Séminaire de Saint-Hyacinthe).

1907

Illustration for competition for the cover of the magazine *Art et Décoration* (fig. 109). Executes sketches of the Chapel of the Convent of the Sacred Heart, Dover, New Hampshire; the Church of Sainte-Marie, Salmon Falls, New Hampshire; the chancel and nave walls of the church in Somersworth, New Hampshire; and the chancel of the church in Stornoway, Quebec. Not known if these projects developed further.

March: Invited to submit a proposal for the decoration of the Chapel of the Congrégation de Notre-Dame, Sorel. Unsuccessful; submitted after contract had already been awarded.

Fig. 108

Fig. 109

Fig. 110

Fig. 107   At the wedding of Marie-Louise Lebrun and Ozias Leduc, August 31, 1906. Seated: Marie-Louise's mother Rosalie Brouillette Lebrun and Ozias's mother, Émilie Brouillet Leduc (photo: Ernest Lebrun?).

Fig. 108   Ozias Leduc and his wife Marie-Louise in the door of the artist's studio Correlieu, with Eugène L. Desautels or Jean-Baptiste Allaire? (standing) and Origène Leduc (seated), about 1906 (photo: Ernest Lebrun?, printed from glass negative No. 81, BNQ 327/13/1.15).

Fig. 109   Ozias Leduc, Illustration for a competition held by the magazine *Art et Décoration*, 1907 (whereabouts unknown; photo by Ozias Leduc, printed from glass negative No. 96, BNQ 327/12/6.16).

Fig. 110   Albina Gagné (née Darche) and her daughter Alice in front of the house designed by Ozias Leduc, July 12, 1936 (photo: Paul Gagné [1898-1980]; private collection).

September: Undertakes decoration of Church of Saint Mary, Dover, New Hampshire (fig. 134).
December: Plans for the Chapel of the Couvent des Sœurs, Manchester, New Hampshire. Not known if project developed further.

1908
March: Undertakes decoration of the Chapel of Notre-Dame-de-Bonsecours, Montreal (fig. 135).
July: Executes several measured plans and sections of the Church of Saint Anne, Manchester, New Hampshire. Not known if project developed further.
August: Inquires about the possibility of decorating Saint Michael's Cathedral, Chatham, New Brunswick. Thomas F. Barry, Bishop of Chatham Diocese, responds that the church is not ready for such a project.
October: Executes cartoons for two stained glass windows for the Church of Saint John the Baptist, New York (fig. 136).

Other works executed in 1908: *Profile in Cloud* (cat. 134).

1909
April(?): Proposal for the decoration of the Church of Saint-Pierre, Montreal, in collaboration with J. August Rho. Unsuccessful(?).
April: Undertakes further decorations of the Chapel of Notre-Dame-de-Bonsecours, Montreal.
April-May: Proposal for a painting for the Church of Saint-Norbert, in collaboration with J. Auguste Rho. Unsuccessful.
April-August: Proposal for Church of Saint-Mathieu, Belœil, in collaboration with J. Auguste Rho. Unsuccessful(?).
October: Requested by the sisters of the Monastery of Le Précieux Sang, Notre-Dame de Lévis, to donate the painting *Jesus in Bethany*, executed for them.

Other works executed in 1909: *Self-portrait*, about 1909 (cat. 108).

1910
January: Starts work on *The Martyrdom of Saint Barnabas* (cats. 136-137) commissioned by Joseph-Urgèle Charbonneau, Curé of Saint-Barnabé-Sud.
March: Continues with the decoration of the Church of Saint-Romuald, Farnham (cat. 135).
October: Undertakes decoration of the Cathedral of Saint-Hyacinthe, for which Msgr. Alexis-Xyste Bernard had invited Leduc to submit a proposal.

1911
February: Undertakes decoration of the Church of Saint-Edmond, Coaticook (fig. 137).

Other works executed in 1911: *Portrait of Raoul Ducharme*, plaster plaque (private collection); *Portrait of Guy Delahaye* (cat. 138).

1912
March: Exhibits at the Art Association of Montreal
September: Alerted by Georges Desautels, house painter, that the churches of Saint-Hughes and Saint-Louis(?) are both scheduled for decoration. Not known if Leduc pursued either project.
October: Gives drawing lessons to members of the Convent of La Présentation de Marie, Saint-Hyacinthe. (Leduc served in this capacity again in 1913, 1915, 1922, 1923 and 1929.)
November: Exhibits with the Royal Canadian Academy, Ottawa.

Works executed in 1912: *Portrait of Guy Delahaye* (fig. 149); nine tailpieces for Guy Delahaye's *"Mignonne, allons voir si la Rose…" est sans Épines* (see cats. 140-142).

1913
Paints the private chapel of the Bishop of Saint-Hyacinthe.
Collects information with a view to building his own house; the house includes a new studio, which he occupies from the late twenties until the forties (fig. 110).
March: Exhibits at the Art Association of Montreal.
November: Exhibits with the Royal Canadian Academy, Montreal. *Day's End* (cat. 144) is selected as part of the RCA exhibition tour to Winnipeg in January 1914.

Other works executed in 1913: *Blue Cumulus* (cat. 143).

1914
March: Exhibits at the Art Association of Montreal.
June-July: Works on a pilgrimage monument for Notre-Dame de l'Assomption, in Rogersville, New Brunswick, for Msgr. Marcel-François Richard, on the recommendation of the Montreal statue maker J. Carli.
August: Exhibits at the *Exposition Provinciale du Québec*, Quebec City, and at the Canadian National Exhibition in Toronto.
November: Exhibits with the Royal Canadian Academy, Toronto.
November: Starts planning his *Portrait of Canon J.-M. Laflamme* (cat. 165).
December: Contributes *Grey Effect (Snow)* (cat. 146) to a travelling exhibition organized by the Patriotic Fund to raise money for Canadian victims of World War I.

Other works executed in 1914: *Judith*, about 1914 (cat. 147); *Green Apples*, completed 1915 (cat. 148).

1915
Winter: Leduc is introduced to Olivier Maurault by Robert LaRoque de Roquebrune.
Gives drawing lessons to the Sisters of La Charité de l'Hôtel-Dieu, Saint-Hyacinthe. (Leduc served in this capacity again in 1923, 1925, 1926, 1929, 1931 and 1933.)
January: Contributes two works to an exhibition for the *Fonds de secours national français*, Ottawa, organized to raise money for wives and children of French World War I soldiers.
March: Exhibits at the Art Association of Montreal.
August: Exhibits at the Canadian National Exhibition in Toronto. *Green Apples* (cat. 148) is purchased by the National Gallery of Canada.
November: Exhibits with the Royal Canadian Academy, Montreal.

Other works executed in 1915: *The Concrete Bridge* (cat. 149); *Autumn Landscape* (cat. 150); *Autumn Landscape*, about 1915 (cat. 151); *Portrait of Robert LaRoque de Roquebrune*, about 1915-1916 (cat. 155); *Portrait of Josée LaRoque de Roquebrune*, about 1915-1916 (whereabouts unknown; see cat. 156).

1916
Executes a painting for the Chapel of the Convent of Les Sœurs de la Présentation de Marie, Saint-Hyacinthe.
February 20: First solo exhibition, *Quelques peintures et dessins de O. Leduc*, opens at the Bibliothèque Saint-Sulpice, which had been inaugurated the previous September 15.
March: Exhibits at the Art Association of Montreal.
June: Participates in the exhibition of the Société des Artistes de Québec, Quebec City.
August: Exhibits at the Canadian National Exhibition in Toronto.
October: Invited by Viau & Venne, architects, Montreal, to submit a proposal for the decoration of the Church of Saint-François-Xavier, West Shefford. Leduc apparently failed to meet the November 15 deadline.
November: Undertakes decoration of the Church of Saint-Enfant-Jésus, in the Mile-End neighbourhood of Montreal (cats. 166-167, fig.138). Exhibits with the Royal Canadian Academy, Montreal. His entry, *Golden Snow* (cat. 152), is purchased by the National Gallery of Canada.
November 17: Elected Associate of the Royal Canadian Academy. (Leduc was nominated by Maurice Cullen, seconded by J. W. Beatty, in December 1915.)

Other works executed in 1916: *Afterglow* (fig. 52); *Landscape (Mountain Road)* (cat. 154); *Madame Louise Lecours, née Higgins* (cat. 157); *Portrait of J. E. Wilfrid Lecours* (cat. 158); *Portrait of Olivier Maurault, p.s.s.*, completed 1924 (cat. 163).

1917

January-May: Displays five works at Henry L. Auger, General Broker, Montreal.

March: Exhibits at the Art Association of Montreal.

Proposal for the tomb of Msgr. Prince in Cathedral of Saint-Hyacinthe, on the invitation of Abbé Charles-Philippe Choquette (fig. 104). Unsuccessful.

Plans the decoration of the Sacred Heart Chapel in the Church of Saint-Enfant-Jésus, Mile-End, Montreal (work starts in July) (cats. 166-167).

March-April: Cartoons for three stained glass windows for the Pauline Chapel, Cathedral of Saint-Michel, Sherbrooke, commissioned by the architect Louis-N. Audet (cats. 168-169). (Despite Leduc's slowness in carrying out the work, Audet engaged the artist in November 1918 to design a stained glass window for his home, illustrating the song "À la claire fontaine" [not executed]).

June: Declines invitation to hear a talk on Napoléon Bourassa (d. 1916) at the artist's studio but expresses admiration and respect for Bourassa's contribution to the development of Canadian art.

November: Executes cover illustration for the magazine *Le Nigog* (first published January 1918) (fig. 111). Contributes to the Exposition permanente des œuvres d'art canadiennes, Municipal Library, Montreal.

Other works executed in 1917: *Portrait of Fernande Choquette-Clerk* (cat. 159); *Head of a Man Shading His Eyes* (cat. 164); *The Good Shepherd* (whereabouts unknown; fig. 56).

1918

April 25: Death of Leduc's mother Émilie (née Brouillet), aged seventy-eight.

July: Elected president of the Saint-Hilaire Parish School Board (cat. 172). (Re-elected in 1919, 1920 and 1921.)

Autumn: Proposal for the decoration of the Church of Sainte-Marie-de-Monnoir, Marieville (fig. 112), submitted in collaboration with Fortunat Rho, painting contractor. Unsuccessful.

Other works executed in 1918: *Portrait of Léo-Pol Morin*, about 1918 (cat. 160).

1919

February: Receives from Montreal stained glass artisans Perdriau & O'Shea a photo of the interior of the Chapel of Les Pères du Sacré-Cœur, Quebec City. Not known if Leduc pursued project.

March: Invited to illustrate a series of impressions of the countryside by author Albert Laberge. Leduc's response not known.

September: Undertakes the decoration of the Church of Saint-Raphaël, Île Bizard (fig. 139).

October: Executes *En Route pour la Messe de Minuit à Saint-Hilaire*, an illustration for "La Noël à Saint-Hilaire", a short story published October 15 in *Au Pays de l'Érable*, a collection of stories from the fourth literary contest sponsored by the Société Saint-Jean-Baptiste.

December: Submits to Perdriau & O'Shea a sketch for three windows in the private chapel of the Bishop of Saint-Hyacinthe. The subjects are: *The Good Shepherd*, *Resignation* and *Prayer* (not executed).

Other works executed in 1919: *Posthumous Portrait of Évangéline Cheval-Lahaise*, mother of Guillaume Lahaise (private collection).

1920

February: Informed by Adélard Trépanier, painter-contractor, that the curé of the Church of Saint-Louis-de-Gonzague, Montreal, is interested in a meeting.

April: Organization and production of a booklet on the Sacred Heart Chapel of the Church of Saint-Enfant-Jésus written by Louis Deligny (pseudonym of Olivier Maurault [cat. 163]) in consultation with Leduc. (Completed in January 1921 and published the following month.)

June: *Portrait of the Honourable Joseph-Napoléon Francœur*, Speaker of the Quebec Legislative Assembly (completed March 1922; cat. 171).

July: *Apotheosis of Saint Joan of Arc* commissioned by the Church of Saint-Raphaël, Île Bizard.

September: Executes two sketches of and takes notes on interior of the Church of Saint-Constant, in preparation for a proposal for decoration in collaboration with Adélard Trépanier. Leduc had been recommended to the curé by Alfred Nantel. Not known if proposal drafted.

November: Works included in an exhibition of Canadian artists at Maison Morency Frères, Ltée, Montreal. Also exhibits with the Royal Canadian Academy, Montreal.

1921

April: Exhibits at the Art Association of Montreal. Begins collaborating with Louis-N. Audet on a proposal for the decoration of the private chapel of the Bishop of Sherbrooke (cats. 175-182).

April-October: Designs bookplates for Yves Tessier-Lavigne. (Leduc also designed bookplates for Olivier Maurault [fig. 55], Joseph Barcelo and Paul Lavoie.)

May: Elected vice-president of the Saint-Hilaire Convent Bazaar and Parish Works.

Fig. 111

Fig. 112

Fig. 111   Cover of the magazine *Le Nigog*, from a design by Ozias Leduc, 1918 (private collection).

Fig. 112   Ozias Leduc, Study for *The Immaculate Conception* (model accompanying the submission for the decoration of the Church of Sainte-Marie-de-Monnoir, Marieville), 1918, graphite on paper, 49.4 x 17.5 cm (BNQ 327/10/24).

Fig. 113

Fig. 114

Fig. 115

Fig. 113   Municipal council of the parish of Saint-Hilaire, April 3, 1934. Left to right: Deputy Mayor Ozias Leduc, Councillors Léopold Boissy, J. A. Desautels, L.-Henri Boucher and Charles-E. Watts (Mayor Bruce F. Campbell is not pictured.) (private archive).

Fig. 114   Arch designed by Leduc for Saint Jean-Baptiste Day, set up on the Chemin des Trente, 1925 (photo by Ozias Leduc, printed from glass negative No. 234, BNQ 327/12/12.35).

Fig. 115   Cover of Adélard Dugré's novel *La campagne canadienne*, illustrated by Ozias Leduc, 1925 (private collection).

August 29: Death of Leduc's father, at the age of eighty-four.
October 25: Invited as delegate to the Liberal convention in Saint-Hilaire.
November: At the request of Vigor Rho, executes a large *Sacred Heart* for the Chapel of Saint Joseph, Hospital of Les Sœurs Grises, Saint-Boniface, Manitoba.

Other works executed in 1921: *Mauve Twilight* (cat. 173)

1922

May: Declines invitation to a dinner for artists, intellectuals and friends, in honour of the Honourable Athanase David, Secretary of the Province.
While in Quebec City for his portrait of J.-N. Francœur, goes to see Charles Huot's *Glorification of Our Great Men* in the Legislative Assembly.
Executes a painting of two angels and a dove, and monograms, requested by Vigor Rho, Winnipeg, for an altar dedicated to the Blessed Virgin Mary in Winnipeg. In June, executes a painting of *The Sacred Heart*, also for Rho.
June: Makes sketches for a *Raising of Lazarus* and a *Nativity*, two of four works intended for the chancel at Saint-Raphaël, Île Bizard. Not completed, owing to lack of sponsorship. Paul-Émile Borduas arrives in Sherbrooke to assist Leduc on the decorations of the Bishop's private chapel (cats. 175-182).

Other works executed in 1922: *Mountainside in Cloud* (cat. 174).

1923

March: Invited by Curé J. Hubert Nadeau of Saint-Denis-sur-Richelieu to submit a proposal by May for the decoration of the church. Not known if proposal submitted.
June: Designs a theatre curtain of a Canadian landscape at the request of A. E. Boulay on behalf of the Municipal Council of Acton-Vale for the town's theatre.
September: Donates a work (title unknown) to a bazaar (Belœil?).
October: Donates two paintings to the bazaar for Notre-Dame Hospital, Montreal, at the request of Athanase David's wife Antonia.
November: Becomes a member of the Association Sportive de Saint-Hilaire. (Leduc remained a member until 1927.)

1924

January: Elected Municipal Councillor for the Saint-Hilaire parish. Supervises street renovation, installation of electrical lines, planning of roads. Proposes and founds, April 7, 1924, the Comité d'Embellissement de la Paroisse de Saint-Hilaire. (As Deputy Mayor, Leduc occasionally acted as Mayor.)

He resigned as Municipal Councillor on March 8, 1937.) (Fig. 113.)
May: Invited by Montreal architects Viau & Venne to submit a proposal to P. Hébert, curé of the Church of Saint-Laurent, for the decoration of the church. Not known if proposal submitted.
September-October: Designs a theatre backdrop ("royal room") for the Collège Mathieu, Gravelbourg, Saskatchewan, at the request of Georges Boileau, o.m.i. (Leduc later created three more curtain backdrops for the Oblates in Gravelbourg.)
October: Undertakes restoration of the decoration executed in 1903 in the Chapel of the Convent of the Ladies of the Sacred Heart, Halifax. While in Halifax, consults with the Sisters of the Monastery of Le Bon Pasteur about the possibility of decorating their chapel with two paintings and ornamentation. Offer declined for financial reasons.

1925

Elected chairman of the Saint Jean-Baptiste Day Celebration Committee in Saint-Hilaire. Designs an arch for the festivities; delivers a speech June 19 (fig. 114).
January: Helps to restore a painting by Joseph Dynes (1825-1897) in the Chapel of Hôtel-Dieu, Saint-Hyacinthe.
May-June: Takes photographs of Pointe-du-Lac (Trois-Rivières region) as research for illustrations of a new edition of Adélard Dugré's *La campagne canadienne* (fig. 115).

1926

March-May: Consultations with J. R. Dion, decorator and general contractor, and Curé Bourassa of Church of the Sacré Cœur de Jésus, Montreal, regarding the decoration of the sacristy and the construction and decoration of two crypt chapels, dedicated to Our Lady of Lourdes and Saint Anne. Execution "postponed"; no evidence proposal ever carried out.
March: Becomes artistic director for decoration of the Church of Sainte-Geneviève, Pierrefonds.
June: Becomes member of the Cercle Artistique de Saint-Hilaire.
July: Undertakes decoration of the Chapel of the Convent of Les Saints Noms de Jésus et de Marie, Saint-Hilaire.

1927

January: Undertakes decoration of the baptistry, Church of Notre-Dame, Montreal (fig. 140).
June: Undertakes decoration of the Church of Saint-Jude.
October 1: Attends lecture by the French painter Maurice Denis on religious art, held at the Cercle universitaire of the University of Montreal (fig. 116). Denis is later shown

Leduc's decoration of the Sacred Heart Chapel at Saint-Enfant-Jésus (cat. 167) and the Church of Notre-Dame Baptistry.
November: Notified that his biography and photograph have been accepted for publication in *Prominent Men of Canada* (Montreal: National Publishing Co. [1928?]). Leduc delays their inclusion pending his proposed revisions.
December: Declines invitation from Charles Maillard, Director of the École des Beaux-Arts, Montreal, to adjudicate student works on the grounds that the presence of Borduas among those being assessed is a source of conflict of interest. (In May 1932, Maillard again invited Leduc, who declined owing to his excessive workload.)

1928

Undertakes restoration at the Church of Saint-Hilaire.
March/April: Publication of an article on Leduc by Arthur Lemay in *Le Terroir*.
Executes sketches (cats. 188-189) for the scenery of Dr. Choquette's five-act play *Madeleine*, performed in Saint-Hilaire July 1 and August 18. Borduas, Church and Raoul Viens work on the production.
September: Publication of Jean Chauvin's *Ateliers*, a study of twenty-two Quebec painters and sculptors, which devotes a chapter to Leduc.
October: Presides over the Saint-Hilaire meeting of the Union catholique des cultivateurs, conjointly with their President General, Aldéric Lalonde.

Other works executed in 1928: *Portrait of Bishop Alphonse-Osias Gagnon*, completed 1933 (cat. 183).

1929

Executes scenery designs for *La Bouée*, a play by Dr. Choquette (sets apparently not executed) (cats. 190-191).
Summer (?): Gives a talk to the Union catholique des cultivateurs of Saint-Hilaire. Uses an artistic-agricultural production analogy to convey his belief that art is at once intellectual virtue, expression of beauty and useful, and that every aspect of human existence should be directed towards the pursuit of beauty.
September: Designs a light fixture for the Church of Saint-Hilaire.
November 20: Encouraged by the publication of his letter to the editor of *La Terre de Chez Nous*, the artist proposes (unsuccessfully) a series of articles on art for the magazine.

Other works executed in 1929: *The Blessed André Grasset* (cat. 192).

Fig. 116

1930

April: Undertakes decoration of the Chapel of Saint Theresa of Lisieux in the Church of Notre-Dame, Montreal.
July: Undertakes decoration of the Church of Les Saints-Anges, Lachine (fig. 141).
Declines invitation from Maillard to participate in a national exhibition in Toronto in August.

1931

January: Elected warden at the Church of Saint-Hilaire.
April: Proposal for the Church of Saint-Pierre, Montreal. Unsuccessful.

Other works executed in 1931: *Portrait of Florence Bindoff*, completed 1935 (cat. 194).

1932

April: Invited to become a member of the Association des Auteurs Canadiens (French section), an organization of Canadian authors and artists. Admitted as a member in May.
November 5-12: Two photographs of the decoration of the Bishop's private chapel, Sherbrooke, are included in the exhibition of La Semaine du livre et de l'art canadien, organized by the Association des Auteurs Canadiens, at the Bibliothèque Saint-Sulpice. The photos are from a full set taken of the Bishop's Chapel decoration by the photographer Paul Gagné of Sherbrooke. This marks the beginning of a long friendship between Leduc and Gagné (fig. 117).

1933

Undertakes decoration of the Church of Saint-Michel, Rougemont (fig. 142).
January: Prepares sketches for the decoration of the Chapel of the Novitiate of Les Pères de Sainte-Croix (Sainte-Geneviève, Pierrefonds). Project not executed.

1934

July: Loses bid for the contract to decorate the Church of Notre-Dame, Granby, to Guido Nincheri.

Fig. 117

Fig. 118

Fig. 119

Fig. 116   Maurice Denis at the Cercle universitaire, Montreal. Front row: Mr. Lerolle, Jean Désy, Maurice Denis, Charles Maillard; second row: Canon Émile Chartier, Ernest Cormier, Olivier Maurault, Ozias Leduc; third row: Adrien Hébert (photo: *La Presse* [Montreal], October 3, 1927, p. 4).

Fig. 117   Ozias Leduc and his wife Marie-Louise in Saint-Hilaire, July 12, 1936 (photo: Paul Gagné; private collection).

Fig. 118   Ozias Leduc, *Portrait of Dr. James John Edmund Guerin*, 1935 (whereabouts unknown; printed from acetate negative No. 447, BNQ 327/12/3.41).

Fig. 119   Albert Tessier and Ozias Leduc in the studio of the artist, August 1936. On the back wall: *Portrait of a Woman* (cat. 109), *Madame Louise Lecours, née Higgins* (cat. 157) and a photo of Édouard Monpetit (Archives du Séminaire de Trois-Rivières, Albert Tessier papers, FN-0014).

Fig. 120

Fig. 121

Fig. 122

Fig. 120   Rodolphe Duguay and Ozias Leduc in Leduc's orchard in Saint-Hilaire, 1938 (photo: Albert Tessier, Archives du Séminaire de Trois-Rivières, Albert Tessier papers, FN-0014-P2-34a-68).

Fig. 121   Ozias Leduc receiving an honorary doctorate from the University of Montreal, 1938 (photo: *La Presse* [Montreal], May 27, 1938).

Fig. 122   Geological excursion to Mount Saint-Hilaire, with members of the Séminaire de Saint-Hyacinthe's first-year philosophy class gathered around Ozias Leduc, fall 1940 (Centre d'archives du Séminaire de Saint-Hyacinthe).

Fig. 123   Ozias Leduc, *Still Life (with Michelangelo's "Dusk")*, 1940, oil on canvas, 40.7 x 61 cm (whereabouts unknown; printed from acetate negative No. 363, BNQ 327/12/2.25).

Fig. 123

Works executed in 1934: *The Ecstasy of Saint Theresa* (cat. 196).

1935

March: Named honorary member of the Club de Palets de Saint-Hilaire. (At a later unknown date, Leduc gave a lecture to the Club's officers.)
June: Visits the Chapel of the Convent of La Présentation de Marie, Granby, regarding a potential contract for its decoration. Not known if proposal submitted.
July: Advises the Director of the Normal School, Saint-Hyacinthe, on the installation of a painting.

Works executed in 1935: *Portrait of Frederick Bindoff* (cat. 195); *Portrait of Dr. James John Edmund Guerin* (whereabouts unknown; fig. 118).

1936

Introduced to Abbé Albert Tessier (fig. 119) of Trois-Rivières through Olivier Maurault and the artist Rodolphe Duguay (fig. 120). Begins a series of small pencil and charcoal drawings called "Imaginations". (Continued until 1942; cats. 199-223.) Begins writing poetry.
August: "Remarques sur l'Art" broadcast on CKAC Radio's *L'Heure provinciale*, in which Leduc discusses the artist's role in the pursuit of perfection. Uses the metaphor of Jacob wrestling with the Angel to express the artist-creator's challenge and ultimate domination of matter, thus attaining Beauty and Truth.
December: Executes a *Portrait of Sir John Coape Sherbrooke* (Sherbrooke City Hall), after an engraving by Robert Field. Commission received with the help of Paul Gagné. Teaches drawing at the Collège Saint-Maurice, Saint-Hyacinthe. (Leduc served in this capacity again in 1940.)

Other works executed in 1936:
Père Jacques Buteux, s.j., completed 1937 (cat. 197);
Père Jacques Buteux, s.j., completed 1937 (cat. 198).

1937

February: Misses the opportunity to bid for execution of a Way of the Cross for the church in Lachute Mills.

May 12: Founding of the Société d'histoire régionale de Saint-Hyacinthe. (Leduc designed their emblem in February 1938.)
September: Jules Bazin and Gérard Morisset document the Church of Saint-Hilaire and visit Leduc at his studio.

Other works executed in 1937: *Moonlit Twilight*, about 1937 (cat. 224).

1938

May: Receives honorary doctorate from the University of Montreal (fig. 121).

Works executed in 1938: *Old Man with Apples* (cats. 225a and b); *The Ferryman's House*, completed 1939 (cat. 226); *Portrait of Madame St-Cyr*, completed 1939 (cat. 227).

1939

April 25: Death of Leduc's wife Marie-Louise (née Lebrun), at the age of seventy-nine.
Autumn: Schoolteacher Thérèse Brouillette, of whom Leduc would make a number of portraits (cats. 229-231), starts helping him with his correspondence.
December 11: Delivers talk "Dires sur le symbolisme" at the Seminary of Saint-Hyacinthe. Advocates embracing the language of symbolism in religious art as a means of attaining spiritual fulfilment and truth.

Works executed in 1939: *Snowscape* (Musée Pierre-Boucher, Trois-Rivières); *Portrait of Aline Audet* (cat. 228).

1940

Gabrielle Messier becomes Leduc's student and, in 1942, his assistant.
September/October: Conducts one of the annual geological excursions on Mount Saint-Hilaire for students from the Philosophy I course at the Saint-Hyacinthe Seminary. (These excursions were initiated in the late nineteenth century.) (fig. 122.)

Works executed in 1940: *Still Life (with Michelangelo's "Dusk")* (whereabouts unknown; fig.123); *Portrait of Gertrude Leduc (The Lady in Green)* (private collection).

1941

Begins a friendly correspondence with Claire Lavoie of Montreal.
February 23: Receives a visit from the Dominican Marie-Alain Couturier, an advocate of religious art.
March 4: Attends a lecture by Couturier in Montreal, on the subject of the gulf between modern art and the general public.
Creates an image of *Saint Vincent Ferrier*, published in *Le Rosaire*, periodical edited by the Dominicans.

Other works executed in 1941: *Mater Amabilis* (cat. 232); *Return from the Fields* (cat. 233); *Portrait of Gabrielle Messier* (private collection; fig. 124); *Portrait of Florence Ducharme (The Lady in Yellow)*, completed 1943 (whereabouts unknown; fig. 32).

1942

March: Undertakes decoration of the Church of Notre-Dame-de-la Présentation, in Almaville-en-Bas (today Shawinigan-Sud), on which he continues to work until his death (cats. 237-253). First evidence of Leduc's acquaintance with René Bergeron, who was the organizer of the Conférences Sociales. (In April 1946, Bergeron suggested that he write Leduc's biography. In 1949, he became Leduc's dealer, selling his works out of his gallery L'Art canadien in Chicoutimi.) At the request of Albert Tessier, executes several studies for a *Holy Family* to be reproduced as a holy picture (the project was not completed) (cat. 234).

1943

Leduc's studio is frequented by young Montreal artists (friends of Borduas). November: Informed that his name has been presented as a possible candidate for the decoration of a private chapel at Mont-Tremblant. Not known if project developed.

Works executed in 1943: *Head of the Virgin* (Ottawa, National Gallery of Canada).

1944

Commissioned to execute a portrait, which is refused; he titles it *Portrait of Madame Labonté* (cat. 235).

1945

January: Contracted to restore his paintings at Notre-Dame-de-Bonsecours, Montreal. December 1945-January 1946: Twenty-five items by Leduc included in a joint exhibition with sculptor Elzéar Soucy and painters Joseph Saint-Charles and Edmond Dyonnet at the Musée de la Province de Québec (now the Musée du Québec). (The exhibition was planned in 1943.) (Fig. 125.)

1946

April 27: Death of his sister Adélia (wife of Ernest Lebrun [cat. 109]), aged seventy-six. September: Informed that he will be commissioned to execute two large paintings (each about 12' x 9' [366 x 274 cm]) for the Chapel of the Seminary of Saint-Joseph, Mont-Laurier. It appears the project was never realized, owing to lack of sponsorship.

1948

January 4: CBC broadcast of "L'Envolée mystique", a composition for organ by J.-J. Gagnier (fig. 93) inspired by the high altar painting at Notre-Dame de-la-Présentation, Shawinigan-Sud.
October: Consulted regarding three painted rondels with inscriptions for the Church of Saint-Germain, Grantham. Undertakes decoration of the Church of Saint-Guillaume, Upton, where he also makes suggestions for the completion of the Stations of the Cross.

1949

July: Contacted for future consultations regarding the decoration (painting) of the Church in Pointe-du-Lac (Saint-Maurice county).
Church of Saint-Hilaire declared a Historical Monument after pleas by Victor Morin on behalf of Olivier Maurault and Ozias Leduc.
September: Executes a Way of the Cross for the Chapel of the Convent of Les Saints Noms de Jésus et de Marie, Saint-Hilaire (cat. 254).

1953

Begins selling of his works to museums and private collectors.
February: Borduas sends Leduc a typescript of his article "Quelques pensées sur l'œuvre d'amour et de rêve de M. Ozias Leduc", to be published in the summer issue of *Canadian Art*.

1954

June 19: Exhibition of works by Leduc at the Lycée Pierre-Corneille, Montreal, organized by Gilles Corbeil.
July/August: Entire issue of *Arts et pensée*, devoted to the artist.
Sketches designs for the Canadian flag (fig. 126).
December 24: Falls ill. Hospitalized two days later at the Hôtel-Dieu, Saint-Hyacinthe, where he remains until his death.

1955

June 16: Leduc dies. Buried in the cemetery at Saint-Hilaire.

Fig. 124

Fig. 125

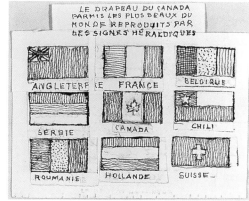

Fig. 126

Fig. 124   Ozias Leduc, *Portrait of Gabrielle Messier*, 1941, oil on cardboard, 25.5 x 20.3 cm (private collection).

Fig. 125   Installation photo of the *Exposition de Edmond Dyonnet, Ozias Leduc, Joseph Saint-Charles, Elzéar Soucy*, Musée de la Province de Quebec, Quebec City, December 1945 - January 1946. Left to right: *Golden Snow* (cat. 152), *Portrait of a Young Woman, The Good Shepherd* (fig. 56), *Return from the Fields* (cat. 233), *Fall Plowing* (cat. 120), *Afterglow, Still Life* (1940), *Portrait of Guy Delahaye* (1912), *Mater Amabilis* (cat. 232), *Portrait of Abbé Olivier Leduc* (cat. 131), *The Concrete Bridge* (cat. 149) (neg. 29811, BNQ 327/13/8.1d).

Fig. 126   Ozias Leduc, *Study for a Proposal for the Canadian Flag*, 1954, black ink on paper, 12.3 x 15.5 cm (BNQ 327/10/31).

List of Church Decorations

Fig. 127

Fig. 128

Fig. 127   Chapel of Saint Francis Xavier (first Basilica of Sainte-Anne-de-Beaupré), 1886 (photo: Jules-Ernest Livernois [1858-1933], Archives de la basilique de Sainte-Anne-de-Beaupré).

Fig. 128   Leduc's assistants for the decoration of the Church of Saint-Hilaire, about 1896-1897. Standing at rear: Honorius Leduc, Ozias Leduc, Raoul Tétro Ducharme, unidentified, Ernest Lebrun(?); standing in front: Louis-Philippe Martin, unidentified; seated in front: Dollard Church and two unidentified workers (private collection).

Chapel of Saint Francis Xavier, Basilica of Sainte-Anne-de-Beaupré

1886
Ornamental (fig. 127)
With Adolphe Rho
Chapel and decoration destroyed

Church of Saint-Paul-L'Ermite (Joliette county)

1892
NAVE VAULT: *Angel Heads* (rondels)
Painted over

Cathedral of Saint-Charles-Borromée, Joliette
Curé Prosper Beaudry
Theme: Mysteries of the Rosary

Summer 1893-end of 1894
CHANCEL VAULT: *Resurrection* (see cat. 18), *Ascension, Pentecost, Assumption, Coronation of the Virgin*
NAVE VAULT, right: *Annunciation, Visitation, Nativity of Jesus, Presentation of Jesus in the Temple, Jesus Found in the Temple*; left: *Agony in the Garden, Flagellation, Crown of Thorns, Carrying of the Cross, Crucifixion*
TRANSEPT, left: *Adoration of the Magi, Flight into Egypt, Jesus Calming the Waves* (fig. 6), *Miraculous Draught of Fishes*; right: *Holy Family in Egypt, The Good Shepherd, Christ at the House of Martha and Mary, Christ Giving the Keys to Saint Peter*

1896
ORGAN LOFT, left: *Saint Cecilia*; right: *King David*
$50
Whereabouts unknown

Church of Saint-Hilaire, Mont-Saint-Hilaire
Curé Joseph-Magloire Laflamme
Theme: The Seven Sacraments

About 1894
Saint Hilary Raising the Child Who Died without Baptism (see cats. 24-26)

1896-1899
CHANCEL: *Adoration of the Magi, Ascension*, two groups of *Adoring Angels*
SIDE ALTARS, right: *Assumption*; left: *Saint Hilary Writing His Treatise*
NAVE, right: *Baptism of Christ, Christ at the House of Simon, Supper at Emmaus*; left: *Angel Head, Marriage of the Virgin, Christ Giving the Keys to Saint Peter*; beneath balcony, at right: *Saint Matthew, Saint Mark*; beneath balcony, at left: *Saint Luke, Saint John*; back wall: *Pentecost, Death of Saint Joseph* (see cats. 27-56)
Emblems, Stations of the Cross
$915
Assistants: Émery Martin, Félix Martin, Louis-Philippe Martin, Ulric Martin, the artist's brothers Honorius and Origène Leduc, Louis Bélisle, C. Millette, Eugène L. Desautels, Edmond Lemoine, Raoul Tétro Ducharme and Dollard Church (fig. 128)

1928
Church restored; stained glass windows ordered for chancel: (left) *Christ the King*, (right) *Pietà* (installed 1931)

September 1929
Lamplight design by Leduc, executed by his brother Ulric

Church of Saint-Michel, Rougemont
Curé Narcisse Latraverse

March 1901-July 1902
CHANCEL CEILING, centre: *Saint Michael Subduing Satan* (after Raphael)
CHANCEL VAULT, left: *Angels Appearing to the Shepherds*; right: *Agony in the Garden*; five emblems (five centre panels)

CHANCEL WALLS, left: *Nativity of Jesus*
(inspired by Feuerstein), *Resurrection*; right:
Ascension (after E. Deger), *Pentecost*
SIDE ALTARS, left: *Assumption* (after Leduc's
Saint-Hilaire *Assumption*); right: *Saint Joseph*
NAVE VAULT, right: *Transfiguration, Christ
Giving the Keys to Saint Peter, Saint Anthony
of Padua, Education of the Virgin, Saint
Cecilia*; left: *Jesus among the Doctors, Supper at
Emmaus, Saint John the Baptist, Saint Dominic
Receiving the Rosary, Saint Isidore*
Emblems (fig. 129)
$475(?) for nineteen paintings; $90 for eigh-
teen emblems
Church and decoration destroyed by fire
November 30, 1930

Saint Ninian's Cathedral, Antigonish, Nova Scotia
Father Joseph MacDonald
Theme: Love of God for Humanity
    September 1902-June 1903
CHANCEL, vault: *God the Father*; over chancel
arch: two *Angels*, each holding a Table of the
Law (both destroyed for reconstruction, 1937)
NAVE, ceiling towards chancel: *Adoration of
the Shepherds, The Good Shepherd, Crucifixion,
Ascension* (after Dobson, Plockhorst, Bonnat
and Hofmann); back wall, at left, towards
chancel: *Saint John the Baptist*; back wall, at
right, towards chancel: *Saint Cecilia*; arcade,
at left, towards chancel: *Saint Bartholomew,
Saint Philip, Saint John, Saint James the Great*
(fig. 130), *Saint Andrew, Saint Peter*; arcade, at
right, towards chancel: *Saint Matthias, Saint
Thaddaeus, Saint Simon, Saint James the Less,
Saint Thomas, Saint Matthew*
Imitation marble, imitation relief moulding,
stencilled ornaments
$3,000
Assistants: Raoul T. Ducharme and Louis-
Philippe Martin
    April 1903 (contracted)
MAIN ALTAR: Stations of the Cross, with
decoration of imitation relief, gilding and
framing
$1,463
Installed by November 8, 1904, by Ernest
Lebrun (Leduc's cousin and brother-in-law)

Chapel of Mount Saint Bernard Convent, Antigonish, Nova Scotia
Sister Saint Joseph le Juste
    April-July 1903
Ornamental (including altar decoration),
gilding
$272

Fig. 129

Fig. 130

1909
Asked his fee to complete the programme
with two paintings, Leduc submitted a price
of $100 per painting and sketches of *The
Immaculate Conception* and *Joseph in His
Glory*. These were accepted, but there is no
evidence the contract was formalized or
carried out.

Chapel of the Ladies of the Sacred Heart, Halifax
Mother Reid, Superior
    August-December 1903
Emblems, monograms, ornament in imita-
tion relief, gilding, painted frames of Stations
of the Cross (fig. 131)
$1,200
Assistants: Louis-Philippe Martin, Raoul
Tétro Ducharme and Honorius Leduc
    October-late December 1924
Mother Wauters, Superior
Restoration of the decoration
$1,900
Chapel demolished

Church of Saint-Romuald, Farnham
Curé Joseph-Magloire Laflamme
    October 1905-February 1907
CHANCEL, behind main altar: *God the Father*
and *Glorification of the Cross, Sermon on the
Mount* (fig. 132); left of altar: *Temperance*;
right of altar: *Justice*
CROSSING: *Transfiguration, Pentecost, Christ
Giving the Keys to Saint Peter, Raising of the
Son of the Widow of Nain, Adoration of the
Magi*
NAVE, above confessionals: rondels of *Saint
John, Saint Luke* (right), *Saint Mark, Saint
Matthew* (left)
Stations of the Cross (installed July 1907)
$2,965
Assistants: Origène Leduc, Honorius Leduc,
Jean-Baptiste Allaire
    March 1910
SIDE ALTARS, right: *Holy Family in the
Carpenter's Shop*; left: *Coronation of the Virgin*
(see cat 135)

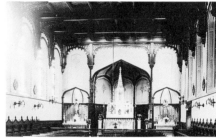

Fig. 131

Fig. 132

Fig. 129   Interior of the Church of Saint-Michel,
Rougemont, 1901-1902 (Centre d'archives du
Séminaire de Saint-Hyacinthe, Sec C, série 2, dos 53.3,
tir 2).

Fig. 130   Ozias Leduc, *Saint James the Great*,
1902-1903 (Saint Ninian's Cathedral, Antigonish, Nova
Scotia; photo by Ozias Leduc, printed from glass negative No. 21, BNQ 327/11/3.9).

Fig. 131   Interior of the Chapel of the Ladies of the
Sacred Heart, Halifax, 1903 (Public Archives of Nova
Scotia, Photographic Collection, Pans H-4648).

Fig. 132   Ozias Leduc, *The Sermon on the Mount*
(behind the main altar of the Church of Saint-
Romuald, Farnham), 1906-1907 (photo by Ozias
Leduc, printed from glass negative No. 339,
BNQ 327/11/3.21).

Fig. 133   Interior of the Church of Sainte-Marie,
Manchester, New Hampshire, 1906 (photo: F.X.
Durette Studio; Centre d'archives du Séminaire de
Saint-Hyacinthe, ESE8 dos.5).

Fig. 133

Fig. 134

Fig. 135

Fig. 136

Fig. 137

Fig. 134   Ozias Leduc, *Angel* (Church of Saint Mary, Dover, New Hampshire), 1907-1908 (photo by Ozias Leduc, printed from glass negative No. 53, BNQ 327/11/4.2).

Fig. 135   Ozias Leduc, *Coronation of the Virgin*, 1908 (Montreal, Chapel of Notre-Dame-de-Bonsecours; photo by Ozias Leduc, printed from glass negative No. 128, BNQ 327/11.4.9).

Fig. 136   Ozias Leduc, *Saint Francis Xavier Baptizing the Indians* (cartoon for a stained glass window for the Church of Saint John the Baptist, New York), 1908-1909 (whereabouts unknown; photo by Ozias Leduc, printed from glass negative No. 313, BNQ 327/11/4.6).

1911-1912
NAVE: *Presentation of the Virgin, Saint Francis Receiving the Stigmata, Saint Aloysius Gonzaga Receiving Communion, Saint Anthony of Padua*
Curé Laflamme continued to involve Leduc in decoration projects and decisions intermittently to 1926.

Church of Sainte-Marie, Manchester, New Hampshire
Curé Pierre Hévey
April-late July/early August 1906
Emblems, ornamental, imitation relief and gilding (fig. 133)
Assistants: Eugène L. Desautels (Leduc's cousin and business partner), Louis-Philippe Martin, Jean-Baptiste Allaire and Honorius Leduc
Painted over 1960

Church of Saint Mary, Dover, New Hampshire
Father Daniel Murphy (to whom Leduc was recommended by Curé Hévey)
September 1907-March 1908
SIDE ALTARS, left, above statue of our lady: *Two Angels Supporting an Inscribed Tablet*; right, above statue of Saint Joseph: *Two Angels Supporting an Inscribed Tablet*
ORGAN ARCH: *Two Angels Supporting an Inscribed Tablet* (fig. 134)
Emblems, ornamental, gilding
Assistants: Sylvio Ouellette, Dondero, L. Précourt, L. E. Jackson, G. W. Gould, Fred Bourque, J. A. Clark, H. Eyres, Dollard Church, W. Bilodeau, Raoul Tétro-Ducharme, A. Noël
Destroyed; church interior remodelled 1945-1946

Chapel of Notre-Dame-de-Bonsecours, Montreal
March-September 1908
CHANCEL, VAULT: *Coronation of the Virgin* (fig. 135); side walls: two groups of *Three Angels in Adoration*
Subcontracted by D.-Adolphe Beaulieu
Restored by Alphonse L'Espérance in 1949
April-June 1909
AT SIDE OF SANCTUARY DOOR, left: *Paul Chomedey de Maisonneuve, Founder of Ville-Marie*; right, *Marguerite Bourgeoys, Founder of the Grey Nuns*
Subcontracted by D.-Adolphe Beaulieu
January-October 1945
Leduc contracted to restore his paintings

Church of Saint John the Baptist, New York
October 1908-January 1909
STAINED GLASS WINDOWS: *Pope Pius V, Saint Francis Xavier Baptizing the Indians* (fig. 136)
In collaboration with D.-Adolphe Beaulieu

Cathedral of Saint-Hyacinthe
Msgr. Alexis-Xyste Bernard (who solicited the submission and selected the decorative programme)
October 1910-spring 1912
CHANCEL, VAULT: *God the Father*
Ornamental, emblems, gilding of relief of statues of *Four Evangelists*
$5,000 ($2,250 subcontracted to Eugène L. Desautels)
Painted over except for *God the Father*; cathedral redecorated 1942

Church of Saint-Barnabé
Curé Joseph-Urgèle Charbonneau
January 1910-April 1912
MAIN ALTAR: *Martyrdom of Saint Barnabas* (cat. 137)
$200
Removed 1950

Church of Saint-Edmond, Coaticook
Curé François-Napoléon Séguin
February-August 1911
CHANCEL: *Four Evangelists* (see fig. 137); two scenes from the *Life of Saint Edmund*
Emblems, stencilling, gilding, repainting and decorating of statuary
In collaboration with Louis-N. Audet, Sherbrooke
$3,150 (additional $450 for the chancel decoration)
Painted over

Private Chapel of the Bishop of Saint-Hyacinthe
Msgr. Alexis-Xyste Bernard
1913
Ornamental

Church of Saint-Enfant-Jésus, Mile-End (Montreal)
Curé Philippe Perrier
October-December 1916
CROSSING, DOME PENDENTIVES: *Annunciation, Nativity of Jesus, Holy Family in Nazareth* (see cat. 166), *Jesus among the Doctors*
In collaboration with D.-Adolphe Beaulieu
March 1917
PULPIT: *Attributes of the Evangelists, The Old and New Law* (fig. 138)
ALTARS: In collaboration with Louis-N. Audet, of Audet & Charbonneau, architects

Sacred Heart Chapel (Baptistry)

July 1917-December 1919
MAIN ALTAR: *Head of Christ, The Good Shepherd*; above: *Sacred Heart of Jesus Surrounded by Angels Carrying Instruments of the Passion, with a Glorification of Labour* (see cat. 167)
ABOVE DOOR TO SANCTUARY: *Adam and Eve Expelled from Paradise and the Promise of a Redeemer*
ABOVE DOOR TO SACRISTY: *Baptism of Christ* (centre), *Angels* (one left, one right)
ROTUNDA: *Christ on the Cross, Two Thieves, Signs of the Zodiac*
Emblems
In collaboration with Louis-N. Audet
Repainted by Alphonse L'Espérance

Chapel of the Convent of Les Sœurs de la Présentation de Marie, Saint-Hyacinthe

1916-1919
Notre-Dame du Bon Conseil

Pauline Chapel, Cathedral of Saint-Michel, Sherbrooke

Msgr. Paul Larocque
March 1917 - April 1919
Cartoons for three stained glass windows:
Conversion of Saint Paul (cat. 168), *Saint Paul Preaching before the Areopagus, Martyrdom of Saint Paul* (cat. 169)
Commissioned by Louis-N. Audet

Church of Saint-Raphaël, Île Bizard

Curé Alfred Nantel
September 1919
Ornamental
In collaboration with Adélard Trépanier, who contacted Leduc on the basis of his renown as an "artist-painter"
July 1920
Apotheosis of Saint Joan of Arc (fig. 139)
$450, raised through subscription
(This painting was a pendant to an *Apparition of the Sacred Heart to Saint Marguerite*, signed by Suzor-Coté but executed by Rodolphe Duguay, for which at least $2,000 was paid. Both paintings were unveiled August 21, 1921.)
Removed, private collection

Chapel of the Bishop's Palace, Sherbrooke

Msgr. Paul Larocque
March 1921-1932
Decorative borders
CHANCEL: *Litanies of the Virgin*; vault: *Mystic Rosebush*
NAVE, left: *Mary Hailed as Co-redeemer, Annunciation*; right: *Jesus Found in the Temple; Crucifixion* (cats. 175-182); back wall: *Tree of Jesse, Two Angels*

In collaboration with Louis-N. Audet
Paul-Émile Borduas, assistant in 1922; Raoul Viens, in 1926

Chapel of Saint Joseph, Hospital of Les Sœurs Grises, Saint-Boniface, Manitoba

November 1921
The Sacred Heart
For Vigor Rho, Winnipeg; based on an image he sent
(In 1922, Leduc painted two angels, a dove and monograms at Rho's request, for an altar dedicated to the Blessed Virgin in Winnipeg. In June, he executed a painting of *The Sacred Heart*, also for Rho.)

Chapel of Hôtel-Dieu, Saint-Hyacinthe

January-February/March 1925
The Sacred Heart (whereabouts unknown) installed
Advises the painter Sister Albina Lanthier for Stations of the Cross; restores Joseph Dynes's painting *Christ Healing the Sick* (about 1875)

Church of Sainte-Geneviève, Pierrefonds

Curé Joseph-Rodolphe Granger
March 1926-October 1927
In charge of decoration
REREDOS, centre, above main altar: *Apotheosis of Saint Genevieve*; left: *Saint Genevieve Meets Saint Germain at the Gates of Paris*; right: *Death of Saint Genevieve*
Emblems, monograms, illuminated cross and triangle
At least $1,000
Project executed in collaboration with Adélard Trépanier, painting contractor, subject to approval by Viau & Venne, architects

Chapel of the Convent of Les Saints Noms de Jésus et de Marie, Saint-Hilaire

July-late August 1926
CHANCEL, VAULT: *The Cross and the Fountain of Grace*
Assistants: Dollard Church, Jean-Baptiste Allaire and Paul-Émile Borduas
Painted over
September 1949
Stations of the Cross (cat. 254)
$1,200, raised by the alumni of the convent

Baptistry, Church of Notre-Dame, Montreal

Curé Olivier Maurault (project initiated in July 1926, when Leduc approached Curé L. Perrin about the restoration of a painting; discussion taken over by Maurault in October. Contract for the full decoration of the baptistry signed November 1926, with Leduc given carte blanche.)

Fig. 138

Fig. 139

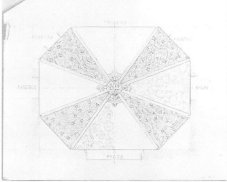

Fig. 140

January 1927-1929
VAULT: *Theological Heaven* alternating with *Material Heaven* (fig. 140)
WALLS: *Four Evangelists, Christ on the Cross, Sources of the Jordan, Tree of Good and Evil*
Restoration of *Baptism of Jesus* (anonymous copy after Carlo Maratta)
$800

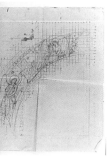

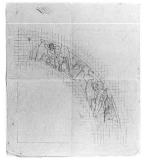

Fig. 141a

"SICUT

Fig. 143

Fig. 138 Interior of the Church of Saint-Enfant-Jésus, Mile-End (photo [undated]: Archives de l'archevêché de Montréal).

Fig. 139 Ozias Leduc, *The Apotheosis of Saint Joan of Arc* (Church of Saint-Raphaël, Île Bizard, 1920-1921) (photo by Ozias Leduc, printed from glass negative No. 139, BNQ 327/11/5.34).

Fig. 140 Ozias Leduc, *Studies for Decorative Motifs* (for the vault of the baptistry of the Church of Notre-Dame, Montreal), 1927-1928, graphite on beige paper, 20.3 x 25.9 cm (BNQ 327/10/14).

Figs. 141a-b Ozias Leduc, *Studies for the Organ Arch* (Church of Les Saints Anges, Lachine), 1930, graphite on brown paper, 40.7 x 37.8 cm and 42.7 x 38.5 cm (BNQ 327/10/24).

Fig. 142 Ozias Leduc, *Saint Michael Appearing to Abraham*, 1933-1935 (Rougemont, Church of Saint-Michel; printed from acetate negative No. 9, BNQ 327/11/6.17).

Fig. 143 Ozias Leduc, *The Temptation of Adam and Eve* (detail), about 1945, oil on canvas, glued in place, 355 x 338 cm (Shawinigan-Sud, Church of Notre-Dame-de-la-Présentation).

June 1929 - February 1930
At Olivier Maurault's request
Three stained glass window designs: *Symbols of the Apostles in Correspondence with Those of the Prophets* (allegorical figures and inscriptions)
$1,200

Church of Saint-Jude
Curé Henri Bélisle

June 1927
Funerary hangings for the main altar, altars of the Blessed Virgin and Sacred Heart of Jesus, chancel pilasters and columns, nave columns
Ornamental symbols, emblems and monograms
Stations of the Cross
Backdrop for Nativity scene
Statue repairs

Chapel of Saint Theresa of Lisieux, Church of Notre-Dame, Montreal
Curé Louis Bouhier

April-June 1930
ALTAR PANEL: *Death of Saint Theresa of Lisieux*
ABOVE ALTAR, BEHIND STATUE: *Mystic Rosebush*
COLUMNS: ornamental decoration, emblems, monograms

Church of Les Saints-Anges, Lachine
Curé J.-Victor Thérien
THEME: Adoration of the Mystic Lamb (Apocalypse)

July 1930-March 1931
(contract signed July 3, 1930, stipulating completion of decoration by December 15)
CHANCEL VAULT, CROSSING: *Mystic Lamb*; centre: *Triumph of Saint Michael*; left: *Jophiel, Uriel, Gabriel*; right: *Raphael, Chamael, Zadkiel*
CHANCEL AND TRANSEPT WALLS: pairs and trios of *Angels Bearing the Instruments of the Passion*
NAVE AND TRANSEPT VAULT: forty-four *Adoring Angels* (two per panel), with monograms and emblems of Christ
ORGAN ARCH: *Concert of Angels* (figs. 141a-b)
$20,980
Under Viau & Venne, architects
Assisted by Paul-Émile Borduas
Decoration retouched by Alphonse L'Espérance, 1959

Church of Saint-Michel, Rougemont
Curé Arsène Nadeau

1933-1935
CHANCEL VAULT, centre: *Saint Michael Subduing Satan*; left: *Saint Michael Appearing to Hagar, Saint Michael Appearing to Abraham* (fig. 142), *Saint Michael Painting the Doors of the Houses of Egypt*; right: *Saint Michael Appearing to the Aged Virgin, Saint Michael Appearing to the Bishop on Mount Gargano, Saint Michael Appearing to Joan of Arc* (at least $815)
CHANCEL ARCH: two *Kneeling Angels* with inscriptions and emblems ($800)
Border decoration around windows ($215)
SIDE ALTARS, left: *Presentation of Mary*, after an unidentified artist; right: *Christ Blessing Little Children*, after Vogel von Vogelstein, executed by Borduas
TRANSEPTS: *The Four Evangelists*
Stations of the Cross after those in the Church of Saint-Hilaire

1943
Stencil touch-ups

Church of Notre-Dame-de-la-Présentation, Shawinigan-Sud
Curé Arthur Jacob (to whom Leduc was recommended by Olivier Maurault)

March 1942-1955
CHANCEL, centre: *Holy Trinity Adored by Angels*; lower right: *Sacrifice of Isaac*; lower left: *Offering of Melchizedek*; two groups of *Angels Carrying Phylacteries*
NAVE, ceiling: *Presentation of the Virgin, Coronation of the Virgin* (finished by Gabrielle Messier); upper section, left: *Annunciation, Holy Spirit* (emblem), three *Angels, The Cross, Temptation of Christ in the Desert* (emblem); upper section, right: *Holy Family in the Carpenter's Shop, Hand of Benediction* (emblem), three *Angels, Temptation of Adam and Eve* (fig. 143), *Eye of God* (emblem); left wall: *Clearing the Land, Père Jacques Buteux at the Foot of Shawinigan Falls, March 28, 1651; The Sower*, right wall: *The Paper Mill Workers, Père Jacques Buteux Put to Death by the Iroquois, May 10, 1652, The Metal Foundry Workers*
Emblems, inscriptions, ornament (cats. 237-253)
$4,625 (In 1947, an additional $350 was paid for six drawings and $3,100 for the finished paintings.)
Assistants: Honorius Leduc, Gabrielle Messier, Roch Doucet, M. Gadbois.

Church of Saint-Guillaume, Upton

October 1948-January 1949
Painting contractor and consultant for Stations of the Cross

List of Exhibitions of Works by Ozias Leduc

Works included in the exhibition *Ozias Leduc: An Art of Love and Reverie* or illustrated in this catalogue are indicated in parenthesis.

Titles have been transcribed as they appeared in exhibition checklists when such documents were available. (A few obvious minor errors have been rectified without mention.)

1890

Montreal: *Exposition des Beaux-Arts*, Salle Cavallo, September 1 - October 6
Mater Dolorosa (cat. 6)
Christ en croix, d'après Bonnat (fig. 105)

1891

Montreal: 12th Annual Spring Exhibition, Art Association of Montreal; April 20 (preview), April 21 - May 9
No. 79: *Nature morte, violon*, $40
No. 80: *Mater Dolorosa*, not for sale (cat. 6)

1892

Montreal: 13th Annual Spring Exhibition, Art Association of Montreal; April 18 (preview), April 19 - May 14
No. 93: *Nature morte, livres*, $40 (cat. 11)

1893

Montreal: 14th Annual Exhibition of the Royal Canadian Academy of Arts, Art Association of Montreal; February 28 (preview), March 1-18
No. 92: *Nature morte, Oignons*, $60 (cat. 16)
No. 93: *Nature morte, Etude à la lumière d'une chandelle*, $90 (cat. 17)

Toronto: 21st Annual Exhibition, Ontario Society of Artists; April 24 (preview), April 25 - May 10
No. 195: *Still Life* [not included in auction], $50 (cat. 13)

Chicago: World's Columbian Exposition; May 1 - October 30
No. 73: *Nature morte, Oignons* (cat. 16)
No. 74: *Nature morte, Étude à la lumière d'une chandelle* (cat. 17)

1894

Ottawa: 15th Annual Exhibition of the Royal Canadian Academy of Arts, National Gallery of Canada; March 29 (preview), March 30 - April 6(?)
No. 73: *Still Life, "Open Book"* (cat. 20)

Montreal: 15th Annual Spring Exhibition, Art Association of Montreal; April 23 (preview), April 24 - May 19
No. 102: *Liseuse*, not for sale (cat. 21)

Toronto: 22nd Annual Exhibition, Ontario Society of Artists; April 24 (preview), April 26 - May 12(?)
No. 66: *Candle Light Study*, $55 (cat. 17)

Toronto: 23rd Annual Exhibition, Ontario Society of Artists; December 14 (preview), December 15-?
No. 172: *Young Boy Studying*, $60 (cat. 23)

1895

Montreal: 16th Annual Spring Exhibition, Art Association of Montreal; March 6 (preview), March 7-30
No. 74: *Still Life*, $50 (fig. 98)

Montreal: *Kermesse Notre-Dame*, Notre-Dame Hospital; after October 9
La liseuse (cat. 21)

1897

Ottawa: 18th Annual Exhibition of the Royal Canadian Academy of Arts, National Gallery of Canada; March 9-20
No. 89: *Books and Skull* (fig. 98)

Montreal: 17th Annual Spring Exhibition, Art Association of Montreal; March 31 (preview), April 1 - May 1
No. 88: *The young Student*, $75 (cat. 23)

1898

Montreal: 18th Annual Spring Exhibition, Art Association of Montreal; April 4 (preview), April 5-23
No. 76: *Still Life*, $40 (cat. 90)

1899

Montreal: 20th Annual Exhibition of the Royal Canadian Academy of Arts, Art Association of Montreal; April 7 (preview), April 8-29(?)
No. 84: *Portrait of a Woman* (cat. 109)

1900

Ottawa: 21st Annual Exhibition of the Royal Canadian Academy of Arts, National Gallery of Canada; February 15 (preview), February 16-24
No. 69: *Still Life* [Raphael Album?] (fig. 11)

Montreal: 19th Annual Spring Exhibition, Art Association of Montreal; March 16 (preview), March 17 - April 7
No. 71: *Pigeons*, $40 (cat. 103)

1901

Quebec City: Magasin Louis Morency; mid-June
Fall Plowing (cat. 120)
The Choquette Farm, Belœil (cat. 121)
The Hayfield (cat. 122)

1902

Toronto: 30th Annual Exhibition, Ontario Society of Artists; February 27 (preview), February 28 - March 14(?)
No. 49: *Still Life (Open Book)* (cat. 20?)

1912

Montreal: 29th Annual Spring Exhibition, Art Association of Montreal; March 14 (preview), March 15 - April 6
No. 236: *Portrait of the Poet, Guy Delahaye* (fig. 49)

Ottawa: 34th Annual Exhibition of the Royal Canadian Academy of Arts, National Gallery of Canada; November 28 (preview), November 29-?
No. 147: *Portrait of Guy Delahaye* (fig. 49)

1913

Montreal: 30th Annual Spring Exhibition, Art Association of Montreal; March 25 (preview), March 26 - April 19
No. 243: *Cumulus bleu*, $25 [sic] (cat. 143)

Montreal: 35th Annual Exhibition of the Royal Canadian Academy of Arts, Art Association of Montreal; November 20 (preview), November 21 - December 20 (travelled to Winnipeg Museum of Fine Arts, Winnipeg Industrial Bureau, January 16-?, 1914)
No. 174: *Fin de Jour* (Winnipeg, No. 73, $90) (cat. 144)

1914

Montreal: 31st Annual Spring Exhibition, Art Association of Montreal; March 26 (preview), March 27 - April 18
No. 244: *Effet Gris (Neige)*, $125 (cat. 146)

Quebec City: *Exposition provinciale du Québec*, August 31 - September 5
Le Cumulus bleu (cat. 143)

Toronto: Canadian National Exhibition, Department of Fine Arts; August 29 (preview), August 31 - September 12(14?)
No. 290: *Fin de Jour*, $100 (cat. 144)
No. 291: *Effet Gris (Neige)*, $125 (cat. 146)

Toronto: 36th Annual Exhibition of the Royal Canadian Academy of Arts; November 19 - (preview), November 20 - December 19
No. 126: *Le Cumulus Bleu* (cat. 143)

Toronto: *Patriotic Fund*, Royal Canadian Academy of Arts, December 30 (travelled to Winnipeg, Halifax, Saint John, Quebec City, Art Association of Montreal, March 15-27, 1915, Ottawa and Hamilton)
No. 37: *Effet gris (neige)* (cat. 146)

1915

Ottawa: *Contributions des artistes canadiens au fonds de secours national français*, Maison A.C. REA & Co; January - February
No. 33: *Etude d'expression - Study of Expression*
No. 34: *Sous-bois - Wood Interior*

Montreal: 32nd Annual Spring Exhibition, Art Association of Montreal; March 25 (preview), March 26 - April 27
No. 219: *Pommes Vertes*, $225 (cat. 148)

Toronto: Canadian National Exhibition, Department of Fine Arts; August 28 (preview), August 30 - September 13
No. 194: *Pommes Vertes*, $225 (cat. 148)

Montreal: 37th Annual Exhibition of the Royal Canadian Academy of Arts, Art Association of Montreal; November 18 (preview), November 19 - December 18
No. 128: *The Concrete Bridge* (cat. 149)

1916

Montreal: *Quelques peintures et dessins de O. Leduc*, Bibliothèque Saint-Sulpice; February 19 (preview), February 20 - March 15
No. 1: *Nature morte.* A Mme J.E.W. Lecours (fig. 5)
No. 2: *Ciel de rêve* crayon noir. A Mr R. LaRocque de Roquebrune
No. 3: *Dessin pour une couverture de livre* Au Dr. Choquette (fig. 103)
No. 4: *Le pont de béton.* (cat. 149)
No. 5: *Etude de tête* (mine de plomb).
No. 6: *Nature morte* [McCord Museum of Canadian History, Montreal?]
No. 7: *Fin de jour.* (cat. 144)
No. 8: *Pommes vertes.* A la Galerie Nationale du Canada (cat. 148)
No. 9: *Le Père Eternel.* (Croquis à la mine de plomb.) [for Saint-Hyacinthe Cathedral]
No. 10: *Dessin d'illustration.* (Fusain.)
No. 11: *Portrait de femme.*
No. 12: *Sous Bois, soleil couchant.* (Crayon noir.) (cat. 116)
No. 13: *Figure décorative.* (Fusain.) [Angel]
No. 14: *Portrait de Guy Delahaye.* (cat. 138?)
No. 15: *Un soir.* (Fusain.)
No. 16: *Projet de décoration.* (Gouache,)
No. 17: *Etude,—Une ferme.*
No. 18: *Nature morte* (cat. 103)
No. 19: *Pommiers, le soir.* (Fusain.) [private collection]
No. 20: *Crépuscule.* (Crayon noir.)
No. 21: *L'Etudiant.* (cat. 23)
No. 22: *Portrait du peintre.* (cat. 107)
No. 23: *Nature morte.* (cat. 1)
No. 24: *Le Solitaire.* (Crayon noir.) A Mme J.E.W. Lecours
No. 25: *Le Cumulus bleu.* (cat. 143)
No. 26: *Nuit d'été.* (Crayon noir.)
No. 27: *Paysage d'automne.* (cat. 150)

No. 28: *Projet de vitrail.* (Aquarelle.) (fig. 136?)
No. 29: *Dessin d'illustration.* (Fusain.) (cat. 102)
No. 30: *Portrait d'un poète.* (Fusain.) (cat. 139)
No. 31: *Croquis pour un Couronnement de la Vierge.* (cat. 135)
No. 32: *Etude,–soleil couchant.*
No. 33: *Liseur.* (Fusain.) (cat. 22)
No. 34: *Projet de décoration.* (Gouache.)
No. 35: *Dessin d'illustration.* (Fusain.) (cat. 127)
No. 36: *Projet de décoration.* (Gouache.)
No. 37: *Etude,–teintes d'automne.* (cat. 131?)
No. 38: *Ornements symboliques pour fin de pages.* (Dessins à la plume.) (cats. 140-142)
No. 39: *Mater Dolorosa.* (cat. 6)
No. 40: *Christ en croix* (fig. 105)

Montreal: 33rd Annual Spring Exhibition, Art Association of Montreal; March 23 (preview), March 24 - April 15
No. 182: *Lueurs du Soir*, $80 (fig. 52)

Quebec City: Société des artistes de Québec; June 10-24
No. 56: *Le Pont de béton*, (P. à l'huile.) $80 (cat. 149)
No. 57: *Portrait de Guy Delahaye* (fig. 49)
No. 58: *Lueurs du soir*, $80 (fig. 52)
No. 59: *Paysage d'Automne*, $150 (cat. 150)
No. 60: *Liseur*, (fusain) $50 (cat. 22)

Toronto: Canadian National Exhibition, Department of Fine Arts; August 26 (preview), August 28 - September 9
No. 382: *The Concrete Bridge*, $80 (cat. 149)

Montreal: 38th Annual Exhibition of the Royal Canadian Academy of Arts, Art Association of Montreal; November 16 (preview), November 17 - December 16
No. 134: *Neige dorée* (cat. 152)
No. 296: *Mme Josie [sic] la Roque de Roquebrune*, charcoal

1917

Montreal: Henry L. Auger, Courtier général; January - May
[No. 7]: *La carrière* (cat. 144)
[No. 12]: *Sous-bois*
[No. 23]: *Les Pommes* [McCord Museum of Canadian History, Montreal]
[No. 26]: *Nuit d'été*
[No. 32]: *Etude* [Sunset]

Montreal: 34th Annual Spring Exhibition, Art Association of Montreal; March 22 (preview), March 23 - April 14
No. 200: *The Good Shepherd*, $75 (fig. 56)
No. 201: *L'Orage*, b/w, $15
No. 202: *Pommiers en fleurs*, $15
No. 368: *Mme Louise Lecours*, medallion (cat. 157)

Montreal: Exposition permanente des œuvres d'art canadiennes, Bibliothèque municipale; November 25-?
The Good Shepherd(?) (fig. 56)
Two unidentified works

1918

Halifax: Nova Scotia Museum of Fine Arts
No. 15: *Pommes Vertes* (cat. 148)

1920

Quebec City: *L'exposition de peintures et de dessins*, Académie commerciale; October 25 - November 1
Fall Plowing (cat. 120)
The Choquette Farm, Belœil (cat. 121)

Montreal: *Exposition de quelques peintures et sculptures d'artistes canadiens*, Maison Morency Frères Ltée; November 2-11
Portrait of Guy Delahaye (fig. 49)
Day's End (cat. 144)

Montreal: *42nd Annual Exhibition of the Royal Canadian Academy of Arts*, Art Association of Montreal; November 18 (preview), November 19 - December 19
No. 320: *Head of Christ*, Study. (Charcoal) (cat. 164?)
No. 321: *The Good Shepherd.* (Charcoal)
No. 322: *The Elm, Night effect.* (Crayon)
No. 323: *Nuit d'été.* (Crayon)

Saint John, New Brunswick: *Paintings by Canadian Artists*, Saint John Art Club Loan Exhibition, Provincial Exhibition
No. 11: *Neige dorée* (cat. 152)

1921

Montreal: *38th Annual Spring Exhibition*, Art Association of Montreal; March 31 (preview), April 1-23
No. 140: *"L'Heure Mauve"*, $350 (cat. 173)

Montreal: Bibliothèque municipale
The Good Shepherd(?) (fig. 56)

New Westminster, British Columbia, *Provincial Exhibition*, Fine Art Gallery
No. 6: *Neige dorée* (cat. 152)

1922

Montreal: Maison Morency Frères; March
Portrait de Joseph-Napoléon Francœur (cat. 171)

1923

Montreal: Kermesse de l'Hôpital Notre-Dame; October 13-25(?)
Octobre [drawing]

1924

Wembley: *The British Empire Exhibition*, Canadian Section of Fine Arts, Wembley Park; April 23 - March 31, 1925 (circulated elsewhere in England, Scotland and Belgium)
No. 125: *Golden Snow* (cat. 152)
No. 126: *Green Apples* (cat. 148)

1926

Toronto: *French Canada*, Art Gallery of Toronto
No. 214: *Neige dorée*

1927

Paris: *Exposition d'art canadien*, Musée du Jeu de Paume; April 11 - May 11
No. 106: *Neige dorée* (prêtée par la National Gallery du Canada.) (cat. 152)
No. 107: *Pommes vertes* (idem.) (cat. 148)

1931

Buenos Aires: *Contemporary Canadian Art Exhibition*, The British Empire Trade Fair; March 14 - May
No. 36: *Neige dorée* (cat. 152)

Wembley: *Exhibition of Canadian Art*, British Empire Trade Exhibition
Neige dorée (cat. 152)

1932

Montreal: Semaine du Livre et de l'Art canadien, Bibliothèque Saint-Sulpice; November 5-12
Dessin, O. Maurault collection

Four photos of the decoration of the Bishop's Chapel, Sherbrooke (BNQ)

1938

London: *A Century of Canadian Art*, Tate Gallery; October 15 - December 15
No. 132: Pommes vertes (cat. 148)

Montreal: École du Meuble; June 2-?
L'Heure mauve (cat. 173)

1944

Montreal: *Exposition d'art canadien*, College André-Grasset; October 29 - November 7
No. 13: *Nature morte* [McCord Museum of Canadian History, Montreal]
No. 14. *Mlle Pierrette Langevin* [private collection]
No. 15. *Le lecteur de journal* (cat. 22)
No. 16. *Rois de la forêt* (cat. 213)

1945

Toronto: *The Development of Painting in Canada, 1665-1945*, Art Gallery of Toronto, January (travelled to Art Association of Montreal in February; National Gallery of Canada, Ottawa, in March; and Musée de la Province de Québec, Quebec City, in April)
No. 123: *Pommes vertes* (cat. 148)

Quebec City: *Exposition de Edmond Dyonnet, Ozias Leduc, Joseph Saint-Charles, Elzéar Soucy*, Musée de la Province de Québec; December 1945 – January 1946
No. 23: *Pommes vertes* (cat. 148)
No. 24: *Neige dorée* (cat. 152)
No. 25: *Labour d'automne* (cat. 120)
No. 26: *Nature morte* (fig. 123)
No. 27: *L'Heure mauve* (cat. 173)
No. 28: *Lueurs du soir* (fig. 52)
No. 29. *Le Bon Pasteur* (fig. 56)
No. 30: *Le Petit Liseur* (cat. 23)
No. 31: *Portrait de Mme Lebrun* (cat. 109)
No. 32: *Mater Dolorosa* (cat. 6)
No. 33. *Nature morte* [Raphael Album]
No. 34. *Nature morte* (fig. 5)
No. 35: *Mère Aimable* (cat. 232)
No. 36: *Le Père Buteux* (cat. 197)
No. 37: *Le Père Buteux* (cat. 198)
No. 38: *Retour des champs* (cat. 233)
No. 39: *Portrait de Mlle B...* (cat. 231)
No. 40: *Le pont de béton* (cat. 149)
No. 41: *Mon Portrait* (cat. 105)
No. 42: *Tête penchée* (cat. 86)
No. 43: *Portrait de M. l'abbé L...* (cat. 131)

No. 44: *Sainte-Famille à l'atelier*
No. 45: *Les batteurs au fléau* (cat. 96)
No. 46: *Guy de Lahaye* (cat. 139)
No. 47: *Madame W. L.* (cat. 157)

1947

Montreal: *La peinture montréalaise des dix dernières années*, Cercle universitaire, 515 Sherbrooke Street East; February 15-?
Still Life, Books(?) (cat. 11)
Mauve Twilight (cat. 173)

Windsor: *French Canadian Art, 1850-1947*, Willistead Art Gallery; November 3-30
No. 4: *Neige dorée* (cat. 152)

1952

Montreal: *Ten Montreal Collectors*, Montreal Museum of Fine Arts; February 7 (preview), February 8-24,
Afterglow (fig. 52)
Still Life [Raphael Album]
Still Life (cat. 185)

1953

Ottawa: *Exhibition of Canadian Painting to Celebrate the Coronation of Her Majesty Queen Elizabeth II*, National Gallery of Canada; June 2 - September 13
No. 37: *Mme Lebrun* (cat. 109)

1954

Saint-Hyacinthe: *Exposition régionale des Jeunesses Musicales du Canada*; April 29 - May 9
No. 70: *Etude pour: "Papillon"*
No. 71: *Ste Famille*
No. 72: *Enfant de chœur*
No. 73: *Étude de têtes*
No. 74: *Claude Paysan* (cat. 93)

Montreal: *Retrospective Ozias Leduc*, Lycée Pierre-Corneille; June 19
Les trois pommes (cat. 1)
Cupidon poursuivant un papillon
Nature morte, livres (cat. 11)
Nature morte, oignons (cat. 16)
Garçon lisant (cat. 23)
Portrait de Mme Lebrun (cat. 109)
Autoportrait (cat. 106)
Mon Portrait (cat. 107)
Madeleine repentante (cat. 125)
Nature morte (mannequin qui pleure) (fig. 5)
Fin de Jour (cat. 144)
Judith (cat. 147)
Portrait de Léo-Pol Morin (cat. 160)
L'Heure mauve (cat. 173)
Le liseur (cat. 22)

Exhibitions held after the death of Ozias Leduc

1955

Ottawa: *Ozias Leduc, 1864-1955*, National Gallery of Canada, December 9-19 (organized with Musée de la Province de Québec; travelled to University of Montreal, January 13-25, 1956; Musée de la province de Québec, Quebec City, February 2-?; Centre des Loisirs Saint-Germain, Rimouski, February 29 - March 5; Art Gallery of Hamilton, March - April; Winnipeg; Art Gallery of Toronto, May

No. 1: *LES TROIS POMMES* (cat. 1)
No. 2: *NATURE MORTE AUX OIGNONS* (cat. 16)
No. 3: *LE REPAS DU COLON* (cat. 17)
No. 4: *LE PETIT LISEUR* (cat. 23)
No. 5: *PORTRAIT DE MADAME LEBRUN* (cat. 109)
No. 6: *MON PORTRAIT* (cat. 107)
No. 7: *NATURE MORTE: ALBUM DE RAPHAËL*
No. 8: *PORTRAIT DE L'ABBÉ CHOQUETTE*
No. 9: *MARIE-MADELEINE REPENTANTE* (cat. 125)
No. 10: *LES LABOURS D'AUTOMNE, A SAINT-HILAIRE* (cat.120)
No. 11: *LA BELLE TÊTE NOIRE*
No. 12: *PORTRAIT DE LA MÈRE DE L'ARTISTE* (cat. 4)
No. 13: *LES LIVRES ET LA LOUPE* (cat. 185)
No. 14: *PAYSAGE*
No. 15: *PAYSAGE* (cat. 151)
No. 16: *JUDITH* (cat. 147)
No. 17: *MUSE DANS LA FORÊT* (cat. 130)
No. 18: *PORTRAIT DE GUY DELAHAYE* (fig. 49)
No. 19: *FIN DU JOUR* (cat. 144)
No. 20: *POMMES VERTES* (cat. 148)
No. 21: *LE PONT DE BÉTON* (cat. 149)
No. 22: *LUEURS DU SOIR* (fig. 52)
No. 23: *PAYSAGE A L'AUTOMNE* (cat. 150)
No. 24: *LE BON PASTEUR* (fig. 56)
No. 25: *ENDYMION ET SÉLÉNÉ* (cat. 129)
No. 26: *NEIGE DORÉE* (cat. 152)
No. 27: *L'HEURE MAUVE* (cat. 173)
No. 28: *PAYSAGE DE NEIGE*
No. 29: *PORTRAIT DE MADEMOISELLE B.* (cat. 231)
No. 30: *PORTRAIT DE MADAME LABONTÉ* (cat. 235)
No. 31: *LE LISEUR* (cat. 22)
No. 32: *TÊTE DE SAINT-HILAIRE* (cat. 24)
No. 33: *LE CHAUSSEUR* [*sic*]
No. 34: *BANC DE NEIGE* (cat. 187)
No. 35: *PAYSAGE*
No. 36: *PORTRAIT DE ROBERT ROCQUE-BRUNE* (cat. 155)
No. 37: *THE IMMACULATE CONCEPTION* (cat. 176)
No. 38: *THE ANNUNCIATION* (cat. 178)
No. 39: *PRESENTATION IN THE TEMPLE* (cat. 180)
No. 40: *CRUCIFIXION* (cat. 182)
No. 41: *NUAGES DOMINANTS*

1956

Montreal: Galerie l'Art français, 370 Laurier Avenue West; February 6-18

(List compiled from newspaper articles)
Open Window (cat. 118)
Portrait of Abbé Olivier Leduc (cat. 131)
Portrait of Abbé Joseph-Zéphirin Vincent (cat. 132)
Portrait of Josée LaRoque de Roquebrune (cat. 156)
Study for the *Portrait of Olivier Maurault, p.s.s.* (cat. 161)
My Mother (fig. 3)
My Father (fig. 2)
Pot de fleurs [Geraniums], oil
Les chasseurs, watercolour
Head of a Woman, charcoal
Pompon, charcoal
Portrait of a Bishop
Seated Nude
Le petit penseur, crayon (reproduced in *The Gazette* [Montreal], February 4, 1956)
A Priest Holding a Book, drawing
Le rouet, small pencil drawing
A Man in a Shipyard, small drawing
Portrait of the Artist's Sister, drawing
Preliminary drawings for *The Nativity* for Saint-Enfant-Jésus, Mile-End
Studies of hands, heads, angels and apples on a branch
Self-portrait
Le faucheur
Still Life with Glass and Onions
Study for a Still Life with Magnifying Glass
Study for *Endymion and Selene*(?)

Arvida: Studio Fantasia au centre récréatif d'Arvida, organized by the Société Saint-Jean-Baptiste d'Alma under the auspices of the Comité des Arts et Métiers; March 9-11
About sixty works, on loan from René Bergeron of L'Art Canadien, Chicoutimi, including:
Girl Reading (cat. 21)
Hand of Abbé Joseph-Zéphirin Vincent (cat. 133)
The Assumption (Head of an Angel)
Study of a Head
The Death of Attala
Self-portrait

1957

Montreal: Galerie l'Art français
Seated Cleric (cat. 131)

1958

Victoria, British Columbia: *Opening Exhibitions*, Centennial Gallery of the Art Gallery of Greater Victoria; September
No. 11: *NEIGE DORÉE* (cat. 152)

1960

Mexico City: *Mexican Exhibition*, October 5
No. 51: *Les trois pommes* (cat. 1)
No. 100: *Neige dorée* (cat. 152)

Montreal: *Onze artistes à Montréal, 1860-1960/Eleven Artists in Montreal, 1860-1960*, Montreal Museum of Fine Arts; September 8 - October 2
No. 31: *The Three Apples/Les Trois Pommes* (cat. 1)

No. 32: *Still-Life: Phrenology/Nature Morte: Phrenologie* (cat. 12)
No. 33: *L'Enfant au Pain/L'Enfant au Pain* (cat. 15)
No. 34: *My Mother in Mourning/Ma Mère en Deuil* (cat. 4)
No. 35: *Portrait of Mrs. Lebrun/Portrait de Mme Lebrun* (cat. 109)
No. 36: *Portrait of Father C. P. Choquette/Portrait de L'Abbé C. P. Choquette* (fig. 104)
No. 37: *Still-Life: Books/Nature Morte: Livres* (cat. 11)
No. 38: *End of the Day/Fin de Jour* (cat. 144)
No. 39: *The Good Shepherd Seeks the Lost Lamb/ Le Bon Pasteur Cherchant la Brebis Perdue* (fig. 56)
No. 40: *L'Heure Mauve/L'Heure Mauve* (cat. 173)

1961

Montreal: *Doctors and Art*, Montreal Museum of Fine Arts; June 7 - July 4
Nature morte, livres (cat. 11)

1962

Montreal: *New Accessions II*, Montreal Museum of Fine Arts, May 9 - 27
L'Heure Mauve (cat. 173)

Saint-Hilaire: *Exposition Osias Leduc*, École Desrochers, Festival Saint-Hilaire; October 7
According to Gabrielle Messier, this exhibition included, among other works:
Mater Dolorosa (cat. 6)
Boy with Bread (cat. 15)
Bending Head (cat. 86)
Erato (Sleeping Muse) (cat. 89)
"Mais elle, ceci l'amusait ce grand garçon si brun…" (cat. 95)
My Portrait (cat. 105)
My Portrait (cat. 107)
Study for a *Portrait of Guy Delahaye* (cat. 139)
The Concrete Bridge (cat. 149)
Still Life (with Books and Magnifying Glass) (cat. 185)
Portrait of Guy Delahaye (fig. 49)
Portrait of Charles-Philippe Choquette (fig. 104)

Bordeaux: *L'Art au Canada*, Galerie des beaux-arts, May 11 - July 31
No. 20: *PHRÉNOLOGIE* (cat. 12)

1967

National Gallery of Canada (organized by):
Canadian Painting, 1850-1950/La peinture canadienne, 1850-1950, (travelled to Windsor, January 8 - February 12; London, Ontario, February 17 - March 26; Hamilton, April 1 - May 7; Kingston, May 12 - June 10; Stratford, June 16 - July 30; Saskatoon, August 9 - September 9; Edmonton, September 15 - October 10; Victoria, October 20 - November 18; Charlottetown, November 30 - December 30; Saint John, New Brunswick, January 1968; Fredericton, February; Quebec City, March)
No. 19: *PORTRAIT DE MADAME LABONTÉ/PORTRAIT DE MADAME LABONTÉ* (cat. 235)

Ottawa: *Three Hundred Years of Canadian Art/Trois cents ans d'art canadien*, National Gallery of Canada; May 12 - September 17

(travelled to Art Gallery of Ontario, Toronto, October 20 - November 26)
No. 160: *The Farmer's Supper/Le Repas du colon* (cat. 17)
No. 187: *Pommes vertes/Pommes vertes* (cat. 148)
No. 221: *The Immaculate Conception/L'Immaculée Conception* (cat. 176)

Quebec City: *Exposition Borduas – Ozias Leduc*, Musée du Québec; June - ?
No. 1: *L'Enfant au pain* (cat. 15)
No. 2: *Le liseur* (fig. 14)
No. 3: *Ma mère en deuil* (cat. 4)
No. 4: *Tête penchée* (cat. 86)
No. 5: *La nuit* (cat. 19)
No. 6: *Oncle Théophile*
No. 7: *Tante Aglaé*
No. 8: *Christ en croix* (fig. 105)
No. 9: *Autoportrait* (cat. 107)
No. 10: *Marie-Madeleine repentante* (cat. 125)

Montreal: *Ozias Leduc*, Maison des Arts La Sauvegarde; September 2 - October 25
No. 1: *27 petits dessins dans un grand cadre* (cats. 57-83)
No. 2: *Sous-Bois*
No. 3: *La liseuse* (cat. 21)
No. 4: *Le Bon Pasteur* (fig. 56)
No. 5: *5 petits dessins*
No. 6: *Les trois pommes* (cat. 1)
No. 7: *Chasse aux canards par un matin brumeux*
No. 8: *Croquis pour un tableau (une sainte famille pour l'abbé Albert Tessier)* (cat. 234)
No. 9: *Etude – portrait de Mgr Olivier Moreault*
No. 10: *Etude de lèvres*
No. 11: *Etude de nus*
No. 12: *Pomme*
No. 13: *Vieillard*
No. 14: *4 Etudes*
No. 15: *Portrait de jeune fille* (cat. 231)
No. 16: *Ange*
No. 17: *Paysage*
No. 18: *Village St-Hilaire*
No. 19: *Apôtres*
No. 20: *St-Joseph*
No. 21: *Vieillard*
No. 22: *Tête de jeune homme*
No. 23: *Madame Bindoff*
No. 24: *Tête d'ange*
No. 25: *Lac Hertel*
No. 26: *St-François d'Assise*
No. 27: *Moulage en plâtre "Madame Lecours"*
No. 28: *Tête de jeune homme en habit d'époque* (œuvre de Borduas et son maître Ozias Leduc)
No. 29: *Portrait de Mme Lebrun* (cat. 109)
No. 30: *Tête de jeune homme*
No. 31: *Tête d'enfant*
No. 32: *Portrait du poète Guy Delahayse*
No. 33: *Même portrait* (cat. 139)
No. 34: *Arbres à St-Hilaire*
No. 35: *La Pêche miraculeuse*
No. 36: *L'Extase de Ste-Thérèse*
No. 37: *Etude pour un portrait de Dr T. Guerin, ancien maire de Montréal*
No. 38: *Le jardin enchanté* (cat. 184)
No. 39: *La muse* (cat. 88)
No. 40: *Judas*
No. 41: *Voix de Jeanne d'Arc*
No. 42: *Les oignons rouges* (cat. 16)

1970

Ottawa: *The Mr. and Mrs. Jules Loeb Collection/La collection de M. et Mme Jules Loeb*, National Gallery of Canada, October 15 - November 15 (travelled to Sir George Williams University, Montreal, September 1-30; Winnipeg Art Gallery, January 15 - February 15, 1971; University of British Columbia, Vancouver, March 1-31; Mendel Art Gallery Saskatoon, April 15 - May 15; Art Gallery of Windsor, June 1-31; Université de Sherbrooke, July 15 - August 15; Beaverbrook Art Gallery, Fredericton, September 1-30)
No. 28: *The Visitation/La Visitation*
No. 29: *The Coronation of the Virgin/Le Couronnement de la Vierge*

1971

Toronto: *Festival québécois*, University of Toronto, November 13-21
Labour d'automne (cat. 120)

1973

Madison: *Canadian Landscape Painting, 1670-1930: The Artist and the Land*, Elvehjem Art Center, University of Wisconsin; April 12 - May 23 (travelled to Hopkins Center Art Galleries, Dartmouth College, Hanover, New Hampshire, June 15 - August 1; University Art Museum, University of Texas, Austin, August 20 - October 7)
No. 32: *Neige dorée* (cat. 152)

Ottawa: *Peintres du Québec – Collection Maurice et Andrée Corbeil/Painters of Quebec: Maurice and Andrée Corbeil Collection*, National Gallery of Canada, May 11 - June 10 (travelled to Montreal Museum of Fine Arts, March 30 - April 29)
No. 42: *La phrénologie/Phrenology* (cat. 12)
No. 43: *Nature morte aux œufs/Still Life with Eggs*
No. 44: *Couronnement de la Vierge/The Coronation of the Virgin* (cat. 135)
No. 45: *Guy Delahaye/Guy Delahaye* (cat. 138)
No. 46: *Nature morte à la bouilloire/Still Life with Kettle*
No. 47: *Paysage à l'automne, lac Saint-Hilaire/Autumn Landscape, Lac Saint-Hilaire* (cat. 150)
No. 48: *Lueurs du soir/Afterglow* (fig. 52)

1974

Ottawa: *Ozias Leduc: peinture symboliste et religieuse/Ozias Leduc: Symbolist and Religious Painting*, National Gallery of Canada; January 31 (preview), February 1 - March 2 (travelled to Canadian Cultural Centre, Paris, March 28 - April 28; Canadian Embassy, Brussels, June 1-30; Art Gallery of Hamilton, August 1-28; McCord Museum of Canadian History, Montreal, September 15 - October 15)
No. 1: *LES TROIS POMMES/THE THREE APPLES* (cat. 1)
No. 2: *MA MÈRE EN DEUIL/MY MOTHER IN MOURNING* (cat. 4)
No. 3: *L'ENSEVELISSEMENT DU CHRIST/ENSHROUDING OF CHRIST* (cat. 9)
No. 4: *ESQUISSE POUR LA DÉCORATION DE L'ÉGLISE DE SAINT-HILAIRE: SAINT HILAIRE RESSUSCITANT L'EN-FANT MORT SANS BAPTÊME/STUDY FOR THE DECORATION OF THE CHURCH OF SAINT-HILAIRE: "SAINT HILARY RAISING THE CHILD WHO HAD DIED WITHOUT BAPTISM"* (cat. 26)
No. 5: *ESQUISSE POUR LA DÉCORATION DE L'ÉGLISE DE SAINT-HILAIRE: SAINT HILAIRE RESSUSCITANT L'EN-FANT MORT SANS BAPTÊME (TÊTE)/STUDY FOR THE DECORA-TION OF THE CHURCH OF SAINT-HILAIRE: "SAINT HILARY RAIS-ING THE CHILD WHO HAD DIED WITHOUT BAPTISM" (HEAD)* (cat. 24)
No. 6: *NATURE MORTE, VIOLON/STILL-LIFE WITH VIOLIN*
No. 7: *NATURE MORTE (LES TROIS SOUS)/STILL-LIFE WITH THREE PEN-NIES* (cat. 13)
No. 8: *LA PHRÉNOLOGIE/PHRENOLOGY* (cat. 12)
No. 9: *L'ENFANT AU PAIN/CHILD WITH A PIECE OF BREAD* (cat. 15)
No. 10: *NATURE MORTE (ÉTUDE À LA LUMIÈRE D'UNE CHANDELLE)/STILL-LIFE (STUDY BY CANDLELIGHT)* (cat. 17)
No. 11: *LE PETIT LISEUR/THE LITTLE READER* (cat. 23)
No. 12: *LE LISEUR/THE READER* (cat. 22)
No. 13: *NATURE MORTE AU MASQUE MORTUAIRE DE BEETHOVEN, AVEC LIVRES ET FEUILLES/STILL-LIFE WITH BEETHOVEN'S DEATH MASK, BOOKS, AND LEAVES*
No. 14: *NATURE MORTE AUX ŒUFS/STILL-LIFE WITH EGGS*
No. 15: *ÉTUDE POUR LA DÉCORATION DE L'ÉGLISE DE SAINT-HILAIRE: L'ASSOMPTION DE LA VIERGE (TÊTE)/STUDY FOR THE DECORA-TION OF THE CHURCH OF SAINT-HILAIRE: "ASSUMPTION OF THE VIRGIN" (HEAD)* (cat. 32)
No. 16: *ÉRATO (MUSE ENDORMIE)/ERATO (SLEEPING MUSE)* (cat. 89)
No. 17: *AU CIMETIÈRE/"IN THE CEME-TERY"* (cat. 102)
No. 18: *AUTOPORTRAIT/SELF-PORTRAIT* (cat. 107)
No. 19: *FERNANDE ET CLAUDE/"FERNANDE AND CLAUDE"* (cat. 99)
No. 20: *PORTRAIT DE Mme LEBRUN/PORTRAIT OF MRS LEBRUN* (cat. 109)
No. 21: *ÉTUDE POUR LES LABOURS D'AU-TOMNE À SAINT-HILAIRE/STUDY FOR "FALL PLOUGHING AT SAINT-HILAIRE"* (cat. 119)
No. 22: *NATURE MORTE AU LIVRE ET À LA LOUPE/STILL-LIFE WITH BOOK AND MAGNIFYING GLASS* (cat. 185)
No. 23: *PORTRAIT DE L'ABBÉ C. P. CHOQUETTE/PORTRAIT OF ABBÉ C.P. CHOQUETTE*
No. 24: *ÉTUDE POUR PORTRAIT DE Mgr JOHN CAMERON/STUDY FOR "POR-TRAIT OF MSGR JOHN CAMERON"* (cat. 126)

No. 25: *L'ÎLE ENCHANTÉE/THE ENCHANTED ISLE* (cat. 184)

No. 26: *PORTRAIT DE L'HONORABLE L. P. BRODEUR/PORTRAIT OF THE HON. L.P. BRODEUR* (cat. 123)

No. 27: *ÉRATO (MUSE DANS LA FORÊT)/ERATO (MUSE IN THE FOREST)* (cat. 130)

No. 28: *PORTRAIT DE L'ABBÉ J.-Z. VINCENT/PORTRAIT OF ABBÉ J.-Z. VINCENT* (cat. 132)

No. 29: *PROFIL DANS UN NUAGE/ PROFILE IN CLOUD* (cat. 134)

No. 30: *ENDYMION ET SÉLÉNÉ/ ENDYMION AND SELENE* (cat. 129)

No. 31: *ÉTUDE POUR LA DÉCORATION DE L'ÉGLISE SAINT-BARNABÉ DANS LE COMTÉ DE SAINT-HYACINTHE: LE MARTYRE DE SAINT BARNABÉ/STUDY FOR THE DECORATION OF THE CHURCH OF SAINT-BARNABÉ, SAINT-HYACINTHE COUNTY: "THE MARTYRDOM OF SAINT BARNABAS"*

No. 32: *PORTRAIT DU POÈTE GUY DELA-HAYE/PORTRAIT OF THE POET GUY DELAHAYE* (fig. 49)

No. 33: *LE CUMULUS BLEU/BLUE CUMULUS* (cat. 143)

No. 34: *EFFET GRIS (NEIGE)/GREY EFFECT (SNOW)* (cat. 146)

No. 35: *POMMES VERTES/GREEN APPLES* (cat. 148)

No. 36: *JUDITH/JUDITH* (cat. 147)

No. 37: *PAYSAGE D'AUTOMNE (LAC HER-TEL)/AUTUMN LANDSCAPE (LAKE HERTEL)* (cat. 150)

No. 38: *LE PAIN DE SUCRE/"THE SUGAR LOAF"* (fig. 51)

No. 39: *NEIGE DORÉE/GOLDEN SNOW* (cat. 152)

No. 40: *LUEURS DU SOIR/AFTERGLOW* (fig. 52)

No. 41: *ESQUISSE POUR LA DÉCORATION DE L'ÉGLISE SAINT-ENFANT-JÉSUS DU MILE-END DE MONTRÉAL: L'ANNON-CIATION/STUDY FOR THE DECORATION OF THE CHURCH OF SAINT-ENFANT-JÉSUS, MILE-END (MONTREAL): "ANNUNCIATION"*

No. 42: *PORTRAIT DE ROBERT LAROQUE DE ROQUEBRUNE (DANS LA POSE DU MONTESQUIOU DE BOLDINI)/POR-TRAIT OF ROBERT LAROQUE DE ROQUEBRUNE IN THE POSE OF BOL-DINI'S "MONTESQUIOU"* (cat. 155)

No. 43: *LE BON PASTEUR/THE GOOD SHEPHERD* (fig. 56)

No. 44: *ÉTUDE POUR LA DÉCORATION DE LA CHAPELLE DU SACRÉ-CŒUR DE L'ÉGLISE SAINT-ENFANT-JÉSUS DU MILE-END DE MONTRÉAL: LE CHRIST EN CROIX (TÊTE)/STUDY FOR THE DÉCORATION OF THE CHURCH OF SAINT-ENFANT-JÉSUS, MILE-END (MONTREAL): "CHRIST ON THE CROSS" (HEAD)*

No. 45: *PORTRAIT DE NOËL LEDUC/ PORTRAIT OF NOËL LEDUC*

No. 46: *PORTRAIT DE GERTRUDE LEDUC/PORTRAIT OF GERTRUDE LEDUC*

No. 47: *L'HEURE MAUVE/MAUVE TWILIGHT* (cat. 173)

No. 48: *ÉTUDE POUR LA DÉCORATION DE L'ÉGLISE SAINT-RAPHAËL DE L'ÎLE BIZARD, L'APOTHÉOSE DE JEANNE D'ARC: LES VOIX/ STUDY FOR THE DECORATION OF THE CHURCH OF SAINT-RAPHAËL, ÎLE BIZARD: THE "VOICES" IN "THE APOTHEOSIS OF JOAN OF ARC"*

No. 49: *ESQUISSE POUR UN PROJET DE DÉCORATION DE L'ÉGLISE SAINT-RAPHAËL DE L'ÎLE BIZARD: NATIVITÉ/STUDY FOR A PROPOSED DECORATION FOR THE CHURCH OF SAINT-RAPHAËL, ÎLE BIZARD: "NATIVITY"*

No. 50: *NUAGE À FLANC DE MON-TAGNE/MOUNTAINSIDE IN CLOUD* (cat. 174)

No. 51: *ESQUISSE EN COULEURS POUR LA DÉCORATION DE LA CHAPELLE PRIVÉE DE L'ÉVÊQUE DE SHER-BROOKE: ANNONCE DE MARIE CO-RÉDEMPTRICE/ COLOUR STUDY FOR THE DECORATION OF THE PRIVATE CHAPEL OF THE BISHOP OF SHERBROOKE: "MARY HAILED AS CO-REDEEMER"* (cat. 176)

No. 52: *ESQUISSE EN COULEURS POUR LA DÉCORATION DE LA CHAPELLE PRIVÉE DE L'ÉVÊQUE DE SHER-BROOKE: L'ANNONCIATION/COLOUR STUDY FOR THE DECORATION OF THE PRIVATE CHAPEL OF THE BISHOP OF SHERBROOKE: "ANNUNCIATION"* (cat. 178)

No. 53: *ESQUISSE EN COULEURS POUR LA DÉCORATION DE LA CHAPELLE PRIVÉE DE L'ÉVÊQUE DE SHER-BROOKE: JÉSUS RETROUVÉ DANS LE TEMPLE/COLOUR STUDY FOR THE DECORATION OF THE PRIVATE CHAPEL OF THE BISHOP OF SHER-BROOKE: "CHRIST DISCOVERED AMONG THE DOCTORS"* (cat. 180)

No. 54: *ESQUISSE EN COULEURS POUR LA DÉCORATION DE LA CHAPELLE PRIVÉE DE L'ÉVÊQUE DE SHER-BROOKE: AU PIED DE LA CROIX/COLOUR STUDY FOR THE DEC-ORATION OF THE PRIVATE CHAPEL OF THE BISHOP OF SHERBROOKE: "AT THE FOOT OF THE CROSS"* (cat. 182)

No. 55: *PORTRAIT DE L'ABBÉ OLIVIER MAURAULT/PORTRAIT OF ABBÉ OLIVIER MAURAULT* (cat. 163)

No. 56: *ESQUISSE POUR LA DÉCORATION DE L'ÉGLISE DE SAINTE-GENEVIÈVE DE PIERREFONDS: SAINT GERMAIN D'AUXERRE BÉNISSANT SAINTE GENEVIÈVE/ STUDY FOR THE DECO-RATION OF THE CHURCH OF SAINTE-GENEVIÈVE-DE-PIERRE-FONDS, PARISH OF SAINTE-GENEVIÈVE: "SAINT GENEVIEVE BEING BLESSED BY SAINT GERMAIN OF AUXERRE"*

No. 57: *ESQUISSE POUR LA DÉCORATION DU BAPTISTÈRE DE L'ÉGLISE NOTRE-DAME DE MONTRÉAL: LA RÉDEMPTION/ STUDY FOR THE DEC-ORATION OF THE BAPTISTERY OF THE CHURCH OF NOTRE-DAME, MONTREAL: "THE REDEMPTION"*

No. 58: *ÉTUDE POUR LA DÉCORATION DU BAPTISTÈRE DE L'ÉGLISE NOTRE-DAME DE MONTRÉAL: ATTRIBUT DE SAINT LUC (TAUREAU)/STUDY FOR THE DECORATION OF THE BAPTIS-TERY OF THE CHURCH OF NOTRE-DAME, MONTREAL: ATTRIBUTE OF SAINT LUKE (BULL)*

No. 59: *ÉTUDE POUR LA DÉCORATION DU BAPTISTÈRE DE L'ÉGLISE NOTRE-DAME DE MONTRÉAL: ATTRIBUT DE SAINT MATHIEU (ANGE)/STUDY FOR THE DECORATION OF THE BAPTIS-TERY OF THE CHURCH OF NOTRE-DAME, MONTREAL: ATTRIBUTE OF SAINT MATTHEW (ANGEL)*

No. 60: *ÉTUDE POUR LA DÉCORATION DU BAPTISTÈRE DE L'ÉGLISE NOTRE-DAME DE MONTRÉAL: ATTRIBUT DE SAINT MARC (LION)/STUDY FOR THE DECORATION OF THE BAPTISTERY OF THE CHURCH OF NOTRE-DAME, MONTREAL: ATTRIBUTE OF SAINT MARK (LION)*

No. 61: *ÉTUDE POUR LA DÉCORATION DU BAPTISTÈRE DE L'ÉGLISE NOTRE-DAME DE MONTRÉAL: AILES POUR LES ATTRIBUTS DES QUATRE ÉVANGÉLISTES/ STUDY FOR THE DEC-ORATION OF THE BAPTISTERY OF THE CHURCH OF NOTRE-DAME, MONTREAL: WINGS FOR THE ATTRIB-UTES OF THE FOUR EVANGELISTS*

No. 62: *ÉTUDE POUR LA DÉCORATION DU BAPTISTÈRE DE L'ÉGLISE NOTRE-DAME DE MONTRÉAL: ATTRIBUT POUR SAINT JEAN (AIGLE)/STUDY FOR THE DECORATION OF THE BAPTIS-TERY OF THE CHURCH OF NOTRE-DAME, MONTREAL: ATTRIBUTE OF SAINT JOHN (EAGLE)*

No. 63: *ÉTUDES POUR LA DÉCORATION DU BAPTISTÈRE DE L'ÉGLISE NOTRE-DAME DE MONTRÉAL: ATTRIBUT DE SAINT JEAN (AIGLES)/STUDY FOR THE DECORATION OF THE BAPTISTERY OF THE CHURCH OF NOTRE-DAME, MONTREAL: ATTRIBUTE OF SAINT JOHN (EAGLES)*

No. 64: *CROQUIS POUR LA VOÛTE DU BAPTISTÈRE DE L'ÉGLISE NOTRE-DAME DE MONTRÉAL/STUDY FOR THE DECORATION OF THE BAPTIS-TERY OF THE CHURCH OF NOTRE-DAME, MONTREAL: VAULT*

No. 65: *ÉTUDE POUR LE CIEL THÉOLOGIQUE DANS LE BAPTISTÈRE DE L'ÉGLISE NOTRE-DAME DE MONTRÉAL/STUDY FOR THE DECO-*

RATION OF THE BAPTISTERY OF THE CHURCH OF NOTRE-DAME, MONTREAL: THEOLOGICAL HEAVEN

No. 66: *ÉTUDE POUR LES COLONNES ET LES NERVURES DE LA DÉCORATION DU BAPTISTÈRE DE L'ÉGLISE NOTRE-DAME DE MONTRÉAL/STUDY FOR THE DECORATION OF THE BAPTISTERY OF THE CHURCH OF NOTRE-DAME, MONTREAL: COLUMNS AND MIDRIBS*

No. 67: *CROQUIS POUR L'ÉLÉMENT GAUCHE DU DÉCOR DE LA PIÈCE « LA BOUÉE » D'ERNEST CHOQUETTE/ STUDY FOR SET FOR CHOQUETTE'S PLAY "LA BOUÉE": LEFT SIDE* (cat. 191)

No. 68: *LE PASTEUR DES ATTIKAMÈGUES/ THE SHEPHERD OF THE ATTIKAMEK*

No. 69: *LE PÈRE BUTEUX/FATHER BUTEUX* (cat. 198)

No. 70: *LA MEULE/THE HAYSTACK* (cat. 211)

No. 71: *CRÉPUSCULE LUNAIRE/MOONLIT EVENING* (cat. 224)

No. 72: *LA MAISON DU PASSEUR/THE FERRYMAN'S HOUSE* (cat. 226)

No. 73: *PAYSAGE DE NEIGE/SNOWSCAPE*

No. 74: *MÈRE AIMABLE/DEVOTED MOTHER* (cat. 232)

No. 75: *PAYSAGE SOMBRE/DARK LANDSCAPE*

No. 76: *LA SAINTE-FAMILLE À L'ATELIER/HOLY FAMILY IN THE CARPENTER'S SHOP*

No. 77: *LA TÊTE DE LA VIERGE/HEAD OF THE VIRGIN*

No. 78: *ÉTUDE POUR LE MUR DE CHEVET DE L'ÉGLISE NOTRE-DAME-DE-LA-PRÉSENTATION D'ALMA-VILLE-EN-BAS: LA SAINTE TRINITÉ/ STUDY FOR THE DECORATION OF THE CHURCH OF NOTRE-DAME-DE-LA-PRÉSENTATION, ALMAVILLE-EN-BAS: "HOLY TRINTY"* (cat. 237)

1976

Montreal: *Trois générations d'art québécois, 1940-1950-1960,* Musée d'art contemporain
No. 101: *« Madame Labonté »* (cat. 235)

Montreal: *Arts et Culture/Arts and Culture,* Organizing Committee for the Games of the XXI Olympiad
L'Enfant au pain (cat. 15)

Sherbrooke: *Portraits et paysages… avant Borduas,* Galerie d'art de l'Université de Sherbrooke; June 6-27
Cinq enfants au lit, crayon
L'ange et la Vierge, crayon
Nature morte à la rocaille, huile sur carton
Neige dorée, dessin au crayon
Paysage, dessin au crayon (cat. 214)
Saint-Joseph, huile sur toile
Saint-Pierre et le Christ, dessin au crayon (cat. 44)

Ottawa: Galerie Rodrigue Lemay
A "considerable number" of sketches and drawings, including:
Two studies for *Madame Labonté* (one a hand study)
Studies for the chapel of the Bishop's Palace, Sherbrooke

1977

Shawinigan-Sud: *Le dernier grand œuvre d'Ozias Leduc* (preparatory sketches for the decoration of the Church of Notre-Dame-de-la-Présentation), Church of Notre-Dame-de-la-Présentation, July 27-28 (travelled to Centre culturel de Shawinigan, Salon Pic, August 1-30; Galerie du Parc, Pavillon Saint-Arnaud, Trois-Rivières, September 13-25)
1.1 *Cinq études de coiffures* [for *The Presentation of Mary in the Temple*]
2.1 *La sainte Trinité*
2.2 *Le Père éternel*
2.3 *Projet d'autel et Christ en croix*
2.5 *Corpus*
2.6 *Cinq études anatomiques de bras*
2.7 *Étude anatomique d'un bras*
2.10 *L'offrande de Melchisedech* (cat. 239)
2.11 *Le sacrifice de Melchisedech*
2.12 *Abraham immolant son fils* (cat. 240)
2.13 *Tête de bélier*
2.14 *Étude pour le sacrifice d'Abraham*
3.4 *Annonciation et colombe*
4.2 *Saint Joseph et main divine* (cat. 246)
5.2 *Adam et Ève, et œil de Dieu* (cat. 244)
5.3 *Adam et Ève, et Dieu omniscient* (cat. 242)
5.5 *Adam et Ève* (cat. 241)
5.7 *Tentation d'Adam et Ève* (cat. 243)
5.8 *La tentation d'Adam et Ève*
6.2 *Tentation de Jésus, no. 1* (cat. 245)
6.3 *Jésus, Satan, la Croix*
6.5 *Étude de nu du Christ*
6.6 *Deux études de main*
6.7 *Quatre études anatomiques de bras*
6.8 *Deux études anatomiques de jambe gauche*
6.9 *Deux études anatomiques de jambes*
6.10 *Étude de jambe et esquisse de tête mitrée*
6.11 *Trois études de jambes*
7.1 *Texte de Leduc*
7.2 *Le Père Buteux chez les Attikamègues*
7.4 *Le Père Buteux chez les Attikamègues*
7.6 *Textes de Leduc* et *Petit dessin pour Buteux*
7.7 *Personnage bénissant*
7.14 *Le Père Buteux au pied des chûtes de Shawinigan, le 28 mars 1651* (cat. 247)
7.15 *Étude du Père Buteux au pied des chûtes…*
7.16 *Étude pour Père Buteux au pied des chûtes, tête et torse*
7.17 *Le Père Buteux Jésuite*
8.1 *Étude du Père Buteux*
8.2 *Étude du Père Buteux*
8.4 *Mort de Buteux*
8.5 *Étude d'un bras d'indien bandant l'arc*
8.6 *Deux croquis d'indiens*
8.7 *Croquis d'indien effrayé*
8.8 *La mort du Père Buteux*
8.11 *La mort du Père Buteux* (cat. 249)
9.1 *Défrichement, Le Sol, no. 1*
9.2 *Croquis de charrue*
10.1 *Les semailles*

10.4 *Texte "La Saison des semailles", de Victor Hugo et dessin*
11.1 *Chargement des meules, no. 4*
11.4 *Chargeurs de meules*
12.1 *Le métal, no. 6*
12.2 *Le métal* (cat. 253)
12.10 *Le fondeur*
12.12 *Modèle pour cuviste*
12.16 *Métal fondu*
12.17 *Lingots d'aluminium*

1978

Montreal: *Dessins inédits d'Ozias Leduc/Ozias Leduc the Draughtsman,* Sir George Williams Art Galleries, Concordia University; October 6-24 (travelled to Norman Mackenzie Art Gallery, University of Regina, December 1-31; Vancouver Art Gallery, January 13 - February 11, 1979; Agnes Etherington Art Centre, Kingston, February 27 - March 29; Art Gallery of Ontario, Toronto, April 7 - May 6; Musée régional de Rimouski, May 18 - June 18; Musée du Québec, Quebec City, August 9 - September 5; Rodman Hall Arts Centre, Saint Catharines, September 15 - October 15; Art Gallery of Windsor, October 25 - November 24)
No. 1: *Élie dans le désert/(Elijah in the Desert).*
No. 2: *Tête de vieillard/Head of an Old Man.*
No. 3: *Assomption/Assumption.*
No. 4: *Portement de la croix/The Bearing of the Cross.*
No. 5: *Paysage avec chute d'eau/Landscape with water fall.*
No. 6: *Adolescent endormi/Young Man Asleep.*
No. 7: *Quatre maquettes pour des rideaux de scène/Four maquettes for stage sets.* (fig. 99)
No. 8: *Figure allégorique féminine/Female allegorical figure.*
No. 9: *Nu endormie, étude pour* Le Sommeil d'Endymion */Sleeping female nude, study for the* Sommeil d'Endymion.
No. 10: *Portrait d'Ozéma Leduc/Portrait of Ozema Leduc.* (cat. 31)
No. 11: *Nu endormi sur un rocher/Sleeping Female Nude in a landscape.* (cat. 88)
No. 12: *Nu assis, la tête appuyée sur la main/Seated female nude, her head resting on her hand.*
No. 13: *Paysan appuyé sur une clôture/Farmer leaning against a fence.*
No. 14: *Le Bal/Country Dance* (cat. 97)
No. 15: *Chambre de convalescente/Convalescent Girl in her Room.*
No. 16: *La noyade de Claude Paysan/The Drowning of Claude Paysan.* (cat. 101)
No. 17: *Deux études et deux photographies pour le portrait de l'abbé Charles-Philippe Choquette/Two studies and two photographs for the portrait of abbé Charles-Philippe Choquette.*
No. 18: *Auto-portrait/Self-portrait.* (cat. 106)
No. 19: *Deux anges portant une palme et une couronne/Two angels holding a palm frond and a crown.*
No. 20: *Esquisse et trois photographies préparatoires pour le portrait de l'honorable Louis-Philippe Brodeur/Preparatory drawing and three photographs for the portrait of Louis-Philippe Brodeur.* (figs. 39-40)

No. 21: *Illustration pour "Le Réveillon" dans* Les Contes vrais *de Pamphile Lemay/Illustration for "Le Réveillon" story in* Les Contes vrais *by Pamphile Lemay.* (cat. 127)

No. 22: *Portrait de Mgr Alexis-Xyste Bernard/ Portrait of Mgr. Alexis-Xyste Bernard.*

No. 23: *Portrait de Guy Delahaye/Portrait of Guy Delahaye.* (cat. 139)

No. 24: *Effet gris, neige/(Grey effect, snow).* (cat. 145)

No. 25: *Paysage de tempête avec arc-en-ciel/Stormy Landscape with Rainbow.*

No. 26: *Lueurs du soir/(Afterglow).* (cat. 153)

No. 27: *Tête d'homme se protégeant les yeux du soleil/Head of a man shading his eyes.* (cat. 164)

No. 28: *Portrait de jeune fille (Mademoiselle Jeanne Lecours)/Portrait of a young girl (Miss Jeanne Lecours).*

No. 29: *Portrait de Monsieur Olivier Maurault, p.s.s./Portrait of Olivier Maurault, p.s.s.* (cat. 161)

No. 30: *Dessin préparatoire pour le carton du vitrail* Le Martyre de s. Paul*/Preparatory drawing for the cartoon for the stained glass window,* Le Martyre de s. Paul.

No. 31: *Feu de forêt/Forest fire.*

No. 32: *Carton pour une bande décorative: pommes et feuilles d'érable/Cartoon for a decorative band: apple and maple leaves.*

No. 33: *Ex-libris de la Commission scolaire de Saint-Hilaire/Ex-libris for the Schoolboard of Saint-Hilaire.* (cat. 172)

No. 34: *Portrait de Monsieur Olivier Maurault, p.s.s./Portrait of Olivier Maurault, p.s.s.*

No. 35: *Deux études pour les ex-libris de Monsieur Olivier Maurault, p.s.s. et de Joseph Barcelo/Two studies for the ex-libris of Olivier Maurault, p.s.s and Joseph Barcelo.* (fig. 55)

No. 36: *Le jardin enchanté/(The Enchanted Garden).*

No. 37: *Quatre études pour l'ex-libris d'Yves Tessier-Lavigne/Four studies for the ex-libris of Yves Tessier-Lavigne.*

No. 38: *Cinq feuilles d'études pour le décor de la chapelle de l'évêché de Sherbrooke/Five sheets of studies for decoration of the bishop's palace of Sherbrooke.*

No. 39: *Ex-libris de Paul Lavoie/Ex-libris for Paul Lavoie.*

No. 40: *Torse d'un Christ en croix/Torso of Christ on the cross.*

No. 41: *Deux dessins préparatoires pour des illustrations de* La Campagne canadienne*/Two preliminary drawings for the illustrations to* La Campagne canadienne.

No. 42: *Troisième station du chemin de la croix pour le couvent de Saint-Hilaire/Third Station of the Cross, Convent of St. Hilaire.*

No. 43: *Le Jourdain, étude pour le décor du baptistère de l'église Notre-Dame de Montréal/The Jordan, study for the decoration of the baptistry, church of Notre-Dame, Montreal.*

No. 44: *Banc de neige/(Snow bank).* (cat. 187)

No. 45: *Femme assise dans un paysage/Seated woman in a landscape.*

No. 46: *Cinq études préparatoires pour l'Apparition de s. Michel au Mont Gargano/Five preparatory drawings for the Apparition of St. Michael at Mount Gargano.*

No. 47: *Paysage/Landscape*

No. 48: *Montagne au loin/(Mountain from a distance).* (cat. 199)

No. 49: *Crépuscule lunaire/(Moonlit evening).*

No. 50: *Quatre études et blason de la Société d'histoire régionale de Saint-Hyacinthe./Four studies and emblem of the Société d'histoire régionale de Saint-Hyacinthe.*

No. 51: *Nature morte au livre ouvert/Still life with open book.*

No. 52: *Homme nu debout/Standing nude male.*

No. 53: *Les chargeurs de meules/The Paper mill workers.*

No. 54: *Étude (Le métal) et deux photographies pour* Les travailleurs du métal*/Sketch (The metal) and two photographs for* The metal workers.

Musée du Québec (organized by): *L'art du paysage au Québec (1800-1940)*, (travelled to Mount Saint Vincent University Art Gallery, Halifax, October 27 - November 19; Memorial University Art Gallery, Saint John's, December 28 - January 29, 1979; Beaverbrook Art Gallery, Fredericton, February 15 - March 15; Musée du Québec, Quebec City, April 5 - May 13)
No. 32: *LA MAISON DES CHOQUETTE À BELŒIL/THE CHOQUETTE HOUSE AT BELŒIL* (cat. 121)

1980

Saint-Jérome: Galerie d'art du Vieux Palais; August 1 to September 1

Works by twenty artists, including Leduc, born in the second half of the nineteenth century
Unidentified work

1981

Quebec City: *À la découverte du patrimoine avec Gérard Morisset*, Musée du Quebec; February 4 - March 1
Unidentified work

Montreal: *Ce qui ne meurt pas*, Musée de l'Oratoire Saint-Joseph, August - November 2
Two pencil studies for the Stations of the Cross for the Church of Saint-Jude: *Christ Condemned to Death, Jesus on the Cross*

1982

Ottawa: *Les Esthétiques modernes au Québec de 1916 à 1946/Modernism in Quebec Art (1916-1946)*, National Gallery of Canada; April 23 - June 13 (travelled to Art Gallery of Windsor, July 4 - August 15; Musée d'art contemporain de Montréal, September 2 - October 17; Rodman Hall Art Centre, Saint Catharines, November 5-30; Musée du Québec, Quebec City, ?- February 27, 1983)
No. 6: *L'Heure mauve* (cat. 173)
No. 101: *The Sacred Heart of Jesus*, retouched photograph (fig. 58)

Trois-Rivières: *Galerie de portraits de femmes*, Galerie d'art du Parc, manoir de Tonnancour; October - November 7

Berlin: *OKanada*, Akademie der Künste; December 5 - January 30, 1983
No. 26: *Les Trois pommes* (cat. 1)
No. 27: *L'enfant au pain* (cat. 15)
No. 28: *Nature morte* (cat. 90)
No. 29: *Les Foins* (cat. 122)
No. 30: *Erato (Muse dans la forêt)* (cat. 130)
No. 31: *Cumulus bleu* (cat. 143)
No. 32: *Neige dorée* (cat. 152)

1983

Quebec City: *Cinquante années d'acquisition*, Musée du Québec; November 2 - March 4, 1984
No. 146: *La liseuse* (cat. 21)
No. 153: *Labours d'automne à Saint-Hilaire* (cat. 120)
No. 164: *Portrait de Guy Delahaye* (cat. 138)
No. 176: *Chasse aux canards par un matin brumeux*
No. 328: *Adolescent endormi*
No. 345: *Portrait de Léo-Pol Morin* (cat. 160)

London, Ontario: *The Hand Holding the Brush: Self Portraits by Canadian Artists/La main qui tient le pinceau*, London Regional Art Gallery; November 4 - January 8, 1984 (travelled to Macdonald Stewart Art Centre, Guelph, January 20 - March 4; Art Gallery of Hamilton, March 19 - April 29; McCord Museum of Canadian History, Montreal, May 14 - June 24; Beaverbrook Art Gallery, Fredericton, July 9 - August 19; Mount Saint Vincent University Art Gallery, Halifax, September 3 - October 14; Agnes Etherington Art Centre, Kingston, October 29 - December 16)
No. 27: *Mon Portrait* (cat. 107)

1984

Quebec City: *Le Grand Héritage: l'Église catholique et les arts au Québec*, Musée du Québec; September 10 - January 13, 1985
No. 107: *Monsieur Olivier Maurault, p.s.s.* (cat. 163)
No. 217: *Le Martyre de saint Paul*, stained glass (cat. 169)

1985

Sherbrooke: *Musée de nos maisons I*, Musée des beaux-arts de Sherbrooke; April 28 - May 27
Étude de ciel (cat. 2)

Trois-Rivières: *Ozias Leduc*, Musée Pierre-Boucher; October - November 11

About thirty works, of which the following were lent by the Musée du Québec:
La maison grise des Choquette à Belœil (cat. 121)
Paysage, porte de Clignancourt
Paysage
Chasse aux canards par un matin brumeux
Madame Labonté (cat. 235)
Tragédie
La Comédie
Allégorie
Allégorie

Etude du Père Buteux
Etude du Père Buteux
Etude du Père Buteux au pied des chutes
Etude du père Buteux au pied des chutes
Le père Buteux au pied des chutes Shawinigan le 28 mars 1651 (cat. 248)
Le père Buteux chez les Attikamèques
La mort du Père Buteux
Le père Jacques Buteux tombant sous les coups des Iroquois, le 10 mai 1652 (cat. 249)
Lampe portant un monogramme du Christ
Ange portant des fruits
Le Fondeur
Les Fondeurs de Métal (cat. 253)

1986

Montreal: *Les paysages d'Ozias leduc, lieux de méditation/Contemplative Scenes: The Landscapes of Ozias Leduc*, Montreal Museum of Fine Arts; February 14 - March 23 (travelled to MacDonald Stewart Centre, Guelph, April 18 - May 18; Art Gallery of Windsor, July 25 - August 24; Ring House Gallery, Edmonton, September 12 - October 12; Beaverbrook Art Gallery, Fredericton, January 15 - February 15, 1987)
No. 1: *LE CUMULUS BLEU/BLUE CUMULUS* (cat. 143)
No. 2: *PAYSAGE/LANDSCAPE* (cat. 186)
No. 3: *FIN DE JOURNÉE/DAY'S END* (cat. 144)
No. 4: *POMMES VERTES/GREEN APPLES* (cat. 148)
No. 5: *PAYSAGE D'AUTOMNE, LAC HERTEL/AUTUMN LANDSCAPE, HERTEL LAKE* (cat. 150)
No. 6: *PAYSAGE D'AUTOMNE/AUTUMN LANDSCAPE* (cat. 151)
No. 7: *NEIGE DORÉE/GOLDEN SNOW* (cat. 152)
No. 8: *L'HEURE MAUVE/MAUVE TWILIGHT* (cat. 173)
No. 9: *L'ÎLE ENCHANTÉE/ENCHANTED ISLAND* (cat. 184)
No. 10: *CRÉPUSCULE LUNAIRE/MOONLIT TWILIGHT* (cat. 224)
No. 11: *LA MAISON DU PASSEUR/THE FERRYMAN'S HOUSE* (cat. 226)
No. 12: *PAYSAGE DE NEIGE/SNOWY LANDSCAPE*

1987

Sherbrooke: *Ozias Leduc parmi nous*, Centre d'exposition Léon-Marcotte, Musée du Seminaire de Sherbrooke; March 6 - April 12

A selection of works from the 1986 MMFA travelling exhibition *Contemplative Scenes*, along with works from the Archdiocese and private collectors in the region, including:
Portrait of Msgr. Alphonse-Osias Gagnon (cat. 183)
Old Bonsecours Church, Montreal (cat. 201)
Landscapes and portrait studies in pencil and charcoal
Four Evangelists, stained glass
Dove, stained glass

1988

Montreal: *Voies/Voix Intimes*, Galerie d'Art Lavalin; May 11 - July 9
« *Chasse aux canards par un matin brumeux* »
« *Nuage à flanc de montagne* » (cat. 174)
« *Portrait de Léo-Pol Morin* » (cat. 160)

Toronto: *Collector's Canada: Selections from a Toronto Private Collection*, Art Gallery of Ontario; May 14 - July 10 (travelled to Musée du Québec, Quebec City, September 21 - October 30; Vancouver Art Gallery, January 20 - March 5, 1989; Mendel Art Gallery, Saskatoon, March 23 - May 7)
No. 44: *The Hayfield* (cat. 122)

1990

Montreal: *L'art d'acquérir: acquisitions récentes 1988-1990/The Art of Acquisition: Recent Acquisitions, 1988-1990*, Montreal Museum of Fine Arts; November 2 - December 2
Les trois pommes/The Three Apples (cat. 1)

1991

Quebec City: *La collection des dessins et estampes: 80 œuvres choisies*, Musée du Québec; May 16 - September 8
No. 28: *Portrait de Léo-Paul Morin* (cat. 160)
No. 29: *Étude pour effet gris (neige)* (cat. 145)

1993

Montreal: *Un beau geste: les nouvelles acquisitions/The Graceful Gesture: New Acquisitions, Part I*, McCord Museum of Canadian History; June 19 - November 7
Portrait de Madame St-Cyr (cat. 227)

1994

Montreal: *La collection Lavalin au Musée d'art contemporain/Lavalin collection at Musée d'art contemporain*, Musée d'art contemporain de Montréal; April 30 - October 23
La phrénologie (cat. 12)

Sherbrooke: *Musée de nos maisons X*, Musée des beaux-arts de Sherbrooke, September 24 - October 30
Étude de ciel (cat. 2)

1995

Montreal: *Lost Paradise: Symbolist Europe*, Montreal Museum of Fine Arts; June 8 - October 15
No. 243: *Erato (Muse in the Forest)* (cat. 130)
No. 244: *End of the Day* (cat. 144)

Mont-Saint-Hilaire: *Ozias Leduc, peintre et citoyen de St-Hilaire*, Maison de la Culture (organized by Musée d'art de Mont-Saint-Hilaire), November 15 - January 7, 1996
Landscape [Boulders]
Un saint
Portrait de l'Abbé Joseph-Zéphirin Vincent (cat. 132)

Nature morte
Paysage [Dark]
Paysage de neige
Alphonse Tessier (cat. 233)
Brume matinale (cat. 203)
Mère Aimable (cat. 232)
Le chemin de croix du couvent de Mont-Saint-Hilaire (three Stations)
Three pencil drawings (man wearing a suit, horses, dog)
Mgr Olivier Maurault (cat. 161)
Tête et cou
Nuages dominants (cat. 204)
Portrait de mon père (cat. 3)
Couverture de Claude Paysan (cat. 93)
Feuilles d'automne
Fleurs dans un verre
Étude pour le portrait de Mgr (Charles-Philippe) Choquette
Paysage (rivière)
Pochoir
Étude de plusieurs visages
Portrait de jeune fille
Les deux anges
Ange
Étude pour *Érato (Muse endormie)* (cat. 87)
Portrait de Mgr (Charles-)Philippe Choquette
Érato (Muse endormie) (cat. 89)
Fernande et Claude (cat. 99)
Étude tête penchée (cat. 86)
Batteurs au fléau (cat. 96)
La Sainte Famille à l'atelier
Paysage d'automne, lac Hertel (cat. 150)
Chat couché
Corbeille de fruits d'automne
Verre et gobelet
Nature morte à la cruche et au tabouret
La pluie
Fenêtre ouverte (cat. 118)
Portrait de Rodolphe Brunet (cat. 85)

Selected Bibliography

DUMONT, G. A. "L'Exposition des beaux-arts III". *Le Monde illustré* [Montreal], October 11, 1890, pp. 374, 376.

DOMINO. "Exposition de peinture". *Le Monde* [Montreal], April 23, 1892, p. 1.

"Chronique artistique – O. Leduc", *L'Opinion publique* [Montreal], April 14, 1893, p. 284.

"The Spring Exhibition: 'Still Life', Leduc", *Montreal Daily Star*, March 11, 1895, p. 5, ill.

DANDURAND, Mme [Joséphine]. "Le 'Salon' de Montréal". *Le Coin du feu* [Montreal], April 1895, pp. 97-102.

WERTHEMER, G. de. "L'Exposition annuelle de peintures à L'« Art Association » – Revue complète du Salon", *Les Nouvelles* [Montreal], April 4, 1897, pp. 2-3.

FRÉCHETTE, Louis, "Le Salon", *La Presse* [Montreal], April 10, 1897, p. 4.

FRANÇOISE [pseudomyn of Robertine Barry]. "Chronique du lundi", *La Patrie* [Montreal], April 12, 1897, p. 2.

CHOQUETTE, Dr. [Ernest]. "Un artiste de mon pays". *La Patrie* [Montreal], December 3, 1898, p. 2.

F[ABRE], H[ector]. "Revue Littéraire – *Claude Paysan*, par le docteur Choquette, illustré par Leduc". *Paris-Canada* [Paris], December 1, 1899, pp. 3-4.

RÉMUNA, Jean [pseudonym of Arsène Bessette]. "M. Osias Leduc". *Le Canada-Français* [Saint-Jean], May 3, 1901, p. 2.

LEDUC, Ozias. "The Decorations of St. Ninian's Cathedral". *The Casket* [Antigonish, Nova Scotia], September 3, 1903, p. 2.

ROQUEBRUNE, Robert de. "L'exposition Leduc". *L'Action* [Montreal], February 19, 1916, p. 1.

VÉZINA, Émile. "Notes d'art – L'Exposition Leduc". *Le Devoir* [Montreal], February 21, 1916, p. 1.

BOHÈME, Ruth [pseudonym of Fernande Choquette]. "Un peintre de 'chez nous'". *La Patrie* [Montreal], March 11, 1916, p. 19.

LABERGE, A[lbert]. "L'oeuvre d'un artiste". *L'Autorité* [Montreal], March 11, 1916, p. 2.

DELIGNY, Louis [pseudonym of Olivier Maurault, p.s.s.]. *La chapelle du Sacré-Coeur, église du Saint-Enfant-Jésus, Montréal – Une décoration du peintre Ozias Leduc*. Montreal: Imprimerie du Messager, 1921. 17 pp., ills.

"Nos églises catholiques – deux édifices religieux dont notre province peut s'enorgueillir avec raison". *La Presse* [Montreal], July 9, 1921, p. 13.

CHAUVIN, Jean. *Ateliers: études sur vingt-deux peintres et sculpteurs canadiens*. Montreal and New York: Louis Carrier & Co., Éd. du Mercure, 1928. 266 pp. (pp. 118-126).

LEMAY, Arthur. "Un artiste du terroir à St-Hilaire de Rouville: l'œuvre du peintre Osias Leduc". *Le Terroir* [Quebec City], vol. 8, nos. 11-12 (March-April 1928), cover and pp. 186-187.

LEDUC, O[zias]. "Un concours – une fête à St-Hilaire de Rouville". *La Terre de chez nous* [Montreal], November 20, 1929, p. 12.

"La chapelle Pauline apparaît, après un travail de huit ans, comme un bijou artistique". *La Tribune* [Sherbrooke], October 22, 1932, p. 3.

MAURAULT, Olivier, p.s.s. "Un inédit de Mgr Olivier Maurault p.s.s., recteur de l'Université de Montréal – Ozias Leduc, peintre mystique". *Le Mauricien* [Trois-Rivières], vol. 2, no. 2 (February 1938), pp. 4-5, 29.

GAGNON, Maurice. *Peinture moderne*. Montreal: Éd. B. Valiquette, 1940. 214 pp. (pp. 185, 187, 189, 199-201; ills. 52-54).

—. "Poèmes philosophiques du peintre Ozias Leduc". *Technique*, vol. 16, no. 9 (November 1941), pp. 640-643, 660.

BERGERON, René. *Art et Bolchévisme*. Montreal: Fides, 1946. 135 pp. (pp. 90-96).

DORVAL, Suzette. "Interview d'Osias Leduc". *Amérique française*, vol. 7, no. 3 (March-May 1949), pp. 21-23, plates.

GUINDON, Henri-M., s.m.m. "Une somme mariale – la peinture d'Ozias Leduc". *Messager de Marie Reine des Cœurs*, vol. 46, no. 7 (March 1949), cover and pp. 77-8.

BORDUAS, Paul-Émile. "Quelques pensées sur l'œuvre d'amour et de rêve de M. Ozias Leduc". *Canadian Art*, vol. 10, no. 4 (Summer 1953), pp. 158-161, 168. Published in English in Paul-Émile Borduas, *Écrits/Writings 1942-1958*, trans. François-Marc Gagnon and Dennis Young (Halifax: The Press of the Nova Scotia College of Art and Design, 1978), pp. 131-134.

GLADU, Paul. "L'ermite de Saint-Hilaire: le peintre Ozias Leduc". *Le Petit Journal* [Montreal], November 29, 1953, p. 61.

LEDUC, Ozias. "Pensées". *Amérique française*, vol. 11, no. 6 (December 1953), pp. 3-4.

—. "Pensées en liberté". *Arts et pensée*, vol. 3, no. 15 (January-February 1954), p. 91.

—. "Le Drapeau canadien" (letter to the editor). *Le Devoir* [Montreal], April 19, 1954, p. 4.

—. "Assomption". *Arts et pensée*, vol. 3, no. 17 (May-June 1954), p. 139.

—. "Antipodes". *Amérique française*, vol. 12, no. 2 (June 1954), p. 130.

REPENTIGNY, Rodolphe de. "Le plus canadien et le plus universel de nos peintres". *La Presse* [Montreal], June 23, 1954, p. 48.

"Hommage à Ozias Leduc". Special issue of *Arts et pensée*, vol. 3, no. 18 (July-August 1954): L[ouis]-J[oseph] BARCELO, "Leduc tel que je l'ai connu", p. 172; Paul-Émile BORDUAS, "Paul-É. Borduas nous écrit au sujet de Ozias Leduc", pp. 177-179; Gilles CORBEIL, "Plaisir à Leduc" and "Ozias Leduc, peintre de natures mortes", pp. 162, 169-171; Claude GAUVREAU, "Leduc, un indépendant", p. 173; Noël LAJOIE, "Ozias Leduc, poète", p. 180; André LECOUTEY, "Les décorations religieuses d'Ozias Leduc", pp. 184-186; Fernand LEDUC, "Ozias Leduc, peintre exemplaire", pp. 176; Ozias LEDUC, "L'histoire de S.-Hilaire – On l'entend, on la voit" and "Rythmes intimes", pp. 165-168, 181-183; Olivier MAURAULT, p.s.s.,

"Monsieur Ozias Leduc, homme-artiste", pp. 174-175; Gilles ROUX, "Ozias Leduc – Esquisse biographique", pp. 163-164.

LEDUC, Ozias. "Demain?". *Amérique française*, vol. 12, no. 3 (September 1954), p. 162.

—. "Dactylo". *Amérique française*, vol. 12, no. 5 (November-December 1954), p. 325.

CORBEIL, Gilles. "Un hommage au peintre Ozias Leduc, 1864-1955 – Rencontres avec Ozias Leduc". *Le Devoir* [Montreal], January 14, 1956, pp. 8, 16.

LAJOIE, Noël. "Un hommage au peintre Ozias Leduc, 1864-1955" and "Quelques poèmes". *Le Devoir* [Montreal], January 14, 1956, p. 8.

REPENTIGNY, R[odolphe] de. "Images et plastiques – Il faut connaître Ozias Leduc" and "œuvre prestigieuse d'Ozias Leduc". *La Presse* [Montreal], January 14, 1956, p. 66.

CHOQUETTE-CLERK, Fernande. "À la mémoire d'Osias Leduc". *Le Clairon maskoutain* [Saint-Hyacinthe], June 15, 1956, pp. 9, 11.

JACOB, Arthur. *Légendes des tableaux de la décoration en l'église Notre-Dame de la Présentation d'Almaville, (aujourd'hui Shawinigan-Sud) comté de Saint-Maurice, P.Q.* Trois-Rivières: Imprimerie du Bien Public, October 11, 1960. 45 pp.

OSTIGUY, Jean-René. "Ozias Leduc, peintre indépendant". *Vie des Arts*, vol. 7, no. 29 (Winter 1962-1963), pp. 16-21.

—. "Étude des dessins préparatoires à la décoration du baptistère de l'église Notre-Dame de Montréal", *National Gallery of Canada Bulletin*, no. 15 (1970). 40 pp. Summarized in English as "The Preparatory Drawings for the Decoration of the Baptistry of Notre-Dame Church in Montreal", p. 39.

ÉTHIER-BLAIS, Jean, and François[-Marc] GAGNON. *Ozias Leduc et Paul-Émile Borduas.* Montreal: Presses de l'Université de Montréal, 1973, "Conférences J.A. DeSève" 15-16. 152 pp. (pp. 7-59, 97-152; ills. 1, 4, 7).

LACROIX, Laurier. "La décoration religieuse d'Ozias Leduc à l'évêché de Sherbrooke", Master's thesis, University of Montreal, 1973. 379 pp.

OSTIGUY, Jean-René, *Ozias Leduc: Symbolist and Religious Painting*, exhib. cat. Ottawa: National Gallery of Canada, 1974. 224 pp.

LACROIX, Laurier. "La chapelle de l'évêché de Sherbrooke: quelques dessins préparatoires d'Ozias Leduc" (summarized in English as "The Chapel of the Bishop's Palace in Sherbrooke: Some Preparatory Sketches by Ozias Leduc"). *National Gallery of Canada Bulletin*, no. 30 (1977), cover and pp. 3-18.

LACROIX, Laurier, *et al. Ozias Leduc the Draughtsman*, exhib. cat. Montreal: Concordia University, 1978. 168 pp.

LACROIX, Laurier. "The Dream Mountain of Ozias Leduc". *ArtsCanada*, vol. 35, no. 3 (October/November 1978), cover and title pages, pp. 9-15.

ÉHIER-BLAIS, Jean. *Autour de Borduas.* Montreal: Presses de l'Université de Montréal, 1979. 199 pp. (pp. 45-74).

DION, Jean-Noël. "(1864-1955) Pour souligner le 25ᵉ anniversaire de la mort du peintre Ozias Leduc". Six articles published in *Le Courrier de Saint-Hyacinthe*, September 24 - October 29, 1980.

LEDUC, Ozias. "Quelques mots sur l'Art par Osias Leduc, peintre, 1939". Text of the lecture "Réflexions sur l'Art" given by Leduc before the Société d'histoire de Saint-Hyacinthe, December 1939, published in five articles in *Le Courrier de Saint-Hyacinthe*, November 12 - December 10, 1980.

STIRLING, J. Craig. "The St-Hilaire Church Interior Decorations (1896-1900) of Ozias Leduc", Master's thesis, Concordia University, 1981, 298 pp. Published in French as *Ozias Leduc et la décoration intérieure de l'église de Saint-Hilaire*. Quebec City: Ministère des Affaires culturelles, "Civilisation du Québec" series, 1985. 279 pp.

OSTIGUY, Jean-René. *Modernism in Quebec Art, 1916-1946*, exhib. cat. Ottawa: National Gallery of Canada, 1982. 168 pp. (pp. 14-21, 26-31, 42-43, 60-63, 142-143, 150-151).

BEAUDRY, Louise, "Une analyse formelle et iconographique de quatre paysages (1913-1921) d'Ozias Leduc (1864-1955)", Master's thesis, University of Montreal, 1983. 183 pp.

—. *Contemplative Scenes: The Landscapes of Ozias Leduc*, exhib. cat., Montreal: Montreal Museum of Fine Arts, 1986. 63 pp.

GEHMACHER, Arlene. "In Pursuit of the Ideal: The Still Life Paintings of Ozias Leduc", Master's thesis, University of Toronto, 1986. 61 pp. and catalogue.

LANTHIER, Monique. "Le Portrait d'homme d'Ozias Leduc au MBAM retrouve son identité", *The Journal of Canadian Art History*, vol. 9, no. 2 (1986), pp. 164-177, ills.

—. *Portrait et Photographie chez Ozias Leduc*, Master's thesis, University of Montreal, 1987, 190 + XXXI pp.

LANTHIER-LEBEAU, Monique. "Amitié Olivier Maurault-Ozias Leduc", *Cahier de la Société historique de Montréal*, vol. 7, no. 1 (December 1988), pp. 347-354.

GLADU, Paul. *Ozias Leduc.* Laprairie: Broquet Inc., 1989, "Signatures" series. 103 pp.

WINTERS, Barbara Ann. "The Work and Thought of Ozias Leduc in the Intellectual and Social Context of His Time", Master's thesis, University of Victoria, May 1990, 447 pp.

LANTHIER, Monique. "Ozias Leduc et Louis-Philippe Brodeur, ou Le Portraitiste et son modèle". *Cahier d'histoire de la Société d'histoire de Belœil – Mont-Saint-Hilaire*, no. 38 (June 1992), cover and pp. 3-16.

GEHMACHER, Arlene. "The Mythologization of Ozias Leduc, 1890-1954", Ph.D. dissertation, University of Toronto, 1995. 315 pp.

List of Works Exhibited

PHOTO CREDITS

EXHIBITED WORKS

Agnes Etherington Art Centre, Kingston, Ontario,
cat. 102
The Art Gallery of Greater Victoria, Victoria,
British Columbia
cat. 238
Art Gallery of Ontario, Toronto
Carlo Catenazzi
cats. 10, 18
The Beaverbrook Art Gallery, Fredericton, New
Brunswick
cat. 143
Bibliothèque Nationale du Québec - Fonds
Ozias Leduc
cats. 167, 172, 237
Centre d'Archives du Séminaire de Saint-
Hyacinthe, Institut canadien de conservation
cat. 165
La Corporation Archiépiscopale C.R. du
Diocèse de Sherbrooke
cats. 168-169, 183
House of Commons, Ottawa
cat. 123
McCord Museum of Canadian History, Montreal
cats. 132, 227
Mendel Art Gallery, Saskatoon
cat. 103
The Montreal Museum of Fine Arts
Christine Guest
cats. 57-77, 79-83, 124, 149, 157, 200, 208, 212,
216, 220, 224, 234
Brian Merrett
cats. 1-3, 8-9, 11, 13, 16, 19-20, 22, 28, 30, 32, 78,
84-87, 89-96, 98-99, 101, 104-105, 109-119, 126,
128, 131, 135, 139-140, 142, 144, 150, 151, 153-154,
158-159, 161, 163-164, 170-171, 173, 184, 186,
188-193, 195-197, 199, 204-207, 209, 211, 213-215,
217-219, 221-223, 225-226, 228-231, 236, 252, 254
Musée d'art contemporain de Montréal
Richard-Max Tremblay
cat. 12
Musée d'art de Joliette
cats. 7, 166

Musée de la Civilisation, Quebec City
Pierre Soulard
cat. 146
Musée des beaux-arts de Sherbrooke
cats. 44, 45,
Musée du Québec, Quebec City,
cats. 136-137, 155, 174
Patrick Altman
cats. 5, 40, 121, 125, 141, 145, 160, 187 239-240,
245-247, 249, 250-251, 253
Claude Bureau
cats. 127, 156, 162, 187, 194
Jean-Guy Kérouac
cats. 21, 88, 108, 120, 125, 138, 147, 194, 235,
241-244, 248
Musée du Séminaire de Sherbrooke
cat. 201
Musée Pierre-Boucher du Séminaire de
Trois-Rivières
cats. 198, 203, 232-233
The National Gallery of Canada, Ottawa
cats. 4, 6, 14-15, 17, 23-27, 29, 33-39, 41-43,
46-56, 97, 100, 106-107, 129-130, 148, 152,
175-182, 185, 202, 210

FIGURES

Photographers of period photographs are named in
the figure captions.

We are grateful to the Bibliothèque nationale du
Québec for granting permission to reproduce the
following documents from the Fonds Ozias-Leduc:
figs. 1, 4-5, 10-12, 15, 31, 37-38, 40, 43-45, 47-49,
55-56, 58, 61, 69, 72, 75-76, 91, 93, 96-97, 103,
105, 108-109, 112, 114, 118, 123, 125-126, 130, 132,
134-136, 139, 140-142
Stephen Clerk
fig. 14
Guy Couture
fig. 127
Michel Dubreuil
figs. 78-90, 143
Paul Gagné
figs. 110, 117

Arlene Gehmacher
fig. 62
Laurier Lacroix
figs. 6, 59
Robert Lebeau
figs. 13, 33, 39, 73-74, 100, 124
André Morain
fig. 51
Archives de l'archevêché de Montréal
fig. 138
McCord Museum of Canadian History, Montreal
fig. 99
The Montreal Museum of Fine Arts
Marilyn Aitken
fig. 68
Christine Guest
figs. 16-30, 64-67, 94
Brian Merrett
fig. 36, 50, 70, 104
Musée du Québec, Quebec City
Patrick Altman
figs. 93a-b
Jean-Guy Kérouac
figs. 2-3
Musée régional de Vaudreuil-Soulanges
fig. 102
Philadelphia Museum of Art
Graydon Wood
fig. 34
Public Archives of Nova Scotia,
Photograph Collection
fig. 131
Réunion des musées nationaux, Paris
fig. 8, 53
Saint Francis Xavier University, Antigonish,
Nova Scotia
Bernice MacDonald
fig. 41